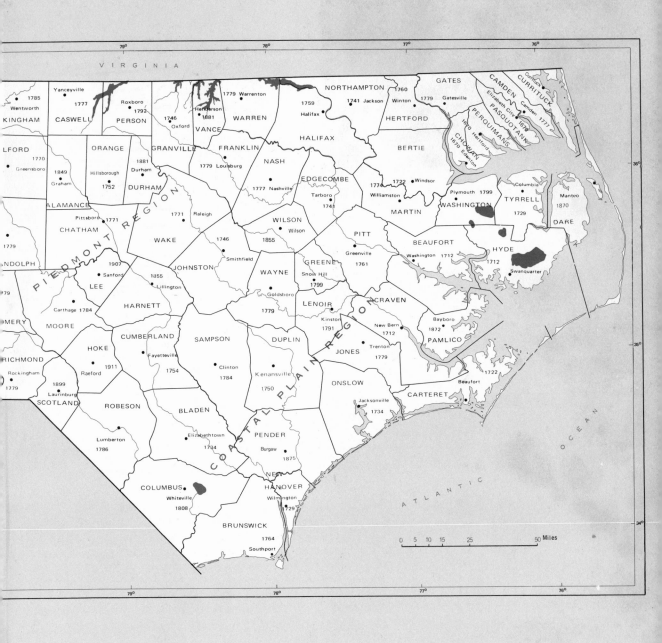

NORTH CAROLINA

The History of a Southern State

NORTH CAROLINA

THIRD EDITION

*by Hugh Talmage Lefler
and Albert Ray Newsome*

The University of North Carolina Press • Chapel Hill

Manufactured in the United States of America
Text edition, ISBN 0–8078–1202–1
Trade edition, ISBN 0–8078–1207–2
Library of Congress Catalog Card Number 72–81330
First printing, August 1973
Second printing, August 1976
Third printing, August 1979

To the Memory of

WILLIAM KENNETH BOYD
ROBERT D. W. CONNOR

and

ALBERT RAY NEWSOME

whose lives exemplified the state motto
Esse Quam Videri

Contents

Preface

Almost two decades have passed since the first edition of this book appeared, and nearly ten years since the second edition. In the 1963 revision, I completely reorganized and rewrote that portion of the book dealing with North Carolina history after 1896. Insofar as the twentieth century is concerned that was a "new book." The first edition contained only sixty-six pages on the period after 1900. The second edition contained more than twice that amount. Many new maps, charts, and appendixes were also added, and the 1950 statistics were replaced by those of 1960. Additions were also made to Significant Dates, and many new books were added to the Chapter Bibliographies.

During the past decade a great deal of new history has, of course, been made—new history both in the sense of factual events and in the sense of scholarly writings. To keep abreast of these changes, I have again extended this history to encompass recent developments. I have also reconsidered, revised, and enlarged certain portions of the volume. The last four chapters have been completely rewritten.

The overall organization of this revision remains the same as that of the second edition, but numerous changes have been made in the content. A number of persisting errors, mostly small but nonetheless vexatious, have been corrected. Alterations or additions have been made in order to bring my interpretation, as far as possible, into line with the most recent scholarship. There is much more about the role of Negroes in the state's history than appeared in the earlier editions.

All of the appendixes have been brought up to date, and the Chapter Bibliographies have been revised so as to incorporate significant books recently published.

This volume, like the two earlier editions, is designed to meet the requirements of the general reader who desires a comprehensive view of the state's history within reasonable compass. I have also tried to write a book that may serve as a text for college courses in North Carolina history. For the student and the general reader, it is hoped that the Chapter Bibliographies on pages 729–66 may point the way to more extended studies.

A modern, scholarly, up-to-date history of North Carolina must include developments in agriculture, industry, transportation, communication, trade, education, literature, religion, and social life, as well as the state's military and political history. I have therefore tried to present a balanced narrative of the state and its leaders in every field but above all else to show how the millions of North Carolinians have lived and made a living during the course of three centuries.

North Carolina has never lived to itself. From its first discoveries by the French in 1524 and the Spanish two years later, and from the first English efforts to plant a colony in the New World—at Roanoke Island in 1585—North Carolina's history has been a part of the history of Western civilization. Before 1776 North Carolina was a colony in the British Empire. Since that date it has been part of the American Union—with the exception of a short period, 1861–65, when it was a member of the Confederate States of America. Therefore I have attempted to portray the role of North Carolina and its people in national and international affairs—a role more significant than many North Carolinians realize. But I have not overlooked the historic role of the state's component parts—its counties, towns, and cities; its educational and religious institutions; its political parties and governmental agencies at all levels.

I am indebted to literally hundreds of authors and editors, living and dead, who have published books and articles relating to North Carolina. Many of these are listed in the Chapter Bibliographies. I am also indebted to a number of authors of unpublished theses and dissertations at The University of North Carolina and Duke University.

Space does not permit me to name all the people who rendered assistance in the preparation of this revision. I am deeply indebted to scores of individuals who answered countless letters I wrote in an effort to get the most up-to-date facts about North Carolina. This is particularly true of the many dedicated public servants in the state government who supplied me with reports of various governmental agencies.

I owe a debt of gratitude to Jerry C. Cashion and Michael G. Martin for pointing out errors in the second edition and to William S. Powell for many valuable contributions to this revision.

Acknowledgments are made to Denoyer-Geppert Company and the World Book Company (now a part of Harcourt Brace Jovanovich, Inc.) for permission to reproduce maps that had been prepared by the late Albert Ray Newsome and published in the *North Carolina Social Science Maps* and *The Growth of North Carolina.*

Acknowledgments are also made to Dena Neville, Robin Melton, Dianne Taylor, Mrs. Linda Stephenson, Mrs. Hallie Allen, and Mrs. Erline Nipper for their assistance in typing the manuscript.

I owe much to the tolerance and patience, and even more to the active assistance of my wife, Ida Pinner Lefler, who listened, read proof, helped with indexing, and in every way shared the strains and pangs of authorship. I am solely responsible for any errors of fact or interpretation which may appear in the volume.

Hugh T. Lefler

NORTH CAROLINA

Chapter 1

EXPLORATIONS AND
ATTEMPTS AT SETTLEMENT

The founding of North Carolina was not an isolated event. It was simply a step in the discovery, exploration, and settlement of the New World. The discovery of America by Columbus in 1492, followed by the Papal Bull of 1493 and the Treaty of Tordesillas between Spain and Portugal in 1494, granting a virtual monopoly of the Western Hemisphere to Spain, aroused interest and envy in England and France, which were just beginning to emerge as national states. Neither of these nations paid much heed to the Spanish monopoly and they did not hesitate to send out explorers to emulate Columbus.

In 1497–98 John Cabot, sailing under a charter granted by Henry VII, discovered North America, thus giving England its claim to the New World. Some writers have claimed that Cabot touched the Carolina coast, but it is almost certain that he never sailed south of New England, and probably not south of Nova Scotia or Labrador. England failed to follow up his discovery by actual settlement and almost a century elapsed before English colonization began.

French Exploration of the Coast

The first European who is known to have explored the coast of present North Carolina was Giovanni da Verrazzano, a Florentine navigator in the service of France. In 1524 Verrazzano explored the North Carolina coast from Cape Fear northward to present Kitty Hawk (he called it Arcadia), and on July 8 of that year sent to Francis I the "earliest description known to exist of the Atlantic coast north of Cape Fear." This account was published in 1582 in Richard Hakluyt's *Divers Voyages touching the Discoverie of America and the Islands Adjacent* and probably influenced Walter Raleigh in formulating his plans for "planting the English nation" in the New World.

Verrazzano's narrative, like most promotional literature of the time, gave

3

an interesting but somewhat exaggerated description of the country, with its "faire fields and plains," its temperate climate and "good and wholesome aire," its huge and beautiful trees—"greater and better than any in Europe," its "sweet and odoriferous flowers," its great bounty of game and fowl of every kind, and its natives who were "charmed by their first sight of white men." Verrazzano concluded that the country was "as pleasant and delectable to behold, as is possible to imagine."

Despite this glowing report of North Carolina's first press agent, France was too busily engaged in European politics, diplomacy, and war to undertake colonization. In the 1560s, however, two unsuccessful efforts, under the leadership of Jean Ribaut and René de Laudonnière, were made to plant French colonies in the present South Carolina–Florida area, after which France shifted its colonizing efforts to Canada, the Mississippi Valley, and Louisiana, placing major emphasis on fisheries and fur trade rather than on agriculture.

Spanish Exploration and Attempted Settlement

Spain was the most active and persistent nation in the early exploration of what is now North Carolina and the South Atlantic region generally. In 1520 Pedro de Quexoia led an expedition from Santo Domingo to the Carolina coastal area. One distinguished member of this expedition was Luís Vazquez de Ayllón, Spanish official, slave trader, and explorer. In July, 1526, a group led by Allyón consisting of over five hundred men, women, and children, including a few Negro slaves and ninety horses, entered the "Río Jordán" and planted a colony. There is some doubt as to the exact location of this river, but Ayllón's own description of the coast and the entrance to the river, with other observations, indicates clearly that it was the Cape Fear. As the expedition entered the mouth of the river a ship was wrecked; one was built to replace it and a second was also built, probably the first ships built by Europeans in what is now the United States. The rest of the history of this short-lived colony is a story of disappointment, illness, mutiny, and failure. The large number of deaths from fever and starvation caused Allyón to move the colony southward to a place called San Miguel de Guadalupe, in present South Carolina. But disease and starvation continued to take their toll, and after Ayllón's death on October 18 the colony, now reduced to about 150 persons, returned to Santo Domingo.

Spanish Exploration of the Mountain Region

In 1540 Hernando de Soto, marching northward from Florida in quest of "gold-bearing mountains" which the Indians had told him were to be found to the north, penetrated the mountains of southwestern North Carolina in present Jackson, Macon, Clay, and Cherokee counties, and on his trip westward crossed the Little Tennessee River, the first Mississippi tributary discovered by Europeans. In 1561 Angel de Villafañe led a Spanish expedition from Vera Cruz as far north as Cape Hatteras, but this expedition was "driven in distress" to Santo Domingo. In 1566–67 an expedition, led by Juan Pardo and Hernando Boyano, marched northward from the Gulf region and reached the mountains of North Carolina, establishing garrisons along their route. Left with one of these garrisons, Boyano explored the mountain area and then marched to the southwest, where he was joined by Pardo, and they both returned to the Gulf coast.

Spain made no further efforts to colonize the Carolina region, although the Spanish government later protested against English colonization of the area and made several unsuccessful attempts to destroy Engish colonies. Spain was too much interested in the gold and silver of Mexico and Peru and in the tropical and semitropical regions to the south to expend its efforts in colonizing what appeared to be an unprofitable country. As a Spanish writer declared, "To the South, to the South, lay the riches." So the Carolina country was left to the Indians and to eventual colonization by the English.

The First English Efforts to Plant a Colony in the New World

The first English colony planted in the New World was sent out by Walter Raleigh, soldier, courtier, historian, poet, and recipient of lands and other favors from Queen Elizabeth. Although his efforts to "plant the English nation" in the New World were doomed to failure, "the idea remained," and Raleigh has been justly called the "Father of English America," and Roanoke Island "the birthplace of English America." On March 25, 1584, Raleigh obtained a patent from Queen Elizabeth I—essentially a renewal of the 1578 charter to his older half-brother Sir Humphrey Gilbert—conveying to him, his heirs, and assigns the title to any lands that he might discover "not actually possessed of any Christian prince, nor inhabited by Christian people." Raleigh was authorized to plant colonies and to establish a government, in which the settlers were to have "all the priviledges of free Denizens, and persons native of England," but no laws could be passed "repugnant to the laws of England."

Walter Raleigh Sends Amadas and Barlowe Expedition, 1584

Raleigh's immediate interest was discovery, for he believed that men "would be well content to goe in the voyage if they might onely be assured that there is such a Countrey, & that their money would not be wasted to nothing in the preparations." Within a month after receiving his charter, he dispatched Captains Philip Amadas and Arthur Barlowe to explore the country and to recommend a suitable site for settlement. With the Portuguese Simon Fernández as pilot and "with two barkes well furnished with men and victuals,"

Arrival of the English at Roanoke

North Carolina Collection, The University of North Carolina at Chapel Hill

they sailed to the Canaries and thence westward along the same route which Columbus had followed, reached the West Indies, and then drifted with the Gulf Stream. On July 2, after a voyage of sixty-seven days, they came to "shole water" along the present North Carolina coast, where they "smelt so sweet and so strong a smel, as if we had bene in the midst of some delicate garden abounding with all kind of odoriferous flowers." After sailing along the coast for "a hundred and twentie English miles" before they could find a suitable entrance, they finally entered Pamlico Sound at Wococon (present Ocracoke Inlet), on July 4.

A few days later Barlowe and seven of his men "went twenty miles across the sound," where they came to an island, "which the Indians called Roanoke, distant from the Harbour by which we entered, seven leagues." One of the native chieftains, Granganimeo, received the whites cordially and "made all signs of joy and welcome, striking on his head and breast and afterwards on ours, to shew wee were all one, smiling and making shewe of the best he could of all love and familiarities." When the English group visited one of the nearby villages, they "were entertained with all love and kindness, and with as much bounties after their manner as they could possibly devise."

Barlowe's Glowing Report about the Roanoke Island Region

Amadas and Barlowe were favorably impressed by what they saw and they "fell to trading with them," exchanging tin dishes, copper kettles, and other English articles for "Chamoys, Buffe, and Deere skinnes." After six weeks of exploring and trading the group returned to England, carrying "two of the Savages being lustie men, whose names were Wanchese and Manteo," as well as a bracelet of pearls for Raleigh. Soon after their arrival Barlowe wrote a glowing report to Raleigh, describing the soil as "the most plentifull, sweete, fruitful and wholsome of all the world," containing the "highest and reddest Cedars of the world," and inhabited by "the most gentle, very handsome and goodly people," who were "loving and faithful, voide of all guile and treason, and such as live after the manner of the golden age."

Barlowe's report was received enthusiastically by Raleigh, Queen Elizabeth, and others interested in "planting the English nation" in the New World. Raleigh was knighted and the land was christened "Virginia," in honor of the unmarried Queen.

About this time the younger Richard Hakluyt prepared a paper for Raleigh's guidance in planting a colony and portrayed for him a settlement of the English in Virginia, which would make Englishmen "lords of navigation," and which would eventually produce grapes for wine and raisins; sugar to relieve England of "a dependence on infidels or our doubtful friends"; olives for oil; anil, woad, saffron, and madder for dyes; silk, flax, and hemp for textiles and cordage; citrous fruits, and many other desirable commodities.

The First English Colony in the New World: The Ralph Lane Colony

Raleigh was enthusiastic about the prospects. He had no difficulty in procuring "a fleet of seven ships well stocked and manned" for his "first colony." The Queen supplied one ship and one of her "Principal Secretaries of State," Sir Francis Walsingham, among others, subscribed money for the undertaking. The expedition of 108 men—no women and children—sailed from Plymouth on April 9, 1585, under the command of Sir Richard Grenville, a cousin of Raleigh's, with Ralph Lane as "lieutenant governor," and Philip Amadas as "Admirall of the Country." The group included John White, a "skillful painter"; Thomas Hariot, preacher, scientist, and Raleigh's tutor in mathematics; and Thomas Cavendish, the "boy wonder," who later circumnavigated the globe. It also included Manteo and Wanchese, but not Barlowe. The fact that apothecaries, a physician, a metallurgist, and several other specialists were also members of the colony is shown in Lane's letters of August and September. Fourteen of the group had the title of "Master" and several had studied law at the Inns of Court—excellent education, to be sure, but not essential training for the conquest of the American wilderness. The rank and file of the "Roanoke Hundred" had probably served in the army.

The expedition came by way of the West Indies. Calls were made at Puerto Rico and on the north side of Hispaniola, where the group bargained for "horses, mares, kine, buls, goates, swine, sheepe, bull hides, sugar, ginger, pearle, tobacco, and such like commodities of the Island." The records show that sugar cane was planted soon after the arrival at Roanoke.

Lane's Report about Roanoke Island

On July 27 the expedition reached Hatteras "and there rested." On August 17 it arrived at Roanoke Island, where Lane soon built "Fort Raleigh," modeled after a fort that he had previously constructed in Puerto Rico, and "sundry necessary and decent dwelling houses." These were not log cabins but were frame houses similar to those in England. On September 3 Lane wrote Richard Hakluyt the elder from the "New Fort in Virginia" the first letter in English from the New World. This letter, which was carried to England by Grenville, who left Roanoke Island about this time, said: "We have discovered the maine to be the goodliest soile under the cope of heaven, so abounding with sweete trees, that bring sundry rich and most pleasant gummes, grapes of such greatnes, yet wild, as France, Spaine, nor Italy hath no greater, so many sorts of Apothecarie drugs, such several kinds of flaxe, & one kinde like silke. . . . For this alreadie we find, that what commodities soever Spaine, France, Italy, or the East parts doe yeeld unto us in wines of all sortes, in oiles, in flaxe, in rosens, pitch, frankensence, currans, sugers, and such like, these parts do abound with ye growth of them all, but being Savages that possess the land, they know no use of the same. And sundry other rich commodities, that no parts of the world, be they West or East Indies, have, here we finde great abundance of."

But Lane exaggerated the wealth of the country, and his men spent too much time and energy in their quest for gold, for a better inlet, and for a passage to the South Seas, and too little time in cultivating the soil and building houses. Lane considered the exploration of the mainland to be his primary task, and one of his parties penetrated the wilderness about 130 miles west and northwest from Roanoke Island. This group explored the Chowan River region and spent some time among the Chowanoc Indians.

Problems of the Settlers

The colony was beset with problems from the start. It suffered from friction among the leaders, Indian hostility, and scarcity of food, tools, and articles necessary to establish settlement on a sound basis. Lane and Grenville were jealous of each other's powers; they had quarreled on the way over and their animosities seemed to increase after landing. Lane finally wrote to Walsingham complaining about Grenville's conduct and saying that he desired to return to England "to be freed from that place where Sir Richard Grenville is to carry authority in chief." This feud ended when Grenville returned to England for supplies. But his departure did not solve all the governmental problems. As governor, Lane was virtually a dictator, and he "set down a discipline which was severely executed." He might have had an informal council, but there are no records of its meeting. In fact, the colony was operated as a semimilitary community, in which the settlers received no individual land grants, and in which they were supposed to labor as paid servants for the commander, Lane.

The problems of "supplies" plagued the colony from the outset. Hariot, in his famous *A Briefe and True Report of the New Found Land of Virginia* (London, 1588), says that when they landed they had only a twenty days' supply of food, a scarcity of clothes, and the lack of "English means for the taking of beasts, birds, and fowl." When some of the settlers could not find gold or silver they "had little or no care for any other thing but to pamper their bellies . . . that lacking fair houses, dainty food, and soft beds, the country was to them miserable." But somehow the colony "managed to pull through the winter," largely because of Indian assistance. In the spring the settlers "sowed, planted, and set such things as were necessary for their relief in so plentiful a manner as might have sufficed them two years without any further labor, and by June the corn would have been ready to harvest." Hariot's little volume, the first book in English by an eyewitness describing an area of part of the present United States, was rushed into print to aid Raleigh in procuring men and money for another expedition before the expiration of his charter.

The Lane Colony Returns to England with Sir Francis Drake, 1586

Before the harvest time of 1586 Indian animosity and hostility had become very serious. As David B. Quinn says in his *Raleigh and the British Empire,* "The settlers had been acceptable as temporary god-like visitors in 1585; in 1586 they had become men who threatened the security of Indian society and aroused savage cupidity by their wealth." The feeling of resentment was accentuated and aggravated by the killing of a native by one of the settlers for the theft of a silver cup. Rumors instantly began to fly that Wanchese was planning a general massacre of the whites. By this time supplies were perilously low and the colony was faced with famine. As luck would have it, at this critical juncture Sir Francis Drake's fleet appeared off the coast. Learning the plight of the settlers, he offered Lane ships to be used in case the colony later found it necessary to return to England. Lane was inclined to accept this offer and remain at Roanoke Island, but a serious storm caused him to change his mind and he decided to take the whole group back to England with Drake. Thus the first English colony in America ended after about ten months of bitter experience.

Arrival of the Grenville Expedition, 1586

An advance ship arrived within a few days after the colony's departure, and two weeks later a number of English ships (three, or perhaps more), outfitted by Raleigh and commanded by Grenville, arrived with supplies and additional men. Grenville searched in vain for the settlers and then set sail for England, leaving behind eighteen men "furnished plentifully with all manner of provisions for two years," in order to hold England's claim to the land—probably a foolish decision, in view of the obvious Indian hostility.

Historical Significance of the Lane Colony

Though Lane's colony had failed, it was not without historical significance. Besides being the first English colony in the New World, it resulted in Hariot's informative book about "Virginia" and in seventy-five surviving famous paintings of Indians, fish, birds, and the like by John White. According to some writers, it also led to the introduction into England of tobacco, potatoes, and corn, but historical records indicate that tobacco was already well known in England, and it is likely that the other products were also known in a limited way.

The John White Colony

Raleigh was determined to send out another colony as quickly as possible, in spite of the efforts of some of Lane's men to thwart this promotional effort. But his "second colonie" was to have a different type of organization and a more specific objective. Since Raleigh's personal fortune was being rapidly dissipated, he associated with him nineteen merchants and thirteen gentlemen of London as "adventurers" on a joint-stock basis. The semimilitary organization was abandoned, and lands were to be allotted to settlers—five hundred acres each, and larger tracts if additional investments were made. The colonists were to take their families, work farms, and develop a settled community life. Raleigh appointed John White as governor and "also appointed unto him twelve assistants, unto whom he gave a Charter, and incorporated them by the name of 'Governor and Assistants of the Citie of Ralegh in Virginea.' "

This colony, which consisted of about 110 settlers, including 17 women and nine children, was instructed to go by the West Indies to replenish its water supply and to collect plants and livestock for the colony; then to sail for Roanoke, pick up the eighteen men left there by Grenville, install Manteo as

Raleigh's representative there, and proceed to deep water on Chesapeake Bay to establish a fort and settlement—as Hakluyt and Lane had previously suggested. Very few of those who had been in the Lane colony were in the expedition. They had had enough.

Raleigh's "second colonie" experienced various misfortunes on the long trip over, which White, in his narrative, attributed to Fernández, master of the *Admirall* and commander of the fleet, who "frequently and lewdly attempted to bring the colony to disaster"—a strange charge, in view of the fact that Fernández was an investor in the enterprise. The expedition arrived off Hatteras, July 22, 1587, and proceeded to Roanoke Island, where White found the houses built by Lane still standing, the fort in ruins, but no sign of the eighteen men left by Grenville except some skeletons and footprints—which might have been those of Indians. According to White, Fernández refused to transport the colony to Chesapeake Bay and "it booted not the governor to contend with him." Whereupon White put his men to work rebuilding the fort and "repayring houses and building new ones."

The Baptism of Manteo and the Birth of Virginia Dare

Within a few weeks two dramatic incidents occurred. Manteo, the "friendly Indian," was baptized and made "Lord of Roanoke and Dasamonguepeuk"—the first recorded Protestant baptismal service in the New World and also the first title of nobility ever granted an American Indian. The best-known incident in the history of the colony was the birth, on August 18, of Virginia Dare, daughter of Ananias and Eleanor White Dare, granddaughter of Governor White, and the first child of English parents born in America. A child was also born to Mr. and Mrs. Harvie, but history has failed to disclose its sex or first name.

Problems of the Settlers

For a short time the colony seemed to be faring well. There was no friction in the government; little time was spent in the quest for gold and silver, or in exploration. There were some minor difficulties with the natives, and George Howe was slain by them. It was too late in the season to plant and harvest crops, and by mid-August supplies had begun to run low, whereupon "the whole company both of the Assistants and the planters came to the governor, and with one voice requested him to return himself into England, for the better and sooner obtaining of supplies, and other necessaries for them." White was not eager to leave the colony, but he was finally "constrayned" to do so, sailing on August 27, but not until after he had obtained a written "bond" from the settlers, safeguarding his own personal property. Shortly before he sailed, the settlers notified him of their intention to move some distance into the mainland, probably about fifty miles, promising that they would leave a sign indicating their location and, if in distress, they would "carve over the letters or the name a Cross † in this forme."

Governor White Fails to Find the "Lost Colony"

White reached England in November, 1587, at the time of a threatened Spanish attack. The following spring Raleigh fitted out a small fleet, commanded by Grenville, to send to Roanoke Island, but the Crown impressed all ships before he could sail. In April of the next year White sailed but was forced back by French ships; he met with the same fate the following year. It was not until August, 1590, that he finally reached Roanoke Island. He found "the houses taken down and the place very strongly enclosed with a high palisado of trees." At the fort he found "many barres of Iron, two pigges of lead, four fowlers; Iron, sacker-shotte, and such like heavier things throwen here and there, almost overgrown with grasse and weedes." About the only traces of the settlers were a few pieces of broken armor and the word "Croatoan" carved on a tree and the letters "cro" on another tree, but with no cross indicating that the settlers were in distress. The colony thus passed out of history, but not from the field of historical speculation.

The Fate of the "Lost Colony."

The fate of the Lost Colony is an intriguing and unanswerable question that has been a favorite subject of romantic antiquarians for centuries. More has been written about Virginia Dare than any other girl in North Carolina history, and the "Lost Colony" has been the theme of articles, books, and plays, and of Paul Green's symphonic drama produced annually at Manteo on Roanoke Island. Some writers have contended that the settlers—or a majority of them—were killed by the Indians; others that they mingled with the natives and that the Lumbee Indians (once known as Croatans) of present day Robeson County are their descendants. Still others have maintained that the Spaniards from Florida destroyed the colony, and there is ample documentary evidence to indicate that the Spanish officials at St. Augustine planned to do just that. One of the most plausible theories—though seldom advanced by writers—is that the group, finally despairing of relief, sailed for England in a boat or boats that had been left with them by White in 1587, and were lost in the Atlantic.

Virginia and North Carolina historians of the early seventeenth century believed that a remnant of the colony was still alive. John Smith, in his *True Relation,* published in 1608, and William Strachey, in his book published a few years later, said it was reported in Jamestown that Powhatan had murdered most of the Roanoke settlers, but that a small number (Strachey says seven) had escaped and had fled to the Chowan River, where they were "preserved by a local chieftain." John Lederer, who made explorations from Virginia into North Carolina in the 1670s, heard about the descendants of the Lost Colony, and commented on their beards, which were not worn by full-blooded Indians. The Reverend John Blair mentioned the Lost Colony in his report of 1704, and about the same time John Lawson wrote that he had met some "Hatteras Indians" who told him that "several of their ancestors were white people."

Significance of Raleigh's Efforts to Plant a Colony

Raleigh had failed to plant a permanent colony in America, thus losing both political prestige and a considerable portion of his fortune—though not all, as some writers have claimed. But his efforts and the publicity given to them by the two Richard Hakluyts and other writers stimulated English interest in the New World and convinced the Crown, as well as many officials, merchants, and others that the Spanish monopoly of the New World could be broken. As Justin Winsor has said, "Baffled in his efforts to plant the English race upon this continent, he yet called into existence a spirit of enterprise which first gave Virginia, and then North America, to that race, and which led Great Britain from this beginning, to dot the map of the world with her colonies."

Permanent English Colonization: Jamestown, Virginia, 1607

Raleigh's failure convinced English leaders that it would take more than the fortune of one man to procure the necessary funds for colonization. Accordingly, the Virginia Company of London was chartered in 1606, and this joint-stock company, organized on the modern corporate principle of limited liability, promoted the establishment of the first permanent English colony in the New World, that at Jamestown, Virginia, in 1607. It is worthy of note that ten of the stockholders of this company had been associated with Raleigh in his last Roanoke Island venture, and also that the first permanent settlers in the North Carolina region some decades later came from the expanding Virginia colony.

Expansion of Settlement from Virginia into the North Carolina Region

Most of what is now North Carolina and all of the Albemarle Sound region were included within the Virginia charter boundaries of 1606 and the expanded grant of 1609, but some years elapsed before Virginia had the desire or need to settle its "southern confines." As early as 1609 a few individuals had pushed westward and southward from Jamestown into the Nansemond River Valley, which borders present North Carolina. As the Jamestown colony began to recover from the "starving time" of 1609–10, and after it had discovered its "gold mine" in the form of tobacco, about 1612, population began to grow and expand. Within a short time most of the good land next to navigable streams was taken up, and complaints were being made about soil exhaustion. The desire for "fertile bottom lands" and fresh hunting grounds caused explorers, hunters, traders, and farmers to follow the streams of southeastern Virginia into the Chowan River–Albemarle Sound area. This movement was a gradual process, and the exact date of its beginning is obscure. The first recorded expedition was made by John Pory, Speaker of the famous first legislature of 1619 and secretary of the Virginia colony, who, in 1622, made a sixty-mile overland journey as far south as the Chowan River through a "very fruitful and pleasant Country, yielding two harvests in a yeere and found much of the silke grasse formerly spoken of Was kindly used by the people and so returned." This region was already attracting some attention in England, for on October 30, 1629, Sir Robert Heath, the Attorney General of Charles I, was granted "A certaine Region or Territory" between 31 and 36 degrees north latitude, and from sea to sea, which was to be incorporated into the "Province of Carolana" ("Land of Charles"). This patent, like most colonial charters, stated the motives for colonization—"a certaine laudable and pious desire as well of enlarging the Christian religion as our Empire & encreasing the Trade & Commerce of this our kingdom."

The question was raised by some leaders of the Virginia colony—and by some historians later—as to whether the king had the legal right to grant land which had been included in the earlier Virginia charters. The answer is that he did, because at the time of the transfer of the Virginia colony to the crown in 1624, all ungranted lands reverted to the crown. So Charles I was within his rights in granting Carolana to Heath in 1629, and Maryland to Lord Baltimore in 1632.

The Heath Charter of 1629

The Heath patent, like the Carolina charter of 1663, was a proprietary grant, using the County Palatine of Durham, England, as a prototype, in which the proprietor was "to have exercise use & enjoy in like manner as any Bishop of Durham within the Bishopricke or County palatine of Durham in our kingdome of England ever heretofore had held used or enjoyed or of right ought or could have hold use or enjoy."

Heath failed to settle his extensive grant and in 1638 he assigned it to Henry, Lord Maltravers, whose plans to colonize failed to materialize. Meanwhile hunters, trappers, and traders continued to filter into the region from Virginia. In 1646 Governor William Berkeley sent two expeditions against the Indians of the Albemarle Sound region—one led by Richard Bennett and the other by Colonel Thomas Dew.

A 1649 Account of the Albemarle Sound Region

The following letter of an anonymous "well-willer," which appeared in *The Moderate Intelligencer* in London, April 26, 1649, is the fullest account of the Albemarle region before its permanent settlement:

"There is A Gentleman going over Governour into Carolana in America, *and many Gentlemen of quality and their families with him.*

"This place is of temperate Climate, not so hot as *Barbado's* nor so cold as *Virginia;* the Winter much like our *March* here in *England.* The Northern latitude begins where *Virginia* ends, at 37, neer Cape *Henry,* and takes in six degrees Southerly; no bounds to the East and West, but the Seas. At Point *Comfort,* neer Cape *Henry,* you enter into a fair Navigable River, called *James* River, about two leagues over: on both sides that River, are the chiefe Plantations in *Virginia,* and their chief Town *James* Town. On the South side of this River, are two Rivers, *Elisabeth,* and *Nansamond,* which convey you into *Carolana;* so that this River is a Haven to both Colonies. This *Carolana,* besides the temperature of the Climate, hath many native Commodities to feed and cloath the body: Deer in abundance, bigger and better meat than ours in *England,* having two young at a time; their skins good cloathing, being better dressed by the *Indians* than ours: Elkes of a large size, admirable meat, having three young at a time; their Hides make good Buffe; besides Hares and Conies, and many other that are good meat: Beasts of prey, that are profitable for their Furres, as Bevers, Otters, Foxes, Martins, Minches, and Musk-Cats, their Cods better sented than those of *East-India,* and more lasting: Fowle of all sorts, Partridges and wild Turkies 100 in a flock, some of the Turkies weighing 40 pounds, Fish there are in great abundance, of all sorts. In the Woods are sundry kinds of Fruits, as Strawberries, Raspices, Gooseberries, Plums, and Cherries; three several kinds of Grapes, large, and of a delicious taste. In these woods are herbes and flowers of fragrant smels, many kinds of singing Birds, which have varieties of sweet Notes. Though this Countrey be for the most part woody, but where the *Indians* have cleared, for their Corne and Tobacco, or where fresh marshes and medowes are, yet they are pleasant and profitable; pleasant, in respect of the stately growth and distance of the Trees one from the other, that you may travail and see a Deere at a great Distance; profitable, being of divers kinds, both for shipping, Pot-ashes, Mulberry trees for Silk-wormes, Walnut trees, and stately Cedars; so that when of necessity you must cut down for Building and other uses, you are recompenced for your labour. You have also many pleasant Ascents, Hills and Valleys, Springs of wholesome waters, Rivers, and Rivolets. Now you see you are plentifully fed and cloathed with the naturall Commodities of the Country, which fall into your hands without labour or toyle, for in the obtaining of them you have a delightful recreation. Now fearing you should out of this abundance, in the excess take a Surfer, you have many Physical herbs and Drugs, *Allom, Nitrum, Terra*

Sigillata, Tarre, Rosin, Turpentine, Oyle of Olives, Oyle of Walnuts, and other Berries; Honey from wild Bees, Sugar-Canes, Mulberries, divers sorts of Gums and Dyes, which the *Indians* use for paint. Within the ground, Mines of Copper, Lead, Tinne, Pearle, and Emroydes. Having the profit and pleasure of the natural Commodities, you shall see what Art and Industry may produce. The Soyle is for the most part of a black mould about two foot deepe. you may trust it with anything. The *Indian* Corne yeelds 200 for one, they have two Crops in six moneths; *English* Wheat, Barley, and Pease, yeeld 30 for one; Hempe, Flax, Rice, and Rape-seed have a large encrease: What *English* Fruits are planted there, improve in quantity and quality. Besides all this is said, we shall shake hands with *Virginia,* a flourishing Plantation, which is not onely able to strengthen and assist us but furnish us with *English* Provision, Cowes, and Oxen, Horse, and Mares, Sheepe and Hogs, which they abound in now, which they and other Plantations were enforced to bring out of other Countries with great difficulty and charge, these are ready to our hands."

Edward Bland's Description of "New Brittaine"

In 1650 Edward Bland, Virginia merchant and fur trader, conducted an expedition into the Chowan, Meherrin, and Roanoke River valleys and, to encourage the settlement of this region, published a promotional tract entitled *The Discovery of New Brittaine.* Bland had been most favorably impressed by the fine tobacco he had seen, sugar canes "twenty-five foot long and six inches round," silver and copper ornaments of the Indians, and the fact that "they have two crops of Indian Corne yearly, whereas Virginia hath but one." He contended that the settlement of "Virginia's Confines" and the conversion of the natives would be beneficial to Virginia traders, and he and his colleagues asked the Virginia legislature for permission to make settlements to the southward. This petition was granted on condition that Bland and his associates would "secure themselves with a hundred able men sufficiently furnished with Armes and Munition," but the records do not indicate that the proposed settlement was made.

Virginia Grants Land in the Carolina Region to Roger Green, 1653

Other Virginia settlers were interested in moving southward, among them Roger Green, "clarke" of Nansemond County, who, in 1653, obtained from the Virginia legislature a grant of ten thousand acres for the first one hundred persons who "should first seat on the Roanoke and on the lands on the south side of the Chowan." As "a reward for his own first discovery and for encouraging the settlement," Green was granted a thousand acres for himself. Documentary evidence does not indicate that Green's project materialized, though some historians believe that it did, and that the actual beginning of North Carolina settlement dates from this time.

In 1654 Francis Yeardley, son of George Yeardley, who had been governor of Virginia three times between 1618 and 1627, visited "South Virginia or Carolina" and wrote boastfully about its "most fertile, gallant, rich soil, flourishing in all the abundance of nature, especially in the rich mulberry and vine, a serene air, and temperate clime, and experimentally rich in precious minerals . . . and parallel with any place for rich land, and stately timber of all sorts; a place indeed unacquainted with our Virginia's nipping frosts, no winter, or very little cold to be found there."

Gradual Settlement of Albemarle Region by People from Virginia

If a 1654 estimate of Virginia's population at 22,000 is correct, it is easy to understand why many people were seeking new lands and economic opportunities in Carolina, Maryland, and elsewhere. By 1660 there seems to have been a steady flow of people from Virginia into what was later known as the Albemarle area, but it was "a movement so natural that the particulars are not recorded in the local annals of the time," and it is difficult to tell exactly when they came. Available records reveal that Nathaniel Batts, Robert Lawrence, Thomas Relfe, Samuel Pricklove, Caleb Calloway, George Catchmaid, John Jenkins, John Harvey, Thomas Jarvis, George Durant, and others had settled in the Sound region before the issuance of the proprietary charter of 1663. At least four of the above-mentioned settlers had brought slaves with them, for which they had been allowed the customary grant of fifty acres per slave.

Nathaniel Batts, the first known permanent white settler in North Carolina, in 1654 or 1655 built a two-room, twenty-foot-square home three miles south of the present Chowan River bridge in Bertie County. "Batts House" is shown on the 1657 Comberford map of "The South Part of Virginia."

The oldest known record of a land grant in North Carolina (found in the records of the county of Lower Norfolk, Virginia) is dated September 24, 1660, from the Chief of the Yansepin [Yeopin] Indians to Nathaniel Batts for "all ye Land on ye southwest side of Pascotank River from ye mouth of ye Sd River to ye head of New Begin Creeke." The oldest land grant on record in North Carolina (Perquimans County) is a deed made to George Durant, March 1, 1662, by "Kilcocanen, King of the Yeopin Indians" for a tract of land in Perquimans County. This deed reveals that there had been some grants earlier than this date, for it refers to previous land sales.

Chapter 2

NATURAL SETTING AND
NATIVE PEOPLES

North Carolina is divided into three rather clearly defined geographic areas: the Coastal Plain, the Piedmont Plateau, and the Mountains, each region having distinct physical features.

The Coastal Plain and Its Subregions

Almost two-fifths of the state's area lies within the Coastal Plain, extending from the Atlantic Ocean to the "fall line" of the Roanoke, Tar, Neuse, and Cape Fear rivers—a distance varying from 100 to 150 miles, and ranging in elevation from sea level to approximately 400 feet. This extensive area may be divided into two subregions, the Tidewater and the Western Coastal Plain. The Tidewater area, from thirty to eighty miles in width, is low and relatively swampy and extends westward as far as the effects of the tide are visible—roughly a line through Gatesville, Washington, New Bern, Jacksonville, Burgaw, and Wilmington. This area contains a large portion of the Dismal Swamp, many natural lakes, and several large savannas.

The "Graveyard of the Atlantic."

Along the coast for a distance of some 175 miles, there is a long chain of islands, or "banks," ranging in height from a few feet to that of Kill Devil Hill in Dare County, which is more than a hundred feet high. From these sandbanks along the coast three capes with awe-inspiring names jut out into the ocean: Hatteras, extending into the "Graveyard of the Atlantic," Lookout, near the entrance to the Beaufort–Morehead City area, and Cape Fear, at the entrance of the river leading up to Wilmington. Between the banks and the mainland proper are two large sounds, Pamlico and Albemarle, and several smaller ones, including Bogue, Croatan, Core, and Currituck—constituting the largest area of inland waters of any state along the Atlantic seaboard. A casual look at the map might indicate that this region would be ideal for navigation and commerce, but the sounds are shallow and the inlets to them—Ocracoke, Topsail, Oregon, and others—are shallow, shifting, and treacherous.

Most of the rivers of the Coastal Plain—the Chowan, Roanoke, Tar-Pamlico, and Neuse-Trent—empty into the shallow sounds, tending to make them steadily more shallow with sediment from the rivers and rendering them unfavorable for commerce. The only large river of this area—and of North Carolina—which flows directly into the Atlantic Ocean within the limits of the state is the Cape Fear, but the sediment deposited at its mouth to form Frying Pan Shoals has made a very dangerous entrance.

Influence of Geographic Factors on North Carolina History

Since the beginning of settlement, writers have commented about the dangers of the North Carolina coast. Over a century ago William Tatham wrote, "On this dangerous coast, beset in all directions with shifting sands and changing currents, all circumstances indicate that reliance on charts, no matter how accurately made, is unsafe." Collier Cobb, noted geologist, declared in the early part of this century, "It is impossible for mere man to overcome these ever-changing phenomena, unless he can control the movement of the sun and moon and nullify the law of gravitation." And in 1952 David Stick published an interesting book about shipwrecks along the North Carolina coast, entitled *Graveyard of the Atlantic.*

The treacherous coast and lack of good ports were major factors in diverting English colonization to the Chesapeake region after the failure of the Raleigh colonies at Roanoke Island. When permanent settlement of North Carolina began almost a century later, the absence of good harbors retarded colonization directly from Europe, and consequently the colony was settled largely "as an overflow from other colonies," notably Virginia, South Carolina, and Pennsylvania. These same geographic factors operated throughout the nineteenth century to the detriment of North Carolina's economic development, and even in the twentieth century the state is still trying to overcome these natural obstacles—by improvements in transportation by highway, rail, and air, as well as by the recent development of port facilities at Wilmington and Morehead City.

It has been truly said, "Nature, which decreed that commerce should not flourish in the Coastal Plain, quite as clearly dedicated that region to agriculture." Its relatively level and light soil was easy to cultivate. Its predominant forest tree, the pine, was easy to cut, which made it relatively simple to clear land for cultivation. The pine also furnished the basis for one of North Carolina's greatest industries before 1870, the production of naval stores. Abundant and well-distributed rainfall and a mild climate made the region well adapted

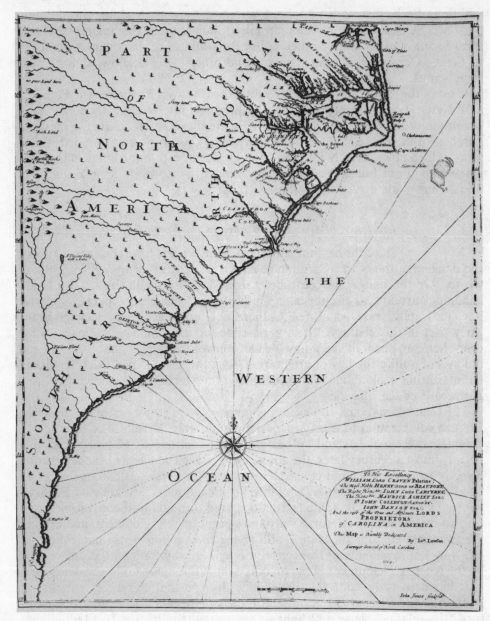

John Lawson's Map of Carolina, 1709

North Carolina Collection, The University of North Carolina at Chapel Hill

to agriculture, while the lack of water power and the scarcity of mineral resources retarded the development of manufacturing until the phenomenal development and use of electric power in recent years.

The North Carolina Piedmont

The Piedmont Plateau embraces almost two-fifths of North Carolina's area and has an average width from east to west of some two hundred miles, ranging in elevation from gently rolling country about 400 feet in height to rugged hills and small mountains of 2,700 feet (Pilot Mountain in Surry County and Pore's Knob in Wilkes County, highest in the Brushy Mountains.) Other small mountains in this area are South Mountain in Rutherford, Burke, and Cleveland counties; Sauratown Ridge in Stokes County, and the Uwharrie Mountains in Montgomery, Randolph, and Stanly Counties. The soil of the Piedmont region is of many types, but red clay predominates, and this makes the land more difficult to farm than the more porous soil of the Coastal Plain. The climate is mild but colder than that of the Coastal Plain; frosts are earlier, winters more severe, and the growing season from a week to a month shorter. The prevalent trees are hardwoods, though pines are abundant. The streams of the Piedmont are narrow, shallow, and swift—not well adapted to navigation and commerce, but excellent for the development of power. Almost from the start the region developed a diversified economy, and it is no accident that the leading manufacturing towns of North Carolina grew up in the Piedmont and that, in recent years, some 80 percent of the state's industrial plants are in that area.

Topography, soil, climate, forests, and other factors tended to retard the cultivation of large tracts of land and caused the Piedmont to develop as an area of small farms cultivated chiefly by white labor, and this led to the development of a more democratic social order than prevailed in the eastern portion of North Carolina.

Transportation Problems of the Piedmont

The major rivers of the Piedmont—the Yadkin, Pee Dee, Catawba, and Broad—all flow into the Atlantic within the borders of South Carolina. This fact has had significance. Lacking adequate water transportation, the early settlers developed a system of land transportation along the river valleys, and communication was largely along northeast-southwest lines, and not east-west to the Coastal Plain. The Piedmont, or "Back Country," was not settled by people moving up stream from the Coastal Plain, but by Scotch-Irish, Germans, Welsh, and others moving along the valleys from Virginia, Pennsylvania, and South Carolina. Once the region was settled, trade routes followed the valleys, and the chief markets for North Carolina Piedmont goods were

Charleston, Camden, Cheraw, Petersburg, and even Philadelphia. There were only limited commercial or social contacts with Edenton, New Bern, Wilmington, and other commercial communities in the Coastal Plain. As a western North Carolina farmer wrote in 1768, in protest against the construction of Tryon's "Palace" at New Bern, "Not one man in twenty of the four most populous counties [Mecklenburg, Anson, Rowan, and Orange] will ever see this famous house when built, as their connections and trade do, and ever will, more naturally center in South Carolina."

The Mountains

The third physical region of North Carolina embraces the mountains of the Southern Appalachians. It has been defined as a "steep, rugged escarpment rising suddenly above the Piedmont, extending from the irregular chain known as the Blue Ridge on the east to that long chain known under the various names of the Iron, the Smoky, and the Unaka Mountains on the west." This beautiful region, characterized by alternations of high mountains and deep valleys, covers an area of about six thousand square miles. It contains the largest area and the highest mountains of the Appalachian system, having forty-nine peaks over 6,000 feet high and 174 others over 5,000. Mount Mitchell, in Yancey County, 6,684 feet in elevation, is the highest peak in the eastern United States.

Wilderness Factors—Forests, Fields, and Streams

Though physiographic factors played a major role in the historical development of North Carolina, another very significant force, especially in early years, was the existence of an unbroken, unlimited, unknown, and mysterious wilderness, which "proved both a blessing and a curse" to the early inhabitants.

Early explorers and later visitors were impressed by the beauties, wonders, and abundance of this wilderness. Verrazzano, in 1524, was charmed by the "many faire fields and plains, full of mightie great woods . . . with divers sorts of trees, as pleasant and delectable to behold, as is possible to imagine." Barlowe, in his report to Raleigh in 1584, referred to the delicious odors of the bay trees, to the "highest Cedars of the world," oaks "farre greater and better" than any in Europe, and to pine, cypress, and other "sweet smelling timber trees." John Lawson, in 1709, and Dr. John Brickell, in 1737, spoke of the forest resources in glowing terms, and half a century later Janet Schaw, writing about the Cape Fear, said, "Nothing can be finer than the banks of this river; a thousand beauties of flowers and sylvan tribe hang over it and are reflected from it with additional lustre." She described the magnificent trees "which might adorn the palaces of kings," and "the noble Magnolias . . . infinitely more beautiful than one could imagine," which resembled "the Glory of a full spread oak covered with white roses."

Problems of Procuring Food, Shelter, and Clothing

The first problems confronting the early settlers were procuring food, clothing, shelter, and tools. After bitter experience they learned that only a few of their "supplies" could be obtained from England—for such obvious reasons as distance, slowness of transportation, smallness of ships, poverty of the settlers, and indifference of the people back home. Naturally the settlers came to depend upon the resources at hand, and they found that the wilderness could supply most of their needs.

The streams and forests furnished a great variety of food—fish, fowl, and game in vast quantities. Barlowe found the waters "alive with the goodliest and best fish in the world." The forests abounded with animals which the settlers found both useful and destructive—rabbits, squirrels, raccoons, beavers, foxes, buffalo, "the largest wild beast of the forest," "monstrous, strong, and swift" elk, deer "in great plenty," and bears, which were "very common."

The whole Carolina region was teeming with birds and wild fowl, especially turkeys "in flocks of 500 or more," pheasants, quail, the now extinct Carolina parakeet, wild geese, ducks, and wild pigeons so numerous that, according to Dr. John Brickell, they would fly "one flock after another for above a quarter of an Hour together," and, according to a Moravian diarist in 1753, a small group of hunters killed eighteen hundred in one day.

The woods and waters of North Carolina furnished an abundant supply of food, clothing, and building materials, without which settlement would have been almost impossible. As R. D. W. Connor says, "It was the presence of an unlimited food supply in the forests that enabled the pioneers to push out into the wilderness and prepare the way for civilization." There are many comments in contemporary writings such as that of the Moravian diarist that "a deer was killed and was very welcome . . . for we had little food left."

The clothing problem was also partially solved by the use of skins and furs, from which many useful articles were made—caps and hats from skins and furs of deer, raccoon, and beaver; shoes, gloves, and leggings, as well as robes, rugs, and bed covering from bearskins; lanterns and powder horns from buffalo horns; oil from bear's fat, and "incomparable fine candles" from deer tallow.

Forest Industries

"Forest industries," notably naval stores—tar, pitch, rosin, and turpentine—provided the leading export of colonial North Carolina. The production and export of boards, shingles, barrels, staves, and other products gave the colony high rank in the lumber industry.

Problems Caused by Birds and "Beastes" of the Forest

While the birds and "beastes" of the forest supplied much of the food and many of the necessities of the settlers, they also posed a problem for the farmer. Birds and fowl, especially wild turkeys, were "great destroyers of Pease, Wheat, and Indian Corn"; parakeets frequently ruined whole apple crops; foxes, raccoons, mink, weasels, and hawks killed many chickens; eagles were "very destructive of Poultry, Lams, young fawns, and pigs," and bears were "great devourers of Swine, and also of potatoes, which they could root out of the ground." A colonial writer estimated that "every grown wolf" did £20 to £30 damage to crops yearly.

The destructive habits of these animals and fowl were a constant source of concern to the people and to colonial officials. In 1736 Governor Gabriel Johnston devoted a great portion of his legislative message to this problem. Bishop Spangenberg, in 1753, declared that "wolves and bears must be exterminated if cattle raising is to succeed" in Wachovia. Laws were enacted to encourage the people to destroy these "pests" and rewards were offered for their "scalps," though this by no means "exterminated the vermin." Despite the destruction of crops, poultry, sheep, and swine caused by these birds and beasts of prey, the good seems to have outweighed the bad. The abundance of fish and game meant a great deal to the inhabitants of early North Carolina, and in modern times some portions of the state have become the "paradise of the hunter and fisherman."

In addition to the meat supply procured from the forests and streams, the woods and fields abounded in such wild fruits and berries as apples, peaches, pears, plums, damsons, and figs. Mulberries were used by the settlers in lieu of raisins; strawberries were found "not only large, sweet and good, but in as great plenty as in any part of the world"; blackberries and huckleberries were to be had almost everywhere and scuppernong grapes "in great profusion." Janet Schaw, in 1774, said "finer grapes cannot be met."

Timber Resources

The forests supplied abundant food for hogs, horses, cattle, and sheep—acorns, nuts, berries, and fruits—which enabled the people to raise large "droves of hogs" at small cost and to support livestock and cattle with a minimum of expense and trouble.

The forests also supplied the settlers with materials for houses and other buildings, furniture, carts, wagons, carriages, tools, and boats of various types. The predominant tree of the Coastal Plain, the pine, was the "most useful Tree in the woods." Pine and oak, of which there were eleven varieties, furnished most of the building materials—boards, clapboards, shingles, and staves—and barrels of various sizes and names. Red cedar, found in abundance, was used for sills and boards; cypress and cedar for cupboards, drawers, and chests; live oak, an extremely hard wood, for "Coggs and milles," walking sticks, mortars, and pestles; walnut, maple, sweet gum, and sycamore for "several domestick necessaries," such as "wainscot, Tables, Chairs, Trenchers, Desks, Stocks for guns and the like," maple for spinning wheels and flax wheels, and red cedar for caskets. Black dye was made from walnut, alder, and gallberry; yellow dye from certain wild flowers. Berries of bay and myrtle were used for making candles.

Shipbuilding

The vast amount of inland water navigable by small craft, plus the great abundance of shipbuilding materials and naval stores, led to extensive shipbuilding in early days. Brickell said that the planters "make very necessary Vessels for carriages of the commodities by water," and that "both sexes were very dextrous with canoes." Most of the sloops, schooners, brigs, brigantines, and other sailing craft were made of white oak timbers for the framework and flooring, while masts, spars, and yards were from tall straight pines or cedars. Live oak was used by some shipbuilders because it made "the best Trunnels of any oak in the world for ships and vessels of any sort." Cypress was used for many of the canoes, "periaugers," and flatboats used in river trade, because of its lightness and durability in water.

Minerals

North Carolina contains a little of nearly all the precious stones and minerals but not very much of any one. The state, which has been called "nature's sample house," is the only known source of hiddenite, a yellow-green gem. Although some three hundred kinds of minerals have been found within its boundaries—and at least seventy of them have definite economic value—the state, in recent years, has usually ranked about thirty-seventh in mineral production. Before 1860, however, it had a much higher rank in this respect, and was the leading "gold state" for half a century.

Early explorers in North Carolina were fascinated by the Indians' tobacco pipes "tipt with silver" and by the copper and gold ornaments they wore. The Lane colony of 1585 had reported the discovery of iron ore at two places, but it was not until 1729 that small shipments of the ore were made to England, and the development of iron mining did not occur for another century, and then only on a limited scale.

In the grant of Carolina to Robert Heath in 1629, the grantee, among other privileges, was to have the products of "all veines, mines or pits . . . of Gold, Silver, Jewels & Precious stones & all other things whatsoever, whether of stones or metalls." Despite this interest in gold, there is no authentic record of its discovery in North Carolina until 1799, when a seventeen-pound nugget was found on the Reed Plantation near present Concord. Between this date and 1860 over $50 million worth of this precious metal was mined in the state.

Copper was discovered by gold prospectors in the early nineteenth century. In 1820 Denison Olmsted reported the existence of coal in the Deep River area. The story of the exploitation of these resources, along with that of iron, manganese, tin, chromium, lead, zinc, nickel, and other minerals belongs to the nineteenth and twentieth centuries, as does the history of "non-metals," such as asbestos, barium, bromine, clays, and kaolin; feldspar, kyanite, lithium, limestone, marble, mica, tungsten, phosphates, and granite, other building stones, as well as crushed stone for highways.

The Indians of North Carolina

A major influence in the colonization of North Carolina and a significant factor at later periods of the state's history was the presence of the Indian.

The first description of an American Indian by an English writer is found in the report of Captain Barlowe to Walter Raleigh in 1584 and relates to the aborigines of North Carolina, whom he found in various portions of the region he visited. He described them as a "very handsome and goodly people, and in their behaviour as mannerly and civill as any of Europe." They were "well featured in their limbes . . . broad breasted, strong armed, their legs and other parts of their bodies well fashioned, and they are disfigured in nothing." This flattering description of their physique is borne out by the paintings of John White and the De Bry engravings of these paintings.

Sources of Information about Indians

Our knowledge of the North Carolina Indians in early days is imperfect, insufficient, and probably inaccurate. The natives had no written language and therefore left no written records. Our knowledge of them is drawn largely from the accounts of travelers, officials, missionaries, land speculators, and others who did not understand their spoken language, characteristics, customs, and institutions. But modern excavations of Indian villages (Keyauwee, near Asheboro; Saponi, near Spencer; Occoneechee, near Hillsborough; Saura, near Eden), mounds (notably Town Creek Indian Mound, near Mt. Gilead in Montgomery County), and burial grounds, resulting in the discovery of various types of Indian "relics," have thrown much light on the aboriginal population of North Carolina.

No census of Indian population was taken in the colonial era, but estimates of the number of tribes and total population were made from time to time by governors, missionaries, and such writers as John Lawson and Dr. John Brickell. Modern scholars have estimated that there were about thirty tribes and from 30,000 to 35,000 Indians at the time of the advent of the whites into the North Carolina region. Lawson listed twenty-nine tribes in 1709, but he added the comment that "there is not the sixth Savage living within two hundred Miles of all our Settlements, as there were fifty Years ago." And John Archdale, writing about the same time, said that "God sends war and sickness like an Assyrian angel" to destroy the Indians and "make room for the English."

Most Significant Indian Tribes

Of the various tribes, only five have been of particular significance in North Carolina history: the Hatteras, with whom the whites had their first contact; the Chowanocs, with whom the settlers had their first war, though a minor one; the Tuscarora, the largest, most important, and most warlike tribe of eastern North Carolina, numbering some six to eight thousand people, with whom the whites had the most deadly Indian war in North Carolina history; the Catawba, the most numerous and important of the eastern Siouan family in North Carolina, and the Cherokee, like the Tuscarora, of Iroquoian stock. The Cherokee, numbering perhaps twenty to thirty thousand in early years, as late as 1735 had "sixty-four towns and villages, populous and full of children." The whites had little contact with either Cherokees or Catawbas in the first century of the colony's history.

How the Indians Lived

The unit of Indian society was the tribe or "nation," apparently based on blood relationships. Each tribe had a chief or head man, sometimes called a king. For protection—and perhaps for social, economic, or religious reasons—the Indians lived in towns. John White mentioned twenty "villages" in the vicinity of Roanoke Island, and most of the later writers usually referred to "towns" or villages of the natives. The Indians lived in tents made of animal skins tied or woven together and usually round—not conical as tradition has it. In some tribes they had houses or huts, frequently built of cypress or pinebark. Sometimes several families lived in one house or tent. Cooking was crude and primitive. Meat was placed upon sharp sticks and broiled over the fire, and roasting food in hot ashes was a prevalent practice. "How They Build Boats," "How They Cook Their Fish," "How They Boil Meat," and "How They Eat" have been preserved for posterity by the paintings of John White. Food included meats of various kinds procured from the forest, particularly deer, bear, and rabbits, as well as birds, fowl, and fish.

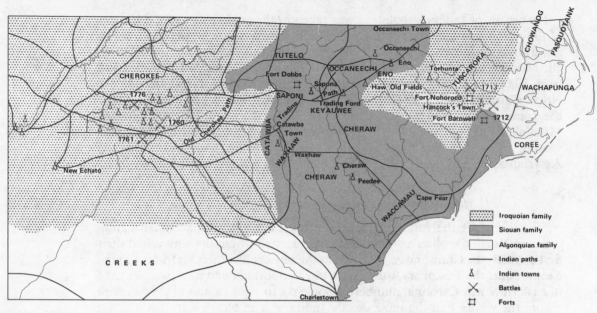

Indian Tribes of Carolina about 1700

Cartography by the Department of Geography and Earth Sciences
The University of North Carolina at Charlotte

In many of the tribes the women did most of the planting, cultivating, and harvesting of crops. They also cooked, made clothes, made mats and baskets from grass, reeds, and rushes, and cared for the children. Farm implements were crude affairs usually formed from wood or bone. Some of the Indians were skilful farmers. They grew corn, potatoes, tobacco, beans, peas, and many other vegetables. In fact, almost every vegetable that we know today was listed by John Lawson in 1709 in his account of the North Carolina Indians.

The primary pursuits of Indian men were hunting, fishing, and fighting. They hunted with bows and arrows, tomahawks, spears, knives, and clubs—later with guns procured from white traders. Boats were made of trees, hollowed out by burning and referred to by whites as "dugouts." The "medicine men" were skilled in the treatment of some types of illness and wounds with herbal medicines and by "conjuring." A few Indian villages had "sweat houses" (physiotherapy), and when smallpox epidemics raged, many Indians died because, after being sweated, they plunged into cold streams. As a rule, women were held in high esteem, monogamy being practiced by most tribes, but the Tuscarora were noted for their "trade women." William Byrd said that the services of an Indian female became an "economic necessity," and declared, "A Princess for a pair of Red stockings can't, surely, be thought buying Repentance much too dear."

De Bry's Engraving of a Painting of an Indian Village by John White

North Carolina Collection, The University of North Carolina at Chapel Hill

The Indians seem to have been very religious; they believed in a "Great Spirit" and a life after death spent in the "Happy Hunting Ground." A considerable number of natives were converted to Christianity and they took genuine interest in the "white man's religion," though they found it hard to reconcile Christian teachings and the settlers' actions.

Relations between Indians and Whites

At first relations between the two races in North Carolina were relatively peaceful, though there were occasional minor conflicts. But the aggressive, if not contemptuous, attitude of the whites and the resentment of the natives, together with conflicting and irreconcilable interests, made hostilities inevitable. The Indians faced the problem of survival, both as a people and as individuals. From the white man's point of view, it was a contest between "civilized man" and the "savage," between the "Christian" and the "heathen." Some white writers praised the physical prowess, courage, endurance, and patience of the Indians; others described them as filthy, cunning, treacherous, deceitful, and cruel. Lawson said that the Tuscarora were "proud, haughty, treacherous, and domineering," that they scorned to treat or trade with weaker tribes, but he added, "They are really better to us than we have been to them, and they always freely give us of their victuals at their quarters, while we let them walk by our doors hungry, and do not often relieve them. We look upon them with disdain and scorn, and think them little better than beasts in human form." Lawson, who held the Indians in higher esteem than other North Carolina writers of the time, was killed by the Indians soon after he had made this observation. Some of the white leaders considered the Indians as "vermin" to be exterminated along with bears, foxes, and other "beastes" of the forest. Legislative rewards were offered for Indian scalps, and Indian prisoners of war were usually sold into slavery.

R. D. W. Connor, at one time Kenan Professor of History at the University of North Carolina, truly said: "The Indians unfortunately took more readily to the vices than to the virtues of the whites. Contacts tended to brutalize both races but the Indians naturally suffered most." The whites taught the natives the use of "firewater"—an easy thing to do, introduced among them smallpox and other "white men's diseases" which they were unable to combat, enslaved many of their children, and "debauched their women."

The whites did not recognize Indian title to the soil, despite the fact that the British government insisted that Indian title to the soil must be "extinguished." The simplest way to carry out this mandate was to extinguish the Indian, and this is precisely what the whites proceeded to do. It has been aptly said that when the English landed in this country "they fell on their knees and then on the aborigines." The whites simply took over the lands which they desired, even though, in many instances, they did go through the formality of purchase or treaty. In addition to appropriating the lands, the settlers cleared the forests and exterminated many of the "wild beastes," thus destroying the basis of Indian civilization. Indian culture and European civilization were simply incompatible, and the former had to yield. As early as 1731 Governor Burrington reported that there were only six "nations" in the province, and of these the Tuscarora was the only one that numbered over twenty families. This report, of course, did not include the Catawba and Cherokee, who were located west of the then settled area. The role of these two tribes in North Carolina history will be treated in a later chapter.

Indian Contributions to White Civilization.

The Indians retarded and affected the course of settlement. They played a significant role in the fur trade, especially in its intercolonial and international aspects. From the natives the settlers learned the techniques of wilderness warfare, as well as the methods of fishing, trapping, and dressing skins and furs. The Indians taught the whites the methods of clearing land, hill cultivation, and fertilization, and contributed such crops as corn, tobacco, potatoes, various vegetables, and many varieties of fruits. Cultural contributions were made by the natives in the form of Indian words, myths, legends, and traditions. In the field of politics and diplomacy the role of the Indian was particularly important. Some Indians were friendly, or even "tributary" to the whites; others were "enemy Indians," like most of the Tuscarora. The attitude of the Indian was most significant in intercolonial relations, as, for example, in the dispute with Virginia over the boundary when it was charged, probably with truth, that Virginians were inciting the Indians of the disputed area to warfare against North Carolina. In the numerous international conflicts of the colonial era, it was a matter of grave concern whether the Indians were allied with the English, or with the French and Spanish.

In addition to Indian contributions to white culture mentioned above, a permanent influence of Indian civilization has been the preservation of hundreds of Indian place names—rivers, towns, and counties (eleven of the present one hundred). Except for the Cherokee, the Indians have disappeared from North Carolina, but "Their name is on your waters—ye may not wash it out."

Chapter 3
THE CAROLINA PROPRIETARY: ALBEMARLE COUNTY

The restoration of Charles II to the throne of England marked a turning point in both English and colonial history. The Age of the Restoration, 1660–85, was characterized by a great demonstration of national energy, intellectual progress, scientific advancement, expansion of the navy and merchant marine, virtual elimination of the Dutch as a commercial rival, and, above all else, a great expansion overseas. During the twenty-five-year reign of the "Merrie Monarch," England rounded out its North American colonies along the Atlantic seaboard by taking New Netherland from the Dutch in 1664 and filling in the gap from New England to the Chesapeake by founding the colonies of New York, New Jersey, Pennsylvania, and Delaware. South of Virginia English colonization extended into the Spanish-claimed region when Carolina was granted to the Lords Proprietors in 1663.

Charles II was happy to be on the throne and did not desire to "go on his travels again." But he was hard-pressed for funds and needed the financial backing and political support of prominent courtiers, merchants, and landowners. The proprietary grant of Carolina was a means of paying a political debt to those who had helped to restore the king and who might be counted on to keep him in power, and it was thoroughly in line with the colonial policy of British statesmen and mercantilist philosophy.

The Eight Lords Proprietors of Carolina

The eight grantees of Carolina were distinguished men. Edward Hyde, Earl of Clarendon, was Lord High Chancellor and the king's first minister; George Monck, newly created Duke of Albemarle, was Master of the King's Horse and captain general of all his forces; William, Earl of Craven, was an old soldier of the king and a man of great wealth; Lord John Berkeley was a member of the Privy Council and active in naval administration; Sir

32

William Berkeley, his brother, was then governor of Virginia; Sir George Carteret was a privy councillor, a vice-chamberlain of the household, treasurer of the navy, and famous for his defense of the Jersey Isles during the English Civil War; Lord Anthony Ashley Cooper, who later became the first Earl of Shaftesbury, was Chancellor of the Exchequer and member of the Special Council for Foreign Plantations, and Sir John Colleton was also a member of this body.

According to Charles M. Andrews, the proprietary grant of 1663 was not a voluntary act on the part of Charles II, but was "put through by others and assented to" by the king. Wesley Frank Craven maintains that Charles "probably opposed the grant but found this skilfully assembled group too many for him." These views have merit, for it is certainly true that all of the proprietors exerted influence on the formulation of colonial policies. The idea of the grant did not originate with the king, but with those of the proprietors who had been associated with "plantations" in America—Colleton, landowner and slave trader in Barbados; William Berkeley, landowner and governor of Virginia; Cooper, landholder in Barbados; and Clarendon, who held property in Jamaica. John Berkeley acted "as agent for the enlistment of more influential men" in persuading the king to make the grant.

Reasons for the Proprietary Charter of 1663

Besides any personal aims or ambitions Charles II might have had, there were at least four motives for issuing the charter: "a laudable and pious zeal for the propagation of the Christian faith," "the enlargement of our empire and dominions," the increase of English commerce—and the increase of the proprietors' fortunes. By the terms of the charter of March 24, 1663, "the true and absolute Lords Proprietors" were granted all territory lying between 36 and 31 degrees north latitude and extending westward to the South Seas (Pacific Ocean), to be held of the king "in free and common socage," for which a nominal payment of "twenty marks of lawful money of England" was to be paid the king annually, as well as one-fourth of all gold and silver found. Proprietary shares were "alienable and heritable." The proprietors were "to have, use, exercise, and enjoy" any power "any bishop of Durham in our Kingdom of England, ever heretofore have held, used or enjoyed."

The Carolina Charter of 1665

The boundaries of Carolina under the 1663 charter were not extensive enough to satisfy the proprietors, and at their "humble request" a second charter was issued by Charles II in 1665, which extended the boundaries one-half degree to the north and two degrees to the south. The boundary was extended northward largely to settle a dispute which had arisen over the Heath

King Charles and Some of His Friends at the Restoration

North Carolina Collection, The University of North Carolina at Chapel Hill

patent of 1629, and in order to place the Albemarle settlements within the limits of Carolina. The southward extension of the boundary far beyond Saint Augustine was a "thrust at Spanish Florida."

The English County of Durham: Prototype of Proprietary Colonies

The County Palatine of Durham served as the prototype for Carolina and all other English proprietary colonies. England simply adapted an old institution to the purposes of colonization. Early in English history the County Palatine of Durham had been created on the northern frontier, as a buffer against Scotland. Unlike the ordinary English shire, Durham was virtually autonomous, owing only nominal allegiance to the crown. The bishop, as ruler of the county, was supreme in civil and military affairs. He raised and directed his own military and naval forces, controlled the tax system, and enjoyed many feudal privileges. In payment for these special favors the bishop was obligated to protect England's frontier against the Scots.

Powers Granted the Proprietors

The proprietors of Carolina, enjoying the powers of "any Bishop of Durham," were granted "full power and authority" to create and fill offices, to erect counties and other subdivisions of government, to incorporate towns, cities, and ports of entry, to erect so many "mannors" as they should think convenient, to establish courts of justice for the punishment of offenders even to the extent of "member and life," to commute punishments and pardon offenses, to collect customs duties, fees, and taxes, to have "the advowsons and patronage of churches," to grant land, to confer titles of nobility—provided they were not the same as those used in England, to raise and maintain a militia and to commission its officers, build forts, suppress and punish rebellion, declare martial law, and wage war against the natives and other enemies by land and sea.

Limitations of Proprietary Powers

There were some significant limitations to the exercise of these vast powers. Laws were to be enacted only with the "advice, assent and approbation of the freemen, or the greater part of them, or of their delegates," and all laws must be "reasonable, and not repugnant or contrary" to those of England. Even more significant was the guarantee to settlers of the "liberties, franchises, and privileges of the king's subjects resident within the realm of England." The people were guaranteed rights of trade and freedom from taxation except "by and with the consent of the free people or the greater part of them." Although churches were to be "dedicated and consecrated according to the ecclesiastical laws" of England, the proprietors were authorized to grant liberty of conscience to all persons who should conform to the practices and beliefs of the Anglican Church.

The Problem of the "Heath Claimants" to Carolina

Within a few months after the issuance of the charter, the proprietors, who had already met and worked out plans for settlement of their grant, were confronted by claimants under the Heath patent of 1629. The Duke of Norfolk, son of Henry Maltravers, claimed that the "province of Carolina" had been assigned to his father in 1632, who in turn had assigned it to him. Likewise Henry Vassall claimed that a portion of Carolina had been assigned to him. These two claims were presented to the Privy Council on June 10, 1663, and after a thorough investigation of "all pretenders" by that body, of which Albemarle and Clarendon were key members, the council found that "no English whatsoever have, by virtue of any such Graunts, hitherto planted in the said Province, and that such Letters (if any were) are become voyd."

Proprietary Plans for Three Carolina "Counties."

The proprietors now had a clear title to Carolina, and in order to show the king that they "slept not with their grant," they made plans for the development of three "Counties": (1) Albemarle, which embraced "all that parte of the province which lyeth on the north east or starboard side entring of the river Chowan now named by us Albemarle river togeather with the Islands and Isletts within ten leages thereof;" (2) Clarendon, which included the lands south of Albemarle and extending into the Cape Fear Valley, and (3) Craven, covering the area south of Cape Romaine.

The early years of the Carolina proprietary were marked by discontent, confusion, ineffective government, and open rebellion. Some of the trouble and unrest was due to the fact that Carolina, unlike other colonies, was controlled by a proprietary board, which held meetings irregularly and which followed a vacillating policy. Most of the proprietors were busy with affairs of state and their personal interests and devoted little time or thought to their province. Only Cooper and William Berkeley took an active interest in Carolina, and that only for a limited time. Of the original grantees, Colleton died in 1666, Albemarle in 1669, and the five others within twenty years after the original charter of 1663. Craven lived thirty-five years after 1663 and was the only proprietor to outlive Charles II.

The "Declaration and Proposals to All That will Plant in Carolina."

Several of the proprietors, notably Cooper, were interested in governmental experiments, and plan after plan was tried and abandoned for some new scheme, with the result that "the inhabitants could not be sure that their government was stable." Shortly after the issuance of the charter, the proprietors began to negotiate with two groups of prospective settlers—one, a company of New England "adventurers" associated with a few men from England, and the other, a group of Barbadians. A petition from the latter, coupled with the eagerness of the proprietors to promote immigration, led to the "Declaration and Proposals to All that will Plant in Carolina." This proprietary document, which had particular reference to the settlement of Clarendon County, outlined the framework of government and laid down the conditions for granting lands. It has been called the "first organic law in Carolina." By its provisions, the "undertakers" of the colony, in advance of settlement, had to submit a list of thirteen names from which a governor and council would be chosen for a three-year term, after which their places would be filled "on nomination by the local freeholders." There would be an assembly, with power to pass laws with the consent of the governor and council, subject to proprietary approval. Lands would be granted on the basis of a headright—each undertaker receiving one hundred acres for himself, fifty additional acres for each manservant capable of bearing arms and equipped to do so, and thirty acres for each woman servant. To stimulate immigration, men and women servants were to be given ten and six acres respectively at the expiration of their indentures. The colony was to finance its own administration out of revenues from quitrents, which were set at one half-penny per acre.

About this time William Berkeley, then governor of Virginia, was authorized by the proprietary board to "constitute and commissionate a governor for Albemarle River" and also to select "6 fitting persons to be of the Councill." The governor and council were to have the power to elect "all officers Military and Civil which shall be convenient and necessary," except the secretary and surveyors, who were to be proprietary appointees. The governor and council "by and with the advice and consent of the freeholders or freemen or the Major parte of them, their deputyes or delligates" were "to make good and wholesome laws ordinances and constitutions for the better Government," these laws to be transmitted to the proprietors within one year, pending which the laws would be in force.

A set of instructions to Berkeley in the same year stipulated the conditions for granting land, which were the same as those laid down in the Declaration and Proposals, except for one new feature. The governor was to have a monopoly of the fur trade in Albemarle, "if he could find no other means of support."

William Drummond Appointed Governor of Albemarle County

In October, 1664, Berkeley, acting on these orders and instructions, commissioned William Drummond, a Scottish merchant residing in Virginia, as "governor and commander in chief" of Albemarle County. This marks the beginning of government in Carolina. It was not until January 11 of the next year that the proprietors commissioned Sir John Yeamans as "Governor of the County of Clarendon near Cape Faire and of all that tract of ground which lyeth southerly as far as the River St. Mathias." But it was not until 1670 that Craven County was established in what later became South Carolina.

The proprietors were eager to promote settlement of both Albemarle and Clarendon counties and made many "proposals" to prospective settlers. One of the most remarkable documents issued by them was the "Concessions and Agreement," drafted in January, 1665, in consultation with Yeamans, and with particular reference to Clarendon County. According to this proposal, there were to be a governor, secretary, register, and surveyor general—all chosen by the proprietors. There was to be a council of any even number from six to twelve appointed by the governor and with its powers clearly defined in the document. A unicameral legislature, composed of the governor, council, and "twelve deputyes or representatives" chosen by the freemen, was to have vast powers. It could select its own time and place of meeting; pass all laws necessary for the government of the county; create courts and determine their jurisdiction, officers, and fees; levy all taxes; erect "barronyes" and manors; erect forts and "constitute trained bands"; make war and peace; pass naturalization laws, and prescribe the amount of land to be allotted to individuals. In language similar to the Maryland Toleration Act of 1649, no person was to be in any ways "molested punished disquieted or called in question for any differences in opinion or practice in matters of religious concernement."

The Short-Lived County of Clarendon

Immediately after the issuance of this liberal document, Yeamans assumed the office of governor of Clarendon County. Very little is known about this short-lived colony. In the fall of 1665 Yeamans landed a group of Barbadians at Cape Fear, but only after losing a ship at the river's entrance. This was but the beginning of Clarendon's misfortunes. Other immigrants were shipwrecked; there was friction between the first settlers and "newcomers"; the few New Englanders present made trouble; there was Indian hostility, and, most significant of all, there were reports by two explorers from Barbados, Robert Sandford and William Hilton, describing the more attractive Port Royal region to the south. Consequently Yeamans abandoned the colony, the proprietors closed the land office, and the settlers moved away—some to Albemarle, some to Virginia, and others to New England. At the time of Clarendon

County's demise in 1667, there were about eight hundred people in the area, and, according to Yeaman's report shortly before his departure, "prospects were good."

The Fundamental Constitutions of Carolina

The proprietors were unhappy about some of the provisions of the Concessions and Agreement, and they were disappointed at the abandonment of Clarendon and the slow growth of Albemarle. To promote settlement and to protect property rights, a new document was prepared for the government of Carolina. This was "The Fundamental Constitutions of Carolina," supposedly written by philosopher John Locke, Ashley Cooper's protégé, who served for a time as secretary to the proprietors.

The Fundamental Constitutions, or "Grand Model," which was dated July 21, 1669, was designed "for the better settlement of the Government of the said Place, and establishing the Interest of the Lords Proprietors with Equality, and without Confusion, and that the Government of this Province may be most agreeable to the Monarchy under which we live, and of which this Province is a part; and that we may avoid erecting a numerous Democracy." This language, as well as other details in the 120 provisions of the document, sounds more like Harrington's *Oceana* than like the later famous "Treatises of Government" by Locke. Yet the original draft of the first edition of this document is in Locke's handwriting.

Joseph Sabin erroneously called the Fundamental Constitutions "the first instrument ever digested and written out, for the entire and perfect government of a political body," while another writer described it as "the most elaborate of seventeenth-century blueprints for regulating the political, social, and religious affairs of colonial America." The document provided for a feudal system in which Carolina would be divided into counties, signories, baronies, precincts, and colonies held by a colonial nobility with curious titles, ranging from palatine to cacique. The proprietors and this nobility were to hold two-thirds of the land, and the rest was to be granted to settlers. Manors, owned by nobility and worked by "leet men" (whose status was perpetual), would be organized on the feudal pattern. Government would be in the hands of the proprietors, whose meetings were to be presided over by the eldest, known as "palatine." A "parliament," consisting of proprietors, nobility, and representatives of the people, was to be established. This was a cumbersome and complex system which might have worked in feudal Europe, but which was not adapted to a wilderness civilization. In spite of the fact that the document was declared to be "perpetual and unalterable," it went through five editions before being completely abandoned early in the next century.

Certain portions of the Fundamental Constitutions were put into effect. The Palatine Court became a reality and played an important—and disturbing

—role in the life of the colony. There were many "landgraves" and "caciques," especially in South Carolina, which had twenty-six of the former and thirteen of the latter. North Carolina had a few landgraves, among whom were Christoph Von Graffenried and Charles Eden.

In spite of its large number of impractical ideas, the Fundamental Constitutions contained many desirable provisions, such as that for registration of births, marriages, and deaths; registration of land titles; biennial parliaments; trial by jury; and religious toleration. John S. Bassett concluded: "Their reactionary features were hardly worse than their generation, and their liberal features were better than their time."

For more than thirty years the proprietors attempted to persuade the colonial legislatures formally to approve the Fundamental Constitutions. Meeting with repeated refusals, they instructed the governors to "come as nigh the Constitutions" as they could. But this did not work, and in 1693 the proprietors declared that the Constitutions "are now ceased." Yet five years later they reissued the document in abbreviated form, reducing the number of articles from 120 to 41.

Governmental Structure of Albemarle County

Although the government was legally headed by the eight proprietary offices provided for in the Fundamental Constitutions—palatine, admiral, chamberlain, chancellor, high constable, chief justice, high steward, and cacique, each of whom was supposed to have a court and also a deputy in Carolina—the actual government of Albemarle was vested in the governor and his council, chosen by the proprietors, in conjunction with the assembly, which was elected by the freeholders.

The Governor

The governors of Albemarle County, 1664–89, and of North Carolina, 1689–1729, were commissioned by the proprietors. Their terms of office were indefinite, though at first there seems to have been a general agreement on three years. Their salary was left to the local assembly, and was to be paid from the revenues from quitrents and land sales, with fees as an additional source of income. The governor had extensive executive, legislative, judicial, and administrative powers. He appointed the council and called and presided over its sessions. He appointed all judicial and administrative officers —including most of the local officials—administered oaths of office and allegiance, and issued and revoked military commissions. He could remove officials, without the council's consent, and could grant pardons and reprieves. He had power to summon, prorogue, and dissolve the assembly, and the right to veto any law. With the advice and consent of the council, he issued writs for election of delegates to the assembly. He also issued warrants for land grants; probated wills; conducted relations with other colonies, with Indian tribes, and with the mother country; headed the military and naval forces of the province; and exercised powers in church affairs.

The Council

The council assisted the governor in executive and administrative matters and sat with the elected members of the assembly as the legislature. Sitting with the governor, it constituted the highest court in the colony until the creation of a supreme court, near the turn of the century. At first the council had six members, then six to twelve, and then ten.

The Assembly

The popular or elective branch of the legislature went through several steps and name changes in its evolution. In the few pertinent documents of the late seventeenth and early eighteenth centuries it is consistently called the "House of Burgesses." By 1707 or 1708 the term "lower house" appears occasionally, but it seems to have been used in a descriptive sense at that time, not as an official name. By the middle of the 1720s, however, "House of Burgesses" and "Lower House" were used interchangeably, as if both were considered official names. Tradition has it that a legislative assembly of all the freeholders in Albemarle was held in 1664, but there are no records of such a meeting. Representative government actually began under the Concessions and Agreement of 1665, which provided that twelve men be chosen annually to sit with the governor and council as a legislature. This system prevailed until 1670, when Albemarle was divided into four "precincts"—Chowan, Pasquotank, Perquimans, and Currituck, each of which was allotted five delegates in the lower house.

Until about 1695, or perhaps as late as 1697, the elected representatives sat with the governor and council as a unicameral body, presided over by the governor or his deputy. After the adoption of the bicameral system, the lower house elected its own speaker and other officers, adopted its own rules of procedure, and exercised many "parliamentary privileges" similar to those of the British House of Commons, such as the right to expel members, enforce their attendance, decide contested elections, and initiate money measures. The House could meet only on the call of the governor and at a place designated by him, since there was no "fixed seat of government." In fact, the legislature was convened biennially, or oftener, because the governor was dependent on that body for his salary. The House was jealous of its "powers of the purse," and largely through this weapon increased its prestige and influence at the expense of the governor and council.

Executive-Legislative Conflicts

Controversies between the lower house, led by the speaker, who held the highest elective office in the government, and the "prerogative party," usually led by the governor, representing the royal prerogative, ran through the history of Albemarle County and through the whole of North Carolina's history to the Revolution. There were prolonged and bitter quarrels over the governor's salary, quitrents, land patents, rent rolls, taxes, paper currency, defense, selection of officials, location of the capital, and many other matters. The "popular party" won many of these contests and the lower house received quite a reputation for its independence. John Urmston wrote in 1717 that "this Lawless people will allow of no power or authority in either Church or state save what is derived from them," and Governor George Burrington declared in 1731, "The Assembly of this Province have always usurped more power than they ought to be allowed." Later he stated that "All the governors that ever lived in this Province lived in fear of the People (except myself) and Dreaded their Assemblyes."

The Court Structure

At the head of the judicial system, both of Albemarle County and later of North Carolina, stood the General Court, which at first consisted of the governor and council and was the appellate court of the colony. In 1685 the proprietors instructed the governor to appoint "four able discreet men" as justices for Albemarle, but as late as 1695 the governor and council were still acting as the highest court of the province. Sometime between that date and 1702 the court was organized as the proprietors had ordered. Finally, in 1712, Christopher Gale was appointed chief justice for North Carolina, holding his commission directly from the proprietors.

There was also a court of chancery, made up of the governor and council, which sat without a jury and probated wills, received and examined accounts of administrators and executors, tried public officials for malfeasance, and perhaps exercised other judicial functions.

Each precinct in Albemarle—and later in North Carolina—had a court, which was administered by the justices of the peace, who were appointed by the governor. The justices not only had limited civil jurisdiction—up to cases of £50 value—and criminal jurisdiction, but they also exercised many administrative powers, such as the creation of road districts; care of roads, bridges, and ferries; and the location of mill sites. The apportionment of taxes was made by the General Court. The executive officer of the precinct (and later the county) court was the provost marshal, an appointee of the governor. In 1738 the title of this office was changed to sheriff. There were also clerks of the precinct courts who kept the "marks" of livestock and did other clerical work.

The Problems of Albemarle County

With the demise of Clarendon County in 1667 Albemarle County remained the only organized government in the North Carolina region. The history of Albemarle as a distinct colony for the next two decades is a story of unrest, confusion, slow growth, and armed rebellion. There were many reasons for this unhappy state of affairs. In the first place, Albemarle was an isolated settlement, largely out of touch with the outside world. Communication by land was almost impossible except with Virginia, and even this was difficult because of forests, swamps, and rivers that made travel a "jungle experience." Albemarle waters admitted vessels of only light draft, and the other Carolina settlement on the Ashley-Cooper rivers was so far away as to be almost completely out of the picture. Secondly, the proprietors, unhappy about the slow growth of Albemarle—for which they were partly responsible—expended more thought, time, and money on the South Carolina settlement, after the founding of Charleston in 1670. They blamed the Albemarle people for their failure to expand southward and complained to the Albemarle legislature about its "people that neither understood your own nor regarded our Interests."

Proprietary Offers to Settlers

One of the most vexatious problems was that of land tenure. The proprietors had tried to formulate a land policy, and on several occasions instructed the governor and council on this matter. They had some maps prepared, the meaning of which they never properly appreciated, and they encouraged the publication of a number of promotional tracts, designed to counter the adverse reports being circulated about Albemarle. In 1666 *A Brief Description of the Province of Carolina* appeared, written at the proprietors' insistence by Robert Horne, who had never seen the country which he so eloquently described. The "fair and spacious Province" of Carolina was portrayed as a region of fertile soil, "freed from the inconstancy of the Weather," and "wonderfully healthy and fruitful," offering freedom from custom on certain articles for a seven-year period, land grants of a hundred acres to freemen, and lesser amounts to servants at the expiration of their indentures, the right of people to participate in making laws, and many other inducements.

In spite of these attractive offers, people did not move to the colony in large numbers. A major reason for this was the confusion and uncertainty about terms of landholding, and the first legislature of Albemarle petitioned the proprietors "praying that the inhabitants of the said County may hold their lands upon the same terms and conditions that the inhabitants of Virginia hold theirs." In Virginia quitrents were one farthing an acre, payable in produce, whereas in Albemarle they were one half-penny an acre, payable only in specie. In support of the Albemarle petition, Thomas Woodward, the surveyor-general, wrote the proprietors saying that the current land policy "discourages many who had intentions to have removed from Virginia hither . . . It bein Land only that they came come for."

The Great Deed of Grant, 1668

To alleviate this situation, the proprietors, on May 1, 1668, signed and sent to Governor Samuel Stephens, who had succeeded Drummond the previous year, a document henceforth known as the Great Deed of Grant, which superseded the land provisions of the Concessions and promised the Albemarle settlers that henceforth they would hold lands "upon the same terms and conditions that the Inhabitants of Virginia hold theirs."

Legislative Efforts to Promote Settlement

To implement this more attractive land policy, the Albemarle legislature of 1669 passed several laws designed to stimulate immigration and otherwise promote the colony's welfare. Tax exemption was granted to all "newcomers" for one year, and new settlers were to enjoy a five years' stay of all suits "on any debt or other cause of action" which had arisen outside the colony. The law which prohibited the ownership of more than 660 acres in one tract—but which did not apply to those receiving grants directly from the proprietors—was designed to democratize landholding, and probably to check speculation. "Strangers from other parts" were excluded from the Indian trade of the colony. As a recognition of the fact that there were no ministers in the province civil officials were permitted to perform the wedding ceremony, and marriage was made a civil contract.

Some of these statutes, notably the stay law, the marriage act, and the Indian trade law provoked Virginia authorities, who began to circulate disparaging remarks about Albemarle, calling it "Rogue's Harbor" and other unflattering names, overlooking the fact that the stay law was a verbatim copy of a Virginia statute of 1642.

Land Problems Retard Settlement

The Great Deed of Grant and the 1669 laws did not produce the anticipated results; they did not promote rapid settlement, and they failed to end land disputes. Although the settlers considered the Great Deed "as firm a document as the Proprietor's own charter from the Crown," the proprietors did not consider it irrevocable, and several governors, following proprietary instructions, raised rents to the old half-penny-an-acre level—or even higher. It was rumored that the proprietors "intended to raise quitrents to two pence and from two pence to six pence per acre." In 1676 Timothy Biggs wrote the proprietors that "the people have no assurance of their lands for that yet never any Patents have been granted under your Lordships to the Inhabitants is matter of great discouragement for men of Estate to come amongst us because those already seated there have no assurance of their enjoyment."

Promotional Literature

Again the proprietors resorted to promotional literature—and more exaggerated than before. In 1682 Joel Gascoyne published in London *A True Description of Carolina,* in which he said:

"The Heavens shine upon this famous Country the soveraign Ray of health; and has blest it with a serene Air, and a lofty Skie, that defends in from Noxious Infection; nor is there any known Distemper. . . . Moreover its a salubrious Air to the sick, and diseased; and a generous retirement to necessitous, and abject Families; as also the assurance of such as study to be rich."

In the same year "R. F." published *The Present State of Carolina,* describing its "florid, and fragrant fields, imbellish't with flowers, that perfume the air; whose sweet scituations, by reason of most delicious and pleasant meadows (and flourishing savanahs) adorns the Continent; and whose benevolent brest sends daily supplies to the planter, and hourly relief to the poor and necessitous native: whose spacious arms (as if circulating the Ocean) proclaims her shores sanctuary to distressed Marriners; and a generous protection to deplorable Seamen, that solicit refreshment from her replenish't Harbours. . . . More-over, this beautiful *Aurora,* or the Rising Sun of America (known only by the name of *Carolina*) is already courted by almost every Country, where note, it begins to depopulate some American settlements. . . ."

Virginia Hostility to Albemarle

Another cause of unrest among the settlers, and a possible deter-rent to immigration, was the rumor that Governor William Berkeley, whom the settlers disliked with a passion, was going to make Albemarle an integral part of Virginia. In 1675 some of the officials of that colony appealed to the proprietors to recognize Albemarle as a part of Virginia. Berkeley, who was having plenty of trouble in his own province, assured the governor and legisla-ture of Albemarle that "wee neither have nor ever will parte with the County of Albemarle to any persons whatsoever But will alwayse maintaine our prov-ince of Carolina entire as itt is." But despite this assurance, relations between the two colonies remained unfriendly. Virginia insisted that the boundary provisions of the 1663 charter, not those of 1665, were effective; hence Albemarle was within the limits of Virginia. The latter had been a royal colony since 1624 and tended to look with contempt on "proprietaries," such as Maryland and Carolina, which were being settled by "draining off" Virginia's population. Virginia authorities resented the Albemarle laws designed to promote immigration, and spread evil reports about Albemarle, which was being settled by "idle debtors," "theaves," "pyrates," and "run-away servants." In 1679 the Virginia legislature translated its animosities into action by prohibiting the shipment of Albemarle tobacco through Virginia ports, and Albemarle officials claimed, perhaps with truth, that the Meherrin and Nottoway Indians along the border were being "incited" by Virginians to make war upon the Albemarle settlement.

Unstable and Inefficient Government

The failure of the proprietors to establish a strong, stable, and efficient government was one of the greatest handicaps to the growth and progress of Albemarle. Some of its governors were weak and ineffective, some were unscrupulous, most were unsatisfactory. The proprietors were forced to admit that it was "a very difficult matter to gitt a man of worth and trust" to accept the office. Hence the governors failed to preserve order, promote the welfare of the people, or defend the colony against Indians, pirates, and other enemies. Constant trouble marked their administrations. One governor, John Jenkins (1672–76), was deposed by a rival faction; a second, Thomas Miller (1677), was overthrown and jailed by "armed rebels"; a third, Eastchurch, was forbidden to enter the colony; and a fourth, Seth Sothel (1683–89), was accused by the assembly of numerous crimes, was tried, convicted, and banished.

From such unstable government, the people could not expect adequate protection from the Indians. Fortunately there were not many powerful or warlike tribes in the immediate vicinity. But there were several small uprisings, and in 1675 there was an attack by the "Chowonocs," which was repulsed "by God's assistance though not without loss of many men."

The Culpeper Rebellion

Soon after the close of this conflict, and while the people were still armed and organized, the so-called Culpeper Rebellion occurred. The causes for this uprising were deep-seated and can be traced almost to the beginning of Albemarle's history. It arose from two somewhat related factors: a factional fight between what might be called the proprietary and antiproprietary parties; and the efforts of England to enforce the Navigation Acts, particularly the Plantation Duty Act of 1673.

In its efforts to carry out the policies of British mercantilism, Parliament had passed the Navigation acts of 1651 and 1660, with the specific object of promoting direct trade between England and its colonies by limiting this commerce to British, Irish, and colonial vessels only. In addition, certain "enumerated articles," including tobacco, could be shipped only to England. Flagrant evasions of this legal requirement, such as the shipment of tobacco to New England labeled as "bait for New England fishermen," led to the passage of the Plantation Duty Act of 1673, which permitted the shipment of tobacco and other enumerated commodities to other colonies, provided a duty were paid—in the case of tobacco, one penny per pound. Tobacco was the chief "money crop" of Albemarle and its leading export. And much of the Albemarle tobacco crop was exported in New England ships belonging to "about half a dozen traders" from Massachusetts and Rhode Island.

Albemarle Resistance to British Trade Laws

The proprietors believed that it was in their interest as well as that of the colony that the Plantation Duty Act be enforced. They felt that the Albemarle colony stood to gain economically by direct trade with England, and that it was "a certain Beggary to our people of Albemarle if they shall have goods at 2d hand and soe much dearer than they may be supplyd from England and with all sell their Tobacco and other Commodities at a lower rate than they could in England." They feared that continued evasions of the law might lead to abrogation of their charter, since the movement against "proprietaries" was gaining momentum in England. The leaders of Albemarle were not too concerned about this problem, and they violated the English trade laws with impunity. A matter of more immediate interest to them, and one related to the problem of law enforcement, was the factional struggle for control of the Albemarle government between the proprietary and antiproprietary parties. The proprietary government had never been popular, or even acceptable, to many settlers, such as George Durant and John Jenkins, who had taken up lands in Albemarle before the proprietary grant of 1663. These men and a number of their supporters were large producers of tobacco, and they opposed the enforcement of the Navigation Acts, which might exclude them from their profitable trade with New England. They were determined that the trade laws should not be enforced, and in 1672 Governor Carteret, realizing this fact, resigned his post, leaving the colony in the hands of Acting Governor John Jenkins.

Factional Struggle for Control of the Government

The situation grew steadily worse. In November of 1673 the king ordered all colonial governors to select officers who would enforce the trade laws, and two years later he repeated this request. At this time the Treasury Board in England appointed a collector and a surveyor for Albemarle, but since the appointees did not reach Albemarle, Governor Jenkins was allowed to select two men of his own choosing. He named Timothy Biggs as surveyor and Valentine Bird as collector. Apparently Jenkins had no intention of enforcing the Plantation Duty Act, and he had the backing of George Durant, the colony's most powerful political leader, and of John Culpeper, who had recently arrived from South Carolina. The opposition to the Durant-Culpeper-Jenkins faction was led by Thomas Eastchurch, Speaker of the assembly, and Thomas Miller. Jenkins, in an arbitrary effort to crush the opposing faction, had Miller arrested and jailed for "treasonable utterances" and tried to prevent Eastchurch from appealing to England about nonenforcement of the law and the "deplorable situation" in Albemarle. He ordered the dissolution of the assembly, but this body, under the thumb of Speaker Eastchurch, refused to be dissolved. Instead, it drew up charges of "several misdemeanors" against Jenkins, deposed him, and threw him into jail. Meantime Miller had escaped jail, and he and Eastchurch went to England to present their case to the proprietors. Apparently their story was convincing, for in November, 1676, Eastchurch was appointed governor and instructed to divert Albemarle trade from New England to England; to establish three ports of entry; to ascertain the depth of water at low tide in the inlets; and to "take all necessary steps" for enforcement of the trade laws. Miller was chosen as secretary and collector of the customs.

The Problems of Governors Eastchurch and Miller

Eastchurch was long delayed at Nevis, in the West Indies, where, "lighting upon a woman yt was a considerable fortune took hold of the opportunity [and] marryed her," sending Miller on to the troubled colony with a commission to act as president of the council and to "settle affayres against his coming." As a customs official Miller made "a very considerable progress." He seized 817 hogsheads of tobacco and goods illegally imported to the value of £1,242, and he reported that he had collected over £8,000 in customs duties. But in his attempts to act as governor he incurred the wrath of his opponents, who charged him with corruption, vindictiveness, tyranny, and "many hanious maters." He interfered with precinct elections, imposed heavy fines, and arrested and imprisoned several prominent men. He also organized a "pipeing guard," ostensibly for defense against the Indians. The proprietors admitted that Miller "did many extravagant things" and soon "lost his reputation and interest among ye people."

Armed Rebellion

Smouldering resistance broke out into armed rebellion in December, 1677, when "a very pretty vessel of force," commanded by Captain

Zachariah Gillam, landed in Pasquotank River. When the captain went ashore, Miller personally arrested him for violating the Navigation Acts and held him in £1,000 bond. "Armed with a brace of pistolls," Miller likewise arrested George Durant, who was on board Gillam's ship, "as a Traytour." Gillam threatened to take his cargo elsewhere, but the people, aroused to action by Durant and John Culpeper, the surveyor general and member of the Durant faction, begged Captain Gillam to stay, promising him their support against Miller.

This incident led to the uprising erroneously known as "Culpeper's Rebellion." Culpeper, Bird, and others conferred with Durant and devised a plan to oust Miller. With the support of about forty citizens of Pasquotank precinct and with arms supplied by Captain Gillam, they surrounded Miller's house, captured and imprisoned him, seized the tobacco which he had collected, and took possession of the customs revenues and records. They then preceeded to arrest other officials and issued a "Remonstrance to all the Rest of the County of Albemarle," defending their actions and demanding that Albemarle have a "free parliament." To achieve this objective, they issued a call for the election of delegates to an assembly which would meet at Durant's home.

The "Rebels" Take Control

The people responded favorably and an assembly of eighteen delegates met and appointed five of their number to join with Richard Foster, the one proprietary deputy on their side, as the council. The council tried Miller and several other prisoners, "clap Miller in irons," and declared that if Eastchurch attempted to take over the governorship "they would serve him ye same sauce." To execute this decision, they sent armed forces to the Virginia border to prevent Eastchurch's entering Albemarle. Meantime, the latter had arrived in Virginia and had been promised the support of the governor of that colony, but Eastchurch became ill and died before reaching Albemarle.

Assuming the powers of government, the "rebels," led by Culpeper, summoned an assembly to meet at Durant's home. Amid "tumoltuous proceedings," a grand jury was impanelled, which returned a true bill against Miller, but upon receipt of news that Eastchurch had arrived in Virginia and was on his way to Albemarle, Miller was retained in jail, and steps were taken to prevent Eastchurch's arrival.

With Miller in prison and Eastchurch dead, the "rebels" conducted the government "by their owne authority & according to their own modell." The assembly appointed Culpeper collector of the customs (the highest office he held in the "rebel" government) and authorized him to take possession of the customs revenues. Timothy Biggs, and later Miller, escaped jail and carried their case to the proprietors, whereupon the assembly sent Culpeper to London to assure the proprietors of their allegiance and to "insist very highly for right against Miller." The upshot of the matter was that Culpeper and Gillam were both arrested and the Privy Council ordered a full investigation of the whole affair, directing the proprietors to present a complete account of the "rebellion," together with "an authentick Copy of their Charter." Fearful of the abrogation of this document, the proprietors minimized the uprising as much as possible. Culpeper, however, was tried before the Court of King's Bench for treason, but the Earl of Shaftesbury (formerly Lord Ashley Cooper), one of the Carolina proprietors, used his influence to secure acquittal, on the ground that there had been "no settled government" in the colony at the time and that Culpeper was guilty only "of riot." The seizure of the royal customs revenues could not be so easily overlooked, and Culpeper threw himself upon the mercy of the king. The British Commissioners of the Customs recommended that Culpeper be tried for embezzlement, but the proprietors promised to make a satisfactory settlement, though they admitted that he had acted "without lawful authority."

Seth Sothel, The Last Governor of Albemarle County

The proprietors deemed it unwise to appoint a new governor of Albemarle who represented either faction and, in 1678, commissioned Seth Sothel, one of their own number, as "Governor and Collector of Customs" for the troubled colony. Sothel had spent some fifteen years in enterprises connected with the province of Carolina and had purchased the original Clarendon share. He had been granted a "seignory," or estate of twelve thousand acres, on the condition that within five years he would establish a town of at least thirty houses and six score inhabitants. His seignory was on the Edisto River in what is now South Carolina. He never fulfilled the conditions and never acquired title to this vast estate. The other proprietors considered Sothel "a sober, moderate man, no way concerned in the factions and animosyties" of Albemarle, and having the ability to "settle all things well."

Sothel embarked for his difficult assignment but was captured on the high seas by Turkish pirates and taken to Algiers, where he was held prisoner for a year.

Meanwhile John Harvey, president of the council, acted as governor and Robert Holden as collector. Both were "Quyetly and cherefully obeyed," but Harvey died within a year and the council selected Jenkins as his successor, a choice approved by the proprietors. This was a clear victory for the Durant faction, and "although Jenkins had the title, yet in fact Durant governed and used Jenkins as his property." But Durant was the ablest leader in the province, and order was restored, laws enforced, customs duties collected "without any disturbance from the people," a specie tax levied to make good the revenues seized "in the tyme of the disorders," and an Act of Oblivion passed pardoning the "rebels." A few die-hards of the opposing faction tried to make trouble, but to no avail, and it was reported in 1680 that "all things are in quyet."

Sothel Banished by the Albemarle Legislature

Again commissioned as governor in 1681, Sothel finally arrived in Albemarle in 1683. His arrival changed the whole picture. If the accusations made against him were true—and most of them were—he was one of the most arbitrary and corrupt governors in all the English colonies. It was charged that he imprisoned a large number of his opponents without trial; detained some on the false charge that they were pirates; illegally seized several estates; "detained" cattle, slaves, and even lace and "seven pewter dishes" belonging to individuals; and that he accepted bribes. When Thomas Pollock threatened to appeal to the proprietors, Sothel had him jailed, and when Durant protested against his "misdemeanors and other oppressions," he was jailed "without any process or collor of law" and "all of the estate of the said George Durant" was converted to Sothel's "owne use."

By 1688 the people could tolerate their proprietor-governor no longer. The following year he was tried by the General Assembly. Trial by the assembly, rather than by the Lords Proprietors, was at his own request. He was found guilty on thirteen charges—including oppression, tyranny, extortion, and bribery—and was compelled "to adjure the Country for 12 months and the Government for ever." Soon after this Philip Ludwell was appointed by the proprietors as governor of Carolina "north and east of Cape feare." With the banishment of Sothel and the appointment of Ludwell, the history of Albemarle as a distinct colony ended and that of "North Carolina" began.

Chapter 4

THE EMERGENCE OF
NORTH CAROLINA, 1689-1729

The situation confronting Governor Ludwell was none too promising. Except for a small area fringing Albemarle Sound, the colony was sparsely settled by about three thousand people, the northern boundary was in dispute with Virginia, and the settlers were dissatisfied with the system of granting lands.

Ludwell's Instructions

Ludwell assumed office with specific proprietary instructions "to take care of the quiet and safety of the province under our Government," to see that the letter notifying Sothel of his dismissal was "carefully delivered to his own hands," to ascertain "the reasons of the late disturbances," and to select three of "the honestest and ablest men" he could find to "hear and determine all causes both Civill and Criminall according to Law." If he should "finde anything deficient or Inconvenient to ye Inhabitants," the proprietors promised "to take due care therein."

Gibbs's "Rebellion"

Hardly had the new governor arrived in the colony before he faced an incipient rebellion, which was "inconvenient" to both the inhabitants and himself. A certain Captain John Gibbs, claiming that he had been appointed governor by Sothel at the time of the latter's banishment, issued on June 2, 1690, a "Declaration" in which he denounced Ludwell as a "Rascal, imposter & Usurper," and commanded "all Persons to keep the King's peace, to consult ye ffundamentals, and to render me due obedience, & not presume to act or do by Virtue of any Comission or Power whatsoever derived from ye above sd Ludwell, as they will answer it, att their utmost perill." If any

Ludwell adherent desired to "fight it out with the sword," Gibbs promised to "fight him in this Cause, as long as my Eyelids shall wagg."

Four days later Gibbs and a band of his "armed men" broke up the Currituck precinct court, took two of the magistrates prisoner to Gibbs's house, and issued an order forbidding any court "to sitt or act by any Commission but his." In spite of the rumor that Gibbs had "near eighty men in armes att his house in Currituck," when most of the inhabitants "immediately putt themselves in Armes to secure ye Country from farther outrages," Gibbs fled to Virginia, where Governor Francis Nicholson, at Ludwell's request, "quieted these stirs," though the Virginia governor declared that the people were still mutinous and it was uncertain how long they would remain peaceful. At the request of the Lords Proprietors—perhaps at Nicholson's suggestion—Ludwell and Gibbs went to London to present their respective claims, with the result that Gibbs was repudiated.

North Carolina Governed by a Deputy of the Governor of "Carolina"

Meanwhile, between November, 1690, and November, 1691, Thomas Jarvis was "acting governor" by Ludwell's appointment. At the latter date the proprietors appointed Ludwell as "Governor of Carolina" and gave him instructions that largely ignored the Fundamental Constitutions in an effort to make the government "sutable to our Charter from the Crowne." Henceforth there was to be a governor of "Carolina," resident at Charles Town, with power to appoint a deputy governor for the northern portion of the colony. A "single parliament" was recommended for Carolina, but it was found impracticable for the Albemarle region to send delegates to Charles Town; so the North Carolina region continued to have its own legislative body. Another significant change in government was the elimination of the five members of the council who had been elected by the assembly.

A New Era in North Carolina History

Ludwell's administration inaugurated a new era in North Carolina history. For the next fifteen years the people enjoyed orderly, well-administered, peaceful government, a situation partially due to capable deputy governors and "acting governors"—Thomas Jarvis, 1691–94; Thomas Harvey, 1694–99; and Henderson Walker, 1699–74. Ludwell "understood the character and prejudices of the people thoroughly; and as he was possessed of good sense and proper feeling, he had address enough . . . gradually to restore a state of comparative peace." Ludwell's proclamation of November, 1693, recognizing the validity of the Great Deed of Grant of 1668, made him popular with the people, but the proprietors took offense at his action and promptly removed him from the governorship. The sagacity, prudence, and sound judgment of John Archdale, governor of Carolina, 1695–96, together with his experience in colonial administration, made him particularly acceptable to North Carolina. Archdale spent a winter personally directing the government of the "northern portion of Carolina," and the assembly declared that "his greatest care is to make peace and plenty flow amongst us."

Able Governors

Both Jarvis and Harvey, deputies of Ludwell and Archdale respectively, had long been leaders in Albemarle. They understood and sympathized with the ideals and feelings of the people and were men of sterling character and sound judgment. Henderson Walker, the next deputy governor, had been in Albemarle for seventeen years and had served as attorney general, justice of the General Court, and member of the council. A man of education, a lawyer of proved ability, and a sincere churchman, he was deeply interested in the welfare of the colony, jealous of its good name, and quick to resent the "imputation of evil neighborhood" which some Virginians had tried to fix upon it.

Expansion of Settlement

About the time that Ludwell became governor of Carolina, settlers began to settle on lands south of Albemarle Sound, the first recorded settlement being made on Pamlico River about 1690–91 by "a few French families" from Virginia, seeking a milder climate, better range for their cattle, and more religious freedom. In 1694 the proprietors, in an effort to encourage settlement, instructed Archdale to erect as many counties as he deemed necessary "for ye better regulating and ye encouragement of ye people." Accordingly Bath County was created in 1696, embracing the region from Albemarle Sound to Cape Fear.

French Huguenots Arrive from Virginia

Settlers now began to move into the colony at a more rapid rate. A large portion of the newcomers were from Manakin Town, a French Huguenot settlement a few miles above the Falls of the James River near present Richmond. Hoping to escape persecution in France, the Huguenots had started this settlement in 1700 under the leadership of Marquis de la Muce and Charles de Sailly. But the English had taken up most of the good lands, so that the French "were hemmed in on all Hands from providing more Land for themselves and their Children." Reports of the salubrious climate and abundant and cheap lands to the south caused many of them, including their minister, C. P.

de Richebourg, to migrate to the Neuse-Pamlico section. According to John Lawson, writing in 1709, these new settlers were "much taken with the Pleasantness of that Country," and were "a very industrious People . . . good neighbors amongst us, and gives Examples of Industry, which is much wanted in this Country."

So large was the influx from Virginia that the government of that colony, as well as the British Board of Trade, directed an inquiry into the causes and possible means of prevention. And Governor Henderson Walker indignantly denied the charge that Virginia runaways were being harbored in North Carolina. He wrote the Board of Trade: "I assure you that neither our laws nor our practice deserves such imputation of evil neighbourhood. Neither are there runaways harbored here that one can discover by diligent inquiry nor shall any such thing be suffered so far as it is in our power to prevent it."

Bath, the First Town in North Carolina

About 1704, on a bluff overlooking the Pamlico River, a town was formally laid off by John Lawson, surveyor general of the province, who with Joel Martin and Simon Alderson, was its founder. On March 8, 1706, the legislature incorporated Bath, the first town in North Carolina. Bath grew very slowly and never became very populous, but it was a place of considerable political and commercial importance for a number of decades. Several sessions of the legislature met in the little town, and in 1715 Port Bath was created—the first official port of entry in the province.

In 1709 William Gordon, an Anglican missionary wrote: "Here is no church, though they have begun to build a town called Bath. It consists of about twelve houses, being the only town in the province. They have a small collection of books for a library, which were carried over by the Reverend Doctor Bray, and some land is laid out for a glebe; but no minister would ever stay long in the place, though several have come hither from the West Indies and other plantations in America . . . in all probability it will be the centre of trade, as having the advantage of a better inlet for shipping, and surrounded with pleasant savannas, very useful for stocks of cattle."

The newcomers from Virginia, "at vast labour and expense recovered and improved great quantities of land thereabouts," and the council, in 1706, "taking into their serious consideration" the fact that Bath County had "grown populous and daily increasing," divided it into three precincts—Archdale, Wickham, and Pamptecough (Pamlico). About 1707 a group of Huguenots from Virginia, "considerable in numbers," crossed the Pamlico River and took up lands along the Neuse and Trent. Lawson wrote that most of the French who lived at Manakin Town "are removed to Trent River, where the rest are daily expected."

By 1710 settlements extended from the Virginia border to Albemarle Sound and along the banks of the Roanoke, Pamlico, and Neuse, extending as far as thirty miles from these rivers in some places. In 1694 the number of taxables for the whole province was reported as 786, which probably meant a total population of over 3,000. Eight years later, the taxables of Chowan precinct alone were 283, and in 1708 the estimated population of Pasquotank was more than 1,300. Virginia officials complained about the loss of population to North Carolina, and in 1708 the president of that colony's council wrote that "many of our poorer sort of Inhabitants daily remove themselves into our neighboring colonies, especially to North Carolina, which is the reason the number of our Inhabitants doth not increase proportionately to what might be expected . . . the chief cause of this Removal is want of land to plant and cultivate."

New Bern Founded, 1710

The largest and most significant settlement in the Neuse-Trent area was made at New Bern in 1710 by a colony of German palatines, along with some Swiss and a few English. The French Huguenot migration to the province had been the result of individual initiative, while the founding of New Bern was the result of the promotional activity of a Swiss land company, headed by Baron Christoph von Graffenried and Franz Louis Michel. The baron had long been interested in planting in America a colony of persecuted palatines and Swiss, and had made extensive inquiries about mines, agriculture, forest resources, and the best means of making a settlement. He had read Joshua Kocherthal's glowing account (1706) about Carolina where the "English live with the Indians there in complete friendship and good understanding," and he had gone to London, where he talked with the Duke of Albemarle, who told him about "the beauty, goodness and riches" of Carolina. About this time, 1709, Parliament passed a law for the naturalization of foreign Protestants, with the result that some thirteen thousand palatines landed in England within the next two years. Most of these poor immigrants came to London, which was already burdened with its own poor and could hardly cope with the situation. Queen Anne agreed with the views of Graffenried and a number of English capitalists that colonization was the solution, and the queen consented to assume the expense of transportation, £4,000, if the baron took one hundred families of Palatines to America. After conferring with John Lawson, surveyor general of Carolina, then in London to arrange for the publication of his book entitled *A New Voyage to Carolina,* Graffenried decided to plant his colony in North Carolina. Accordingly he purchased 17,500 acres of land, to be located on the Neuse and Trent rivers, for £175. He was also given a twelve-year option on 100,000 acres, and a "lease of all royal mines and minerals in Carolina" for thirty years.

Careful Selection of Settlers

In choosing settlers for his colony, Von Graffenried selected only "young people, healthy, laborous and of all kinds of avocations and handicrafts in number about 650." Tools, implements, and ships were all chosen with great care. The first group selected was placed under the control of "three persons, notables from Carolina, who happened then to be in London and who had lived already several years in Carolina." Two of these "notables" were Lawson and Christopher Gale. The baron remained in England, awaiting the arrival of a Swiss group from Bern, while Lawson and Gale prepared to lead their group to Carolina.

Problems of the Palatines

The palatines left England in January, 1710. After a disastrous and stormy voyage of thirteen weeks, during which about one-half of the settlers died, the transports reached Virginia, and as they entered the James River a French privateer plundered one of the vessels and deprived the passengers of everything they had. The group, greatly reduced in numbers, set out overland and finally reached the Chowan River, where Thomas Pollock, provided them "certain necessities" and furnished ships to transport them to their ultimate destination. As Graffenried wrote, "that colony was shattered before it was settled."

Lawson had been given the privilege of locating the site for a town, and he chose a point between the Neuse and Trent rivers. No preparations had been made for the new settlers, who found themselves in a wilderness during the hot and unhealthy season without food or shelter. They were in such dire circumstances that they were forced "to sell all their clothes and movables to the neighboring inhabitants in order to sustain their life."

The Town of New Bern Laid Out

The proprietors had instructed Gale, receiver general of the province, to use such public revenues as could be spared for the support of the settlers, but the Cary Rebellion was in full swing and Governor Cary withheld all funds from Gale. When Graffenried arrived on September 10 with one hundred Swiss settlers, he found the settlement in a wretched condition, "sickness, want and desperation having reached their climax." The baron immediately began to organize affairs. Land was surveyed, forests cleared, houses built, and a water mill erected for grinding grain. A town was laid out between the two rivers "in the form of a cross, one arm extending from river to river, and the other, from the point, back indefinitely." The new town was named New Bern, in honor of the Swiss city Bern.

For the first year and a half the settlers were happy and prosperous. According to their leader and historian, Graffenried, "within eighteen months they managed to build houses and make themselves so comfortable, that they made more progress than the English inhabitants in several years. . . . There was a fine appearance of a happy state of things," when suddenly, in September, 1711, disaster struck and the colony was almost wiped out by the Tuscarora Indians.

The Cary Rebellion

The effort to establish the Church of England was a divisive and disrupting issue in North Carolina—as it was in several other colonies—and kept the province in a state of turmoil and confusion for almost a decade, finally culminating in a "rebellion."

The Question of the Established Church in North Carolina

According to the royal charters of 1663 and 1665, the Anglican Church was the only one that could have official encouragement, and the intentions of the proprietors to establish the church were clearly revealed in the Concessions of 1665, in the Fundamental Constitutions of 1669, and in repeated instructions to governors. The fact that dissenters were allowed to practice their own forms of worship did not mean that there could not or would not be an Establishment, but the neglect and inaction on the part of the Anglicans, or Church party, played into the hands of dissenting groups, notably the Quakers. The latter became active in Albemarle about 1672 and continued to increase in numbers and influence until the close of the century. The Quakers constituted only about one-seventh of the total population, but they were strong in Pasquotank and Perquimans precincts and were better organized than any other religious body.

Writing in 1704, John Blair, an Anglican missionary, said: "For the country may be divided into four sorts of people: first, the Quakers, who are the most powerful enemies to Church government, but a people very ignorant of what they profess. The second sort are a great many who have no religion, but would be Quakers, if by that they were not obliged to lead a more moral life than they are willing to comply to. A third sort something like Presbyterians, which sort is upheld by some idle fellows who have left their lawful employment, and preach and baptize through the country, without any manner of orders from any sect or pretended Church. A fourth sort, who are really zealous for the interest of the Church, are the fewest in number, but the better sort of people, and would do very much for the settlement of the Church government there, if not opposed by these three precedent sects: and though they be all three of different pretensions, yet they all concur together in one common cause to prevent any thing that will be chargeable to them, as they allege Church government will be, if once established by law."

Another Anglican missionary, John Urmston, referred to the Quakers of Perquimans as "very numerous, extremely ignorant, insufferably proud, and consequently ungovernable," while those in Pasquotank were "factious, mutinous, and domineering."

The Quakers Hold the Balance of Power

The Quakers held the balance of power in the province and under the governorship of John Archdale, a Quaker proprietor with offices in Charles Town, controlled all branches of the government. This alarmed the Anglicans, who were determined to gain control by a law establishing the church. The Church party was aided by two developments: the appointment of Henderson Walker, able and zealous churchman, as governor in 1699, and by the sending of missionaries to the colony from England. Walker was disturbed by the fact that the colony had gone forty years "without priest or altar," and he urged the Bishop of London, who had religious jurisdiction over all the colonies, to send a missionary to the province. Accordingly, Daniel Brett was sent in 1700, but he turned out to be "ye Monster of ye Age," and Walker complained to the Bishop of London: "It hath been a great trouble and grief to us who have a great veneration for the Church that the first minister who was sent us should prove so ill as to give the Dissenters so much occasion to charge us with him."

The First Church Law: The Vestry Act of 1701

But the Church party did not abandon the idea of an Establishment, and Walker, by "a great deal of care and management," secured the passage of a Vestry Act in 1701—the first church law in North Carolina. This act provided for the laying out of parishes, the organization of vestries, the erection of churches, and for a poll tax on all tithables for support of clergymen. The churchmen were happy and proceeded to implement the law by the creation of Chowan parish, December 15, 1701, followed shortly by the organization of Pasquotank and Perquimans. The Quakers, Presbyterians, and even some Anglicans protested against this law—on principle and because it increased taxes—and they determined to repeal it at the next session of the assembly, which would have a Quaker majority. The Quakers were relieved when the proprietors rejected the law, though not because of principle, but because the law gave too much authority to the vestry and did not provide adequate salaries for the clergy.

The Vestry Act of 1703

Quaker jubilation, however, was short-lived. In spite of the fact that the Quakers had a large representation in the lower house, Walker got a Vestry Act passed in 1703, which provided that all members of the assembly must take an oath that they were communicants of the Church of England, in addition to the Oath of Allegiance to Queen Anne. This requirement denied the right of affirmation, which Quakers had enjoyed for many years. Governor Daniel, who became governor in 1704, and some Anglican leaders contended that the oath had nothing to do with the question of the Established Church, but the Quakers maintained that it was aimed directly at them and that they were being denied their rights. Daniel's action was so unpopular with Presbyterians that they united with the Quakers and secured his removal from office in 1705.

Thomas Cary Becomes Governor

Thomas Cary, a Charleston merchant, who succeeded Daniel, had been considered friendly to dissenters in South Carolina, but his conduct in North Carolina was even more offensive to Quakers than that of his two predecessors. Not only did Cary enforce the oath and deprive Quakers of their seats in the legislature but he imposed a fine of five pounds on those who should enter an office without taking such oath. He also got a law enacted which voided the election of anyone who had "promoted his own candidacy." According to the Anglican missionary, William Gordon, "this so nettled the Quakers" that in 1707 they sent John Porter to London to protest to the proprietors. Through the influence of Proprietor Archdale, who was a Quaker, Porter returned with an order to suspend all laws regarding oaths and to remove Cary from office. When Porter arrived, Cary was in South Carolina, and William Glover, president of the council, was acting in his stead. At first Porter and the Quakers accepted Glover, but when the latter refused to accept new members of the council until they took the oath, Porter and his followers formed an alliance with Cary to turn Glover out. But Glover refused to give up the office and the two factions prepared for military action. The leaders of the two groups, however, agreed to submit their respective claims to the voters, and an election was held for members of the assembly. In a bitter contest the Cary party carried Bath, Perquimans, and Pasquotank; Glover carried Currituck; and Chowan was about evenly divided. When the legislature convened in October, 1708, there were two sets of delegates from each county. Glover's followers lost out to the Cary men, led by the powerful Edward Moseley, Speaker of the House. Whereupon Glover, still claiming the governorship, fled to Virginia. The Cary party, in power from 1708 to 1711, declared void all laws of the Glover regime, and appointed numerous Quakers to office.

Edward Hyde Becomes First Governor of "North Carolina"

The Lords Proprietors in England, unhappy about the chaotic conditions in their province, decided on December 7, 1710, to appoint a governor of North Carolina "independent of the Governor of Carolina." They selected Edward Hyde, who falsely claimed to be a cousin of Queen Anne, for that position, but a full year passed before his appointment was approved by the crown. Hyde's commission was not issued until January 24, 1712. Meanwhile he had come to North Carolina and acted as the "deputy governor." His first legislature, which was described by John Urmston, an Anglican missionary, as "a strange mixture of men of various opinions and inclinations; a few Churchmen, many Presbyterians, Independents, but most anythingarians," began its session on March 11, 1711. It passed a law for the punishment of "seditious words or speeches" or "scurrilous libels" against the government, levied a £100 fine on all officials who refused to qualify "according to the strictness of the laws of Great Britain now in force," provided that "all such laws made for the establishment of the Church" were effective, and nullified all the laws of Cary's second administration.

Cary's Armed Forces Defy Governor Hyde

This was too much for Cary, who gathered his followers at his house, which was supplied "with great Guns and other warlike stores," and defied Governor Hyde. Cary also had a "Brigantine of six Guns" and some other ships "equipp'd in a warlike manner." Graffenried, a member of the council at the time, wrote that Cary "became an open and declared rebel and brought together a gang of tramps and rioters by means of promises and . . . by means of good liquor, rum, and brandy, to which he treated the rabble, he secured many adherents and they finally came to an open rebellion against Mr. Hyde." On June 30 Cary attacked the governor's forces, which were assembled at Thomas Pollock's plantation, but he was repulsed. Shortly thereafter Richard Roach reorganized Cary's followers for another attack, but by this time Governor Alexander Spotswood of Virginia had sent a company of "royal marines" to Hyde's relief, and these so "frighted the Rebellious party" that Cary and many of his supporters fled to Virginia. Cary was sent to England for trial, but was released "for lack of evidence." Thus ended the "Cary Rebellion."

Aftermath of the "Cary Rebellion"

The Cary Rebellion collapsed with the flight of its leader, but three years of internal strife, plus a series of bad crop years, had left the colony so weakened, divided, and demoralized that it gave the Tuscarora Indians and their allies a glorious opportunity to launch a deadly attack against the whites in September, 1711. The Tuscarora, the sixth nation of the Iroquois, had migrated southward from the New York area at some remote period and in the early eighteenth century occupied lands along the Roanoke, Pamlico, Neuse, and Trent rivers, with their chief towns along the Neuse and its tributaries, and with hunting grounds extending into the Cape Fear Valley. Numbering about twelve hundred "fighting men" and a total population of perhaps four thousand, they were more numerous, more advanced, better organized and governed, and more hostile to the whites than any other Carolina tribe.

Background of the Tuscarora War: Tuscarora Resentment against Whites

Some contemporary observers commented about the amicable relations between these Indians and the whites. The Swiss Settlers found the natives "clever and sociable." When John Lawson declared, "They are really better to us than we have been to them," he added the significant comment: "The Indians are very revengeful, and never forget an injury done, till they have received Satisfaction." Thomas Pollock, president of the council and later acting governor, declared that the Indians struck in 1711 "without any cause that we know of," though he later admitted that "our own divising hath been the cause of all our troubles." Governor Spotswood of Virginia said that the Tuscarora uprising had come "without any previous show of discontent." The history of Indian-white relations during the decade following 1701 did not warrant such optimism.

The Indians resented white encroachments on their hunting grounds, very wisely believing that it would not be long until the "newcomers" would take possession of all their lands. When the settlers purchased lands, in many cases they failed to pay what the natives asked, as is revealed by various statements and court records of the time. In 1701 the Indians along the Pamlico complained to Lawson that the English "were very wicked people and that they threatened the Indians for hunting near their plantations." Two years later the Corees staged a minor uprising, which was easily repulsed. In 1706–7 Thomas Pollock marched against the Meherrins along the disputed Virginia-Carolina border, seized thirty-six Indians and imprisoned them for two days without food or water, wrecked their cabins, and threatened to destroy their crops if they did not surrender their lands. When the North Carolina authorities appealed to Virginia regarding the Meherrins, Spotswood and the Virginia legislature refused to act on the ground that the whites were the aggressors and that North Carolina was "the author of its own misery." In 1710 the Tuscarora sent a petition to the governor of Pennsylvania protesting against the seizure of their lands and the enslavement of their people. The white practice of kidnapping Indians, particularly women and children, was one of the greatest grievances of the natives, and it was carried on so extensively that the Pennsylvania legislature of 1705 passed a law against "the further importation of Indian slaves from Carolina."

"Sharp" Practices of Whites Who Traded with the Indians

Almost every writer of the time mentioned the "sharp" and "irregular" practices of the Carolina traders who "dealt too hard" with the natives and cheated them in many ways. Graffenried, who considered this a major cause of the Tuscarora uprising, wrote that the whites "cheated these Indians in trading, and would not allow them to hunt near their plantations, and under that pretense took away from them their game, arms, and ammunition," and that "these poor Indians, insulted in many ways by a few rough Carolinians, more barbarous and unkind than the savages themselves, could not stand such treatment much longer, and began to think of their safety and of vengeance, what they did very secretly." William Byrd II, of Virginia, referring to the Carolina traders said: "These petty Rulers don't only teach the honester Savages all Sorts of Debauchery, but are unfair in all their dealings, and use them in all kinds of Oppression." He maintained that the traders had abused the Indian women and mistreated the men "until the Indians grew weary and tired of the Tyranny and Injustice with which the whites treated them and resolved to endure the bondage no longer."

Settlement of the New Bern Region: Immediate Cause of the War

The immediate cause of the Tuscarora War may be traced to the settlement of New Bern in 1710. The execution of John Lawson, September 10, 1711, when he and Graffenried were exploring the Neuse Valley, gave evidence of a determination to exterminate anyone who tried to deprive the Indians of their lands. Some contemporary writers blamed Cary for inflaming the natives by "slanders and instigations" against Governor Hyde, and Spotswood said this was "the only occasion of this Tragedy." Both Cary and his opponents had been negotiating with Tuscarora leaders, but the Indian massacre of September did not occur until after the Cary Rebellion had ended, and the Indians told John Barnwell later that they had not been incited to action by white leaders of either faction. Yet the dissension and internal weakness of the colony resulting from the Cary uprising provided an opportune moment, and apparently the Indians decided early in September to launch an all-out attack. The day after Lawson's death Tuscarora leaders told Graffenried that some five hundred Tuscarora, Mattamuskeet, Pamlico, Neuse, Coree, and Bay River Indians intended to make this attack, but Graffenried, a prisoner of the Indians, could not convey this tragic news to his people.

The Massacre of September 22, 1711

About dawn on September 22 the Indians, who were better armed than the whites—thanks to white traders—dividing into small groups, attacked white settlements all the way from the Neuse to the Pamlico, killing, scalping, and burning. Christopher Gale, writing to the governor of South Carolina, said, "One hundred and thirty people massacred at the head of Nuse, and on the south side of Pamtaco rivers, in the space of two hours; butchered after the most barbarous manner that can be expressed, and their dead bodies used with all the scorn and indignity imaginable; their houses plundered of considerable riches (being generally traders), then burned, and their growing and hopeful crops destroyed." Women were laid upon the house floors and stakes driven through their bodies. It was reported that more than eighty infants were slaughtered. Men, women, and children lay mutilated and dead in the hot sun, "a prey to dogs, wolves, and vultures." Those fortunate enough to escape fled to Bath or to fortified homes for protection, and one survivor wrote: "We are forc'd to keep garrison and Gard, day and Night."

The Country Laid Waste

Thomas Pollock described the uprising vividly: "The people of this country are greatly impoverished; them at News and Pamtico having most of their houses and household goods burnt, their stock of cattle, hogs, horses, &c. killed and carried away and their plantations ruined by the Indians." The greatest tragedy in colonial North Carolina was described as "almost depopulating a whole County," which was "totally wasted and ruined." Fortunately the Albemarle Sound area escaped, thanks to Tom Blunt, leader of the "friendly Tuscaroras," who had agreed to remain neutral, but which he and his followers were rewarded by a large grant of land, later known as "Indian Woods," located in present Bertie County.

Governor Hyde Calls on South Carolina and Virginia for Aid

Governor Hyde faced a very grave situation. Much of the colony lay in ruins; food was scarce and ammunition scarcer; trade was almost nonexistent except for small shipments of naval stores, and the colony was without money or credit. In addition, the Quakers refused to take up arms, and desertions from the militia were numerous "to ye great weakening of its strength."

The governor acted with vigor and speed. He summoned the legislature and obtained the passage of laws to emit £4,000 in paper currency—first in the colony's history—and to draft all men between sixteen and sixty into the militia (those who could not fight were required to pay £5 each to prosecute the war). He reorganized the militia and had forts built at strategic points. But the task was too great for the impoverished colony. So he called on Virginia and South Carolina for aid. The Virginia legislature voted six blankets for every Tuscarora captured and authorized £1,000 and nine hundred yards of cloth. Spotswood ordered his militia to the border, but refused to send them farther unless North Carolina promised to support his militia and also agreed to surrender the area in dispute between the two provinces—a promise North Carolina refused to make.

South Carolina Sends Aid: The Expedition of "Tuscarora Jack" Barnwell

South Carolina sent timely assistance. Its legislature voted £4,000 and sent troops at once without asking "for a mortgage or other security." With some 30 whites and about 500 "friendly Indians," chiefly Yemasees, Colonel John Barnwell ("Tuscarora Jack") marched 300 miles through the wilderness and defeated the Indians in two battles hear New Bern, in January, 1712. Then, reinforced by about 250 North Carolina militia, he attacked the main Tuscarora stronghold, led by King Hancock, at Cotechny. The Indians were "terrified by the cannon," but held out for ten days, when Barnwell agreed to a truce, in order to save the lives of white women and children held prisoners in the fort. According to the terms of this truce, the Indians henceforth were "to plant only on Neuse River, the creek the fort is on, quitting all claims to other lands. . . . To quit all pretensions to planting, fishing, hunting or ranging all lands lying between Neuse River and Cape Feare."

Barnwell was criticized by North Carolina officials for his failure to win a more decisive victory. Governor Spotswood of Virginia said that Barnwell had "clapt up a peace upon very unaccountable conditions" and that he should have broken "entirely the power of that enemy." The North Carolina Assembly refused to grant Barnwell's request for a grant of land, though he had suffered "inexpressible torments," had lost five of his own horses and several hundred pounds sterling, and had been wounded besides. He resented "such unkind usage" and, determined to reap some profit from his dangerous and costly expedition, he and his men seized some Indians and took them as slaves to South Carolina.

The War Resumed: Colonel James Moore's Expedition from South Carolina

The Tuscarora were offended by this action and claimed that the whites had violated the truce. So they resumed their attacks in the summer and fall of 1712. North Carolina was in a desperate plight again, a situation made worse by a yellow fever epidemic that took many lives, including that of Governor Hyde. But Thomas Pollock, the acting governor, immediately called on South Carolina for assistance and received a favorable response, in spite of North Carolina's ingratitude to Barnwell. In December, 1712, Colonel James Moore, with thirty-three whites and about a thousand "friendly Indians," marched to the Neuse, and, cooperating with Pollock's forces, won a "glorious victory" at Fort Nohoroco on Contentnea Creek, March 25, 1713. Pollock reported his and Moore's losses as 57 killed and 82 wounded; "Enemies Destroyed is as follows—Prissoners 392, Scolps 192, out of ye sd. fort-& att Least 200 Kill'd & Burnt In ye fort—& 166 Kill'd & taken out of ye fort." As Governor Spotswood put it, North Carolina had destroyed a number of captives with "exquisite tortures." An undetermined number of prisoners were sold as slaves, the current price being £10 each.

The power of the Tuscarora in North Carolina was broken by this decisive defeat, though there was a Coree uprising in 1714, and as late as 1718 rangers were used to police the Neuse-Pamlico area against Indian attacks. The Tuscarora who were fortunate enough to escape death or slavery began to migrate to New York, and by 1802 most of them had rejoined their "Iroquois brethren." In 1715 North Carolina partially repaid its debt to South Carolina, when it sent troops to aid that province in crushing the power of the Yemassees.

Aftermath of the Indian Wars

The colony emerged from the Cary Rebellion and the Indian uprisings in pitiable condition. Many people had been killed, many had left, and immigration had practically ceased. A large proportion of houses and barns had been burned, much of the livestock and cattle killed or carried away, and vast stretches of land laid waste. Trade had almost ceased to exist and there was little specie. According to Pollock, the public debt incurred to finance the war was greater than "we will be able to pay this ten or twelve years." Altogether £36,000 in bills of credit had been issued in 1712, 1713, and 1714, and revenues from taxes and other sources were not enough to retire these bills. In 1729 £10,000 of them were still outstanding. The paper bills had depreciated rapidly and were soon passing at five to one. When the proprietors refused to accept such bills in payments of fees and quitrents, the situation of the people became extremely critical.

A Period of "Peace and Quietness"

But there was a brighter side to the picture. The removal of the Indian menace, the separation from South Carolina, the virtual elimination of personal factions under Thomas Pollock's effective leadership, and the strengthening of the authority of government prepared the way for an era of growth and progress. Pollock, president of the council and acting governor

(1712–14), said that the wars had extinguished "the fire of difference and division among the people," and Giles Rainsford, an Anglican missionary, thanked God that "we have no disturbances among ourselves, but all people's hearts unite and every Member of the Government is as happy as the times will admit of under the wise and prudent administration of our good President." When Pollock was succeeded by Governor Charles Eden in May, 1714, the colony had begun to enter a period of "peace and quietness."

Revision of the Laws

The legislature of 1715 did much to pave the way for this era of progress, when it revised and codified "the ancient standing laws of this Government" and passed about sixty new laws designed to promote the welfare of the province. Many of these statutes were designed to improve administration and to avoid the confusion that had existed. The law "for the more effectual observing of the Queen's Peace, and establishing a good and lasting Foundation of Government in North Carolina" provided severe punishment for anyone found guilty of spreading "false news" or "scurrilous Libels" against the government, or participating in conspiracies, riots, and rebellions. Other statutes defined the powers and duties of precinct officials, regulated the fees of officers, and required the bonding of all officials who handled public monies, prescribed the details for holding elections, and provided for biennial sessions of the legislature. A new Vestry Act, unchanged until 1741, established the church on a sound footing. This law was accompanied by an "Act for Liberty of Conscience," which placated the Quakers by allowing them the right of affirmation and gave all dissenters what they had long demanded—legal protection. To stimulate immigration, the old laws of 1669 were reenacted. Cognizant of the scarcity of specie, sixteen commodities were "rated" as money (later the list was increased to twenty-two). Laws were also passed to encourage the establishment of sawmills and gristmills. A comprehensive plan was adopted for the laying out of roads, the construction of bridges, and the establishment and maintenance of ferries, with the result that trade and travel increased, especially after Governor Burrington laid out a road in 1724 "from Nuse to Cape Fear River about one hundred miles in length." A pilotage law, which provided for pilots at Roanoke and Ocracoke to "constantly and diligently make it their business to search & find out the most convenient channels," to keep them properly marked, and to pilot vessels safely over the sandbars, led to an increase in trade.

New Towns

Bath and New Bern had suffered much as a result of the Tuscarora War. The former, which had only twelve houses when this conflict began, had been reduced to nine houses, and New Bern had suffered to a much greater proportionate extent. In order to promote the founding of towns, a law was passed to allow representation in the legislature of any group settlement with as many as sixty families. The results were gratifying. Under Thomas Pollock's leadership New Bern was rebuilt and was incorporated in 1723. The year before the "Towne on Queen Anne's Creek," which had been started some years earlier, was incorporated as Edenton, in honor of the governor. Although Bath had been made a port of entry, it failed to develop as a great commercial center. Some fifteen years later, Burrington described it as "a town where little improvements have been made." Beaufort was begun about 1713 and in 1722 was made a port of entry. Within a few years Roanoke (Edenton), Currituck, and Brunswick were also made ports.

The "Golden Age of Piracy"

Several of the laws passed in the period following the Indian Wars were designed to stimulate legitimate trade and to check smuggling and piracy, which were so prevalent that the colony acquired an unsavory reputation. As early as 1683 the Lords of Trade complained of the "harboring and encouraging of Pirates in Carolina and other Governments and Propriety, to the great damage that does arise in his Majesty's service." It was charged that Governor Sothel had issued commissions "to Pyrates for rewards," that Governor Archdale had "sheltered them," and, years later, that Governor Eden and his secretary, Tobias Knight, shared their ill-gotten booty.

It is not too difficult to explain why smuggling and piracy were so prevalent from 1689 to 1718, and why this period has been called "The Golden Age of Piracy." And it should be borne in mind that the attitude toward these questionable and illegal practices was different then from that which developed later. English trade laws were extremely unpopular in the colonies, and it was smart, proper, and profitable to evade them. Hence smuggling prevailed almost everywhere. Piracy was not considered an unmitigated evil and many of the pirates were regarded as respectable men and were sheltered and protected by the people. After all, they brought in many highly desirable articles which they usually sold at reasonable prices; they also helped to keep out French and Spanish vessels, and thus enabled England to expand its trade with the colonies. England was involved in wars during a great portion of this period (1689–97 and 1701–13), and this tended to stimulate smuggling and to promote privateering on a very large scale. The borderline between privateering and piracy is a slender one, and the "case history" of many a pirate reveals that he began his thieving career in a legal manner as a privateer, and then, when the war ended, he continued to prey upon the commerce of the enemy—as well as upon that of England and the colonies—as a pirate. There were other reasons for piracy: the natural yearning for adventure; the possibility of "getting rich quick"; unemployment and the desire for profitable occupation; and the weakness, inefficiency, and even collusion of port and other officials with these "sea robbers." The peculiar nature of the North Carolina coast, with its bars of shifting sands and shallow sounds, made it difficult to police, and this affords some explanation of North Carolina's primacy in piracy.

"Blackbeard" and Stede Bonnet

The most notorious of North Carolina's pirates were Edward Teach, alias Thatch, better known as "Blackbeard," and Major Stede Bonnet. Blackbeard, "a swaggering, merciless brute," native of Bristol, England, had moved to Jamaica, where he operated a successful privateer during Queen Anne's War, bagging a number of French and Spanish ships. When the war ended in 1713, he became a pirate, with headquarters at New Providence Island in the Bahamas. When the British authorities drove the pirates from that island in 1718, the "whole remnant of the scoundrels" transferred their operations to the Carolina coast. Blackbeard located at Bath, where he boasted that he could be invited into any home in North Carolina.

From his new base of operations Blackbeard seized ships, including English and colonial, along the coast. When the king offered pardon to all pirates who surrendered and promised to cease their piratical operations, Teach promptly took the pardon. Within a few weeks, however, he was back at his old trade. Whereupon a British expedition, headed by Woodes Rogers, was sent to break up "the nest of pirates." Rogers failed to capture either Blackbeard or Bonnet, and the former soon returned to Bath with a cargo of sugar and spices, citrous fruits, and other articles, taken from a French ship.

Some of this booty, particularly the sugar, was stored in the barn of Tobias Knight, secretary of Governor Eden. This angered many North Carolinians, especially Edward Moseley, Maurice Moore, and Jeremiah Vail, who searched Knight's property and found the evidence. Governor Eden denounced this "unlawful and improper action" and defended Knight. When Moseley and Moore broke into Knight's house at Sandy Point, near Edenton, to examine the public records, the governor had them arrested for breaking and entering, which evoked from Moseley the statement that "the governor could find men enough to arrest peaceable citizens, but none to arrest thieves and robbers." The council tried the case, and exonerated Knight, but the General Court tried Moseley and Moore for "stirring up sedition," fining the former £100 and declaring him ineligible for public office for three years; Moore was fined £5 and was not disqualified.

Bonnet and Other Pirates Hanged; Blackbeard Killed

Stede Bonnet, a man of wealth and education, had retired from the British army and settled in Barbados, where he had a fine home and a good

Edward Teach, or "Blackbeard"

North Carolina Collection, The University of North Carolina at Chapel Hill

reputation. For some reason he joined Blackbeard's gang; then separated from him, and went into piracy on his own, with headquarters along the Lower Cape Fear. His ravages against South Carolina shipping were so destructive that Governor Robert Johnson fitted out an expedition, headed by Colonel William Rhett, which came into the mouth of the Cape Fear River, and after a furious five-hour battle, captured Bonnet, who was taken to Charleston, tried, convicted, and hanged on December 10, 1718, along with twenty-nine other pirates. During November and December of that year no fewer than forty-nine "Carolina pirates" were hanged at Charleston.

A few weeks after Bonnet's capture, Governor Spotswood of Virginia, hearing that Blackbeard was off the Carolina coast with a prize, sent out two sloops, manned with British sailors from ships in the James River and commanded by Lieutenant Robert Maynard of the Royal Navy, in quest of the notorious pirate and his famous ship *Adventure*. Encountering Blackbeard near Ocracoke Inlet on November 22, Maynard, in a fierce hand-to-hand combat, killed the pirate and half of his crew of eighteen; the other nine were taken to Virginia, convicted, and hanged. There were a few sporadic outbreaks of piracy after this, but the "Golden Age of Piracy" had ended.

Immigration and Expansion

The removal of the Indian menace, the suppression of piracy, and the energetic, if arbitrary and controversial, administration of Governor George Burrington, 1724–25, all tended to stimulate the growth and expansion of the colony. Burrington may have been headstrong, despotic, vain, selfish, and even guilty of excessive drinking as his enemies charged; yet he did much for the welfare of the province. Immediately after assuming office he aligned himself with the "popular party," led by Moseley, Chief Justice Gale, and Thomas Pollock, and for a short time these men gave him their enthusiastic support. But it was not long until they turned against him, denounced his "great Incapacity and Weakness," and made charges against him, many of which were later proved false and malicious, but which nevertheless caused the proprietors to remove him from office.

If one considers the passage of laws as the standard by which to judge a governor, Burrington was a complete failure. Three times he convened the legislature and three times he sent that body home without a law being enacted. On the other hand, Burrington built roads and improved harbors, and, partially as a result of his activities, immigration reached a new high. In 1724–25 alone, it was reported that over a thousand families had moved into the province. The creation of four new counties between 1722 and 1730 bears testimony to the expansion of population—Bertie in 1722 from "that part of Albemarle County lying on the West side of Chowan River," Carteret in 1722 from the eastern part of Bath County, Tyrrell in 1729 from the north end of Bath, and New

Hanover, the same year, to take care of the newly begun settlement on the Lower Cape Fear.

Beginning of Settlement of the Lower Cape Fear Valley

The broad and fertile Cape Fear Valley had remained unsettled since 1667, when the proprietors had closed the land office in "Clarendon County," because of the dangerous coast, hostile Indians, and greater interest in other portions of Carolina. But the whole picture was changed after the Tuscarora War. James Moore, his brother Maurice, and other South Carolina leaders had been impressed with this region as they marched through it during the Indian Wars, and they, along with some people from Albemarle, became interested in settling it. About 1723 a few individuals who were familiar with the area ignored the proprietary injunction against granting lands and began to stake out claims, clear land, and erect houses. Governor Burrington, realizing a *fait accompli,* and being personally interested in these lands himself, yielded to the request of the assembly and, in spite of his royal instructions, reopened the land office. He took a large tract himself, and lands were granted to a considerable number of newcomers from South Carolina and Albemarle, as well as to a few people from other colonies.

In contrast with the history of Albemarle, which had no town for a half century, the Lower Cape Fear settlement may be said to have begun with the founding of the town of Brunswick, laid off by Maurice Moore about 1725, some fourteen miles above the mouth of the river. About 1733 the town of Wilmington was begun, sixteen miles farther up the river. These two towns became the shipping points of the Lower Cape Fear, and both were included in the official Port of Brunswick.

Settlement of the Boundary "Betwixt Virginia and North Carolina"

While this development was taking place, the North Carolina–Virginia boundary dispute, which had been going on for half a century to the detriment of both colonies, was being settled. This controversy began with the 1665 charter extension of the Carolina boundary 30 minutes north of the original 36 degrees provided for the 1663 charter. This 36th parallel runs a little south of the present Edenton, Durham, and Greensboro, and if the Virginia contention had been upheld that the 1665 extension northward was invalid, it would have given a large block of territory to that colony. Virginia officials, from the start, considered the 36th parallel as the "dividing line betwixt Virginia and Carolina," and from 1681 to 1728 there was intermittent controversy about land grants, quitrents, Indians, and law enforcement in the region between 36 degrees and 36 degrees, 30 minutes. This disputed area was the most densely populated portion of North Carolina, and it was a matter of primary importance that the boundary be adjusted in that colony's favor. As early as 1681 the proprietors petitioned the crown for an official survey, but Virginia action prevented its being made. In 1699 a royal order to survey the line was unheeded by Virginia and Governor John Harvey was informed that it was "not convenient with us to treat with any persons by you appointed." In 1705 the Virginia Council had a secret survey made, to ascertain how much land Virginia might lose. Four years later Queen Anne ordered the two colonies to adjust the boundary, but again Virginia refused to treat with the Carolina commissioners. In 1716 Governors Eden and Spotswood entered into negotiations, but no survey was made. It was not until 1727, when George II was on the verge of buying the shares of the Carolina proprietors, that an order to survey the line was obeyed.

Running the Boundary Line

In 1728 Governor Richard Everard of North Carolina appointed four commissioners—Christopher Gale, Edward Moseley, William Little, and John Lovick—to work with representatives of the Virginia government, the leading member of whom was William Byrd II, who not only helped to "run the line" but wrote the classic *History of the Dividing Line Betwixt Virginia and North Carolina*. The commissioners met at Currituck Inlet on March 5, 1728, and, after some arguments as to the "starting point of the line," ran the boundary westward. When they reached "Hycoote River," 161 miles from the starting point—and fifty miles beyond the settled area—the North Carolina commissioners, weary, and having "drunk up" all of Byrd's liquor—according to his story—quit and went home. The Virginia delegation protested against this action, insisting that their instructions were "to complete the Line," and that it would not be long until all of the area in dispute would be settled. Accordingly they extended the survey seventy-two miles westward to present Stokes County. The North Carolina commissioners were happy over the final results, and reported that "there was taken by the Line into Carolina a very great Quantity of Lands and Number of Families that before had been under Virginia." Governor Gooch of Virginia said: "To the great surprise" of Virginia "it is now found that instead of gaining a large Tract of Land from North Carolina, the line comes rather nearer to Virginia than that which Carolina has always allowed to be our bounds."

The Crown Purchases Carolina from the Proprietors

The official report of the boundary line commissioners was made to the king, not to the proprietors, because meantime the sale of Carolina to the crown had been consummated, and North Carolina became a royal colony,

July 25, 1729. South Carolina had become royal in 1719 and for ten years thereafter North Carolina had been on the verge of following suit. Meantime the king was exercising a closer supervision than ever by requiring that governors be approved and instructed by him. Proprietary and corporate colonies had never been very satisfactory to the crown or to other English governmental agencies, and as early as the 1680s a strong trend toward "royalization and centralization" was evident. The transfer of Carolina to the crown was simply a part of the process which saw the revocation of the Massachusetts charter in 1684, the creation of the Dominion of New England in 1686, and the royalization of New Jersey, New York, and New Hampshire.

The Lords of Trade had suggested in 1689 that all the proprietary colonies be brought "under a nearer dependence on the crown." Two years later Governor Francis Nicholson of Virginia declared that the "properties would remain unsettled and disturbed" until the crown sent governors to these colonies. In 1706, at Queen Anne's request, the Board of Trade formulated charges against all proprietary and corporate colonies, declaring that these colonies had "in no ways answered the chief design" for which they had been created, and were guilty of "several misfeances, and Illegal proceedings." They had violated the laws "for Regulating Trade and Navigation"; had passed laws repugnant to those of England, "and directly prejudicial to Legal Trade"; had denied appeals from their courts to the Privy Council; had been a "refuge and retreat of Pirates and Illegal Traders"; had exported and imported goods illegally; had given protection to people who had fled from other colonies to escape punishment or taxes; had debased the currency; had failed to furnish their quotas in wars; had neglected their "own Defense & Security against an Enemy, either in Building Forts or in providing their Inhabitants with Sufficient arms and ammunition against an attack: which is every day more and more to be apprehended considering how the French power increased in those parts"; and made "ill use . . . of the powers intrusted to them by their Charters and the Independency which they pretend to." Therefore the board recommended "the reuniting to the Crown the Government of all these Colonies."

For several decades the Carolina proprietors resisted the royal efforts to take over their colony, and when legal action was begun in 1686, Shaftesbury, one of the proprietors, declared that it was "not in any perticular man's power to dispose of it." The proprietors realized, however, that they were fighting a losing battle and that sooner or later they would lose their colony. The South Carolina revolution of 1719 and the transfer of that portion of Carolina to the crown gave them warning of things to come. Besides, they had never made any profits from North Carolina, which had been little more than a source of worry and irritation. Accordingly, in January, 1728, seven of the proprietors drew up a memorial, in which they offered to sell their interests to the crown. An agreement was finally reached and an act of Parliament was passed to make it effective. By this agreement seven of the proprietary shares were sold to the Crown for £17,500 (or £2,500 each). The king also allowed the proprietors a lump sum of £5,000 to satisfy their claims for arrearages to quitrents due them. The Carteret share was not sold and later became the Granville District.

Chapter 5

THE COMING OF THE HIGH-LANDERS, SCOTCH-IRISH, AND GERMANS, 1729-1775

The transfer of the province from the Lords Proprietors to the crown marked the beginning of a significant era in North Carolina. The history of the colony for the next forty years was characterized by a steady and rapid growth in population; the settlement of the Cape Fear Valley and the Piedmont; the expansion of agriculture, industry, and trade; some improvement in transportation and the beginnings of a crude postal system; a higher standard of living, reflected in better homes, finer furniture, more and better tools and implements, and more comfortable living conditions; the rapid growth of dissenting religious sects; the founding of many churches, a few schools, and some libraries; and the publication of the first books and newspapers in the colony.

The royalization of North Carolina caused no significant change in governmental structure or powers. The powers and duties of the governor, the council, the assembly, the courts, and local officials such as sheriffs and justices of the peace remained much the same as they had been. The crown simply replaced the proprietors as the fountainhead of authority in government and in administration of land policy. Henceforth the king and Privy Council, rather than the proprietors, controlled the selection of the governor and other royal officials, instructed the governors on the conduct of their office, formulated policies, and heard complaints from the colony, which were usually voiced by an official agent resident in England. North Carolina was among the last of the colonies to establish a regular agency, and the lower house of the legislature (assembly) asserted its authority over that agent. The colony had sent special agents to London as early as 1676, but it was not until an act of October, 1768, that a permanent agent, James Abercromby, was appointed. He served the assembly as agent for more than a decade.

The proprietors had been primarily concerned with profits; the crown, although not indifferent to "returns," put major emphasis upon the promotion of the naval-stores industry and other economic activities which fitted into the British mercantile system. More and more, North Carolina, like other English colonies, became an integral part of the "Old Colonial System"—with all of its advantages and such disadvantages as responsibility for imperial defense. More and more North Carolina came to have closer contact with the various agencies of colonial administration—king, Privy Council, Board of Trade, Treasury Board, Commissioners of the Customs, Admiralty Board, and Navy Board. And more and more the assembly became jealous of its powers and engaged in controversies with the governors over salaries, paper currency, Indian policy, defense, and other matters of vital concern both to England and to the province.

Royal government was characterized by greater stability, stronger administration, and better enforcement of law and order than had prevailed under the proprietary regime. The royal governors of North Carolina—George Burrington, 1731–34; Gabriel Johnston, 1735–52; Acting Governor Nathaniel Rice, 1752–53; Acting Governor Matthew Rowan, 1753–54; Arthur Dobbs, 1754–65; William Tryon, 1765–71; and Josiah Martin, 1771–75, were of higher caliber, better character, and more experience than the proprietary governors, and they compared favorably with the governors of other colonies. Although some of the chief executives, notably Burrington and Martin, have been criticized and almost villified, both by contemporary writers and by some modern historians, and although all of the governors had prolonged and bitter quarrels with their assemblies—an experience not peculiar to North Carolina—these men, by and large, had the interests of the colony at heart. All of them tried to promote policies for the settlement and expansion of North Carolina, for improvements in transportation, trade, communication, education, religion, and other movements for the general welfare of the colony as well as for the best interests of the British Empire. Most of the policies they advocated were beneficial to both mother country and colony, though the execution of these policies caused much executive-legislative conflict. The colonial governor had the difficult, if not impossible, task of trying to serve two masters, one of whom commissioned him while the other paid his salary.

Population Growth and Expansion

The royal period of North Carolina history, 1729–75, was one of rapid growth and expansion of population. At the close of proprietary rule there were only about thirty thousand whites and fewer than six thousand Negroes in the province. At this time North Carolina was perhaps the most sparsely settled of all the English continental colonies, and most of its population, chiefly of English stock, lived largely in the Tidewater. By 1740 there were "a few families" along the Hyco, Eno, and Haw rivers, and six years later a few settlers "west of the Yadkin." In 1751 the governor reported that "inhabitants flock in here daily, mostly from Pennsylvania and other parts of America, and some directly from Europe. They commonly seat themselves toward the West and have got near the mountains." By 1752 the colony's population had increased to more than 50,000; three years later it was 80,000; and by 1765 it had jumped to 120,000. By 1775 the white population was estimated at 265,000 and the Negro population at 80,000. North Carolina had become the fourth most populous English continental colony, exceeded only by Virginia, Pennsylvania, and Massachusetts.

There were many causes for this ninefold increase in population in less than half a century. One of the most obvious factors was a high birth rate. Lawson and Brickell, contemporary writers, observed that "marriages were early and frequent, most houses being full of little ones." But the death rate was also high, infant mortality being estimated at 40 percent. North Carolina's birth rate was probably no higher than that of other colonies whose population increased at a much slower rate. Immigration is the real explanation of its phenomenal increase in population. The most impelling motives for emigration from Europe to the English colonies were wars, past, present, and anticipated; poverty, unemployment, and general economic unrest; religious persecution, legal discriminations, and harsh and vindictive penal systems; love of adventure and the desire to start life anew and "become somebody" in the New World. As Curtis Nettels has said: "To the poor peasants and workers of Europe, immersed in poverty, war, and religious persecution, the English colonies beckoned with an irresistible appeal. There at least one might enjoy peace and security, freedom of Protestant worship, and the economic opportunity of cheap land and high wages: there perhaps one might pass beyond the grasp of the tax-collector and the sound of marching armies."

During the royal period Scotch-Irish, Germans, Scottish Highlanders, Welsh, English, and a few other national stocks poured into the Upper Cape Fear Valley and into the backcountry. Settlements reached the foot of the mountains by 1760 and soon pushed across the mountains. A vast area, hitherto almost unbroken wilderness, was turned into farms and homes. Roads, bridges, and ferries were built; sawmills and gristmills were established; lumber, naval stores, potash, shipbuilding, and other industries were developed; some river channels were improved and a few lighthouses constructed. Old towns such as Edenton and New Bern took on new life, while many new towns were begun, the most significant of which were Wilmington, Halifax, Hillsborough, Salisbury, Salem, Charlotte, and what is now Fayetteville. The creation of twenty-six new counties during this period is ample evidence of the growth and expansion of population.

In the 1730s the most rapid population growth was in the Coastal Plain and particularly in the Lower Cape Fear Valley, extending from fifty to a hundred miles inland. This was a natural development. Brunswick, which had been founded about 1725, was one of the best ports in the province; and Wilmington, destined to outrank all other ports, was begun about a decade later. Both towns were included in the "Port of Brunswick," for a colonial port was an area rather than a specific town. As early as 1732 forty-two vessels cleared from Brunswick and there were about twelve hundred people in this area. The next year Governor Burrington reported, "The reputation this Government has lately acquired, appears by the number of People that have come from other Places to live in it. Many of them are possessed of good American estates . . . a thousand men have already settled here since 1731." He estimated the colony's population at thirty thousand whites and six thousand Negroes. By 1740 an estimated three thousand lived in the Lower Cape Fear region.

Settlement was moving slowly and steadily up the Cape Fear and other eastern rivers. In 1733 there were twenty families near the "Falls of Tar," some one hundred families "thriving" on New River, and a small group of Highland Scots on the Upper Cape Fear. By 1734 population increase led to the creation of three new counties, Onslow, Edgecombe, and Bladen. In 1744 Governor Gabriel Johnston reported that the Cape Fear Valley was being settled by "a sober and industrious set of people" who were noted for "amazing progress in their improvements," and that this region was "the place of greatest trade in the whole province."

The Scottish Highlanders

"The earliest, largest, and most numerous settlement of Highlanders in America" was the one in North Carolina in the years between 1732 and the American Revolution. The Highland Scots were the only large group to come to North Carolina directly from their native land. As early as 1732 a few Scots had settled on the Upper Cape Fear and were enthusiastic about the "salubrious climate, fertile soil, and liberal government." In 1736 Alexander Clark, of Jura in the Hebrides Isles, brought a shipload of his fellow countrymen to the colony, where he found "a good many Scotch." Four years later 350 Highlanders landed at Wilmington under the leadership of Neil McNeill. They left that town because, according to tradition, the settlers made fun of the peculiar costumes and unusual language and settled in the present Fayetteville region. These newcomers, pleased with their new location and future prospects, petitioned the assembly in February, 1740, saying, "If Proper encouragement be given them, they'll invite the rest of their friends and acquaintances over." The assembly, interested in promoting immigration, and probably prodded by Governor Johnston, who was a native of Scotland, voted to exempt the new settlers from all taxation for ten years. A similar exemption from payment of any "Publick or County tax for Ten years" was offered to all Highlanders who should come to North Carolina in groups of forty or more, and the governor was requested "to use his Interest, in such manner, as he shall think most proper, to obtain an Instruction for giving Encouragement to Protestants from foreign parts, to settle in Townships within this Province."

Meantime conditions in Scotland were becoming more distasteful to the Highlanders. Since the Act of Union in 1707, Scotland had been resisting the enforced alliance with England. Smouldering unrest finally broke out into open warfare, and on April 16, 1746, at Culloden, the Scots were decisively defeated by a British army led by the "Bloody Duke" of Cumberland. The aftermath of this battle created a situation that led thousands of Scots to come to North Carolina. The clan system—so dear to the hearts of the Highlanders—was broken up, estates were confiscated, and the Scots were forbidden to bear arms and to wear the costumes of their clans. Many estates were taken over by British officers and soldiers, who substituted sheep raising for ordinary agriculture, and thus threw many Scots out of work. Rents were increased and there was economic distress throughout the Highlands.

There was one way out of this unhappy situation. After Culloden the king offered pardon to all "rebels" who would take the oath of allegiance to the House of Hanover and emigrate to America. Thousands hastened to take advantage of this offer, and there developed "a Carolina mania which was not broken until the Revolution." A chorus of a dance hall song was "Going to seek a fortune in North Carolina."

Within a few years there were Highland settlements throughout the Upper Cape Fear in the region now embracing Anson, Bladen, Cumberland, Harnett, Hoke, Moore, Richmond, Robeson, Sampson, and Scotland counties. In 1754 the legislature created Cumberland County, ironically named for "Butcher Cumberland." At the head of navigation on the Cape Fear a town was begun, which was incorporated as Campbellton in 1762, named for Farquhard Campbell. In 1778 Campbellton and the adjacent trading center of Cross Creek were consolidated as Lower and Upper Campbellton, respectively. The name was changed to Cross Creek, so named because of the phenomenon of two creeks which apparently crossed without their currents mixing.

Soon after Cumberland County was created, the legislature authorized the construction of a road from the Dan River on the Virginia border to Cross Creek, and another road leading to it from Shallow Ford in Surry County. Thus Cross Creek became a significant river port and the center of a "wagon trade" for a vast region extending westward as far as the Moravian settlement at Salem.

The French and Indian War (1754–63) interrupted immigration to the colonies, but with the advent of peace it was renewed on a larger scale than ever. Thousands of Scots came to America—from the Scottish mainland and also from the "Western Isles" of Jura, Islay, Argyleshire, Stonoway, Skye, Lewis, Lochabar, Ross, and Sutherland, as well as from other islands. Between 1763 and 1769 the *Scots Magazine* mentioned four different migrations from Islay to North Carolina. From 1768 to 1771 some sixteen hundred Highlanders came into the Cape Fear area, and in the summer months of 1770 fifty-four shiploads migrated from the Western Isles to the province. In 1772 Governor Martin wrote Lord Hillsborough, secretary of state for the colonies: "Near a thousand people have arrived in Cape Fear River from the Scottish Isles since the month of November with a view to settling in this province whose prosperity and strength will receive great augmentation by the accession of such a number of hardy, laborious and thrifty people."

The year 1773 witnessed the heaviest emigration, approximately four thousand leaving that year, a goodly portion of whom came to North Carolina, where they found "the largest and most important settlement of Highlanders in America." In 1775 Governor Martin estimated that he could raise a loyalist army of three thousand Highlanders, which indicates that there were probably as many as twenty thousand in the province.

The Highlanders who came to North Carolina were among the most substantial and energetic people of Scotland. Scottish journals referred to them as men "of wealth and merit," as "the most wealthy and substantial people in Skye," and "the finest set of fellows in the Highlands" who carried "at least £6,000 sterling in ready cash with them." In the 1772–73 migration it was claimed that each person carried an average of £4, and it was estimated that the fifteen hundred emigrants from County Sunderland during these two years carried with them £7,500, "which exceeds a year's rent of the whole county."

The Scots continued to use Gaelic, and in 1756 Hugh McAden reported that many of them "scarcely knew one word of English." But Gaelic gradually gave way to English, although there were survivals of the ancient tongue for more than a century.

Most of the Highlanders became farmers, and they were particularly important in the production of naval stores from the vast forests of longleaf pines. Quite a number became merchants and, according to Governor Tryon, many were "skilled mechanics." Some entered the professions and made distinctive contributions in politics, religion, education, and military affairs.

Scotch-Irish

At the same time that the Highland Scots were settling the Cape Fear Valley large numbers of Scotch-Irish and Germans were moving into backcountry North Carolina, chiefly from Pennsylvania, but also from New Jersey, Maryland, and Virginia.

The term Scotch-Irish is a misnomer. It is geographical and not racial and does not imply a mixture of the two national stocks. It refers to Scots, chiefly Lowlanders, who settled in Ireland, or to the descendants of these people. In Ireland they were usually called "Irish Protestants" or "Irish Presbyterians," while in the colonies they were called Scotch-Irish or Irish, although they scorned the latter designation.

The story of how James I of England "planted" the "six escheated counties" of Ulster with Lowland Scots in an effort to make "Ireland a civil place" is well known and need not be recounted here. During his reign and for the greater part of the seventeenth century thousands of Scottish Lowlanders moved into North Ireland. By their energy and skill they transformed Ulster into a prosperous region; they built up extensive cattle and sheep industries and developed woolen and linen manufactures on a large scale. English woolen interests, feeling the pressure of competition, succeeded in getting the Woolen Act of 1699 passed to prohibit the exportation of Irish wool and woolen cloth to any places except England and Wales. This was a serious blow to the Ulsterites, but it was only one of many problems confronted by these energetic and determined people. The Test Act of 1704, passed through the influence of the High Church party, excluded Ulster Presbyterians from all important civil and military offices, made it illegal for them to practice law or to teach school, and denied them many other civil and religious rights. Presbyterians were fined and imprisoned for exercising their form of worship and the doors of many of their churches were nailed shut.

Perhaps the most potent and constant causes of Ulster migration to the English colonies were agrarian and economic. The first large exodus of 1717–18 was caused primarily by the destruction of the woolen industry, disabilities arising from the Test Act, and the doubling and trebling of rents by rack-renting landlords. The great migration of 1727–28 was caused by the same forces, plus a series of poor harvests, culminating in a great famine. The *Pennsylvania Gazette* of November 20, 1729, referring to the people of Ulster, said, "Poverty, wretchedness, misery, and want are become almost universal among them." And Jonathan Swift, in his famous *Irish Tracts,* wrote: "Whoever travels throughout this country . . . would hardly think himself in a land where either law, religion, or common humanity was professed. . . . The old and sick . . . every day dying and rotting by cold and famine and filth and vermin." In 1740 and 1741 another severe famine, in which an estimated 400,000 died of starvation, and an economic crisis caused by overproduction of silk weaving, led to a tremendous exodus. The tide of emigration slackened during the French and Indian War and did not become large again until 1771–73. This, the last large migration to the English colonies, was brought about by the usual causes, plus a sharp decline in the linen industry and a new outburst of rack-renting.

Still another reason for large Ulster emigration was the activity of ship captains, agents of land companies, and other promoters interested in procuring indentured servants for the colonial labor market. As Abbot Emerson Smith has pointed out, thousands of servants were brought from Ireland to the English colonies. An Irish archbishop in 1728 stated that "above 3,200" Irish had been shipped to America in the previous three years, and "that only one in ten could pay his own passage." A writer in an Irish magazine calculated that from

3,000 to 6,000 annually emigrated in the years between 1725 and 1768, and the naval records reveal that 5,835 "Irish servants" landed at Annapolis, Maryland from 1745 to 1775.

The causes of the large exodus of Ulster Scots to America have been described in eloquent language by the great English historian, James A. Froude: "Men of spirit and energy refused to remain in a country where they were held unfit to receive the rights of citizens. . . . Religious bigotry, commercial jealousy, and modern landlordism had combined to do their worst against the Ulster settlement. . . . Vexed with suits in ecclesiastical courts, forbidden to educate their children in their own faith, treated as dangerous in a state which but for them would have had no existence, and associated with Papists in an Act of Parliament which deprived them of their civil rights, the most earnest of them at length abandoned the unthankful service. They saw at last that the liberties for which their fathers had fought were not to be theirs in Ireland. . . . During the first half of the eighteenth century, Down, Antrim, Armagh, and Derry were emptied of their Protestant families, who were of more value to Ireland than California gold mines."

Some Ulster Scots were to be found in almost every English colony, but Pennsylvania received by far the largest number, mainly because of its reputation for political, religious, and economic freedom and the glowing reports received of its fertile soil and healthful climate. Philadelphia became the chief port of debarkation, and Pennsylvania became the chief distributing point for the Scotch-Irish population in the English colonies.

From 1717 to 1735 thousands of Ulsterites poured into Pennsylvania and took up lands in the central and back country. By 1730 the vanguard of settlers had reached the foothills of the Alleghenies and in the summer of that year migration began to be deflected southwestward into the Valley of Virginia. As population increased, land prices and rents advanced to such an extent that they were soon twice as high in Pennsylvania as in Virginia or North Carolina, whose land agents were beginning to advertise their real estate with a "come-south-where-it's-cheap" appeal.

There were a few scattered Scotch-Irish settlers in North Carolina long before the great influx from Pennsylvania began. In the 1670s William Edmundson mentioned James Hall, a native of Ireland who had moved to Virginia and thence to Albemarle. John Urmston, Anglican missionary, early in the next century had been disturbed by some "vehement Scotch Presbyterians" in his parish. Some members of the wealthy and influential Pollock family had migrated from Ulster to North Carolina. But the first group settlement of Scotch-Irish occurred after 1735, when Arthur Dobbs, "some other gentlemen of distinction in Ireland," and Henry McCulloh, an Ulster Scot who was then a prominent London merchant, presented a memorial to the North Carolina council "representing their intention of sending over to this Province several poor Protestant familys with design of raising Flax and Hemp." The following year they were granted some 60,000 acres of land in what are now Duplin and Sampson counties. In 1737 "Dobbs, McCulloh, Murray Crymble and James Huey and Company" were granted 1,200,000 acres on the Yadkin, Catawba, and Eno rivers, provided they settle within this grant "substantial people" who would "carry on the Pot Ash trade" and produce hemp and other naval stores. The company failed to obtain the requisite number of 3,625 persons, and as late as 1754 it had brought in only 854 people. In 1767, after years of turmoil about boundaries, land titles, and quitrents, the company surrendered its grant to the crown.

As early as 1740 there were a few Scotch-Irish families along the Haw and Eno rivers and by 1764 there were some "west of the Yadkin." In 1752 Moravian Bishop Spangenberg wrote that many people were moving into North Carolina from England, Scotland, and the Northern colonies, "as they wished to own lands and were too poor to buy in Pennsylvania or New Jersey." Three years later Governor Dobbs stated that as many as ten thousand immigrants had landed at Philadelphia in a single year, many of whom were "obliged to remove to the southward for want of lands to take up" in Pennsylvania. The observant Frederick William Marshall, of the Wachovia settlement, realized the truth of the governor's statement, but he added the interesting comment, "The migration of men are like the movements of a flock of sheep, where one goes the flock follows, without knowing why."

The "Great Wagon Road"

How did these thousands of Pennsylvania émigrés—Scotch-Irish, Germans, Welsh, and others—"with horse and wagon and cattle," reach their destinations in the North Carolina backcountry? They made their southward trek over "The Great Philadelphia Wagon Road," frequently called "the bad road," which began at the Schuylkill River Ferry opposite Philadelphia, ran west through Lancaster to Harris's Ferry on the Susquehanna, thence through York to Williams' Ferry on the Potomac, where it entered the "Great Valley of Virginia," passing through Winchester, Strasburg, and Staunton, crossing the James River at present Buchanan, and turning almost due south to the site of present Roanoke; thence eastward through the Staunton Gap of the Blue Ridge, then southward, crossing the Blackwater, Irvine, and Dan rivers, and thence to Wachovia on a tributary of the Yadkin—and, after about 1756, on to Salisbury.

The North Carolina legislature, cognizant of the "new immigration," created five counties—Johnston and Granville in 1746, Anson in 1750, Orange in 1752, and Rowan in 1753. By 1755 it was reported that the last three of these had "at least three thousand people, for the most part Irish Protestants and Germans," and that they were "dayley increasing." Immigrants continued to pour in from Pennsylvania, and "they commonly seated themselves toward the west and got near the mountains." Accordingly Mecklenburg County was created in 1763. The next year the exaggerated claim was made that there were more white inhabitants able to bear arms in one of these six "back counties" than there had been in the whole province seven years before. In 1767 there were 14,599 taxables in these counties, which probably meant a total population of 60,000. Within twenty years the number of Orange taxables increased from 20 to about 4,000.

During the French and Indian War (1754–63) many people moved from Virginia to North Carolina because of French and Indian attacks in "The Valley," and because of the eagerness of dissenters to escape taxes for the Anglican Church. This migration was accelerated at the close of the war, as was that from Pennsylvania. In 1766 Governor Dobbs wrote, "I am of opinion this province is settling faster than any on the continent, last autumn and winter, upwards of one thousand wagons passed thro' Salisbury with families from the northward, to settle in this province chiefly; some few went to Georgia and Florida, but liked it so indifferently that some of them have since returned." A writer in the *South Carolina and American General Gazette* in 1768 declared, "There is scarce any history either ancient or modern, which affords an account of such a rapid and sudden increase of inhabitants in a back frontier country, as that of North Carolina."

Scotch-Irish Traits

The Scotch-Irishman was described by some writers as "clannish, contentious, and hard to get along with." He was usually well "set in his ways," as illustrated by the prayer attributed to him, "Lord, grant that I may always be right, for Thou knowest that I am hard to turn." His thrift was proverbial, and it was said of him, "The Scotch-Irishman is one who keeps the commandments of God, and every other good thing that he can get his hands on." In spite of these ascribed qualities—or perhaps because of them—the Scotch-Irish made a great contribution to the growth, expansion, and development of North Carolina. They established Presbyterian churches throughout a wide area. Within a short time they established schools. They had a flair for politics, and in this, as in religion, they were not given to compromise. They developed agriculture and a variety of local industries, having among their numbers capable weavers, coopers, joiners, wheelwrights, wagon-makers, tailors, blacksmiths, hatters, rope-makers, fullers, and other skilled workers. They had fighting qualities acquired in their rough, hardy, outdoor life, which stood them in good stead on the frontier. All in all they exerted a tremendous influence in shaping the history of the colony and the state.

German Settlements

Moving from Pennsylvania along the same route at the same time as the Scotch-Irish, and settling in the same general area of the North Carolina Piedmont, were many Germans. In the early years of the eighteenth century thousands of Germans had been forced to flee their native land because of intolerable political, religious, and economic conditions. So large a number of these people migrated to Pennsylvania that by 1775 one-third of its population was German, or so-called Pennsylvania Dutch. The same reasons which prompted the Scotch-Irish to move from Pennsylvania southward also motivated the Germans; and in addition there was the desire on the part of some of the German sects to establish economically independent communities on a religious basis, and to do missionary work among the Indians.

Most of the Germans who came to North Carolina belonged to three religious sects—Lutheran, Moravian, and Reformed. Few of the "plain people," as the Germans called the Dunkards and other Pietist sects, settled in North Carolina as they had in the Shenandoah Valley of Virginia. Morgan Edwards listed only three Dunker settlements in North Carolina in 1772, but a modern scholar has identified three other Dunker congregations. No other Pietist sect was represented in the colony. The Lutherans came to be the largest German religious element in North Carolina, and the Reformed group also had considerable numbers, but the most significant and largest of these sects in the first stages of settlement was the Moravians.

About 1747 there were a few Lutherans along the Haw River and perhaps as far west as present Catawba County. By 1750 there were German settlers in Rowan, and three years later it was reported that there were at least three thousand fighting men in Anson, Orange, and Rowan counties, "for the most part Irish Protestants and Germans, brave, industrious people." Rowan County was created in 1753, Salisbury was founded in the same year and incorporated two years later, and St. John's Lutheran Church in that town was organized in 1768. Three years later it was reported that "near three thousand German protestant families" had settled in Rowan, Orange, Mecklenburg, and Tryon counties.

Moravian Settlement of Wachovia

In 1752 Lord Granville suggested to the Moravian Brethren, who had already planted a settlement at Bethlehem, Pennsylvania, that they purchase from him such land as they desired in North Carolina. In the fall of that year Moravian Bishop August Gottlieb Spangenberg, with a party of Brethren from Pennsylvania, visited the colony to select a place for settlement. They traversed North Carolina from Edenton to the Blue Ridge and finally chose a site in what is now Forsyth County. Spangenberg, well pleased with the land, climate, abundant game, and other resources, regarded it "as a corner which the Lord had reserved for the Brethren." In August he purchased 98,985 acres of land in "the three forks of Muddy Creek" for £500 sterling and an annual quitrent of £148 9s. ½ d. Spangenberg named the tract "Wachovia," supposedly from two German words, "Wach" and "Aue," which mean "meadow-stream." It is likely that the name was taken from "Wachau," the name of the estate in Saxony of Count Zinzendorf, European leader of the Moravians.

The first group of settlers for Wachovia set out from Bethlehem on October 8, 1753, and on November 17 they arrived at a spot where now stands the community of Bethabara ("Old Town"). This party consisted of fifteen unmarried men—minister, warden, physician, baker, tailor, shoemaker, tanner, gardener, three farmers, and two carpenters. Their first shelter was the deserted cabin of a German trapper, Hans Wagoner. Within a short time they had begun a town and before the end of the following year they had in operation a carpenter shop, a flour mill, a pottery, a cooperage works, a tannery, a blacksmith shop, and a shoe shop. On March 26, 1758, these Moravians held the first Easter sunrise service in Wachovia. In 1759 Bethania, or "New Town," was founded, some three miles from Bethabara. The town of Salem, in the center of Wachovia, was begun in 1766. Within a decade a number of Bethabara people moved to Salem and the latter continued to receive additional settlers from Pennsylvania.

The Moravians tended to segregate themselves from other settlements. They were determined to preserve their religious, social, and economic customs. They emphasized community cooperation and common ownership of property. It was not until 1849 that the congregation abandoned its supervision of business, and not until 1856 that the lease system was dropped. By the time of the outbreak of the Revolution Salem had at least thirty dwelling houses and also a "congregation house," a "single brethren's house," a community store, and an excellent tavern. A visitor in 1786 reported that "every house in Salem is supplied with water brought in conduits a mile and a half." They also had waterworks and fire fighting equipment.

It is impossible to state with accuracy the number of German settlers in colonial North Carolina. A. B. Faust, a leading authority, estimates the number in 1775 at eight thousand. Governor Dobbs's statement that the frontier families usually had "from five to ten members each" leads one to conclude that the German population of the province was probably as high as fifteen thousand. The 1790 census estimated that only 2.8 percent of the North Carolina population was German. It is likely that the "population experts" have been misled by the Anglicizing and shortening of German names, such as Müller to Miller, Schwartz to Black, Behringer to Barringer, Braun to Brown, Fischer to Fisher, Zimmerman to Carpenter, Albrecht to Albright, and Schmidt to Smith.

By habit and training, the German—Moravian, Lutheran, or Reformed—was industrious, thrifty, and law-abiding. Unaccustomed to slavery and unacquainted with Negroes, he was inclined to rely on his own labor. He became the best farmer in the province. A traveler in 1783 described the Germans as "distinguished above the other inhabitants for their industry and diligence in agriculture and the crafts . . . which is recognized by most of their fellow-citizens, but tempts very few to imitate."

Chapter 6

AGRICULTURE AND INDUSTRY, 1729-1775

Agriculture is generally the principal economic pursuit of all new and underdeveloped countries, and colonial North Carolina was no exception to this rule. At least 95 percent of its early settlers were engaged in agriculture or related industries. This was a natural development favored by the abundance, fertility, and cheapness of land; by the imperative need of the people for self-sufficiency; by the desire, if not the necessity, for articles of export, and by the application of British mercantilist principles, which insisted on "returns" from the colonies of goods that did not compete with British manufactures.

The abundance of land, the ease of acquiring it, and the relative scarcity of capital and labor were fundamental factors in determining the economy, social order, and political character of North Carolina. Land and slaves were the chief forms of wealth, and the possession of slaves was inextricably related to the ownership of land. Everything affecting land tenure—the size of grants, registration of titles, accuracy of surveys, amount and mode of quitrent payments, and laws governing forfeiture and escheats—was of immediate concern to the people. In North Carolina, as in other southern provinces, the headright system of granting lands prevailed. In the early years a hundred acres were granted to each "undertaker" and fifty acres were allotted to others. Later fifty acres were allotted to each individual who paid his way to the colony and settled, provided he made improvements on his grant and fulfilled other conditions. The headright system, most prevalent in the seventeenth century, continued throughout the colonial era, but after 1730 the customary mode of acquiring land was by purchase. Land values were low at first, and the available figures are unsatisfactory; but there was a tendency for prices to increase, so that land was selling as high as fifteen pounds sterling per one hundred acres before the Revolution. The purchase of land and the law of primogeniture, by which all the real property of those dying intestate descended to the oldest son, helped to build up and perpetuate large estates. The law of entail made it possible to prevent the division of large estates, and thus tended to preserve vast tracts of land in the same family.

Land was so plentiful and the desire so great to get the colony settled that some very large tracts were granted to individuals and to companies. Complaints were made at an early date about making large grants to those individuals who had "not nigh enough people to manure and people the same," and the Albemarle legislature of 1669 passed a law forbidding the taking up of tracts larger than 660 acres without special permission of the Lords Proprietors. But this permission was easy to obtain and some tremendous grants were made. Several planters owned from 5,000 to 10,000 acres each. Roger Moore was granted more than 10,000 acres, and in 1732 Thomas Pollock, of Bertie, devised 22,000 acres of land, besides ten other plantations and seventy-five slaves. Edward Moseley, Cullen Pollock, Gabriel Johnston, and other individuals received large acreages, and the Moravian Brethren in Wachovia received nineteen deeds for a total of 98,985 acres. But large grants were the exception rather than the rule, and only in the Lower Cape Fear were most tracts very large. The colonial government followed the general policy of restricting the size of grants, with the result that North Carolina came to be a "colony of small landowners" who lived on and cultivated their own soil. Consequently, less of a plantation aristocracy developed than in the neighboring colonies of Virginia and South Carolina.

Land was not held in fee simple, but a quitrent was paid—to the proprietors until 1729 and after that date to the royal governor as agent of the crown. The quitrent was a relic of feudalism transported to America. As a part of the manorial system, it was a feudal due, which originated in money payment required by the lord from the tenant in place of payments formerly made in produce or labor. By the payment of a fixed money rent, the payee was "quit" or freed from all other annual feudal charges.

The rate of quitrents in North Carolina varied and increased in the eighteenth century. The usual rent before 1730 was two shillings per one hundred acres per annum on "rental" land and one shilling per one hundred acres on purchase land. After 1730 the rates were doubled. These rents were not based on the value of land or ability of the owner to pay, and they were always odious, unpopular, and poorly collected.

The method of taking up land in North Carolina was described by a writer in 1773: "The method of settling in Carolina, is to find out a space of King's land, or unpatented land, and to get an order from the governor, which order is given to a surveyor; when the survey is finished, he draws a plan of that space of land, which plan is returned into the office for recording patents. Then he gets his patent signed by the governor, which is good forever after; the expense of all this is commonly about ten guineas, and sometimes not so much: supposing the run of land taken up to be 640 acres, only there is 2s. 6d. quit rents paid yearly for the hundred acres."

The legal fee for surveyors at this time was £1 13*s.* 4*d.* for each one thousand acres or under and 2 shillings extra for each one hundred acres above a thousand acres.

The great importance of water transportation, the poor facilities for land transportation, and the fertility of bottom lands led the early settlers to select sites along the rivers, particularly where there was a good "landing." Lawson observed in 1709 that "most of the Plantations in Carolina naturally enjoy a Noble Prospect of large and spacious Rivers, pleasant Savannas, and fine Meadows." The proprietors tried to cope with this problem by specifying the amount of land which might be acquired by each grantee along the watercourses, but their efforts were futile, and within a short time most of the good bottom lands had been taken up, forcing newcomers to settle in areas removed from natural "landing places."

Throughout the colonial era North Carolina landholders, like those in other English colonies, were handicapped by confusion in the land system. The carelessness of land surveys, plots described, and boundaries marked retarded settlement of some areas in the province and caused unrest almost everywhere. Such phrases in deeds as "beginning at a sweet gum on the east side of log pine branch and running to a pine tree on the west side of White Oak Swamp," led to confusion, controversy, and frequently to litigation. This problem and many others relating to land tenure handicapped agriculture, though there were other problems of greater magnitude.

Crops

At first North Carolina farmers, like those in other colonies, experimented with a variety of European crops. Olives, silk, French grapes, and a few others failed; wheat, oats, and some others succeeded. The settlers finally adapted many Indian crops, notably maize or Indian corn, tobacco, different varieties of beans and peas, white potatoes, sweet potatoes, and several crops of lesser importance. The major crops of the colony were corn, tobacco, peas, beans, wheat, and rice. Tobacco became the leading "money crop" and was grown extensively in the Albemarle Sound region, in the Roanoke Valley, and later in Granville and the whole tier of counties along the Virginia border. The culture of tobacco—seed-beds, transplanting, worming, priming, suckering—was much the same as it is today, but it should be noted that "the weed" was of the burley type and that, in contrast with the present flue-cured method used in the "bright leaf" industry, it was air-cured or sun-cured—a process which took from five to six weeks; after this the tobacco was taken down, the leaves cut off the stalks, and assorted and packed into hogsheads. The hogsheads were then hauled, or more frequently rolled, to a landing and put on board for shipment—usually to England, since tobacco was one of the "enumerated commodities" listed in the Navigation Act of 1660. The North Carolina law required that all tobacco exported be packed in hogsheads containing a minimum of one thousand pounds each, and that the tobacco be approved by an official inspector.

North Carolina produced and exported a great variety of foodstuffs, of which corn, wheat, peas, and beans were the most important. Next to naval stores, these "provisions" constituted the largest item of export. Corn was grown in all parts of the province, although not as extensively in the Cape Fear Valley as in the Sound region and the Piedmont. Yields were usually high, and it was reported that an industrious person could produce seven hundred bushels a season. Peas, usually "Indian peas" or the black-eyed variety, and beans, chiefly kidney beans and bushel beans (supposed to yield a bushel of green beans per vine) were grown in large quantities, especially in the Sound region, and were exported in large amounts to the West Indies and to other continental colonies. Wheat, which was broadcast by hand, cut with reap-hooks or sickles, threshed with flails or treaded out by oxen, and ground in water-driven mills, was produced in all parts of the colony, but in large quantities only in the Cape Fear Valley, and later in the Piedmont. In 1764 Governor Dobbs proudly reported that the Cape Fear was supplying its own wheat needs and had exported several hundred barrels of flour to the West Indies. Some rice was grown in the Lower Cape Fear, but it was not a crop of major importance and its significance has been overemphasized by some writers. North Carolina farmers also produced some hemp, flax, indigo, and cotton, the latter in very small amounts. Honey, wine, sorghum, hops, timothy grass, white potatoes, sweet potatoes, and a wide variety of fruits and vegetables were also grown, chiefly for home consumption.

Agricultural Policy

In its agricultural policy North Carolina followed the pattern of Virginia and some other colonies by enacting laws to promote crop production and to improve agricultural practices. The printed *Colonial Records of North Carolina* contain some thirty references to laws pertaining to corn, twenty-five to tobacco, fifteen to wheat, and a lesser number to other crops. Agricultural legislation was discussed by every General Assembly. Bounties were offered for the production of flax, hemp, indigo, silk, and several other commodities. Wheat and tobacco culture were encouraged by law. In 1715 sixteen commodities, chiefly agricultural, were legally authorized as media of exchange; a later law extended this list of "commodity money" to twenty-two articles, which included all the principal farm crops and tended to stabilize the price of these articles. Small tracts of land, usually fifty acres, and the right to use timber from adjacent lands, as well as exemption from public taxes and militia service, were given for the operation of sawmills, corn mills, and flour mills. Scores of laws were enacted for the inspection, grading, and standardizing of tobacco, pork, and other exports and making it illegal to ship any articles except those of the best grades. There was legislation requiring that fields be fenced against livestock and wild animals. Laws were passed for the destruction of "vermin" which were destroying crops; for the branding and marking of horses, cattle, and hogs; for regulating the shipment of hides; for improving the breed of livestock, and there were many other laws aimed at the betterment of agriculture.

Methods of Farming

Methods of farming were generally backward and unscientific. As a rule land was tilled year after year until the soil was exhausted and yields greatly diminished; then "new ground" was cleared and the "old fields" were turned out to "rest" and to grow up in trees. There was little or no crop rotation; fields were rotated instead. Barnyard manures were not used, commercial fertilizers were unknown, and "green manures" were seldom employed. Land was abundant and cheap, and it was considered easier and more profitable to clear new grounds than to increase the productivity of old fields, especially for the cultivation of tobacco, which was supposed to flourish on fresh lands. European travelers were annoyed by the slovenly and indolent methods of the settlers. One writer declared that the farmers "depend altogether upon the Liberality of Nature; without endeavouring to improve its Gifts by Art or Industry They sponge upon the Blessings of a Warm Sun and a fruitful Soil and almost grutch the pains of gathering."

In 1775 the anonymous author of *American Husbandry* said: "The mode of common husbandry is to break up a piece of wood land, a work very easily done . . . this they sow with Indian corn for several years successively, till it will yield crops no longer . . . when the land is pretty well exhausted they sow it with peas and beans once a year . . . and afterwards sow it with wheat for two or three years. . . . In this system of crops they change the land as fast as it wears out, clearing fresh pieces of wood land exhausting them in succession."

Agriculture was retarded by this conventional method of cropping, which was passed on from father to son, as well as by the prevalent practice of planters in paying overseers part of the crops as compensation for their services. Prevalent superstitions, which led planters to plow land, plant and harvest crops, and slaughter hogs according to phases of the moon or other "signs," were also detrimental. Agricultural improvement was delayed, too, by the failure of farmers to pay enough attention to proper drainage, seed selection, deep plowing, and other practices that might have increased crop yields.

One of the greatest handicaps to good farming was the inadequacy of tools and implements. Skilled workmen were few. Lack of trade with the outside world made it difficult to import farm equipment. Plows were scarce, and those in use were awkward and cumbersome, operating "something like a shovel pulled through the earth." Crude makeshifts were used for hoes, harrows, forks, spades, and other implements. What tools the farmers had were passed on from one generation to another—if they had not been broken or worn out. Bishop Spangenberg, in a 140-mile journey in the summer of 1752, reported that he saw "not one wagon or plough, nor any sign of one."

Crop Pests and Other Farm Problems

The colonial farmer "talked about the weather," and he suffered from droughts, floods, hailstorms, and other vagaries of the weather. But his flood problem was not as acute as it became after most of the forests were destroyed. Like the farmer today, he faced the perennial problem of crop pests: the smaller variety consisting of worms, bugs, and weevils (but not the boll weevil), and the larger variety, usually called "vermin," which embraced most of the wild animals and fowls of the forest. Perhaps the most destructive "pests" were crows, wild pigeons, doves, wild turkeys—"great destroyers of peas, wheat, and Indian corn"—eagles, which were "very destructive of poultry," and bears, which were "great destroyers of swine and inordinately fond of potatoes."

The "vermin" problem was so serious that in 1736 Governor Johnston devoted a great portion of his legislative message to this matter and suggested, "For the better preserving your Cattle, Corn, and other grains, I believe you will find it highly necessary to provide a sufficient reward for the Killing of Vermin which I am informed have done great Mischief in most parts of the Province." The legislature followed his advice and passed a law offering rewards for the "scalps" of various destructive animals.

One of the most serious and constant problems was that of overproduction and falling prices, especially of tobacco. The price of this article fluctuated greatly from year to year, and averaged little more than two pence per pound after 1700. As early as 1666 "tobacco-stinting" negotiations were carried on between the governor of Albemarle and the governors of Virginia and Maryland, but this first effort at intercolonial regulation of tobacco production failed. So did various attempts of the North Carolina legislature to regulate acreages, in order to bolster tobacco prices.

Livestock and Cattle

At first North Carolina farmers had only a scant supply of livestock, cattle, and hogs, but by the eighteenth century domestic animals were numerous throughout the settled areas. The principal draft animals were oxen, used for such heavy work as plowing and hauling. The horse, "the indispensable animal," was employed primarily for riding, though some horses were used for heavier work in the fields and for transportation of goods to and from market. There were no mules in North Carolina—or in any of the English colonies. The farmers had milk cows, beef cattle, hogs, chickens, geese, and other kinds of fowl. Most of the cattle and livestock were of the "scrub variety" and had "a lean and hungry look." These animals were smaller than our present varieties, largely because of the prevalent custom of allowing them to run at large on the almost unlimited range, thus preventing any scientific improvement of the breed. Horses and cattle were branded by their owners and turned loose to fend for themselves. This practice worked satisfactorily in summer, but in winter the stock suffered from lack of food to such an extent that by spring they were "so reduced by hunger and cold that they hardly recover before fall." The inaccessibility of markets made it unprofitable to devote much attention to the improvement of the breed.

Great numbers of hogs, usually of the "razor-back" or "wind-splitter" species, their ears notched with the owner's mark, roamed the unfenced woods, growing fat on "mast" until five or six weeks before "killing time," when they were penned and fed corn, in order to improve the quality of meat. Enormous quantities of hog meat were consumed locally, probably to the injury of the people's health; large droves of hogs—sometimes as many as five hundred— were marketed on foot in Virginia, or even Pennsylvania; and vast quantities of pork were exported to the West Indies and other foreign markets. Because of its shorter winters, it was claimed that North Carolina could "send its salted hog meat to market at a third or half cheaper" than the northern colonies. About one-eighth of the pork and beef shipments from the English continental colonies were from North Carolina.

With the settlement of the Cape Fear Valley and the Piedmont about the middle of the eighteenth century, there was a marked increase in the quantity and quality of cattle and livestock. This was particularly true in the areas settled by the Germans, who usually had large barns and housed their stock in winter. "Black cattle" became famous in the backcountry, and one writer, in 1775, observed: "It is not an uncommon thing to see one man the master of from 300 to 1200, and even 2000 cows, bulls, oxen, and young cattle; hogs also in prodigious numbers. Their management is to let them run loose in the woods all day, and to bring them up at night by the sound of a horn: sometimes, particularly in winter, they keep them during the night in inclosures, giving them a little food, and letting the cows and sows to the calves and pigs; this makes them come home the more regularly. Such herds of cattle and swine are to be found in no other colonies." This and many other contemporary accounts about livestock holdings were greatly exaggerated. Large holdings were rare rather than common. No holdings of over three hundred head of cattle are found in extant inventories and even records of one hundred head are rare.

A contemporary writer described the huge herds of cattle which pastured on the "wild pea-vines, buffalo grass," and other natural pasturage of the Piedmont. A system of ranching, annual roundups at "cowpens," and branding, followed by "long drives" to the coast, to Charleston, to Virginia, and to points as far distant as Philadelphia and Lancaster, was a forerunner of the later cattle industry of the "Wild West." And, like the western cattlemen of the next century, colonial farmers faced the problem of "cattle rustling." All owners of livestock and cattle were required by law to brand their animals, but this did not solve the problem of thievery. Efforts were also made to stamp out disease among cattle by the passage of a quarantine law in 1752. A few cattlemen attempted to improve the breed of cattle by importing better stock from Virginia and Pennsylvania. By 1775 North Carolina had the highest rank in beef cattle production it has ever held, and an estimated fifty thousand head were exported annually.

North Carolina Industry

The North Carolina farmer was a self-sufficient and versatile jack-of-all-trades. He was a combination farmer, engineer, hunter and trapper, carpenter, mechanic, and businessman. The colony had two general types of industry: (1) household manufactures, or the production of articles by members of the family, largely for their own use; and (2) commercialized manufactures, which produced goods for sale within the colony or for the export market. The relative scarcity of capital and skilled labor, the inadequacy of transportation facilities, the lack of good ports, and high freight rates on imports and exports retarded the development of large-scale commercialized industry. At the same time these factors, plus the abundance of raw materials and the bountiful supply of unskilled labor, especially that of women and children, tended to stimulate household industries.

The colonial household supplied itself with nearly all foodstuffs—bread, dairy products, pork and beef, and many other articles for the table. Surplus grains and fruits were manufactured into beer, wine, brandy, whiskey, and other "intoxicating beverages" by the people who had no inclination toward prohibition and who believed that such drinks were healthful. Cloth-making was a major household industry and almost every home had cards, spinning wheels, and looms which converted wool, flax, and perhaps a small amount of cotton into cloth. Cattle hides were tanned and converted into shoes, breeches, and other items of clothing, and also into harness and other essential articles. Deerskins were made into leggings, caps, and moccasins. Most of the farmers made their own furniture, farm implements, and household utensils from local materials. Firewood from the forest provided the fuel for heating and cooking—and to a certain degree for lighting—and almost every household moulded its own candles and made its own soap. It has been truly said that the colonial household was a "soap factory and a laundry."

The Naval Stores Industry

Though most of North Carolina's industries were of the household type, the colony developed two major industries—naval stores and lumber—as well as several lesser industries based on forest products. The most significant commercial industry was naval stores—tar, pitch, rosin, and turpentine. The most valuable of the colony's exports were these stores, and this was the only industry in which North Carolina held first place among the English colonies. In fact, North Carolina led the world in the production of naval stores from about 1720 to 1870, and it was this industry which gave to North Carolina its nickname, "Tar Heel State." In the eighteenth century seven-tenths of the tar, more than one-half of the turpentine, and one-fifth of the pitch exported from all the colonies to England came from the longleaf pine forests of North Carolina.

At the opening of the century England, involved in war, found itself at the mercy of the monopolistic Swedish Tar Company from which it was purchasing nearly all of its tar, pitch, and other "stores" so badly needed by the navy and merchant marine. In line with the current mercantilist philosophy of making England self-sufficient by getting the colonies to produce those articles which England was importing from "enemy nations," Parliament passed the Naval Stores Bounty Act of 1705, authorizing the payment of a bounty of four pounds sterling per ton on tar and pitch, and three pounds per ton on rosin and turpentine. To be doubly sure that England procured these articles from the colonies, naval stores were placed on the "enumerated list" in 1706.

This British policy proved to be a boon to North Carolina and enabled it to develop a great export crop, which in no way interfered with ordinary agricultural pursuits. In fact, naval stores production dovetailed into the whole agricultural economy. Farmers could carry on naval stores operations when the weather prevented ordinary farm work; the use of the trees for tar aided the farmer in the process of clearing land; and, since all these stores were shipped in barrels or hogsheads, a very important cooperage, or barrel-making, industry was developed. Early observers had commented about the barrenness of the soil of North Carolina's Coastal Plain. One traveler said that the region was "hardly fit for human habitation," while another expressed the view that the "vast forests of pitch trees" would retard the development of agriculture. These forests, however, turned out to be the greatest single economic asset the colony had, "yielding more profit to the occupier, from the smallest capital imaginable, than can be well conceived was it not so well authenticated."

The methods used in making naval stores were described by many contemporary writers, the following account being written in 1710: "Rosin is obtained by cutting Channels in the standing green Trees, that meet in a Point at the Foot of the Tree, where two or three small Pieces of Board are fitted to receive it. The Channels are cut as high as one can reach with an Axe, and the Bark

Scraping Turpentine
North Carolina Collection, The University of North Carolina at Chapel Hill

is peeled off from all those Parts of the Tree that are expos'd to the Sun, that the Heat of it may all the more easily force out the Turpentine, which falling upon the Boards placed at the Root, is gather'd and laid in Heaps, which melted in great Kettles, becomes Rosin.

"Tar is made thus: First they prepare a circular Floor of Clay, declining a little towards the Center, from which is laid a Pipe of Wood, whose upper Part is even with the Floor, and reaches 2 Foot without the Circumference; under this End the Earth is dug away, and Barrels placed to receive the Tar as it runs. Upon the Floor is built up a large Pile of dry Pine-wood, split in Pieces, and surrounded with a Wall of Earth, which covers it all over, only a little at the Top, where the Fire is first kindled. After the Fire begins to burn, they cover that likewise with Earth, to the End there may be no Flame, but only Heat sufficient to force the Tar downward into the Floor. They temper the Heat as they please, by thrusting a Stick through the Earth, and letting the Air in at as many Places as they see convenient.

"Pitch is made either by boiling Tar in large Iron Kettles, set in Furnaces, or by burning it in round Clay-holes, made in the Earth."

Within a few years after the bounty system became effective, tar, pitch, rosin, and turpentine were among the major North Carolina exports. Production increased steadily, although there were some temporary setbacks caused by wars, falling prices, and other factors. The table below, based on the manuscript customs records in the Public Record Office in London, reveals the volume and value of North Carolina naval stores exports to England in the late colonial period.

Tar ranked first in the value of these shipments, pitch second, turpentine third, and rosin a poor fourth. The average annual value of naval stores exported from the colony in the late colonial period was about £50,000, in addition to the bounties paid.

	Tar and Pitch (bbls.)	Turpentine (bbls.)	Total	Value
1752–53	73,580	10,429	84,009	£42,000
1768–69	116,886	10,793	127,679	73,164
1769–70	62,386	17,428	79,814	39,713
1770–71	84,411	17,955	102,366	27,922
1771–72	111,967	15,202	127,169	63,324
1772–73	105,581	11,647	117,228	56,923
1773–74	84,048	18,891	106,049	53,098
1774–75	66,232	30,031	99,703	49,345
1775–76	106,086	73,043	179,129	94,003
1776–77	3,706	10,704	14,410	8,275

The Lumber Industry

The lumber industry was more widespread than that of naval stores and in some respects more important and of greater monetary value. Since the only statistics available for colonial manufactures are export figures, it is impossible to grasp the magnitude of lumber products in colonial North Carolina. In every community there was a great demand for wood in the construction of houses, barns, and other buildings, as well as for making furniture, farm implements, and a variety of wooden utensils for home use. Almost all articles were exported in casks, barrels (thirty-one and a half gallons until 1766, and then thirty-two gallons), hogsheads, or some other type of wooden container. In some years, as many as 100,000 barrels were used for the exportation of naval stores, and more than half this number for the shipment of "provisions" and other articles. The cooperage industry was one of the colony's largest industries.

Lumbering, which began as a household industry, had assumed commercial proportions by the beginning of the eighteenth century. At an early date saw-mills were established. These were usually water-powered, and were encouraged by colonial and local authorities in the form of land grants, tax exemption, and other favors. By the middle of the century they were in operation throughout the province, and in 1766 there were over fifty in the Cape Fear Valley alone. Lumbering, like naval stores, was usually carried on in connection with ordinary farm operations, and these two industries supplemented the income of some individual operators as much as £1,000 a year.

Lumber was exported in various forms, chiefly barrel staves, headings, and hoops of oak; shingles, largely from cypress, and boards, mainly of pine. These articles as well as other wood products were exported to various points, over one-half being shipped to the British West Indies. C. C. Crittenden estimates that about two-fifths of the shingles, one-seventh of the barrel staves, and one-eleventh of the pine boards exported from the continental colonies were from North Carolina. In one year, 1753, the colony exported 762,000 barrel staves, and in 1764 Governor Dobbs wrote that the colony exported "above 30,000,000 feet in lumber and scantlings." In terms of value, about one-seventh of the total lumber products from the continental colonies originated in North Carolina.

There was some shipbuilding in the colony from the beginning, but it never became a major industry, and only New Jersey and Georgia ranked below North Carolina in this respect. Of 229 vessels built between 1710 and 1739 and trading with North Carolina only 38 were launched in that colony. And of the 38 all but 5 were small sloops and schooners. Approximately 70 percent of all tonnage trading to North Carolina and one-third of the colony's own merchant fleet came from New England shipyards.

The records relating to potash, hemp, flax, flour, and several other products are meager, although there are abundant references to efforts to encourage the production and exportation of these articles. England was most eager to procure potash from the colonies, in order to "render itself independent of the Baltic." And in 1736 Henry McCulloh proposed to send over "a considerable number of Workmen to carry on the Pott Ash trade and for the raising Hemp." This industrial experiment was not successful, and the potash industry never developed in the colony on a large scale, though small quantities were probably produced. Bounties for the exportation of flax and hemp were voted by the legislature, but these industries never developed on a commercial scale, though flax and linen production was important as a household industry.

Chapter 7

TRANSPORTATION, TRADE, AND COMMUNICATION, 1715-1775

The handicap of a dangerous coast and lack of good harbors did not prevent North Carolina from developing foreign and coastwise commerce, though its trade was far below that of Virginia, South Carolina, and several other colonies. Although geographic factors were not as favorable as they might have been—or as they appeared from a casual glance at a North Carolina map—it should be remembered that most of the ships trading with the colonies were less than three hundred gross tons, that many of them were less than one hundred tons burden, and that ships as small as this could anchor at most of the North Carolina ports.

The ships trading in the colony's coastal waters were of many types. The most common were the two-masted schooner and the one-masted sloop, vessels usually of less than fifty tons. The two-masted brig or brigantine, of about one hundred tons burden, was one of the major carriers of naval stores, especially from Brunswick and Edenton. The largest vessels operating along the coast were the "ship," a three-masted vessel, and the two-masted scow. These two types of craft averaged about 150 tons, and the ship, in particular, was important in the trade with the mother country. Both people and goods travelled by water. It was cheaper and usually faster than land transportation. Favorite names for ships of all kinds were *Sally, Betsy, Nancy,* and other feminine names.

Most of the sailing craft carried passengers as well as freight, although conditions on such small craft were most uncomfortable. A group of Moravians sailed from Philadelphia to Wilmington in 1762 on a twenty-three-ton sloop which had "a tiny cabin in which at a pinch six Sisters can sleep, but the rest, including the Captain and two sailors, must do the best they can in the hold, on top of the barrels and boxes." Janet Schaw, a decade later, had a happier experience and found the ship "neat, clean, and commodious."

102

The speed of sailing ships was very slow by modern standards. A trip from North Carolina to New York usually took from four to five days, to the West Indies about two weeks, and to England from three to eight weeks—depending to a great extent on whether winds were favorable or not.

Though North Carolina had a few good outlets for ocean commerce, it had an excellent system of inland waterways—sounds, rivers, and creeks. These waterways were adapted to small craft and became the chief arteries of trade and travel. Most of the large plantations and many of the small farms were located on or near navigable waters; all of the important towns in the Coastal Plain were situated on watercourses; and along some of the rivers, especially the Roanoke and Cape Fear, travelers reported that there were "many warehouses and stores." The emphasis placed on waterways was clearly revealed in the numerous road laws, like the one of 1745, which provided that roads be built "to the nearest landing."

The most prevalent types of craft used on inland waters were canoes, periaugers, scows, and flats, or flat-bottomed boats. Most of the canoes were made of hollowed logs, usually cypress, and were propelled by paddles or oars. Periaugers were made and propelled in the same fashion but were much larger than ordinary canoes. Occasionally canoes and periaugers used masts and sails. Scows and flats, propelled by poles, were used extensively and carried large cargoes of freight, especially in the lower stretches of the eastern rivers. Some yawls, sloops, and shallops were also employed in the river trade.

Crooked and uncharted channels, sand bars, logs, fish dams, and other obstructions in streams caused many accidents and led to legislation making it the duty of the overseers of roads and their companies of men to clear streams of obstructions and otherwise improve river channels. These laws were never effectively enforced, and the difficulties of trade and travel became so serious that inland waterways had ceased to be of major importance by the time of the Revolution.

Meanwhile the backcountry was being settled, and here, from the outset, there was little emphasis on water transportation because of the swift and rocky rivers and also because of early interest in road-building.

Roads

The colony had many so-called roads, but good roads were few and far between. The proximity of early settlements to watercourses, the sparseness of population, the lack of capital, aversion to taxes, the inertia of the people, and other factors delayed the development of an effective highway system. The first roads in the colony were Indian trails or "trading paths," usually well located along the shortest and best routes. As population grew and expanded, these narrow trails were widened—and deepened— by constant usage, and some of them were made into "roads" by order of provincial or local authorities. While travel accounts of this era contain conflicting reports about many aspects of North Carolina life, all agreed on one thing—that the roads were bad. Such terms as "poor," "wretched," "exceeding bad," and "miserable" appear repeatedly in contemporary writing. Roads were not graded, surfaced, drained, or adequately marked. There were few bridges, and ferries were inadequate, inconvenient, and expensive. Janet Schaw declared that "the only making they bestow upon the roads in the flat part of the country is cutting out the trees to the necessary breadth, in as even a line as they can, and where the ground is wet, they make a small ditch on either side." In the Coastal Plain particularly, many of the roads were lined with dead trees, which had been killed as a result of naval stores operations, and observers declared that travel along such routes was "attended with great danger."

Road Laws

Almost every session of the legislature after 1730 considered the transportation problem, and scores of road laws were passed. The Act of 1764, the most detailed of these, empowered the county courts "to order the laying out of Public Roads, and establish and settle Ferries, and to appoint where Bridges shall be built, for the Use and Ease of the Inhabitants of this Province; and to clear navigable Rivers and Creeks." The court was to name "Overseers of the Highways or Roads," who were to summon all male taxables, ages sixteen to sixty, to work the roads a certain number of days each year. All public roads were to be laid out by juries appointed by the court, and were to be cleared of trees and other obstructions to a width of twenty feet, while the limbs of trees on the sides of the roads were to be cut away so as not to obstruct carriages or horsemen. The overseers were to have mileposts set up and signposts wherever roads forked or crossed. Bridges and causeways over small streams and swamps were to be constructed of pieces of wood "at least fourteen feet long, laid across the road, well secured and covered with earth." Bridges over larger streams were to be "at least twelve feet wide, made of sawed plank at least two inches thick, with strong posts, rails, and beams, all well fastened together." Ferry keepers were to be licensed by the county court and required to provide "good and Sufficient Boats," subject to a heavy penalty for failure to do so.

If the road laws had been enforced, North Carolina might have developed a satisfactory system of land transportation, but this was not the case. As late as 1778 it was reported that the main post road running through the state "has become so bad, through the neglect of the Overseers of it, as greatly to delay the Post Riders and Travellers in general. Trees have fallen across it, and are not removed; the Roots are not cut up; a number of the Causeways are Swampy and full of Holes, and many of the Bridges are almost impassable."

Important Roads

The last two decades of the colonial period witnessed an increase in the number of roads and perhaps a slight improvement in their quality. Old maps, especially those by John Collet in 1770 and Henry Mouzon in 1775, reveal a network of roads in North Carolina. There were several important north-south roads leading from Virginia to South Carolina, such as the one running through Edenton, Bath, Wilmington, and Brunswick. Another extended from Halifax to Tarboro, and a third led from Cross Creek to the north. East-west road construction was delayed, chiefly because of the northwest-southeast direction of the rivers and the natural trade connection of the Piedmont with Virginia, Pennsylvania, and South Carolina. The "Great Trading Path"—rough, long, and circuitous—ran from the Sound region to the mountains, and there were a few other roads that ran from east to west for shorter distances, but these were not major factors in trade. North Carolina did not establish a stage line until 1789—long after most of the other states.

Bridges and Ferries

In some respects the sounds and rivers of the province handicapped land transportation more than the bad roads themselves. A few of the streams had bridges, built by individuals and operated on a toll basis; some streams had ferries, authorized and regulated by local authorities, and also operated for toll by individuals. One of the first drawbridges in America was built over the northeast branch of the Cape Fear shortly before the Revolution. There were never enough bridges and ferries to develop an effective transport system; at best they were inconvenient and expensive. The absence of bridges or ferries over some rivers and creeks made many a traveler risk life and limb in "fording the shallows," especially hazardous after a freshet.

Vehicles

Travel and transport over the roads was slow, difficult, frequently unpleasant, and at times positively dangerous. Two-wheel carts, which could transport about a thousand pounds, and four-wheel wagons, which could haul twice that amount, probably averaged about twenty miles a day. Such "pleasure vehicles" as gigs, chairs, post-chaises, chariots, phaetons, and coaches could probably travel thirty to forty miles a day, though the average speed was much less. Riders on horseback frequently made as much as fifty miles a day, with the average nearer thirty. The horse was indispensable for land travel and transport and people rode horseback for long distances. This was particularly true of Anglican missionaries, itinerant preachers, peddlers, and certain government officials. Travel on foot was the slowest but surest and safest form of travel, and people walked great distances. A group of Moravians walked from Bethlehem, Pennsylvania, to Wachovia, a distance of some four hundred miles, in thirty days.

Lodging

There are scores of contemporary narratives that indicate that many travelers lost their way because the blazes on the trees had become indistinct or because of the lack of signposts or other markers. Travelers were impressed by the loneliness and desolation of the roads; one of them declared that "nothing can be more dreary, melancholy and uncomfortable than the almost perpetual solitary dreary pines, sandy barrens, and dismal swamps." Lodgings and other accommodations along the routes of travel were few, and when lodgings were obtainable, they were usually of poor quality. Wagoners often spent the nights "upon dry leaves on the ground with the feet towards a large fire, which they made by the road side wherever night overtakes them, and are covered only with a blanket." Travelers fortunate enough to obtain lodging in the home of a planter fared very well; those who stopped at the homes of small farmers usually found "miserable conditions," and those who stayed at the inns, or "ordinaries," faced a real experience. Though innkeepers were licensed by the county court and required to give bond to make adequate provision for travelers and their horses, most of these places, with the exception of a few located in the towns, offered dismal accommodations. The following description of a "Carolina ordinary" by an English traveler was probably not exaggerated:

"They were mostly long-huts, or a frame weatherboarded; the better sort consisting of one story and two rooms; the more numerous having no internal divisions. . . . One corner of the room would be occupied by a 'bunk' containing the family bed; another by a pine-wood chest, the family clothes press and larder; a third would be railed off for a bar, containing a rum-keg and a tumbler. The rest of the furniture consisted of two chairs and a table, all in the last stage of palsy. . . . If hunger and fatigue compelled you to remain, a little Indian corn for your horse, and a blanket on the hearth, with your saddle for a pillow, to represent a bed, were the most you could obtain. . . . As to edibles, whether you called for breakfast, dinner, or supper, the reply was one—eggs and bacon. . . . Ten to one you had to cook the meal yourself. . . . No sooner were you seated than the house-dog (of the large wolf breed) would arrange himself beside you and lift his lank, hungry jaws expressively to your face. The young children, never less than a dozen (the women seeming to bear them in a litter in those regions), at the smell and sight of the victuals would let up a yell enough to frighten the wolves."

Commercial Regulations

North Carolina commerce was subject to British trade laws and to regulations imposed by its own legislature. Its trade was probably aided more than it was hampered by the Navigation Acts, especially those of 1660 and 1673, which required that (1) oceanic trade could be carried only in British or British colonial vessels; (2) that all European goods exported to the colonies must be shipped via England; and (3) that certain enumerated commodities, including tobacco and naval stores (after 1705), could be exported from the colonies only to ports of the British empire. C. C. Crittenden, in his excellent book, *The Commerce of North Carolina, 1763–1789,* has shown that shipbuilding and naval stores were stimulated by the first of these apparent restrictions; that the second requirement hampered North Carolina very little, and that the trade of the colony actually profited by the enumeration.

North Carolina Trade Regulations

There were scores of legislative enactments to regulate the duties and fees of pilots, to provide for the marking of channels, and for the inspection of all articles exported. Occasionally duties were levied on such articles as rum and wine, for revenue purposes, and on rice, in order to discourage its importation from South Carolina. The lax enforcement of these laws and regulations injured North Carolina commerce and was a subject of constant complaint by the governors and by certain British agencies, notably the Navy Board. In the case of naval stores shipped from North Carolina, Governor Tryon wrote that "the most probable method an Inspector can take to lose his office is being faithful and diligent in the execution of it," and Governor Dobbs maintained that there were "many frauds" in the collection of the provincial duty on wines and spirits.

Ports of Entry

British trade laws were much better enforced than were the colonial regulations. This was largely due to the zeal of the British naval officers appointed for the province, who were required to keep a record of imports and exports, make lists of all ships entering and clearing, examine certificates of bond and registration, and in other ways enforce British trade regulations. Each port of entry had a collector, appointed by the British commissioners of the customs. The colony had five official ports. In the order of their importance— but not of their creation—they were Brunswick, which comprised the whole Cape Fear basin and included the towns of Wilmington and Brunswick; Roanoke, including the Sound region, with Edenton as its central point of shipment; Beaufort, embracing the area from Topsail Inlet to the Lower Neuse Valley;

Bath, the first port of entry created, which, after 1730, included only the Pamlico Region; and Currituck. The bulk of the colony's oceanic trade passed through the first three of these ports; the last two had dwindled into insignificance by the time of the Revolution.

North Carolina Exports and Imports

The chief exports of North Carolina were: (1) naval stores, shipped mainly to England, though considerable quantities went coastwise to New England; (2) provisions, shipped mainly to the West Indies and to other continental colonies; (3) lumber products, over one-half of which were shipped to the West Indies; and (4) tobacco, shipped mainly from Port Roanoke to England, though large quantities went overland and by water to Virginia. These four items of export averaged about £80,000 value annually in the late colonial period, with another estimated £20,000 of exports of deerskins, rawhides, leather, livestock, and a variety of miscellaneous articles.

From Great Britain, North Carolina imported such manufactured goods as cloth, wearing apparel, hardware, household utensils, leather goods, farm implements, paints, cast iron, steel, lead, pewter, brass, and miscellaneous articles ranging from anchors to playing cards.

The major imports from the West Indies were sugar, molasses, rum, salt, and slaves. Other articles included coffee, ginger, citrus fruits, and mahogany.

A great variety of articles imported from other continental colonies—many of which were re-exports—included sugar, molasses, rum, salt, chocolate, wine, tea, coffee, raisins, and pepper, alcoholic drinks of various kinds, and fish—cod, mackerel, salmon, sturgeon, herring, and shad.

The following advertisement, by Jonathan Dunbibin, of goods for sale at his "ready money store near the Market-House" in Wilmington, which appeared in the *Cape Fear Mercury*, December 29, 1773, illustrates the great variety of articles for sale by one merchant, though it was hardly typical of the stores of colonial North Carolina: "COARSE and fine salt, rum, loaf & brown sugar, molasses, window glass 10 by 8, short and long pipes, salt-petre, Anderson's pills, Turlington's balsam, Glauber-salts, Tin quart and pint measures, tin funnels, pewter basons, dishes, soup and flat-plates, table and tea-spoons, copperas, mens and boys coarse felt hats, mens and boys fine beaver do, ladies riding hats, childrens hats and feathers, ladies silk hats and shades, Cotton and wool cards, common and white chipple needles, pins, horn jacket button-moulds, cambricks, lawns, plain, flowered and strip'd black and white gauze, figured plain and tinsell ribbands 2 d and 4 d do, broad sash do, ladies velvet collars, ladies silk-mitts, muslin, fans, printed and check handkerchiefs, sewing silk of different colours, gold and silver spangled buttons, pink and black duranto, pink and black calimanco, black cravats and barcelona handkerchiefs, black ruffell, corded and flowered dimity, coarse and fine white threads, coloured and oznabrigs do, thread jacket and shirt buttons, tapes, long and pistol lawns, coat bindings, worsted damask, lindsey woolsey, buckram, cassamires with trimmings, mohair buttons, silk, twist, nutmegs, cinnamon, cloves, mace, black-pepper, ladies wash-leather and white kid gloves, mens do, ladies newest fashioned full suits of gauze, also caps, fillets & flys, paris-nett, chip-hats, ermine, skeleton-wire, earings and necklaces blond-lace-and edging, plain and striped lustring, sattin do, taffety, mode, persian and silk damask, brass cocks, candlesticks, scales, powder, shot, lead, hemp-lines, scein twiner, Glouster-cheeze, table-knives and forks, cuttoe and pen knives, scissars, thimbles, ivory and horn combs, ladies tortoise shell crooked, hair-combs, large & small fishing hooks, writing-paper, marble-covered blank-books, letter files, Dyches spelling-books, quills, sealing-wax, waters, ink-powder, glass quart decanters, wine glasses, tumblers, pint and quart china and delph bowls, stone tea cups and saucers, womens and mens saddles, bridles, saddle cloths, womens and girls stuff and leather shoes, men & boys shoes, horse-whips, silk sashes, oil skin and silk umbrellas, meal sifters, duffell blankets, rugs; superfine bread cloths with trimmings, negro cloths, womens and mens thread & worsted hose yarn ditto, silk plain and ribbed ditto; bearskin, wilton cloth, white & red flannels, german serge, bath beaver coating and trimmings; ready made jackets, great coats, womens red cardinals plain and trim'd with ermine; Russia drab, checks and stripes, oznabrigs, callicoes and chintz's, garlix, brown Holland, Russia drilling, dowlass, huckaback, striped holland; coarse and fine irish linens, Irish and Russia sheeting, doylies, sadlers tacks, bosses, stirrup irons, bridle bitts; 4d, 6d, 8d, 10d, & 20d, nails; bohea tea; stock, chest and padlocks, HL hinges from 7 to 12 inches, curry combs and brushes; broad and narrow axes, carpenters hammers, marking irons, broad and narrow hoes, coopers froes, shoemakers hammers, shoe and heel knives, iron and steel plate hand saws, tap borers, sad irons, shoe nippers and pincers, 100 foot rules, shoe & knee buckles, best pinchback ditto; cart boxes, neat fowling pieces, bridle and plain gun locks; jack plains, frying pans, iron pots; skillets, and baking pans, steel snuffers; hand mill stones, and sundry other articles."

Trade of the Backcountry

The records relating to trade of the back country are meager and so was the trade. During the first century of the colony's existence, the Piedmont region was virtually unsettled, but with the influx of thousands of Scotch-Irish, Germans, and others after 1750, there was an increasing need for markets for their surplus goods as well as a considerable demand for goods which they could not produce. The region was seriously handicapped by lack of navigable waters, slow and expensive land transportation, the fewness and smallness of towns, and the consequent paucity of merchants. Hillsborough, one of the largest towns in the area, had only about forty inhabitants as late as 1764;

Salisbury was begun in 1755 with the construction of a courthouse and eight "crude dwellings," and Charlotte was described as late as 1771 as "an inconsiderable place hardly deserving the name of village." Salem, founded in 1766, was probably the largest town and certainly the chief commercial center of the Piedmont. The meticulously kept records of the Moravian Brethren, which constitute our best source of information on the trade of the backcountry, clearly reveal that the bulk of the trade of the North Carolina Piedmont followed the roads down the valleys of the Yadkin, Catawba, and other rivers into South Carolina, eventually reaching Charleston. There was a small trade with Philadelphia, some with Salisbury, and even a little with Edenton, New Bern, Cross Creek, and Wilmington.

The leading exports of the backcountry were deerskins, cattle, hides, corn meal, wheat, flour, butter, flax, hemp, herbs, and a few other products of the farm and forest. In a two-months period in 1774, more than a thousand head of cattle were driven through Wachovia to Pennsylvania.

The major imports of this region were manufactured goods—cloth and clothing, kitchen and other household articles, farm tools, and such items of food and drink as sugar, salt, molasses, and run.

For many years there was very little trade between the Piedmont and the Coastal Plain, because of conditions previously described. But the long and expensive trips to South Carolina, Virginia, and Pennsylvania led the Moravians and other shippers of the Piedmont to seek markets closer home. The merchants of Cross Creek and Wilmington welcomed this effort to divert trade to their communities and heartily supported legislative enactments to construct east-west roads. A law of 1755 authorized the building of a road from Orange Court House (later Hillsborough) to the Cape Fear. Later laws provided for roads from Mecklenburg and Rowan counties to the same river, and also from the Guilford-Chatham area. The effects of these laws were felt only slightly before the advent of the Revolution.

North Carolina Merchants

In contrast with the paucity of merchants in the backcountry, the commercial communities of the Coastal Plain had a large number of merchants, many of whom were prominent in the economic, social, religious, and political life of the colony. Among the most important merchants in Wilmington were Cornelius Harnett and the firm of Hogg and Campbell, which also operated stores in Bladen County, Cross Creek, and Hillsborough. New Bern led the east central section—and perhaps the whole province—in the number of merchants, the most significant of whom were Samuel Cornell and the firm of Edward Batchelor and Company. The Blount, Hewes, and Blair firm did a large business at Edenton, the mercantile center of the Sound region. The colony had many independent merchants, but some of the largest stores were branches of Scottish firms, the most important being the Glasgow firm of John Hamilton and Company, which operated stores at various points between the Virginia border and the Cape Fear and extending into the Piedmont. The Glasgow house of Buchanans, Hastie and Company had stores at Halifax and Windsor in the East and at Deep Creek and in Orange County in the Piedmont. Several other Scottish firms did business in the Albemarle, Cross Creek, and Wilmington communities.

The colonial merchant was not a specialist. Many of them were both wholesalers and retailers; many were both exporters and importers; some were planter-merchants; some, such as the Blount brothers, owned and operated ships; a number were money lenders and the main source of credit in their community. The extent and variety of their business pursuits are well illustrated by the firm of John Hamilton and Company, which owned numerous stores and warehouses; held a large and varied stock of local and imported goods, ships, and wagons; operated a cooperage works, a hatters' shop, a tailors' shop, a blacksmith shop; besides owning numerous plantations, horses, cattle, and hogs. Many of the merchants owned land which they cultivated or rented; some owned town lots, sawmills, and gristmills.

Character of Business Transactions

Most of the merchants tried to operate on a cash basis and some advertised that they would not give credit—"In God we trust, all others pay cash." But the scarcity of specie, the use of produce for payments, and other factors made cash transactions difficult, and the merchants became creditors of the planters and farmers. Some of the larger firms "carried on very extensive business without any funds of their own, but altogether upon the credit which they had abroad." British merchants sold them goods on credit and thus indirectly financed various North Carolina enterprises.

North Carolina merchants, like those in other colonies, might make payments to their British creditors in coin—usually English shillings or Spanish milled dollars, in products such as naval stores and tobacco, or in bills of exchange.

Scarcity of Specie

Specie was extremely scarce in the province, for the settlers brought little of it with them and no coins were minted in the colony. Spanish dollars and "pieces of eight" and other Spanish, French, and Portuguese coins found their way into North Carolina as a result of trade with the West Indies, but the balance of trade was frequently against the colony and it was being drained of its specie supply. To cope with this problem, the colonists resorted to several expedients, such as the legalization of "commodity money" and the issuance of paper currency, neither of which was ever wholly satisfactory. Gresham's law tended to operate, and people paid debts and other obligations with "cheap currency" and inferior commodities, thus tending to drive the "dear money" into hiding.

Prices of Goods

Prices for imported goods were higher in North Carolina than in most of the English colonies, which had better commercial outlets. In the early eighteenth century prices charged for British imports were as high as 2,000 percent above the first cost in Great Britain, but by 1760 merchants were selling goods in the Coastal Plain at a wholesale markup of about 50 percent and a retail markup of about 100 percent above the first cost in Britain. Prices in the backcountry were considerably higher than in the Tidewater for obvious reasons. Some merchants amassed "considerable fortunes," but some became bankrupt. Risks incidental to shipping, bad debts, overproduction of goods, unsystematic purchasing by merchants, and other economic factors tended to hold profits to a minimum, though a few merchants and firms made large profits. John Hamilton and Company probably netted from £4,000 to £5,000 annually.

The Postal System

Means of communication were slow, uncertain, and expensive. In the early days letters were sent by ship captains, traders, planters, or any other means that seemed convenient. Legally the regulation of mails was a function of the General Assembly, and as early as 1715 a law was passed ordering that all "public despatches" be carried promptly from plantation to plantation until they reached their ultimate destination, under penalty of five pounds sterling for each default. This law made no provision for private letters and was ineffective as to public letters, which were usually sent by private messengers. In 1755 the legislature, on recommendation of Governor Dobbs, made an agreement with James Davis, the public printer and newspaper publisher, by which for the sum of £106 6s. 8d. annually he "would forward public despatches to all parts of the province" and send messengers every fifteen days from New Bern and Wilmington to Suffolk, Virginia, and bring back official communications. The delivery of private letters seems to have been optional. In 1757 Davis and two other men were appointed for one year to "carry the post" once every two weeks from Wilmington to and from Suffolk. This arrangement was continued in 1758, with Davis having the entire contract.

Improvements in the Postal System

Governor Tryon was disturbed about the colony's poor postal service and repeatedly urged the legislature to increase appropriations and take other measures to improve the system. In 1764 he succeeded in getting a legislative appropriation of £67, but this sum was thoroughly inadequate to do the job. Three years later the governor complained that the province still had no postal system "from want of the means to support the expence." To Lord Hillsborough, he wrote, "It is a disagreeable reflection, My Lord, that the chain of communication through the Continent should be broke within this province." The governor's efforts finally met with a modicum of success and, writing in 1771, he informed the legislature that the postmaster general for the colonies had "for some months past opened a communication by post, between the Southern and Northern Provinces on this Continent, by establishing a regular intercourse between Charles Town and Suffolk in Virginia." Hugh Finlay, who spent over three months in North Carolina in 1774 investigating the postal system for British authorities, found that "the only post road in the province" was the one which ran through Edenton, Bath, New Bern, and Wilmington, and that each of these towns had a postmaster. Finlay arranged for a fortnightly mail service between Wilmington and Cross Creek, and he suggested many improvements in the postal system which were not made. Mail service continued to be irregular, slow, and unsatisfactory. In 1773 it took two weeks for a New Bern letter to reach Salem, and the next year post riders took twenty-seven days to carry mail from Charleston to Suffolk—an average of sixteen miles a day.

Chapter 8

THE SOCIAL ORDER

The social order of early North Carolina, like that of other English colonies, was the product of two conflicting forces: European ideas of class distinctions and pioneer conditions that tended to produce a more democratic society. The early settlers, largely of English stock, brought with them inherited ideas of class distinctions—nobility, gentry, yeomanry, and peasantry. During the proprietary era (1663–1729) an incipient aristocracy, based on extensive landholdings and the use of slave and indentured labor, began to emerge. At the same time a social diversity and fluidity resulted from the leveling influence of wilderness conditions, the ease of acquiring land, political disturbances, and "unregulated liberty." The period of royal rule (1729–75) witnessed an increasing tendency toward social and economic stratification, which was due in part to the orderly settlement of the Cape Fear Valley and the Piedmont, to improvements in economic conditions, and to extensive land speculation on the part of the "better sort."

Social Classes

In order of social standing, the white population of colonial North Carolina consisted of three elements: (1) gentry or planter aristocracy, (2) farmers, and (3) indentured "Christian servants." The gentry, the smallest, most wealthy, best educated, and most influential of these groups, was composed mainly of large landholders, but it also included public officials, wealthy merchants, Anglican ministers, and the leading lawyers, doctors, and other professional men. In all probability less than 5 percent of the North Carolina families belonged to the gentry, and very few of the planters owned as many as fifty slaves each.

Thomas Pollock, one of the wealthiest men in the colony, owned one plantation of about forty thousand acres and nearly a hundred slaves. Roger Moore owned over two hundred slaves. But such wealth was rare. The majority of the planters owned less than five hundred acres and fewer than twenty slaves.

The planters occupied the best sites along the Roanoke, Tar, Cape Fear, and other eastern rivers, and here and there along the valleys of the Piedmont were some agricultural holdings approaching the plantation scale. Brickell observed that the planters "live after the most easie and pleasant manner of any People I ever met with." They cultivated manners carefully and prized formal education as further evidence of social distinction. Possessing more wealth, influence, leisure, education, and contacts with the outside world, the gentry gave tone and direction to society and politics and contributed more toward the development of agriculture, industry, and trade than their numbers justified.

Influence of Law and Custom

Social distinctions were set up at first by law, but later depended largely on custom and imitation of the English social system. The charter of 1663 envisioned the creation of a colonial nobility and actually provided for noble titles, as long as they were not the same as those used in England. Likewise the Fundamental Constitutions, designed to "avoid a numerous democracy," classified society into strata, ranging from degrees of "nobility" such as palatine, landgrave, and cacique down to the lowest social class of "leet men," and provided that "all children of leet men" should remain leet men "to all generations." The Fundamental Constitutions also required large property qualifications for officeholding and jury service. The Act Concerning Orphans, of 1715, required that guardians should have their wards educated and provided for "according to their rank and degree."

The Planter Class

Members of the upper social class prided themselves on such titles as Planter, Gentleman, and Esquire, and they frequently had family crests and/or coats-of-arms as badges of social rank. They were jealous of their social position and some of them had bitter quarrels with each other and with the governors over social precedence; one of these "social fights," that of Sir Nathaniel Duckenfield in 1771, was referred to the Court of Heraldry in England for settlement. But society was more fluid than the laws and customs, and in many instances the classes tended to mix and even to merge into one another. There was always opportunity for a small farmer, or even a freed servant, to acquire land and ascend the social ladder. By native ability, proper marriage, or lucky land deals, a number of small farmers and artisans, including at least one blacksmith, passed into the ranks of the aristocracy. Many of the wealthy planters and merchants were self-made men.

Members of the various social classes were frequently thrown together at inns, churches, militia musters, court sessions, and other public gatherings.

There was always a degree of friendliness and good fellowship between people in various walks of life, but by the middle of the eighteenth century there had developed some feeling of class hatred because the privileged minority, who dominated provincial and local politics, were appropriating more than their share of the lands and were ruling in the interest of their class and to the detriment of the "meaner sort," who constituted the bulk of the colony's population.

The Planters' Homes

The planter's home and its furnishings, and even his personal appearance, all reflected his influence and superior social status. Numerous references in contemporary writings to "great houses" and "elegant mansions" as well as drawings and later photographs of Orton, Hayes, and other exceptionally fine houses, have created the impression that every colonial planter lived in a magnificent dwelling, led a leisurely life, and spent a great portion of his waking hours sipping mint juleps and dispensing hospitality in true "southern style." A careful examination of colonial writings reveals a different and much less attractive picture of the planter's home and social routine. His house was usually a plain, unpainted wooden building, lacking architectural grace, sacrificing beauty to comfort and convenience, and frequently without much landscaping.

In the early days the one-story house, sided with unpainted boards that had been sawed or rough-hewed, was the prevalent type among the less prosperous planters. Before 1700 there were few or no log dwellings in the colony or anywhere else in the English colonies, except in the areas settled by the Swedes —although this type later became common among the poorer people of the Coastal Plain and was the "typical house" of the people on the frontier. There were some story-and-a-half houses, and after 1730 there was an increasing trend toward the two-story structure. In many cases the house had a wing, perhaps a loft, and generally a small front porch and a "shed-room" kitchen—for reasons of comfort, safety, and sanitation.

The "Mansions" of North Carolina

The increase of wealth among the planters and the general upswing in economic conditions were reflected in architecture and in social life generally. Governor Burrington, writing in 1735, said, "There are many good Brick and wood Mansion Houses." Some of the wealthier planters were beginning to copy or adapt the Georgian style of architecture and were building more comfortable and beautiful houses, but most planters' homes were not very large or imposing, and only a small number were of brick. Some modern writers have thus misinterpreted the colonial meaning of the word "mansion." The prevail-

The Residence of John Penn, Granville, N.C.

North Carolina Collection, The University of North Carolina at Chapel Hill

ing types of architecture were determined by building materials, tradition, foreign influence, and, of course, the taste of the builder. Most of the houses were constructed of locally produced materials, although there were occasional importations of fine wood and ornamental brick and stone.

A few large and imposing houses, some of which have become show places in modern North Carolina, were built in the fifty years preceding the American Revolution. Among these was Orton, the home of "King Roger" Moore, near Wilmington, which has been called "the finest colonial residence in North Carolina." The original building at Orton was a one-story, plain, rectangular structure, but this was later "completely transformed into a great Classic Revival Mansion." Other unusually fine residences were Lillington Hall, the home of Alexander Lillington; Lilliput, the residence of Eleazer Allen in Brunswick County; Castle Haynes, the home of Hugh Waddell; the Cupola House, at Edenton, "the finest framed Jacobean-type house south of Connecticut"; and the John Wright Stanly House at New Bern, with "the finest colonial stairway in North Carolina."

These finer homes were well adapted to warm weather. They had wide halls and rooms with high ceilings, usually wainscoted to the top and ornamented with artistic balusters and beautiful mantels. Many of the houses had four large rooms on each floor, with a large fireplace in each room. There were often two or three large beds in one room, but small children usually slept in a low "trundle bed," which was kept under a big bed in daytime and rolled out at night. A warming pan was frequently used to warm beds in cold rooms.

Numerous outbuildings—including office, laundry, and kitchen—"planned as a symmetrical whole," made for greater comfort, privacy, convenience, and sanitation. Cooking was done in open fireplaces, well equipped with cranes, hooks, pots, pans, and kettles. At a short distance from the "big house" were the barn, granary, crib, stables, and poultry houses, and still farther away, hidden by the trees, were the slave quarters. Most of the planters' homes had "a most beautiful prospect" by some "Noble River or Creek," and the approach to the "Mansion" was along an avenue of stately trees, such as "might adorn the Palaces of Kings." Many of the houses were surrounded by flower gardens and mazes and walks of boxwood or other shrubs.

Furniture and Furnishings

Most of the planters lived comfortably, some luxuriously. Brickell wrote that "the better sort have tollerable Quantities of Plate, with other convenient Ornamental and valuable Furniture." Wills and inventories reveal that many of the homes were furnished with beautiful things imported from Europe or New England as well as many articles that had been made on the plantation. The planters had fine draperies, tapestries, linens, featherbeds, quilts, and counterpanes; chairs, tables, desks, sideboards, cupboards, chests of drawers, and bedsteads, usually four-posters made from mahogany, walnut, pine, maple, or cherry; brass or copper andirons, tongs, shovels, and fenders; silver services, platters, tea and coffee pots, knives, forks, and spoons; wineglasses, decanters, punch bowls; and such "necessary articles" as cards, spinning wheels, and looms, as well as a great variety of kitchen utensils.

Dress of the Planters

The dress of the planter and his family was quite similar to that of the gentry of England and of the upper class in the other colonies and was considered "a badge of social rank." The upper class did not want the "meaner sort" to wear the symbols of aristocracy—and this frequently led to extravagance in dress. The men let their hair grow long and tied it in little tails down their backs. Some planters powdered their hair or wore powdered wigs, especially when they "dressed for social functions." They wore long frock coats, usually made of imported broadcloth, sometimes black but frequently of bright colors; tight-fitting knee-length trousers made of either brocade, velvet, silk, or plush; silk stockings and slippers with large ornamental silver or gold buckles. The planters' wives and daughters often dressed in silk, satin, taffeta, muslin, or fancy calico. There were variations in style from time to time, as there have always been, but throughout most of the colonial era, the hoop skirt was the vogue, as well as wasp waists, laced corsets, and high hats adorned with feathers or plumes. Shoes had wooden heels and pointed toes (no open work). Most of the women wore rings, bracelets, necklaces, lockets, and other ornaments.

Food of the Planters

The colonial planter "lived at home" and he lived well. His table was filled with a great abundance and variety of food. Beef, pork, and other meats were produced on every plantation; fish and game were plentiful, and on many of the plantations a trusted servant or slave would be used for the special purpose of supplying the planter's table. A traveler, lost in North Carolina about 1760, reported that he was hospitably received at a planter's home where he found "a large table loaded with fat roasted turkies, geese and ducks, boiled fowls, large hams, hung-beef, barbecued pig . . . enough for five-and-twenty men." Great quantities of fresh and salt meat were eaten the year round. Fresh fruits and vegetables were scarce except in summer. Most of the planter's food came from the plantation, but his nonalcoholic or "sober liquors"—tea, chocolate, and coffee—were imported. Some of his intoxicating beverages were made on the place, but there were importations of fine whiskies, brandies, wines, and other liquors. It was "very much the custom" in North Carolina "to drink Drams of some kind or other before Breakfast," and the frequent references in wills and inventories to decanters, wineglasses, and punch bowls indicate the planter's fondness for drink and also reflect his hospitality.

Hospitality

The planters liked company and considered hospitality to travelers a patriotic and social duty because of the scarcity of inns and taverns. They also had few means of hearing news from the outside world. Letters were rare and much delayed by the slowness of transportation and the lack of a good postal system. There were no newspapers in the colony before 1751, and even after that date their circulation was very limited. Travelers were thus the planter's mail, newspaper, and radio—and "upon many a lonely plantation, a person who brought news from the outside world, was a welcome guest, for whom the housekeeper gladly brought out her finest silver and china, her best linen and her most tempting food, and for whom the planter set out the choicest drinks which his cellar afforded." Stories of North Carolina hospitality were carried to distant regions early. John Lawson, writing about 1701, observed: "As the land is very fruitful, so are the planters hospitable to all that come to visit them; there being very few Housekeepers, but what live very nobly, and give away more provisions to Coasters and Guests who come to see them, than they expend amongst their own families." Brickell, writing two decades later, said that "the better Sort, or those of good Economy," kept "plenty of Wine, Rum and other Liquors at their own Houses, which they generously make use of amongst their Friends and Acquaintances, after a most decent and discreet Manner." And in 1786 Elkanah Watson wrote, "Travellers with any pretensions to respectability seldom stop at the wretched taverns; but custom sanctions their freely calling at the planter's residence, and he seems to consider himself the party obliged by this freedom."

Sports and Recreation

The planters led a busy life but most of them found opportunities for games, other "diversions," and social functions of various kinds. They had occasional house parties and "set suppers" to which other planters and their families were invited. Weddings were not as important socially as they became in later years, but there were numerous "handsome weddings," usually attended by "a large company of people" who enjoyed the feasts and merrymaking lasting sometimes as long as a week. Funerals were also festive events that were well attended, with food and drink consumed in large quantities. At wheat harvests, corn-shuckings, house-raisings, barn-buildings, quilting parties, and other gatherings work and play were combined.

Despite the poor roads and other transportation difficulties, most of the planters traveled a great deal—usually on horseback—to attend religious meetings, militia musters, court sessions, and other public meetings. Traveling ministers were usually greeted by large congregations, and people flocked to militia musters—perhaps for social rather than military reasons.

Dancing

Dancing was the favorite amusement of the planters. Brickell observed, "Dancing they are all fond of especially when they can get a Fiddle, or Bagpipe; at this they will continue for Hours together, nay, so attach'd are they to this darling Amusement, that if they can't procure Musick, they will sing for themselves." The square dance, the Virginia reel, and the minuet were danced to music furnished by a Negro slave who played the fiddle. In 1737, George Whitefield disgustedly reported that he found "a dancing master in every little town."

Horse Racing and Cockfighting

The planters were much addicted to horse racing and cockfighting and frequently laid large wagers on their favorite horse or gamecock. Race tracks and cockpits were found in many communities and the "intolerable itch" for gambling on these sports was denounced by clergymen and other moralists. James Iredell observed that "an intolerable itch for gambling prevails in all companies at Wilmington." This was probably true of other towns and communities, especially in the Tidewater. In 1753 a law was passed "to prevent excessive and deceitful Gaming," but this did not stop the practice. The importation of playing cards reached tremendous proportions during the next twenty years, and gambling seemed to be on the increase.

As the Revolution approached, it became necessary for the American people to gird up their loins for the struggle, and in 1774 the Continental Congress, setting a precedent for the Congress of 1942, urged the people to forego all "expensive diversions and entertainments" in the interest of economy and morale; and the Wilmington Safety Committee complied by prohibiting all card-playing, horse-racing, billiards, and dancing, declaring "that nothing will so effectively tend to convince the British Parliament that we are in earnest in our opposition to their measures, as a voluntary relinquishment of our favorite amusements. Those who will take the trouble of making observations on mankind, must soon be convinced, that the people who abandon their pleasures for the public good, are not to be biased by any other consideration. Many will cheerfully give up part of their property to secure the remainder. He only is the determined patriot who willingly sacrifices his pleasures on the altar of freedom."

The Small Farmers

Small farmers and artisans constituted by far the largest element of the colony's white population. This social class had its origin in free immigrants and freed servants, who usually obtained fifty acres of land upon acquiring their freedom, but it also included small merchants, overseers, tavern keepers, fur traders, workers in naval stores, blacksmiths, gunsmiths, and workers in a variety of industrial pursuits. Members of this social group possessed a certain degree of class consciousness and were proud of such titles as "farmer," "husbandman," and "yeoman," and those who could write frequently attached one of these titles, usually the last, to their names. The small farmer seldom owned more than two to three hundred acres of land; perhaps the majority held fifty acres or less. The average farm was a small clearing in the forest, which provided the owner with food, fuel, and materials for shelter and clothing. Connor has aptly described these small farmers as "a strong, fearless, independent race, simple in taste, crude in manners, provincial in outlook, democratic in social relations, tenacious of their rights, sensitive to encroachment on their personal liberties, and, when interested in religion at all, earnest, narrow, and dogmatic."

Subsistence Farming

The small farmer and his family were engaged in self-sufficient or subsistence farming. They cleared the forest, tilled the soil, produced the bare necessities of life, and eked out a living—sometimes successfully and in an orderly way, but frequently "in the most slovenly manner." Most of them held no bond servants or slaves, though a few possessed a small number. According to Brickell, most of the farmers worked hard and "equalized[ed] with the Negro's in hard Labour." Farming on a small scale and producing few articles for sale, they had little money with which to purchase goods or to pay taxes and quitrents. They had few conveniences and no luxuries; what they could not produce they simply did without. Only a few necessities, such as salt and iron, were purchased, and money for buying these was usually obtained by selling hogs or cattle which the farmer drove on foot to market. Some of the more industrious farmers made money by selling beeswax, tallow, hides, and furs; and quite a number supplemented their farm income by seasonal employment in the naval stores industry.

Homes of the Farmers

The homes of "the meaner sort" were likely to be small, crude, and unattractive structures. They were usually located near a stream or a fresh-water spring and were built of wood from the nearby forest. Most of the houses were one-story, some were a story-and-a-half, and a few were two-story, especially among the Germans in the Piedmont. Many of the farmhouses, especially in the Coastal Plain, were built of clapboards, while after 1700 some houses in this region, and perhaps a majority of those in the backcountry, were built of logs. The Scotch-Irish farmers of the Piedmont usually built a house of "logs neatly squared and notched, lapping over at the four corners, the interstices filled up with little blocks of wood plastered over and whitewashed." A few of the Scotch-Irish houses were plain, rectangular, two-story structures, not unlike the houses in Ulster. Some of the finer houses, such as that of Michael Braun, near Salisbury, were of "rough, sturdy masonery, end chimneys, arched windows, no porch, and no classic doors." The typical house of the Piedmont farmer was described as having "one room, one door, and one window closed with a wooden shutter . . . built of hewn logs, the interstices stopped with clay, the roof covered with riven boards." Frederick William Marschall, writing from Salem in 1768, said: "I found three family houses ready for use, all made of framework covered with clay, or framework filled with brick

A Backcountry Home

North Carolina Collection, The University of North Carolina at Chapel Hill

and clay. I imagine we shall have to cover the walls with weather-boards, which in this country is the most expensive method and not a good one on account of the sharp lightning and other danger of fire but without lime it seems to be the only thing to do."

Many of the farmhouses had only one room, but some had two rooms, the most important as well as the largest being the kitchen, which served as a combined parlor, living room, dining room, and workshop. Some of the houses had a "lean-to" or "shed-room," and a loft, which served as a storage room or as a bedroom for children, though in many cases the whole family slept in one room. Few of the houses had glass windows, brick chimneys, or even plank floors. Eli W. Caruthers, writing in *Revolutionary Incidents: and Sketches of Characters, chiefly in the "Old North State"* (1854), said that old men told him at the time of the War of the Regulation (1768–71), that "there was not a plank floor, a feather bed, a riding carriage nor a side saddle within the rounds of their acquaintance."

House Furnishings

The farmer's furniture, made by hand of wood from the nearby forest, was designed for utility and space saving. A few stools and benches, a crude table or two, shelves or a "larder" for provisions, and a few pots and pans constituted the major portion of the house furnishings. For beds people used mattresses of leaves, shucks, or straw, which they put on the floor. Animal skins and handmade quilts were used for covering. Knives, forks, and spoons were scarce and were usually made of bone, wood, or iron. Most of the dishes were wooden, though there was a little china in some of the homes and some pewter dishes and crude earthenware.

Food and Drink of the Farmer

Corn bread, hominy, and pork—fresh or salt—were the staple foods of most of the farmers. It was said of the average eighteenth-century North Carolinian that "if he could raise enough corn and pork for subsistence, he cared for nothing more." John Lawson considered North Carolina pork "fed on peaches, maize, and such other natural produce" to be "some of the sweetest meat that the world affords." William Byrd II, while surveying the "Boundary Line Betwixt Virginia and Carolina," "made a North Carolina Dinner upon Fresh Pork." A Frenchman traveling through the province in 1765 dined one day on venison "in a poor farmer's house," but at another home several days later "dined on fat Bacon, greens, and Indian bread and had good sider to Drink."

The farmers had garden vegetables and fruits in season. Some of them used native herb teas as substitutes for real tea. Apple cider, peach brandy, persimmon beer—and hard liquors when they could afford them—were favorite drinks.

"Christian Servants"

The lowest social stratum among the white population of colonial North Carolina consisted of several classes of unfree workers—voluntary servants, involuntary servants, and apprentices. Perhaps the largest proportion of these "Christian servants" who came to the colony were "redemptioners," that is, poor people who voluntarily "bound" themselves by a written contract, or indenture, to some master for a fixed number of years, in order to redeem their passage to the New World. North Carolina also had some involuntary servants, a class that included felons, paupers, political prisoners, and others sentenced to terms of service in the colonies by British courts in lieu of more severe punishment in England. Perhaps a few kidnapped persons were also brought into the province and sold into servitude.

North Carolina never had as many servants as did some colonies, particularly Virginia, Maryland, and Pennsylvania. This was because of its limited contacts with the outside world, its indirect settlement from other colonies, and the introduction of Negro slavery at an early date. It is likely that a few servants came into Albemarle during the first decade of settlement. As early as 1665 the proprietors offered all masters eighty acres of land for each male servant imported, and forty acres for each "weaker servant as women, children, and slaves." From the close of the century to the American Revolution the general practice of the colonial government was to grant fifty acres to each master for every person, bond or free, whom he imported.

Legal Provisions of "Indentures"

The period of service for a voluntary servant depended on the terms of the indenture and was usually three or four years. An involuntary servant usually served five years, though occasionally seven years was the prescribed term, and there are numerous references in the extant records to "His Majesty's Seven Years' Passengers." The law of 1715 provided that those above sixteen years of age without indenture serve five years; those under sixteen, until they were twenty-two years of age. The law of 1741 fixed no specific number of years, but left the matter to agreement between master and servant, with the provision that all disputes concerning length of service be settled by the county court.

Many of the indentures provided that the servant be taught a trade and also be taught to read and write. The rights of the master and servant were fixed by law. The act of 1715 made it the duty of the master to provide "Competent Dyet, Clothing & Lodging," and not to "exceed the Bounds of Moderation" in correcting servants. If a servant had "just cause of complaint," he could "repair to the next Magistrate," who was required to "bind over such Master or Mistress to Appear & answer the Complaint the next Precinct Court." There were heavy penalties for the brutal flogging of servants, and, according to the law of 1741, a servant could not marry without the written consent of the master.

"Freedom Dues"

"Freedom dues," which were given all servants at the expiration of their terms, varied from time to time. At first the custom was to grant the same number of acres—but not the same land—as had been granted the masters for importation of the servant, and also "two suits of apparel and a set of tools." The law of 1686 allotted fifty acres for freedom dues. The law of 1715 dropped the land grant and allowed three barrels of Indian corn and two new suits "of a value at least £5," and the 1741 law set the figure at £3 proclamation money and a "sufficient suit." The latter policy prevailed to the close of the colonial era.

Runaway Servants

The problem of runaway servants must have been serious. The Reverend John Urmston observed in 1716 that "white servants are seldom worth the keeping and never stay out the time indented for." To cope with the problem, the North Carolina law provided that for each day absent the runaway must serve two days extra. (In South Carolina it was seven days and in Maryland, ten.) Perhaps more serious than the problem of the state's own runaways was the almost constant complaint by Virginia officials that North Carolina was harboring Virginia's runaway servants, a charge made by Governor Francis Nicholson in 1691 and repeated by several later governors. North Carolina officials resented these accusations, and the legislature of 1715 passed a law providing a fine for harboring a runaway—"10 shillings per day to the master, together with all costs of returning the servant."

Apprentices

Apprentices belonged to the same social class as "Christian servants." Dependent orphans, illegitimate white children, and "children of vagrants" were apprenticed to masters and served until the age of maturity —eighteen for a girl and twenty-one for a boy. No fewer than thirty different trades have been noted in the North Carolina apprenticeship records. Those most frequently mentioned were mechanic, blacksmith, carpenter, cooper, cordwainer, weaver, tailor, joiner, mariner, wheelwright, fisherman, silversmith, ditcher, and barber.

Significance of White Servitude and Apprenticeship

The system of servitude and apprenticeship, although not as important in North Carolina as in some colonies, was of significance. It provided an opportunity for the poor in Europe to settle in the province; it helped recruit a supply of labor, both skilled and unskilled; and it was an educational agency of great value and import. The careers of servants after freedom in North Carolina are difficult to follow, but it is certain that many of them rose in the social scale, first of all becoming successful farmers, and finally, in some cases, entering the planter class.

Free Negroes

At the bottom of the social pyramid were the Negroes—free and slave. There may have been slaves in the colony many years before there were "free persons of color," and the former usually outnumbered the latter about twenty to one. There were a few free Negroes in Albemarle as early as 1701, and the legislation of the time indicates that their number was constantly increasing. Most of the free Negroes acquired their freedom by legal manumission, but some had a free status because they were the children of either white or Indian mothers. In slavery the child took the legal status of the mother.

Laws Relating to Free Negroes

There was much legislation pertaining to the free Negro. The law of 1715 prohibited them from voting or intermarrying with whites. It also prohibited the master from setting free any Negroes who had been "Runaways or Refractory," but this was not designed to prevent "any man from setting his Negro free as a Reward for . . . honest and Faithful service, provided that such Negro depart the Government within six months after his freedom." The law of 1741 provided that "no Negro or mulatto slave shall be set free except for Meritorious Services to be adjusted and allowed by the County Court," and the slave thus manumitted must leave the colony within six months. Somewhat similar legislation was enacted by the independent state in 1777.

Apparently these laws were not rigidly enforced, especially the provisions about leaving the colony. Free Negro population continued to increase, so that by 1790 there were nearly five thousand in the state, largely in the eastern counties.

As early as 1733 the children of free Negro parents were being bound out as apprentices, and as time went on a larger and larger number of free Negro children were brought within the apprenticeship system. This practice may have been harsh, but the training these children received helped prepare them to earn a living when they had completed their apprenticeship. A large number of free Negroes earned a livelihood at various unskilled types of labor. Quite a number, however, were skilled artisans such as carpenters, coopers, bricklayers, blacksmiths, spinners, weavers, and wheelwrights. Perhaps the majority of free Negroes were farmers, some of whom amassed small properties, and a limited number acquired considerable wealth.

Increase of Negro Population

The royal period witnessed a marked increase in the Negro population, both slave and free. There were some Indian slaves as late as 1715, but they were never very numerous or satisfactory, and in order to solve the labor problem Negro slavery was introduced, perhaps by settlers moving into

Albemarle from Virginia. Slavery was legal in the province from the beginning. The Lords Proprietors recognized the institution in the Concessions of 1665 by granting land to the master for each slave imported, and the Fundamental Constitutions gave to the owner "absolute power and authority over his Negro Slaves." The proprietors had offered to the master fifty acres of land for every slave imported, and as early as 1694 five whites claimed headrights for the importation of eight slaves. Doubtless a number of planters recruited a labor force in similar fashion. But slavery did not grow as rapidly in the province as in the neighboring colonies of Virginia and South Carolina, partially because of the lack of good ports. As Governor Burrington later wrote: "Great is the loss this Country has sustained in not being supply'd by vessells from Guinea with Negroes; in any part of the Province the People are able to pay for a ships load; but as none come directly from Affrica, we are under a necessity to buy the refuse, refractory and distemper'd Negroes, brought from other Governments; It is hoped some Merchants in England will speedily furnish this Colony with Negroes, to increase the Produce and its Trade to England."

Numbers and Location of Slave Population

Most of the slaves before 1730 were in the tobacco-growing region of the northeastern portion of the colony. In 1710 there were reported 308 Negroes and 1,871 whites in Pasquotank and Currituck counties. Two years later the estimated number for the whole colony was 800. The law of 1715 required masters to report the number of slaves above fourteen years of age for taxation, and in 1721 the Board of Trade reported about 1,600 "tythables" for the colony, "of which about one-third were blacks."

The slave population continued to increase at about the same rate as the white population until around 1763. Before that date the Negroes constituted from one-sixth to one-fifth of the colony's population; after 1763, from one-fifth to one-fourth. After 1740 there was a rapid rise in slavery in the rice-growing areas of the Lower Cape Fear and the naval stores region of Craven, Edgecombe, and adjoining counties. Janet Schaw, the "Lady of Quality," describing the routine of a rice plantation in 1775, observed: "The labor required for the cultivation is fit only for slaves, and I think the hardest work I have seen them engaged in."

The heaviest concentration of slaves was always in the counties east of the fall line. In 1756 Governor Dobbs reported to the Board of Trade that there were 77,561 "blacks" in the province, of which 1,420 were in New Hanover, 1,091 in Edgecombe, and 934 in Craven. On the other hand, Orange County had only 50 Negroes of a total population of 1,000, and Rowan had 54 of a total of 1,170. In 1767 Brunswick County had 1,085 black taxables and 224 whites. A return of the North Carolina taxables for 1765 lists 28,542 whites

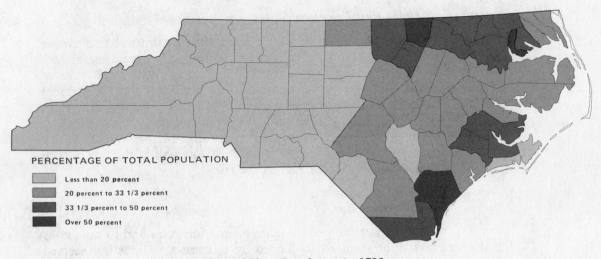

Distribution of Slave Population in 1790

Cartography by the Department of Geography and Earth Sciences
The University of North Carolina at Charlotte

and 17,370 Negroes. Ten years later it was estimated that there were 50,000 Negroes east of the fall line and only 15,000 west of it. The Census of 1790 reported the state's white population at 288,204 and the slave population at 100,572, or about one-fourth of the total.

Prices of Slaves

There was no standard price for a slave, and values varied from time to time and place to place, depending on such factors as the age, sex, physical condition, and temperament of the slaves. The prices of tobacco, naval stores, rice, and other staples also had a bearing on slave values. According to Bassett, the price of a North Carolina slave after 1730 averaged from £15 to £26 sterling. In 1745 an old woman was sold for £100, a boy for £150, and a "prime field hand" for £250, but the average price of slaves was usually much lower than these figures.

Dr. Brickell, writing about 1731, observed that there were two classes of Negro slaves in the province: (1) those who had recently been brought in from Guinea, (2) and those who had been raised in the colonies. The latter, he said, were much "more manageable" and commanded a higher price than "fresh Africans."

Legal Restrictions on Slaves

As the number of slaves increased, their treatment became more severe and the laws concerning them stricter. In the early days some owners allowed their slaves to keep hogs and cattle and to cultivate small plots of grounds for their own use, but the abuse of these privileges and the frequent stealing of cattle led to the passage of a law in 1741 that provided that no slave should on any pretext raise horses, cattle, or hogs, and that all such stock as was found in the possession of slaves six months after the passage of the law was to be seized and sold by the church wardens, one-half of the proceeds to go to the informer and the other half to the parish.

Plantation Rules

Slaves were subject to many plantation rules and to numerous legal restrictions that seem harsh judged by modern standards but seemed reasonable and necessary to eighteenth-century planters and legislators. Legally the slave was a chattel, and as such had no legal rights. He could not be tried in the same court as a freeman, and he could not testify in court against a white man. Naturally the movement of slaves was carefully watched, and there were many plantation rules and acts of the legislature against slaves traveling without proper passes, hunting, or possessing firearms. In general, slaves were forbidden to attend gatherings of Negroes and were not allowed to communicate with other slaves at night.

Harsh Treatment of Slaves

Burrington, the first royal governor, was instructed to get a law passed "for the restraining of any inhuman severity which by ill masters or their overseers may be used towards their Christian servants and their slaves and that provision be made therein that the wilful killing of Indians & Negroes may be punished with death and that a fit penalty be imposed for the maiming of them."

Despite this royal instruction, which was repeated to later governors, the treatment of slaves became more harsh, and many brutal punishments were inflicted on those guilty of breaking plantation rules or provincial laws. Brickell wrote that he had seen "Negroes whipped until large pieces of skin were hanging down their backs," and yet he had "never observed one of them shed a tear." The law of 1741 provided that a slave convicted of perjury should be ordered by the court "to have one Ear nailed to the Pillory, and there stand for the space of One Hour, and the said Ear to be cut off, and thereafter the other Ear nailed in like manner, and cut off at the Expiration of one other Houre; and moreover, to order every such Offender Thirty Nine Lashes well laid, on his or her bare Back, at the Common Whipping Post."

Runaway slaves were outlawed by the same act, which provided that "It shall be lawful for any Person or Persons whatsoever to kill and destroy such Slave or Slaves by such Ways and Means as he or she shall think fit, without Accusation or Impeachment of any Crime for the same."

There were several legal penalties for enticing slaves to leave their masters, and the death penalty was prescribed for consulting, advising, or conspiring "to rebel, or make insurrection." In a few instances Negroes convicted of murder were burned at the stake by court order. It was not until 1774 that a law was passed making the "wilful and malicious killing" of a slave by a white person a crime, and even then the penalty for the first offense was only "twelve months imprisonment."

Religious Opposition to Slavery

At first the North Carolina whites, like those in other English colonies, felt it was immoral to hold a Christian in bondage, but "lawful to enslave heathen." Accordingly some of the slaveowners refused to allow their slaves to be baptized. The Reverend James Adams, an Anglican missionary in Pasquotank, reported in 1709 that he had instructed Negro slaves in the principles of the Christian religion, "but their masters will by no means permit their slaves to be baptized, having a false notion that a Christian slave is, by law, free." Gradually this attitude changed, and reports of missionaries and church records reveal a steady increase in the number of slaves baptized. Apparently Negroes were allowed to attend or even join "white churches," but they were not allowed to have churches of their own, because of white fears of "conspiracies" and insurrections.

The Quakers and Moravians seem to have been the only religious groups to oppose slavery openly, but a number of individuals questioned its morality and its "evil effects" on both slave and owner. Janet Schaw believed that slavery lowered the moral standard of the whites, where masters often "honour their black wenches with their attention," prompted "by no other desire or motive but that of adding to the number of slaves." Few contemporary writers accepted this view, and there is no conclusive evidence that "slave breeding" was practiced in the province. In J. Bryan Grimes's *Wills and Inventories,* however, there are frequent provisions in wills for the buying or devising of young female slaves, and occasionally such phrases as "soon likely to breed" are added.

Developing Opposition to Slavery

In the last decade of the colonial era a trend toward slaveholding was noticeable in the interior, especially in Granville and other tobacco-producing counties along the Virginia border. At the same time opposition also began to develop against slavery, as indicated by the resolution of the "Freeholders in Rowan County," August 8, 1774: "That the African Trade is injurious to this Colony, obstructs the Population of it by freemen, prevents manufacturers, and other Useful Emigrants from Europe from settling among us, and occasions an annual increase of the Balance of Trade against the Colonies." And the first Provincial Congress at New Bern, August 27 of that year, resolved "that we will not import any slave or slaves, nor purchase any slave or slaves imported or brought into this province by others from any part of the world after the first day of November next."

Chapter 9

RELIGIOUS AND CULTURAL DEVELOPMENT, 1730-1776

The increase in population, wealth, and political stability after 1730 was accompanied by the slow growth of Anglicanism, the rapid increase of dissenting Protestant sects, the beginning of formal schools, the establishment of the printing press, the founding of newspapers, the organization of a few libraries, and a general upward trend in social progress.

Organized religion had made little headway in North Carolina during the proprietary period, and as late as 1717 Governor Eden had referred to the "deplorable state of religion in this poor province." The Anglican Church had been established by law, but it was weak and without adequate support, while dissenting groups, notably Quakers, had considerable power. The crown was now determined to establish the church on a sound footing and at the same time to grant religious toleration—but not equality—to all Protestants. Every royal governor received official instructions from England similar to those given to Burrington in 1731: to get laws passed which would give adequate support to the Established Church; to "permit a liberty of conscience to all persons (except Papists)"; to "take especial care that God Almighty be devoutly and duly served," that churches already built "be well and orderly kept and that more be built," and that "no Schoolmasters be permitted to keep school in that our said Province without the license of the Lord Bishop of London."

Burrington tried in vain to get the legislature to translate these instructions into law. His successor, Gabriel Johnston, reported to the Assembly of 1739 that only at Bath and Edenton were church services regularly held, that the state of religion was "really scandalous," and that there was a "deplorable and almost total want of divine worship throughout the province," a condition he urged the legislature to remedy "without loss of time."

The assembly accordingly passed a Vestry Act in 1741, but the British Privy Council disallowed the law because it gave the sole right of presentation (selection of the rector) to the vestries, which the council said was "incompatible with the rights of the Crown and ecclesiastical jurisdiction." Governor Dobbs renewed the fight and a Vestry Act was passed in 1754, but it was disallowed on the same grounds as the 1741 law. According to Stephen B. Weeks, the leading authority on this subject, "This was the beginning of a triangular fight between Dissenters, democratic Churchmen, and supporters of the rights of the Crown. The ecclesiastical history of the next ten years is of interest chiefly because of the stubborn resistance to the enforcement of Church laws by the Dissenters, the stubborn determination of the Churchmen to have an establishment with the right of presentation, and the steady opposition of the Crown to both parties."

Four other Vestry Acts—1758, 1760, 1761, and 1762—were disallowed by the Privy Council on the same grounds. Finally, in 1765, Dobbs succeeded in getting a Vestry Act passed which met with the approval of the Bishop of London and of the crown—a law exactly like the previous ones except there was no reference to the method of selecting the clergy. At the time Dobbs reported that there were only six clergymen in the province, only "four of which are pious and perform their duty," and he expected the new law to improve the state of religion. Governor Tryon, a zealous churchman, reported in 1765 that the Church of England "have the majority of all other sects," but he added, "No British colony on this continent stands more, or so much in need of regular moral clergymen as this does." He believed that if enough clergymen were sent to the colony, "the larger number of every sect would come over to the established religion." Tryon underestimated the strength and zeal of the dissenting sects, and he was too optimistic about the growth of the Establishment, though the number of Anglican ministers and missionaries had increased to eighteen and there had been a small increase in the number of communicants.

The Anglican Church was never very strong or popular in North Carolina. It was unpopular because it had been established by the royal government and had a close relation to it. Non-Anglicans resented its support by public taxes, its control of education, and its other special privileges, particularly the law that permitted only Anglican clergymen to perform the marriage ceremony. The forms and doctrines of the church, the "Anglican squat," the church's aristocratic outlook and apparent lack of interest in the common people, its lack of emphasis on preaching, and its lack of emotional appeal met with popular disfavor. The Anglican Church also had a fundamental weakness in having no American bishop. An episcopal organization that lacked a bishop to confirm members, ordain ministers, and discipline the clergy was an anomaly that handicapped the church in many ways. According to the late Bishop J. B. Cheshire, "the Church in North Carolina was helpless, blind, and paralyzed."

The lack of a resident bishop retarded the development of a native clergy, since prospective ministers had to go to England for ordination. Consequently there was always a scarcity of ministers. In 1727–28 the colony had eleven parishes and not a single clergyman. Tryon wrote in 1754 that "more ministers were required" for the thirty-two parishes, and he deplored the fact that "for lack of ministers, justices of the peace marry people and bury them." In 1765 Governor Dobbs was buried by a magistrate, since there was not a clergyman within a hundred miles. North Carolina had a smaller number of Anglican clergymen than any other colony of comparable size—only forty-six clergymen during the whole colonial period, and the Society for the Propagation of the Gospel in Foreign Parts, founded in 1701, supplied thirty-three of these. Of the forty-six preachers and missionaries, five were casual visitors; six either died soon after arrival or made a hasty return to England; and three or four were considered "bad men" by the church authorities themselves. Stephen B. Weeks, a leading authority on religion in North Carolina, referred to "the pernicious activities" of the SPG missionaries, and Governor Tryon urged the society not to send to North Carolina "the sweepings of the Universities but some clergy of character." It is true that one missionary "behaved himself in a most horrid manner" and was labelled "ye Monster of ye Age," another was accused by a fellow missionary of falling "into the sin of fornication," while a third was referred to by Governor Eden as "that rum soaked missionary." These were exceptional cases, but the conduct of these "bad men" hurt the church and, as one missionary wrote, "proved a great stumbling-block to many of our persuasion." Most of the missionaries were moral, devoted, zealous, hard-working, and self-sacrificing men. John Boyd, in his labors in the Brunswick region in 1735, traveled on horseback and on foot as much as 260 miles a month and baptized 1,030 people during the year. Clement Hall, 1744–55, traveled over fourteen thousand miles, baptized about ten thousand persons, and published one of the first books in North Carolina, *A Collection of Many Christian Experiences* (1753). The major part of missionary work was among the whites, but considerable religious activity was carried on among the Negro slaves, several thousand of whom were baptized and hundreds admitted to church membership. Alexander Stewart was the only missionary who reported that he had baptized a large number of Indians.

There was always a scarcity of churches and "chapels of ease," and some of those which existed were in wretched physical condition. Tryon, in 1754, said that there were only five church buildings in the province—at Brunswick, Wilmington, Bath, Edenton, and New Bern, and only the one at New Bern was "in good repair." Parson Daniel Earl reported the church at Edenton in "a very ruinous condition."

Anglican clergymen and lay leaders constantly complained about the apathy of church members, who were "disheartened and dispersed like sheep" and were "in a leaderless and chaotic state." This condition was partly due to the neglect of some of the parishes to hold vestry elections and to the failure of the vestries to collect taxes and to purchase glebes, the only glebe house in the colony being the one erected at Bath in 1763. The apathetic attitude was also caused, in large measure, by the failure of the governors and other high officials, most of whom were Anglicans, to enforce the existing church laws and, perhaps most significant of all, by the British disallowance of Vestry Acts which might have solved many of the church's problems.

The increasing opposition of Baptists, Presbyterians, and other dissenters also hurt the Anglicans. These groups demanded separation of church and state, repeal of compulsory taxation for the church, and complete religious equality. The Presbyterians, in particular, attacked the Marriage Act of 1741, which gave virtual control of the performance of the marriage ceremony to Anglican clergymen. Opposition to this law and flagrant disregard of it finally led to the law of 1766, which legalized prior marriages by Presbyterian and other "dissenting ministers."

The most significant development in the religious life of colonial North Carolina after 1730 was the growth and spread of dissenting sects, notably Quakers, Baptists, Presbyterians, Lutherans, Moravians, German Reformed, and Methodists. Writing from New Bern in 1760, Parson Reed, an Anglican minister, said: "The anabaptists are obstinate, illiterate & grossly ignorant, the Methodists ignorant, censorious & uncharitable, the Quakers rigid, but the Presbyterians are pretty moderate except here & there a bigot or rigid Calvinist. As for papists, I cannot learn there are above 9 or 10 in the whole Country. I have estimated the number of Infidels & Heathen to be about 1,000."

The Quaker church or the Society of Friends, which was its official name, was the only important religious sect in the colony before 1700. The first Quaker preacher visited the colony in 1672; there was a monthly meeting as early as 1678, a quarterly meeting in 1681, and a yearly meeting organized in 1698. As late as 1708 William Gordon, an Anglican missionary, reported: "There are few or no dissenters in this Government but Quakers." The Cary Rebellion, which occurred about this time, ended Quaker domination of the government and hurt their prestige, though they were not active participants in the uprising. Although they had lost much of their political power, the Quakers continued to be the most potent force in the religious life of the colony until the close of the proprietary period. From 1700 to 1729 no fewer than seventeen Quaker missionaries visited the province, much to the annoyance of Anglican clergymen and to that of some of the government officials. In 1729 Sir Richard Everard, the last proprietary governor, wrote that the Quakers were "very busy making Proselytes and holding meetings daily in every part of this Government." He attributed their success to the lack of Anglican clergy, overlooking the fact that the Friends had a great appeal to the "unchurched classes" because of what Burrington called "the regularity of their lives, hospitality to strangers, and kind offices to new settlers."

Quaker power and influence in the Albemarle region declined after 1730, but there were new settlements of Friends in the central part of the colony, especially after 1750, when many migrated from Pennsylvania and New Jersey and settled in the present counties of Guilford, Randolph, Alamance, and Chatham. In 1751 the Cane Creek Monthly Meeting was organized in Orange County (present Alamance), and in 1754 the New Garden Meeting in Guilford County. The latter became the parent of other monthly meetings. The Quakers continued to grow in numbers in the Piedmont, especially after 1771, when there was a migration from Nantucket, New England, which probably outnumbered the earlier influx from Pennsylvania. The growth of Quakerism continued until the outbreak of the Revolution, when Quaker immigration almost stopped, and when the sect's opposition to war caused the Friends to go through "a time of suffering," and a decline in membership.

Presbyterians

There were some individual Presbyterians in North Carolina before 1700, but no organized church group. John Blair, an Anglican missionary writing in 1704, referred to a group "something like Presbyterians," and John Brickell, in 1737, wrote that "after Quakers, Presbyterians succeed [come] next in numbers" and that they were chiefly "settled in and about the River Neus."

The coming of the Highlanders, and to an even greater degree the influx of the Scotch-Irish, gave a great impetus to Presbyterianism, though both these Scottish groups came into the colony without ministers. There were a few Presbyterians in the Cape Fear Valley as early as 1736, especially on the McCulloh grants in Duplin and New Hanover counties, and in the region of present Fayetteville. At least two churches were organized—Cross Creek and Goshen—but they were without pastors for several years.

After 1740 the Synod of Philadelphia, representing the "old side" doctrines, received numerous petitions "from many people of North Carolina . . . showing their desolate condition," in response to which the synod sent William Robinson to North Carolina in 1742–43 and John Thomson in 1744. For the next two decades missionaries made periodic visits, the most significant being that of Hugh McAden, the "father of Presbyterianism in North Carolina." McAden made a missionary tour of the colony, April 3, 1755-May 6, 1756, and recorded in his interesting journal that he found at least seven meetinghouses between the Hyco and Yadkin rivers. In 1758 the Philadelphia Synod sent the Reverend James Campbell, who became the first regular Presbyterian pastor in North Carolina, serving three churches in the Cape Fear Valley—the only Presbyterian minister in that region until 1770.

Alexander Craighead, in 1758, became pastor of the Sugar Creek Church in Mecklenburg County, and from that time until his death in 1766 he was the only regular Presbyterian minister between the Yadkin and the Catawba.

In 1755 the Synod of New York, representing the "new side" beliefs, organized the Hanover Presbytery, which included the Virginia and North Carolina churches. This presbytery held at least four meetings in North Carolina, the last of which met at Buffalo Church, near present Greensboro, in March, 1770, and petitioned the New York Synod for the creation of a presbytery for the Carolinas. This request was granted and in May, 1770, the Orange Presbytery was organized, consisting of eight congregations in North Carolina and four in South Carolina. The first meeting of the newly organized Orange Presbytery met at Hawfields Church, in present Alamance County.

J. P. Maclean, in his *Scotch Highlanders in America,* gives the names and dates of forty-four Presbyterian churches in North Carolina before 1780. Perhaps as many churches as that were built or planned, but there were not enough ministers to serve so many congregations adequately. The Presbyterians, however, exerted an influence out of proportion to their numbers, for their preachers and educators included such famous men as David Caldwell, Henry Patillo, Samuel E. McCorkle, and James Hall.

Baptists

According to Morgan Edwards, early Baptist historian, there were some individual Baptists or "Anabaptists" in North Carolina as early as 1695. There were a few Baptists among the early settlers who came into Albemarle from Virginia, and perhaps there were some who came to the colony from other places. But there was no organized Baptist congregation until 1727, when a church, located on the Pasquotank River in present Camden County, was founded by the Reverend Paul Palmer, the earliest recorded Baptist preacher in North Carolina. Two years later Shiloh Church, in present Camden County, was begun by Palmer. For several years this "Baptist teacher," as Governor Everard called him, traveled, preached, baptized, and held meetings "daily in every part of this Government." The Anglicans tried to stop Palmer's religious activities, but he appealed to the English Toleration Act and, in 1728, was granted a license to preach by the governor. The next year Everard reported that Palmer had made hundreds of converts.

During the next two decades other Baptist missionaries, notably Joseph Parker, Josiah Hart, Robert Williams, and William Sojourner carried on the work Palmer had so industriously and effectively begun. All of these preachers were General Baptists, who preached the Arminian doctrine of "a salvation free to all, asking no other evidence of repentance, than a desire to be baptized." Their major activity was in the Albemarle Sound region and the lower Roanoke Valley. So successful were they in their labors that by 1752 they had established sixteen congregations and claimed several hundred members.

The Kehukee Baptist Association

The most significant Baptist Church in the eastern portion of the colony was that at Kehukee, Halifax County, organized in 1742 by William Sojourner. By 1755 this church reported 125 members, while all the other Baptist churches in that area had fewer than 100. In 1769 the Kehukee Association was organized "out of churches which had been reformed to an orthodox standard" and included congregations in Halifax, Edgecombe, Martin, Washington, Beaufort, Carteret, and several other eastern counties. This association had a phenomenal growth, and even some of the South Carolina churches united with it. By the time of the Revolution the Kehukee Association had sixty-one churches and an estimated five thousand members.

About this time, the Particular Baptists, who emphasized "particular election" and other Calvinist doctrines, became active in the colony, primarily through the activities of John Gano and other missionaries sent to North Carolina by the Philadelphia Association in 1754 and the years following. Gano's activity in the "Jersey Settlement" and surrounding vicinity in the Piedmont led to the establishment of several churches.

The Separate Baptists: Sandy Creek Church

The most significant landmark in Baptist history, however, was the founding of Sandy Creek Church in what is now Randolph County in 1755 by the Reverend Shubal Stearns, who had recently arrived with eight families from Boston. This marked the beginning of the Separate Baptists, who emphasized the "doctrine of the new birth," "believer's baptism," "free justification," and the autonomy of each congregation. The Separate Baptists "discovered, in their estimation, the nine following rites, viz.; Baptism—the Lord's Supper—love-feasts—laying-on-of-hands—washing feet—anointing the sick—right hand of fellowship—kiss of charity—and devoting children." This last rite was satirically called "dry-christening." The Separates also emphasized "*weekly* communion" and evangelical religion. They established camp meetings "from motives of convenience and necessity, and relinquished them as soon as they were no longer needful." The Reverend George Pope, pastor of Abbott's Creek Church, said that "the fantastic exercise of jerking, dancing &c. in a religious way, prevailed much with the united body of Methodists and Presbyterians, towards the close of the revival; but they were not introduced at all among the Baptists in these parts. But falling down under religious impressions was frequent among them. Many were taken with these religious epilepsies, if we may so call them, not only at the great meetings where those scenes were exhibited which were calculated to move the sympathetic affections, but also about their daily employment in the fields, some in their houses, and some when hunting the cattle in the woods. . . . And besides falling down there were many other expressions of zeal, which, in more moderate people, would be considered enthusiastic and wild." Mr. Pope claimed that he baptized about five hundred persons "in the course of the revival, and that large numbers were also baptized by John Culpeper, William McGregore, and many others." Another contemporary, writing about a camp meeting, said: "My pen cannot describe the one half I saw, heard, and felt. I might fill a volume on this subject, and then leave the greater part untold."

The Sandy Creek Church, "the Mother of all the Separate Baptists," had a phenomenal growth, increasing from 16 to 606 members within a few years. Within seventeen years 42 churches and 125 ministers had "sprung from the parent church." In 1758 the Sandy Creek Association—oldest Baptist association in the state and fourth oldest in the United States—was organized, and for the next twelve years all Separate Baptist Churches in Virginia and the Carolinas were affiliated with this association, which had yearly meetings.

By the time of the outbreak of the Revolution in 1775 the Baptists of one variety or another had come to be the most numerous religious sect in the colony, and are said to have had at least one church in each county, with a total of more than forty churches. The Baptists had become the leading opponents of the Established Church. Their democratic organization and government, their local autonomy and religious democracy, had a great appeal to the common people and a marked influence on the growth of political democracy.

Moravians

As stated earlier, the Germans who settled in the North Carolina Piedmont included three religious sects: Lutheran, Reformed, and Moravian. These groups had some similarities—a common racial origin and language, plus the fact that their increase was largely due to new arrivals from Pennsylvania or Germany. But there were marked differences, especially between the Moravians and the "Church People," as the Lutheran and Reformed groups were called.

The Moravians, or United Brethren (*Unitas Fratrum*), were the best organized of these German sects. From their first settlement at Bethabara, in 1753, they came as a congregation, accompanied by a minister. They made no efforts at proselyting and increased their membership only as a result of natural increase and by new arrivals from Pennsylvania and Europe. They practiced a modified form of communism, under which a congregation board supervised both religious and civil matters such as trades and industries. The store, tavern, bakery, pottery, brickyard, tannery, distillery, and other industries were operated for the benefit of the "congregation fund." Always numerically small, the Moravians were very influential, and made distinctive contributions in education, agriculture, science, and medicine. Only the language barrier prevented them from making an even greater contribution. The *Records of the Moravians in North Carolina,* meticulously kept since 1753, and translated and edited in volumes by the late Adelaide L. Fries and others, constitutes "the most remarkable literary corpus of the colonial South." These records consist of diaries, reports, letters, memoirs, obituaries, hymns, poetry, and many other documents which throw light on the Moravians of Wachovia and give valuable information on North Carolina in the eighteenth century.

Lutherans and German Reformed

The Lutherans, who eventually became the largest sect among the Germans in North Carolina, settled in a much wider area, centering in the present counties of Rowan, Cabarrus, Stanly, Davidson, and other counties of the central Piedmont. The German Reformed groups usually settled in the same communities as the Lutherans and the three oldest Reformed churches, Grace (later named Lowerstone) in Rowan, and Leonard's (Pilgrim) and Beck's in Davidson, were "union churches," where the two sects worshipped on alternate Sundays. In contrast with the Moravians, both groups came into the colony without pastors. The Reverend Christian Theus, a Reformed minister from South Carolina, preached in the North Carolina Piedmont in the 1750s and early 1760s, but it was not until 1768 that there was a Reformed preacher in charge of a particular church. In that year the Reverend Samuel Suther, native of Switzerland, who had been teaching school in Philadelphia since 1739, became the pastor of Grace Church and also officiated at the two other Reformed churches. It is interesting that it was not until 1853 that Lowerstone Church had a minister who preached "entirely in English."

Suther preached to a number of Lutheran congregations, and it was not until 1773 that this sect had a regular minister. Meantime three Lutheran congregations had been organized—Zion (Organ) Church near Rockwell in Rowan County, St. John's in Salisbury, and St. John's in Cabarrus County. In 1773 the members of Organ and St. John's sent two delegates to Germany to secure a minister and a schoolmaster. Their mission was successful and the Reverend Adolph Nussman and Johann Gottfried Arndt took over the spiritual and educational leadership of the North Carolina Lutherans. For the next twenty-one years Nussman "labored faithfully in poverty and privations," serving congregations in Rowan, Cabarrus, Iredell, Catawba, Lincoln, Davidson, Guilford, and Stokes counties.

Methodists

The Methodists were the last Protestant sect to appear in colonial North Carolina. Methodism originated as a reform movement within the Church of England and it had no organization as a distinct church until after the American Revolution. Several "Methodist" preachers, however, visited North Carolina to preach the doctrines of the "Methodist Society" to "the dear Americans," as John Wesley called his followers. George Whitefield, the great oratorical preacher, "who could make hell so vivid that one could locate it on an atlas," came to North Carolina several times between 1739 and 1765, where, according to the Anglican Parson Reed, "this surprising Minister had very numerous congregations," because "people were very desirous to hear him" and came many miles to do so. Whitefield condemned "rebaptizing of adults and the doctrine of irresistible influence of the spirit & likewise recommended infant Baptism." Reed declared in 1761 that "the Methodists of late have given me a great deal of trouble . . . by preaching up the inexpediency of Human Learning & the practice of moral virtue & the great expediency of Dreams Visions & immediate Revelation." He thought that "the poor ignorant people were being deluded" by their "pernicious doctrines," and that many were "tinctured with the principles of Methodism." He remarked, however, that "the fervor of the Methodists . . . is very much abated" and believed "it would be totally lost in a few months."

The Anglican parson was too optimistic. If the Methodist fervor abated in the 1760s, it increased very much in the next decade, partly because of the organization of "Methodist Societies" in Virginia and North Carolina. The first of these was founded by Joseph Pilmore (or Pilmoor) at Portsmouth, Virginia, November 14, 1772. Pilmore preached the first "Methodist sermon" in North Carolina at Currituck Court House, September 28 of that year. He also conducted religious services at several other points in the eastern part of the colony. Shortly thereafter Robert Williams, Thomas Rankin, Devereux Jarratt, and perhaps other ministers of the Methodist faith preached at various places in northeastern North Carolina. The first Methodist Circuit in the colony was organized in 1774 and included congregations "which extended from Petersburg to the Roanoke River some distance into North Carolina." As a result of this renewed Methodist activity a great revival swept the northern counties in 1775, continuing for weeks and bringing 683 members "into the fold."

Organization of the Methodist Episcopal Church

A conference held at Baltimore, May 21, 1776, established the first "North Carolina Circuit" with Edward Dromgoole, Francis Poythress, and Isham Tatum as preachers. The formal organization of the Methodist Episcopal Church in the United States took place at Baltimore in 1784, and the first annual conference of this new church organization was held in Green Hill's home at Louisburg, North Carolina, April 20, 1785, with Superintendents Francis Asbury and Thomas Coke present.

Education

Education in early North Carolina, as in the other colonies and in England, was closely associated with the church. Most of the teachers were clergymen, lay readers, or candidates for the ministry. The pioneer educational agency in North Carolina was the Society for the Propagation of the Gospel, whose missionaries "brought with them the first parish or public libraries," and whose "lay readers were the first teachers."

First Schoolteachers in North Carolina

The first North Carolina schoolteacher mentioned in the extant records was Charles Griffin, or Griffith, a "reader" in the Anglican Church, who came into the colony in 1706 and opened a school in Pasquotank County. Governor William Glover praised Griffin for his "industry and unblemished life," but James Adams, an SPG missionary, said that Griffin did well for a short time and "then fell into the sin of fornication & joined with the Quaker interest." Whereupon Adams took over the school and Griffin moved to Chowan County and opened another school, which was attended "by a number of students, especially Quakers." It is not known how long Griffin taught in Chowan County. By 1714 he was living in Virginia, where in January, 1715, he was employed by Governor Alexander Spotswood to educate Saponi Indian children for a salary of £50 a year, which the governor paid out of his own pocket. Three years later Spotswood hired Griffin as master of the Indian school at the College of William and Mary, a position carrying the title of "Brafferton Professorship."

Another teacher mentioned in the records was "one Mr. Mashburn," who, according to a 1712 report by Anglican missionary Giles Rainsford, "keeps a school at Sarum [in present Gates County] on the frontier of Virginia," where both white and Indian children were taught to "write and read very distinctly" as well as being trained in the "grounds and principles of the Christian religion."

The Planters' Interest in Education

Most of the small farmers were too busy clearing the forests, tilling the soil, and eking out a living to pay much attention to education, formal or otherwise. In 1716 Governor Eden wrote to England that the planters would "willingly pay most of the salaries of teachers" if the SPG could procure them. The wills and inventories of the time reflect a zeal for education. Not only did the planters provide in their wills for the education of their own children and relatives, but a few of humanitarian and philanthropic bent made provision for the training of underprivileged children, through bequests and endowments. Some of the wills gave specific instructions that the boys should be trained in trades and professions, the girls in "those things which would make them a good wife and housekeeper." In 1697 Alexander Lillington willed "that my Executors carry on my son, John, in his learnings as I have begun, and that

All my Children be brought up in learning, as conveniently can bee." Thomas Bell, in 1733, provided that the profits from his estate be devoted to the education of a niece and nephew, "in as handsome and good a manner as may be." In 1734 John Baptista Ashe provided that one son be trained in law, one in merchandise, and a daughter "be taught to write and read & some feminine acccomplishments which may render her agreeable; and that she be not kept ignorant in what appertains to a good house wife in the management of household affairs."

Education of the Poorer Classes

The children of the wealthier were usually given some instruction in the home and then sent outside the colony for advanced training—perhaps to a college in this country or in England. The children of the poor, and especially orphans and illegitimate children, received some education through the agencies of indentured servitude and the apprenticeship system. Masters and guardians were required to give their wards the "rudiments of learning" and teach them a "useful trade." Orphans were to be taught according to "rank and degree." Public education was foreshadowed in numerous wills of the time, such as that of James Winwright, who in 1744 provided that after his death and that of his wife the "yearly rents and profits of all the Town Land and Houses in Beaufort Town" be used "for the encouragement of a sober discreet Quallifyed Man to teach a School at least Reading Writing and Common Arithmetic" in the town of Beaufort, and that fifty pounds sterling be used "for the Building and furnishings of a Creditable House for a School and a Dwelling house for the Master." The provisions in the will of James Innes led to the establishment of an academy at Wilmington—chartered in 1783 and opened after 1800.

Attitude of Governors and Assembly toward Education

The coming of the Scotch-Irish and Germans into the North Carolina Piedmont gave a great impetus to education, as these two elements established schools in most of their communities soon after settlement. Governor Dobbs wrote the Board of Trade in 1755 that the Scotch-Irish desired "A Teacher of their own opinion and choice." As early as 1756 the Moravian records refer to schoolteachers, a "day school," and a "school for older boys."

As early as 1736 Governor Johnston had urged the legislature to do something about education. "In all civilized Societys of men," he said, "it has always been looked upon as a matter of the greatest consequence to their Peace and happiness, to polish the minds of young Persons with some degree of learning, and early to instill into them the principles of virtue and religion, and that the Legislature has never yet taken the least care to erect one school, which deserves the name in this wide extended country, must in the judgment of all thinking men, be reckoned one of our greatest misfortunes."

The assembly replied: "We lament very much the want of Divine Publick Worship (a crying scandal in any, but more especially in a Church Community;) as well as the general neglect in point of education, the main sources of all Disorders and Corruptions, which we should rejoice to see removed and remedied, and are ready to do our parts, towards the reformation of such flagrant and prolifick Evils." But it took no immediate action to correct these "evils."

Movement for Public Schools

Although the idea of education as a public duty was held by all of the royal governors and by some of the legislators, it was left to church groups and individuals to establish schools. Governor Johnston made an eloquent appeal to the assembly in behalf of schools, and Dobbs urged legislative "provisions for the education of youth." Bills for the establishment of free schools were introduced into the legislatures of 1749 and 1752, but they were defeated. Finally, in 1754, an act was passed which, among other things, appropriated £6,000 "for founding and endowing a Public School" in the colony, but shortly thereafter this money was "borrowed and employed" for military purposes. R. D. W. Connor thought that this law envisioned the founding of a college and has called it "the first legislative effort to establish a college in North Carolina at public expense." In 1758 the General Assembly petitioned the king for authority to use North Carolina's quota of the money Parliament had reimbursed the province for its recent military expenditures "for purchasing glebes & erecting a Free School in each County." The Board of Trade refused to approve this proposal. Apparently the plan of 1754 for "a Public School for the Colony" had given way to that of a "Free School in each County," an entirely different thing.

In 1759 Governor Dobbs made a clear-cut distinction between the free county schools, which should be "only for English scholars to learn to read, write, and account with some other branches of the Mathematicks," and the "one Public Provincial school" for the languages and higher branches of learning, which would be endowed.

North Carolina's First College

The first successful effort to establish a college in North Carolina was made by the Presbyterians of Mecklenburg County, who in 1770 persuaded Governor Tryon to recommend to the assembly that it establish "a public seminary in some part of the back country of this Colony for the education of youth." This led to the passage of an act on January 15, 1771, incorporating

Queen's College at Charlotte. This was the first time that the word "college" appeared in the records. The institution was authorized to grant degrees, and it was to be financed by a "duty of six pence per gallon on all rum brought into and disposed of in Mecklenburg County for ten years following the passage of the act." The law specified that the president, who might have "three or less tutors," must be "learned, pious, exemplary," and that he be a member of the Established Church. The law did not require that the tutors be licensed by either the Bishop of London or by the governor. Supposedly, the act incorporating Queen's College was disallowed by George III, April 22, 1772, in spite of Tryon's urgent plea for its approval. The college, however, had begun operations before Governor Martin, who had just succeeded Tryon, received official word of the law's disallowance, and it continued to operate as a "private school" without a charter until 1777, when it was chartered as Liberty Hall by the General Assembly of the independent state. The school operated for the next three years, with no church control, but by 1780 it had fallen into "an entire state of decay," because of the financial stringency resulting from the Revolution, and it closed its doors. A new charter was obtained in 1784, and the school was transferred to Salisbury and renamed "Salisbury Academy."

Constitutional Provision for Education

The agitation for public education, though not meeting with immediate success, finally bore fruit in Section 41 of the State Constitution of 1776, which provided "that a School or Schools shall be established by the Legislature for the convenient Instruction of Youth, with such Salaries to the Masters paid by the Public, as may enable them to instruct at low Prices; and all useful Learning shall be duly encouraged and promoted in one or more Universities." This was considered by many people as a constitutional mandate for public schools and state-supported higher education. But the state was slow in establishing a university and even slower in setting up a public school system.

The failure of colonial North Carolina to promote formal education did not mean that its people lacked interest in "the finer things of life." Such cultural indices as books, libraries, and newspapers, or even the training of lawyers, doctors, and other professional men are, in a sense, a part of the story of education.

Books and Libraries

Books were not very numerous in the colony, and their very scarcity gave added importance to libraries—private, semiprivate, and "public." The earliest collections of books mentioned in extant records were those sent to the colony by the Society for the Propagation of the Gospel, the most important of which was the so-called "free public library" sent to St. Thomas Parish, Bath County, by the Reverend Thomas Bray about 1701. This library seems to have been poorly managed in its early days, and a law of 1715 provided "for the more effectual preservation of the same."

After 1730 libraries became common among planters, clergymen, lawyers, doctors, and others who could afford them. Books were often listed in wills and inventories of estates, usually from twenty to fifty per family, but a few planters and professional men had large collections. The Reverend James Reed had 266 books, Edward Moseley 400, and Samuel Johnston, at Hayes, more than 1,000 volumes—the largest library in the province. These libraries usually contained books in the fields of theology, philosophy, political economy, history, literature, law, and medicine, among others. Greek and Roman writers were represented, as well as Shakespeare, Milton, Bacon, Locke, Voltaire, Swift, Addison, Steele, and many others. A few of the libraries had copies of leading English periodicals, notably *The Spectator, The Tatler,* and *The Annual Register.*

Printing and Newspapers

The press made a late entry into North Carolina, nine other continental English colonies having priority in this field. Like the press in other colonies, its establishment arose from the necessity of printing and circulating the laws of the provincial legislature. The revisal and printing of the laws had been agitated for a long time. In 1736, 1739, 1740, and 1744 Governor Johnston reminded the assembly about "the shameful condition" of its laws and urged that something be done. In 1746 the legislature was told that "for want of the Laws of this Province being revised and printed, the Magistrates are often at a loss how to discharge their Duty, and the People transgress many of them through want of knowing the same." Accordingly a law was passed to appoint commissioners to "Revise and Print the Laws of this Province." A committee was appointed, consisting of Edward Moseley, Samuel Swann, Enoch Hall, and Thomas Barker. The revisal was completed, almost wholly by Swann, and laid before the 1749 assembly for approval. As this work neared completion it was obvious that the colony would need a printer. Accordingly the assembly appointed James Davis as "Public Printer," to print the laws and other official documents, at a salary for five years of £160 proclamation money (increased to £200 in 1760) to be raised by a tax of four pence "on each and every Taxable Person within this Province." Davis, who had learned his trade at Williamsburg, set up his printing press at New Bern on June 24, 1749, and the earliest known imprint from it was the fourteen-page journal of legislative proceedings, September 26–October 18, 1749, entitled *The Journal of the House of Burgesses, of the Province of North-Carolina.* In 1751 he published *A Collection of all the*

Public Acts of Assembly, of the Province of North Carolina: Now in Force and Use, sometimes called Swann's Revisal. The book, usually considered "the first book published in North Carolina," was also known as "The Yellow Jacket" because of the color of its binding. Davis also founded the first newspaper in the colony, *The North Carolina Gazette.*

Chapter 10

ROYAL GOVERNORS AND THEIR PROBLEMS, 1730-1775

The transfer of the colony to the crown in 1729 marked no significant change in the structure of government, at either the provincial or local level. The powers and duties of governor, council, assembly, courts and local officials were unchanged, though the crown, instead of the proprietors, now commissioned and instructed the governor. As a royal colony North Carolina became more closely identified with the imperial system and had a much closer relationship to the king and Privy Council and to various British administrative agencies, notably the Board of Trade, the Secretary of State for the Southern Department, the Treasury Board, War Board, Admiralty Board, and Commissioners of the Customs.

The Relation of North Carolina to the Mother Country

Though North Carolina was royalized during the era of "salutary neglect" and in the reign of a weak sovereign, George II, the general policies of the crown were definite and consistent, though not rigidly enforced. The major objectives were the mercantilist ideas of an economically self-sufficient empire and closer connection of the colonies with the mother country and with each other. To achieve these objectives it was imperative that the governors, councillors, and judges be subservient to imperial control and as independent as practicable of popularly elected assemblies. To guarantee this independence, the crown deemed it essential that the governors and judges be paid "fixed salaries out of a permanent fund"; that the tenure of judges be "during pleasure" of the governor as the official representative of the crown; that the governor have the exercise of "royal prerogatives": to issue writs of election; to summon, prorogue, and dissolve legislatures; to determine a quo-

149

rum in these legislative bodies, and to veto laws. The governor was also required to enforce the Navigation Acts and other British trade laws.

North Carolina Opposition to British Policies

These imperial policies and the efforts to enforce them met with considerable opposition in North Carolina and the other colonies. There was a fundamental clash between some British policies and local interests; and there was a basic constitutional conflict between the royal prerogatives and royal instructions, on the one hand, and the "charter rights" of the people, on the other.

The king and his ministers maintained that the charter of 1663 had been a royal grant to the Lords Proprietors and not to the people, and that the charter had ceased to be effective after the crown's purchase of the proprietary interests. North Carolina leaders, especially in the assembly, took a different view. They maintained that the charter had a dual character: first, it was a grant of title to the soil and of certain governmental powers to the proprietors; and second, it was a guarantee of the rights of the people. The proprietors had surrendered their own powers to the crown, but not the rights of the people. Hence the king must govern according to the terms of the charter. This view was clearly stated by Governor Dobbs in a report to the Board of Trade in 1760 in which he said, "The Assembly think themselves entitled to all the Privileges of a British House of Commons and therefore ought not to submit to His Majesty's honorable Privy Council further than the Commons do in England, or submit to his Majesty's instructions to this Governor and Council here." And the governor asked for royal support so that he might "oppose and suppress a republican spirit of Independency rising in this Colony."

The "Popular Party" versus the "Prerogative Party"

The fundamental issue was the royal power versus people's rights, a conflict that gave impetus to the growth of the "prerogative party," headed by the governor and usually supported by the council, representing the imperial point of view, and the "popular party," championed by the Speaker of the assembly or the treasurer. Divergent points of view on many matters led to perennial disputes between the executive and legislative branches of the colonial administration, and to controversies that "ran through the events of the period not like a silver thread but like a knotted cord."

The Problem of the Governor's Salary

Many of the executive-legislative conflicts had to do with finance, and the assembly consistently and persistently used its "power of the purse" to force concessions from the governor and from the council. In a sense the governor was not responsible to the assembly or the people. He was commissioned and instructed by the crown. But the assembly controlled his salary, and this control proved to be a most effective weapon.

The practice during the proprietary era had been for the legislature to vote "presents" to the governor, such as the £500 to Everard in 1729, so that he would approve a bill authorizing the emission of £40,000 paper currency, in violation of his royal instructions. The first royal governor, George Burrington, was forbidden to accept presents and was instructed to get the legislature to provide "a fixed salary out of a permanent fund without limitation in point of time." Burrington hoped to receive an annual salary of £700 out of quitrent revenues, but the assembly refused to adopt a plan for the successful collection of these rents. At the time Burrington assumed office William Byrd II of Virginia wrote him: "I think, by some samples I have known of that country, it would cost a pretty deal of trouble to bring it into order, and a less spirit than yours will never be able to effect it. People accustomed to live without law or gospel will with great Reluctance Submit to either. . . . In the meantime I wish you all the success in the world in bringing the chaos into form and reducing that Anarchy into a regular Government. In so doing you will deserve to have your statue erected, or, which perhaps is better, to have your salary doubled."

Burrington's "spirit" was not equal to the task, and he got neither statue nor salary. In disgust he wrote that no governor could have carried out his instructions and kept the peace with a people who were "subtle and crafty to admiration, who could be neither outwitted nor cajoled, who always behaved insolently to their Governors, who maintained that their money could not be taken from them save by appropriations made by their own House of Assembly, a body that had always usurped more power than they ought to be allowed."

Johnston fared little better, in spite of his boasted "management" of the legislature. Writing to the Board of Trade in 1746, he said that he had received no salary for eight years. At the time of his death his salary was in arrears for fourteen years.

Dobbs had about the same experience. In March, 1764, he informed the Board of Trade that the lower house had refused "to settle a salary on him" or to pay the rent of a house for his use. Two years later he wrote: "I can see no prospect of getting a fixed salary to the Governor and His Successors. There seems to be an established maxim fixed in the several Assemblies in the colonies to keep the Governors and Government as much in *their* power as they can."

Dobbs petitioned the authorities in England for an annual allowance from another source. Accordingly, upon an order of the Privy Council's plantations committee, the Treasury Board awarded Dobbs a yearly salary of £1,000 sterling from the 4.5 percent customs revenues of Barbados and the Leeward Islands. The authorities made this arrangement permanent and for the remainder of the colonial era North Carolina governors had an annual source of income from the crown. The Townshend Revenue Act of 1767 put all royal governors on the "civil list" by providing that part of the revenues to be derived from the taxes would be applied to the salaries of royal governors and judges. Despite these actions by the British government, the governors still insisted that the legislatures vote them a salary.

By clever diplomacy and tact Governor Tryon obtained all the funds he desired from the legislature. His survey of the Cherokee Boundary Line in 1767 added £1,490 to the colony's debt and his military expeditions against the Regulators in 1768 and 1771 cost the colony £44,844. He likewise persuaded the assembly to appropriate £15,000 for the construction of the palace at New Bern. He is usually considered the best of all the North Carolina colonial governors, in spite of the fact that he spent large sums of money and increased the indebtedness of the colony by more than £50,000.

"Control of the Purse": Controversies over Money Matters

Control of taxation was in many respects the most serious of all conflicts between the assemblies and the governors. There were three aspects of this problem: amount, purposes, and methods of expenditure. The governor claimed that legislative appropriations were "aids to the king," and hence he had control of all expenditures. He maintained that he was accountable for all fiscal matters to the king and not to the assembly. The latter insisted on its "control of the purse" and claimed "the sole right of Framing and Modelling all Bills of Virtue of which Money has been Levied on the Subjects for an Aid to his Majesty." It was determined not to surrender this power to either governor or council. It contested the right of the latter body to amend money measures, and it won its point.

There was a prolonged and bitter controversy between the governor and the assembly, and also between the assembly and the council, about attaching "riders" to appropriation measures. This was particularly true during the French and Indian War, 1754–63. This question came up in every session, and there was so much wrangling over it that little legislation resulted. Dobbs reported to the Board of Trade that the 1758 assembly had been as "obstinate as mules," and he requested greater authority for "supporting his Majesty's prerogative." The board rebuked the assembly for its "unfortunate and ill-timed disputes," but to no avail. The controversy over "money matters" continued until North Carolina became an independent state. The reaction of the people to their experiences was reflected in the Constitution of 1776, which provided that the people were "not to be taxed . . . without the consent of . . . their Representatives in General Assembly," and also that the governor should "have power to draw for and apply such sums as shall be voted by the General Assembly, for public purposes, and be accountable to them for the same."

The Judiciary

The royal governors, as agents of the crown, were authorized to erect courts and to appoint judges. Before 1700 the governor and his council constituted the highest court in the province, and there was little controversy about the judiciary, but when a Supreme Court was created about 1700 controversy developed. The assembly recognized the right of the crown to appoint the chief justice, but denied its power to select the associate justices. Within a short time controversies developed over the appointment and tenure of judges of the various courts and also over the creation and jurisdiction of particular courts. Some special courts were created by the governor, such as the Exchequer Court (in Johnston's administration), for the trial of cases arising from the crown's revenues, which were to a large extent obtained from lands. The Chancery Court, also a "prerogative court," was the creation of the crown, not of the legislature of the colony. This court, which was in a general way a court of equity, not of law, was established in the early years of proprietary rule. As early as 1696 an Admiralty Court for North Carolina was created by the crown, with all of its officials—judge, register, marshal, and advocate—appointed by and responsible to the Board of Admiralty in England. This court, usually called the Vice-Admiralty Court, never had juries. It was designed to administer law "maritime and civil" and played a dual role in North Carolina ports. It was, in one capacity, the arbitrator of all conflicts involving ocean commerce. It was also the agency that heard and determined cases involving infringements of the British Navigation Acts.

Although these special courts were created by the governor or by the crown itself, the assembly won its fights to establish regular courts, and the judicial structure in the province was grounded on laws enacted by the legislature. The governor, following royal instructions, insisted that the Supreme Court have "original jurisdiction" in many matters, and that it exercise the combined powers of the English courts of King's Bench, Common Pleas, and Exchequer. The assembly opposed such a vast exercise of power, and on numerous occasions, especially in 1746, attempted to extend the jurisdiction of the county courts. But the council, upholding the governor, killed this proposal, insisting that such extension of power was contrary to the rights of the crown.

The chief justice and the associate justices of the Supreme Court sat as a prerogative Court of Oyer and Terminer and Gaol Delivery. In 1762 the council, sitting as the upper house of the legislature, claimed that the king had the right to appoint all courts of oyer and terminer, a view which was opposed by the assembly. The result was that no legislation ensued and the matter was left in the hands of the governor.

Controversy over the Tenure of Judges

The tenure of judges was a bone of contention throughout the period. The governor insisted that judges, appointed by him, should hold office for life. The legislature of 1759–61 enacted a law providing that judges should hold office during good behavior, claiming that the legislature should enjoy the same powers as Parliament in this respect. This law was promptly disallowed by the Privy Council as an encroachment on the royal prerogative. And in 1761 instructions were sent to all colonial governors authorizing them to veto any laws that regulated the tenure of judges. But the legislature consistently refused to vote judges' salaries unless their tenure was "during good behavior." To sum up the situation, the judiciary system of colonial North Carolina—appointment of judges, creation of courts, and jurisdiction of the courts—was largely in the hands of the governor. Through control of the purse the assembly was able to exercise a certain measure of control.

The Quorum Controversy

There were almost constant quarrels between governors and assemblies over what constituted a quorum in the assembly, and here again there was a conflict between royal instructions to governors and the "charter rights" of the people. The charter had provided that laws should be passed "by and with the advice, assent and approbation of the freemen . . . or the greater part of them, or their delegates and deputies," and the legislature of 1715 had passed a law providing that the "Quorum of the House of Burgesses shall not be less than one full half of the House." The crown objected to this law as "very extraordinary and liable to great inconvenience," and, following the example of the British House of Commons, instructed Governor Dobbs to consider fifteen members a quorum of the assembly. But on four successive occasions, 1760–1764, this body refused to legislate with less than a majority present, "denying His Majesty's right of constituting fifteen to be a quorum." The Privy Council denounced the assembly's action as "an indecent opposition to the authority of the Crown."

The quorum controversy continued to the end of royal rule. When Governor Martin ordered the 1773 assembly to organize and proceed to business, Speaker John Harvey replied that there was no quorum present. Martin told Harvey, "I am to inform you that by His Majesty's Royal Instructions to me fifteen members of the House of Assembly make a Quorum and I am ready to proceed upon the business with such a Quorum." Harvey replied, "I am to inform you that it is the opinion of the Members of Assembly now in Town that it is not consistent with the duty they owe their constituents to proceed to make a House unless there be a majority of the Representatives of the People to constitute the same." Whereupon Martin dissolved the assembly, declaring that the members "had deserted the business and Interests of their constituents, and flagrantly insulted the dignity and authority of Government." This was the last quorum fight. The State Constitution of 1776 settled the question by stating that a quorum in each house shall consist of a "majority of all the members." This has remained the requirement.

The Land Problem and Quitrent Controversy

The most stubborn and persistent controversies between governors and legislatures concerned quitrents and other matters relating to land tenure. These problems were closely associated with salaries for officials and with the whole problem of government.

Burrington, the first royal governor, inherited a chaotic quitrent situation. There was general confusion regarding land tenure. The terms of the Great Deed of Grant of 1668 had been "honored in the breach," and rents had been increased beyond the minimum figure provided for in this document. There was no accurate rent roll indicating the names of landholders and the acreage on which rents were due, despite the law of 1715 that had provided for the registration of all land titles. There was uncertainty and confusion concerning the medium of payment, whether it should be in specie, commodity money, or paper currency. Most confusing of all was the problem of "blank patents," which had been issued by proprietary governors, particularly the last one, Sir Richard Everard. Some 500,000 acres had been granted to persons who received patents signed by the proper officials, but with the date, exact location of the land, and the amount of purchase money left blank.

Rent Laws

Burrington assumed the governorship with instructions to increase rents from two shillings to four shillings per one hundred acres, and to have payments made only in proclamation money. He believed that the proposed increase in rents would retard settlement, for he knew that the people preferred to pay these rents in "country pay"; nevertheless he laid his instructions before the legislature and advised the passage of a rent law embodying these ideas. The assembly, led by Edward Moseley, who was both Speaker of the House and treasurer of the province, strongly opposed the proposals, but finally enacted a law that permitted payments in either proclamation money, or "rated commodities," as established by the law of 1715 and later statutes, or by paper currency. The law had no satisfactory provision for the registration of land titles, and thus the problem of "blank patents" was not solved. The governor angrily prorogued the assembly. Again in 1732 and 1733 he tried to obtain a rent law, but to no avail. He told the assembly that his instructions forbade the payment of quitrents and fees "in any other specie but in proclamation money." But the assembly insisted that it would be "impossible for them to make payments in proclamation money," and they would not "burthen them [the people] with such a proposal." Burrington's reply was that "if the King's Instructions are contrary to some Laws of this Province, the Government must act in Obedience to the King's Commands, therefore you must not be Surprized that whatever Your Law directs contrary to my Instructions is not taken Notice of [by] me." Moseley and other "popular" leaders wrote the Board of Trade complaining about Burrington's conduct and presenting their side of the question. The upshot was that Burrington resigned as governor in 1733, perhaps at the suggestion of the Board of Trade.

Problem of Collecting Rents

His successor, Gabriel Johnston, attacked the problem immediately and boasted of his "management" in handling this and other matters. In many respects, however, he was more arbitrary and less sympathetic with the people's views than Burrington had been. Johnston added the annoying requirements that rents be paid at "specified places" and "not on the land," as had been the custom hitherto; that property be "distrained" for nonpayment of rents; and that rents be paid in "gold and silver," or in bills of exchange approved by the council. He reorganized the system of collections by appointing a separate receiver for North Carolina—hitherto under the administration of officials located at Charleston—and two receivers for each precinct. This general system prevailed until 1754, when the sheriffs were assigned the task of collection at 10 percent commission for themselves and 5 percent for their deputies.

Johnston succeeded in getting a rent law through the legislature in 1738, but it was disallowed by the Privy Council, probably because it allowed payments in commodities. Johnston's determined efforts to get a rent law failed in 1741, but in 1748 he was successful, mainly because the legislators from the Albemarle counties, angry at the governor because of his alignment with the Neuse–Cape Fear region, had absented themselves from the legislative session. The new law provided for the registration of all land grants and required that payments be made either in proclamation money or in officially inspected tobacco at one pence per pound. Again the Privy Council disallowed the law.

The Granville District

The quitrent problem was made more acute by the creation of the Granville District, a grant made to Lord Carteret, Earl Granville, as compensation for his one-eighth share in "Carolina," which he had refused to sell the crown in 1729. The district included the upper half of present North Carolina and extended from the Virginia boundary to 35° 34', a strip sixty miles wide, including about two-thirds of the colony's population. The boundaries were established from the coast to Bath in 1744, west to the Haw River in 1746, and west to Cold Water Creek, a tributary of Rocky River, in 1766.

The existence of a "private proprietary grant" within a royal colony meant a loss to the government of badly needed revenue and also introduced a new element of discord into the already troubled political situation. The Granville District proved to be unsatisfactory to all parties concerned and in the colony as a whole. Granville failed to realize much revenue from his holdings, partly because of the conduct of his agents, notably Francis Corbin. These agents failed to prepare accurate rent rolls or to keep satisfactory accounts of monies collected. In many cases they were accused of exacting illegal fees and extortionate rents, acts which precipitated several mob actions. The agents insisted that the rents be paid in specie and "distrained" property for nonpayment.

Effects of Granville District on the Colony

With the colony as a whole suffering from loss of revenues as a result of the Granville District Governor Martin complained to England in 1773 that the Granville District had divided the colony, had "fatally embarrassed its policies," and was "not only profitless to the Proprietor, but a nuisance to this colony." The only solution seemed to be purchase by the crown, a proposal advanced by Tryon in 1767, repeated by Martin in 1771, and suggested by the legislature in 1773, when the assembly petitioned the crown to purchase the Granville District, "that the said Land may be held of him as other lands are held of his Majesty in his District in this Colony." The king did not act, the Revolution broke out within a short time, and the new state solved the problem by confiscating all of the ungranted lands in the Granville District.

The Paper Currency Controversy

The scarcity of specie in North Carolina constituted a major problem, and the efforts of the legislature to find a solution by authorizing "commodity money" and the emission of paper currency precipitated many clashes with the governor, who was instructed not to approve laws for the use of such "currency."

Commodity Money and Paper Currency

From the beginning specie had been extremely scarce. The settlers brought little specie with them; no gold, silver, or copper was mined, and the limited trade of the province brought in inadequate amounts of specie. Accordingly the chief form of exchange had been commodities, on a barter basis. The law of 1715 "rated" as money sixteen commodities—tobacco, corn, wheat, tallow, leather, beaver skins, wildcat skins, butter, cheese, buck and doe skins, feathers, pitch, whale oil, pork, and beef, and at a higher rate than the prevailing market price. A later law increased the number of these commodities to twenty-two. Beginning in 1748 the legislature limited commodity payments for taxes. After 1748 tobacco notes could be used to pay all provincial, county, and parochial taxes. This was also true of indigo notes after the end of 1755. But barter and commodity money failed to meet the currency needs, especially in times of emergency, such as that occasioned by the Indian wars and the Anglo-French wars of the late colonial era. In 1712 the crisis resulting from the Tuscarora War led the legislature to issue £4,000 in bills of credit. A poll tax was levied to provide a sinking fund for these bills, but collections were so poor that the Assembly of 1713 was forced to issue £8,000 more. This issue was to be redeemed by a tax on land as well as on polls. Again collections fell below expectations, and depreciation soon amounted to 40 percent or more. So in 1714–15, the legislature, over the protest of the proprietors, authorized the issuance of £24,000 to sink the bills of former emissions and to pay off outstanding indebtedness. To redeem this new emission of currency, a fifteen–shilling poll tax was levied, which was reduced to ten shillings in 1720, and to five shillings in 1722. Outstanding bills of credit were reduced to £16,000 in 1717 and to £12,000 in 1722.

Burrington, the first royal governor, had instructions against the emission of paper currency, and promptly notified the assembly of this fact. But the legislators were not perturbed and proceeded to authorize the emission of £40,000, one-fourth of which was to be applied to redeeming outstanding bills of credit, and £20,000 to be loaned to the precincts.

The assembly told Burrington that there was not enough specie in the province to meet the demands of the people and to pay rents and fees, and insisted that "all such payments be made in some valuable commoditys, or in the Bills now currant in this Province at proper Rates." It said that "for nearly twenty years the Officers' fees have been paid in Paper Currancy at the Rate mentioned in the Acts of Assembly." Because of this and other controversies, Burrington summoned and prorogued three successive legislatures without a single law being passed.

More Paper Currency and Increase in Poll Taxes

Soon after Gabriel Johnston became governor the legislature voted £14,150 3s. 2d. "for the service of the Public of this Province" and "laying a tax on the inhabitants" for its payment. No mention was made of the amount of the tax, but four years later a poll tax of five shillings per taxable was levied.

The demands of England upon North Carolina for men and money during the War of Jenkins' Ear (1739–44) and King George's War (1744–48) led to increased taxation and further demands for paper currency. In 1740 £12,000 was appropriated for troops and a poll tax of three shillings proclamation money was levied, but no paper currency was issued in spite of a demand for it. Spanish attacks on the coastal area in 1741, 1744, 1747, and 1748 led to further demands for money. In 1743 a poll tax of eight pence proclamation money was voted for providing proper magazines of ammunition in the several counties of this province." Two years later a tax of one shilling proclamation money was levied for an eight-year period for the purpose of making some "new current Bills of Credit." In 1748 £6,000 in bills of credit were voted to build two forts at Cape Fear and Ocracoke, to aid "in repelling the Spanish enemy," and a levy of one shilling proclamation money for retiring these and other bills.

A law was passed in 1749 "to fix a Place for the seat of Government, and for keeping Public Offices; for appointing Circuit Courts, and defraying the Expence thereof," and to finance this a poll tax of four pence proclamation money was placed on all taxables for a three-year period—continued for three more years by an act of 1753. In 1750 a poll tax of two pence for four years was levied to defray expenses of the circuit courts.

The outbreak of the French and Indian War in 1754 led to the emission of £40,000 in bills of credit for building forts, raising troops, and dispatching them to Virginia. A one-shilling poll tax was voted as a sinking fund for this emission. The next year a poll tax of two shillings per taxable for a five-year period was levied, and in 1756 the assembly granted £3,400 to "His Majesty" for erecting a fort and for raising two companies for the defense of North Carolina's western frontier, the amount to be raised by a tax on liquors and a poll tax of two shillings for the ensuing year. In 1757 a tax of four shillings six pence per poll was levied for military expenses and for paying the principal and interest on outstanding bills. This law remained effective until 1760, when another poll tax of two shillings was authorized for retiring bills of credit. In 1758 and 1759 a poll tax of four shillings six pence and a liquor tax were levied to pay troops and for garrisoning coastal forts. At the same time a special poll tax of one shilling eight pence was levied for a four-year period to pay the salaries of the chief justice and the attorney general, "and other contingent charges of government." There was also a 1759 poll tax of one shilling and eight pence to be collected annually in 1761, 1762, and 1763, for replacing the £5,500 which had been used to pay the colonial militia. There was a 1760 poll tax of one shilling, to continue until all outstanding bills of credit should be paid. The next year this tax was increased to two shillings and continued for five years.

A law of 1761, granting the crown £20,000 in proclamation money for the upkeep of the military forces, was to take effect in 1764, when a poll tax of two shillings was to be collected until the entire sum should be paid. Also voted in 1764, to continue for two years, was a poll tax of one shilling and six pence, for paying the salary of the chief justice and the attorney general. In 1771 a two-shilling poll tax was levied.

Other Controversies

Besides their frequent clashes over money matters, there were many other controversies between governors and legislatures. Some were merely trivial, personal, and petty quarrels, but some concerned fundamental principles of self-government—government by royal prerogative or by constitution; that is, by provisions express or implied in the Carolina charter and laws passed in pursuance thereof. The assembly's statement in 1773 expressed the situation clearly: "It is the blessed distinction of the British Code of Laws that our Laws are regulated by the Constitution. . . . The rules of right and wrong, the limits of the prerogatives of the Crown and the privileges of the people, are . . . well known and ascertained: to exceed either of them is highly unjustifiable."

This was a most significant statement and had far-reaching implications. It indicated that the constitution and laws were binding on both king and people; that the king, when acting within the constitution, was entitled to obedience; that the king owed to the people the protection of their rights; and that violations of these rights by the king justified resistance by his subjects. Here was clearly enunciated the basic principles of the American Revolution—principles succinctly and clearly stated in the Declaration of Independence and the first state constitutions. The preamble of the North Carolina Constitution of 1776 declared, "Allegiance and Protection are in their Nature reciprocal, and the one should of Right be refused when the other is withdrawn. And whereas George the Third . . . by an Act of the British Legislature declared the inhabitants of these States out of the Protection of the British Crown . . . all government under the said King . . . hath ceased, . . . And . . . the Thirteen United Colonies are of Right, wholly absolved from all Allegiance to the British Crown."

The North Carolina-South Carolina Boundary Dispute

A different type of controversy, but a cause of unrest, confusion, disorder, and even bloodshed, was the boundary dispute between North Carolina and South Carolina.

Edward Hyde was commissioned, May 9, 1712, as governor of "ye province of Carolina that lyes N⁰ & Eᵗ of Cape ffeare Called N⁰ Carolina." The word "river" did not appear in this commission, and North Carolina officials maintained that Cape Fear—or a line drawn due west from that cape—should be the boundary. The South Carolina authorities contended that the Cape Fear River was the proper dividing line and proceeded to grant lands along the southern banks of the river. As early as 1713 South Carolina officials complained that illegal grants were being made south of the Cape Fear River and asked the proprietors to have the boundary settled, but nothing was done. In

1720 the South Carolina legislature complained to the British Board of Trade "how much this province suffers by the Inhabitants and slaves running away there where they are succored," and in 1727 certain South Carolina merchants complained to London of "a desertion of debtors" to the Cape Fear "where they think their Credit[rs] can't reach them," and they declared that it was imperative that a definite boundary be fixed.

Both George Burrington and Governor Robert Johnson of South Carolina met with the Board of Trade in London in 1730 and reached an agreement that the line should be run thirty miles southwest of the Cape Fear River and "to be run at that parallel distance the whole course of the said river." But no sooner had Burrington reached North Carolina than he begin to insist that such a survey would be too expensive—that it would cost at least £3,000, and that the Pee Dee River was a "natural and proper division." The Board of Trade, in 1732, took exception to this view and insisted that the original agreement be observed. Burrington refused to budge and when he resigned and Gabriel Johnston succeeded him as governor, in April, 1733, nothing had been done to establish the boundary.

The 1735 Survey

Governor Johnston acted promptly on the dispute, and in 1735 both he and Governor Johnson of South Carolina appointed commissioners to make a survey. These commissioners met in March, 1735, at Lilliput, the home of North Carolina Commissioner Eleazer Allen, on the Cape Fear. After a six weeks' conference they reached an agreement, probably the result of Johnston's personal intervention, that the line should begin "at the Sea, thirty miles from the West side of the mouth of the Cape Fear River, to run on a northwest course to the thirty-fifth parallel of north latitude, and from thence due west to the South Seas," provided that at no point should the line "approach nearer to Cape Fear River than thirty miles," and if the said westward line should include any part of the Cherokee or Catawba lands, these should be "set off" so as to leave them in South Carolina. At intervals between May and November the commissioners ran the line "thro' Desert and uninhabited Woods in many places absolutely impassible" without first cutting a passage— thirty miles west and southwest of the Cape Fear River and then northwestward for about seventy miles, to the Little Pee Dee River.

Later Surveys

The survey was resumed in September, 1737, at a point two miles northwest of one of the branches of Little Pee Dee, and the line was extended in the same northwestward direction for a distance of twenty-two miles to a stake in a meadow "erroneously supposed to be the point of intersection with the 35th parallel of north latitude." No further official surveys were made until 1764, though Johnston "did . . . press the Settling and adjusting of that Boundary Line," and the boundary dispute was subordinated to the more important question of defense during the wars that raged intermittently from 1739 to 1763.

Confusion and Disorder in the Disputed Region

Meanwhile settlers began to move into the area west of the Little Pee Dee, especially into the Waxhaws region, leading to the creation of Anson County in 1750. Confusion and disorder reigned throughout the region. As early as 1753 some of the residents "in the Waxhaws" complained to the North Carolina council that "the property of several persons within this province" had been granted to intruders from South Carolina by officials of that province, "to the great Disturbance of their Peace and Quiet." The council advised Governor Dobbs to take action to prevent further South Carolina land grants in the "debatable land." But the practice continued, and in 1755 Dobbs complained that Governor James Glen had "spirited up some settlers" on Dobbs's own lands "to take out Warrants of survey from him, and he would support them." The next year it was charged that Glen was "daily granting warrants of survey" for lands that had been granted to Henry McCulloh by Governor Dobbs. The result of this situation was ill feeling, confusion, disorder, loss of revenue to both colonies, and riots to such an extent that the whole area became "a kind of Sanctuary allowed to Criminals and Vagabonds, by their pretending it serves their purpose that they belonged to either Province." Dobbs reported to the Board of Trade in 1759 that there was such confusion that "the bordering Counties can't be settled."

The land problem in the disputed area was most acute, but there were many other difficulties. Both colonies were eager to win Indian friendship, and in 1754 Governor Glen urged King Haiglar of the Catawbas to drive off all white men who came on their lands. They probably followed this advice, because North Carolina settlers complained that the Catawbas were killing their stock and destroying their crops. Dobbs maintained that Glen had "buoyed up" these Indians by granting them nine times as much land (2,500 acres per person) as had been granted the Tuscaroras by North Carolina (227 acres each).

"Outrages" in Anson County

The South Carolina governor commissioned justices of the peace in the disputed area, imposed fines on residents who would not obey his summons to attend militia musters, and, according to Dobbs, encouraged the settlers not to pay taxes or quitrents to North Carolina authorities. The sheriff of Anson County, while collecting taxes, was seized and jailed, and Governor

Dobbs admitted that he was powerless to prevent such "outrages." Glen, in turn, blamed North Carolina officials for the disorderly situation and complained to Dobbs about several "outrages" against South Carolina inhabitants by North Carolinians, "which having been committed under the colour of authority by persons pretending to be officers of our Government, the offense was the more intolerable."

Dobbs replied that the local officials in North Carolina had "only repelled an invasive force" who were surveying land, collecting rents and taxes, and imposing fines within North Carolina territory. He further declared that if the situation did not improve he would be "obliged to use force, & consequently throw both provinces into a flame."

Effects of Dispute on Trade

The bitter dispute had its effects on government and on commercial relations between the two colonies. There had been considerable trade along the Catawba, Yadkin, and other rivers leading from North Carolina to South Carolina—trade that culminated at Charleston. But the friction between the two colonies had led the South Carolina legislature to place heavy duties on goods brought in from North Carolina. The latter retaliated in 1751 by a heavy duty on spirituous liquors imported into Anson County from South Carolina and a law against South Carolina cattle ranging in North Carolina. It is noteworthy that the act of 1762 incorporating Campbellton, at the head of navigation on the Cape Fear River, expressed the hope that "the trade of the counties of Anson and Rowan which at present centers in Charlestown, South Carolina, to the great prejudice of this Province, will be drawn to the said town."

Surveys of 1764 and 1772

Following the termination of the Great War for Empire in 1763, the Board of Trade instructed the governors of the two colonies to appoint commissioners to extend the line of 1737 "so far north as the thirty-fifth parallel, thence due westward to the eastern limits of the Catawba lands." In 1764 the boundary line was run from the terminus of the 1737 line to the old Salisbury-Charlotte road, a distance of about sixty-two miles. An error in astronomical observations led to running the line at 34° 49', or eleven miles south of the 35th parallel.

Tryon was eager to get the remainder of the line surveyed and to obtain a "proper final Boundary." For several years negotiations took place between the two colonies, and finally in 1772, after Josiah Martin became governor, the line was extended from the termination of the survey of 1764, along the Salisbury Road, around the Catawba Lands to the forks of the Catawba River, thence due westward (supposedly) to the Cherokee Mountains—a total of about sixty-five miles.

A glance at the map reveals that the line did not follow the 35th parallel, but that east of the Catawba River it runs south, and west of the river it runs north of that parallel. This curious notch in the border was due to new instructions from the Board of Trade, which ignored the 1735 agreement, and not to drunken surveyors or the desire of a patriotic lady to have her apple orchard in South Carolina! By this survey South Carolina gained the region between the 35th parallel and the line from the forks of the Catawba to the Cherokee boundary, and extending from the Catawba River and Catawba Indian lands to the Cherokee line—a region South Carolinians termed the "New Acquisition."

North Carolina Opposition to the "Compromise Line"

North Carolinians disliked the "compromise of 1772," and the legislature refused to vote any money for the expenses of the survey, giving as an excuse the £60,000 debt resulting from the War of the Regulation.

The boundary question was one of the first problems to confront the independent states of North Carolina and South Carolina. The latter accepted the 1772 survey as final, but the Bill of Rights of the North Carolina Constitution of 1776 declared: "In order to avoid future disputes that the limits of the State should be ascertained with precision; and as the former temporary line between North and South Carolina was confirmed and extended . . . that line, and that only, should be esteemed the southern boundary of this State, that is to say, beginning at the sea at a cedar stake, at or near the mouth of Little River (being the southern extremity of Brunswick County) and running from thence a northwest course through the boundary house, which stands in thirty three degrees fifty six minutes to thirty five degrees north latitude, and from thence a west course so far as is mentioned in the Charter of King Charles II to the late proprietors of Carolina."

North Carolina's Role in Anglo-French Wars

The struggle between Britain and France for control of North America, which began in 1689 and reached its grand climax in the Great War for Empire (1754–63), had a vital bearing on North Carolina history and accentuated the importance of the controversies described above. War emergencies, the need for men, money, and supplies from the colonies and more intercolonial cooperation forced England to grant many concessions as the price of cooperation. There was a degree of laxity in the enforcement of the Navigation Acts and other trade laws and, on the other hand, and as a natural result, a growing feeling of "separatism" within the colonies, though there was no evidence of any movement for independence.

The year 1689, a turning point in diplomatic history, inaugurated a series of six wars between England and France during the next century and a quarter. The first of these conflicts, known in America as King William's War (1689–97), was precipitated by European causes, led to little fighting in America and none in North Carolina, and effected no transfer of territory by the Treaty of Ryswick.

French and Spanish Attacks on the North Carolina Coast

The second Anglo-French conflict, Queen Anne's War (1702–13), though caused primarily by European issues, was of vital concern to North Carolina. Though most of the American fighting was in the Canada–New England–New York sector, French and Spanish "frequently landed and plundered" the North Carolina coast, and, according to Governor Burrington, put the colony to "great expense in establishing a force to repel them." Two of the Lords Proprietors asserted that "in 1707 when Carolina was attacked by the French it cost the Province Twenty Thousand Pounds and that neither his Majesty nor any of his predecessors had been at any charge from the first grant to defend the said Province against the French or other enemies." Edward Randolph, British Surveyor General of the Customs, had earlier reported that the colony "lies open and exposed to every invasion, being an easy prey to their merciless and insulting Enemys the French and Spaniards." The situation was made more acute by the impoverished condition of the colony resulting from the Cary Rebellion, followed soon thereafter by the disastrous Tuscarora War. In 1715 North Carolina went to considerable expense to help South Carolina defeat the Yemassees, whom the Spaniards in Florida supposedly were arming to rise against that colony. There were a few minor attacks on the North Carolina coast during Queen Anne's War and, though these were not devastating, they revealed the colony's defenseless condition.

North Carolina Troops in the War of Jenkins' Ear

The third Anglo-French war, which began as an Anglo-Spanish War known as the War of Jenkins' Ear (1739–44) and later merged into an Anglo-French War called King George's War (1744–48), saw North Carolina troops in action for the first time as part of the British army. The king asked the colony for troops, and the assembly replied that "no Colony hath with more chearfullness contributed than we shall to forward the intended descent upon some of the Spanish Colonies." Accordingly it authorized the raising of four companies of a hundred men each, and appropriated £1,200. North Carolina troops, led by Captain James Innes, reached Jamaica in November, 1740, and later took part in the ill-fated expedition against Cartagena. Of the one hundred men in the Cape Fear Company, only twenty-five returned. The fate of the other three hundred men from North Carolina is unknown.

Spanish Attacks on the North Carolina Coast

The most serious problem confronting North Carolina at this time was the constant threat of Spanish attacks on shipping and on towns along the coast. In 1741 no fewer than a dozen North Carolina vessels were seized by Spanish privateers. These seizures continued until after the close of the war in 1748 and almost paralyzed the colony's ocean-going commerce, especially that between the Brunswick-Wilmington area and Charleston. The *South Carolina Gazette* reported that during the years 1735–39 eighty ships had cleared between Charleston and North Carolina, while during the five years ending in 1748, only twenty-one cleared. In June, 1747, it was reported "that there are now no less than 9 Spanish Privateers cruizing on this coast," and perhaps a score of vessels trading with North Carolina were taken as prizes in that one year. In July, 1748, three ships were "cut out of Ocracoke Inlet" by Spanish privateers.

All parties concerned tried to stop these attacks. The governor, sanctioned by the king, issued letters of marque and reprisal to privateers, and a few were fitted out at Wilmington, but they proved ineffective. The assembly authorized the construction of forts at Ocracoke, Bear Inlet, Core Sound, and Cape Fear, and appropriated funds for their construction. But these forts, if they were ever built, were of no value. The assembly, in desperation, hired Commodore George Walker to defend the coast against the Spanish ships and later voted him £10,000 for his work. The British navy sent some patrol ships to the coast, but open charges were made by North Carolina shippers that "the Spaniards were so encouraged by the Indolence, if not the c[owardi]ce of the English commander that they ravaged the coast with impunity."

Spanish Attacks on Beaufort and Brunswick

The truth of this charge and the inability of the colony to protect itself were demonstrated in 1747, when the Spaniards attacked and plundered Beaufort. It was shown more dramatically on September 3, 1748, when a Spanish force landed, attacked, and captured Brunswick, and "plundered and destroyed everything without fear of being disturbed." But the inhabitants rallied, returned to the town, and recaptured it.

The "Great War for Empire," 1754–1763

The Treaty of Aix-la-Chapelle (1748) settled nothing as far as America was concerned, since England and France agreed to a *status quo ante-bellum.* The return of peace to Europe did not settle nationalistic and economic rivalries in America. Indeed the situation was further complicated by increasing colonial interests in the Ohio Valley, already claimed and partly settled by the French. Both nations had come to realize that this valley was the key to the control of the continent. It was the "gateway to the West," and the shortest link between New France and Louisiana, not to mention its vast acreage of fertile lands and its potential wealth in furs. The English formed a number of speculating companies, the most conspicuous of which was the Ohio Company of Virginia (1749), with a grant of 500,000 acres in the Ohio Valley. Soon the agents of this company were pushing into the disputed region. In answer to these challenges, the French speeded their construction of forts at strategic points—usually at river junctions.

Diplomatic Background of the War

The diplomatic maneuvering between France and England reached a climax in the summer of 1753, when the British Secretary of State for the Southern Department sent a letter to various colonial governors, including Dobbs of North Carolina, advising the governors "not to take the offensive, but if the enemy invades the undoubted limits of British territory, you must repel force by force." Shortly thereafter, young George Washington, acting on orders of Governor Robert Dinwiddie of Virginia, who was also a promoter of the Ohio company, warned the French commander in the region to evacuate English territory. The French officer's reply was short and to the point: "We are here, and by God, we expect to stay here." Both sides now realized that the problem could not be solved by diplomacy or compromise, nor concluded until one party had been driven completely from the continent.

In preparation for what was hoped to be the final struggle, Great Britain understood the necessity of strengthening the alliance with the Iroquois Confederacy and of securing the full cooperation of all the colonies. Long allied with the English, the Iroquois were restive because of their sufferings in the three previous wars and the fact that the English had done very little to help them. The colonies were also a doubtful factor, for they felt, among other things, that all their efforts of men and money in the previous war had been wasted and that England was sacrificing colonial interests to the Anglo-French conflict.

To remedy this situation, the Board of Trade in September, 1753, asked the governors of seven colonies—North Carolina was not included—to send delegates to Albany, New York, to obtain a more effective alliance with the Iroquois or, failing that, to gain a promise of neutrality. The Albany Congress, which convened in June, 1754, failed to obtain either of these cherished objectives, but when the war broke out, the Iroquois gave the English much valuable assistance.

The Albany Plan of Union and North Carolina's Reaction

This congress is best known because of a plan of union, presented by Benjamin Franklin, which provided for a centralized form of government for all the colonies, supervised by a president general to be appointed by the crown, and having a legislature, or grand council, to consist of delegates chosen by each colonial legislature on the basis of wealth and population of the colony. Although this plan had many good features, it was not approved by the colonial assemblies or by England. Governor Dobbs laid the plan before the legislature in December, 1754, saying that the king had advised him "to promote a happy union among the provinces for their General Union and Defence." The assembly ordered the plan to be distributed among its members "for their Mature Consideration," but it was never brought up for a vote.

Just as the Albany Congress was adjourning the French and Indian War began as George Washington, heading a small detachment of Virginia militia, defeated a small body of French troops at Great Meadows. Washington's defeat at Fort Necessity shortly thereafter marked the beginning of a series of British reverses, which included the defeat and death of General Edward Braddock of the regular British army in the campaign against Fort Duquesne, July 9, 1755, and the French conquest of Lake Champlain and the eastern Great Lakes sector.

England Defeats France

In 1756 the Seven Years' War began in Europe. The broadening of the conflict, together with British defeats in America, brought William Pitt to leadership in the British ministry in 1757, and he quickly brought order out of chaos. He unified the military command in America and replaced old and incompetent commanders with younger and abler men, such as Wolfe, Amherst, and Boscawen. He also put more reliance upon proved colonial leaders like George Washington and William Shirley. He tried to prevent illicit trade with the enemy, both by appeals to patriotism and by parliamentary legislation. In addition, he promised English financial assistance to the colonial war chest, and substituted an offensive strategy for the defensive one which had been followed during the "years of defeat." Moreover, his alliance with Frederick the Great of Prussia helped weaken France's military complement in America by keeping large French forces tied down in Europe, enabling Pitt to boast later, "America was conquered in Germany."

With these changes, the tide of war began to turn. One by one, French possessions fell into English hands. The most memorable battle, Wolfe's decisive defeat of Montcalm at Quebec in 1759, was followed by the capitulation of Montreal in 1760, thus ending the major fighting on the American mainland.

North Carolina's Role in the French and Indian War

North Carolina, like other colonies, was totally unprepared for war. In spite of the fact that war had been imminent for years, no adequate preparations had been made. Governor Dobbs reported to George II in 1754 that the militia was almost completely unorganized and untrained. "Not half [were] armed, and what arms they had were very bad; there is not one pound of [public] gunpowder or shot in store in the Province, nor any arms—nor twelve barrels of gunpowder in . . . Traders hands." He appealed to the king for assistance because "at present we have no credit and must pay double price if any is imported by Merchants." The king responded to his request by sending one thousand stand of arms, much of which was lost the next year after Braddock's defeat in Pennsylvania, when North Carolina troops "deserted in great numbers," taking their arms with them.

North Carolina's Contribution of Men and Money

Early in the war Governor Dinwiddie of Virginia wrote Acting Governor Matthew Rowan for aid. Rowan laid this matter before the assembly, which voted £12,000 "for raising and providing a regiment of 750 effective men to be sent to the Assistance of Virginia," with the understanding that that colony would support them after their arrival. When Rowan learned that Virginia had refused to do this, he concluded that the money appropriated was insufficient to support 750 men; so he reduced the number to 450. Colonel James Innes was placed in charge of these troops and marched them to Winchester, Virginia. When they arrived they had no money or supplies and were disbanded and sent home. But Innes proceeded to Wills Creek, Maryland, where he built Fort Cumberland and took charge of all colonial troops there.

In December, 1754, the assembly voted £8,000, fifty men for North Carolina defense and a hundred men, exclusive of officers, to join Braddock in his expedition against Fort Duquesne. Edward Brice Dobbs, son of the governor, was placed in command of these troops. This North Carolina company missed action at the battle of Fort Duquesne because it was on a scouting expedition at the time. After the battle Dobbs joined Innes at Fort Cumberland.

When Governor Dobbs received news of Braddock's crushing defeat, he convened the legislature and asked that a proper sum be "cheerfully granted at once." Whereupon the assembly authorized £10,000 and three new companies of a hundred men each "to protect the Frontier of this Province and to assist the other Colonies." These companies were sent to New York and participated in the British defeat at Oswego and the unsuccessful efforts to take Fort Niagara and Crown Point from the French.

The Problem of Home Defense

The problem of home defense had now become very acute, and Lord Loudoun, commander of all British forces in North America, notified the governors of all the southern colonies to prepare to defend their own borders. On March 15, 1757, at a conference in Philadelphia attended by Loudoun, Dobbs, and the governors of the colonies from Pennsylvania southward, the delegates decided to send 5,000 men for defense of the southern frontier—1,200 British regulars and 3,800 colonial militia. North Carolina's quota was only 400. At this time the assembly voted £5,300 and 200 men—not 400 as had been requested—"to be imployed for the service of South Carolina or at home in case not demanded or wanted there." These troops were to serve in the army of British Colonel Henry Bouquet.

Hugh Waddell and North Carolina Troops at Fort Duquesne

In December, 1757, Pitt called on all the colonies for "as large a Body of Men . . . as the Number of Inhabitants may allow" for an expedition to reduce Fort Duquesne. The assembly voted £7,000 and three hundred men, to be sent to General John Forbes, in charge of the Duquesne expedition. Major Hugh Waddell, in command of the three North Carolina companies, raised, organized, and marched these men to the Pennsylvania front, where they acquitted themselves well. Governor Dobbs wrote that Waddell "had great honour done him being employed in all reconnoitering parties; and dressed and acted as an Indian; and his Sergeant John Rogers took the only Indian prisoner who gave Mr. Forbes certain intelligence of the Forces in Fort Duquesne upon which they resolved to proceed." The Indian had said that if the British forces pressed on, the French would evacuate the fort. This advice was followed, and the strategic post fell into British hands without a shot being fired; it was immediately renamed Fort Pitt, in honor of the "great war minister."

North Carolina's Indian Problem

After their defeat at Fort Duquesne the French concentrated their intrigues upon the southern Indians, notably the Cherokees and Creeks, whom the English now began to call "French Indians." As early as 1754 the assembly had provided for a company of rangers, commanded by Hugh Waddell, to protect the western frontier. The next year the legislature ordered a fort to be built, and this work was entrusted to Waddell, who constructed the fort near present Statesville and named it Fort Dobbs. By this time the assembly had voted approximately £66,000 for military purposes, more than £38,000 of which had been used outside the province.

In the spring of 1759 reports were widely circulated about "many horrid murders" perpetrated by the Indians along the Catawba and Yadkin rivers. On the night of February 23, 1760, the Cherokees surrounded Fort Dobbs, but were decisively beaten off by Waddell and his forces. About this time the governor of South Carolina called on North Carolina and Georgia for aid against the Indians and Waddell was ordered to lead the troops under his command, with five hundred men to be raised from Anson, Rowan and Orange counties to assist South Carolina.

Final Victory over the Indians

Meanwhile Colonel Archibald Montgomerie, with an army of sixteen hundred Highlanders and several hundred colonial militiamen were defeated by the Cherokees, June 27, 1760, at Echoee, near the present town of Franklin. As a result, Indian depredations and white reprisals increased. The assembly was much concerned, and in March, 1761, voted money to raise, clothe, and pay five hundred men to be used as the governor or British commander deemed best.

The British officers and leaders in Virginia, North Carolina, and South Carolina now planned a campaign in which troops from the three colonies, assisted by Colonel James Grant and his regiment of Highlanders—some 2,600 men altogether—would march into Indian country and end the depredations. Within two miles of the spot where Montgomerie had been defeated a year earlier Grant and his forces decisively defeated the Indians, June 10, 1761, "drove them into recesses in the mountains, burned their granaries, laid waste their fields, and pushed the frontier seventy miles farther west." The Cherokees signed a treaty that ended the war and threw open to white settlement a very extensive area.

The Augusta Conference of 1763 and Its Results

Peace was made with the Catawbas at the Augusta Conference, November 5–10, 1763, when the governors of Virginia, North Carolina, and South Carolina, along with John Stuart, British Indian Superintendent for the Southern Colonies, met with twenty-five Indian chiefs and seven hundred warriors, and after six days of oratory, eating, drinking and distributing presents costing £5,000 sent by George III, a "Treaty of Perfect and Perpetual Peace and Friendship" was made, in which the Catawbas acknowledged the king as the "Great White Father"—and in which they surrendered all of their lands, except a reservation of about fifteen square miles!

British Supremacy in the New World

As a result of the Great War for Empire and North Carolina's own war with the Indians, the French and Spaniards were expelled from the southern frontier as an effective threat; the Cherokees were removed (for the time being) as an obstacle to westward expansion; the Catawbas had been assigned a reservation in South Carolina; and there was assurance that the region south and west of the Ohio and east of the Mississippi was to be British territory. Significant for the future was the fact that North Carolina had had some experience in intercolonial cooperation, which went far toward breaking down prejudices through the realization of common interests and common destiny. The French were now removed as a threat to British supremacy, and there was an increase in the colonies of a spirit of independence, though no move for separation as yet. In some respects the war that was concluded by the Treaty of Paris in 1763 made possible the revolt of 1775. And the French defeat, provoking as it did a desire for revenge against England, was later to help America win its independence.

Chapter 11

SECTIONAL CONTROVERSIES

Sectionalism, which has been defined as "unusual devotion to a particular section of the state or country rather than to the whole," was a natural development in North Carolina, composed as it was of sections differing in climate, soil, and geography. Sectionalism became manifest on a small scale soon after settlement expanded south of the Albemarle region into the valleys of the Neuse and Pamlico. It increased with the movement of population into the Lower Cape Fear after 1726 and into the Upper Cape Fear after 1739. It reached its highest peak and most bitter form with the settlement of the Piedmont after 1750. Sectional controversies were the natural product of forces described in earlier chapters: geographical differences, various religious sects, and differing types of social life grounded on differences in economy. In addition there were political factors which became increasingly potent causes of sectional rivalry and strife. Related to these factors were personal ambitions, family jealousies, and local rivalries, especially among those towns that were eager to be come ports of entry, court towns, or the site of the permanent capital.

All these causes were interrelated. Geographical factors contributed to economic differences in agriculture, industry, and trade in the various regions. Economic differences created social distinctions. Racial and social factors were involved in religious rivalries. And all of these factors contributed to political controversies.

The Representation Controversy—Sound versus Cape Fear

The first important sectional controversy was that which developed between the Albemarle counties and the Lower Cape Fear. As stated earlier, the first of these areas had been settled largely by an overflow of colonists from Virginia; the second, by an overflow from the Charleston region. The most obvious cause of their conflict was political and centered around the question of representation in the legislature. But economic forces had a distinct bearing on the dispute. The Albemarle Sound region depended on Virginia ports for much of its trade, while land rents in this area, held under terms of the 1668 Great Deed of Grant, were only about half those charged in the Neuse-Pamlico and Cape Fear sections. The Lower Cape Fear had direct trade connections with the outside world and little commercial intercourse with Albemarle.

Overrepresentation of the "Northern Counties"

The Sound region had a virtual monopoly of the government at all levels. The governor and most of the council lived there and showed more interest in the development of that area than in the rest of the province. The "Northern Counties" of Chowan, Pasquotank, Perquimans, Currituck, and Tyrrell had five delegates each in the assembly and Bertie three, while the Cape Fear counties had only two each. Every session of the assembly before 1736 was held in the Albemarle region, usually at Edenton, the "unofficial capital," and every Speaker of the House prior to 1740 was an Albemarle resident.

After 1730, as the Neuse-Pamlico region grew more rapidly and its trade began to outstrip that of the Albemarle, a few complaints were made against political and commerical discriminations by the Northern Counties, which in 1735 had thirty-one members to twenty-three for the other counties.

Governor Gabriel Johnston's "Management"

As has been pointed out earlier, Governor Gabriel Johnston, taking office in 1734, had a prolonged quarrel with the assembly over quitrents, the preparation of an accurate rent roll, and the location of a permanent capital. A compromise measure was passed in 1739, but this law was disallowed by the British Privy Council the next year. Johnston, whose major interest—and personal landholdings—lay in the Cape Fear region, used "management" to align the Neuse and Pamlico representatives against Albemarle by calling the assembly to meet in Wilmington in the winter of 1741, hoping, as he said, "to keep at home the northern members" so that he could get his cherished rent law and an act for the location of the capital which he desired passed. The Albemarle delegates surprised him by attending and blocking the passage of his proposed legislation. The next three sessions of the legislature met in New Bern in 1744, 1745, and 1746, and in June of 1746 a bill was introduced fixing the capital at New Bern. The bill was defeated by the vote of the Albemarle delegates. Finally, at Wilmington in November of that year, with only fourteen of fifty-four elected delegates in attendance and with all of the Albemarle representatives absent, the assembly, led by Speaker Samuel Swann of Onslow County, passed a law fixing the seat of government at New Bern and reducing the representation of the Albemarle counties to two each.

The Northern Counties Denounce the "Rump Assembly"

The Albemarle counties protested to Governor Johnston and to the authorities in England against the "trickery, fraud, and illegality" of these acts of the "rump assembly," and in the elections of February, 1747, these counties elected the customary five delegates each. But the assembly refused to seat them, declared the election null and void, and asked that a new election be held. Whereupon the Albemarle counties appealed to the king, asking for a decision on the right of the assembly to determine county representation, the number necessary for a quorum, and the validity of the laws passed by the previous session. Governor Johnston also appealed to England, stating the case for himself and for the "Southern Counties."

North Carolina's "Long Parliament"

For some unexplained reason the king and Privy Council delayed their decision on this controversial matter for seven years. During this time Johnston called no new elections and the "Long Parliament" held no fewer than thirteen sessions, eleven of them at New Bern, one at Bath, and one at Wilmington. The Albemarle people were on the verge of revolt and conditions were approaching anarchy. Many citizens refused to pay quitrents or taxes, to obey the laws of the 1746 legislature, to serve on juries, or even to use the paper currency which had been authorized by the assembly. According to Johnston, "Tho' they do not appear in Arms, they are really in a State of Civil Rebellion." He declared that if the problems were not soon solved, "I don't see how we can long keep up the face of Government."

Disorder and Confusion in Albemarle

Writing about conditions in the Albemarle region, September 12, 1752, Bishop August Gottlieb Spangenberg, noted Moravian leader, who was in Edenton at the time, said: "If I am to say how I find things in North Carolina I must admit that there is much confusion. There is discord between the Counties, which has greatly weakened the authority of the Legislature, and interferes with the administration of justice. . . . So in some respects anarchy reigns in these older Counties; there are many cases of murder, theft, and the like, but no one is punished. The men will not serve as jurors, so when Court is held for the trial of criminal cases no one is there. If a man is imprisoned the jail is broken open; in short 'fist law' is about all that is left. But the County Courts are held regularly, and matters within their jurisdiction are attended to as usual. Land matters in North Carolina are also in unbelievable confusion. . . . A man settles on a piece of land and does a good deal of work on it (from the Carolina standpoint), then another comes and drives him out,—and who is to definitely settle the matter?"

Finally in April, 1754, the Privy Council disallowed the two 1746 laws that had been responsible for this critical situation. The new governor, Arthur Dobbs, brought with him instructions upholding the Albemarle view on representation, declaring that this was a matter for the crown and not for legislative decision. Therefore the 1746 law, which had ruled against the Albemarle contention on the quorum question, was illegal, but the session which had passed the law was legal, since "the Crown had the right to determine a quorum." The Capital Act of 1746, which had been passed by "management, precipitation, and surprise," was disallowed, and a new election of assemblymen was ordered on the basis of former representation. According to the governor's royal orders, the new assembly should have sixty members, five from each of the Albemarle counties, three from Bertie, two each from the remaining counties, and also one from each of the borough towns.

In the 1754 election, the first since 1747, the Albemarle counties elected five members each, and in the legislature that convened at New Bern all counties and boroughs were represented—for the first time since June, 1746. This marked the end of the representation controversy, the reunion of the "popular party" in the two sections, and the virtual end of the quarrel between the northern and southern counties.

By this time the increase of population in the backcountry began to threaten eastern control, which tended to promote an alliance of various Tidewater interests against the growing power of the West.

Basic Causes of East-West Sectionalism

East-West sectionalism has been one of the most important and most enduring factors in the history of North Carolina. As has been indicated, there were fundamental differences between East and West—in geography, national stocks, religion, social life, and economy. The East was settled largely by English and by Scottish Highlanders; its plantation economy was based on slave labor and aristocratic ideals. The West was largely Scotch-Irish and German in stock, with an economy that emphasized small farms, free labor, and democratic ideals. There were also religious differences, with the Anglican Church relatively strong in the East, but almost nonexistent in the backcountry. The commercial outlets of the East were largely with England, the West Indies, New England, and, to a lesser extent, with Virginia and Charleston. The backcountry trade contacts were more difficult and fewer, being largely restricted to overland trade with Pennsylvania, Virginia, and South Carolina.

Before 1760 there was little commercial intercourse between the East and the West and naturally little conflict, because of the sparseness of backcountry population and inadequate East-West transportation facilities. But the growth and expansion of the Piedmont population after 1750 created problems of new counties, raised the old question of representation, and brought forth complaints against eastern domination.

Controversy over Location of the Capital

The first significant controversy arose from the problem of locating a permanent capital. The system of "migratory legislatures" and "itinerant government" was unsatisfactory. The governor usually lived at one place, the assembly met at another, the treasurer lived at still another, and the councillors at various places. Governors Johnston, Dobbs, and Tryon all urged the legislature to establish a "fixed seat of government." Nearly all of the towns, most of which were located in the East, were eager to become the capital. In 1744 Johnston declared that "we have now tried every Town in this Colony and it is high time to settle somewhere. It is impossible to finish any matter as it ought to be while we go on in this itinerant way." After years of agitation and legislative debate a law was passed in 1746 fixing New Bern as the "seat of government," but this question was linked with the representation controversy and, as already seen, the law was disallowed by the Privy Council.

Dobbs was determined to get the matter settled and his efforts seemed to be meeting with success when in 1758 the legislature authorized the establishment of the capital at Tower Hill (near present Kinston), on the Neuse River about fifty miles above New Bern. When the Privy Council learned that this site was located on lands owned by Dobbs personally and that there had been charges of speculation and corruption in getting the statute passed, the law was promptly disallowed and Governor Dobbs was rebuked for having signed it.

New Bern Becomes the Capital

The East was apprehensive that the capital might be located at Hillsborough, and this led delegates from the Sound region and the Cape Fear to unite in favor of a compromise site. Tryon recommended New Bern as a "central location" and the assembly passed, in November, 1766, "an Act for erecting a Convenient Building within the town of New Bern for the residence of the Governor," and appropriated £5,000 for its construction, a sum increased by an additional £10,000 the next year. Since the colonial treasury was virtually bankrupt, the legislature ordered that the original £5,000 be paid "out of the Money appropriated by Act of Assembly for erecting of Public Schools, and purchasing glebes." But this sum was to be repaid from revenues to be derived from a tax of two pence a gallon on all wine, rum, and distilled liquors imported from any place except Great Britain, and from a poll tax of eight pence proclamation money for the next two years. The next year another tax of two shillings per poll was levied for three years.

The "Governor's Palace"

Work was begun on the palace in 1767, under the supervision of John Hawks, whom Tryon had brought from England "to superintend this work in all its branches." The Hawks plan included a brick house of two main stories, eighty-seven feet wide and fifty-nine feet deep, with two wings of two low stories each, connected with the main building by semicircular colonnades. The palace was the governor's residence and capitol, containing assembly hall, council room, and public offices. Over the vestibule door, in Latin, was the beautiful and hopeful, if somewhat ironic, inscription: "A free and happy people, opposed to cruel tyrants, has given this edifice to virtue. May the house and its inmates, as an example for future ages, here cultivate the arts, order, justice, and the laws."

When the structure was completed in 1770, it was considered the finest "government house" in English America.

The construction of the palace met with general approval in the East, although some thought it a waste of money. But the people in the backcountry were vehement in their opposition. One irate citizen of Mecklenburg County wrote in 1768: "Not one man in twenty of the four most populous counties [Orange, Rowan, Mecklenburg, and Anson] will ever see this famous house when built, as their connections and trade do, and ever will more naturally center in South Carolina." The westerners resented all poll taxes, but the one levied for this "unnecessary building" was particularly odious. They contended that this tax operated "to the prejudice" of the western counties, which had more white people but less wealth than those of the East. As one westerner said: "A man that is worth £10,000 pays no more than a poor back settler that has nothing but the labor of his hands to depend upon for his daily support." Some Orange County farmers boldly told their sheriff in 1768: "We are determined not to pay the tax for the next three years, for the Edifice or Governor's House. We want no such House, nor will we pay for it."

The East-West Representation Controversy

The building of Tryon's Palace was a serious irritant to the backcountry people, but there were many other and more critical western grievances. Perhaps the major cause of discontent and unrest in the western counties was the domination of provincial government by the eastern planter aristocracy. The county was the unit of representation in the assembly and there were many more counties in the East than in the West. As has been seen, the Albemarle counties had five representatives each. Nine borough towns also had one representative each in the assembly (Edenton after 1725, Bath and New Bern after 1731, Wilmington after 1739, Brunswick after 1754, Halifax after 1760, Campbellton and Salisbury after 1766, and Hillsborough after 1770). Of these, only the last two were in the West. The practice of creating new counties by act of the General Assembly was such as to guarantee political domination by the East. In the fifteen years after 1740 seven new western counties and six eastern counties were formed, though nearly all of the population increase was in the West. In 1754 the six westernmost counties (Anson, Granville, Johnston, Orange, Cumberland, and Rowan) had 22,000 people and only twelve representatives. The remaining counties had 43,000 people and forty-five representatives. By 1771 about one-half of the colony's estimated 250,000 population lived in Granville, Johnston, Orange, and Cumberland counties and in Mecklenburg County, which was created from Anson and Rowan in 1762. Yet these counties had only seventeen members (including three borough members) to sixty-one for the other counties. The ratio for eastern representation was one representative for each 1,700 people, and for western representation, one for each 7,300 people.

Not only did the East dominate the legislature, but it had complete control of the other branches of provincial government. From 1765 to 1771, the "Regulator period," the governor, all councillors, all the judges, the treasurer, and the Speaker of the House lived in the East.

Undemocratic Character of Local Government

The undemocratic character of local government was even more irritating than eastern domination to the people of the backcountry; it was also a cause of unrest and complaint among the "meaner sort" throughout the province. The common people resented the fact that not a single officer was chosen by popular vote. The county court, consisting of the justices of the peace of the county, appointed by the governor, controlled almost every aspect of local government and administration. It appointed, or nominated to the governor for appointment, the sheriff, constables, overseers of roads, searchers, patrolers, inspectors, town commissioners, and almost all local officers except the clerk of court, who, after 1762, was appointed by a royal official known as "Principal Clerk of the Pleas." The sheriff, the major executive official of the court and chief administrative officer of the county, was appointed by the governor for a two-year term, from a list of three names sent him by the county court. But the persons thus nominated must be justices of the peace at the time of their nomination, though they were not allowed to serve as justices and sheriff at the same time. The election machinery was in the hands of the "courthouse ring," the sheriff being the chief election official.

The "Courthouse Ring"

It is significant that, as a rule, about two-thirds of the assemblymen were justices of the peace. Thus there was an alliance between the political leaders of the colony and the self-constituted "courthouse rings." Though this system met with bitter criticism in various quarters, it had its ardent defenders among the planter-aristocracy. The idea of a popularly elected county court was dreaded by many conservatives, particularly in the East. James Iredell, commenting about the proposed state constitution in 1776, expressed the view held by many conservatives when he wrote: "God knows when there will be an end to this trifling here. . . . A draft of the Constitution was presented to the house yesterday, and lies over for consideration. . . . There is one thing in it which I cannot bear, and yet I am inclined to think it will stand. The inhabitants are empowered to elect the Justices in their respective counties, who are to be judges in the county courts. . . . Numberless inconveniences must arise from so absurd an institution."

Colonial "Carpetbaggers"

Many of the local officials were natives of the counties in which they served, but some, especially those most hated, such as Edmund Fanning and Henry Eustace McCulloh, were outsiders. As one contemporary observer wrote, "To it [the county] come the merchant, the lawyer, the tavernkeeper, the artisan, and the court officials, adventurers all in the perennial pursuit of gain."

Another writer declared, "They [the officials] were, all of them, or nearly all, of Northern or European birth, who came to the Southern provinces to make their fortunes, in what place, or by what means, they cared not." At a later date these political opportunists would have been called "carpetbaggers."

Multiple Officeholding

Multiple officeholding was one of the most deplorable results of this system and a constant source of irritation and complaint. The practice was permitted by law, but this did not make the westerners like it, particularly when the officeholders were "foreigners," who seemed to hold the natives in contempt. Fanning, a native of New York, personal friend of Governor Tryon, Yale graduate, and holder of honorary degrees from Oxford and other colleges, was the best educated man in the province—and its most hated citizen. Between 1766 and 1768 Fanning, who was a lawyer by profession, was assemblyman from Orange County, registrar, superior court judge, and colonel of the militia. He hated the common people and they reciprocated on many occasions. Francis Nash, a native of Orange, during the same period served as assemblyman, clerk of court, justice of the peace, member of the county court, and captain of the militia. John Frohock of Rowan was assemblyman, clerk, justice of the peace, member of the county court, and colonel in the militia. These were only a few of the instances of multiple officeholding and alliances between local "court-

"house rings" and eastern politicians.

Eighteenth-Century Concept of Public Office

In defense of these officials and of this system, it should be observed that the eighteenth-century concept of public office was quite different from what it is—or should be—today. A public office then was considered as the gift of the crown and the property right of the officeholder. Hence one could buy and sell offices and military commissions. For example, Frohock sold his clerkship to Samuel Spencer for £150. Local officials were paid by fees and received no salaries. These fees were regulated by law, but most people were ignorant of the amounts prescribed and were always suspicious that illegal fees were being exacted, as in fact they were in too many cases. In 1768 ninety-nine people signed a protest against Clerk Spencer that said, "As to the Clerk his extortions are burthensome to all that fall in his power as he takes double and sometimes treble his due. And tho' it is true he purchased his office from Colonel Frohock and gave to the amount of £150 for it yet it's unreasonable we should bear the expense by way of extortion."

Poetic Attacks on Officials

Fanning and Frohock in particular were satirized and lambasted in "ambling epics and jingling ballads" by Rednap Howell, the "poet of the Regulation," in a broadside, "When Fanning First to Orange Came":

> Says Frohock to Fanning, to tell the plain truth,
> When I came to this country I was but a youth.
> My father sent for me; I warn't worth a cross,
> And then my first study was to steal for a horse.
> I quickly got credit and then ran away
> And haven't paid for him to this very day.
>
> Says Fanning to Frohock, 'tis folly to lie;
> I rode an old mare that was blind of an eye.
> Five shillings in money I had in my purse;
> My coat it was patched but not much the worse.
> But now we've got rich and it's very well known
> That we'll do very well if they let us alone.

Another verse ran as follows:

> When Fanning first to Orange came
> He looked both pale and wan,
> An old patched coat upon his back,

> An old mare he rode on.
> Both man and mare warn't worth five pounds
> As I've often been told;
> But by his civil robberies
> He's laced his coat with gold.

Some historians have accepted as wholly true the charges of Howell, Husband, and other Regulators, but Carl Bridenbaugh, one of the leading authorities on colonial history, writing in 1952 about Howell and his fellow propagandists, said: "By pamphlet, ballad, and stump speech they made Colonel Fanning the symbol of misgovernment and extortion, although his crime seems to have been only that he was Tryon's friend." This author goes on to say that Howell's broadside "has probably blackened a name forever. The Regulators may have lost the war, but they certainly won the history."

Complaints against Granville's Land Agents

Howell and perhaps others writing about this troubled period of North Carolina history took liberties with the truth, but the fact remains that the scarcity of money, the incidence of taxation, and the land policy of the Granville District caused general unrest throughout the backcountry and evoked many charges of corruption, illegal fees, and excessive rents and taxes. As early as 1755 a legislative committee reported that Francis Corbin, Lord Granville's agent in the province, and his subordinates, were "exacting exhorbitant fees on all grants." But nothing was done to redress the grievances of the landholders. In November, 1758, the legislature received a petition against the excessive fees and general maladministration of Granville's land office. An investigation was ordered, but the only immediate result was the publication of the fees charged by Granville's agents. Corbin was eventually dismissed, but too late to avert several unpleasant situations. Late in January, 1759, a group of malcontents rode to Edenton, seized Corbin, and carried him to Enfield, where they made him promise to appear at the next term of Granville Court to stand trial on charges of extortion.

Meantime "The Petition of Reuben Searcy and Others" was presented to the county court of Granville on March 23, 1759. In this document, representing the views of "Sundry of the Inhabitants," the attorney general of North Carolina was accused of taking extortionate fees, of preventing the appointment of justices of the peace for the northern part of the county, and "through his wiles and false insinuations to which art and chicanerie he owes his great success and high perferment in this province" of imposing both "on the inferior class of mankind," and on Governor Dobbs. Herman Husband, in his *Impartial Relation* (1770), implied that Searcy was prosecuted for libel, but the court records reveal no such action.

The Enfield "Riot"

On May 14, 1759, the so-called Enfield Riot in Halifax County occurred, and Governor Dobbs ordered the arrest of several of the "rioters," who were jailed, but were promptly released when irate citizens broke into the jail. Whereupon Dobbs wrote the Board of Trade that "these mobs, riots and insurrections" were all confined to the Granville District and had been provoked by "Corbin's maladministration as Granville's agent." But Dobbs and the assembly sided with the agents, and the law of 1760 to establish courts in the disaffected counties was enacted to control "disaffected and evil disposed persons." Two years later the council ordered that proclamation be issued "for quelling the riotous disorders in the western frontiers of this province."

The "War of Sugar Creek"

One of the most dramatic of these "riotous disorders," which, like the uprising at Enfield, was in the nature of a rent riot, flared up in Mecklenburg County in the spring of 1765 and reached a grand climax at "the war of Sugar Creek." On May 7 John Frohock and six other surveyors on the lands of Henry Eustace McCulloh and George A. Selwyn were severely whipped by a group of more than one hundred farmers, "many of whom were Armed with Guns," led by Thomas Polk. McCulloh, writing to Edmund Fanning two days later, said that "had I been present—I most assuredly & without ceremony had been murdered," and that this mob had "declared solemnly—publicly, they will put me to death." He also described in colorful language how one surveyor had been "striped from the nape of his neck to the Waistband of his Breeches, like a draft-Board," while another nearly had his "skull cracked open."

When Governor Tryon heard about this "Great Breach and Disturbance of His Majesty's Peace and Government," he issued a proclamation, May 18, 1765, offering pardon to "any two persons concerned in the said Riot," who would give the names of "the several Rioters" to the governor or the attorney general. The records fail to show that either official received the desired information.

The Nutbush Address

The next act in a series of protests and demonstrations against the malpractices of local officials was "An Address to the People of Granville County," June 6, 1765, by George Sims, schoolmaster of Nutbush community. This document, usually called "The Nutbush Address," described the "notorious and intolerable abuses" the people were suffering, such as excessive taxes, high rents, extortionate fees, and fraudulent accounting of public funds, and declared that it was "Not our mode or form of Government, nor yet the body of our laws, that we are quarreling with, but with the malpractices of the Officers of our County Court, and the abuses which we suffer by those empowered to manage public affairs."

The first organized effort to redress these "abuses" took place in October, 1766, at a mass meeting at Sandy Creek in Orange County, with the issuance of what has been called "Regulator Advertisement Number I." This document appealed to all the people of North Carolina to resist local oppression and to put an end to the extortion of county officials. The purpose of the meeting was to inquire "whether the true men of the county labour under any abuses of power and in particular to examine into the public taxes," and to demand an accounting of officials. The county officers of Orange took the position that they were not responsible to the people, and Fanning declined to refer his conduct to "the shallow understanding of the mob." The indignant citizens of Orange then appealed to the assembly, but this body turned a deaf ear to their appeals and the agitation continued.

The Cherokee Boundary Line

The running of the boundary line "between the Frontiers of North Carolina and the Cherokee Hunting Grounds" in the summer of 1767, at a cost of £1,490, irritated many people in the back country. The need for this survey had been felt for many years, but westerners saw no reason for Governor Tryon to do the job in person. They certainly saw no need for him to march from Salisbury to the Indian lands and back (May 18–June 13), with a retinue of about a hundred people, including two regiments of Rowan and Mecklenburg militia, sixteen "servants and assistants," and only two surveyors. These two men and their Indian helpers were paid only £30, but presents worth £175 were given to the Indians. The actual running of the line took place after Tryon, his officers, and most of his cavalcade had returned to their homes. The backcountry people condemned the "pompous, ridiculous, unnecessary and wasteful expenditure" of public funds in time of peace. They were greatly disturbed by the rumor—which turned out to be false—that Fanning, who had accompanied Tryon as his adjutant general, had been paid £1,000.

The following petition, signed by thirty citizens of Orange and Rowan and presented to the legislature of 1768, expresses well the abuse of power exercised by local officials: "Your poor Petitioners having been continually Squez'd and oppressed by our Publick Officers both with Regard to their fees as also in the Laying on of Taxes as well as in Collecting together with Iniquitous appropriations, and wrong applications. . . . We humbly supplicate your Worships to take under your serious consideration, we labor under Extreme hardships about our levies, Money is very scarce [and] hardly . . . to be had would we Purchase it at ten times its value & we exceeding Poor & lie at a great distance from

Trade. . . . for Gods sake Gentlemen be not negligent or unconcerned in an affair of such importance. On your breath depends the Ruin or Prosperity of thousands of poor Families, & tho' to Gentlemen Rowling in affluence, a few shillings per man, may seem triffling yet to Poor people who must have their Bed and Bed Clothes yea their Wives Petticoats taken sold to defray these charges, how Tremendious judge ye must be the consequences, an only Horse, to raise Bread or an only cow to give milk to an Helpless family by which in a great measure are otherwise supported seized and sold and kept for a single levy. . . . Good God Gentlemen, what will come of us when these demands come against us Paper Money we have none Gold and Silver we can Purchase none. . . . To be concluded, it now depends [on you] whether we shall be made happy or miserable. Save us Save us from Inevitable Destruction for the Lords sake Gentlemen Exert yourselves this once in our favour & your Petitioners as in duty bound shall ever pray."

Organization of the "Regulators"

The year 1768 was the turning point in the controversy and marked the formal organization of the Regulator movement. "Regulator Advertisement Number 6," March 22, 1768, used the word "Regulator" for the first time and stated in unmistakable language what these aggrieved people proposed to "regulate." They agreed: "(1) To pay no more taxes until they were satisfied that they were agreeable to law, (2) to pay no more fees than the laws required, (3) to subscribe to a fund for defraying necessary expenses, (4) to meet as often as they conveniently could, and (5) to allow a simple majority to rule in case of differences."

The keynote of the Regulation agreement was: "An officer is a servant of the publick, and we are determined to have the officers of this county under a better and honester regulation than any have been for some time past." In 1767 Tryon wrote the Earl of Shelburne that "The Sheriffs have embezzled more than one-half of the public money ordered to be raised and collected by them . . . [about 40,000 pounds] . . . not 500 of which will possibly ever come into the Treasury as in many instances the Sheriffs are either insolvent or retreated out of the province." Parson James Reed said the Sheriffs "very frequently spend the Public money not one in 10 I believe I might say in 20, can ever make up their accounts, by which means the Clergy are frequently left for a long time out of their stipends."

The Regulators had just cause for complaint. Governor Tryon admitted in 1767 that at least 50 percent of the taxes collected by the sheriffs was unaccounted for, and that some of the sheriffs were in arrears for many years, especially in Rowan and Anson counties. The situation had become so bad in Anson that the people took matters into their own hands and pledged themselves not to pay taxes for the current year. As of October, 1768, only 1,017 of 3,059 taxables in Rowan had paid their 1766 levies, and a year later 1,833 "refractory Regulators" still remained in arrears. The Regulators said much more about taxation than they did about paying taxes.

Regulators' Attempts to Solve Their Problems by Peaceful Means

"Regulator Advertisement Number 8," May 21, 1768, perhaps the best-written and calmest of the Regulator documents, and signed by nearly five hundred residents of Orange, was the climax of the Regulator attempts to obtain justice by peaceful and legal means. This document began with an apology to Tryon for anything that might "be construed as derogatory" to the king or the law, and assured the governor that neither disloyalty nor disaffection was the cause of their troubles, but "the corrupt and arbitrary practices of nefarious and designing men who being put into posts of profit and credit among us, use every artifice, every fraud, and where these fail, threats and menaces are not spared to squeeze and extort from the wretched poor." It rebuked the "heated, unruly spirits" who had fired several shots into Fanning's house a short time before.

Hunter and Howell carried this document to Brunswick and presented it to Governor Tryon. After consulting with his council, the governor replied to the petition, stating that the Regulators' grievances did not justify their course of action, and ordering them to give up the name of Regulators, cease organized activities, pay their taxes, and not molest officers. As Herman Husband later said, Tryon was "inclined to the other side, multiplying all our faults to the highest pitch he was capable of."

Tryon realized that the Regulators had grounds for many of their complaints and issued a warning to all officials and lawyers against charging excessive fees, ordered the publication of a list of legal fees, and directed the attorney general to prosecute officers and lawyers charged with extortion. He promised to go to Hillsborough in July, where he hoped to "find everyone at peace."

The governor kept his word and went to Hillsborough in August. Rumors were flying that he was raising the militia to suppress the Regulators and also calling on the Indians to attack from the rear.

The Trials at Hillsborough, 1768

Meanwhile Fanning had been indicted for taking excessive fees as register of deeds and his trial had been set for the September session of court. Disorders continued throughout the summer. The Orange sheriff had "distrained" a Regulator's horse for nonpayment of taxes; the horse was recovered by a group of Regulators, and the "mob" marched to Hillsborough, threatening officials and lawyers. Herman Husband and William Butler had been arrested on charges of "inciting the populace to rebellion," and they were scheduled for trial at the coming session of court. Threats of their rescue and reports about the rising of the Regulators prompted Tryon to call out the militia, and a force of 1,461 marched to Hillsborough. This only angered the Regulators—and increased the debt of the colony £5,000.

What took place at Hillsborough in September, 1768, was a perfect illustration of the centralization of power in the "courthouse ring." Fanning, the defendant to be tried, and Richard Henderson, the presiding judge, were both colonels in the militia. Six other militia officers were members of the governor's council, and eighteen assemblymen were also officers in the militia. This was one-fourth of the assembly to which the Regulators had recently appealed for redress of grievances.

On the other side of the picture, there were present—according to Herman Husband—about 3,700 Regulators, four of whose leaders were to be tried for "inciting the populace to rebellion" or for "resisting the sheriff." Husband was acquitted; the other three were convicted, but were pardoned by Tryon. There was no serious disorder and the threatened "Battle of the Eno" did not materialize. Fanning was convicted of taking a six-shilling fee for registering a deed when the legal charge was two shillings and eight pence and was fined "one penny and cost." Though he promptly resigned his office, the Regulators were not appeased by this obvious miscarriage of justice.

Regulator Case Carried to Legislature

Again the Regulators decided to carry their case to the legislature and this time they hoped for better results because in the 1769 elections Orange, Anson, Granville, and Halifax had elected solid Regulator delegations, including two of their outstanding leaders, Herman Husband of Orange and Thomas Person of Granville. Ironically enough, Fanning was chosen from the "pocket borough" of Hillsborough, which had recently been created through the influence of Tryon to get his friend a seat in the legislature—or so the Regulators charged.

The Regulators' grivances were presented to the assembly, but the dissolution of that body by Tryon after a four-day session, supposedly because of other issues, prevented any positive action. Meantime the Regulator organization was gaining new recruits and spreading into new areas. There were disorders in Edgecombe County, in Anson and Johnston, and mob action at the Hillsborough Court, September 24 and 25, 1770, when approximately 150 Regulators marched into the courthouse, assaulted lawyer John Williams, dragged Fanning through the streets, and caused Judge Henderson to flee for safety. As Henderson described it, they left "poor Colonel Fanning and the little Borough in a wretched situation." The next day the Regulators conducted a mock court, filling the docket with many bitter, sarcastic, and profane remarks, usually ending with "plaintiff pays costs." There were widespread rumors of an intended Regulator descent on the legislature that was to meet at New Bern in December.

The Johnston "Riot Act"

Panic was running through the colony. Tryon hastily summoned his council, which urged him to use military force to quell the disturbances. When the assembly convened, the governor denounced the "seditious mob" at Hillsborough and urged the legislature to adopt measures to cope with the situation. The creation of four new counties in "Regulator Country" was the only victory the "insurgents" won in this session. In a state of high tension and faced with reported uprisings, the assembly passed the Johnston Riot Act, which provided that prosecutions for riots might be tried in any county, even though the riots did not occur there; outlawed any person resisting or avoiding arrest; and authorized the governor to put down the Regulators by military force. Bassett observed of this assembly that, "born as it was in terror, it is not surprising that it should have passed away in blood." Efforts to oust Person from the assembly failed, but Husband was expelled on charges of libel, and as not being "a credit to the Assembly." Tryon and the council were afraid to let Husband go back to Orange and they jailed him at New Bern on charges of libel. The Grand Jury failed to find a true bill against him and he was released. About this time reports reached Tryon that the Regulators were marching on New Bern to rescue Husband and to burn the town.

Regulator reaction to the "Bloody Johnston Act" was swift and defiant. The organization increased in numbers and many strong resolutions were drawn up, such as those in Rowan and Orange, which denounced this "riotous act," and in which the Regulators promised to pay no more taxes, declared Fanning an outlaw to be killed on sight, forbade any sessions of court, and threatened to kill all lawyers and judges. The situation seemed to be getting out of hand.

Tryon's Expedition against the Regulators; the Battle of Alamance

Tryon, who had already been appointed governor of New York, decided to take drastic and dramatic action. He issued orders for a special term of court to be held at Hillsborough in March, 1771, and, as his council had advised, called out the militia "with all expedition" to protect the court and to suppress the Regulators. The militiamen responding numbered 1,452, of whom 1,068 were from the East, and the remainder from Orange, Rowan, and a few other western counties. Tryon marched from New Bern to Hillsborough and on May 14 encamped on Great Alamance Creek, a few miles west of Hillsborough, where he was met by a force of about 2,000 Regulators. The latter petitioned the governor for an audience, but he refused to communicate with them "as long as they were in arms against the government." He gave them one hour to lay down their arms and disperse. At the end of the hour, he gave the order to fire, and after a two-hour battle the Regulators were defeated and scattered. Tryon's losses were nine killed and sixty-one wounded; the Regulators lost twenty killed and about one hundred wounded. Tryon's terse report about the battle was that "a signal and glorious victory was obtained over the obstinate and infatuated rebels."

Twelve Regulators were tried for treason and all were convicted. Six were hanged and the rest were pardoned by the governor. Tryon offered clemency to all who would lay down their arms and submit to authority. Within six weeks 6,409 submitted and later received pardons from the king through Governor Martin.

Governor Josiah Martin wrote the Earl of Hillsborough, Secretary of State for the Colonies, August 30, 1772, that he saw most clearly that the Regulators "had been provoked by insolence and cruel advantages taken of the people's ignorance by mercenary tricking attorneys, clerks, and other little officers who have practiced upon them every sort of caprice and extortion" and that "the resentment of government was craftily worked up against the oppressed and the protection which the oppressors treacherously acquired where the injured and ignorant people expected to find it, drove them to desperation."

Many Regulators Leave North Carolina

Husband, Howell, and several other leaders of the Regulation had left North Carolina before the Battle of Alamance. Many Regulators, perhaps thousands, moved to the Tennessee country within a short time after their crushing defeat. Morgan Edwards, noted Baptist preacher, traveler, and author, writing in 1772, said that these people "despaired of seeing better times and therefore quitted the province. It is said that 1,500 families have departed since the battle of Alamance and to my knowledge a great many more are only waiting to dispose of their plantations in order to follow them." Tryon and Fanning, the Regulators' archenemies, had also left North Carolina for good.

An Appraisal of the Regulation Movement

There is a vast literature on the War of the Regulation and the Regulators. Scores of poems, songs, articles, pamphlets, and books have either praised or damned these "simple and greatly abused farmers." Many myths have grown up around the movement, its leaders, and the rank and file of Regulators. Some writers, past and present, have described the Regulation as a "great democratic movement." Others have called Alamance "the first battle of the American Revolution." It was not a democratic movement in the modern sense of that term. Its leaders insisted that they were not fighting for a change in the "Form or Mode of Government," but were contending for relief from the malpractices of judges, sheriffs, and "mercenary tricking Attornies, Clerks, and other little Officers," who were usually American-born adventurers of English descent, and "who had sniffed from afar opportunities for wealth and power in a new country." One Regulator writer had referred to the court officials and lawyers as "these cursed hungry Caterpillars, that will eat out the very Bowels of our Commonwealth, if they are not pulled down from their Nests in a very short time."

It is claiming too much to maintain that Alamance was "the first battle of the American Revolution." It was simply the climax of a revolt of the western people against oppressive laws and corrupt local officials. And there was not a single British redcoat at Alamance Creek in 1771. Nor was North Carolina the only colony where discontented people in the backcountry organized, agitated, and even fought for a redress of their grievances against provincial and local officials. South Carolina, for instance, had a Regulation movement by the same name and at the same time as North Carolina. Its *Plan of Regulation* was adopted in June, 1768, and the organization continued its activities for two years after the North Carolina movement had subsided.

Another myth associated with the Regulation movement is the idea that all, or even most, of the Regulators became Tories in the Revolution, which broke out four years after the Battle of Alamance. An examination of the records reveals that of 883 of the known Regulators, 289 were Whigs, 34 Tories, and 560 Revolutionary status unknown.

The Regulation movement in North Carolina collapsed in 1771, but not the cause for which the Regulators had been fighting. Alamance was only a temporary defeat in a revolt against sectional political domination and maladministration in local government. The movement for justice to the backcountry was interrupted by the American Revolution and its aftermath, but the later renewal of the East-West controversy reached its grand climax and victory for the West in the Constitutional Convention of 1835.

Chapter 12

THE APPROACH OF THE AMERICAN REVOLUTION, 1763-1775

The seeds of the American Revolution existed in the British Empire from the beginning of settlement in the New World. The numerous protests of various colonies on many occasions, particularly from 1673 to 1689 and after 1763, revealed a "spirit of separatism," which eventually culminated in revolution and independence. It was inevitable that antagonism and cross-purposes should have developed between England and her "plantations" overseas. The colonies had been settled largely by dissenters and radicals seeking change and freedom from interference by church or state. Most of the seventeenth-century settlers had come from England proper; most of those in the eighteenth century were Scotch-Irish, Germans, and Scottish Highlanders—people who had no inherited affection for English institutions, policies, or laws, and who manifested a spirit of independence to a great degree in their relations to any government—local, colonial, or English.

British Mercantilism and Its Application to the Colonies

The basic principle on which English colonization was grounded, that of mercantilism, caused resentment on the part of colonial leaders, especially merchants, from the start. Throughout the colonial era English leaders, including the "friends of America," accepted the principle that "all plantations endamage the mother kingdom, where the trades of such plantations are not confined to the mother kingdom by good laws and severe execution of them." It is a well known fact that the series of Navigation Acts (1651–96) and other acts of trade that translated mercantilist principles into law were not rigidly enforced before 1763. The phrase "salutary neglect" has been applied to the half century after 1713, during which the colonies had been allowed to go their own way, to develop their own institutions, to work out their own destiny, with scarcely more than a gesture of supervision from the crown, or occasional annoyances from easily evaded trade restrictions. Naturally sharp differences of opinion developed in England and the colonies, especially in regard to such fundamental issues as taxation and representation.

England's New Colonial Policy

When, therefore, England inaugurated its "New Colonial Policy" in 1763, a clash of interests developed. Colonial protests that were ignored or overruled eventually fanned the spirit of revolt. As Edmund Burnett wrote: "The colonies had reached that state in their development where they felt they no longer had need of a doting parent—and they resented subjection to a domineering one."

To cope with such new problems as western lands, Indians, defense, and war debts, resulting from England's victory over France in 1763, the imperial system was reorganized to extend protection, government, and opportunity for profitable exploitation. To achieve more effective control over the old colonies and the four new ones (Quebec, East Florida, West Florida, and Grenada), the Grenville ministry decided to keep a standing army of ten thousand men in the colonies; to tighten the mercantile system by stricter enforcement of the old trade laws and by the enactment of new laws; and to guarantee financial independence of royal officials, particularly governors and judges, by salaries obtained from colonial revenue by parliamentary taxation, instead of by colonial legislative appropriations. While this new policy was designed to cope with the problem of "imperialism," it never abandoned the principles of mercantilism. British trade laws were upheld to the last, even by Pitt and other defenders of colonial liberty in England. A London newspaper as late as January 5, 1775, declared: "If we allow France and Holland to supply them with fabric, we may as well give up all ideas of having colonies at all." Some of the Grenville policies were old, some were new, but all became odious to the colonials, because England now meant to enforce the laws and to make the imperial system work.

Effects of the New Colonial Policy on North Carolina

The impact of the new policies relating to land, trade, taxation, and defense was felt by all the colonies, less perhaps by North Carolina than most. The Royal Proclamation of 1763, with its Proclamation Line along the crest of the mountains reserving lands west of that line for "Indian Country," was designed to solve the problems of the lands and turbulent peoples recently acquired from France. Since North Carolina settlement had not reached the reserved area, there was little reaction in the colony to this new land policy.

The Sugar Act of 1764, designed to raise revenue for "protecting, defending, and securing the said colonies," was a minor irritant to North Carolina importers of sugar, molasses, and other articles listed in this law, but the act met with little organized opposition in the province, in contrast with the violent reaction of Massachusetts, Rhode Island, and other commercial colonies. The Currency Act of 1764, which forbade the issuance of bills of credit in the colonies, caused little difficulty in North Carolina and was evaded by the issuance of treasury notes and debenture notes. The impact of the Quartering Act of 1765 was not felt in the colony at all, because not a single redcoat was sent to North Carolina before 1776.

Parliament Passes the Stamp Act

The general opposition to the above-mentioned parliamentary enactments was mild compared to the outbursts against the Stamp Act. This law, originally drafted for the Grenville ministry by Henry McCulloh—perhaps the one of North Carolina land-speculation fame—had been brought before the House of Commons in 1764, and was tabled for one year to enable the colonies to suggest a better means of raising revenue. Since only petitions against the proposed tax and suggestions for a return to the old requisition system—but no constructive suggestions—were forthcoming, Parliament passed the Stamp Act, March 1, 1765, to become effective on November 1 of that year. This act was the first direct or "internal tax" levied by Parliament on the colonies. It provided that stamps or stamped paper must be used on a variety of legal documents, commissions, ship's clearance papers, bills of lading, newspapers, pamphlets, almanacs, dice, playing cards, college diplomas, and many other items. The cost of stamps varied from a half-penny to ten pounds sterling, the average being less than a shilling. The taxes were lower than similar ones in England, and the revenues were to be spent wholly in "defending, protecting, and securing . . . the British colonies and plantations in America." Violators of the law might be tried in either an ordinary "court of record" or in a vice-admiralty court.

North Carolina's Opposition to the Stamp Act

News of the passage of the Stamp Act brought forth storms of protest from Maine to Georgia. The tax affected all colonists to some degree, but it hit lawyers, editors, and printers hardest, and the influence and vocal power of these groups were out of all proportion to their numbers.

North Carolina, like other colonies, resisted the Stamp Act from the first, on the ground that it was a tyrannical violation of the traditional principle of English liberty that there must be no taxation without representation. As early as 1760 the assembly of the province had stated that "it was the indubitable right of the Assembly to frame and model every bill whereby an aid was granted to the King, and that every attempt to deprive them of the enjoyment thereof was an infringement of the rights and privileges of the Assembly." And four years later the assembly had denied the power of Parliament to levy direct taxes on the colony.

One of the ablest literary attacks on the British theory of taxation and representation was a sixteen-page pamphlet, *The Justice and Policy of Taxing the American Colonies in Great Britain, Considered,* by Maurice Moore of North Carolina, published in 1765. Moore maintained that the colonists could legally "be taxed only with their own consent"; that they were not and could not be represented in Parliament; and, that, therefore, they could not "with the least degree of justice, be taxed by the British Parliament." He challenged "the notion of virtual representation," which might be satisfactory to the people of the British Isles, but which would never work in its application to the colonies.

The Stamp Act Congress, 1765

There was some unorganized opposition to the Stamp Act during the summer of 1765, and on June 8 of that year the Massachusetts legislature sent out a letter to the legislatures of the other colonies inviting them to send delegates to a congress to be held in New York in October to consider the whole question of British policies regarding the colonies, and particularly the Stamp Act. North Carolina, along with three other colonies (New Hampshire, Virginia, and Georgia), was not represented at the Stamp Act Congress, because Governor Tryon refused to summon the legislature in time to choose delegates—for which he was reprimanded when the assembly met the next year.

The Stamp Act Congress was the first meeting of its kind on an intercolonial scale not called by crown, Parliament, or governor. The resolutions of this body, which proclaimed loyalty to the crown, but objected to certain acts of Parliament, especially the Stamp Act, set off organized resistance in all the colonies. When Governor Tryon asked Speaker Samuel Ashe what North Carolina's reaction to the law would be, Ashe replied that the colony would "fight it to the death." In the summer and fall there were public demonstrations against the law at Cross Creek, Edenton, New Bern, Wilmington, and perhaps at other places, and agreements were reached not to use the stamps, which had not yet arrived. But there was violent opposition to the Stamp Act only on the Lower Cape Fear. Governor Tryon and several members of his council lived here, as well as the newly appointed Stamp Master for the province, Dr. William Houston. And here were the chief ports, Wilmington and Brunswick, where stamps were expected to arrive soon after November 1.

Stamp Act Riot at New Bern

North Carolina Collection, The University of North Carolina at Chapel Hill

Wilmington Demonstrations against the Stamp Act

The first significant demonstration against the Stamp Act in North Carolina occurred at Wilmington on the evening of October 19, when about five hundred people assembled, hanged the effigy of Lord Bute—whom they erroneously blamed for the passage of the hated law—and burned it in a large bonfire of tar barrels near the courthouse, called the gentlemen of the town from their homes to the celebration, where amid cheers they drank toasts to "Liberty, Property, and No Stamp Duty," and "otherwise disported themselves until midnight."

On the evening of October 31, which was Halloween, and also the day before the Stamp Act was to become effective, another large Wilmington crowd marched to the doleful music of the muffled town bell and a drum draped in mourning toward the churchyard for the burial of an effigy of Liberty carried in a coffin. At the grave a final examination revealed a faint pulse-beat in the effigy. Rejoicing that Liberty still lived, the crowd bore the effigy to a large bonfire, placed it comfortably in an armchair, and spent the evening celebrating.

When Stamp Master William Houston visited Wilmington on November 16, three or four hundred Sons of Liberty, with drums beating and flags flying, escorted him to the courthouse where he signed a resignation of his office and then treated the crowd to "the best liquors to be had." With Liberty placards in their hats, they drank toasts "in great form" and then they extorted a promise from Andrew Steuart, the public printer and newspaper editor, to issue the *North Carolina Gazette* on unstamped paper. When the paper appeared it bore on the margin: "This is the place to affix the Stamp," just above a skull and crossbones.

Governor Tryon was alarmed by the turn of events and, eager to avert further trouble, invited "near fifty merchants and gentlemen of New Hanover and Brunswick" to dine with him on November 18, when he "urged to them the expediency of permitting the circulation of Stamps." The next day he received their reply that they thought it was the "securer conduct" to prevent the operation of the Stamp Act. The situation was becoming critical. No ships had cleared since November 1, and legally no ships could leave port, no cargoes be landed, no courts of law be open, no newspapers, books, or pamphlets printed, unless stamps were used. But none were purchased, and officials were afraid to enforce the law. Business and trade were at a standstill; financial ruin faced some of the people.

Armed Resistance at Brunswick

On November 28 the British sloop *Diligence* arrived at Brunswick with an assignment of stamps and stamped paper, but as there was no Stamp Master in the province, the stamps remained aboard ship. The situation became more acute in January, 1766, when two merchant ships, the *Dobbs* and the *Patience,* came into Brunswick and were seized by Captain Lobb of the British *Viper,* because their clearance papers were not stamped. Indignant at this seizure, the people of Wilmington refused to sell supplies to the king's ships, seized a "contractor's vessel," and threw its crew into jail. The attorney general's decision in February that Lobb's seizures were legal and that the two vessels he had detained should be sent to Nova Scotia for legal proceedings, was the signal for armed resistance. On February 18 a meeting in Wilmington of "the principal gentlemen, freeholders, and inhabitants" of several counties of the Province elected leaders and signed an agreement that "We will at any risque . . . unite . . . in preventing entirely the operation of the Stamp Act." Among the leaders were Hugh Waddell, John Ashe, and Cornelius Harnett. The next day several hundred armed patriots marched to Brunswick, posted a guard around the governor's residence, and after an altercation with him, broke open the collector's desk and took the papers of the seized vessels, and so threatened Fort Johnston that its guns were spiked.

On February 20, after armed reinforcements had augmented their forces to nearly a thousand men, a group of "insurgents" boarded the *Viper* and compelled the captain to release the seized merchant vessels. Thenceforth ships entered and cleared the Cape Fear without hindrance—and without stamps.

On the morning of February 21 a large armed body approached the governor's house to secure Comptroller Pennington, who had taken refuge there—supposedly under Tryon's bed. At first Tryon declined to part with his guest, but Cornelius Harnett, courageous leader of the Patriots and the "Pride of the Cape Fear," standing face to face and eye to eye with the governor, declared that the people would take Pennington by force if he were longer detained. Tryon was firm, but Pennington resigned his office, went with Harnett and the "inhabitants in arms" into the main part of town, and in a circle of cheering patriots took oath, along with all other public officials there, except the governor, that he would never issue any stamped paper in North Carolina.

These armed Sons of Liberty, comprising the gentlemen, planters, and merchants of Brunswick, New Hanover, Duplin, and Bladen counties, returned in triumph to their homes. They had preserved their liberties by organized, open, orderly, and successful resistance to the enforcement of the Stamp Act. In no other colony was the resistance by force so well organized and executed. American protests, armed resistance, the failure of the tax to bring in the anticipated revenue, and the protests of British merchants and manufacturers led Parliament to repeal the Stamp Act in 1766.

The Declaratory Resolution of 1766

In their joy over the repeal of this hated law North Carolina and other colonies seem to have overlooked the Declaratory Act of March 18, 1766, passed shortly after the repeal of the Stamp Act, in which Parliament declared that it "had, hath, and of right ought to have, full power and authority to make laws and statutes of sufficient force and validity to bind the colonies and people of America . . . in all cases whatsoever." Parliament still retained the right to tax, but colonial leaders were beginning to challenge this right. Before 1765 some North Carolina leaders had questioned the expediency of parliamentary taxation, but they had not denied the right.

The Townshend Act, 1767

The new British ministry, dominated by Charles Townshend, Chancellor of the Exchequer, was determined to raise at least £40,000 in revenue from the colonies, in order to reduce taxes in England a shilling in the pound. This was to be done by an indirect or external tax, which Townshend thought would be more palatable to the colonials than the direct Stamp tax had been. But the Townshend Duty or Revenue Act of 1767, which placed import duties on wine, tea, paper, glass, lead, and painters' colors, reopened the controversy with the colonies and inaugurated what was "little more than a series of deplorable blunders" that led directly into revolution. Although opposition to this new tax was most bitter in the commercial colonies, two new features in the act met with criticism in every colony. Part of the revenue to be derived from the taxes was to be applied to payment of the salaries of colonial governors and judges, and violators of the law were to be tried in courts of vice-admiralty, which had no juries.

This statute and the determined efforts of the British ministry to enforce all the trade laws, through its reorganized customs administration, gave a new impetus to intercolonial cooperation, which was highlighted by the issuance of the Massachusetts Circular Letter of 1768. This document, written by Samuel Adams, "the father of the American Revolution," and sent to all the colonial assemblies, informed them of the measures the Massachusetts legislature had taken in opposition to the Townshend Acts. The British ministry was becoming alarmed at the growing sentiment for colonial union and fearful of economic resistance by the Americans. Hoping to forestall colonial opposition, Lord Hillsborough, Secretary of State for the Colonies (a position created that year) sent an order to the Massachusetts legislature to rescind the Circular Letter and a mandate to the other provincial governments ordering them to treat the Massachusetts letter with contempt. When Governor Francis Bernard dissolved the Massachusetts legislature because it refused to retract, several colonies adopted resolutions declaring that the Bay colony was suffering in a "common cause," and pledged their support to the idea of economic pressure against the mother country. The Virginia legislature proposed a "nonimportation" program, which gradually met with general approval in most of the colonies.

The North Carolina assembly, led by Speaker John Harvey, adopted an address to the king on November 11, 1768, in which attention was called to the fact that the assembly in the past had "cheerfully and liberally" voted money for service of the public when needed and promised to do so in the future, but it added the significant note "that their representatives in Assembly can alone be the proper judges not only what sum they are able to pay, but likewise of the most eligible method of collecting the same. . . . This [Townshend Act] is a taxation which we are firmly persuaded the acknowledged principles of the British Constitution ought to protect us from. Free men cannot legally be taxed but by themselves or their representatives, and that your Majesty's subjects within this province are represented in Parliament we cannot allow, and are convinced that from our situation we never can be."

North Carolina Opposes the Townshend Taxes

When the next General Assembly convened in October, 1769, Harvey laid the matter of nonimportation before it. But Governor Tryon, anticipating unfriendly action by the legislature, promptly dissolved that body. Whereupon Harvey called for a meeting "independent of the governor." Accordingly a "convention" met in the courthouse at New Bern, with Harvey as "moderator" and with sixty-four of the seventy-seven members of the assembly in attendance. In a two-day session, this body drew up a "nonimportation association," which was circulated throughout the colony and which led to the formation of several local associations.

The precise effects of this action on North Carolina's commerce is difficult to determine. Governor Tryon thought it amounted to little more than talk. In 1771 he wrote to England that "notwithstanding the boasted associations of people who never were in trade, and the sham patriotism of a few merchants to the southward of the province, the several ports of this province have been open ever since the repeal of the Stamp Act for every kind of British manufactures to the full extent of the credit of the country."

The Townshend Duty Act did not yield the anticipated revenues, and this fact, plus the mounting opposition to the law both in America and in England, led to repeal in 1770 of all the taxes, except that on tea. The three pence per pound tea tax was retained, partly because of the king's insistence that one tax must be kept in order "to retain the principle."

The Calm before the Storm

There was an "interval of calm" for the next three years, during which trade between England and the colonies reached its highest point—about £4 million a year. But the radicals in the colonies felt that an agency for communication and common action was needed; they wanted to be prepared for any emergency; and they wanted to wrest control from the conservatives. At best, the assemblies were largely dependent on the governors and were too conservative to please the radicals. An independent agency of some kind was needed for propaganda purposes. On November 2, 1772, the Boston town meeting, under Samuel Adams's guidance, organized a committee "to state the rights of the colonists and of Massachusetts in particular," and to carry on correspondence with other towns in that province.

In March, 1773, Josiah Quincy of Massachusetts, while on a southern tour, spent a night with Cornelius Harnett and wrote that he and Harnett, whom he called "the Samuel Adams of North Carolina," agreed that "the plan of continental correspondence [was] highly relished, much wished for, and resolved upon as proper to be pursued." During the same month the Virginia legislature inaugurated the centralized committee system when it created a standing Committee of Correspondence and Inquiry "to obtain the most early and authentic intelligence of all British Colonial Acts or proceedings of the Administration which might relate to or affect the British Colonies in America and to keep up and maintain a Correspondence with the sister colonies respecting these considerations."

North Carolina Sets Up a Committee of Correspondence

In December the North Carolina assembly created its first Committee of Correspondence, consisting of John Harvey, Robert Howe, Richard Caswell, Edward Vail, John Ashe, Joseph Hewes, and Samuel Johnston. This body was authorized "to obtain early information of any acts of the British government in regard to the colonies, and to correspond with committees of other colonies as to their plans of resistance." The committee's first action was the issuance of a statement declaring that the inhabitants of all the colonies "ought to consider themselves interested in the cause of the town of Boston as the cause of America in general"; that they would "concur with and cooperate in such measures as may be concerted and agreed on by their sister colonies" . . . and that in order to promote "conformity and unanimity in the councils of America . . . a continental congress was absolutely necessary."

The committees of correspondence in all the colonies spread radical propaganda, combated conservative control, and revealed the value of cooperation. John Fiske said that this system "was nothing less than the beginning of the American Union. . . . It only remained for the various intercolonial committees to assemble together, and there would be a congress speaking in the name of the Continent."

The Tea Act of 1773 and the Boston Tea Party

The events of late 1773 and early 1774 accelerated the revolutionary movement. The decision of the Lord North ministry to come to the aid of the East India Company by passage of the Tea Act in 1773, giving that company a monopoly of the tea trade in the colonies, precipitated several "tea parties." The most dramatic of these was at Boston on the night of December 16, 1773, when £15,000 worth of tea belonging to the East India Company was dumped into the sea by citizens of Boston, disguised as Indians. In other ports, notably New York and Philadelphia, there were mass meetings protesting the proposed sale of English tea and the "tea ships" were allowed to return to England without landing their cargoes. In Charleston, South Carolina, the tea was seized by the collector of the port and was stored in local vaults, where three years later it was sold at public auction, the proceeds being used to help the Revolutionary government.

Carolina had its own "tea party," but of a different nature. On October 25, 1774, fifty-one women from at least five counties, and led by Mrs. Penelope Barker (wife of Thomas Barker, North Carolina's colonial agent), met at the home of Mrs. Elizabeth King and agreed "to do everything, as far as in us lies, to testify our sincere adherence to [whatever] . . . appears to affect the peace and happiness of our country." The "Edenton Tea Party" has been called the "earliest known instance of political activity on the part of women in the American colonies."

The deliberate destruction of private property at Boston led Parliament to pass the Boston Port Bill and the other so-called Coercive Acts of 1774. As soon as the news reached Boston that the port was to be closed on June 1, the city's Committee of Correspondence immediately inquired of other colonies whether they would consider Boston as "suffering in the common cause," suggesting at the same time that the colonies unite in a nonimportation, nonexportation agreement. The replies of the colonies were almost instantaneous. North Carolinians took the position that the "cause of Boston is the cause of all" and sent the sloop *Penelope* with 2,096 bushels of corn, 22 barrels of flour, and 17 barrels of pork to Salem, Massachusetts, which was still open to trade.

The Call for a Continental Congress

About this time, May, 1774, a town meeting in Providence and the committees of correspondence in New York and Philadelphia suggested a general congress of the colonies to bring about united action in the emergency. The Virginia House of Burgesses, meeting informally and unofficially on May 27, sent a letter to all the colonies asking for a congress "to deliberate on those general measures which the united interests of America may from time to time require." But it was the Massachusetts legislature, on June 17, which issued the formal call for a congress, when it resolved "that a meeting of Committees from the several Colonies on this Continent is highly expedient and necessary," and suggested Philadelphia as the place and September 1 as the time.

When Governor Josiah Martin—who had succeeded William Tryon in 1771—heard about this proposed meeting, he indignantly refused to summon the legislature in time to elect delegates to the Philadelphia congress. This aroused the wrath of Speaker Harvey, who said, "In that case the people will hold a convention independent of the Governor." Some of the leaders held conferences to discuss the proper means of calling such an extralegal meeting, and at a mass meeting in Wilmington on July 21 Cornelius Harnett, William Hooper, Edward Buncombe, and others issued a statement declaring it "highly expedient that a provincial congress independent of the governor" be called, and invited delegates to meet at New Bern on August 25. Many local meetings were held and thirty of the thirty-six counties and four of the six borough towns elected a total of seventy-one delegates.

North Carolina's First Provincial Congress

The Congress assembled on the appointed day and elected Harvey, who had been Speaker of the lower house of the General Assembly five times, as moderator. The body remained in session for only three days, but during that time "it fully launched North Carolina into the revolutionary movement." It adopted a resolution that criticized the acts and policies of the British ministry, though professing loyalty to George III; it declared that "any act of Parliament imposing a tax is illegal and unconstitutional. That our Provincial Assemblies . . . solely and exclusively possess that right." It expressed sympathy for the inhabitants of Massachusetts, who had "distinguished themselves in a manly support of the rights of America in general" and said "that the cause in which they suffer is the Cause of every honest American"; it endorsed the idea of a general congress and pledged North Carolina to support its actions; it adopted a nonimportation and nonexportation agreement; it elected William Hooper, Richard Caswell, and Joseph Hewes as delegates to this congress; and it authorized Harvey to call another provincial congress when he deemed it necessary.

The First Provincial Congress of North Carolina was a significant meeting. It gave a practical demonstration of self-government, originating in the people. It tended to give cohesion and unity to the Whigs. And it was an example of intercolonial cooperation by the people's chosen deputies, in defiance of royal authority.

The First Continental Congress, 1774

The work of the First Continental Congress, which met in Philadelphia, September 8—October 26, 1774, is well known and may be briefly summarized. The purpose of this gathering was to make a clear statement of colonial rights, to put economic pressure on Parliament, and to develop a stronger colonial union. The congress pledged the support of the twelve continental colonies represented (Georgia had no delegates present) to Massachusetts; it rejected the proposed Galloway Plan of Union, a proposal quite similar to the Albany Plan of Union of 1754; it drew up a Declaration of Rights and Grievances, a Petition to the King, and Addresses to the People of Great Britain and also to those of British America. More significant was the adoption of the Continental Association, a complete nonimportation, nonexportation, nonconsumption agreement, which would be enforced by a system of "Committees of Safety" in each colony. The effects of this economic boycott were soon apparent. Trade between England and the colonies dropped about 97 percent within a year, and the imports from Britain to the Carolinas fell from £378,116 in 1774 to £6,245 in 1775.

The Continental Congress completed the union of the colonies, established it on a permanent basis, and used the significant term "The United Colonies." It launched something of a political and economic revolution which soon led to the overthrow of royal governments in most provinces. And the Continental Association was tantamount to an economic declaration of war on the mother country.

North Carolina's Second Provincial Congress

Governor Martin tried to stem the tide of revolution in North Carolina. He summoned the assembly to meet at New Bern on April 4. Meantime Harvey had issued a call for the Second Provincial Congress to meet at the same place on April 3, the purpose of the meeting being "to act in union with our neighboring colonies" and to elect delegates to the Second Continental Congress.

The composition of the two bodies that assembled at New Bern was almost identical. Harvey was elected Speaker of the assembly and moderator of the Congress. Every one of the fifty-two members of the assembly, except one who later became a Tory, was a member of the Provincial Congress of sixty-seven members. The congress met at 9 A.M. and the assembly an hour later. Governor Martin denounced both bodies, and both groups denounced Martin. In an address to the assembly he urged resistance to "the monster, sedition, which has dared to raise his impious head in America." He declared that the congress was an insult to the assembly and called on the people to repudiate it. He wrote the Earl of Dartmouth, Secretary of State for the Colonies, that ten counties had sent no delegates (only nine had not); that in many others the committees arrogated the choice of delegates to themselves; and that in the remainder they were chosen by not one-twentieth of the people. He insisted that "the inhabitants of the western counties who were for the most part concerned in the late insurrection" were especially likely to remain loyal.

The Second Provincial Congress adopted resolutions stating the right of the people to hold meetings and to petition the king for redress of grievances; it approved the Continental Association and urged all people to support it; it reelected Hooper, Caswell, and Hewes to the Continental Congress, and it authorized the ailing Harvey to call another congress when necessary, or Samuel Johnston to do so in case of Harvey's death. In line with the recommendations of the Continental Congress, it endorsed the idea of safety committees and authorized the creation of one committee for each county, one for each town, one for each of the six military districts, and a council of safety for the whole province.

North Carolina's Last Royal Assembly

The assembly accomplished very little. It approved the Continental Association and thus made it official. It endorsed the actions of the Continental Congress and approved the reelection of the North Carolina delegates. Governor Martin, becoming angrier all the while, dissolved the assembly on April 8, after a fruitless session of four days. This was the last royal assembly that ever met in North Carolina.

Martin reported to the Earl of Dartmouth that the authority of the royal government "is here as absolutely prostrate as impotent, and nothing but the shadow of it is left." Unless "effectual measures" were taken, the governor said, "there will not long remain a trace of Britain's dominions over these colonies." Martin declared that his own situation was "most despicable and mortifying." "I daily see indignantly the Sacred Majesty of my Royal Master insulted," he said, "the Rights of His Crown denied and violated, His government set at naught, and trampled upon, his servants of highest dignity reviled, traduced, abused, the Rights of His Subjects destroyed by the most arbitrary usurpations, and the whole Constitution unhinged and prostrate, and I live alas ingloriously only to deplore it."

The "Shot Heard Round the World"

By the spring of 1775 the opponents of reconciliation were in control both in England and in America, and each was determined not to compromise. Radicals controlled public opinion and dominated the committees of correspondence and safety committees in all the colonies. Only a slight incident was needed to turn rebellious opposition into open warfare. That incident occurred in Massachusetts on April 19, 1775, when General Gage's attempt to seize military stores the Whigs had gathered led to the battles of Lexington and Concord—the "shot heard round the world." War had come; royal government had collapsed, and there was urgent necessity for some agencies to enforce the measures of the Provincial Congress and the resolutions of the Continental Congress. Safety committees seemed to afford the best solution for this problem, especially at the local level.

Safety Committees and Their Work

In 1774 and 1775 eighteen counties and four towns set up safety committees, whose members were usually chosen by mass meetings. These committees, which Martin denounced as "motley mobs" and "promoters of sedition," were active in spreading Whig propaganda, in making military preparations, and in enforcing the Continental Association. The Wilmington–New Hanover committee regulated trade by seizing British cargoes, fixing the price of imported goods, urging all merchants not to sell or export gunpowder, and calling on all householders in Wilmington to "sign the association." The Halifax County committee resolved to have no more dealings with a certain loyalist merchant; in Edenton the property of a loyalist was seized; in Pitt County the price of salt was set; and the Rowan County committee regulated all prices. The Tryon County committee referred to "the unprecedented, barbarous and bloody actions committed by British troops on our American Brethren near Boston on April 19."

The "Mecklenburg Declaration of Independence"

The most significant, as well as the most controversial, action of any safety committee, was that of Mecklenburg County in May, 1775. According to a statement written from memory by John McKnitt Alexander in 1800 (because his minutes of the meeting had been burned), a meeting was held in Charlotte on May 20, 1775, which declared the citizens of that county "a free and independent people." According to a June, 1775, newspaper account, a meeting was held in Charlotte on May 31 at which a set of Resolves was adopted declaring that all commissions granted by the king in the colonies were "null and void" and calling upon the people of Mecklenburg to meet and elect military officers who should hold their powers "independent of Great Britain." Any person accepting office from the crown was declared to be "an enemy to his country." Governor Martin sent a newspaper account of the Resolves to England and wrote that they "surpass all the horrid and treasonable publications that the inflammatory spirits of this Continent have yet produced." Without a doubt, the spirit of independence was strong in Mecklenburg. The Convention of 1861 placed the date May 20, 1775, on the state flag in honor of the "Mecklenburg Declaration of Independence."

Governor Martin Flees

Governor Martin issued a proclamation against the "depredations" of the various safety committees, but to no avail. The governor was becoming angrier all the while. As early as March, 1775, he had written to

General Gage, commanding officer of all British forces in North America, for arms and ammunition, but his letter had been intercepted by the Whigs. Meanwhile he planted the half dozen cannon he had before the palace, but these were carried off, as he said, by a "mob stimulated with liquor." Rumors were flying of plans of the New Bern Committee to seize the palace. Martin, fearful for the safety of his family, had already sent his wife to New York. Finally, on the night of May 24, the governor spiked the palace cannon that had not been carried off, hid the ammunition, and fled to Fort Johnston on the Cape Fear, arriving there on June 2. When he heard reports that the Wilmington and New Hanover committees were planning to attack the fort and seize him, he took refuge in the British ship, the *Cruizer,* lying offshore. He had fled to safety in the nick of time, because on July 18 the militia and minutemen of this region, led by Robert Howe, John Ashe, and Cornelius Harnett, burned the fort or, as Martin put it, they "wantonly in the dead hour of night set on fire and reduced to ashes the houses and buildings within the Fort." The governor insisted that all the troubles were caused by "evil, pernicious and traiterous councils and leaders of seditious committees" and said he felt sorry for the "innocent, misguided and deluded people," whom he considered "the blind instruments of their atrocious leaders."

The Need for Provisional Government

The flight of Governor Martin, the downfall of royal authority in North Carolina, and the outbreak of war with the mother country in April 1775, made it imperative for North Carolina to establish some form of provisional government. On June 19 the colony's delegates in the Continental Congress sent an address to the county and town committees, urging them to support the revolutionary movement and declaring that the "fate of Boston was the common fate of all." The address continued: "North Carolina alone remains an inactive Spectator of this general defensive Armament. Supine and careless, she seems to forget even the Duty she owes to her own local Circumstances and Situation. . . . Do you ask why then you are exempted from the Penalties of the Bill restraining Trade? The Reason is obvious—Britain cannot keep up its Naval Force without you; you supply the very sinews of her strength. Restrain your Naval Stores and all the Powers of Europe can scarce supply her; restrain them and you strengthen the hands of America in the glorious contention for her liberty. . . . We conjure you by the Ties of Religion Virtue and Love of your Country to follow the Example of your sister Colonies and to form yourselves into a Militia. . . . Study the Art of Military with the utmost attention, view it as the Science upon which your future security depends. . . . Carefully preserve your small quantity of gunpowder. . . . Reserve what Ammunition you have as a sacred Deposit. . . . In one word fellow subjects the Crisis of America is not at a great distance."

On July 5 Lord Dartmouth wrote to Governor Martin saying, "Almost every other Colony has catched the flame, and a spirit of Rebellion has gone forth, that menaces the subversion of the Constitution," and he urged the governor to make "vigorous efforts to reduce his Rebellious Subjects to obedience."

The General Assembly was due to meet at New Bern on July 12, but Martin prorogued this body until September 12; later he decided not to call it at all. Harvey had died in May, and Samuel Johnston, who had been authorized to call another congress, was slow to act. Meantime the people were becoming alarmed and restive. Many petitions were sent to Johnston urging him to call the congress. The Wilmington Safety Committee wrote him on July 13: "Our situation here is truly alarming, the Governor collecting men, provisions, warlike stores of every kind, spiriting up the back counties, and perhaps the Slaves, finally strengthening the fort with new works, in such a manner as may make the Capture of it extremely difficult. In this Situation, Sir, our people are Continually clamoring for a provincial Convention. They hope every thing from its Immediate Session, fear every thing from its delay."

Revolutionary Sentiment in North Carolina

In April, 1775, Parliament, in order to punish the colonies for the "disorders that prevailed" in them, passed an act cutting off their trade with Great Britain and the West Indies, declaring that it was "highly unfit that they should enjoy the same privileges and advantages of trade that his Majesty's faithful and obedient subjects enjoyed." The fact that North Carolina was excluded from this act caused apprehension and even indignation in the colony. On July 20, the day this "restraining act" was to take effect, the Wilmington Safety Committee denounced it as "a base and mean artifice, to seduce them into a desertion of the common cause of America," and declared that North Carolina would not accept "advantages insidiously thrown out" by the law, but would continue to adhere strictly to the plans of the Continental Congress. On another occasion this committee declared the act to be "low, base and flagitous, a wicked attempt to enslave America," and denounced the whole ministry as "profligate and abandoned."

Doubtless many North Carolinians shared these views. Perhaps many agreed with the sentiments expressed in a letter of July 31 from "a gentleman in North Carolina and one of the Delegates of the Congress" to an Edinburgh merchant: "Every American, to a man, is determined to die or be free. We are convinced that nothing can restore peace to this unhappy country, and render the liberties of yours secure, but a total change of the present Ministry, who are considered in this Country as enemies to the freedom of the human race, like so many Master devils in the infernal regions, sending out their servant furies, to torment wherever they choose their infernal vengeance should. . . . We do not want to be independant; we want no revolution, unless a change of Ministry and measures would be deemed such. We are loyal subjects to our present most gracious Sovereign in support of whose crown and dignity we would sacrifice our lives, and willingly launch out every shilling of our property, he only defending our liberties. This Country, without some step is taken, and that soon, will be inevitably lost to the Mother Country. We say again, for the love of Heaven, for the love of liberty, the interest of posterity, we conjure you to exert yourselves."

Governor Martin's "Fiery Proclamation"

Governor Martin was cognizant of the rapid growth of revolutionary sentiment in the colony, which he attributed largely to the propaganda of the safety committees. On August 8 he issued his "Fiery Proclamation," in which he denounced all of these committees, especially the one at Wilmington, for circulating "the basest and most scandalous Seditious and inflammatory falsehoods," calculated to "mislead the people" and turn them against His Majesty. He deplored the "malice and falsehood of these unprincipled censors" and their "evil, pernicious and traiterous Councils and influence," although "my immediate vengeance [is] restrained by pity for the innocent, misguided and deluded people whom I consider as the blind instruments of their atrocious leaders." He went on to say that he had seen "a most infamous publication in the *Cape Fear Mercury* importing to be resolves of a set of people stiling themselves a Committee for the County of Mecklenburg most traiterously declaring the dissolution of the Laws Government and Constitution of this country and setting up a a system of rule and regulation repugnant to the Laws and subversive of His Majesty's Government." He thought the majority of the people in North Carolina were still loyal to England, but he feared that "the assembling Convention at Hillsborough will bring the Affairs of this Country to a Crisis which will make it necessary for every man to assert his principles."

The Hillsborough Provincial Congress

The convention mentioned by Martin assembled at Hillsborough on August 21, with 184 delegates present out of the 207 who were elected, representing every county and town. Samuel Johnston, who had called the meeting, was chosen "president." Before proceeding to business, every member signed a "test oath," professing allegiance to the crown, but declaring that "neither Parliament, nor any Member or Constituent Branch thereof," had a right to impose taxes on the colonies. A committee of secrecy was appointed to procure arms and ammunition and to report to the congress what sums would be necessary to purchase these. Two committees were appointed, whose work was designed to checkmate the propaganda efforts of Governor Martin. One of these was to confer with Scottish Highlanders who had recently migrated to North Carolina, "to express to them the Nature of our unhappy controversy and to advise and urge them to unite," while the other was to confer with the Regulators to try to win their support for the Whig cause.

On August 25 the congress drafted a reply to Governor Martin's "Fiery Proclamation," resolving "that the said Paper in a false, Scandalous, Scurrilous, malicious and sedicious Libel, tending to disunite the good people of this province, and to stir up Tumults and Insurrections, dangerous to the peace of His Majesty's Government, and the safety of the Inhabitants, and highly injurious to the Characters of several Gentlemen of acknowledged Virtue and Loyalty; and further, that the said paper be burnt by the common Hangman."

The congress also prepared an address to the people of North Carolina and another to the "inhabitants of the British Empire." The body resolved that, since Martin had "deserted" the colony, it was necessary to establish a temporary government, and for that purpose a committee of forty-five members was chosen for the "regulation of the Internal Peace, Order and Safety of this Province." A resolution was adopted saying that all people in the colony "are bound by the Acts and resolutions of the Continental and Provincial Congresses, because in both they are freely represented by persons chosen by themselves."

Provisional Government in North Carolina

The Congress then proceeded to establish what Allan Nevins has called "the most elaborate provisional government on the continent." Provision was made for a provincial congress, with five members from each county and one from each of the six borough towns, to be chosen by the freeholders of their respective units. There was to be a provincial council, consisting of thirteen members, one "at large" elected by the provincial congress, and two from each of the six military districts, elected by the qualified voters. The council was to be the chief executive and administrative authority, and in a sense would replace the royal governor and council. There were to be safety committees in each military district as well as in each county and town, chosen annually by popular vote.

Preparations for War

The chief concern of the Hillsborough Congress was preparations for war. "Our principal debates," wrote Johnston before the meeting convened, "will be about raising troops." The Congress issued what might be termed a declaration of war: "Resolved, that hostilities being actually commenced in the Massachusetts Bay by the British Troops under the Command of General Gage. . . . And whereas His Excellency Governor Martin, hath taken a very active and instrumental share in opposition to the means which have been adopted by this and the other United Colonies for their common safety as well to disunite this from the rest as to weaken the Efforts of the Inhabitants of North Carolina to protect their Lives, Liberties and Properties against any force which may be exerted to injure them . . . defending this Colony, preserving it in safety against all attempts to carry the said Acts into Execution by Force of Arms, this Colony be immediately put into a state of defence."

Two regiments were authorized for the Continental Line, each regiment to have five hundred men, and to be commanded by Colonel James Moore of New Hanover County and Colonel Robert Howe of Brunswick. Six battalions of "minutemen," of five hundred men each, were also authorized, one from each of the six military districts, and Edward Vail of Edenton, Nicholas Long of Halifax, Thomas Wade of Salisbury, James Thackston of Hillsborough, Richard Caswell of New Bern, and Alexander Lillington of Wilmington were appointed field officers of these regiments. Each battalion was to have ten companies of fifty men each. The fifteen least populous counties were to raise one company each; fifteen other counties, two companies each; while Halifax, Edgecombe, Dobbs, Orange, and Granville were to supply three companies each. It was also recommended that all inhabitants procure bayonets for their guns "as soon as possible, and be otherwise provided to turn at a minute's warning." A bounty of twenty-five shillings was allowed every private soldier and noncommissioned officer to purchase a uniform, consisting of a "hunting Shirt, Leggins, or Splater dashes and Black Garters, which shall be the Uniform; and that the Manual exercise for the said Minute Men be that recommended by His Majesty in 1764." The minutemen were to train successively for fourteen days. Guns were scarce and an allowance was made at the rate of ten shillings per annum "for a good smooth bore or Musket, and twenty shillings for a Rifle, to the owners for the use of their Guns." The pay for men ranged from fourteen shillings a day for colonels to one shilling ten pence for privates.

The congress also adopted financial measures to attempt to meet the emergency. It ordered the immediate collection of all back taxes and it authorized the issuance of 125,000 dollars in "bills of Credit," in denominations ranging from one-fourth of a dollar to ten dollars. The form of the paper currency reflected more optimism than realism, as the following shows: "This Bill entitles the Bearer to receive . . . Spanish milled dollars or the value thereof in Gold and Silver according to the Resolution of the provincial Congress held at Hillsborough the 21st day of August 1775." To redeem these bills a poll tax of two shillings was levied every year on each taxable, to commence in 1777 and to continue for nine years unless the "money should be sooner sunk." Social ostracism was threatened and severe penalties were imposed for refusal to accept the bills or for counterfeiting them.

Party Divisions: Whigs versus Tories

North Carolina was not prepared for war, and public opinion was sharply divided. The thought of fighting the mother country was abhorrent to many, even to some who had a thorough distaste for British laws and policies. There were three groups, or parties, in the province. First, Whigs, probably embracing half the people, who were willing to fight England for a "redress of grievances" and even for independence, if necessary. Most of the small farmers and artisans belonged to this group, but the Whigs also included many large landholders and were far from being "a rabble in arms." Second, there were the loyalists, commonly called Tories, but also known as King's Men, Royalists, and occasionally referred to as "these dam rascals." This group supported the idea of peaceful opposition to British policies and opposed war at all cost. It included many of the wealthy merchants, most of the old official class, some of the wealthy planters and professional men, and those conservatives who dreaded despotism, on the one hand, and feared anarchy on the other. This party likewise included a large number of Scottish Highlanders and some of the Regulators, who were still aggrieved over their defeat at Alamance in 1771 by the eastern militia. A third group, much smaller than either of the other two, might be classified as "neutrals," and included Moravians, Quakers, and a large number of the German settlers in the Piedmont counties.

In the early stages of the war, the two major parties seemed to be about evenly divided, with the Whigs having a slight majority. They certainly controlled the governmental machinery at all levels, and from this vantage point, tried to win support of the Tories. On the other hand, Governor Martin and the Tory leaders tried to win converts to their side—by offers of rewards and threats of reprisals. The Whig policy of conciliation proved to be ineffective, and by 1777 the Whig-dominated legislature adopted a strict policy of coercion, which became more severe as the war progressed and which eventually led to the confiscation of many estates and to a sizable migration from the state, especially among Highlanders and Regulators.

Military Aid to South Carolina and Virginia

It was about a month before news of the Battle of Lexington and other military engagements in Massachusetts reached North Carolina. It was another six months before armed conflict began in the southern colonies. But North Carolina was making military preparations, and it was watching the Tories and keeping an eye on the Cherokee Indians, who were becoming restive and giving the Whigs cause for worrry.

In November, 1775, Virginia asked North Carolina for military assistance against the British in the Norfolk area, where Governor Lord Dunmore was burning houses, ravaging plantations, and carrying off slaves. Dunmore seized

Norfolk and issued a proclamation emancipating slaves if they would join the British forces. This proclamation, as well as the governor's construction of a fort on the road leading from Norfolk south, alarmed North Carolina Whigs, and the regiments of Colonels Howe, Long, and Sumner were ordered to Virginia. Long's regiment shared in the American victory at Great Bridge on December 14. Howe's men reached Virginia later and played a significant role in driving the British from Norfolk.

When the South Carolina Whigs found themselves unable to suppress the "Scovellites," a group of South Carolinians who had become ardent Tories, they called on North Carolina for aid. Some seven hundred North Carolinians, led by Colonels Griffith Rutherford, Thomas Polk, Thomas Neel, and Lieutenant Colonel Alexander Martin joined the forces of General Richardson of South Carolina and on December 22 crushed the Scovellites—or, as Governor Martin said, "disarmed the loyal people"—in what has been called the Snow Campaign, because of the inclement weather at the time of the battle.

The War Begins in North Carolina

Meantime Governor Martin had worked out a grandiose scheme for the British conquest of North Carolina. In a letter to Lord Dartmouth, Secretary of State for the Colonies, June 30, 1775, he outlined his plan for the restoration of the entire South to royal control. First, he would get arms and ammunition from General Gage, to arm at least three thousand Highlanders (he claimed he could raise twenty thousand fighting men), and he wrote the general asking him for ten thousand stand of arms, six brass six-pounders, and other military supplies; he also asked for the restoration of his commission as lieutenant colonel, which he had sold in 1769 because of ill health—a request which Dartmouth flatly refused to grant. Second, he sent Alexander Schaw, brother of the "Scotch Lady of Quality," to London to present the scheme to Dartmouth. Dartmouth must have thought well of the idea, because it was discussed and approved by the Privy Council.

Martin's plan called for: (1) a North Carolina army of three thousand Highlanders, three thousand Regulators, and three thousand other Tories; (2) Lord Charles Cornwallis with seven regiments of British regulars; (3) Sir Peter Parker with a powerful fleet of fifty-four ships; and (4) Sir Henry Clinton with two thousand British soldiers from Boston. All these forces were to be concentrated at Brunswick by February 15, 1776. The British ministry approved the plan and orders were sent to the several commanders.

On January 10 Martin issued a proclamation calling upon all loyal subjects to "unite and suppress the rebellion" in the province. A place of rendezvous was to be selected and troops were to march in a body to Brunswick, to arrive there not later than February 15.

In July General Gage had ordered Lieutenant Colonel Donald McDonald and Captain Alexander McLeod to North Carolina to recruit men for a battalion of the Royal Highland Emigrant Regiment. Governor Martin appointed McDonald as brigadier general of the militia and McLeod as lieutenant colonel; and the British government promised to all Highlanders who joined the service of the crown two hundred acres of land, remission of arrears in quitrents, and twenty years' tax exemption. These attractive offers and Martin's untiring labors resulted in a large number of recruits. Most of the Highlanders who "turned Tory" came from those who had arrived in the colony since 1770 and whom Martin had forced to swear "their readiness to lay down their lives in defence of His Majesty's government" before he would grant them lands. Johnston wrote Joseph Hewes, March 10, 1776, that with the exception of the Tory leaders, "not one owned property worth £10."

North Carolina Whig leaders, aware of Martin's plan for a British invasion and disturbed by the recruiting of soldiers and by reports of Tory activity in various places, began to mobilize their forces. Two regiments of the Continental Line, under the command of Colonel James Moore and Colonel Robert Howe, were already being organized. Local minutemen and militia units were hastily formed in many counties. The Wilmington patriots threw up breastworks, declared martial law, seized some twenty "professed Tories," and sent women and children to safety outside the town. The New Bern Safety Committee ordered out the district's militia and minutemen, led by Colonel Richard Caswell, equipped with artillery and authorized to buy necessary provisions and wagons along the line of march. The military units of Dobbs, Johnston, Pitt, and Craven counties were instructed to join Caswell.

The Battle of Moore's Creek Bridge

About the middle of February some sixteen hundred Highlanders met at their rendezvous at Cross Creek, where, under the leadership of General Donald McDonald, they began their march toward Wilmington. Colonel James Moore, who directed the strategy of all the Whig forces, was determined to keep the enemy from reaching Wilmington. A secondary objective was to take possession of Cross Creek, the Tory place of rendezvous. To achieve these objectives, Moore marched his own forces to Elizabeth Town; Caswell was sent to take possession of Corbett's Ferry on Black River; Colonels James Martin and James Thackston, to occupy Cross Creek; while Colonels Alexander Lillington and James Ashe were to reinforce Caswell, and if a junction could not be effected, they were to secure Moore's Creek Bridge, some eighteen miles above Wilmington, and the place where the Tory forces had to cross on their way to that town.

By a series of skillful maneuvers, directed by Moore and executed by his subordinates, the bulk of the Whig forces, numbering about eleven hundred under the immediate leadership of Caswell, reached Moore's Creek Bridge (the creek flows into Black River about ten miles above the Black's confluence with the Cape Fear), on the evening of February 26. The Highlanders, now numbering about sixteen hundred after marching all night through swamps and dense underbrush, reached the bridge about sunrise on February 27 and immediately launched an attack. The Whigs had removed much of the flooring of the bridge and had greased the log sleepers with soft soap and tallow. This made the crossing extremely difficult and added to confusion in the Tory ranks. Falling into the neatly set trap of Caswell and Lillington, the Highlanders were met by a whining storm of swan-shot and bullets. For three minutes they faced the devastating fire and attemped to cross the bridge; then, leaving their commander, McLeod, dead, the survivors hastily left the scene of carnage. The Whigs lost only one killed and one wounded; the Tories had about fifty killed and wounded. Moore reached the scene soon after the battle was over, pursued the Tories, and captured 350 guns, 1,500 rifles, 150 swords and dirks, 13 wagons, £15,000 in gold, 850 soldiers and several officers, including General McDonald.

This overwhelming Whig victory, which has been called the "Lexington and Concord of the South," was applauded throughout the colonies. Ezra Stiles, president of Yale, recorded in his diary: "The Colonels *Moore, Martin, Caswell, Polk, Thackston, Lillington & Long,* have great Merit; any one of these Gent. in this Country would be an over match for a *Howe, Burgoyne,* or a *Clinton.* Their knowledge of the Country and necessary Modes of Attack would frustrate any Attempt fallen upon by the Characters last mentioned. The Whole Province in general considers Regulars in the Woods an easy Conquest."

The British press either ignored or minimized the significance of the battle. The *Gentleman's Magazine* said it was of little consequence as "they only reduced a body of their own, supported by no one company of regular troops." The *Annual Register* took a more realistic view when it declared that the North Carolina Whigs "had encountered Europeans (who were supposed to hold them in the most sovereign contempt, both as men and soldiers) and had defeated them with an inferior force."

Who deserves credit for the Moore's Creek victory? Was Lillington or Caswell in command? The evidence clearly indicates that Caswell was the commanding officer, but the Lillington champions stated their views in the well-known poetic lines:

> Moore's Creek field, the bloody story,
> Where Lillington fought for Caswell's glory.

The real hero of the whole campaign was James Moore, although he did not take part in the actual battle. It was Moore who maneuvered the Whig forces so that he compelled the Tories to give battle on ground of his own choosing.

Clinton, Cornwallis, and Parker with a powerful force arrived in North Carolina in May, but found nobody to welcome them but a beaten and dispirited governor. They sailed away to Charleston to beat in vain against the log walls of Fort Moultrie. The tide of war had turned away from North Carolina, and during the next four years the state was free from invasion from without and insurrection from within.

Chapter 13

TRANSITION FROM COLONY TO STATEHOOD

The Problem of Independence

Before 1776 most Whig leaders in North Carolina—and in all the colonies—denied that they were aiming at independence and constantly expressed loyalty to "the best of Kings" Yet when Royal Governor Josiah Martin dissolved the assembly on April 8, 1774, he wrote Lord Dartmouth, Secretary of State for the Colonies, "Government is here as absolutely prostrate as impotent, and nothing but the shadow of it is left." Two weeks later William Hooper privately declared that the colonies were "striding fast to independence," and on September 23 Samuel Johnston referred to the controversy with England as a "dispute between different countries" and predicted a complete separation unless the mother country relented. Perhaps a few North Carolina Whigs agreed with the sentiments of an anonymous writer that the only way "to escape the threatened ruin" was by "declaring an immediate independency." But a careful scrutiny of contemporary records reveals that these views were not held by the rank and file of people, or even by their leaders, in either North Carolina or the colonies in general.

North Carolinians, like other colonials, seemed proud of their membership in the British Empire. The Provincial Congress at New Bern in 1774 voted its intention "to maintain and defend the succession of the House of Hanover as by law established" and avowed its "inviolable and unshaken fidelity" to George III. The real objective of the Whig leaders was the preservation of the "rights of Englishmen" within the empire, not separation from it. Their quarrel after 1763 was with Parliament, not with the king, and their opposition to Parliament, expressed in scores of documents, always concluded with a declaration of loyalty to the crown.

The Compact Theory

Their position was based on the "compact theory." They owed obedience to the king; the king owed protection to his subjects. This was stated in many resolutions, nowhere better than in the Granville County Resolves of 1774, which said that by "civil compact subsisting between our king and his people, allegiance is the right of the first magistrate, and protection the right of the people." Hence a violation of the compact by either would release the other. North Carolina Whig leaders placed responsibility for the controversy with the mother country on Parliament and repeatedly petitioned the king for protection against parliamentary tyranny. This was the same position taken by the Continental Congress in its resolutions in 1774—and even in 1775 after hostilities had begun—and it was a view generally accepted by most colonials up to the time of the Declaration of Independence in 1776.

Talk of Reconciliation with England

There was much talk of "reconciliation," in both England and America before 1776, and a "peace mission" was sent to America as late as 1778. But military events in 1775 and 1776 caused a shift in colonial opinion. The Battles of Lexington, Concord, and Bunker Hill in New England, in the spring of 1775, the fighting in Virginia in early winter, the Snow Campaign in South Carolina early the next year, and finally the Battle of Moore's Creek Bridge, February 27, 1776, gave momentum to the movement for separation from the empire. Moreover, the attitude of George III seemed to close the door to reconciliation. His refusal to receive colonial petitions and his rejection of the "Olive Branch" proposal of the Continental Congress convinced Whig leaders that the king supported the parliamentary policy of American taxation. His address opening Parliament in February, 1775, took the view that the colonies were "in rebellion," and he called for troops to enforce obedience. His proclamation of October, 1775, put the colonies "out of his protection." The Whigs now maintained that the king's acts were no longer binding on them, and in such resolutions as the Mecklenburg Resolves of May 31, 1775, all commissions theretofore issued by the crown were declared "null and void."

More and more the king's ideas and acts were denounced, and there was increasing advocacy of separation from England, "unless grievances were redressed." These revolutionary ideas were first expressed in private letters; then in newspapers and local mass meetings; and finally in official resolutions of the Provincial Congress. Repeatedly the king was charged with violating the "charter rights" of the colonies, and hence they were no longer bound to support the king or Parliament. William Hooper, writing from the Continental Congress at Philadelphia, declared "it would be Toryism to hint the possibility of future reconciliation." John Penn, who had just come from the Continental Congress wrote: "The recent events in the colony have wholly changed the temper and disposition of the inhabitants that are friends of liberty; all regard or fondness for the king and nation of Britain is gone. A total separation is what they want. Independence is the word most used. They ask if it is possible that any colony after what has passed can wish for reconciliation. The convention have tried to get the opinion of the people at large. I am told that in many counties there was not one dissenting voice."

The Fourth Provincial Congress and the Halifax Resolves

When the Fourth Provincial Congress assembled at Halifax, April 4, 1776, all the delegates favored independence. Samuel Johnston, writing from that town the next day, declared "All our people here are up for independence," and Robert Howe said, "Independence seems to be the word. I know not one dissenting voice." On April 8 a committee of seven, headed by Cornelius Harnett, was appointed "to take into consideration the usurpations and violences attempted and committed by the King and Parliament of Great Britain against America, and the further measures to be taken for frustrating the same, and for the better defence of this Province." On April 12 this committee submitted a report that was adopted unanimously by the 83 delegates present of the 148 who had been elected from thirty-four counties and eight towns. The last paragraph of the famous Halifax Resolves reads: "Resolved, That the delegates for this Colony in the Continental Congress be impowered to concur with the delegates of the other Colonies in declaring Independency, and forming foreign alliances, reserving to this Colony the sole and exclusive right of forming a Constitution and laws for this Colony, and of appointing delegates from time to time (under the direction of a general representation thereof), to meet the delegates of the other Colonies for such purposes as shall be hereafter pointed out."

This was the first official *state* action for independence, and it was not a declaration for North Carolina alone, but a recommendation to the Continental Congress that independence should be declared by all the colonies, that is, by the Continental Congress as their representative.

A copy of the Halifax Resolves was sent to Joseph Hewes in the congress at Philadelphia. Newspapers in other colonies printed the document and urged their congresses to "follow this laudable example." Elbridge Gerry of Massachusetts considered it a "noble and decisive measure," and John Adams observed that "there is little probability of our ever again coming under the yoke of British regulation of trade."

On May 15 the Virginia Provincial Congress instructed its delegates in the Continental Congress to "propose" independence. On May 27 the North Carolina and Virginia delegates laid their instructions before the congress, and on June 7 Richard Henry Lee moved "that these United Colonies are and of right ought to be free and independent States. . . ." Congress adopted this resolution on July 2, and two days later approved the final draft of the Declaration of Independence written by Thomas Jefferson, with some assistance from John Adams and Benjamin Franklin. Hooper, Hewes, and Penn signed this "immortal document" for North Carolina.

The North Carolina Council of Safety, meeting at Halifax, received news of the national Declaration on July 22 and immediately adopted a resolution declaring that the "good people" of the colonies "were absolved from all Allegiance to the British Crown." It ordered that the safety committees of the counties and towns in North Carolina have "the same to be proclaimed in the most public Manner." Cornelius Harnett first read the Declaration of Independence publicly in the state to a large crowd at Halifax on August 1. Within a few months it was read in every county and town in North Carolina.

The Provincial Congress Decides Not to Adopt a State Constitution

The day after the adoption of the Halifax Resolves the Provincial Congress selected a committee of twenty members to draft "a temporary Civil Constitution." Two days later Hooper and Hewes, who had arrived from Philadelphia, were added to the committee. After many delays this committee, on April 25, reported the "outline" of a constitution, which called for a legislative council of one member from each county to constitute the upper house, and a lower "house of the representatives of the people," to be chosen by the free householders of each county. There was to be an executive council, consisting of a president and six councillors "to be always sitting" and "to do official business of Government." It is noteworthy that this prematurely drafted constitution contained no bill of rights. Five days later the congress voted not to adopt a state constitution, and a committee of nine members was chosen "to form a temporary form of government until the end of the next congress." Meantime, on May 10, the Continental Congress authorized the states to draft constitutions, but the next day the Provincial Congress—obviously before it had received this mandate—voted "That from the end of this present session," the Council of Safety should have "full power and authority to do and execute all acts and things necessary for the defence and protection of the people of this Colony."

The Council of Safety Rules the State

The Provincial Council and the six district committees of safety, which had been none too active for the past year, were abolished and in their stead was substituted a Council of Safety for the whole state. This was a permanent body continuously in session. The county safety committees remained unchanged in structure and powers, though they became less active.

The Council of Safety became the supreme power in the state, "about the only power," as E. W. Sikes has said. Cornelius Harnett, the "Pride of the Cape Fear," its president, was for all practical purposes the governor of the state. The chief work of the council was to procure men, money, and military supplies, but it established a kind of political censorship and exercised centralized governmental authority.

It was generally understood, when the Halifax Congress adjourned on May 15, 1776, that another congress would meet the following November. With the proclamation of the Declaration of Independence, however, and the authorization by the Continental Congress that states draw up constitutions, the Council of Safety, on August 9, ordered an election to be held October 15 for choosing delegates to a Fifth Provincial Congress to meet at Halifax. The voters were asked "to pay the greatest attention" to the election of delegates who were "not only to make Laws for the good Government of, but also to form a Constitution for this State, that this last as it is the Corner Stone of all Law, so it ought to be fixed and Permanent, and that according as it is well or ill Ordered it must tend in the first degree to promote the happiness or Misery of the State."

Conservative and Radical Views on State Government

An exciting and bitter campaign ensued. The Whigs, who had appeared unified in their prosecution of the war, were sharply divided on the nature of the new government. The Conservative Whigs, led by Samuel Johnston, James Iredell, William Hooper, and Archibald Maclaine, wanted few changes from the old royal government. They favored a strong executive, an independent judiciary with life tenure, adequate protection of property rights, and property qualifications for voting and officeholding. Johnston said he had no confidence in any of the proposed forms of government—"that numbers had now started in the race for popularity and were condescending to the usual meanness." He did not think that government could solve the problem of "how to establish a check on the representatives of the people, to prevent their assuming more power than would be consistent with the liberties of the people."

The Radicals, led by Willie Jones, Thomas Person, and Griffith Rutherford, advocated "a simple democracy" in which there would be a strong legislature, a weak executive subordinate to the legislative, and religious freedom with no established church.

In a bitter contest for delegates, accompanied by "Tumult and disorderly Behaviour" and even "fraud and debauchery" at the polls in several counties, 169 delegates were elected, representing thirty-two counties and nine towns. Only Bladen County did not elect delegates. The Conservatives and Radicals won about an even number of seats with the "Moderates" holding the balance of power. Samuel Johnston, who was burned in effigy and defeated at the polls, shortly thereafter wrote, "Everyone who has the least pretensions to be a gentleman is borne down *per ignobile vulgus*—a set of men without reading, experience, or principles to govern them."

State Constitution and Bill of Rights Adopted, 1776

The congress met at Halifax on November 12, 1776, with only 79 of the 169 elected delegates present the first day, though 33 were seated the next day, and 37 others before the session adjourned on December 23. The congress decided that vote should be by "voice," instead of by "Counties and Towns," that is, a majority of members should govern—which was a reversal of policy of the previous congresses. Richard Caswell was the unanimous choice for president. On November 13 a committee of eighteen members was appointed to draw up a "Bill of Rights and Form of a Constitution." It was only the pressure from a few county delegations, notably Orange and Mecklenburg, that compelled the congress to add a bill of rights to its constitution. Thomas Jones of Edenton, spokesman for the committee, though Caswell was its chairman, reported the constitution on December 6 and the bill of rights on December 15. Apparently these two documents were read and discussed paragraph by paragraph, but no record was made of these debates. The Declaration of Rights was adopted on December 17 and the constitution the next day. Both were ordered printed and distributed throughout the state. It is significant that they were not submitted to popular vote. The war was the paramount problem, and there was no time for another bitter political campaign. Other states put their constitutions into effect without submission to the electorate; and, besides, it was not eighteenth-century practice to submit such matters to popular vote.

Sources of Ideas in the Bill of Rights and Constitution

Sikes has said about the constitution: "It can lay claim to originality neither in conception nor expression."

The North Carolina bill of rights, consisting of twenty-five articles, enumerated the rights of the people against any government. It contained statements of rights that the colonials had asserted under English laws but that had been denied by the king and Parliament; it reaffirmed ideas enunciated in the Magna Charta of 1215 and the English Bill of Rights of 1689; it contained statements—some verbatim—from the Maryland and Virginia bills of rights and, above all, it reflected the experiences of North Carolina as a colony.

The political theory of the new constitution, stated in Articles 1, 2, and 4, emphasized popular sovereignty, separation of powers, and three separate branches of government.

The political rights of the people, stated in Articles 6, 16, 17, 18, and 20, guaranteed freedom of elections, freedom from arbitrary taxation, supremacy of civil power over the military, right of assembly, and frequent elections.

The legal rights of the individual, enumerated in Articles 7–11, 13, and 24, stressed the individual's rights in criminal trials, trial only upon indictment, presentation, or impeachment; trial by jury; immunity from excessive bail and "cruel or unusual punishment"; immunity from general search warrants; the right to a speedy trial; and immunity from ex post facto (retroactive) laws.

Personal liberties of the individual, found in Articles 15, 17, and 19, guaranteed freedom of the press, "one of the great Bulwarks of Liberty"; freedom of conscience and religion; and the "right to bear arms for the defence of the State," but standing armies in time of peace were declared "dangerous to Liberty."

The preamble of the constitution, based on the compact theory, gave reasons for revolt against the crown and stated that George III and Parliament had "declared the inhabitants of these States out of the Protection of the British Crown"; "that Continental Congress had declared the colonies independent"; and that "in order to prevent Anarchy and Confusion" it had become necessary to establish a government which was derived from the people.

The Legislative Department

The "Legislative Authority" was vested in a General Assembly, consisting of a senate and house of commons, "both dependent on the people." Members of each house were to be chosen annually by ballot, one senator from each county and two commoners from each county, plus one commoner from each of the six "borough towns." Qualifications for senators were: residence in the county for one year and a freehold of not less than three hundred acres. Senatorial suffrage was granted to all "freemen," white or Negro, who had lived in the state one year and in the county one month, and who possessed a fifty-acre freehold. Qualifications for commoners were the same as for senators, except that only a hundred-acre freehold was required. The privilege of voting for commoners was restricted to freemen of one year's residence, upon payment of "public taxes."

The constitution enumerated in a series of articles all who were barred from holding a seat in the legislature: all receivers of public monies, members of the Council of State, the chief justices, the major executive officials, all regular military officers, and all military contractors.

Each house was to elect its own speaker and other officers, pass on the qualifications and elections of its own members, pass bills into law; and both houses, sitting jointly each year, were to elect the governor, council of state, attorney general, and other executive officials, as well as judges and high-ranking military officers. A quorum in each house was to be a majority of *all* the members.

The Executive

The executive department of the government was to consist of the governor, Council of State, secretary, treasurer, and attorney general—the same general setup as in the colonial period.

The qualifications for the governor were that he should be at least thirty years of age, have five years' residence in the state, and own a freehold "in lands and tenements above the value of one Thousand Pounds." He was to be chosen annually, by joint ballot of the two houses, for a one-year term, and to be eligible for reelection three years in any six successive years. His ordinary executive powers, such as appointments to public office, were to be restricted by the "advice" of the council. He and the other officials were to be paid "adequate salaries."

The seven members of the Council of State were also to be elected by joint ballot of the two houses—and for a one-year term. This body was to have power to "advise the Governor in the execution of his office" and was to be independent of the governor. Members of the council could not be members of either Senate or House of Commons.

Other executive officers to be elected by the assembly were a secretary of state for a three-year term, a treasurer for one year, and an attorney general to serve "during good Behavior."

Judiciary

The Judiciary consisted of "Judges of the Supreme Courts of Law and Equity, Judges of Admiralty, and Attorney General"—all appointed by joint ballot of the General Assembly and commissioned by the governor to hold office during good behavior; justices of the peace, on recommendation by "county representatives in the General Assembly," were appointed and commissioned by the governor to hold office during good behavior.

Local Government

The structure of local government remained much as it had been in the colonial era. The constitution provided for creation by legislative provision of the offices of sheriff, coroner, and constables in each county. Election, tenure, and duties were to be fixed by legislative enactment.

Representation in the Continental Congress

The framers of the constitution, realizing the necessity for continuance of the Continental Congress, provided that the state's delegates to this body be chosen annually by joint ballot of the General Assembly; they were to be eligible for three successive terms and subject to recall by the General Assembly.

Miscellaneous Provisions

The constitution contained many provisions that reflected colonial experience, such as those relating to religion, education, qualifications and disqualifications for officeholding, multiple officeholding, imprisonment for debt, and naturalization. There was to be no established church; no compulsory attendance at religious worship or compulsory support of any religious organization; "but all persons shall be at liberty to exercise their own mode of worship." No clergyman, "while he continues in the exercise of the pastoral Function," could be a member of the General Assembly. No person "who shall deny the being of God, or the Truth of the Protestant Religion, or the Divine Authority of the Old or New Testament, or who shall hold Religious Principles incompatible with the Freedom and Safety of the State," was eligible for any public office. Section 41, copied from the Pennsylvania Constitution, provided "that a School or Schools shall be established by the Legislature for the convenient Instruction of Youth, with such Salaries to the Masters paid by the Public, as may enable them to instruct at low Prices; and all useful Learning shall be duly encouraged and promoted in one or more Universities." Section 35 provided that "no person in this State shall hold more than one lucrative office at any one time." The bill of rights was "declared to be part of the Constitution of this State, and ought never to be violated on any pretense whatsoever." The constitution contained no provision for amendment, an omission that was to cause much controversy and conflict in years to come.

Salient Features of the New Constitution

The North Carolina Constitution of 1776, like other state constitutions of this period, was short, simple, and obscure. It was simply a general outline of governmental machinery. Details were to be supplied later by legislatures. The constitution carried over many ideas from the colonial government, but there were some significant changes.

The salient feature of the constitution was the shift to legislative predominance and away from the executive supremacy of colonial days. The governor and the whole executive department were definitely under legislative control—subject to election, removal, short term of office, and restricted powers. The governor's powers were checked by the General Assembly and by the Council of State. In contrast with colonial executives, he had no control over elections, or over the time and place of legislative sessions; no power to summon, prorogue, or dissolve a legislature; and no veto power. William Hooper observed that the only power the governor had was "to sign a receipt for his own salary."

On the other hand, the governor had the power to initiate policies and recommend measures. He had power of pardon and reprieve; he was commander-in-chief of the military and naval forces of the state; and he had general authority to "exercise all other executive powers of government" subject to the constitution and laws of the legislature. There was the prestige of the office as head of the state, and there were opportunities for great service by a strong executive through personal leadership. He had influence rather than constitutional power.

Character of the New Government

The constitution provided for a government that was relatively democratic in theory but not in practice. Members of both houses of the General Assembly were to be elected, but the county, not population, was the basis of representation; there were property qualifications for suffrage and officeholding—which meant a government by the landowners; there were also religious disqualifications for officeholding—which largely eliminated all non-Protestants; executive and judicial officials were elected by the legislature, not by popular vote. As already stated, there was no provision for amendment of the constitution, and the constitution was not submitted to popular vote.

Nevertheless the new government under the constitution was far more democratic in spirit and objectives than the former royal government. It was a forward step in the evolution of political democracy. And the constitution was in force for almost sixty years without change. It was not revised until 1835, and this change came as a result of the democratic movement of the time—the rise of the common man, Jacksonian Democracy, and the revolt of the democratic West against the aristocratic East.

Authorship of the 1776 Constitution

The North Carolina Constitution of 1776, like the United States Constitution of 1787, was "a bundle of compromises" and the result of the labors of many men. The journal of the congress that drafted the document contains no debates and sheds little light on its authorship. Most of the credit should probably go to the committee members who drafted it, especially to Richard Caswell, its chairman, and to Thomas Jones of Edenton, the spokesman for the committee, who presented both the bill of rights and the constitution on the floor. Samuel Johnston called the completed document "Jones' Constitution."

But the constitution was the work of many men and the ideas in it came from many sources. First of all, some of the members were familiar with the constitutions of Virginia, Maryland, New Jersey, and Pennsylvania. The North Carolina delegates in the Continental Congress, particularly Hooper and Penn, were interested in the meeting at Halifax. Hooper had sent a copy of the Pennsylvania Constitution to the North Carolina Congress, describing it as "a motley mixture of limited monarchy, and an execrable democracy—a Beast without a head, the Mob made a second branch of legislation." Many provisions in the North Carolina Bill of Rights and quite a few in the constitution were taken in whole or in part from the constitutions of other states, notably Virginia and Maryland. Then, too, some of the framers were familiar with John Adams's "Thoughts on Government," a copy of which had been sent to Thomas Burke of Orange County. The completed constitution resembled Adams's "outlines of government" in many respects. Still another source of ideas may be found in the instructions to the delegates of Orange and Mecklenburg counties, the first written by Burke, and the latter in the handwriting of Waightstill Avery. These two documents resembled the Adams plan in many details and were reflected in the constitution. The 1776 Constitution of North Carolina thus resembled not only the constitutions of Virginia and Maryland but also the colonial governments of the royal period. Above all, it reflected the reaction of North Carolina to experience.

Chapter 14

THE NEW STATE AND
ITS PROBLEMS

The fifth Provincial Congress completed its labors on December 23, 1776, its last official action being "an Ordinance for appointing a Governor, Council of State, and Secretary until next General Assembly." It appointed Richard Caswell as governor at a salary of £1,500 per annum and James Glasgow as secretary with the "same Fees, Privileges and Emoluments as the Provincial Secretary heretofore held and enjoyed." The Council of State selected by the congress consisted of Cornelius Harnett, Thomas Eaton, William Dry, William Haywood, Edward Starkey, and Joseph Leach, with Harnett as president. Compensation for the councillors was set at twenty shillings per diem.

The Inauguration of Governor Caswell

The executive branch of the new government began operation in January, 1777, when Caswell and the other officials took the oath of office. Caswell's inauguration was a great occasion. The *Virginia Gazette* reported: "On Friday last, (January 10), his Excellency Richard Caswell, Esqr. Governor of this State, arrived here. He was met about six miles from town by about thirty gentlemen on horseback, who accompanied him to New Bern, the bells ringing as soon as he entered the town. Being conducted to Mr. Edward Wrenford's tavern, where a handsome collation was prepared, he received from the Continental officers and soldiers (drawn up for the purpose) a salute with small arms; the fort, *Pennsylvania Farmer,* and the other vessels in the harbour, fired many guns, under a display of the colours of the United States, and in the evening the town was highly illuminated. On Monday the 13th instant the inhabitants assembled, and waited upon his Excellency with a congratulatory address."

The New State's First General Assembly

The first General Assembly of the independent state convened at New Bern on April 7. Samuel Ashe of New Hanover was elected Speaker of the Senate, Abner Nash of Craven, Speaker of the House of Commons. James Glasgow and members of the Council of State were formally elected by joint ballot of the two houses, and on April 18 Caswell was elected governor.

The new legislature faced many problems and enacted many laws to conform to the provisions of the 1776 constitution. Since the state was at war, many of these statutes dealt with military matters. A new militia law was passed and a special act for the "Encouragement of the militia and Volunteers employed in prosecuting the Indian War." A statute "for preventing the Dangers which may arise from Persons disaffected to the State" defined treason and prescribed the death penalty for this offense. A law to prevent domestic insurrections, especially among slaves, was enacted, and the "forging or counterfeiting Bills of Credit and lottery tickets" was made a felony punishable by death. The General Assembly reenacted the ordinance declaring what parts of the common law and former statutes were still in force. After considerable debate, a statute was passed—essentially a copy of the Court Law of 1767—that divided the state into six judicial districts. Six judges were elected, as well as marshals, inspectors, and naval officers of the state's five ports, and brigadier generals for its six military districts. Laws were passed for the creation of county courts, the regulation of their procedure, and the appointment by the legislature of sheriffs, justices of the peace, registers, constables, and coroners in the counties. Three new counties—Caswell, Camden, and Burke—were created and Liberty Hall (formerly Queen's College) was incorporated.

The new state government went into operation during "one of the darkest hours" of the American Revolution. Though North Carolina was not the scene of active military operations again until 1780, military problems transcended all others. Troops had to be raised, organized, trained, equipped, and maintained. Military aid had to be rendered other states and requisitions of the Continental Congress for men and money had to be met. Loyalists had to be watched—though their ardor had been cooled by defeat at Moore's Creek Bridge a year earlier. Indians had to be subdued, notably the Cherokees, who were keeping the frontier settlements in a state of constant alarm. There were the problems of maintaining a "state navy" and privateers, and the acute questions of taxes, paper currency, and inflation. There were problems of unifying the state politically, of conciliating diverse political interests, and of making a constitution work, which emphasized *decentralization* of power, in a situation that necessitated *centralization* of power in the prosecution of a war.

Defects in the State Constitution Become Apparent

The defects of the 1776 constitution soon became apparent. Its undemocratic features, especially its property and religious qualifications for officeholding, disappointed and disillusioned the masses, especially in the West. What were they fighting for, after all? There was a decline of popular interest in the constitution and evidence of decline in support of the new government.

The chief defect—certainly the cause of most complaint for the next half century—was the inequitable distribution of seats in the General Assembly. The county basis of representation gave the East control of the government and created dissatisfaction in the backcountry. During the latter part of the Revolution eastern counties had thirty-three representatives; the West, nineteen; eastern boroughs, four; western, two. This meant that there were thirty-three eastern senators to nineteen from the West and seventy eastern commoners to forty from the West, despite the fact that there was a greater *white* population in the western counties. Western dissatisfaction and complaints did lead to the creation of a few western counties, but too few to allay discontent —and, besides, more new counties were formed in the East. As late as 1799 there were forty-six eastern counties and thirty-four western counties. The result of this inequity led to revival of sectional controversies, which tended to retard effective government.

Weakness of the State Executive

Another defect in the constitution—and one that became more obvious and critical as the war progressed—was the weakness of the state executive. The constitution subordinated the executive to the legislature by limiting a governor to a one-year term and granting him little power. In 1778, when Harnett, member of the Continental Congress, urged Governor Caswell to take more "spirited measures" to fill up the state's quota of soldiers, Caswell replied "that by the Constitution of this State, nothing can be done by the executive power of itself towards this desirable purpose," and he blamed the framers of the constitution (he had been chairman of the drafting committee!) for "cramping so much the powers of the executive."

The executive power failed completely in the military crisis of 1780–81, and the legislature attempted to cope with the problem by creating a Board of War or Council Extraordinary of three members who were to exercise every power necessary to the "security, defense, and preservation of this State."

Governor Nash, elected in 1780, criticized this action, which took authority from the governor and further decentralized executive authority instead of centralizing it. He observed that executive authority had been divided and subdivided until "men, not knowing whom to obey, obeyed nobody," and he declared that the governorship was "but an empty title." In his message to the General Assembly of 1781 Nash said: "When you elected me governor of this state, you presented me the Bill of Rights and the Constitution, at the same time you presented me with the Sword of the State as an emblem of the power I was invested with for the protection of the Constitution and the rights of the people, and in a solemn manner you bound me by an oath to preserve the Constitution inviolate; and yet four months after my election the same Assembly deprived me of almost every power, privilege and authority belonging to my office. . . . I have no doubt that the secret enemies of our Free Constitution exult at the introduction of such innovation and rejoice at seeing the first office in the State rendered useless and contemptible." So disgusted was he that he refused to accept reelection, and Thomas Burke was chosen.

The situation became worse as the war progressed. With the capture of Governor Burke at Hillsborough in 1781 by David Fanning and his band of Tories, state government collapsed and for a few years there was virtual anarchy and civil war, accompanied by violence, lawlessness, murder, and arson, with "every man for himself." Perhaps the chief reasons for this alarming state of affairs was the governor's lack of authority.

Party Division and the Rise of Party Spirit

The weakness of the executive was, in a sense, both a cause and an effect of dissension and controversy within the dominant Whig party. Common dangers, fear of invasion, and effective leadership had created a spirit of unity in the early part of the war. During the first General Assembly in 1777 Abner Nash had declared, "We are all harmony," and he expected to see "a perfect good agreement" prevail throughout the session. He was to be sadly disappointed. Within a short time all semblance of unity among the Whigs had disappeared, and the two factions—Conservatives and Radicals—that had cooperated in the first days of statehood, again emerged, grounded largely on economic and sectional bases. Most of the planter-slaveholders were Conservatives; most of the small farmers, Radicals. The East was the stronghold of the Conservatives, while the Radicals drew their greatest strength from the backcountry. There were exceptions to this classification. Willie Jones and Thomas Person, two of the outstanding Radical leaders, were aristocrats, the former from Halifax and the latter from Granville County.

Party divisions produced friction, bitterness, and many acrimonious controversies. This was clearly demonstrated in the election of delegates to the Continental Congress in 1777, when John Penn defeated Hewes, and William Hooper, who barely escaped defeat, disgustedly refused to accept his seat. Samuel Johnston, one of the leading Conservatives, was not surprised at the action of a legislature made up of "fools and knaves." He said that he expected nothing good from men of such "contemptible abilities" and he resigned his post as state treasurer. In the gubernatorial contest of 1782 Alexander Martin, a Radical, defeated Samuel Johnston; and Richard Caswell, formerly considered a Conservative, shifted his support to Martin. This led to his denunciation as "a man who had basely abandoned his important trusts, and deserted his colors in the hours of distress." The next year the Conservatives got their revenge when they supported Martin, the Radical, for reelection and defeated Caswell, a "political turncoat," who was seeking to stage a political comeback. Caswell's comment was that "Martin was re-elected by 66 votes against 49 for me. . . . The Edenton and Halifax men voted for Governor Martin, saying I had crammed him down their throats last year and they were determined to keep him there."

Politics was also manifest in the election of army and militia officers. The General Assembly elected colonels and generals, and in too many instances politics rather than ability was the major consideration. This resulted in the selection of men with no military experience and in eventual inefficiency and failure. Governor Caswell had been cognizant of this situation as early as 1777, when he declared: "The recruiting service goes slowly due to the negligence, incapacity and lack of experience of the officers"—a situation he attributed to partisan politics.

The Loyalist Problem and the Tory War

The Loyalists were encouraged by divisions among the Whigs and resumed their activities in various parts of the state. The Revolution thus became a civil war—Whigs against Tories, neighbor against neighbor, and sometimes brother against brother—for example, William Hooper and his Tory brother.

There were many conflicting reports about the number, wealth, influence, and activity of Tories. Samuel Johnston thought they were not very numerous and said that "not one man of any influence" had any part in the Tory uprisings. George III and some of his advisers, on the other hand, thought that the state was literally swarming with "loyal men" and that North Carolina was his "most loyal colony." Governor Martin, in 1776, claimed that he could raise an army of six thousand Tories—though there were fewer than two thousand at Moore's Creek. As late as 1780 he said that at least fourteen hundred North Carolinians had joined the British forces.

The loyalists used many techniques to oppose the Whig prosecution of the war and to undermine Whig morale. They spread all kinds of propaganda: exaggerated reports of American defeats (frequently they had no need to exaggerate), reports of slave insurrrections, of Indian uprisings (actually true), and of threatened British invasion. They poked fun at the state government and its officials, and at the members and activities of the Continental Congress. They made threats of "dire punishment" for the "rebels," "upstarts," and "foolish deluded men" as soon as the "rebellion" was suppressed, which they assumed would be within a few years. They also opposed voluntary enlistments and other methods of recruiting soldiers for the Continental armies and found numerous occasions "to prevent the militia from being drafted." When General Griffith Rutherford requested the Council of Safety for troops from the Hillsborough military district to march against the Cherokees in the summer of 1776, he met with refusal because of "the many disaffected persons in that district and neighborhood." The Surry County Tories were actually in arms at this time against the provisional government. In April, 1777, "many evil persons" in Edgecombe and adjoining counties "joined in a most wicked conspiracy" against the new government. Two years later Tories in that section formed an association by which they "obligated themselves to prevent the Militia from being drafted," to aid deserters from the American army, and to resist civil officials. A Cape Fear militia officer reported to the governor that he was "alarmed by these dam rascals, the Tories."

There were Tory raids, neighborhood fights, and destruction of property, even of life. And there were numerous enlistments in the British army. Of course the loyalists endeavored to destroy confidence in state finance, by refusing to pay taxes or to accept paper currency, and by circulating counterfeit money, thereby further increasing the already grave problem of inflation. Activities of the Tories menaced the peace and safety of the state, contributed to the instability of government, and weakened the financial, military, and human resources of North Carolina.

Legislation against Tories

What was the state government's policy toward loyalists and their leaders? At first the Whig leaders favored a policy of conciliation and persuasion. The Provincial Congress at Halifax in May, 1776, ordered the imprisonment of loyalist leaders who had fought at Moore's Creek Bridge. At the same time the congress lamented the actions of "these misguided people," but declared that "we shall hail their reformation with increasing pleasure, and receive them to us with open arms." The next Provincial Congress in the fall of that year hoped that the Tories had "now become sensible of the Wickedness and Folly" of their ways, and offered to pardon all who took an oath of allegiance to the state within ninety days. When few or no Tories subscribed this oath, the Whigs adopted a sterner policy.

A law of April, 1777, defined treason and required Tories to take the oath of allegiance or suffer banishment. All persons found guilty of giving aid and comfort to the enemy were to be imprisoned for the remainder of the war and half their estates were to be confiscated. Loyalist merchants were given three months to dispose of their goods and leave the state. An act of 1779 listed the names of sixty-eight persons whose estates were to be confiscated, including William Tryon, Josiah Martin, Edward Brice Dobbs, Henry E. McCulloh, Justice Martin Howard, and many other large landholders of loyalist sympathies. It is noteworthy that John Carteret, Earl Granville, the largest landholder in North Carolina, was not mentioned. Yet his vast property was confiscated. Commissioners were chosen by the legislature to take possession of all confiscable property. This harsh law met the approval of most Whigs, though Willie Jones and fourteen other members of the House of Commons denounced it as an act not worthy of a "set of hog drovers."

These punitive laws and the increasing social ostracism of many "disaffected persons" caused many Tories to leave the state. It was reported in the summer of 1777 that "a great number of Tories" were sailing from New Bern, and a Whig colonel reported that "two thirds of Cumberland County" were leaving. This mass migration continued throughout the war and accelerated after the British surrender at Yorktown, in October, 1781.

Financial Chaos

One of the most serious obstacles to the success of the Whig cause in North Carolina—perhaps the most critical problem of all the states—was inflation.

Inflation might triumph where British armies had failed. A Hessian officer said in 1779 that the collapse of American currency was "worth forty thousand men to the British." The phrase "not worth a Continental" is still one of the most quoted statements from the Revolution. It might easily have been the epitaph of the short-lived American republic. One Whig leader declared that "America is safe, but from the damned Situation of our Money. Every person seems afraid of it." And General Washington, in May, 1779, lamented that "our Money does but Pass."

When the war began, the state treasury was empty. The new state was without money, without credit, and with little prospect of gaining it. Foreign trade had almost disappeared; trade with England had dropped off to a mere trickle; British bounties on naval stores were lost; and trade with the British West Indies declined sharply. Manufactures were almost nonexistent. And there was an unprecedented demand for funds.

To raise and equip armies, the Continental Congress and the states resorted to issues of paper currency—an apparently easy but uncertain and disastrous expedient. During the course of the war the provincial congresses and state legislatures authorized the following sums of paper currency, largely in the form of bills of credit:

1775	$ 125,000
1776	£ 500,000
1778	£ 850,000
1779	£ 500,000
1780	£ 1,240,000
1781	$26,250,000

Inflation

Many laws were passed to prevent depreciation of the currency and to curb inflation. The bills of credit were made legal tender, and it was a death penalty to counterfeit them. Poll taxes were levied to provide a sinking fund for their redemption. But all in vain. Many people refused to accept paper money; it was ridiculed by the Tories and even by some Whigs; and there was a flood of counterfeit currency. The result was depreciation and a blighting inflation. By December, 1778, depreciation of bills of credit was more than 5 percent; in June, 1779, it was estimated at 8 percent; by December it had reached 30 percent, and by the end of 1780 the legislature recognized by law a depreciation of 800 percent!

Inflation had a disastrous effect on the morale of the army and was one of the major causes of desertion. It is surprising that more men did not desert —only about 10 percent did—since a soldier's pay during the latter part of the war amounted to only about six cents a month in specie—enough to "buy one drink of grog." Depreciation also had a calamitous effect on the purchase of military supplies.

While soldiers and officers complained bitterly about the effects of inflation, the civilian population raised the loudest clamor against prices as they rose to dizzy heights. In 1780 corn was £100 a bushel, corn meal £120 a bushel, and beef £48 a pound. Richard Cogdell, a New Bern merchant, wrote: "A string of fish which used to cost 12 d. is now 1920 d. or 20 dollars. What a terrible prospect this exhibits."

Public officials complained that they could not live on their salaries. A judge's annual salary of £20,000 in paper amounted to only £25 in specie. On March 26, 1781, it was reported in the press that a "Gentleman paid 4,000 dollars per week for his board at New Bern."

Taxes

In spite of the aversion of the people to taxation, the General Assembly was forced to resort to a general property tax. In April, 1777, it authorized a general assessment of all property and levied a tax of one half-penny on each pound value of all "lands, lots, houses, slaves, money at interest, stock in trade, horses and cattle." This was the first ad valorem tax ever levied in North Carolina and introduced a new principle of taxation.

As depreciation of the currency continued and as financial demands of the war mounted, the legislature was forced to increase taxes. In November, 1777, the rate was two pence on every pound value; in April, 1778, it was increased to three pence; in May, 1779, it was fixed at five shillings on each £100 value; and in April, 1780, at six pence for every pound value. In June, 1781, the rate was "four shillings currency on every pound value of taxable property," and also a tax of £150 currency on all single men whose taxable property did not amount to £1,000 currency.

It might appear that these taxes should have raised large sums, but they did not. As Connor says, "Loose methods of assessment, inefficiency of administration, and corruption among officials consumed a large percentage of the revenues." A legislative report of 1786 estimated that the total annual receipts from all taxes was only £65,000—and by this date "prosperity was beginning to return."

With the threat of British invasion in 1780, followed by actual invasion in 1781, the state was in desperate financial straits. Governor Nash reported to the General Assembly of 1780 that the treasury was empty and the state's financial resources exhausted. The General Assembly reported that the emission of paper had a "tendency to increase the price of necessaries" and was "greatly injurious to the public." The next year Governor Burke reported to the assembly: "The public money is unaccounted for, the taxes uncollected and unproductive . . . and the Treasury totally unable to make payment."

Taxes in Kind and Other Sources of State Revenue

To cope with this emergency, the legislature, on September 5, 1780, adopted a new policy of taxation—a "specific Provision tax on all the inhabitants of this State," which provided that for every £100 value of property each inhabitant was required to "contribute and pay to the commissioner of his respective county, one peck of Indian corn, or half peck of wheat, or five pounds of good flour, or one and one fourth pecks of clean oats, or three fourths of a peck of rye, or one peck of rough rice, merchantable, or three pounds of good pork, or two pounds of fatted do., or four and a half pounds of good beef . . . that the inhabitants of Carteret county may deliver one gallon of salt in lieu of any one of the enumerated articles."

Warehouses were established at convenient places where these supplies were stored for distribution to the military forces. This policy remained in effect through 1782 and must have brought in large quantities of badly needed commodities, though there are no figures indicating the exact amounts received.

But the state government was hard-pressed for funds. So the legislature of September, 1780, adopted another new device—a loan system, under which the state treasury issued loan certificates bearing 5 percent interest and exempt from all taxes. A special tax of "12 pence in the pound" was levied for their redemption.

Still another source of revenue, one quite popular with the Whigs, was the sale of confiscated Tory property. A legislative report of November, 1783, reveals that such property to the amount of £583,643-8-0 had been sold. Much confiscated Tory land remained unsold at the close of the war, and between 1784 and 1790 this property was divided into 640-acre tracts and sold at public auction to the highest bidder—netting £284,452-4-0. This total of £868,095-12-0 was perhaps the largest single source of the state's revenue—but it came too late to help in financing military operations.

War and North Carolina Commerce

The nonimportation agreements adopted in 1774 had their effects on trade, both foreign and domestic. In some cases local safety committees, as at Wilmington, interfered with trade more than royal officials ever had. Cargoes of British goods were seized and sold at public auction, and prices of imported goods were fixed by the committee.

The dangerous coast, previously a handicap to commerce, now became a valuable asset. The British navy found it almost impossible to stop the trade carried on by numerous small craft, American and foreign, which sailed through the shallow inlets and shifting channels. Ocracoke, "the contemptible port," was particularly well adapted to this wartime trade. The British navy made no sustained effort to blockade the North Carolina coast, though many British ships and some French vessels were wrecked along the "Graveyard of the Atlantic."

Trade in the backcountry was "unusually difficult" during the war. By the end of 1775 most of the stores had sold out their entire supply of goods, and it was almost impossible for merchants to replenish their stocks.

The effects of the war on the merchants of the state were many and varied. Many, perhaps most, of the loyalist merchants left; a few of them shifted to the Whig cause. Some merchants got rich, others went broke, but nearly all became unpopular and were accused of profiteering. They were denounced along with Tories in general as "jointly pernicious to the public good' and well being of the state."

Considerable trade was carried on by agents of the government, who purchased articles for export, chartered ships, and arranged for the importation of arms, ammunition, and salt; within the state they bought pork, flour, shoes, clothing, and many military supplies.

Effects of the Revolution on Exports and Imports

The Revolution brought an end to the old commercial order in North Carolina, though a small trade continued with Great Britain and the West Indies for a few months after hostilities began.

Old regulations of the British Navigation Acts, and other trade laws were swept away—as were British bounties for naval stores and indigo. British markets for naval stores and tobacco were lost, as were the British West Indian markets for lumber and provisions. The presence of British military and naval forces in the state or along the coast disrupted trade with other continental colonies. North Carolina was therefore compelled to seek new commercial outlets—with the non-British West Indies, France, and other countries.

There was a great change in the nature of North Carolina's export trade. Naval stores shipments almost ceased; shipments of foodstuffs declined— mainly because they were needed at home; shipments of lumber decreased and were limited largely to barrel staves and headings, whereas before the war boards and shingles had been two of the largest items of export. There was an increase in tobacco exports from North Carolina ports, especially Edenton, because of a rise in price, ease of shipment, and the fact that the British blockade of Virginia ports led Virginia, the leading producer of tobacco, to export considerable quantities of it via Albemarle Sound.

Shipments of goods were naturally more irregular than before the war. Trade was also disrupted by inflationary conditions and sharp fluctuations in prices.

The war also caused a marked change in the nature of imports. War supplies had to be obtained; and quantities of arms, ammunition, and other "sinews of war" were procured from France and Spain via the Dutch island of St. Eustatius, St. Croix, French Martinique, and Spanish-French Hispaniola.

The State Navy and Privateers

The war gave an impetus to shipbuilding. A number of advertisements of newly built North Carolina ships for sale appeared in the *North Carolina Gazette* of May 15, 1778. Of seventy-eight ships clearing from Port Roanoke from June to September, 1788, forty-four had been built in shipyards at Edenton, Beaufort, New Bern, and Wilmington.

The state government attempted to build up a navy to protect shipping and to keep Ocracoke Inlet open. In 1776 it fitted out the brig *Pennsylvania Farmer* with a complement of 16 guns and 110 men; the same year Virginia and North Carolina cooperated to equip two large galleys, the *Washington* and the *Caswell,* for defense of Ocracoke Inlet. These galleys were built at "Key Bay on Black Water." The *Pennsylvania Farmer* was sold to a privateer at the time the *Caswell* was put into commission. A 1781 law authorized the construction of two vessels of ten to twelve guns each and two row-galleys, but the records do not indicate that they were built.

North Carolina privateers were much more numerous, active, and effective than the state's navy. These privately owned ships, the *Sturdy Beggar, Chatham, Bellona, Rainbeau, Fanny, Betsey, General Nash, Lydia, Nancy,* and others ravaged British commerce and brought in many valuable cargoes. The more successful ships made fortunes for their owners. In 1777 the *Lydia* captured a British prize valued at £30,000; the next year, the *Bellona* captured at least four British merchant ships, and in 1780 the *General Nash* seized two armed ships, one from the island of St. Kitts, carrying sugar, rum, and fruit, and the other from Scotland, with a £10,800 cargo of tea, sugar, wine, dry goods, and hardware. The last recorded prize taken by a North Carolina privateer was in February, 1783, more than a year and a half after the British surrender at Yorktown, but a half year before peace was officially proclaimed.

Chapter 15
THE STATE AT WAR

The state's most pressing problems throughout the war were those of raising, organizing, training, equipping, and supplying an army.

North Carolina Regiments in the Continental Line

North Carolina's military organizations consisted of troops in the Continental Line, state militia, and independent companies of so-called "partisans." In 1775 the Continental Congress called on all the states for troops, fixing North Carolina's quota at nine regiments. (A regiment consisted of eight companies of seventy-six men each.) The Provincial Congress in August of that year had already provided for two regiments, commanded by Colonels James Moore and Robert Howe. Four more regiments were authorized in April, 1776, officered by Colonels Jethro Sumner, Thomas Polk, Edward Buncombe, and Alexander Lillington. Three more regiments were raised in November, headed by Colonels James Hogun, James Armstrong, and John Williams. The Continental Congress in the meantime had increased the state's quota, and a tenth regiment was authorized in April, 1777, headed by Colonel Abraham Shepperd.

Because of the weakness of executive power, divisions among the Whigs, loyalist activities, inflation, and a lack of military ardor so great that "men quit volunteering for the war," the state's regiments in the Continental Line never had a full complement. Accurate statistics on the number of North Carolina soldiers in the Continental Line, that is, on Continental pay, were not kept and the available figures are not entirely reliable. The reports to Congress of Henry Knox, secretary of war, came nearest to being the official count of soldiers in the Continental service. The following table, based on these reports, reveals North Carolina's quota and its soldiers on Continental pay:

Year	Quota	Soldiers on Continental Pay
1775	none	none
1776	—	1,134
1777	6,120	1,281
1778	4,698	1,287
1779	3,132	1,214
1780	3,132	—
1781	2,304	545
1782	2,304	1,505
1783	2,304	697

These figures reveal that North Carolina had 7,663 soldiers on Continental pay during the whole course of the war. R. D. W. Connor placed the number at 5,454, and a more recent scholar, who counted the names of North Carolina troops in Continental service, came up with the figure of 6,086, of which 661 deserted (a smaller percentage than that of most of the states). It is impossible to cite with accuracy the total number of North Carolinians in the Continental army or the number for any particular year. It is significant, however, that of 235,000 enlistments in the Continental Line from all the states during the whole war, such a small number came from North Carolina. Massachusetts, with a population only a little larger than North Carolina, had about 97,000 men on Continental pay. On the other hand, North Carolina had a vast number of militiamen, who were on state rather than Continental pay. It is impossible to ascertain the exact number of the militia, but some estimates place the figure as high as ten thousand. In other words, North Carolina probably furnished as many as seventeen thousand soldiers for the Revolution.

The State's Military Problems

There were two methods of recruiting soldiers for the Continental Line. The system of volunteering was fairly successful at the beginning of the war, because of enthusiasm and fear of invasion, but as the tide of war rolled away from North Carolina, military ardor cooled, and after 1778 there was a sharp decline in enlistments and an increase in desertion—a situation that existed in many other states as well. The state finally resorted to the bounty system and to the draft of soldiers. The Continental Congress had adopted the bounty system early in the war, and North Carolina adopted this policy in an act in 1780, which gave a bounty of $500 currency upon enlistment and another $500 at the end of each year's service, plus two hundred acres of land in the Military Reservation in the Tennessee country.

State Militia

Realizing that the militia was the "first line of defense," in 1777 the first General Assembly of the new state passed an Act to Establish a Militia in This State, under which all free white males, sixteen to fifty inclusive, were subject to militia service. Soldiers were recruited for the militia both by voluntary enlistments and by draft. No accurate records of the militia were preserved, though various estimates were made from time to time. Henry Knox estimated 2,706 North Carolina militiamen in service in 1779 and 3,000 in 1780. Governor Martin, in 1782, placed the figure of state militia at 26,822, but he did not say how many of these were in service. In some years the number of state militiamen in service was higher than the number in the Continental Line, but throughout the war this was not the case. Some authorities believe that the usual ratio of militiamen to Continental soldiers from North Carolina was about one to four.

Militiamen were generally poor soldiers, who were poorly armed, poorly organized, untrained, and led by inexperienced officers. Many Continental officers, particularly Nathanael Greene, had a low opinion of them. In a letter to General George Washington, January 31, 1781, he said: ". . . it is impossible to carry on the war any length of time with the militia. The wastes of stores, and the consumption of provision and forage, must ruin any nation in the universe, whose revenue is not greater than ours."

Writing to Governor Abner Nash on February 9, 1781, Greene declared: ". . . I think it an endless task to attempt to arm and equip all your militia. Such a waste of arms and ammunition as I have seen in different parts of this state, is enough to exhaust all the arsenals of Europe. Nor ought arms, in my opinion, to be put into the hands of doubtful characters; for you may depend upon it, such will never be useful in this hour of difficulty."

On March 18 Greene wrote Joseph Reed, president of the Continental Congress: "North Carolina has been as nearly reduced as ever a state was in the universe and escape. Our force was so small, and Lord Cornwallis' movements were so rapid, that we got no reinforcements of militia, and therefore were obliged to retire out of the State, upon which the spirits of the people sunk, and almost all classes of inhabitants gave themselves up for lost. They would not believe themselves until they found danger at their doors. The foolish prejudice of the formidableness of the militia being a sufficient barrier against any attempts of the enemy, prevented the Legislature from making any exertions equal to their critical and dangerous situation. Experience has convinced them of their false security. It is astonishing to me how these people could place such a confidence in a militia scattered all over the face of the whole earth, and generally destitute of everything necessary to their own defence. The militia in the back country are formidable, the others are not, and all are very ungovernable and difficult to keep together. As they have generally come out, twenty thousand might be in motion, and not five hundred in the field." In another letter to Reed on the same day Greene said, "Our army is in good spirits, but the militia are leaving us in great numbers to return home to kiss their wives and sweethearts."

Writing to General Washington after the Battle of Guilford Court House, Greene declared: "Our prospects were flattering; and had the North Carolina militia seconded the endeavors of their officers, victory was certain. But they left the most advantageous position I ever saw, without scarcely firing a gun. None fired more than once, and near one half not at all."

Of course there were exceptions, especially when the militia was well led, as at Moore's Creek, Kings Mountain, Eutaw Springs, and the "gallant fight" of Dixon's regiment of North Carolina militia at Camden. A week after this battle, Governor Nash, writing about "that unhappy affair," said, "The militia, except one North Carolina regiment, commanded on the occasion by Colonel Dixon, of the regulars, gave way on the first fire and fled with the utmost precipitation."

"Partisans" and Irregular Bands

In addition to Continental and militia soldiers, there were many independent companies of irregular troops, privately organized and armed, serving as a sort of home guard, but fighting effectively when needed. These bands of "partisans" were very effective, especially in the campaign of 1781. It should be noted, however, that some so-called "partisan leaders," especially William R. Davie and William Lee Davidson, were officers of the Continental army and thus were hardly more than "semi-partisans."

Military Activities of North Carolina Troops

As has been indicated earlier, North Carolina gave a good military account of itself during the first year of the Revolution. In 1775 it sent Howe and his regiment to Virginia, where they aided in defeating a British army and driving the enemy, including Governor Dunmore, from Norfolk. Early in the next year state troops, sent to South Carolina, defeated the Scovellites in the "Snow Campaign," and in February the overwhelming Whig victory at Moore's Creek Bridge thwarted British plans for an invasion of the South. North Carolina had fourteen hundred men under Robert Howe, now a brigadier general, in the defense of Charleston in 1776. From 1777 to 1780 North Carolina troops saw action under Washington in New York, Pennsylvania, and New Jersey, and more than a thousand North Carolinians suffered the hardships at Valley Forge in the winter of 1777–78.

After General Charles Lee's successful defense of Charleston in 1776 he was recalled to the Northern Department and Robert Howe of North Carolina was promoted to major general and placed in command of the Southern Department—the highest post held by a North Carolinian during the war. Howe was later removed from this command, when he was forced to surrender Savannah to the British.

Francis Nash's brigade was active at the Battle of Brandywine, September 11, 1777, and at Germantown, October 4, where he was killed. Edward Buncombe was mortally wounded in this engagement. North Carolina troops, notably Hogun's brigade, helped Washington chase Clinton across New Jersey and fought at Monmouth, June 29, 1778.

In 1778 and 1779 North Carolina became the "recruiting ground for the entire South." There was some complaint that South Carolina was raising men in North Carolina, but Cornelius Harnett thought it was a proper and desirable procedure. Writing to Governor Caswell, November 28, 1778, he said: "I am one of those old Politicians who had much rather see my neighbor's house on fire than my own, but at the same time would lend every assistance in my power to quench the flame."

Griffith Rutherford's Campaign against the Indians

There was little military activity in the state from 1776 to 1781, except for a campaign against the Cherokee Indians in the summer of 1776, when Griffith Rutherford, with approximately 2,400 men aided by forces from South Carolina and Virginia, marched into the Cherokee country, destroyed thirty-six of their towns, and laid waste a great portion of "Indian country." As a result of Cherokee defeats, followed by the Treaty of Long Island (in the Holston River), July 20, 1777, the Cherokees ceded to the whites all lands east of the Blue Ridge and also lands along the Watauga, Nolichucky, Upper Holston, and New rivers.

The Second British Invasion of the South

Having failed to conquer Washington's army in the North, and encouraged by reports of strong loyalism in the South, Sir Henry Clinton, who in 1778 had replaced General Howe in command of all British forces in America, transferred the seat of war to the South, where the British once more hoped that a show of force would arouse the dormant Tories to action and thus enable them "to roll up the war from the South." If this new military strategy proved successful, the southern states would be cut off, as had been planned for New England early in the war. With this objective in mind, the British launched their new offensive against Georgia, militarily the weakest of all the states, and within a short time, led by Colonel Archibald Campbell, they captured Savannah on December 29, 1778. They overran Georgia and restored royal rule. General Robert Howe, the commanding officer of the Southern Department, was court-martialed and removed from command, though his defeat at Savannah had been due to the overwhelming superiority of British military and naval strength.

General Benjamin Lincoln, who succeeded Howe in charge of the Southern Department's army of about seven thousand men, had some two thousand North Carolinians under his command, made up largely of Sumner's brigade of Continentals and John Ashe's brigade of about fifteen hundred state militia. Ashe led an expedition against Augusta, but was surprised and routed at Briar Creek, March 3, 1779. Lincoln, the right wing of whose army was Sumner's brigade, was defeated by General Augustine Prevost at Stono Ferry on June 20. After this defeat Lincoln changed his strategy and, supported by Count d'Estaing's French fleet, began an attack on Savannah. After a siege of two months, September-October, Lincoln gave up the siege and retreated to the prepared defenses of Charleston. Gideon Lamb's North Carolina Whigs and John Hamilton's North Carolina "Legion of Tories" were actively engaged in the Savannah campaign—of course on opposite sides.

Meanwhile the Continental Congress, on September 20, had directed the North Carolina brigades in the North to march southward to reinforce Lincoln, but General Washington countermanded this directive, and not until November 19 did he send Hogun and Clark orders to march. As a result the North Carolina troops rendered no assistance in the unsuccessful siege of Savannah.

British Conquest of South Carolina

Clinton was eager to take Charleston and to avenge his defeat at Fort Moultrie in 1776. With an army of about eight thousand men and five warships—an estimated total of thirteen thousand men—he sailed from Savannah to Charleston December 26, 1779, accompanied by the new British Commander in the South, Lord Cornwallis. The expedition reached Charleston on February 26, 1780.

Lincoln's army in the city numbered about six thousand, including the two North Carolina brigades of Sumner and Hogun and about one thousand North Carolina militiamen. Lincoln would have been wise to have evacuated the city and thus have preserved his army intact—and he favored such a course of action, but he yielded to the civil authorities and tried to defend the city. The result was disastrous, for on May 12 both city and army were forced to capitulate. Seven generals, 290 other officers, and more than 5,000 men, including 815 North Carolina Continental soldiers and officers and about 600 North Carolina militia became British prisoners-of-war.

Clinton then sailed away on June 5 for New York, leaving Cornwallis in command at Charleston with 8,345 men and with orders to complete the conquest of South Carolina. The British already held Charleston, Beaufort, Georgetown, and Savannah. Their next objectives would be Augusta, "the gateway to Georgia"; Ninety-Six, "the key to communication" between Augusta and Piedmont North Carolina; and Camden, "the key between North and South," located about eighty miles from Ninety-Six. Cornwallis's double task was to hold South Carolina and Georgia and then to conquer North Carolina and Virginia.

North Carolina Prepares for Invasion

North Carolina, with its organized forces sacrificed in defense of its southern neighbors, its resources exhausted, and its people dispirited and alarmed, would have been powerless to resist invasion if it had come then. But Cornwallis, perhaps overconfident, delayed the invasion of North Carolina until fall, and then again until the summer of 1780. Meanwhile he occupied Rocky Mount and Cheraw, reestablished royal rule in South Carolina, and enjoyed himself in his comfortable headquarters at Charleston—now an "occupied city."

His delay gave North Carolina time to organize its resistance. General Caswell, now in command of all North Carolina militia, concentrated the eastern militia at Cross Creek, and in the West many small daring bands, led by Rutherford, Davie, Davidson, Locke, and other intrepid leaders, unsurpassed in guerilla warfare, waged "a romantic partisan warfare, full of midnight marches, sudden surprises, and desperate hand-to-hand combats." They astonished Cornwallis, intimidated and suppressed the Tories, and kept up the "spirit of independence." The purpose of these partisans was to weaken the British and delay the invasion of the state. Cornwallis had planned to invade North Carolina as soon as South Carolina was "quiet and obedient." But he was delayed all summer by partisan bands in South Carolina, led by Francis Marion, Thomas Sumter, and Andrew Pickens. This delay gave North Carolina time to prepare for invasion. The General Assembly resolved that it would defend the state to the last extremity, and on February 7, 1780, appointed Richard Caswell major general of the entire state militia and directed him to raise a regiment of Light Horse from the Wilmington and New Bern districts while General Butler was to raise a regiment of Light Horse from the Hillsborough District.

Partisan Warfare

Within a short time partisan warfare broke out in all its fury. In cooperation with groups from South Carolina, daring bands of North Carolina partisans won many spectacular small battles and rendered the patriot cause valuable service in a variety of ways. At Ramsour's Mill on June 20, some eleven hundred Tories led by "Lieutenant Colonel" John Moore, a Tory who lived in that vicinity, were defeated by a Whig force of from three hundred to four hundred men, led by Colonel Francis Locke and Major Joseph McDowell, who were under the overall command of General Griffith Rutherford. On

July 2 Davie's band of partisans won a victory at Hanging Rock, South Carolina, and on the same day General Davidson defeated some 250 Tories at Colson's Mill on the Pee Dee. On July 31 Davie's band destroyed three Tory companies.

These daring and successful exploits intimidated North Carolina Tories, hampered British military movements, and made it very difficult for the enemy to forage for supplies. Cornwallis reported to Clinton that he must subdue North Carolina or "give up both South Carolina and Georgia and retire within the Walls of Charleston." But he was not yet ready to invade North Carolina.

General Horatio Gates Takes Command of the Southern Army

In August, 1780, General Horatio Gates, hero of the decisive victory at Saratoga, New York (1777), was placed in command of the Southern Department, succeeding Lincoln, now a prisoner-of-war at Charleston. Gates assumed command at Hillsborough on July 25, 1780, with an army of some three thousand Continentals and twelve hundred North Carolina militia led by Caswell and Rutherford. Within a short time Gates and his army marched into South Carolina, with Camden, now held by Lord Rawdon's forces, as his objective. Cornwallis anticipated this action and, ready to move at last, marched from Charleston to Camden, unknown to Gates—and also to Rawdon. On August 16 Gates, with 3,052 men, arrived at Camden, where he was surprised and routed by a British army of about 2,000. The Americans lost 800 killed and about 1,000 captured, as well as large quantities of arms, ammunition, and supplies. About one-half of the dead were North Carolinians. General Rutherford was captured, but Gates, accompanied by Caswell, fled through Charlotte and on to Hillsborough, covering the great distance in a remarkable time of three days. Gates's "Northern laurels had turned to Southern willows," and within a short time he was relieved of his southern command. Former Governor Josiah Martin, now with Cornwallis, declared that North Carolina was "rescued, saved, redeemed and restored." In England it was reported that "North Carolina was only considered as the road to Virginia."

The Board of War

The crushing American defeat at Camden paved the way for the long-feared British invasion and caused panic in North Carolina. Governor Nash hardly knew how to handle the emergency. On August 23 he reported to the General Assembly that the Council of State would not attend sessions or give him assistance in the conduct of the war. Accordingly he recommended that a Board of War be created to share with him the responsibility of military affairs when the legislature was not in session. On September 13, 1780, the General Assembly created a Board of War of three members, composed of

Alexander Martin, John Penn, and Oroondates Davis. Davie opposed the idea of a special board of this nature; he disliked its personnel even more. He said, "Nothing could be more ridiculous than the manner this Board was filled. Alexander the Little, being a Warrior of great fame, was placed at the head of the board. Penn, who was only fit to amuse children, and O. Davis, who knew nothing but a game of Whist, composed the rest of the Board."

Penn was the most active member of the Board of War and almost completely controlled the military operations of the state's forces. This irritated Governor Nash, and at the next session of the legislature he protested that the General Assembly "had no right to subvert the Constitution of the State in such a manner," and that it had deprived him of his rightful powers and left him with but an empty title, neither serviceable to the people nor "honorable to myself." He said that his "authority as commander in chief of the militia is abolished, and every officer and commissioner of the state . . . is made answerable and subject" to the Board of War, and he threatened to resign his office unless restored to his lawful functions. The board was abolished by legislative action on January 31, 1781, and was succeeded by a Council Extraordinary, consisting of Caswell, Martin, and Allen Jones.

Meanwhile Cornwallis was moving slowly—as he usually did—toward North Carolina. He left Camden, September 8, and after being harassed much of the distance by the partisans of Marion and Sumter in South Carolina, he reached Charlotte on September 26. His original plan had been to occupy the town, fortify it, and enlist Tory volunteers. He wrote that he had the "strongest professions of Friendship" in North Carolina and did not anticipate any trouble. His preponderance of forces enabled him to capture Charlotte although, according to Stedman, "The whole of the British army was actually kept at bay for some minutes" by Davie's band of some twenty "mounted Americans."

Cornwallis's situation before and after his occupancy of Charlotte was "rendered very troublesome" by the close attention paid him by Davie and Davidson, and he reported to Clinton that Charlotte was "an agreeable village but in a d—d rebellious country," and that the people were "more hostile to England than any in America." Lieutenant Colonel Banastre Tarleton, one of Cornwallis's leading subordinates, wrote that "the counties of Mecklenburg and Rohon [Rowan] were more hostile to England than any others in America," and he went on to say: "The vigilance and animosity of these surrounding districts checked the exertions of the well affected, and totally destroyed all communications between the King's troops and the loyalists in other parts of the province. No British commander could obtain any information in that position, which would facilitate his designs, or guide his future conduct."

Josiah Martin was not so pessimistic. On October 3 he issued a proclamation announcing British victory and the "restoration of royal rule" in North Carolina. Then, on October 12, Cornwallis received news of the overwhelming

American victory at Kings Mountain on October 7. So he changed his plans again and retreated to South Carolina.

Cornwallis's Plan of Campaign

Before leaving Camden for Charlotte some months earlier Cornwallis had mapped out his general strategy for the southern campaign. First, Major James Craig was to capture Wilmington to protect the right flank of the British army and to provide a port to insure supplies. Craig captured Wilmington in January, 1781, and held the town until after the surrender of Cornwallis at Yorktown. Second, Cornwallis, with the main British army, was to drive straight up through the state to Hillsborough, where he had instructed the Tories of that area to establish magazines and store supplies. Third, in order to arouse the Tories and to protect his left flank from attack by partisan bands, Cornwallis had dispatched from Ninety-Six to the westward one of his best officers, Colonel Patrick Ferguson, with about nine hundred men. Ferguson pursued the "over-mountain men" as far as Gilbert Town in Rutherford County, whence he sent a verbal message that "if they did not desist from their opposition to British arms, he would march his army over the mountains, hang their leaders, and lay their country waste with fire and sword." The frontier leaders answered this contemptuous challenge by calling on the frontiersmen to seize arms and to rendezvous on September 25 at Sycamore Shoals on the Watauga River. Determined on Ferguson's destruction, 240 frontiersmen from Sullivan County under Isaac Shelby, 240 from Washington County led by John Sevier, and 400 from Virginia under William Campbell marched across the mountains to be joined by some 160 from Burke and Rutherford counties under Charles McDowell and 350 from Wilkes and Surry under Benjamin Cleaveland and Joseph Winston, with others from Lincoln under Frederick Hambright and from South Carolina under James Williams and William Lacey, and a few from Georgia. Campbell was chosen leader of the combined forces, and a picked contingent of some nine hundred mounted riflemen was chosen from the whole force of about eighteen hundred to pursue and attack Ferguson.

The Battle of Kings Mountain

The British commander, while pretending to despise the assembling "mongrels," asked Cornwallis for aid and retreated to the southern extremity of Kings Mountain, now in York County, South Carolina, about one and a half miles from the North Carolina line. Camped atop the steep ascent covered with shrubbery and underbrush, eager for military glory, and confident of his strength, Ferguson boasted that "all the Rebels from hell" could not drive him from the mountain.

The picked band of patriots set out from Cowpens, South Carolina, on

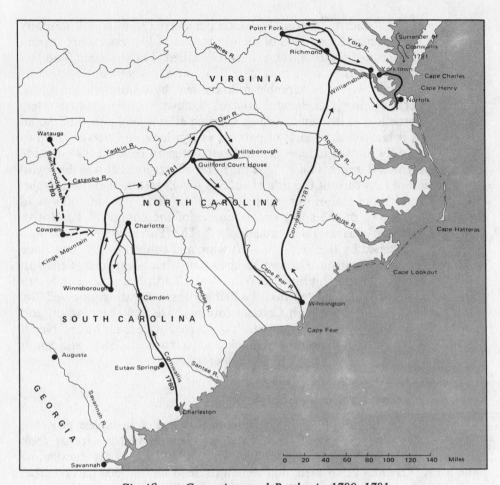

Significant Campaigns and Battles in 1780–1781

Cartography by the Department of Geography and Earth Sciences
The University of North Carolina at Charlotte

October 6, marched all night, and arrived at the foot of Kings Mountain on the afternoon of October 7. Organized in four columns led by Campbell, Sevier, Shelby, and Cleaveland, they were to make immediate and converging assaults. Coolly and quietly scaling the slopes, they attacked the enemy; and for an hour savage combat raged. The patriots, advancing deliberately under shelter of trees and rocks, wrought havoc in the ranks of the enemy by their superb marksmanship. The British and Tories, like a beast at bay, fought desperately, but much of their fire was over the heads of the assaulting patriots. The summit of the mountain proved to be "more assailable by the rifle than defensible with the bayonet." Sounding his silver whistle above the din of battle, and scorning surrender to the "banditti," heroic Ferguson persevered until he fell mortally wounded. His command, deprived of the inspiration of his leadership, surrendered. In addition to Ferguson, there were 119 killed, 123 wounded, and 664 captured. American losses were only 28 killed and 62 wounded.

Kings Mountain was a remarkable military feat by undisciplined militia, under neither state nor Continental control, against a force approximately equal on a battlefield of its own choosing. Coming after a long period of gloom and disaster, it buoyed the hearts of patriots everywhere and nerved them to struggle hopefully toward independence. Later Jefferson recalled that it made a "deep and grateful impression . . . on the mind of everyone. It was the joyful annunciation of that turn of the tide of success which terminated the Revolutionary War with the seal of our independence." General Washington saw in the victory "a proof of the spirit and resources of the country." To British General Clinton it was a "fatal catastrophe." The Tories were cowed into inactivity. Weakened by the loss of his left wing and robbed of his confidence in North Carolina loyalism, Cornwallis abandoned his plans and "fled with great precipitation" from Charlotte to Winnsboro, South Carolina. The North Carolina Board of War reported that the British were retreating, pursued "by Davidson and Davie, who, with Colonel Morgan, are now hanging on and greatly distress them." Kings Mountain had revived American hopes. North Carolina was freed from invasion and quickened to renewed efforts, and South Carolina was fired to rise against her conqueror.

Greene's Southern Campaign

In the fall of 1780, Washington sent one of his ablest generals, Nathanael Greene, to succeed the discredited General Gates. Greene took command at Charlotte, on December 2, of what he said was "only the shadow of an army." He had 2,307 men; half were untrained militia, 300 had no arms and were almost naked, leaving only 800 fit for service. Greene had some brilliant subordinates, such as the Polish Count Kosciusko, William Smallwood of Maryland, and Daniel Morgan, William Washington, and "Light Horse Harry" Lee—all of Virginia. William R. Davie was selected as Greene's commissary general.

Greene did some very careful planning. Rivers were surveyed and mapped, canoes and rafts located. General Davidson remarked that "Greene never saw the Catawba before, but he knows more about it than those who have been raised on its banks."

Though his forces were too weak to attack Cornwallis, Greene audaciously divided his army. With one part he operated along the Pee Dee River with General Isaac Huger, who was stationed at Cheraw; Morgan, with the other portion of Greene's forces, was sent to Ninety-Six with one thousand men, three hundred of whom were North Carolinians. Cornwallis also divided his army.

He remained at Winnsboro, South Carolina, to watch Greene's movements, and sent Tarleton to pursue Morgan, who took position at Cowpens on Broad River, where on January 17, 1781, he routed Tarleton and his forces.

Greene's Historic Retreat

Exasperated at the defeat of his able subordinate and determined to destroy the American forces in the area, Cornwallis set out in pursuit of Morgan, who retreated toward Charlotte, with Cornwallis in pursuit about twenty-five miles in the rear. Greene, now seeing an opportunity to deal the British a deadly blow, ordered Huger to move northward toward Salisbury or Guilford Court House, while he (Greene) raced across country to take command of Morgan's army. Greene marched 125 miles in three days to reach Sherrill's Ford on the Catawba, where he joined Morgan's forces on January 28, the same day Cornwallis arrived at Ramsour's Mill, about twenty-five miles in the rear.

Now followed that masterly and historic retreat of Greene and pursuit by Cornwallis—with three thousand well-armed and well-equipped veterans—across the red hills of Piedmont North Carolina in the dead of winter. Greene had four objectives for his retreat: to draw Cornwallis as far away as possible from his South Carolina bases; to place his own army in safety for recruiting and equipping; to unite the forces of Morgan and Huger; and, finally, to turn on Cornwallis and defeat him.

Superb knowledge of the country, minute preparation, and swollen rivers enabled Green to elude Cornwallis, to cross the Catawba and Yadkin, and after twenty-two days of hard marching, to unite with Huger at Guilford Court House. Cornwallis had reached Salem, about twenty-five miles in the rear—and no nearer Greene than he had been three weeks before. Cornwallis then abandoned pursuit and retired to Hillsborough to rest, refit, and recruit. He issued a proclamation saying that he had come to rescue the loyal subjects of North Carolina "from the cruel tyranny under which they have groaned for several years," and he called on them to join his army at Hillsborough. His proclamation received a cold reception and he failed to obtain a single recruit.

The killing on February 25, 1781, of some ninety Tories, led by Dr. John Pyle, by a force commanded by Henry Lee and Andrew Pickens, in what has been called "Pyle's Massacre," probably cooled the ardor of Tories throughout the Carolina Piedmont.

Meanwhile Greene crossed the Dan River into Virginia on February 13 and, with his army in safety, went through a period of rest and preparation. His retreat had been masterly. The American army had been saved and strengthened. On the other hand, Cornwallis had been pulled 230 miles from his base of supplies at Winnsboro, and now found himself in enemy country in midwinter, and without adequate supplies, among "timid friends and inveterate

Rebels." The pursuit of Greene had cost him 250 men, baggage, wagons, equipment, and heavy cannon. Greene's retreat drew praise—even from the British. Tarleton wrote, "Every movement of the Americans was judiciously designed and vigorously executed." Lord Germain in London declared, "The rebels conduct their enterprises in Carolina with more spirit and skill than they have shown in any other part of America." And General Washington wrote Greene: "Your retreat before Cornwallis is highly applauded by all ranks." War enthusiasm in Virginia and North Carolina reached new heights and recruits flocked to the army. Greene had crossed the Dan into Virginia on February 13 with 1,430 exhausted men; three weeks later he had over 4,000 enrolled. Heavily reenforced by new recruits, he soon marched back into North Carolina. Both he and Cornwallis were eager for battle. A victory was imperative for Cornwallis, but Greene needed only to cripple the enemy. He could replace his losses, but Cornwallis could not.

The Battle of Guilford Court House

Greene took position at Guilford Court House on March 15, and Cornwallis advanced from Hillsborough to meet him. Greene had about 4,400 men, of whom 2,200 were Continentals; Cornwallis had 2,253 men, all seasoned soldiers. Eager to get the best use of his militia, Greene made his tactical disposition conform to the character of his troops, by placing the militia in two lines in front of his Continentals. Three volleys only were asked of the militia, but when the British came in sight the first line gave way, followed shortly by the second. The battle was then given over to the Continentals, many of whom were fighting their first battle. The fighting was furious. Cornwallis was later quoted as saying, "I never saw such fighting since God made me. The Americans fought like demons." Greene's losses were 1,255, but many of these were "wounded or missing." Of this total, 576 belonged to the fleet-footed North Carolina militia, who lost only 7 killed and 6 wounded. Greene's greatest loss was his 290 Continentals. He also lost all of his supporting artillery—his four brass six-pounders. British losses were 93 killed, 413 wounded, and 26 missing—about 25 percent of Cornwallis's army. His greatest loss in personnel was the high casualty among his experienced officers.

Cornwallis remained master of the field, but the battle was a strategic victory for Greene, although it was a tactical defeat. The British army had been so reduced by the march through North Carolina and the battle that Cornwallis was unable to consolidate his gains. News of the battle of Guilford Court House evoked many comments from British political and military leaders, most of them very critical of Cornwallis. Charles James Fox said, "Another such victory would destroy the British army." The *Annual Register* declared, "That victory . . . was productive of all the consequences of defeat." And Horace Walpole declared, "Lord Cornwallis has conquered his troops out of shoes and provisions, and himself out of troops."

Greene's army withdrew from the battlefield and re-formed for another attack, which never came.

Cornwallis was in a dilemma. He was too weak to renew the offensive, but it was disastrous to remain idle. So he announced a victory over Greene and proclaimed the restoration of royal government in North Carolina, calling upon "all loyal subjects to stand forth and take an active part in restoring good order and government." He offered pardon to all rebels who would lay down their arms. His appeal fell on deaf ears and he found himself in a desperate situation. A month later he wrote, "Many of the Inhabitants rode into camp, shook me by the hand, said they were glad to see us, and to hear that we had beat Greene, and then rode home again." His losses of men and supplies must be repaired. But how and where? It was essential for him to have contact with the British fleet, and Wilmington, held by a British force under Major Craig, was the nearest place. So he broke camp and began a slow march to Wilmington. Greene followed as far as Deep River and then called off the pursuit and returned to South Carolina, where he maneuvered the British out of Camden, Augusta, Ninety-Six, and other interior posts—leaving them in possession of only Charleston, Savannah, and Wilmington in the whole South.

Cornwallis Marches to Wilmington and then to Yorktown

Cornwallis reached Wilmington on April 7. His situation was humiliating. He was victorious but helpless. He was confused and exasperated at being ignored by Greene. He wrote that Greene "took advantage of my being obliged to come to this place, and has marched to South Carolina." Cornwallis could return to Charleston and start all over again—a plan that would be an admission of failure and that he said "would be as ruinous and disgraceful to Britain as most events could be." His other alternative was to abandon North Carolina and invade Virginia. This he chose to do, and for the third time he proclaimed the conquest of North Carolina, announced the restoration of Governor Josiah Martin to office, and on April 25 set out from Wilmington to join General Phillips in Virginia. Soon he took position at Yorktown, where, after a siege that began on September 7—hemmed in by the French and American armies and by De Grasse's French fleet—he surrendered to General Washington on October 19, 1781. The war was over, though Major Craig did not evacuate Wilmington until November 18.

When news of the Yorktown surrender reached North Carolina, there were celebrations, bonfires, parades, and salutes. A judge failed to attend court because at "the news of the capture of Cornwallis, we were all so elated, that the time elapsed in frolicking." The majority of North Carolinians had the same feeling of jubilation that the long war was over and that independence had been won.

Chapter 16

AFTERMATH OF THE REVOLUTION

The surrender of Cornwallis at Yorktown on October 19, 1781, followed by Major Craig's evacuation of Wilmington on November 18, ended the military phase of the Revolution in North Carolina, though the "Tory War" dragged on until the departure of the notorious David Fanning in May, 1782. Meantime peace negotiations had been going on in Paris, culminating in the Treaty of September 3, 1783, in which "His Britannic Majesty" acknowledged the United States "to be free, sovereign and independent States."

Conditions in North Carolina in 1783

Several months earlier, on April 19, Governor Alexander Martin laid before the General Assembly a copy of the treaty—"the most important intelligence that has yet arrived on the American continent," optimistically declaring, "Nothing now remains but to enjoy the fruits of uninterrupted Constitutional Freedom." A more realistic view of conditions in the state was presented by Frederick William Marschall of Salem, when he wrote: "This country is in the condition of a patient convalescing from fever, who begins to be conscious of his weakness and still needs medicine and care. The land itself, the people of property, commerce, public and private credit, the currency in circulation all are laid waste and ruined." And Archibald D. Murphey some years later said, "When the war ended, the people were in poverty, society in disorder, morals and manners almost prostrate."

The period from the close of hostilities to the adoption of the United States Constitution in 1789 was a "critical period" for North Carolina and for most of the states comprising the "new nation." The 350,000 people in the state's forty-seven counties were confronted with many grave problems—a weak and inefficient state government, unsatisfactory local government, political strife and bitterness, economic depression, and general social demoralization.

254

The solution to some of these problems could be postponed; others demanded immediate attention. Some matters were purely state or local; others were national in scope, and some were related to international affairs. Problems that demanded immediate action were the demobilization and treatment of veterans of the Revolution; release of prisoners of war; state policy in relation to loyalists and their property; and the location of a permanent capital. The solution of these and other problems was closely related to party politics, the weakness of the executive power, and the general confusion in state government.

Political Strife and Chaos

Mention has already been made of the weakness of the state administration during the war. The situation did not improve after Yorktown. If anything, it deteriorated. Governor Thomas Burke summarized the governmental problem succinctly when he told the legislature, "Neglect of Duty, Abuses of power, Disobedience of Laws, Your monies unaccounted for, and public credit almost sunk, all call for your authority and correction."

In his message to the General Assembly of 1782 Burke emphasized the negligence of officials and the widespread inefficiency in local government. He declared that "the insufficiency of the provisions for the Judges and Attorney General has much embarrassed the Judiciary Department of the Government and threatens to leave the State almost without Courts of Justice." And Governor Alexander Martin, the next year, said that courts could hardly construe the badly drafted laws, and that there was no "regular system of jurisprudence" in the state.

Conservatives and Radicals

During the war there had been political divisions, but there was some semblance of unity among the Whigs. With the cessation of hostilities old party lines tended to disappear and party politics in the state from 1781 to 1789 was characterized by personal factionalism and sectional interests. There were two major groups—as already mentioned—Conservatives and Radicals, a division that bore a close relation to social classes, economic interests, and geography. The Conservatives embraced lawyers, merchants, shippers, large planters and slaveholders, land speculators, and moneylenders. Most of the educated, the wealthy, and the creditor class were in this "party," which constituted a small minority of the population and drew its chief strength from the East and from the towns and commercial centers. This group had the ablest and most distinguished leaders—Samuel Johnston, James Iredell, Hugh Williamson, William R. Davie, Archibald Maclaine, William Hooper, Allen Jones, John Steele, and others.

The Radicals constituted the great bulk of North Carolina people—small farmers and artisans—many of them uneducated, poor, and in debt. They were most numerous in the backcountry, but were found in large numbers throughout the state. Their leaders, such as Willie Jones, Thomas Person, Samuel Spencer, Matthew Locke, and Timothy Bloodworth, were skillful in the arts of manipulating the masses and in gaining control of the machinery of state and local government.

There were other political leaders whose views were between these two extremes. These Moderates included such men as Richard Caswell and Alexander Martin, though at various times these and other Moderates were claimed by one or the other of the political factions. Such was the nature of North Carolina politics in the "critical period."

The Conservatives advocated a stronger state executive and judiciary than did the Radicals; they also favored a stronger national government than that existing under the Articles of Confederation (1781–89). They opposed the issuance of more paper currency, confiscation of Tory property, the outlawing of British debts, and the cession of western lands, all of which were supported by the Radicals. Each group distrusted the other and accused the opposition of holding dangerous views and engaging in dirty politics. William Hooper admitted that he distrusted the "common people," whose votes could "always be purchased by a drink of toddy." And Samuel Johnston denounced the Radicals in the legislature who supported paper money as "a set of unprincipled men, who sacrificed everything to their popularity and private views."

Prisoners of War

When the war ended there were hundreds, perhaps thousands, of North Carolina prisoners of war at Charleston, chiefly those who had surrendered at the capitulation of that city in May, 1780, and including others sent there after the Battle of Camden. Some North Carolina prisoners were also in camps or on prison ships in the British West Indies and off the Florida coast. There had been fruitless negotiations for exchange of prisoners in 1781, but when the General Assembly of 1782 convened, few or no North Carolina prisoners had been released. Consequently the legislature authorized Governor Martin to negotiate with the British commanding officer at Charleston, General Alexander Leslie, for the exchange of these prisoners for "our disaffected Inhabitants guilty of Military offences only." Governor Martin, ably assisted by General Nathanael Greene, completed negotiations in 1783 and announced to the General Assembly of that year that the exchange had been completed.

Veterans' Legislation

The soldiers of the state—Continental and militia—had made tremendous physical and financial sacrifices and the state leaders felt a moral and legal obligation to its veterans. The urgency of relief measures, the empty treasury, and the adundance of vast western lands seemed to point to a solution—land grants to soldiers. Accordingly the Bonus Act of 1780 was passed, setting aside a military reservation, and this was followed two years later by a supplementary act, which granted lands to soldiers and officers, ranging from 640 acres for each private soldier to 12,000 acres for each brigadier general. A commission was appointed in 1782 to survey and lay off lands according to soldiers' claims. Another commission was created to settle in specie the losses of North Carolina officers and soldiers of the Continental Line on account of the depreciation of paper currency and deficiencies of clothing and other supplies due them.

Loyalists and Their Property

The problem of loyalists was not so easily solved, because the war had left its scars, and Tories were considered much as "fifth columnists" would be today. Since the passage of the Confiscation Acts of 1777 and 1779—Griffith Rutherford referred to them as "Imps of Hell"—there had been sharp divisions of opinion concerning the treatment of Tories. The Radical Whigs favored confiscation of their property and demanded stern punitive measures when the war ended. They deplored the article in the Treaty of Paris that advised restitution of confiscated Tory properties by the states, and they were determined that this policy should not be enforced. Some Conservative Whigs, on the other hand, had denounced the Confiscation Acts and demanded leniency after the war—a policy of "forgive and forget." Governor Martin urged the General Assembly to adopt a policy of conciliation. The "Act of Pardon and Oblivion" of 1783 had been called a "compromise," but its provisions seemed harsh to many people. It extended pardon to all Tories, except five classes: "Those who had held commissions in the British army; those sixty-eight men specifically named in the Confiscation Act of 1779; Tories absent from the state during the previous twelve months; those 'guilty of deliberate and wilful murder, rape, robbery, or house-burning'; and Peter Mallet, Samuel Andrews, and David Fanning."

Despite the apparent "pardon" of the rank and file of loyalists, they did not enjoy "oblivion." Many suffered social and political ostracism as well as economic discriminations. Hundreds left the state for new homes in England, Scotland, Canada, and Florida. The petitions of various loyalists for the restitution of their property were rejected, which led William Hooper to remark, "There is not a frenzy of misguided political zeal—avarice clothed in the cover of patriotism—of private passion and prejudice, under the pretence of revenging the wrongs of the country . . . that can give me the least surprise hereafter."

The state government continued to sell confiscated Tory property, the Treaty of Paris provision to the contrary notwithstanding. A report to the legislature of 1783 revealed that such property to the amount of £583,643–8–0 had been sold, and a later report indicated than an additional £284,452–4–0 had been realized from sales between 1784 and 1790. The legislature of 1785 passed a law prohibiting the courts "to entertain suits for the recovery of property," the title to which was based on the Confiscation Acts.

Bayard vs. Singleton, 1786–1787

One of the most famous cases in the history of North Carolina jurisprudence arose under the law of 1785. Mrs. Bayard, the plantiff, brought "ejectment proceedings" against one Singleton for the recovery of some property that had been willed to her by her Tory merchant father, Samuel Cornell of New Bern, but had been confiscated by the state and sold to Singleton. Mrs. Bayard, who was not a resident of the state, was represented by outstanding legal talent—Iredell, Johnston, and Davie. Singleton had able counsel in the persons of Abner Nash and Alfred Moore. The defendant's lawyers stressed the fact that both Cornell and his daughter were "British subjects," and made a motion to dismiss the case. The judges, Samuel Ashe, Samuel Spencer, and John Williams, refused to grant the request, citing Article 14 of the bill of rights, which guaranteed jury trial. Most significant of all, they declared the Confiscation Act, under which the property had been seized and sold, as unconstitutional. The court also held that aliens could not hold land in the state and that alien enemies had no political rights at all. At a trial in November, 1787, the jury found a verdict for the defendant. Twenty-seven other cases of a similar nature were dropped from the court docket at this time.

There was much public criticism of the court's decision, and some lawyers were determined "to write the judges off the bench." The General Assembly authorized "an enquiry into the present state of the administration of Justice in the Superior Courts," and there was talk of impeachment of the judges. But instead of taking such drastic action, the legislature upheld their decision and voted thanks "for their long and faithful service." The significance of *Bayard* vs. *Singleton* is that it was the "first decision under a written constitution" declaring a legislative act unconstitutional—a principle applied by Chief Justice John Marshall in *Marbury* v. *Madison* in 1803, and now considered a fundamental principle of American law.

Location of the State Capital

By the outbreak of the Revolution New Bern, which had been the colonial capital for about a decade, was no longer "the most sentrical town" in North Carolina and there was an increasing demand, especially from the West, for a new capital. Almost every town in the state was eager to be the "seat of government," especially Fayetteville, Tarboro, and Hillsborough. New

Bern remained the capital until 1778, but the pressure for a new "permanent seat of government," which could furnish adequate facilities for legislators and other officials, kept mounting.

Many efforts were made to solve this problem the next few years. Every legislature from 1777 to 1791 discussed the matter. In 1781 Hillsborough was chosen as the site, but there was much opposition to this decision, especially after Governor Thomas Burke was taken prisoner by the Tories in that town. In a political trade by which Alexander Martin was elected governor, the law was repealed in 1782. During the ensuing years the General Assembly met at seven different places—Hillsborough, Halifax, Smithfield, Fayetteville, New Bern, Tarboro, and Wake Court House. The migrations of legislatures from town to town, the residence of the governor and other administrative officials at different places, the location of government records in private homes, and the hauling of these records "in a common cart" from town to town did not make for efficiency in government and were a serious obstacle to business.

The General Assembly finally admitted its failure to solve the capital problem and referred it to the Hillsborough Convention of 1788, which had been called to vote on the Constitution of the United States. This convention adopted an ordinance—considered superior to an act of the legislature and repealable only by action of another convention—which provided that the capital be located within ten miles of Isaac Hunter's plantation in Wake County, leaving the selection of the particular site to the legislature. Almost half of the convention delegates—119 of 268—protested against the majority's decision, contending that a place "unconvenient with commerce" would never "rise above the degree of a village." This dissenting minority maintained that Fayetteville was centrally located "at the head of the best navigation in the State" and that its selection "would have a great and instantaneous effect upon the decayed commerce of this country . . . the principal part of which is now exported from Virginia and South Carolina."

The legislature failed to take action on the capital question at the next session, but in 1791, as a result of a trade between the Wake-Neuse and Albemarle delegates, a legislative commission of nine members was chosen to select the exact site, purchase not less than 640 acres and not more than 1,000 acres, to lay off a city of not less than 400 acres into one-acre lots, to lay out streets, the main ones being 99 and the others 66 feet wide, to reserve 20 or more lots for public buildings, and to sell the remaining lots at public auction. Another commission of five members was chosen to build the "state house" from proceeds of the sale of city lots.

The Joel Lane Plantation Purchased for Capital Site

In March, 1792, a majority of the nine-man commission visited more than a dozen farms in Wake County within ten miles of Hunter's plantation, and after some difficulty, amid the keen rivalry of various farmers eager to sell their land, they purchased Joel Lane's plantation of one thousand acres located near Wake Court House, for the sum of £1,378.

The "New City" of Raleigh

As laid off by the commissioners in 1792—with William Christmas of Franklin County employed as surveyor, the new city contained 400 acres, comprising the streets and 276 lots of one acre each. Five public squares were reserved—Union, Caswell, Burke, Nash, and Moore. The streets were laid off and named—the eight nearest Union (Capitol Square)—after the eight judicial districts, Edenton, New Bern, Hillsborough, Halifax, Salisbury, Fayetteville, Wilmington, and Morgan; nine other streets were named for the commissioners; four others, North, South, East, and West; and the remaining four after Speakers Lenoir and Cabarrus of the General Assembly, Joel Lane, and William R. Davie. The lots were sold at public auction in 1792, and the General Assembly of that year ratified the work of the commissioners and named the city "Raleigh."

The building committee, from the proceeds of the sale of lots, erected a cheap structure, in which the legislature met for the first time on December 30, 1794. Richard Dobbs Spaight was the first governor to occupy the new capitol, which was completed in 1796.

Beginnings of Cultural Recovery

There was a gradual postwar revival of social, educational, and religious activities and institutions. The press, which had been discontinued in 1778, was revived in 1783 when Robert Keith began to print the *North Carolina Gazette* at New Bern. Between that date and 1799 fifteen newspapers were published at Wilmington, Halifax, New Bern, Edenton, Fayetteville, Hillsborough, Raleigh, and Salisbury.

There was also a renewal of literary activity. Scores of pamphlets and newspaper essays were printed, chiefly on political and religious subjects, but occasionally on a purely literary or historical theme. The favorite topics of writers were political—loyalists, soldiers' bonuses, paper currency, state and federal governments, particularly the Constitution of the United States. As was the custom of the day, most writers used a *nom de plume*. Hugh Williamson wrote under the pseudonym of "Sylvius"; Maurice Moore, "Atticus"; James Iredell, "Marcus," "Sully," "Tiberius Gracchus," "True Citizen," and "Plain Farmer"; Archibald Maclaine, "Publicola"; and James Tate, "Honestus."

Religious subjects were second to politics in interest and volume, the favorite topics being immersion versus sprinkling, infant baptism, the dangers of "popery," and separation of church and state.

Apparently writers, publishers, and inventors were eager to have protection for their handiwork, and in 1785 a copyright and patent law was enacted "to encourage genius, to promote useful discoveries and the general extension of arts and commerce."

Other evidences of cultural awakening were the organization of drama clubs, such as the Thalian Association of Wilmington, and the increasing popularity of amateur and professional theatrical performances. Two traveling companies gave shows at no fewer than seven North Carolina towns in the 1787–88 seasons—Edenton, Wilmington, New Bern, Halifax, Windsor, Hillsborough, and Tarboro. Robert Keith established a bookstore at New Bern in 1783 and by 1800 several newspapers were advertising books for sale in local stores. In 1800 a Raleigh paper advertised books in nine categories: religion, novels, law, history and biography, politics and commerce, natural history and geography, voyages and travels, poetry, and juveniles. In 1783 the Society of the Cincinnati was organized at Hillsborough, and in 1787 the Masonic Order was reorganized at Tarboro.

Revival of Interest in Education

There were changes in the educational ideals of North Carolina and other states after 1776. In line with English ideas, which had generally prevailed throughout the colonial era, most people considered education primarily a function of the church and advocated only the education of "gentlemen" and those of the professional classes. Consequently what little education North Carolina enjoyed before the Revolution was controlled by the churches, especially the Church of England and the Presbyterian.

The Revolutionary political philosophy, stressing the principle of religious equality, political democracy, and the right of people to self-government meant —or should have meant—that the success of government depended on educated leaders and citizenry. These ideas broadened the concept of education as the function of the state, as clearly expressed in Article 41 of the State Constitution of 1776: "That a School or Schools shall be established by the Legislature for the convenient Instruction of Youth, with such Salaries to the Masters paid by the Public, as may enable them to instruct at low Prices; and all useful Learning shall be duly encouraged and promoted in one or more Universities."

In spite of this constitutional mandate the legislature failed to establish public schools, and it was extremely slow in taking steps to found a state university. Friends of education interpreted the constitutional provision to mean the establishment of public schools, but the General Assembly contented itself with the incorporation of academies.

Academies

Academies were private schools, although they received legislative charters of incorporation, which created a governing board of trustees and defined its powers and duties. The academies were allowed to grant certificates, but not diplomas or degrees. The trustees usually selected the teachers, prescribed the curriculum, gave the examinations, and, in some instances, administered discipline. A variety of subjects were taught, from reading, writing, and arithmetic to the "ornamental subjects" of needlework, bookkeeping, and astronomy. There were strict rules of conduct and much emphasis on the moral training of students. In some respects the fourth "R" (religion) was more important than reading, writing, and arithmetic.

The academies were operated primarily for education and not for profit. Their financial resources—always meager—came from donations, lotteries, and tuition fees. These fees varied, but usually ran from twelve to twenty dollars a term, which was usually a period of several months. Tuition was charged by all the academies, though occasionally a charter of incorporation required that a certain number of poor children be educated free. It was not easy for some of the academies to procure teachers, because of low salaries. So the legislature gave an "assist to education" by granting teachers exemption from public taxes and militia service.

Forty-one academies, chiefly for boys, were chartered by the General Assembly, 1777–80. New Bern had five academies in 1800; Warrenton had several famous ones, especially the Warrenton Academy, headed by Marcus George, and the well-known "Mordecai Female Seminary." Other famous academies were Hall's Clio's Nursery at Statesville and the Salem Female Academy, which was, in a sense, the forerunner of Salem College.

Founding of the University of North Carolina

The American Revolutionary era witnessed an increasing interest in higher education. There were only nine colleges in the thirteen states at the outbreak of hostilities, and all of these except the College of Philadelphia (later the University of Pennsylvania) were sectarian institutions. With the advent of the Revolution a new ideal in higher education became manifest—that of the state university—best exemplified by the University of Pennsylvania, the University of Georgia, the first state university to be chartered, and the University of North Carolina, the first to open its doors to students (1795).

The origins of the University of North Carolina may be traced back to Section 41 of the state constitution. Perhaps the germ of the idea existed in a proposed college in the colonial era discussed in a previous chapter. But thirteen years elapsed before the state legislature carried out the mandate of the constitution. A long and costly war, a weak and poverty-stricken state at its close, confusion in politics, and other factors explain this delay. Most of the Federalists favored the creation of a state university, but the Antifederalists, who usually controlled the General Assembly, opposed the idea.

In 1784 the Sharpe bill to establish a university was defeated by the legislature. But the Federalists, led by William R. Davie, kept up the fight, and on December 11, 1789, the General Assembly, meeting at Fayetteville, chartered the University of North Carolina, declaring that "in all well regulated Governments, it is the indispensable duty of every Legislature to consult the Happiness of a rising Generation, and endeavor to fit them for an honorable Discharge of the Social Duties of Life, by paying the strictest attention to their Education." Ten days later the legislature passed an accompanying act providing for the erection of buildings and for the support of the university through escheats and arrearages due the state.

One of the major problems was to get funds with which to build and operate a university. The act of incorporation provided for a building fund, but made no appropriation for it, and the trustees were dependent upon private donations, student fees, sale of lands, and the escheats and arrearages due the state. A special meeting of the Board of Trustees was held at Fayetteville on December 18, 1789, to accept Benjamin Smith's offer of twenty thousand acres of Tennessee land. Shortly thereafter Charles Gerrard donated thirteen thousand acres, and Thomas Person $1,025 in cash. Several smaller donations were made. Every person who subscribed £10 towards the university, to be paid within five years, was to be entitled to have one student educated at the institution free from "any expense of tuition." The results were disappointing. Total cash receipts from gifts in 1790 amounted to only $2,700. Consequently the Board of Trustees asked the legislature for a loan and received $10,000—later converted into a gift, largely through Davie's efforts. This was the only legislative appropriation—if it can be called that—which the university received for almost a century.

The charter placed certain restrictions on the location of the university by providing for the "fixing on and purchasing a healthy and convenient situation, which shall not be situate within five miles of the permanent seat of government, or any of the places of holding the courts of law or equity." After consideration of many possible sites, the trustees' committee, headed by Frederick Hargett, selected New Hope Chapel, now Chapel Hill. This place was about the geographic center of the state, where important north-south and east-west roads intersected. The name "Chapel Hill" is found in the report of the Board of Trustees for November, 1792, and a contemporary account gives the following description: "The seat of the University is on the summit of a very high ridge. . . . The ridge appears to commence about half a mile directly east of the building, where it rises abruptly several hundred feet. This peak is called Point Prospect. The flat country spreads out below like the ocean, giving an immense hemisphere in which the eye seems lost in the extent of space."

Donations of 1,380 acres of land by local citizens were accepted by the Board of Trustees and the cornerstone of the first building, now known as Old East, was laid October 12, 1793, in a Masonic ceremony conducted by Davie, then Grand Master of Masons in the state. Formal opening exercises were held January 15, 1795, but the first student, Hinton James of New Hanover (now Pender) County, did not arrive until February 12. For two weeks he was the student body. At the end of the term there were two professors and forty-one students. During the next term the student body numbered about one hundred.

The trustees were given authority to appoint a president and professors and tutors, whom they could "remove for misbehaviour, inability, or neglect of duty." They could also "make all such laws and regulations for the government of the university and preservation of order and good morals therein as are usually made by such seminaries, and as to them may appear necessary: Provided, the same are not contrary to the inalienable liberty of a citizen or to the laws of the State."

No president was chosen for the university. Instead there was a "Presiding Professor," who was responsible for all teaching. He was a "Professor of Humanity," and received a salary of $300 a year and two-thirds of the tuition money. Dr. David Ker, a Presbyterian minister and schoolteacher, was the first presiding professor. In 1804 Dr. Joseph Caldwell, who had been a professor in the university for several years, was selected as its first president.

Religious Developments

The Revolutionary War and independence from England had a profound effect or organized religion. Missionary activity declined among nearly all the churches; that of the Anglican Church, hitherto carried on by the Society for the Propagation of the Gospel, disappeared. There was a cessation of church building and a disorganization of many congregations. Four religious sects lost ground or remained almost static—Anglicans, Quakers, Moravians, and German Reformed.

The Church of England, which had been established by law early in the century and was always unpopular with non-Anglicans, had become anathema to other denominations. Most of its clergy and some of its leading laymen— though not all by any means—were Tories. The Anglican Church was officially disestablished in the state by the Constitution of 1776, although it maintained a skeleton organization to the close of the war, having five ministers and a few hundred members in 1783. Sporadic efforts after the Revolution to organize a Protestant Episcopal Church in North Carolina failed to materialize until 1817, when the Reverend John Stark Ravenscroft became the first Bishop of the Diocese of North Carolina.

Quakers and Moravians also felt the impact of war, especially the Quakers. These were the two chief pacifist sects in the state and their refusal of military service led the legislature to enact laws exempting them from active service, but imposing extra taxation, such as the three-fold tax of 1779. Some Quakers did take up arms, and the three leading Quaker meetings in the "Western Quarter"—Cane Creek, Deep River and New Garden—"disowned" some of their flock for bearing arms. The Moravians took no active part in the hostilities, but their friendly services to the suffering civilians and wounded soldiers on both sides received the commendation of British and American leaders. The Moravian Church held its own or even showed a slight increase in membership during the Revolution, though immigration from Pennsylvania ceased. The Lutheran and German Reformed churches tended to decline as German immigration ceased and language difficulties prevented their extension among non-German-speaking people.

Baptists

The Baptists were the largest and most rapidly growing sect in North Carolina when the war began, with forty-two churches and 3,276 members in 1784. Their growth was temporarily checked by the war, though most Baptists were ardent supporters of the patriot cause. The church revived quickly after the war, and by 1792 there were ninety-four Baptist churches and 7,503 members, making it the largest religious denomination in the state. In fact, it had as many members as all other sects combined.

Methodists

There was no official Methodist Church until after the Revolution, although a large number of Methodist societies had been organized. The war had a disastrous effect on Methodism in North Carolina and other English colonies. John Wesley, founder of the "Methodist movement," had appealed in his "Calm Address" to his American followers and friends to remain loyal to the mother country—advice many heeded. As a result, Methodists were stigmatized and were unpopular. Local churches were closed, missionary activity ceased, and the activities of Methodist societies were greatly restricted. In 1780 Francis Asbury, one of the great personalities in the history of Methodism, made a missionary tour that included North Carolina, and that resulted in renewed activities among the Methodists. By 1783 there were ten Methodist circuits and 2,339 members in the state. The formal organization of the Methodist Episcopal Church in the United States occurred at Baltimore in 1784 when Francis Asbury and Thomas Coke were selected as "superintendents" (later known as bishops). In 1785 the first general Methodist Conference was held by Asbury and Coke in the home of Green Hill at Louisburg. This might be called the official beginning of the Methodist Church in North Carolina.

Presbyterians

The Presbyterian Church also felt the impact of the Revolution. Its chief strength before the war had been among the Highland Scots of the Upper Cape Fear and the Scotch-Irish of the Piedmont. The loyalism of the Highlanders led to a large exodus from the state and temporarily checked Presbyterianism in the Cape Fear Valley. The Scotch-Irish, on the other hand, displayed a fierce hostility to England. The Presbyterian Church was firmly established in the state by 1777, and the two Carolinas, included in the Orange Synod, embraced about forty churches. In the decade following the war, many new congregations were organized, new ministers brought in, and new churches begun. This increase in interest, activity, and membership led to the organization of the Carolina Synod in 1788, when there were twenty-eight Presbyterian pastors ministering to perhaps several thousand members organized into a half hundred or more congregations.

General State of Organized Religion

Thus by 1790 Baptist, Methodist, and Presbyterian churches were well established and growing. There were some Catholics and Jews in the state, but the records throw little light on their numbers or influence. There had been considerable progress among some churches; yet religion was rather backward in the state, hampered as it was by sparseness of population, difficulties of transportation, poverty of the people, and scarcity of ministers. Only a very small percentage of the population belonged to any church. On the most optimistic basis for estimating church membership in 1790, there were not over 14,000 to 15,000 church members in the state's total population of 393,751 —about one out of thirty. Perhaps Asbury was correct when he referred to the North Carolina people as "gospel slighters." There was some deism, especially among the upper classes; among the masses there was much inertia, as well as indifference to organized religion. North Carolina was fertile ground for the "Great Revival," which took place soon after 1800.

Economic Conditions after the Revolution

The war had left North Carolina in debt, its currency worthless, its English markets virtually lost, its West Indian trade greatly restricted, British bounties on naval stores gone, and specie extremely scarce. Agriculture, industry, and trade had languished during the war and did not revive for several years. Most of the state's population led a simple, low-level economic existence and still pursued an extractive colonial economy.

Judged by modern governmental debts and expenditures, it might appear that the state government was not in such bad condition. A legislative committee of 1789 reported the total state debt at $3,480,000, or about nine dollars per capita. State expenses were only about $100,000 a year, but public taxes yielded less than this sum, being only $86,000 in 1786, which was considered a prosperous year. Taxes were very low compared to modern standards. The poll tax rate from 1790 to 1811 was only two shillings; from 1811 to 1813, two shillings and six pence; after 1813, three shillings. The tax on land was eight cents on the $100 valuation before 1817, when it was reduced to six cents. There were a few "miscellaneous taxes," which did not hit the masses—such as the tax on carriage wheels, stores, billiard tables, peddlers, shows, gates, brokers, and slave traders. The paper currency situation was better than it had been during the Revolution, but it was still considered critical, especially by the Conservatives. The legislature, dominated by "cheap money" men, authorized £100,000 of legal tender notes in 1783, and another £100,000 in 1785. This action infuriated the Conservatives, caused "hard money to pass at a fifty percent premium," and led some merchants to leave the state in disgust.

Laws Designed to Improve Economic Conditions

The governors during this "critical period" repeatedly called the attention of the General Assembly to the gravity of the state's economic problems, and much legislation was enacted in an effort to correct some of the difficulties. Laws were passed to provide for "adequate security of titles to property"; to encourage building; "to regulate the value of currency"; for clearing and marking the channels of rivers and sounds; for erecting lighthouses; for regulating pilotage; for building roads, bridges, and ferries; and for reopening the State Land Office. In 1783 a one-year "stay law" was enacted for debts contracted during the current year. The legislature endeavored to encourage industry by offering a bounty of three thousand acres of land for each iron furnace erected. No less than fifty-nine laws were passed between 1783 and 1789, designed to increase the sale of public lands, which resulted in a slow but steady increase of sales. In December, 1786, Virginia and North Carolina commissioners agreed to build the Dismal Swamp Canal from Deep Creek, Virginia, to the Pasquotank River in North Carolina, and a capital of $80,000 was authorized for this purpose.

Transportation and Trade

Water transportation, as in the colonial era, was the most satisfactory and widely used method of trade—and to some extent of travel. Boat ownership was general, and a large number of people, especially in the East, had canoes, periaugers, scows, and flats, engaged in river trade to local markets,

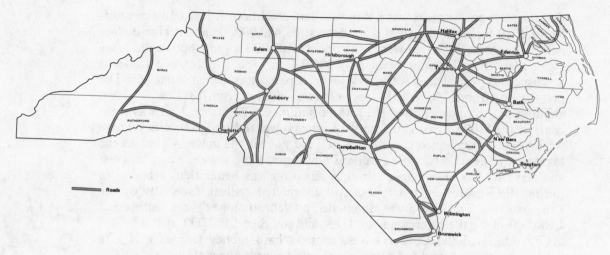

North Carolina in 1783 (Not Including the Territory Ceded to the United States and Later Admitted to the Union as the State of Tennessee), Showing Counties, Roads, and Towns

Cartography by the Department of Geography and Earth Sciences
The University of North Carolina at Charlotte

carrying tobacco, naval stores, and a variety of products. In 1787 on the Tar and Neuse there were some scows and flatboats carrying as many as seventy or eighty hogsheads of tobacco. There were dangers of shoals, logs, snags, currents, and fish dams, and as early as 1780 laws were passed ordering that rivers be cleared of all obstructions, but there was no state aid, and local authorities did not enforce these laws.

Shipbuilding

A considerable number of ships were built from live oak and other timbers at several places in the East. Of seventy-eight small schooners and sloops clearing Port Roanoke in the three summer months of 1788, forty-four were built in North Carolina.

Foreign Trade

External commerce, which had dwindled during the Revolution and the years immediately thereafter, began to revive in the mid-eighties. The port records of 1787 show that in that year 697 vessels came into the state via Ocracoke, and the next year 218 cleared from Wilmington and 78 from Port Roanoke in the three summer months. By 1788–89 more ships came to the Cape Fear than ever before and trade reached a new high. The registered

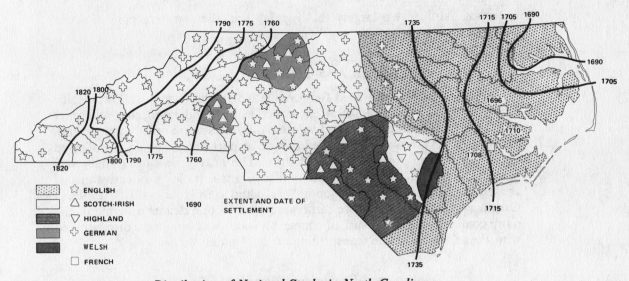

Distribution of National Stocks in North Carolina

Cartography by the Department of Geography and Earth Sciences
The University of North Carolina at Charlotte

tonnage for North Carolina in 1790 was 20,671 in foreign trade and 6,553 in coastwise commerce.

The total tonnage had increased over 100 percent since 1769, and all five ports, especially Brunswick and Roanoke, had increased their volumes of trade. Before the Revolution about one-third of the colony's trade had been to the British Isles and another third to the British West Indies. Now only about one-tenth of the foreign trade of the state went to Great Britain, about one-half to the West Indies, and the remaining two-fifths to other American states. There was also a shift in the type of exports, though naval stores still ranked first, in spite of the loss of the British bounty. New England replaced England as the chief customer for these stores. The export of provisions was greater than before the war—160,000 bushels of corn being exported in 1788 compared to 127,000 in 1769. Lumber shipments reached a new high, especially shingles, 20,000,000 being exported in 1788. The greatest proportionate increase was in tobacco exports—about 6,000,000 pounds being shipped out in 1788, compared to only 360,000 pounds in 1768.

There were changes in the import trade also. The total tonnage almost doubled, and the volume of goods trebled between 1768 and 1788. About 47 percent of the imports came from the West Indies and about 10 percent from the British Isles; most of the remainder came in coastwise. The type of goods imported was about the same as before the war. Trade of the backcountry changed very little from that of the colonial era. The "northern part" of the state was "still drawn largely to Virginia" and the southern part to South Carolina.

Tariff Duties, 1783–1789

The state's need for revenue led to the levying of low specific duties on pepper, sugar, molasses, cocoa, coffee, wine, cider, gin, rum, and other spirituous liquors and to a low ad valorem duty on several other commodities. The law of 1785, however, provided that no import duties should be collected on any articles of American manufacture. The next year a heavy duty was placed on imported slaves in order to discourage a trade "productive of evil consequences, and highly impolitic." It could hardly be said that North Carolina engaged in interstate tariff wars to the same degree as some of the more commercial states. And, of course, all state tariff laws were discontinued with the adoption of the Constitution of the United States.

Growth and Expansion of Population

There was a steady increase in North Carolina population in the postwar generation. The decennial census reports from 1790 to 1820 gave North Carolina's population as 393,751; 478,103; 550,500; and 638,829.

By the time of the outbreak of the Revolution white settlements were being made along the foot of the Blue Ridge. By treaties with the Cherokee Indians in 1777 all lands east of the Blue Ridge were ceded to the state; and, by Indian treaties with the United States in 1785, 1791, and 1798, nearly all lands in North Carolina east of the Alleghenies became state property. These treaties threw open the whole mountain region to the whites, and while there had been a few isolated families in the area before 1783, settlers rushed into the region after that date. In 1784 Samuel Davidson settled in the Swannanoa Valley, and he was followed shortly by John Patton, Charles McDowell, Robert Henry, James Alexander, and others. In 1798 David Vance settled on Reams Creek and Zebulon Baird of New Jersey brought the "first four wheel wagon ever seen in Buncombe County," which had been created a county two years before. In 1795 George Swain came from Massachusetts, and about the same time the Lowries were taking up lands along the French Broad. Asheville was incorporated in 1797.

Settlement of the Trans-Allegheny Region

Though the Carolina charters of 1629, 1663, and 1665 had given North Carolina a valid claim to lands westward to the Mississippi—and actually to the Pacific Ocean—Anglo-French rivalry, sparseness of its own population, and lack of need for expansion kept North Carolina from settling this area prior to the Revolution. A few hunters, Indian traders, and explorers had ventured into Trans-Appalachia, and a few settlements were scattered here and there before 1776. The white population of the whole area was small, but its growth was indicated by the creation of counties in what is now Tennessee—Washington County in 1777, Sullivan in 1779, Greene and Davidson in 1783. In 1787 Sumner County was formed from Davidson, and Hawkins from Sullivan. The next year Tennessee County was carved from Davidson. These seven counties were an organic part of North Carolina until the official act of cession of the Tennessee lands to the United States on December 22, 1789.

Chapter 17

NORTH CAROLINA AND THE FEDERAL UNION, 1777-1789

Perhaps the most urgent postwar problem confronting North Carolina was the state's relation to the federal Union. As has been noted earlier, there had been no intercolonial union except a common bond of allegiance to the British crown; the resistance movement from 1765 to 1775 emphasized colonial rights within the British Empire, not separation from it. But the breakdown of British rule in the colonies, the Declaration of Independence, and the adoption of state constitutions called for a closer union and a stronger central government. Consequently the Continental Congress, after prolonged debate, adopted on November 15, 1777, the Articles of Confederation and sent this document to the states for ratification. In the congress North Carolina delegates John Penn and Cornelius Harnett had favored the Articles, but Thomas Burke had opposed any plan of confederation as "a chimerical project." Harnett wrote Burke at the time: "The child Congress has been big with these two years past is at last brought forth. I fear it [the Articles of Confederation] will by several Legislatures be thought a little Deformed; you will think it a Monster." Harnett thought it "the most difficult piece of Business that was ever undertaken by any Public Body," and he regarded it as "the best Confederacy that could be formed especially when we consider the number of States, the different Interests [and] Customs." Harnett's fears that North Carolina might not approve the Articles were groundless, the General Assembly promptly ratifying unanimously on April 24, 1778.

The Articles required the consent of all thirteen states before the new government could become effective. Eleven states ratified by 1779, but Maryland refused to give its approval until the states with western lands agreed to cede these lands to the central government. Maryland finally ratified in 1781 and the Articles became effective.

The Articles of Confederation, Our First National Constitution

The "Articles of Confederation and Perpetual Union" provided for a federal type of government, rather than a national one. Each state retained its "sovereignty, freedom and independence," but agreed to join with the other states to form the United States of America—"a perpetual union for the common defense and general welfare." There was to be a unicameral Congress, whose members were elected annually by the state legislatures. Each state could have not less than two nor more than seven delegates in Congress, but was granted only one vote. Delegates were to be paid by the states, not by the Confederation government. The executive branch of the government consisted of a committee of Congress—one from each of the thirteen states. There was no president of the United States. There was no provision for a judiciary.

Limited Powers of Congress

Congress was granted very limited powers. It was given control of foreign policy, army and navy, and Indian affairs, but it could not make war or peace without the consent of at least nine states. In fact, no measure could become law until at least nine state delegations approved. Congress could borrow money on the nation's credit, issue currency and regulate its value, establish and maintain post offices; but it was not given direct control of commerce or the power to tax. In raising revenues, the Confederation government was left at the mercy of the states and had to make requisitions on them, with no power to force payments. The chief nationalizing features of the Articles were found in Article IV, which provided that the citizens of each of the states should "be entitled to all privileges and immunities of free citizens in the several States," that "full faith and credit shall be given in each of the States to the records, acts and judicial proceedings of the courts and magistrates of every other State," and that fugitives from justice might be extradited.

Embodied in the Articles was virtually every idea the states had developed politically: Weak executive, important central legislature, the desire to keep taxing power in the hands of the local assembly, the wish to trade without external trade regulations, emphasis on "localism," and fear of a strong central government. All things considered, the Articles of Confederation was a natural product of its time and it was sufficiently binding until a better plan of government could be devised and put into effect.

State Rights Views of North Carolina Delegates in the Continental Congress

The North Carolina delegates in the Continental Congress reflected these traditional "state rights" views. They voted for state control of taxation and commerce; against granting Congress the power to make treaties that would restrict the right of any state to levy tariffs on imports; and against giving Congress the power to fix western boundaries and to erect new states from the "public domain." On the highly controversial question of state quotas for Continental expenses, they favored value of land rather than population. And they voted to make Congress the arbiter of disputes between states over boundaries "or any other cause whatever."

North Carolina's Western Lands

One of North Carolina's most perplexing problems was the disposition of its transmontane lands, claim to which was based on the colonial charter of 1663.

As early as 1779 Congress had recommended the cession of all western lands to the Confederation government "for the common good of the United States," on the ground that these lands were the common property of all the states; that they had been won in a common cause during the Revolution; that the lands would be used for reduction of the public debt; and that ultimately new states would be formed from this domain. But North Carolina opinion on this question was divided. Many people east of the mountains opposed cession and advocated sale of these lands to liquidate the state debt. Some easterners favored cession in order to pay expenses of government in the western region. There was also fear that Congress might adopt the proposal to base taxes and representation in Congress on total population. If such a policy should be adopted, it would be to the state's advantage to cede the western lands. The less territory it owned and the smaller its population, the less would be its part in meeting future Continental expenditures.

Sentiment in the region beyond the mountains—and to some extent in the Piedmont—favored cession. There was unrest in the whole western area of North Carolina and hostility to eastern domination of state and local government. Settlers in the transmontane region complained that the state government had neglected their interests, that they did not have adequate military protection against the Cherokees, and that there were no courts west of Morganton —at the eastern slope of the mountains. The westerners feared that unless North Carolina ceded these lands to the United States the settlement of the region would be retarded, deprived of necessary revenues, and have its Mississippi trade to New Orleans strangled by Spain, which controlled that important port and threatened to stop all American trade in its area.

North Carolina's Conditional Cession of Its Western Lands, 1784

Pressure from Congress and mounting demands of western settlers culminated in the Cession Act of April 1784, when the state legislature agreed to cede its western lands to the United States on condition "that neither the lands nor the inhabitants of the territory . . . shall be estimated after this cession shall be accepted" in counting North Carolina's share of expenses incurred in the Revolution, that the bounties provided for officers and soldiers should be protected, that the lands granted should "be considered as a common fund for the use and benefit" of the states, that one or more states should be created from this region, and that if Congress did not accept the cession within twelve months, the lands should "revert to the State." Meanwhile North Carolina would retain sovereignty. One legislator voted for the Cession Act because the "inhabitants of the western country are the offscourings of the earth, fugitives from justice, and we will be rid of them at any rate." But William R. Davie and thirty-six other legislators voted against the law and signed a vigorous protest against it on the ground that these lands should be used to liquidate the state's Revolutionary debt, that the state's Continental debt was not known with certitude, and that the state had not been given credit for military assistance to other states, notably to Virginia and South Carolina.

The Cession Act was sent to Hugh Williamson in Congress at Philadelphia, but it was received on June 3, 1784, the day Congress adjourned, and no action was taken on it. Williamson expressed surprise at the law and opposed its provisions because it did not give "adequate protection to North Carolina." Meanwhile, this "impolitick Act" was causing "uneasiness and discontent" throughout the state. On the advice of Williamson, Davie, and other Conservatives the General Assembly of October, 1784, repealed the Cession Act "by a great majority."

The "Lost State" of Franklin

News of the Cession Act was received with rejoicing in the western counties. Coming at the time when Congress was considering Jefferson's Ordinance for the admission of new states from the lands ceded or to be ceded to the United States, it seemed logical for the westerners to take steps looking toward separation from North Carolina and to eventual statehood. Accordingly a convention was held at Jonesborough on August 23, 1784, with delegates from all of the Tennessee counties except Davidson. This convention, presided over by John Sevier, charged the North Carolina government with neglect of interests of the people in the Tennessee country and petitioned Congress to accept the Cession Act. Meanwhile the North Carolina legislature repealed this law, and the state officials took a more conciliatory attitude by creating the judicial district of Washington and a military district in the West, with John Sevier as brigadier general. A second convention, called to draft a constitution, was so split between the followers of John Tipton, who opposed separation from North Carolina, and the followers of Sevier, who advocated the creation of a new state, that the meeting broke up in disorder.

At a third convention held on December 14, 1784, two constitutions were drafted by the two factions. One document provided for universal suffrage and popular election of officials for the "State of Frankland"; the other document, championed by Sevier, provided for the "State of Franklin," and was strikingly similar to the North Carolina Constitution of 1776. A convention of November, 1785, adopted the latter constitution. When the legislature assembled, Sevier was chosen governor, local officers were appointed, and a delegate to the Continental Congress elected.

Franklin's success as an independent state depended on three things: the favorable attitude of the Continental Congress; the cooperation of Virginia, whose discontented elements in the frontier county of Washington were asking to be included in the state of Franklin; and the favorable attitude of North Carolina.

Collapse of the State of Franklin

The state of Franklin failed on all three counts. The Continental Congress refused to recognize the existence of the new state, in view of North Carolina's revocation of the Cession Act. The Virginia legislature of 1785 declared that any attempt to "form an independent government within the limits of the state" would be considered "high treason." So incensed was Governor Martin of North Carolina over developments in the Tennessee country that he issued a blistering "Manifesto" against the state of Franklin, in which he asked the people of that area not to be "led away with the pageantry of a mock government, the shadow without the substance, which always dazzles weak minds." He pleaded with the discontented westerners to settle their grievances in a constitutional manner, but if "hurried on by blind ambition" in pursuit of their "unjustifiable measures" which might lead to civil war, "let the fatal consequences be charged on the authors"—the "headstrong, refractory citizens" who were largely responsible for the situation.

Its action repudiated by the Continental Congress, by Virginia, by North Carolina—and even by some of its own citizens—the state of Franklin collapsed, and John Sevier was chosen to a seat in the North Carolina legislature. Meanwhile the counties in the Tennessee country—Davidson, Sullivan, Sumner, Greene, Hawkins, and Tennessee—were torn with civil strife, between the followers of Tipton and those of Sevier. Some of the counties had two rival sets of officers. It is interesting to note that from 1784 to 1789, except for the latter portion of 1784, all of these counties were represented in the North Carolina General Assembly, Washington County by John Tipton. In 1789 North Carolina ceded its western lands to the United States; in 1790 the Territory South of the Ohio was created; in 1794 the Territory of Tennessee was established; and in 1796 the state of Tennessee was admitted to the Union, with a constitution written largely by former inhabitants of North Carolina, including Andrew Jackson.

The Movement for a "More Perfect Federal Union"

The Confederation government, 1781–89, had many accomplishments to its credit. It concluded the Revolutionary War, negotiated a successful peace (Treaty of Paris, 1783), formulated and put into effect a system for the sale of public lands (Grayson Land Ordinance of 1785), and established a policy for the admission of new states (the Northwest Ordinance of 1787). But the Confederation failed to solve many pressing problems of the states and manifested many weaknesses.

The most conspicuous defects in the Articles of Confederation were the lack of independent executive and judicial departments; a dependence on the states for making the resolutions of Congress effective (the states had a moral obligation only); the principle of state equality and sovereignty; and the requirement of the approval of delegations from nine states for any proposals. The ratification of all thirteen states was necessary to amend the Articles. The government's lack of coercive power over states and over individuals led to a decline of its authority and prestige. States failed to maintain their full delegations in Congress. North Carolina was not represented at all at times, and seldom by more than one person. The refusal of the states to meet congressional requisitions for money; state jealousies over boundaries and trade; state tariff wars; difficulties with France, our Revolutionary ally, and with England, our late enemy; the failure of the United States to observe faithfully the provisions of the Treaty of Paris, accompanied by British refusal to withdraw from the northwest trading posts—these and many other problems caused much criticism of the Confederation government.

Extreme dissatisfaction with the Articles was expressed in and out of Congress even before they went into effect. Complaints continued to mount, and literally hundreds of amendments were proposed, though it was virtually impossible to amend the document.

The Annapolis Convention, 1786

The movement for amending the Articles was given impetus by Virginia's objection to Maryland's taxation of Virginia trade on the Potomac River. Largely through the efforts of George Washington, commissioners from these two states met at Mount Vernon in 1785 and reached an amicable agreement. But the commissioners and many people throughout the thirteen states realized that commercial rivalry and interstate tariff wars were properly national problems. Accordingly the Virginia legislature invited all the states to send delegates to a conference at Annapolis, Maryland, the next year to discuss uniform trade regulations. Only five states were officially represented, North Carolina not being among them, though Governor Caswell appointed five delegates. Of these only one, Hugh Williamson, made an effort to go, and he reached Annapolis after the session had adjourned.

The Annapolis Convention, under the lead of Alexander Hamilton of New York and James Madison of Virginia, adopted a resolution introduced by a New Jersey delegate that another meeting be held in Philadelphia in 1787 to "take into consideration the situation of the United States, to devise such further provisions as shall appear to them necessary to render the constitution of the federal government adequate to the exigencies of the Union." All the states except Rhode Island responded favorably, and Congress approved the idea officially on February 21, 1787, and issued the formal call for the convention.

Demands for a Stronger Central Government

Support for amending the Articles and for establishing a "real union" came largely from commercial and business leaders, lawyers, speculators in land and currency, creditors, holders of government securities, and conservatives generally. These groups were in general agreement concerning the proposed changes. They wanted the central government to have complete control over commerce, to end the strife among and within the states, and to have a government that would command the respect of foreign nations and enable the new nation to make commercial treaties. State power and authority, they believed, must be subordinated, but not destroyed.

A stronger central government was demanded by patriotic nationalists, by conservatives who esteemed order and stability and deplored the anarchistic defiance of states and individuals, and by men of property alarmed at the loss of public credit, the chaotic condition of business, and the spreading movement of monetary inflation by state action during the depression of 1785. No longer hopeful of constitutional reform by the amending process, conservative leaders sought quick reform by the circuitous method of a federal convention.

North Carolina has no claim to leadership in this political revolution; it played no appreciable part in the calling of the Federal Convention. In rural, provincial North Carolina the conservative reform strength lay chiefly in the towns and in the plantation and commercial areas of the East. The great mass of poor, democratic small farmers were radicals who had been in bitter conflict with local conservatives for years; they saw no need for a strong, costly, distant national government that might tax them and interfere with their personal liberty and especially their power through the state legislature to regulate trade, issue paper currency, and disregard at will federal laws, requisitions, and treaties. Since 1781 North Carolina had fulfilled its obligations to the Confederation government whenever such action was consistent with its wishes and interests.

North Carolina's decision to participate in the Federal Convention was due to the skill and activity of Governor Richard Caswell, William R. Davie,

Richard Dobbs Spaight, William Hooper, John Gray Blount, Archibald Maclaine—a small group of eastern conservatives—during the last two crowded days of the state legislative session, when Governor Caswell presented a letter from the Virginia governor urging North Carolina's "zealous attention to the present American crisis."

The North Carolina Delegation to the Federal Convention

On January 6, the last day of the session, the General Assembly elected as delegates to the Federal Convention William R. Davie and Richard Dobbs Spaight, Conservative party leaders, Governor Richard Caswell and Alexander Martin, political Moderates who were not hostile to the reform movement, and Willie Jones, recognized Radical leader of the state. Jones declined to serve without giving any definite reason and Governor Caswell appointed Hugh Williamson in his place. In mid-April Caswell declined to serve because of ill health, and he appointed William Blount in his stead.

The North Carolina delegates were from the upper social and economic class—well educated for their day, conservative in political, social, and economic outlook, experienced in public life as successful planters, lawyers, and businessmen, representing the best life of the state and qualified by native intelligence and training to represent the state in the convention. Their average age was a little less than forty, ranging from Davie's thirty to Williamson's fifty-one. Davie, Martin, and Williamson were college graduates. All five had served in the Revolution, Davie with distinction. Davie was a prominent attorney and planter, owner of thirty-six slaves; Blount, a merchant, planter, businessman, owner of thirty slaves; Martin, a lawyer and planter, owner of forty-seven slaves; Spaight, a wealthy planter, owner of seventy-one slaves; Williamson, a physician, merchant, and businessman. All but Martin had served in the Congress of the Confederation and Martin had been governor and judge. But none of the five had had experience in constitution-making. All but Martin were from the East, and no one of the five represented, in personal status, opinions, background, or interest, the small farmer class that constituted the majority of the state's population.

In the work of the convention as revealed in the records Blount and Martin were the silent, inactive members of the delegation. Blount did not offer or second a motion, serve on a committee, or make a speech. The same was true of Martin, except for seconding three motions of minor importance. Williamson wrote sarcastically of Martin that his "great exertions of political wisdom" as governor had so "exhausted his fund, that time must be required to enable him again to exert his abilities to the advantage of the nation."

Davie made five brief speeches, seconded two motions, and served as the North Carolina member of the important "Grand Committee" that finally effected the "Great Compromise" of the convention—a Senate based on equality of states and a House of Representatives based on population. William Pierce, a Georgia delegate, noted that Davie was "silent in the convention" but "his opinion was always respected."

Spaight's activity consisted of four brief speeches, nine motions, and three seconds. Two provisions the Constitution were first proposed by him—the election of United States senators by the state legislatures and the power of the president to make recess appointments. He differed from the rest of his colleagues in his opposition to the Great Compromise.

Williamson was by far the most active, voluble, and influential North Carolina delegate. He made seventy-three speeches, offered twenty-three motions and seconded thirteen, and served on five committees. He was usually the spokesman for the delegation. He first suggested the six-year term for senators, and though he did not originate the proposals finally adopted, he contributed useful suggestions respecting the impeachment of the president, the periodic census, and the method of electoral apportionment.

Drafting the United States Constitution—A "Bundle of Compromises"

The fundamental problem before the convention was federalization or nationalization. Should the Articles be revised or a new constitution written, which would give the central government power to enforce its actions against states and individuals? Most of the delegates believed that a new constitution should be drafted, which would provide for a stronger central government, for on May 30 the convention voted unanimously that "a national Government ought to be established consisting of a supreme Legislative Judiciary and Executive." The major problem of the convention was the nature of that government, and especially the structure of its legislative branch. Should the basis of representation in the Congress be by states or by federal population? This was the major question that had to be resolved; it naturally led to a sharp division between the small states and the large states.

North Carolina was the third most populous state (ranking behind Virginia and Pennsylvania) and its delegates naturally voted with the large states to base representation on population; but at the most critical juncture of the convention they voted with the small states in favor of the Great Compromise, which gave equal state representation in the. Senate. The North Carolina delegates also supported two other compromises made by the convention— the three-fifths compromise, by which Negroes were to be counted as three-fifths of a person in apportioning representation and direct taxes, and the foreign slave-trade and commerce compromise, which prohibited the cessation of the foreign slave trade for twenty years and prohibited the taxation of exports.

In the puzzling task of organizing the national executive, the North Carolina delegation was irreconcilably opposed to the plan finally adopted—that of a single executive, independent of the legislature, responsible to the entire nation, elected indirectly by electors for a short term but with unlimited re-eligibility, and possessed of vast powers enumerated in the Constitution itself.

The North Carolina delegation opposed the compulsory admission of new states on the basis of equality with old states, though it voted with the majority to give Congress permissive authority to admit new states.

On September 15 the completed Constitution—"a bundle of compromises" —was unanimously adopted and was ready to be signed on the seventeenth. Among the thirty-nine signers from all of the delegates were three North Carolinians—Blount, Williamson, and Spaight. Davie and Martin had been absent for several weeks and did not sign. Blount declared at first that he would not sign, but he did so after Benjamin Franklin persuaded him that he was signing for the state and not as an individual.

North Carolina Refuses to Ratify, 1788

Even before the convention had completed its labors, the "plan of Government," as the new Constitution was called, had become an issue in the state. In the words of R. D. W. Connor, "definite and distinctive party names now appeared for the first time in the state's history." To a great degree this was a realignment of former Conservatives and Radicals. The Conservatives, now called Federalists, supported the Constitution because they believed that a strong and efficient federal government was essential to protect property rights; to guarantee a stable, sound national currency; to stimulate domestic and foreign trade; and to support the dignity and rights of the United States in its foreign relations.

As early as July, 1787, Williamson and a few other Federalist leaders urged North Carolina voters to choose capable men for the legislature in the August election. Antifederalists were also active and a bitter campaign ensued. One Federalist leader referred to the Antifederalists as a "blind, stupid set that wish Damnation to their Country," and Archibald Maclaine declared that "we have a set of fools and knaves in every part of this State, who seem to act by concert; and are unfortunately against any man of abilities and virtues." There were charges of irregularities and election frauds in two counties and in the town of Wilmington. William Hooper, a signer of the United States Declaration of Independence, had his "eyes blacked" by an Antifederalist.

Federalist Defense of the Constitution

The publication of the Constitution in full—for the first time in North Carolina—in the *State Gazette of North Carolina,* October 4, intensified the struggle for ratification and brought forth statements from the leaders of both groups. At a meeting in Edenton, November 8, Williamson declared that the Constitution was far from perfect, but it was superior to the Articles. He said that there was need for a strong central government with power to enforce laws over states and individuals, protect property rights, guarantee a stable and sound national currency, stimulate foreign trade, and support the dignity and rights of the United States in foreign relations.

The ablest defense of the Constitution in North Carolina was made by James Iredell. He described conditions under the Confederation—the "disordered and distracted" state of the country, public debts unpaid, the treaty of peace disregarded by both sides, commerce on the verge of ruin, private industry at a standstill. The remedies could be found only in "a united, vigorous government." Congress, under the Articles, had only "the shadow of authority" and little or no real power. All these factors "dictated the necessity of a change." He praised the character and ability of members of the Philadelphia Convention and declared that their proposal was "entitled to utmost respect," and that "local interests ought to give way to the general good."

Iredell analyzed the good points of the Constitution: "popular representation of the people," "useful checks to guard against possible abuses," provision for amendments "which experience might show were needed," and the importance of "those many provisions calculated to make us as much one people as possible." He said: "Our strength consists in union, and nothing can hurt us but division"; Union was "the watch-word of American liberty and safety." Whether "we shall be truly a union, happy in ourselves, and respected by the rest of mankind" or "an irreconcilable scattered people," "doomed to feel the curse of all human discontent," and to be "wretched and contemptible," depended on acceptance or rejection of the proposed Constitution.

Antifederalist Criticisms of the Constitution

The Antifederalists contended that the adoption of the Constitution would lead to the destruction of state rights and to the removal of government from popular control, as illustrated by the methods of selecting the president and United States senators; that capital and industry would be promoted at the expense of agriculture; that the omission of a bill of rights would be disastrous; that a government so far removed from the people was dangerous; and that the state governments would be swallowed up by the national government. Timothy Bloodworth maintained that the Constitution would set up an "autocratic tyranny, or monarchial monarchy." Thomas Person insisted that it would be "impractible and dangerous," and he thought nine-tenths of the people of North Carolina were opposed to it. Lemuel Burkitt, noted Baptist preacher, predicted that if the Constitution were put into effect the district for the capital would become a walled city with a standing army of fifty thousand or more, to be used for "crushing the liberties of the people."

The legislature, which convened at Tarboro on November 19, 1787, had some heated debates on the new Constitution. Thomas Person, state senator from Granville County, attempted to block every move toward ratification. He tried unsuccessfully to prevent the call of a convention to consider the Constitution, and on December 6 the legislature called upon the voters of the state to elect delegates in March, 1788, who should meet in convention at Hillsborough on July 21.

The campaign that followed was vigorous and bitter. As Louise Irby Trenholme says in her excellent monograph on this subject, "No man's character was above attack and no past political or military service could overcome party animosity." Character assassination was common practice, especially on the part of the Antifederalists. Thomas Person denounced General Washington as "a damned rascal and traitor to his country for putting his name to such an infamous paper as the new Constitution," and Willie Jones, who was an aristocrat with a belief in democracy—eighteenth-century style—and the chief leader of the Antifederalists, was forced to deny publicly that he had "called the members of the Grand Convention, generally, and General Washington and Colonel Davie, in particular, scoundrels." Elkanah Watson, prominent Federalist author, recorded with delight how he and some of his Federalist friends, broke up an Antifederalist meeting that was being addressed by Lemuel Burkitt.

The Constitution received its strongest support from the better educated, wealthy, conservative, aristocratic planters, merchants, and professional men in the towns and plantation areas of the East, while the mass of poor, radical, democratic small farmers of the backcountry were hostile to ratification.

The Federalist leaders conducted an able campaign to convince thoughtful voters that ratification would best serve the political and economic interests of North Carolina and the nation. But a few Federalists struck some low blows. Archibald Maclaine referred to the opposition as "a set of fools and Knaves," and Federalists in at least two counties and one town precipitated riots at the polls. In the sweeping Antifederalist victory—184 delegates to 83 for the Federalists—many prominent Federalists were defeated, including Hooper, Caswell, and Alfred Moore, by relatively obscure men.

The Hillsborough Convention, 1788

The convention to vote on the United States Constitution assembled at Hillsborough on July 21, 1788. Although the Antifederalists had an overwhelming majority, they courteously voted with the Federalists to elect Governor Samuel Johnston as president. When the convention began its deliberations, the Constitution had already been adopted by the ratification of one more than the requisite number of nine states; five days later the eleventh state ratified. By extraconstitutional procedure, the old constitution of the United States—the Articles of Confederation—had been scrapped, and now North Carolina was left outside—a sovereign and independent state, in company with only Rhode Island.

The self-confident Antifederalist leaders—Willie Jones, Judge Samuel Spencer, Timothy Bloodworth, Thomas Person, David Caldwell, and others—were not opposed to union or to a central government stronger than the one existing under the Articles, but they did fear that the new Constitution would make possible a central government so strong and consolidated as to impair local self-government, endanger the rights of North Carolina, and threaten the civil liberties of individual citizens. Until individual liberties and state rights were duly safeguarded by the adoption of amendments to the Constitution, they were determined that North Carolina should not ratify. Willie Jones wanted to vote and adjourn on the first day because, he said "all the delegates knew how they were going to vote" and he did not want to be guilty of "lavishing public money." He reluctantly and impatiently permitted Iredell, Davie, and other Federalists to carry on a long, unconvincing, and more or less one-sided discussion in support of the Constitution and its immediate ratification in advance of amendment. Then after eleven days of debate, by a vote of 184 to 83 the Antifederalists carried a resolution, neither rejecting nor ratifying the Constitution, but declaring that a bill of rights "asserting and securing from encroachment the great Principles of civil and religious Liberty, and the unalienable rights of the People, together with Amendments," ought to be laid before Congress and a second Federal Convention, "previous to the ratification of the Constitution" by North Carolina. The convention proposed a bill of rights consisting of twenty parts and also twenty-six amendments.

The geographical distribution of the vote showed that North Carolina was strongly opposed to the Constitution without amendments, except in the area bordering Albemarle and Pamlico sounds and four scattered counties.

The triumph of the Antifederalists was short-lived; the course of events was against them. By a close vote the new legislature in November, 1788, called for the election in August, 1789, of a second convention to meet in Fayetteville on November 16 to consider ratification. A swift reversal of public opinion brought a sweeping victory to the Federalists in the summer of 1789. The Antifederalist minority in the Fayetteville Convention tried vainly to postpone ratification until amendments had been adopted, but by a vote of 195 to 77 the Federalists secured ratification on November 21. Twenty-four counties and twenty delegates had shifted to the Federalist position since the Hillsborough Convention. The vote showed that the Federalists controlled the entire state except Sullivan County west of the mountains, Wilkes County, and three separated groups of counties in the New Hanover, Anson, Granville-Guilford areas where local Antifederalist leaders were particularly influential.

Reasons for North Carolina Ratification, 1789

What influences accounted for this striking reversal of opinion in North Carolina? The censure of its status of independence in company with Rhode Island, with its unsavory reputation for radicalism and paper money, provoked sensitiveness. An effective campaign of education was conducted by Federalist newspapers and leaders, notably Iredell and Davie, who published and distributed the debates in the Hillsborough Convention, which they had hired a stenographer to record. The public read eulogies of Washington, favorable reports of the activities of the federal government in whose organization North Carolina had not participated, and cordial addresses exchanged by Governor Samuel Johnston and President George Washington. The need of increased southern influence in Congress was urged. There was a growing consciousness, especially west of the mountains, of the need of greater protection from the Indians, Spain, and Great Britain. The return of economic prosperity after the depression of 1785–86 was attributed in part to the new federal government, and there was some reaction against the recent paper money excesses of the dominant Radical party. Economic pressure, implicit in the new federal tariff and tonnage acts, in which North Carolina was regarded as a foreign nation, helped to convince Antifederalist farmers that the interests of agriculture and commerce were interdependent; but the admission to the United States of North Carolina–grown or manufactured products free of duty and the suspension of discriminatory tonnage duties on North Carolina vessels until January 15, 1790, showed that the federal government was friendly and conciliatory.

Finally James Madison, influenced by pressure from Virginia and other ratifying states that had recommended amendments, and by the desire to secure the ratification of North Carolina and Rhode Island, took the lead in obtaining the passage by Congress of twelve amendments, chiefly a bill of rights, which were submitted in September to the states for ratification. North Carolina Federalists welcomed them and freely predicted their adoption. But the Fayetteville Convention ratified the Constitution before it was known that any state had ratified any of the proposed amendments. Undoubtedly North Carolina's refusal to ratify the Constitution at Hillsborough was one of the factors in the subsequent submission of amendments by Congress. But even though it did not like the Constitution, the state did not desire to remain independent. Under the pressure of circumstances, it ratified the Constitution and joined the Union before the adoption of the first ten amendments.

Chapter 18

POLITICS AND PERSONALITIES, 1789-1800

The beginning of Washington's administration was character-ized by a lull in the partisanship which had marked the struggle over ratification of the Constitution as Antifederalists cooperated with the Federalists to launch the new government. Within a short time, however, differences of opinion over domestic and foreign policies shattered this temporary peace and created the original two-party system that has persisted as a fundamental part of American life.

President Washington attempted to wipe out party divisions—the "spirit of faction," as he called it, but clash of opinion was certain to arise in his cabinet, which contained Alexander Hamilton (secretary of the treasury) and Thomas Jefferson (secretary of state), who personified opposing schools of political and economic thought, who held different views of the Constitution, and who contended "like cocks in a pit" in cabinet meetings, until both resigned in 1792.

The Political Philosophies of Alexander Hamilton and Thomas Jefferson

Hamilton believed that a strong, powerful national government was necessary to maintain public credit, to forestall anarchy of states and individuals, and to command respect abroad. He thought that this government should be in the hands of the able and intelligent minority—a government by "the rich and the well-born." Although the few might sometimes be selfish, their guidance would be more enlightened than the turbulence of mass control. He favored government *for* the people, but feared that government *by* the people would lead to weakness, insecurity, and anarchy. In this respect he championed the "mixed democracy" theory current in eighteenth-century America.

On the other hand, Jefferson asserted that in a true democracy self-government was the best government. Although the people might make mistakes, these could be corrected more easily than those made by a dominant minority. He placed much less emphasis on stability and order; a revolution now and then would even be beneficial in reviving democratic control. Jefferson said that "the end of life is individual happiness" and "the purpose of the state is to secure and increase that happiness." He believed in a central government which would safeguard state and individual rights, and in a "strict construction" of the Constitution to avoid centralization and perhaps monarchy. The end of government, "at best a necessary evil," was law and order.

Hamilton believed that the central government must be strengthened by a "loose construction" of the Constitution, which he called "a frail and worthless fabric." He emphasized "implied powers" and believed that those powers not expressly delegated to the national government, or not expressly reserved to the states, should be exercised by the national government. Jefferson maintained that "the way to have good and safe government is not to trust all to one, but to divide it among the many." The central government should concern itself with war and peace, foreign policy, and other matters affecting the nation as a whole. He believed in a strict interpretation of the Constitution, under which the powers not delegated to the central government must be reserved to the states, which, being nearer to the people, could be more easily controlled by them. There would be a relatively weak national authority; major dependence would be upon the people of the states. In foreign policy, Hamilton veered toward Britain; Jefferson, toward France.

Followers of the Hamiltonian theory of a strong and powerful central government were known as Federalists—a party somewhat authoritarian in its political theory, nationalistic in its foreign policy, and liberal in its interpretation of the national government's powers under the Constitution.

Sources of Federalist and Republican Support

The chief Federalist support came from the financial, commercial, and industrial classes and included most of the wealthy, aristocratic, and educated people. Its strongest support was in New England, but it found considerable backing in towns and commercial areas in all of the states. Those who supported Jefferson called themselves Republicans, but the Federalists caustically referred to them as Democrats and the name Democratic-Republican became a popular term. The core of Republican strength was in the South, but it drew support from agrarian interests, mechanics, and poor people throughout the Union.

Although the political alignments resembled those in the contest over the ratification of the Constitution, they were not the same as before 1789. Perhaps the bulk of the Federalist party was the same, but the Republicans were held together primarily by their opposition to Hamilton's policies. The Federalists had made some converts in New Jersey and other Middle States, but had lost the support of James Madison and of many planters in the South. The Antifederalists or Republicans contained most of those who had opposed the Constitution, but the party had lost some support, especially in New England. On the other hand, it had gained Madison and many planters who disliked Hamilton's "implied powers" and selfish class program.

The major policies Hamilton advocated were funding the national debt, assumption by the central government of the state debts, creation of a national bank, a protective tariff to protect manufacturers, an excise tax on spirituous liquors, a standing army, and a pro-British foreign policy. All of these policies became party issues, but eventually all were adopted, in whole or in part, by the Congress of the United States.

North Carolina Gives the New Government and Federalism a Chance

North Carolina began its career as a member of the New Nation under the Constitution by giving support but feeling no enthusiasm for the central government. The Convention at Fayetteville in 1789 ratified the Constitution of the United States, and the state legislature, which contained 109 members who had voted for ratification, ceded the state's western lands to the United States, chartered the University of North Carolina, and elected two United States senators, Samuel Johnston and Benjamin Hawkins, both of whom were Federalists. The governor chosen at the same time, Alexander Martin, though not a Federalist, might be called a Moderate. In the first election for members of the national House of Representatives, the electorate of the state chose three Federalists, Hugh Williamson, John Steele, and John Sevier, and two Antifederalists (Republicans), John B. Ashe and Timothy Bloodworth. In 1792 the same representatives were reelected, but in 1794 Martin, now an avowed Republican, was chosen senator and nine of ten seats in Congress went to Republicans.

North Carolina Reacts against Federalism

Though North Carolina voted Federalist from 1789 to 1793, the people of the state were dissatisfied with the extreme nationalistic policies of the Federalist administration. As Henry M. Wagstaff said, "Federalism, as representing a body of political purposes, meaning, in essence, centralization of power in the Federal government, was of slow growth in the state and was never really dominant in its affairs." The legislature instructed the North Carolina senators to vote for open sessions and to oppose "executive sessions" of the Senate, to report to the legislature and to the governor, if the legislature were not in session, to oppose "every excise and direct taxation law," and to work for repeal of the "monstrous salaries" of federal officials. Even the Federalist leaders in the state were lukewarm in their support of most Federalist policies; some they openly opposed.

The Judiciary Act of 1789 and North Carolina Reaction

The first problem to confront Washington's administration was that of governmental organization. The Administrative Act, creating the executive departments of State, Treasury, and War, provoked no criticism. But the Judiciary Act led to bitter controversy. To implement the judicial powers outlined in Article 3 of the Constitution, Congress passed the Judiciary Act of September 24, 1789, stating that the Supreme Court should consist of a chief justice and five associate justices, and creating three circuit courts and thirteen district courts, each with its attorney, marshals, and deputies. The law also prescribed the procedure for transfer of cases from state to federal courts. Suits arising from treaties, or involving conflict of state and federal law, or concerning constitutional interpretation, if left to final adjudication by state courts, might have resulted in conflicting decisions. The Judiciary Act provided that such cases, if decided against the federal government in state courts, might be taken at once on a writ of error to the Supreme Court of the United States for final settlement. Thus state courts and even the state legislature were made subordinate to the federal judiciary, a power deplored by champions of state rights. Even the North Carolina Federalists opposed such an extension of power. Davie said the law was "so defective in point of arrangement, and so obscurely drawn, or expressed, that in my opinion, it would disgrace the composition of the meanest legislature of the States," and Samuel Johnston wrote Iredell that he was determined "to press for a reform of the Judicial system."

So provoked were the members of the North Carolina House of Commons that, in 1790, by a vote of 26 to 55 that body refused to take an oath to support the United States Constitution. At the same time, the legislature voted thanks to the Edenton Superior Court for refusing to obey a writ of *certiorari* of the federal district court ordering a case to be transferred from the state to the federal court.

Chisholm v. Georgia, *and Iredell's Dissenting Opinion*

The question of state rights was brought clearly into focus in the Supreme Court decision, in 1794, of *Chisholm* v. *Georgia.* Alexander Chisholm, a citizen of South Carolina, had brought suit against the state of Georgia for payment of a private claim. The case was carried on appeal to the Supreme Court, although Georgia contended that it could not be sued by a citizen of another state without its permission to bring suit. The majority of the Court upheld the right of the court to hear suits by citizens of one state against another. But Associate Justice James Iredell, a native of Edenton, dissented and wrote a vigorous and brilliant exposition of his views.

Iredell contended that sovereignty was divided, that the states were sovereign as to all powers not expressly delegated by the Constitution to the federal government; that the Constitution was operative on the judiciary only through acts of Congress; and that there was nothing in the Judiciary Act of 1789, or in previous laws, that gave citizens the right to sue a sovereign state. Some scholars of constitutional history believe that Iredell's dissent was based on his belief that this case claimed new power for the Supreme Court not essential to national welfare. Whatever may have been his reasoning, Iredell's dissent was popular in North Carolina and throughout the nation. It was the first significant state rights opinion of the Supreme Court and became the judicial basis of state rights policy. Its principles were incorporated into the Eleventh Amendment to the United States Constitution, in 1798, which provides that "the judicial power of the United States shall not be construed to extend to any suit in law or equity, commenced or prosecuted against one of the United States, by citizens of another State, or by citizens or subjects of any foreign state."

North Carolina's Views on Hamilton's Fiscal Policies

A problem of great immediacy confronting the Washington administration in 1789 was that of providing revenues for the new government. Accordingly a tariff law was passed on July 4, which provided for duties of about 8 percent and was largely a revenue measure. But the fundamental problem confronting President Washington and Secretary of the Treasury Hamilton was that of establishing the credit of the United States at home and abroad. Hamilton believed that the only way to maintain public credit was "by good faith, by a punctual performance of contracts." In a Report to Congress in 1790 he outlined a fiscal program embracing five major policies: (1) Old government bonds and securities should be replaced at face value with new federal bonds at a lower rate of interest, which would fund the national debt. (2) The debts of the states should be assumed at full value by the federal government, and similarly funded. (3) A national bank should be created to market government bonds and to assist in other government fiscal operations. (4) A tariff should be adopted to raise revenue and to furnish adequate protection for American manufactures. (5) An excise tax on spirituous liquors should be levied.

The North Carolina delegates had not taken their seats in Congress at the temporary capital of New York when the tariff law and the funding bill were enacted, but the feeling in the state was one of hostility to the latter policy. To fund the debts in full would mean not only loss to the original investors, but huge profits to undeserving speculators, who had bought certificates of indebtedness at a half or a quarter of their face value.

North Carolina Opposition to Assumption of State Debts

The proposal to assume state debts met with violent opposition in many states, particularly those that had paid their Revolutionary debts in full or in part. North Carolina had little specie and had already levied taxes to meet its Revolutionary debts. Now it would be taxed again to pay the debts of other states. The legislature deplored the proposed law and declared that the assumption of state debts by the federal government without the state's approval would be "an infringement of the sovereignty of this state, and prove eventually injurious and oppressive to the same, dangerous to its interests." The state's delegation in both houses of Congress was therefore directed "to prevent the evil operation of such acts in future assumptions." Federalist Senator Johnston opposed assumption privately, but both he and Senator Hawkins voted for it. Williamson took the view that assumption would increase the burden of taxation in the state; that North Carolina had already taken proper steps to meet its financial obligations; and that no state should be interfered with in the redemption of its paper currency or the liquidation of its securities. So he and his Federalist colleagues in the House voted against assumption. But the policy was adopted by Congress as a result of a political trade, by which northern votes were cast to locate the permanent capital at a site on the Potomac River, in exchange for southern votes to assume state debts.

The United States Bank

In 1791 Congress chartered the Bank of the United States for a twenty-year period, with a capital stock of $10 million of which the federal government was to subscribe one-fifth. Both North Carolina senators voted for the Bank Law; the House delegation was divided, Sevier and Steele voting for, and Ashe, Bloodworth, and Williamson, against. Those who opposed the establishment of the bank maintained that Congress had no right under the Constitution to establish such a fiscal agency, that it was not necessary, that it would benefit only the commercial interests, and that it would create a dangerous financial monopoly for the stockholders. A centralized "money power" might lead to centralized political power.

Opposition to the Excise Tax

The General Assembly protested against Hamilton's proposed excise tax on spirituous liquors, emphasizing the fact that distant markets made money scarce in North Carolina, and that farmers of the state, especially those in the Piedmont and Mountain counties, needed to manufacture and sell whiskey—a "staple crop" of the state, with which the federal government had no right to interfere. The state delegation in Congress was instructed to cast its votes against the proposed tax. The two senators ignored these instructions, but the House delegation voted solidly against the bill. John Steele, a Federalist in the House, declared that "a more exceptional mode of taxation could not be devised than the excise. A direct or poll tax would not be so odious. Such was the aversion of the people to it they would prefer almost any alternative."

After a bitter debate the Excise Tax became law in 1791. Aversion to taxes and governmental interference led to protests, resolutions, and threats of defiance. But the next year the law was revised by reducing the tax and exempting small distilleries from the tax altogether. So North Carolina escaped a possible uprising similar to the Pennsylvania "Whiskey Insurrection" of 1794, which was suppressed by federal forces.

North Carolina and Federalist Foreign Policy

From the beginning of Washington's administration, domestic and foreign problems were complexly intertwined; each depended on the successful solution of the other. The new nation lacked unity, was sparsely settled, heavily in debt, and weak militarily. If it were drawn into war, the result would be disastrous, if not fatal. Washington and his advisers realized that the United States must steer clear of foreign entanglements with England, France, or Spain—the three powers with whom the nation had diplomatic relations of a highly delicate nature. Fortunately the outbreak of war in Europe prevented these three colonial powers from interfering with the United States to any great degree.

Neutrality

Much of the world was affected by the French Revolution of 1789, by which the old regime fell before the onslaughts of the underprivileged, aroused by intellectuals advocating new theories of the rights of man and social justice. Within the next three years, the Revolution swept from domestic reform to violent domestic strife. In Europe sympathy with the Revolutionary movement rapidly changed to apprehension and hostility, fanned by the propaganda of French émigrés. In 1792 Austria and Prussia declared war on France, and soon most of Europe was involved in a general war, with most of the powers aligned against France.

The French Revolution intensified discussion of political principles in the United States. There was considerable pro-French and anti-British feeling in North Carolina. Some of this sympathy was sentimental—England had been our enemy, France our friend. But some of the feeling was motivated by self-interest. The extension of the European war directly affected the United States as both belligerents strove to control the seas and utilize neutral shipping. There was also evidence of strong anti-British sentiment on the part of those such as Thomas Person and others who owed debts to British merchants. And there were many North Carolinians who feared that confiscated loyalist property might be restored to former owners.

Washington's Neutrality Proclamation—1793

French leaders hoped to use the United States to transport products of the French West Indies and to serve as a base of operations for privateers and French military expeditions against British territory in the Western Hemisphere. To achieve these objectives, the new French Republic sent Citizen Edmond Genêt to the United States early in 1793. Genêt arrived at Charleston, where he was received with enthusiasm, and where he organized Jacobin clubs and fitted out some privateers. Although these actions were violations of American neutrality, many Jeffersonians in the South allowed their hatred of England to overcome their better judgment. Genêt passed through Salisbury, North Carolina, on his way to Philadelphia, then the United States capital. Meanwhile, on April 22, 1793, Washington, on the advice of his department heads, issued a formal proclamation saying that the United States proposed to be "friendly and impartial toward the belligerent powers" and warned American citizens "carefully to avoid all acts and proceedings whatsoever which may in any manner tend to contravene such disposition." This declaration of neutrality was unpopular in North Carolina and the legislature refused to endorse the idea. A few Jacobin clubs were organized in the state, in imitation of French revolutionary societies. And the state militia refused to support Governor Spaight in his efforts to punish those who were using North Carolina ports as a base for privateers and prizes. In 1794 Timothy Bloodworth made a campaign issue of the Neutrality Law of 1794 and was elected to the legislature, which appointed him United States senator the next year. There was some talk of war with England and the Fayetteville Light Infantry was organized as the European war situation threatened to involve the United States.

North Carolina Opposition to Jay's Treaty

No policy or action of President Washington caused more bitter criticism in North Carolina than did Jay's Treaty with England, which was negotiated in 1794 and ratified in 1795. The state fought this treaty from start to finish. Both of its senators voted against confirming John Jay as peace commissioner; both voted against ratification of the completed treaty. Meetings were held at Warrenton, New Bern, Wilmington, Charlotte, Edenton, Chapel Hill, and other places to protest certain provisions of the treaty.

Since the treaty called for an appropriation of money, it had to come before the House of Representatives, where every North Carolina delegate except W. B. Grove voted against it. Nathaniel Macon declared that the treaty was more important than the Declaration of Independence, but he had completely different views on these two documents. North Carolinians in Congress and throughout the state complained of "sins of omission and commission" in the treaty; it was a manifestation of executive usurpation of power; there was no provision concerning the return of slaves or indemnity for those carried away by the British armies; it was the result of "Virginia subserviency." Landholders and speculators particularly disliked Article 9, which allowed aliens to hold lands in the United States; this might lead the Granville heirs to reassert their claim to about one-half of North Carolina. North Carolina merchants and shippers disliked the commercial clauses, which would cut the United States off from trade with the British West Indies. And the people of the state disapproved of the provision that a commission be appointed to adjudicate debts to British merchants. Samuel Johnston denounced the whole treaty as "a hasty performance," which reflected no credit on "Mr. Jay's abilities as a negotiator."

North Carolina Politics

The Federalists controlled the national administration for the first twelve years of its existence, during the administrations of George Washington and John Adams. But this was not the case in North Carolina. Of the five governors during this period—Alexander Martin (1789–92), Richard Dobbs Spaight (1792–95), Samuel Ashe (1795–98), William R. Davie (1798–99), and Benjamin Williams (1799–1802), only Spaight and Davie were Federalists, and Spaight later became a Republican. The General Assembly was predominantly Republican, particularly after 1792. After Martin replaced Samuel Johnston and Bloodworth succeeded Hawkins in the United States Senate, the state never had another Federalist senator. In the House of Representatives there was a small Federalist majority from 1789 to 1793, when Steele and Williamson retired. All of the state's representatives from 1793 to 1799, except W. B. Grove, were Republicans, and all were agrarians except Grove and Thomas Blount. Nathaniel Macon, the state's most powerful representative, entered Congress in 1791.

In the presidential election of 1792 there was no opposition to Washington. Perhaps his "southern tour" of the previous year had added to his political strength in North Carolina. In the 1792 election the state's electors manifested its reaction against Federalism by voting for George Clinton rather than John Adams for second place on the ticket. In 1796 the general unpopularity of Federalist policies and the particular dislike of Jay's Treaty led the state to give eleven electoral votes to Jefferson to one for Adams. When President Washington retired from the presidency, the General Assembly voted a "warm address" in his honor. But Washington was not very popular with the North Carolina delegation in Congress. Thomas Blount openly criticized his last message to Congress, and when that body drafted its reply to Washington's Farewell Address, Blount, Macon, Locke, and Holland voted against its adoption on the ground that it was "too adulatory."

Temporary Revival of Federalism in North Carolina, 1798–1800

Strained Franco-American relations from 1793 to 1798, which culminated in the "XYZ" affair of 1797 and the "undeclared war" of 1798; in seizure of American ships by the French; in unfriendly treatment of American sailors; in the undiplomatic and unneutral actions of American ministers in France—all of these developments led to mass hysteria in the state and nation. No less than twenty defense measures were taken by Congress, including the creation of the Navy Department in 1798.

Public opinion in the state was inflamed by French seizure of some North Carolina ships engaged in the West Indian trade and by the death of an American sailor killed in a brawl at Wilmington. The XYZ affair also led to patriotic rallies in support of our "insulted and endangered country." Perhaps the majority of the state's people favored Adams's policy of national defense. But North Carolina congressmen were unresponsive and partisan, in spite of the popular feeling back home. Grove was the only consistent supporter of the administration, though Senator Johnston and Representative Martin voted for the Alien and Sedition Acts of 1798. Macon, leading representative from the state, opposed measures for coastal defense, for completing work on three frigates, for arming merchant vessels, and for enlarging the navy. The general attitude of most of the North Carolina delegation was that there was little danger of war, that defense was costly and unnecessary, that France was the best customer North Carolina had, and that the whole war scare was due to Federalist blundering.

The election of 1798 was the most spirited contest since the adoption of the Constitution. The Federalists made political capital of the French threat to the United States, and the Republicans were put on the defensive. In the congressional election only four of ten incumbents were returned to office—Grove, Macon, Stanford, and Williams. The Federalists claimed they had won seven of ten seats, but in reality there were only four out-and-out Federalists, five Republicans, and one "wavering." In the election for members of the General Assembly the Federalists gained control of the Senate and made considerable gains in the House, though they failed to gain a majority. The speakers of both houses were Federalists, however, and the Federalist-dominated legislature elected William R. Davie governor.

North Carolina's Reaction to the Alien and Sedition Acts of 1798

Criticism of Adams's foreign policy and the vicious partisan attacks on the president, particularly by English and French "liberals" who had recently sought American asylum from European difficulties, led Congress to pass the Alien and Sedition Acts in 1798. The Alien Act empowered the president to deport "all such aliens as he shall judge dangerous to the peace and safety of the United States." The Alien Enemies Act provided for the jailing or deportation of citizens of a country with whom the United States might be at war, and the Sedition Act made punishable by fine or imprisonment all opposition to enforcement of the laws of the United States, and any "false, scandalous, and malicious" utterances against the president or the Congress. The Alien Enemies Act was never invoked, and no one was deported under the Alien Act.

The greatest controversy in the nation and in the state developed over the Sedition Act. Republicans insisted that Federalists were denying constitutional rights of freedom of speech and of the press. The North Carolina Senate rejected a House resolution against the Alien and Sedition Acts, though it voted to instruct the state's congressional delegation to vote for repeal of those obnoxious laws.

The Virginia and Kentucky Resolutions

In 1798 John Taylor of Caroline, Virginia, suggested to Jefferson that Virginia and North Carolina secede from the Union and form a new confederation. Jefferson disapproved this idea and suggested that only a protest be made by the states against the hated laws. After the Federalist upsurge in the North Carolina election Jefferson suggested that Kentucky, rather than North Carolina, join Virginia in making a formal protest. In November and December, 1798, the legislature of Virginia adopted a resolution that had been written by Madison, and Kentucky adopted two series of resolutions prepared by Jefferson. The Kentucky Resolutions maintained that the Union was a compact between the states and if the national government passed a law the states deemed contrary to the Constitution, "a nullification by those [state] sovereignties . . . is the rightful remedy." These resolutions were the first significant statements of the state rights theory.

There was much sympathy in North Carolina for the ideas expressed in the Virginia and Kentucky Resolutions, but the legislature refused to give its formal approval, when the state Senate voted to table the Kentucky Resolutions. Meanwhile the "undeclared war" with France aided the Federalist cause and stimulated the state's spirit of patriotism. In 1799 Benjamin Williams, an Antifederalist, was elected governor but the same Federalist speakers of the two houses of the General Assembly were reelected.

Davie's Mission to France

In 1799 President Adams sent a mission to France to attempt a peaceful solution of the undeclared war. Davie served on this commission (when Patrick Henry declined), along with Oliver Ellsworth and William Vans Murray. In conference with Napoleon they first demanded $20,000,000 for some 2,300 American ships seized by the French and also proposed abrogation of the Franco-American treaties of 1778. After a long bargaining, a Convention was signed in September, 1800, in which the two nations reached an agreement on contraband, on the principle that "free ships make free goods," and that neutral goods on enemy ships might be seized. It was agreed to leave the question of claims and the 1778 treaties for future negotiations, and the famous French "spoliation claims" were not settled until Jackson's administration.

Federalism Begins to Decline in North Carolina

Federalism in North Carolina declined in popularity after 1798 for a variety of reasons—the removal of the war threat, reaction against the Alien and Sedition Acts, the retirement of Davie from active politics, and Spaight's shift to the Republican cause because of the Federalist refusal to repeal the Alien and Sedition Acts. Another potent reason for the decline of Federalism in the state and the great increase in Republican strength was the establishment, in 1799, of the *Raleigh Register,* ably edited by Joseph Gales, a refugee English liberal editor, who had done newspaper work in Philadelphia, and who had been induced by North Carolina Republicans in Congress to establish a paper in Raleigh. The *Register* became the official Republican organ and the best newspaper in the state for the next half century.

The Federalists countered by persuading William Boylan to transfer the *Minerva* from Fayetteville to Raleigh, where the editor stated that the purpose of his paper was "to combat the wild and visionary projects and opinions of Democracy."

The Election of 1800

The election of 1800 was the last serious Federalist bid for control of North Carolina—and of the nation as well. As the election approached, Jefferson considered North Carolina in "the most dangerous state," caused by the political ascendency of lawyers who were "all tories, the people substantially republican, but uninformed and deceived by the lawyers who are elected of necessity because [there are] few other candidates." He hoped to carry North Carolina in the approaching election, but he said, "The medicine for that state must be very mild and secretly administered." The campaign in the state was long and bitter. The two Raleigh newspapers waged a bitter fight for their respective parties, discussing such issues as foreign affairs, the Alien and Sedition Acts, high taxes, low prices of tobacco, Federalist extravagance, religion, and Jefferson's "alleged atheism." The Republican party was accused of "French infidelity" and Jefferson was called a "second-handed varnished Deist." An Orange County minister prayed that "God would send the name of Republicanism to its native Hell."

In the election the Republicans made a clean sweep of the legislature and the Federalists never again threatened to gain control. In the congressional elections, however, four districts voted Federalist—Fayetteville, Wilmington, New Bern, and Salisbury. Jefferson and Burr won eight of the state's twelve electoral votes, and when the House of Representatives broke the tie between Jefferson and Burr, eight of the North Carolina Representatives voted for Jefferson, thus giving the state's total vote to him, since the House of Representatives votes by states in contested presidential elections.

Federalism defeated itself in North Carolina. The reaction against a strong national government, the Federalist alliance with propertied classes, and the party's disregard of public sentiment and contempt for the "common people" helped to drive the Federalists from power forever. From 1791 to 1798 North Carolina turned against the Federalists because of the centralizing tendencies of the Washington and Adams administrations. In 1798–99 the state turned against the Republicans because of threats to the United States. In other words, the state was Republican when state rights were threatened by extreme centralization; it was Federalist when the Union was threatened by extreme state rights doctrine.

Chapter 19

TRIUMPHANT JEFFERSONIAN DEMOCRACY, 1801-1815

Federalism in North Carolina, which had reached a high-water mark in the three years preceding 1801, declined rapidly after that date; it had disappeared as an organized party by 1815.

Decline of Federalism in the State

The explanation for the party's decline and demise lay in the weaknesses of Federalism and the growing strength of Republicanism. From 1789 to 1800 the Federalists had the ablest leaders in the state, but nearly all of these men had disappeared from the political scene by 1801. James Iredell and Archibald Maclaine were dead; Samuel Johnston had retired from active politics; William R. Davie had moved to South Carolina; Richard Dobbs Spaight had turned Republican; Benjamin Hawkins and John Steele had accepted federal appointments from Jefferson. Out of power in both the state and nation, the Federalists had no patronage to dispense. Federalism had become unattractive, with no future. It had never appealed to the masses of people in North Carolina, and its attitude of aristocratic superiority and contemptuous defiance of public opinion did not tend to increase its strength or influence. Federalist senators and representatives violated the instructions of the legislature on several occasions. The General Assembly of 1801 viewed the federal Judiciary Act of 1789 "with concern," found it "inconsistent with the common interest of the United States" on the ground of executive patronage and expense, and instructed the North Carolina delegation in Congress "to use their utmost endeavours to procure a repeal of the said law." But all four North Carolina Federalists in Congress voted against repeal in 1801, and in the course of the debate Archibald Henderson denounced "the spirit of innovation" that permeated the House of Representatives, of which Nathaniel Macon of North Carolina was the speaker. Federalist electors had also defined the public will by voting for Aaron Burr in the presidential election of 1800.

Increasing Republican Strength

The Federalists were weak and growing weaker while Republican strength in the state and nation was increasing steadily. The Republican party had young and aggressive leaders, such as Richard Stanford of Orange County, Willis Alston of Halifax, Richard Dobbs Spaight of Craven, Duncan McFarland of Richmond, Lemuel Sawyer of Camden, and, most influential and conspicuous of all, Nathaniel Macon of Warren. It had the most powerful newspaper in the state, the *Raleigh Register.* It also had a new political weapon —and one which was used to great advantage—federal patronage. Macon, as dispenser of federal jobs in North Carolina, rewarded the Republican faithful, as illustrated by the appointment in 1802 of Timothy Bloodworth, "the Wilmington blacksmith" and archfoe of Federalism, as collector of the port of Wilmington, in which office he was inefficient—and probably dishonest. (He died owing the United States $22,500, but meanwhile he had sent President Jefferson seeds of the Venus Fly Trap and glowing accounts of the progress of Republicanism in North Carolina!) Patronage was likewise used to proselyte Federalists, as demonstrated by the appointment of Benjamin Hawkins as Indian Agent. Another prominent North Carolinian Federalist, John Steele, was appointed comptroller of the treasury in 1796; he was reappointed by both President John Adams and President Jefferson and served until December 15, 1802.

Republican control of state and local patronage was even more effective in building up a strong political machine. The Republicans controlled an overwhelming majority of local offices, notably the county court, which consisted of all the justices of the peace in the county. The General Assembly was preponderantly Republican, and of the congressional districts only New Bern, Fayetteville, and Salisbury voted Federalist occasionally. Federalist aspirations were all but hopeless. When Willis Alston defeated Davie for Congress in 1803, the latter retired in disgust to his South Carolina plantation.

A One-Party System

North Carolina came to have a one-party system, and, as today, this party had some bitter intrafamily quarrels, both in the General Assembly and before the voters. But instead of fights over real issues many of these contests centered on personalities, trades, and demagoguery. John Haywood, state treasurer from 1787 to 1827, thought that he had never seen an assembly "in which there were so few men of talents or of business" as that of 1800, and William Polk, supervisor of revenue for many years after 1790, said that the legislature had "a higher tone of Jacobinism than has ever heretofore appeared." The *Minerva* was alarmed at the "gigantic strides" of the "monster of Jacobinism" in the state, and called Joseph Gales, editor of the official Republican newspaper, an "imported patriot." There was a marked decline in the ability of public officials after 1800. Many a Republican leader shrank from the violence and bitterness of political warfare and proclaimed blatant party loyalty. Duncan McFarland of the Fayetteville District had fist fights; was convicted of rape; was charged with Toryism, murder, perjury, hog-stealing, forgery, and witchcraft; and was rotten-egged in the 1804 campaign; yet he served six terms in the General Assembly and one term in Congress, 1805–7. By and large the North Carolina Republicans in Congress followed the instructions of the legislature, and this body represented the "democracy and plain people" of the state.

Republican Governors

All of the governors of the state from 1801 to 1815, with the exception of Benjamin Williams (1807–8), were Republicans—as might have been expected since they were chosen by joint ballot of the two houses of the General Assembly. John Baptista Ashe, a "firm Republican," was chosen governor in 1802, but he died within a week, and James Turner, a member of the "Warren junto" was selected. Turner was chosen for two more terms and in 1805 the legislature elected him United States senator. Nathaniel Alexander, who succeeded Turner as governor, was an educated and able man. Even the Federalists admitted that he was "an ornament to the predominant party, and, like few of them, a scholar and a true patriot." But the Republican rank and file were not strong for Alexander and in 1807 many of them voted for Benjamin Williams, while enough Federalists supported Alexander for him to be reelected. The Republicans elected David Stone in 1808 and in 1809.

Before 1810 and the approach of the Second War with Great Britain North Carolina Republicans placed more emphasis on state than on national affairs or foreign problems. Economy, the endowing or disendowing of the University of North Carolina, reform of the judicial system, and state banking were the issues around which party struggles were most conspicuous.

The Jeffersonian Republicans in both state and nation believed in economy in theory and practice. The total state government expenditures in 1801 were only $35,000. The governor was given a salary of $1,600 and a house, which Benjamin Smith threatened to leave as indecent and dangerous and not "fit for the family of a decent tradesman." In 1800, in a burst of patriotism and extravagance, the General Assembly authorized Governor Williams to purchase, at a cost of $600, two portraits of George Washington to hang in the unfurnished legislative halls, but no action was taken for many years because of the expense involved. So economy-minded was the legislature of 1804 that it threatened to adjourn to Fayetteville because the Raleigh boardinghouses had advanced the price of board. In 1809 the legislators' per diem was raised from twenty-five to thirty shillings, but the lawmakers refused to increase the salary of the governor, though they did provide for building "a convenient and commodious dwelling house," which was finally constructed in 1816 and used until the close of the Civil War.

National Elections, 1800–1816

In the sixteen years after 1800 the Republicans in North Carolina usually elected nine of the twelve representatives in Congress, the maximum Federalist delegation being five during 1801–3. All of the senators from the state during this period were Republicans—Timothy Bloodworth, Jesse Franklin, David Stone, James Turner, Montfort Stokes, and Nathaniel Macon. In 1804 all fourteen electoral votes were cast for Jefferson and Clinton, and there was no organized opposition to the Republican ticket. In 1808 Madison received eleven electoral votes, and Federalist C. C. Pinckney three. Federalist gains were largely due to the effects of the Embargo Act and to the division within the Republican party between Quids, members of the Republican party led by John Randolph, who opposed some of Jefferson's policies and favored Monroe for president, and the "regular Republicans" in the congressional caucus, who had endorsed Madison. Stanford was a Quid and Macon was one of the leaders of this group. In the 1812 election, under a new electoral law, Madison received all of the state's fifteen electoral votes.

North Carolina's Opposition to the National Administration

The Federalists naturally opposed the policies of Jefferson and Madison, but their opposition was ineffective. The four North Carolina Federalists in Congress opposed the repeal of the Judiciary Act, and three of them were defeated at the next election. The state's two Federalists in Congress voted against war with England in 1812, but to no avail.

There was a small Republican minority in North Carolina which displayed its independence and individualism and voted against the majority of the party on the Yazoo land question, the Embargo and Nonintercourse Acts, and on the declaration of war against England. Nathaniel Macon, the leader of this group of Quids in the state, was a representative in Congress from 1791 to 1815 and a senator from 1815 to 1828. He was speaker of the House of Representatives from 1801 to 1807. This Warren County tobacco planter, honest, simple, economical, courageous, state rights advocate, and guardian of the planter-slaveholders of his district, his state, and the South, supported the interests of the masses as he saw these interests. As a leading champion of strict construction, he opposed Jefferson and Madison on many matters, such as Jefferson's scheme to impeach the federal judges, the policy of "peaceful coercion," and the use of the caucus to select candidates for the presidency. Macon opposed several administration candidates, favoring Monroe over Madison in 1808 and Crawford over Monroe in 1816. As an ardent champion of state rights and strict construction he exerted less influence in national councils after 1815.

Macon believed and practiced economy. He opposed the building of a mausoleum for President Washington, and when the bill was finally passed for this purpose, he said he hoped that this would end "this monument mania." He voted against expenditures for furniture for the White House and frequently reminded Congress of the scarcity of money in North Carolina, a state that had "no splendid luxury or extravagance." As an agrarian he did not believe that the United States could ever become a manufacturing nation "whilst the present Constitution remained to the United States."

Politicalizing the University

Since the opening of the University of North Carolina in 1795, the majority of its faculty and Board of Trustees had been Federalists. Republican leaders and various anonymous writers in the newspapers charged that anti-Republican books were being used, and that the institution had become a hotbed of atheism, which "unsettled the minds of students" and caused them to lose their Republican principles.

North Carolina's "Dartmouth College Case": University vs. Foy

The legislature of 1789 had allotted escheats of the state to the University of North Carolina and the law of 1794 had granted it unsold confiscated Tory lands. The legislature of 1800 passed an act declaring that all previous laws to grant property to the trustees of the university were repealed and made void. Davie called this law, which took away the two most dependable sources of university revenue, the "Gothic law," conceived by "Gothic ignorance and political fanaticism." Under the powers vested in them by the Act of 1789, chartering the University of North Carolina, the trustees brought suit to recover some land escheated before the repealing act of 1800 had been passed. This case, *University* v. *Foy,* came to Raleigh from a lower court at Wilmington and was finally settled by the North Carolina Court of Conference. This court held that the people of North Carolina assembled in constitutional convention desired to have certain rights secured to them beyond the control of the legislature and that among these was "the right to education." The court declared that corporations were established for the advancement of learning, religion, commerce, and for other beneficial purposes, and when established, they acquired identified rights and powers, such as purchasing and holding property. The court also held that the legislature could not deprive the university of its means of support, nor "deprive the institution of funds already vested and refuse to make any additional appropriations, and there never can exist in the state a public school or schools." By establishing the university, appointing trustees, and providing property the trustees were to hold in trust for the institution, the legislature had discharged its duty as the agent of the people and the transfer of property had put that property beyond the jurisdiction of its control.

The next General Assembly refused to repeal the "Gothic law" of 1800 or to make any appropriations, though it authorized the university to hold an annual lottery. The legislators voted that they should not buy tickets, not for reasons of morality but of economy! In 1804 an attempt to restore escheats failed, leading Davie to complain that "friends of science in other states regard the people of North Carolina as a sort of Semi-Barbarian." The next year escheats were restored to the university; the governor was made chairman of the Board of Trustees, the General Assembly was given power to fill future vacancies on the board, and fifteen additional trustees were chosen.

The Republicans had succeeded in politicizing the university. The school, which had 120 students at this time and almost no funds, was in dire straits. Accordingly some of the trustees made personal contributions and authorized President Joseph Caldwell to conduct a statewide campaign for funds. The legislature of 1809 authorized the trustees to recover certain balances in the hands of executors and administrators as well as all debts due to the state before December 31, 1799. This proved to be a productive source of income and probably kept the university alive.

Banks

North Carolina was the last of the original thirteen states to have a bank. The first banks in the state were the Bank of Cape Fear, at Wilmington, and the Bank of New Bern, both chartered in 1804 as private agencies. The former had an authorized capital of $250,000 and the latter of $200,000. The amount of notes and debts of the Bank of Cape Fear was not to exceed $750,000 over the monies on deposit; of the Bank of New Bern not over $600,000. These were private banks, but the laws of incorporation permitted the state government to subscribe 250 shares in each.

The State Bank of North Carolina

There was considerable public hostility to these banks from the start. Though they had been chartered by a Republican legislature, Republicans charged that they were "Federalist projects" and that their unsound notes "had driven every hard dollar out of the state." The banks were unsoundly managed and flooded the state with notes of varying denominations. This caused much complaint, especially in Virginia, where the notes were redeemed at a discount of at least 20 percent, and were even rejected by "Common Oyster Wenches and Fish Mongers," and denounced as "cheats upon society." There was lively discussion in North Carolina on the merits of state versus private banks. As early as 1805 the legislature chartered a state bank, but failure to sell the requisite amount of capital stock led to repeal of the law the following year. Finally, in 1810, the General Assembly chartered the State Bank of North Carolina, believing that this institution would absorb the two existing banks and "equalize the relation between currency and specie." There was to be a central bank at Raleigh and branches at Edenton, New Bern, Wilmington, Fayetteville, Tarboro, and Salisbury. The capital was not to exceed $1,600,000, of which $250,000 was reserved for the state. In subscriptions, preference was to be given to the banks of New Bern and Cape Fear.

Some Federalist leaders attacked the new banking agency and now defended private banks and depreciated currency and pictured the evils of a "moneyed aristocracy" in the hands of Republicans. Other Federalists favored the state bank as a marked improvement over the other two banks. John Stanly, a New Bern Federalist, referred to the "Republican lions and Federalist lambs" on the bipartisan board of directors, while Duncan Cameron of Orange praised the bank for "melting down the violence of party spirit." Banking improved steadily after 1810, and four years later the total authorized capital of all banks in the state had increased from $450,000 to $3,200,000

Republican Manipulation of the Electoral System

In the first presidential election in which North Carolina participated, 1792, electors were chosen by the legislature voting by court districts. This system, which was formalized by the law of 1803, was used in the next four presidential elections and enabled the Federalists to carry three—and occasionally four—congressional districts. This practice was irritating to Republicans, who were eager to have the total electoral vote of the state cast for their candidates. Seizing an opportunity to guarantee North Carolina's undivided support for Madison in the election of 1812, the Republican legislature of 1811 repealed the 1803 law and vested the choice of presidential electors in the General Assembly. Republican leaders were happy that North Carolina would now have its "due and Constitutional weight" to which it was entitled by extent, population, and resources, and which it had never had when "she had suffered her federal minority to divide the electoral vote of the state in the years 1796, 1800, 1804, and 1808." The legislature, proud of its handiwork, even instructed the North Carolina congressional delegation to work for a constitutional amendment to establish a uniform district system throughout the nation.

The new Electoral Law achieved its immediate objective. Madison received all fifteen electoral votes of North Carolina in 1812. But the law provoked violent criticism from the Federalists, who denounced it as "tyrannical," "unrepublican," a "sordid electioneering trick," and a "brazen effort to bolster up the declining fortunes of James Madison." Mounting protests against the law led to its repeal in 1815 and the passage of a new law that retained the district system but provided for a general ticket whereby each voter voted for fifteen electors, one of whom should reside in each congressional district.

Indian Removal and Western Land Policy

In a series of treaties with North Carolina in 1777 and with the United States in 1785, 1791, and 1798, the Cherokee Indians, who had blocked westward expansion for many years, relinquished and threw open to white occupancy all of their lands in North Carolina north and east of a line approximating the present western boundaries of Haywood and Transylvania counties. As a result, the state made hundreds of land grants in this area, most of them for modest acreages, but some being in excess of 100,000 acres to each grantee. Among the largest landholders in the region before 1800 were Charles Gordon in Wilkes, Robert and William Tate in Burke, and David Allison, John Gray Blount, and William Cathcart in Buncombe. Four counties had been created in this area before 1800—Burke, Wilkes, Buncombe, and Ashe. The town of Asheville, founded as Morristown in 1792, was incorporated in 1797.

The basic land law of 1777 required each county court to appoint an entry taker and a surveyor; the claimant to land had to make a written claim to the entry taker, stating the location and approximate boundaries of the land. The county surveyor was required to survey the land and prepare two plots with description of boundaries and acreage, both of which he should transmit to the secretary of state with the warrant of survey. The claimant had to pay the entry taker £2 and 10 shillings per 100 acres for amounts not in excess of 640 acres for himself and an additional 100 acres for his wife and each child, and £5 for each 100 acres above 640. In 1783 the entry taker's fee was increased to four shillings for lands not in excess of 300 acres and four shillings for each additional 100 acres. The surveyor's fee was 16 shillings for each 100 acres. In 1790 the sale price of land was fixed at 30 shillings per 100 acres; in 1794 it was increased to 50 shillings, that is, from 7½ cents to 12½ cents per acre.

The "Walton War"

Soon after settlement of the North Carolina mountain region began, a dispute arose over a section of the Blue Ridge, variously claimed by South Carolina, the United States, Georgia, and North Carolina. When Georgia ceded her western lands (chiefly the Mississippi Territory) to the United States in April, 1802, she received in return that portion of the South Carolina cession (1787) north of her boundary—a twelve-mile strip of land.

Thus North Carolina and Georgia were in possession of adjacent territory, and this "dividing line," or "Orphan Strip," as some called it, was "to occasion more interstate bitterness and violence" than the earlier controversy between the two Carolinas. In 1803 it was incorporated by the Georgia legislature as Walton County. This resulted in violence and bloodshed known as the "Walton War." While the section was a no man's land it became the refuge of renegades and desperate characters seeking to avoid the laws of either state. Confusion characterized the local court system, public officials were "beat and abused," becoming helpless to perform their duties, taxes could not be collected, and citizens of the two states were "warring" among themselves. Imprisonment was common and at one time during the "Walton War" two companies of militia had to be called out, and there were two skirmishes in what is now Transylvania County between North Carolina militia and Georgians in that region.

The whole question was submitted to Congress January 13, 1806. A congressional committee felt that it "had no right to enter into the feeling of either of the parties," but it requested that Congress should define and mark the 35th parallel, which both states proposed to accept when accurately located. No further action was taken, and the matter was dropped.

At the suggestion of North Carolina's Governor Nathaniel Alexander, commissioners from the two states met at Asheville on June 15, 1807. Since it was expected that the location of the 35th parallel would "be the principal subject of debate," the great demand was for "able scientists." Accordingly, Dr. Joseph Caldwell, president of the University of North Carolina and Dr. Joseph Meigs, president of the University of South Carolina, served in this capacity. The commissioners finally signed an agreement that Georgia had no right to claim any territory north or west of the Blue Ridge and east or south of "the present temporary line between the whites and Indians." North Carolina had won the land in dispute, but it was not until 1819 that the Georgia legislature officially confirmed an accurate survey of the 35th parallel, admittedly North Carolina's boundary.

Reorganization of the State Judiciary

One of the most perplexing problems confronting North Carolina was the judiciary—from bottom to top. The 1776 constitution had said very little about courts, inferior or superior. The lower courts of the independent state had about the same structure, power, and weaknesses as their prototypes of the colonial era. There were courts of pleas and quarter sessions held by the collective justices of the peace in each county. This was usually called the county court and had both judicial and administrative powers. Then there were the courts held by the individual justices of the peace—the bottom of the judicial structure—with each justice exercising limited civil and criminal jurisdiction, as it had been in the colonial days. The justices of the peace were appointed officials; they had no salaries, but were paid in fees.

Although there were some complaints about "justice" on the lower level, the most confusion, uncertainty, and dissatisfaction centered around the higher courts.

The Constitution of 1776 had provided that the General Assembly should appoint by joint ballot of the two houses "Judges of the Supreme Courts of Law and Equity—who shall be commissioned by the Governor and hold their offices during good Behaviour." The legislature thus had the power to elect judges, fix their salaries, and erect new courts. To implement the constitutional provision, the law of 1777 provided for three superior court judges and created six judicial districts, each with a court town where a superior court should be held twice a year. In 1782 and 1787 two additional circuits were added, with Morganton and Fayetteville designated as the court towns.

From its inception in 1777 the state's judiciary caused complaint and demands for reform. There were too few courts; distances between court towns were too great and worked a hardship on suitors, witnesses, jurors, lawyers, and judges; the courts should be "brought closer to the people"; there were conflicting opinions of judges, a disturbing lack of uniformity in decisions, and no machinery for appeals. In 1790 the General Assembly provided for east and west ridings of four districts and two judges each. An additional judge was provided for in 1798, and two more were added in 1800. A concession to the growing demand for judicial reform was reflected in the law of 1806, which provided for a superior court to be held in each county twice a year. Federalist leaders criticized this law, perhaps swayed more by the economic interests of their own towns than by political principles, common sense, and simple justice. The Republicans accused those who took this view as basking "in the genial sunshine of the district towns."

The new law made it harder on lawyers and judges who would have to go from one county to another in the performance of their duties. Many lawyers threatened to leave the state; some did leave. Archibald D. Murphey believed that in the future "all lawyers will avoid North Carolina."

Evolution of the State Supreme Court

The greatest weakness in the whole judicial system was the lack of a supreme court. The necessity for such a court was felt from the first because of conflicting opinions of judges of the lower courts. The trial of James Glasgow, secretary of state from 1776 to 1797, for land frauds during 1797–99 focused attention on this problem and led the General Assembly, which had tried Glasgow by a special court in Raleigh, to pass a law requiring that the superior court judges meet twice a year in Raleigh to decide cases disagreed on by the judges. By a law of 1801 this "Court of Conference," as it was now designated, was authorized for a three-year period. In 1804 the legislature made the Court of Conference permanent and in 1805 changed its name to the Supreme Court. In 1810 this court was authorized to choose one of its own number as chief justice and to hear appeals from lower courts.

This system was an improvement on the old system. But there were many obvious defects in it. Judges were put in the position of passing upon their own decisions; it was a hardship for them to come to Raleigh, when they were already overworked in their own judicial districts. Their court dockets were becoming more congested all the while as population and litigation increased. The solution to the problem was to have a separate, independent, full-time supreme court. Finally in 1818 the legislature authorized a supreme court of three judges elected by the legislature, to hold two sessions a year in Raleigh and to hold court day after day until all appeals were decided. This court was authorized to hear appeals only after the decisions of the superior court had been rendered and to review the entire case instead of merely questions of law. Cases in equity were to be instituted *directly* before the Supreme Court. The General Assembly concluded its work on this problem by appointing John Louis Taylor as chief justice and John Hall and Leonard Henderson as associate justices.

National Politics and Foreign Policy

North Carolina Republican senators and representatives gave wholehearted support to most of the Jeffersonian policies. As has been indicated, they favored repeal of the Judiciary Act of 1789. They endorsed and applauded the Louisiana Purchase in 1803 as an "honorable acquisition," in spite of their views on economy and strict construction of the Constitution. They also supported the weak and vacillating foreign policy of the national administration. Republicans in the state resented violations of American rights on the high seas, especially the flagrant incident of June, 1807, when the American *Chesapeake* was fired on by the British *Leopard* in American waters. Mass meetings were held that sanctioned the president's "firm action" in handling this affair, and the General Assembly had a three weeks' debate over a resolution endorsing Jefferson's action. The resolution was finally passed by an overwhelming vote, though the Federalists denounced Jefferson for the purchase of Louisiana, for the decline of the American navy, and for other policies they considered detrimental to American interests. The legislature of 1808 adopted resolutions condemning British diplomatic conduct and the seizure of American ships by the British and French; it endorsed the Embargo Act, which provided that no ship was to leave an American port for a foreign destination, and required the posting of bonds double the value of the cargo for ships engaged in coastal trade.

The economic effects of the embargo were felt most severely in the commercial states, but even North Carolina felt the impact of "peaceable coercion" in a decrease in its West Indian lumber trade and in a sharp decline in prices of tobacco, corn, cotton, and pork. In 1808 Lemuel Sawyer, a North Carolina "War Hawk," demanded the forcible opening of the West Indian trade and early in 1810 advocated war with England and a "bold irruption into Canada." The Nonintercourse Act of 1809 also met the approval of North Carolina Republicans, as did Macon Bill Number Two, which repealed all nonintercourse provisions and stated that American ships could sail to any country; if either France or Britain repealed its Decrees or Orders in Council affecting American commerce, the United States would revive nonintercourse against the other.

The "War Hawks" and Agrarian Imperialism

The failure of "peaceable coercion," the mounting unrest in New England and other commercial areas, and the seizure of some sixteen hundred American vessels and the impressment of some six thousand American sailors by the British increased tension and led to talk of war with Great Britain. Many Americans loudly protested against violations of our neutral rights and insisted on "freedom of the seas." After 1810 Congress was dominated by a group of "War Hawks," chiefly from the West and South, and spearheaded by Henry Clay of Kentucky, Speaker of the House of Representatives. These "agrarian imperialists" publicly proclaimed their intention of annexing Canada. Clay told Congress "The conquest of Canada is in your power," and he asserted that the Kentucky militia could "place Montreal and Upper Canada at your feet." President Madison was not eager for war, but the War Hawks, who stressed nationalism, neutral rights, Canada, and Indian atrocities in the Northwest finally achieved their objective, and Congress on June 18, 1812, declared war on Great Britian by a close vote of 19 to 13 in the Senate and 79 to 49 in the House.

North Carolina had no conspicuous War Hawk. Richard Stanford, who had urged war two years earlier, voted against it along with Representatives Pearson and McBryde. Both senators voted for the war declaration. One group in Pearson's Salisbury District condemned his action as "flagrantly improper," while another group defended his vote by saying that the war was "unwise, premature, and unnecessary." William Gaston, a successful Federalist candidate for the House of Representatives in 1812, declared that the war "was forbidden by our interests, and abhorrent from our honour." Two antiwar Republicans, William Kennedy and Stanford, were also elected to Congress in 1812.

Although the War Hawks had boasted that Canada, their major objective, could be captured easily within two months, there was no sound basis for such optimism. Weakened by Republican economy, the regular army had less than seven thousand men, and many of its top-ranking officers were of Revolutionary vintage. The navy was not much better prepared, containing Jefferson's "mosquito fleet" of about two hundred small ships and sixteen rather formidable frigates. The United States treasury was almost empty when the war began, Congress having failed to recharter the Bank of the United States in 1811. And Congress, in 1812, expecting a speedy victory, did not appropriate additional funds or impose new taxes.

American military, naval, and financial unpreparedness was offset to a degree by the fortunate fact that until 1814 England's main concern was Napoleon Bonaparte—not Canada. The War of 1812 was only the sideshow to the major event in Europe.

Defenseless Condition of the North Carolina Coast

North Carolina's chief military concern was the protection of its own coast. There was fear of British attack, and frequent rumors of British warships off the coast led to the transfer of all specie in the New Bern and Edenton branches of the State Bank to Raleigh and Tarboro. A "Committee of Public Safety" at Wilmington asked Governor Hawkins to protest to the secretary of war about the defenseless condition of the coast. After repeated requests the federal government sent five small gunboats. These proved ineffective, and on July 12, 1813, a British fleet of one large battleship and over one hundred smaller craft, including barges, all under the command of Admiral Cockburn, landed at Ocracoke and Portsmouth; but not considering North Carolina a major objective, the fleet sailed away four days later.

The General Assembly, by a very close vote, adopted a report to President Madison containing "a string of heavy complaints" against the national administration—its gross neglect of North Carolina, which was being left to defend itself while its own troops were being sent away to defend other states; its failure to erect forts or to send warships to protect the coast; and the utter neglect of the North Carolina militia in regard to pay and medical supplies.

The state's quota of militia in 1812 was seven thousand men and was raised largely by volunteers on a county basis. These men were organized into eight companies, four of which were sent to protect the lower Cape Fear and the other four to Beaufort. In 1814 President Madison called for seven thousand more men from the state, and this quota was raised largely by draft. Most of these recruits were sent to aid other states. One detachment under Brigadier General Joseph Graham and Colonel Jesse Pearson was sent against the Creek Indians in Georgia, but arrived just "in time to look on."

In September, 1814, after a British force had burned the national capitol and had threatened the whole Chesapeake area, Madison requisitioned fifteen hundred North Carolina militia of those already in service to "march with all possible dispatch to aid in the defense of Norfolk." They carried out orders, reached that city, where they were soon joined by another thousand from

North Carolina. But they remained idle and North Carolina citizens were called on to supply them with clothing and blankets, since the United States government was unable to do so.

North Carolina's most notable contribution to the war was the exploits of three individuals—Benjamin Forsythe, Johnston Blakely, and Otway Burns.

Lieutenant Colonel Forsythe won honor for himself and his state in battles along the Canadian border, where he was killed at the Battle of Odelltown, Canada, on June 28, 1814. The General Assembly voted to make his young son a ward of the state and to pay for his education. North Carolina's most famous naval hero was Captain Johnston Blakeley, a native of Ireland, who had moved to North Carolina and had attended the University of North Carolina for one year before joining the navy to fight the Barbary pirates. In the war of 1812, in command of the *Enterprise,* he captured the British *Fly;* later, in command of the *Wasp,* a 22-gun, 509-ton vessel carrying 173 men, he ravaged British commerce in the English Channel and won victories over the *Reindeer* and *Avon.* Then the *Wasp* sailed away toward the southwest and was never heard of again.

Blakeley's exploits won universal acclaim. Congress awarded him a gold medal; the state legislature voted him a sword and a $500 silver service, adopted his daughter, and promised to pay for her education—which until 1829 cost the state $7,600.

Otway Burns of Beaufort was captain of a privateer, the *Snap Dragon,* which sailed the seas from Newfoundland to South America, captured many British merchant vessels, and made a fortune for himself. "Notable as were the achievements of Blakeley and Forsythe," says W. K. Boyd, "their most memorable service was to awaken in North Carolina a sentiment of state pride and public spirit."

North Carolina Criticism of the Conduct of the War

At many times during the war, however, national pride, patriotism, and public spirit were at a low ebb. There was criticism of the conduct of the war from beginning to end by some of the state's leading men, chiefly Federalists. Archibald D. Murphey, state senator from Orange, referred to the "incompetent men" in control of the federal administration who were leading the government to the "Brink of Dissolution" and the nation to "Ruin and Desolation." Neither he nor Davie condemned New England for the Hartford Convention of 1814, as a revolt against "the tyranny of Virginia administrations," and Davie was "astonished at the monstrous strides towards depotism made by the party in power." He predicted that "Madison will finish his career amidst the ruins of this country."

Although Republicans had not been very outspoken against the declaration of war, they criticized its management, particularly the "indifferent conduct" of military and naval operations and the failure to protect North Carolina's coast. Macon was not enthusiastic about the war and Stanford and Kennedy were openly hostile. David Stone, former governor and then United States senator, voted against the direct tax and other measures for prosecuting the war. The General Assembly of 1813 drafted resolutions of censure against Stone, but failed to adopt them.

The Federalists were openly against the war and its conduct. They called it "Mr. Madison's War" and charged neglect of the state. In the legislature they attempted a formal censure of the War Department, but failed to get their resolution adopted. They urged the election of "Peace" candidates, expressed sympathy for the "moderation and firmness" of the Hartford Convention, and severely criticized the Treaty of Peace (made at Ghent, Belgium) in 1814. William Gaston said that the treaty, coming after a war where "the visionary hope of planting the 'star spangled banner' in Quebec, had yielded to the necessity of self-defense," that it contained nothing for which the war had been fought and did not even restore the country to "the state which existed before the declaration of war." Pearson declared that the war was "impolitic and disastrous" and that the treaty had not "obtained one single solitary object for which the war had been professedly declared and prosecuted."

The Federalist party in the state was thoroughly discredited by the war. Federalists had failed to capitalize on this situation as they had on the "undeclared war" with France in 1798—and they were now considered unpatriotic, if not disloyal.

The legislature of 1815 rejected the proposals of the Hartford Convention—which seemed silly now that the war was over—and praised Madison for "firmness, energy and wisdom" in prosecuting the war and for an honorable peace. The Federalist party had sounded its own death knell and would never reappear as an organized party, though a few individuals, such as Gaston, were not ruined politically.

There was rejoicing in the state, especially after the news of Andrew Jackson's overwhelming victory at New Orleans in January, 1815—after the war was over officially. North Carolina and the United States were now "free from Europe," and could turn to the solution of their domestic problems.

Chapter 20

THE "RIP VAN WINKLE STATE"

During the first third of the nineteenth century North Carolina was so undeveloped, backward, and indifferent to its condition that it was often called "the second Nazareth," the "Ireland of America," and the "Rip Van Winkle" state.

Problems of North Carolina after 1815

The end of the war with England in 1815 brought to the United States the blessings of prosperity, peace, and freedom from embarrassing foreign problems. The nation and states were free for the first time in a generation to turn their undivided attention and energies to domestic, political, economic, and social development. No state was less developed or had more serious problems relating to agriculture, transportation, commerce, manufacturing, finance, education, and emigration than North Carolina. Nature's resources of climate, soil, and vegetation made it easy for the people of the state to provide a scanty, live-at-home subsistence for themselves and their farm animals, but conditions were such that it was difficult for them to produce enough to live much above the level of mere subsistence. The state was poor, backward, divided—an unattractive place in which to live because of the limited opportunity for advancement. In 1830 a legislative committee reported that North Carolina was "a State without foreign commerce, for want of seaports, or a staple; without internal communication by rivers, roads, or canals; without a cash market for any article of agricultural product; without manufactures; in short without any object to which native industry and active enterprise could be directed." In addition to all of these handicaps, there was general political apathy under a one-party system, which resulted in indifference to all cultural, social, and economic matters.

314

Agriculture

Agriculture was the predominant occupation of the people of North Carolina. In a total population of 638,829, as revealed by the Census of 1820, only 6,800 whites and 6,700 Negroes lived in the six towns of more than 1,000 population each. New Bern had a population of 3,663; Fayetteville, 3,532; Raleigh, 2,674; Wilmington, 2,633; Edenton, 1,561; and Washington, 1,034. The state was almost entirely rural; its economy was highly unbalanced. Primitive methods of cultivation with crude tools and with little fertilization or conservation of the soil, lack of adequate land and water transportation to markets, and high prices of necessary articles which could not be produced on the farm—all these resulted in soil exhaustion, low per capita wealth and income (the lowest of all the states in the nation), a low standard of living, and a reputation and a condition of extreme backwardness. Without profitable staple crops and adequate water outlets to markets, the Mountain and Piedmont areas had little trade, few slaves, and a small-farm subsistence economy based on free white labor and the production of corn, wheat, fruits, cattle, hogs, and whiskey. In the tier of Piedmont counties bordering Virginia tobacco was grown with slave labor as a money crop. In the Piedmont counties bordering South Carolina cotton culture based on slave labor was increasing. Elsewhere in the Piedmont the small-farm economy of diversified crops prevailed. The Piedmont and Mountains were the poorest and most backward sections.

In the Albemarle–Pamlico Sound region agricultural conditions were somewhat better. The chief products—corn, beans, peas, hogs, lumber, and some tobacco and naval stores—could be shipped by water to the eastern towns and through Ocracoke Inlet to outside markets. The density of slave population was greater than in the West. But the swampy soil and the distance and dangers of the water routes handicapped the region. The broad middle eastern section was the most attractive, wealthy, developed, and cultured area in North Carolina. Here were considerable areas of staple crop production on a profitable slave-labor plantation basis. The fertile Roanoke Valley specialized in tobacco, and rice was the staple crop of the lower Cape Fear. Elsewhere corn, pork, and naval stores were the leading staples. Cotton was grown but had not yet become a major crop. In the middle eastern area the slave density in every county exceeded the state average of 32 percent of the population and was more than 50 percent in ten counties. The great assets of this middle eastern section were its climate and soil suited to plantation agriculture, and its navigable rivers leading to markets. In general, however, North Carolina agriculture, without easy access to markets, was backward and unattractive. High farm prices brought a brief period of unusual prosperity after the War of 1812, but the Panic of 1819 brought low prices and hard times for North Carolina agriculture. Despite an increasing acreage in cultivated land, the assessed value of all North Carolina lands dropped from $53,500,000 in 1815 (less than $3 per acre) to $43,000,000 in 1833.

Commerce

North Carolina's internal, coastwise, and foreign commerce was small. The dangerous coast and shallow inlets, sounds, and rivers handicapped coastwise and foreign commerce. In 1816 only one and one-third million dollars worth of produce—chiefly naval stores, lumber, tobacco, cotton, rice, corn, wheat, flour, hams, and bacon—were shipped through all North Carolina ports to the outside world. More than a million dollars worth of this trade was through Wilmington, the chief port in the state. Imports likewise were small. Most of the coastwise and foreign trade of North Carolina was carried by New England shippers. The state had no large trading city and not many merchants. In 1820 there were 174,146 persons engaged in agriculture while only 2,551 were employed in commerce and 11,844 in manufacturing. The merchants had to purchase most of their goods in South Carolina, Virginia, and northern cities. It was difficult and costly for the different parts of the state to trade with each other, for produce to be concentrated at the ports for shipment, and for the imports to be distributed throughout the state. In the East the rivers were navigable for small craft most of the time as far west as the fall line; but the West, which lay above that line, had no navigable rivers and was landlocked and isolated. Not until after 1815 was there any steamboat navigation on the rivers and sounds of eastern North Carolina. *Prometheus,* the first steamboat to operate on the Cape Fear River, was built at Beaufort in 1818 by Captain Otway Burns. The earliest, most regular, and successful steamboat navigation in the state was on the Cape Fear with Wilmington as the chief port. After 1819 there were intermittent efforts to develop regular steamboat shipping on the sounds of northeastern North Carolina, and steamboat lines operating between New Bern and Elizabeth City, and between Edenton and Plymouth, met with limited success.

Roads

Everywhere the roads, which were little more than paths marked out across fields and through forests, were virtually impassable in wet weather. Everywhere and at all times land transportation was slow, difficult, and expensive. In 1842 Governor Morehead said that it cost half the value of a farmer's crop "to transport the other [half] to market." One Wake County farmer declared that "there is no money in raising corn; it costs too much to get it to market." Lack of good transportation facilities discouraged the production of a salable surplus beyond mere subsistence needs and made freight rates high, and these high rates reduced the income of the sellers and raised the price for the buyers. The people near the coastal towns could get flour and other produce more quickly and cheaply by water from Baltimore than from other parts of North Carolina. The high cost of transportation made prices of merchants' goods higher at interior than at coastal towns. But the people in the West and in the East who did not live near navigable water had to get enough money to pay taxes and to buy a few necessary things that could not be produced on their farms. So they drove hogs and cattle on foot to distant markets and hauled their whiskey and other products in wagons over the poor roads at a speed of ten to twenty miles a day to markets fifty to two hundred miles away. Since the farmers made little profit from their sales and had to pay high prices for purchases, they bought and sold very little. Naturally most of them practiced a live-at-home economy of self-sufficiency.

A considerable portion of the state's small commerce was carried on through neighboring states rather than through North Carolina's commercial centers. There was little trade between the West and the East. The people of the northern counties found it easier and cheaper to haul their tobacco and other produce to Petersburg, Richmond, Norfolk, and other Virginia towns and to buy there the goods they needed. They were more closely connected with Virginia than with North Carolina. They traded in Virginia, read Virginia newspapers, visited their Virginia friends, married Virginians, and usually voted as did Virginia in presidential elections. Many North Carolinians resented this dependence upon or subservience to Virginia. The chief trade of the southern Piedmont and the mountains was by wagon down the river valleys to the towns of South Carolina and Tennessee. This flow of trade helped to make other states prosperous and to keep North Carolina poor, backward, and divided. In 1828 a North Carolina writer deplored the fact that "the coastal counties were importing Northern flour, feeding slaves on New York pork," and that the middle and southern counties "were importing droves of hogs from Kentucky and Tennessee." In the same year it was reported that the debts of North Carolinians amounted to $10,000,000.

Manufacturing

Manufacturing on a factory basis did not develop in North Carolina until long after 1815. In that year the state had only one small cotton mill, three paper mills, and twenty-three iron works. There were some small corn and flour mills, whiskey and turpentine distilleries, and establishments for making hats, gunpowder, and a few other products. In thousands of homes throughout the state thread was spun and woven into cloth on hand-operated wheels and looms. The Mountain and Piedmont regions had ample resources of climate, raw materials, water power, and cheap labor for the development of manufacturing; but scarcity of capital, inadequate transportation, and an impoverished home market discouraged the building of factories. Manufacturing was so new and risky that it was unable to compete with agriculture, which dominated the economic life of the state, especially with the spread of cotton culture after 1815 through the eastern and southern counties. The first cotton spinning mill in North Carolina, the Schenck Warlick mill, was established in Lincoln County about 1815. The earliest extant record of this mill is a contract of April 27, 1816, in which Michael Beam agreed to build and install for Michael Schenck and Absalom Warlick a spinning and a carding machine "on a branch . . . below where the old machine" stood. In the next twenty years other small mills were established at Rocky Mount by Joel Battle and Henry A. Donaldson, at Greensboro by Henry Humphries, at Alamance Creek by E. M. Holt, at Great Falls by John W. Leak, at Salem by Francis Fries and Dr. Schumann, and at Leaksville by John M. Morehead. The first cotton mill operated by steam in the state was begun in Greensboro by Humphries in 1830. There were twenty-five cotton mills in the state in 1840, located in twelve counties—Chatham, Caswell, Davie, Davidson, Edgecombe, Guilford, Lincoln, Montgomery, Rockingham, Richmond, Surry, and Stokes. But the people of North Carolina gradually decreased their home manufactures and depended more and more for their factory-made cloth and other articles upon New England, where after 1815 manufacturing became an important industry. The North Carolina mills were small and isolated, and they served only adjacent local areas. As a whole, despite the establishment of small factories, the state was becoming less self-sufficient in manufacturing and increasingly dependent on the North—an economic colony purchasing northern goods with the proceeds of the South's expanding sales of cotton and tobacco.

Finance

Financial conditions likewise were not favorable to the development of the state. Three small banks—the Bank of New Bern, the Bank of Cape Fear at Wilmington, and the State Bank of North Carolina at Raleigh—were adequate for the meager commercial and business needs of a limited area. They issued bank notes which, with the notes of the Second Bank of the United States, constituted the currency or money or medium of exchange. Hard money was scarce and had limited circulation; and this scarcity led to the wide use of barter in local trading. Only the notes of the Bank of the United States were accepted without depreciation outside the state. Purchases of goods in other states drained North Carolina annually of specie. Debts to outside merchants were paid chiefly in state bank notes that were accepted only at a discount—frequently as high as 5 percent—or at a depreciated value. The return of these notes to the state banks for payment in specie compelled the banks to restrict credit, to call loans, and to maintain heavy reserves of specie. In the prosperous inflationary period before 1819, the state banks, operating under liberal charters, made excessive loans and issues of notes in relation to their resources. But the Panic of 1819 brought a period of deflation, falling prices, and lower property valuations, which forced the banks to suspend specie payment of their notes and caused innumerable bankruptcies of individuals. It also caused a fierce political conflict between the creditor and debtor classes and between the advocates of sound and of unsound money, which for more than a decade threatened the stability and even the existence of the privately owned state banks. In 1823 the radical champions of inflation seriously threatened to enact a law establishing a bank with no stockholders and with no capital except the property belonging to the state; this bank would be empowered to issue notes backed by "the faith of the state."

The chief problem of public finance was the impossibility of adequate expenditures for state development from the inadequate public revenues collectible from a poverty-stricken, tax-hating people. Joseph Caldwell, writing in 1832, said: "We sometimes hear it asserted that Taxation is contrary to the genius of a Republican government." State revenue was obtained from taxation chiefly on polls and land, from dividends on state-owned bank stock, and from the sale of public lands. In 1817 the state revenue was $98,000 from taxes; $36,000 from bank stock; and $4,500 from public land sales. The tax-hating public begrudged payment of the state tax of 20 cents a year on each white and black poll and a state tax of 6 cents each year on each $100 valuation of land, which had been levied in 1817 and annually thereafter. Meager revenues permitted an average annual expenditure by the state government for all purposes from 1813 to 1835 of only $132,000. The largest item of expense was the salaries of state officials. In 1834 Governor Swain told the legislature that "the mere expense of the General Assembly have ordinarily exceeded the aggregate expenditures of all other departments of the Government." Nothing was left for roads, schools, and public welfare—evidence, according to Swain, of "the apathy which has pervaded the legislation of half a century." Before 1815 the state had never made appropriations for education, transportation, and public improvements. After 1815 the small state revenue severely limited the legislature in undertaking projects for state development. Sufficient revenues could result only from increased taxation and increased wealth. But after 1815 the taxable valuation of property was declining, and public opinion would not permit tax increases. Furthermore, the administration of the state revenue was inefficient and even corrupt. County sheriffs were slow in collecting and sometimes failed to make complete returns of state taxes. When State Treasurer John Haywood died in 1827 after forty years of service, his accounts were short nearly $70,000.

Intellectual Conditions

Intelligent citizens and visitors were shocked at the colossal ignorance and intellectual degradation of the people of North Carolina. In 1840 one-third of the adult whites were illiterate. If the Negroes and whites under twenty years of age are included, more than half of the population was illiterate. The state was almost entirely without respectable authors, a reading public, libraries, theaters, and other evidences of a cultured civilization. A few newspapers with a small local circulation led a precarious existence. There was no provision for the education of youth. The legislature had chartered 177 academies before 1825, 13 of which were for girls; but no state aid had been given and most of these schools were short-lived. They served only the few children whose parents were able and cared to pay the tuition charges. Some children were taught to read and write by their parents or by hired tutors. But the great mass of children grew up in ignorance, with no opportunity to acquire any education. The University of North Carolina, with less than one hundred students, like the private academies and other schools, served only the small class with sufficient wealth and interest to pay for its own children's education. In 1826 Governor Burton reported that many well-informed observers believed it more difficult to obtain a primary education in North Carolina than it had been fifty years before.

Poverty, sparse population, sectionalism, rurality, and the large number of Negro slaves were in part responsible for educational backwardness, but more important were the attitudes and beliefs of the people. The prevailing philosophy was that education was a private, not a public, matter and was therefore the responsibility of individuals, not the state. The leaders, the masses, and the General Assembly were notoriously indifferent, and there was general contentment with ignorance and mediocrity. The dominant aristocracy of wealth regarded education as a privilege for the favored few who could afford it; education was for gentlemen and the professions only. Its extension to the common people would be costly and even dangerous. Joseph Caldwell, president of the university, referring to the educational inertia of North Carolina, said: "Our habits of legislation have been long established. . . . To provide for the education of the people has unhappily never entered as a consistent part of these habits." He said that people were "sometimes seen glorying in ignorance as their privilege and boast" and that there was a tendency for "ignorance to perpetuate itself."

Emigration

Discouraged by the unpleasant political, social, and economic conditions at home and attracted by the better economic opportunities and the greater degree of social and political democracy of the West, thousands of North Carolinians moved to the new territories and states beyond the mountains every year. Richer soil and better transportation facilities made farming more profitable in the West than in North Carolina; and the region north of the Ohio River, from which slavery was excluded, attracted thousands of antislavery Quakers.

Many of these émigrés became leaders in their new states; some achieved national distinction. Among those who migrated from North Carolina were the families of three presidents of the United States, Andrew Jackson, James K. Polk, and Andrew Johnson; two vice-presidents, Johnson and William R. D. King; three cabinet members, Jacob Thompson, John H. Eaton, and Hoke Smith; two speakers of the House of Representatives, Polk and Joseph G. Cannon; more than a score of congressmen, including the colorful Thomas Hart Benton of Missouri; governors of seven other states, including five of Tennessee, three of Alabama, two of Arkansas, and one of the Oregon Territory; a vice-president of the Republic of Texas, and the first governor of the state of Texas. Among other prominent Americans born in North Carolina and who achieved distinction elsewhere were "Dolley" Madison, famous "first lady"; William S. Porter ("O. Henry"), one of America's best-known short story writers; J. B. Finley, noted Methodist minister; Richard J. Gatling, inventor of the Gatling gun; James Long, who led the first American expedition into Texas; Basil Manly, Jesse Mercer, Leonidas L. Polk, Robert Donnell, and David Purviance, the founders of Furman University, Mercer University, University of the South (Sewanee), Cumberland University, and Miami University (Ohio), respectively; Nathaniel Rochester, founder of Rochester, New York; Edmund Richardson, owner of the largest cotton plantation in the world, who had 25,000 acres in cotton and an annual crop of about 12,000 bales; Isaiah Sellers, the Mississippi River steamboat pilot, whose nom de plume of "Mark Twain" is said to have been appropriated by Samuel Clemens; and Hiram R. Revels, the first Negro to serve in the United States Congress.

The newspapers and letters of the period abound in descriptions of the endless procession of migrating groups. The heaviest migration was from the eastern parts of the state and to Tennessee, Georgia, Alabama, and Indiana. As early as 1815, Murphey estimated that 200,000 North Carolinians were living in other states. Young, energetic, ambitious citizens were leaving; few were coming to take their places. The state dropped in population from fourth place in 1790 to fifth in 1820, and to twelfth in 1860. The 1830s was the decade of heaviest migration—nearly half of the counties actually declined in population and the increase in the state was only 2 percent, whereas the normal increase was 15 percent per decade. A legislative committee reported in 1833 that nine-tenths of the farmers would move away if they could sell their farms. The Census of 1850 revealed that nearly 300,000, or about one-third of all free native North Carolinians, were living in other states—58,000 of them in free states, whereas less than 25,000 natives of other states were residing in North Carolina. The 1860 Census indicated that 405,161 North Carolinians were living elsewhere. This heavy emigration meant a severe loss of population, labor, leadership, progressive citizens, wealth, and trade. Land values declined and so did state revenue from taxes because of the loss of polls and decline of land values. Intelligent men were gravely concerned over making North Carolina sufficiently attractive to check the flood of emigration.

Two fundamental factors accounted in large part for the backward state of affairs in North Carolina: (1) handicaps imposed by nature, and (2) an ill-suited system of government. These were the two chief obstacles to the solution of the state's problems and the development of its resources.

North Carolina's Natural Handicaps

The most important factor in North Carolina's history before the railroad era beginning about 1830 was the poor transportation facilities. Inadequate water routes were an insuperable obstacle to travel and trade. A pitiless nature had all but isolated North Carolina from the seaways of the world. Its coast was the playground of tempests and the graveyard of ships. Sand bars, penetrated only by inlets too shallow for ocean-borne trade, made commerce hazardous, inconvenient, and expensive. On the entire coast there was not a good natural port or harbor. Of the large streams of the East, only the Cape Fear flowed directly into the ocean, but obstacles near its mouth hindered the development of Wilmington. The water of the other navigable rivers of the East reached the ocean through Ocracoke Inlet, whose dangerous shallows were inadequate for ocean-going ships of the nineteenth century. The navigation of the rivers that crossed the Piedmont and Coastal Plain was often obstructed by fallen trees and shallows below the fall line and was always impossible above the fall line because of rocks and shallows. The rivers that drained the West were not navigable until they left the state, on their way through South Carolina or Tennessee to the ocean. The roads were little or no better than they had been in colonial days.

For its inadequate transportation facilities on land and water, the state paid heavy penalties. Among them were high freight rates and restricted commerce; higher prices for goods purchased; lower prices and profits for goods sold; scarcity of capital; low land valuations; low income and standard of living; backwardness of agriculture, manufacturing, and urban development; inadequate revenue for the state and local governments; and a lack of state unity and patriotism. The prevailing regime of isolation and self-sufficiency bred inertia, provincialism, conservatism, individualism, ignorance, and prejudice as characteristics of the people. Moreover, economic dependence upon neighboring states, particularly Virginia, induced intellectual and political dependence. No phase of life escaped the paralyzing effect of nature's curse of poor transportation.

It has already been stressed that nature was the chief factor in the state's sectionalism as well as in its backwardness. Differences in climate, soil, waterways, and topography produced differences in economic development, needs, and interests in the various sections. This, in turn, caused the inhabitants to disagree on public political issues. Before 1835 a bitter political sectionalism between East and West, grounded in the differences in climate and geography, absorbed an undue share of the thought and energy of the people and sacrificed the development of the entire state upon the altar of local and sectional self-interest.

Undemocratic Local Government

In any efforts toward self-development and the overcoming of nature's handicaps, North Carolina was held back by an ill-suited, oligarchic, undemocratic political system.

The county was governed by a county court of justices of the peace appointed for life by the governor upon recommendation of the county's representatives in the General Assembly. The county court not only tried cases but elected the county officers, levied taxes, and exercised wide administrative powers and social and economic controls. Prominent citizens were appointed as justices of the peace and prominence was measured generally by the scale of landholding and wealth. Though respectable, honest, and relatively efficient, the county court was not a democratic institution. It was rather the organ of the dominant propertied class, and it shaped county policy primarily for the interest of the upper class rather than that of the entire population. Leading families often dominated local government as if by feudal or divine right. A "Hawkins" was a member from Warren County in forty of the fifty-eight General Assemblies from 1779 to 1835; members of the Arrington-Boddie family served thirty-five terms in the state Senate and seventeen in the House of Commons; members of the Riddick family of Gates and Perquimans served fifty terms in the Senate and twenty-six in the House of Commons; a "Speight" from Greene County sat in all legislatures except five from 1808 to 1835; Bartlett Yancey was Speaker of the Senate for ten terms, and John Haywood was state treasurer for forty years. Those who controlled county government were not representative of, or responsible to, the people. The justices of the peace were so influential that they generally were able to control the vote of the county in the choice of representatives in the General Assembly and in state and national elections. Though the sheriff and clerk of the court were elected by the people after 1829 and 1832, respectively, the people had little voice in, or control over, their own county government, which was in the hands of the county court.

The Undemocratic State Government

The state government was also undemocratic and not representative of, or controlled by, the people. The Constitution of 1776 established a representative democracy in form but an oligarchy in spirit and practice. Only taxpayers could vote for a member of the House of Commons. Only the owners of fifty acres of land could vote for state senators. Qualifications for state officeholding were: one hundred acres for the House of Commons; three hundred acres for the state Senate; and property to the value of £1,000 or more for governor. The General Assembly, which made the laws and elected the governor and other state officials as well as United States senators, was virtually all-powerful in the state government. North Carolina had a state government by the landlords and for the landlords.

Dominance of the East

The East maintained a perfect domination of the state government from 1776 to 1836, by virtue of the constitutional requirement that each county, regardless of population, size, or wealth, should have two representatives in the House of Commons and one in the Senate. Through its control over the creation of new counties, the East kept a safe lead over the West in the number of counties and therefore an unbroken majority in both houses of the General Assembly. This political supremacy became grossly unjust by 1830, when the West surpassed the East in population. Nevertheless the East furnished an average of three state officials for every one from the West; and thirty-six eastern counties in a total of sixty-four, with only 41 percent of the voting population, chose 58 percent of the members of the General Assembly. The landlocked, undeveloped, but more populous West, where the prevailing regime of small-farm agriculture based on free white labor had produced a greater degree of social, economic, and political democracy, found its every effort for self-development by state action blocked by the dominance of the eastern landlords. These landlords, living a patriarchal life on their plantations in the East, supported chiefly by Negro slave labor, with reasonably satisfactory trade outlets for their produce and enough money for comfortable subsistence and the education of their children, enjoying political control and choice seats at the table of special privilege, looked with an aristocratic air upon the common people. They were pleased with the maintenance of the blessed status quo and were distinctly hostile to such innovations as the extension of political power to the masses or costly improvement projects, for the wealthier East would bear the major cost of these, and the poorer West would reap the major benefit. The undemocratic character of state government and the lack of vision of its leaders before 1835 blocked progress by perpetuating the political dominance of the least progressive section (the East) and the most conservative element of the population (the landed aristocracy).

The One-Party System

Another political obstacle to state development after 1815 was the one-party system. The Republican (or Democratic) party was in unchallenged control, a party whose Jeffersonian philosophy of inaction—that the government which governs least is best—coincided with the interests of the dominant oligarchy in the state. The East dominated the Republican party in

North Carolina because of its control of the General Assembly and party caucuses. Unquestioned allegiance to Jeffersonian principles was the *sine qua non* of political preferment. Archibald D. Murphey had complained about the "evil consequences" of parties, and William Gaston denounced their "vile machinery," but the evils about which they complained were not eliminated by the one-party system. In the absence of open party contests, politics degenerated into personal and factional rivalries involving personal ambition, caucusing, bitterness, and violence, but seldom a political policy or principle. There were at least twenty-seven political duels in the state between 1800 and 1860, and among the participants were legislators, governors, and United States senators. When Montfort Stokes's election to the United States Senate led him to forego a duel with his opponents, he said: "This success prevented me from carrying the matter further. I had gained my object, and felt no disposition to dirty my hands with the blood of the scoundrels." Jobs were more significant than issues; personal rivalries, more imperative than public policies. General Assemblies neglected important legislation while they caucused and balloted over the distribution of offices. Many able statesmen lamented the deadening effect of the one-party system and refused to join or oppose the machine in the unsightly scramble for office. Most of the state's political leaders and officeholders were mediocre in ability.

National politics overshadowed state politics in public interest and discussion. "Mentor," writing in the *Raleigh Register,* said: "It is discouraging to witness the apathy which prevails in North Carolina about all state affairs. There is no subject connected with the operations of the General Government which does not enlist the zeal of our politicians and command the attention of those who have leisure to discuss it; whilst the more immediate concerns of the people of North Carolina are wholly disregarded . . . we leave little or no time, we give no portion of our talents or money to advocate the interests of North Carolina, and establish a policy for the State."

The truth of this statement is borne out by editorials, news items in the press, debates in the General Assembly, messages of governors, and in pamphlets and books before 1840. The eastern majority in the state's congressional delegation enabled the East to control North Carolina's voice in the congressional caucus that nominated the party candidate for president. The legislative caucus for nominating and the general-ticket system for electing the presidential electors hampered the free and full expression of the popular will and enabled the dominant oligarchy of the East to deliver an undivided electoral vote for the Republican nominee. Only four states had a larger electoral vote before 1830; yet North Carolina exercised little influence in the national councils of the party and acquired no cabinet office and few federal positions of importance before 1829. Such was its reward for excessive party loyalty and subservience to Virginia. Davie, in 1814, referred to North Carolinians as the "Vassals of Virginia," who "quietly submit their necks to the Yoke," and Murphey, a year later, declared that North Carolina "bends her neck to Virginia and marches at her nod in all our political movements." North Carolina's representatives in Congress exercised little vision or leadership. Wedded to strict construction of the federal Constitution, to economy, and to inaction, they were obstructionists, out of harmony with the majority of their own national party, which, chastened and changed by a long lease of power, had embarked after the War of 1812 upon a broad construction program of national bank, protective tariff, and internal improvements for the development of the nation.

Nathaniel Macon

Nathaniel Macon was the perfect exemplar of North Carolina Republicanism and the high priest of the status quo. For thirty-seven years this Warren County tobacco planter sat in Congress, and for more than a quarter-century he dominated North Carolina politics—"a man of small parts and mean education, but of rigid integrity, and a blunt though not offensive, deportment," who "votes against all claims and all new appropriations," wrote John Quincy Adams. His personal integrity and simplicity pleased the people; and his views on public questions pleased the East and the dominant landlord group. Earlier he had been Speaker of the House of Representatives; but his rigid adherence to economy, state rights, and strict construction and his consistent opposition to the whole nationalistic program of national defense, protective tariff, national bank, and internal improvements had already lost for him his former great influence in national politics. Seldom did he advocate any policy in Congress or fail to oppose any proposal for national development. In state politics, Macon was a firm believer in the individualistic philosophy of *laissez faire.* Government should be a policeman for the protection of life and property and nothing more. In his view conditions in North Carolina were almost ideal. It was "a meek state and just people" with no "grand notions or magnificent opinions." Therefore he opposed the "grand notions" of public schools, internal improvements, and constitutional reform. In state and national politics he served faithfully the interests of the planter aristocracy of the East, beyond the confines of whose world he was never able to see. He was not a leader, but he personified the North Carolina of his day.

From 1815 to 1835, while New York, Pennsylvania, Virginia, South Carolina, and other states were engaged in programs of state development, North Carolina carried through no great constructive policy for the economic, social, intellectual, or political betterment of the people. In the nation North Carolina was known as the Rip Van Winkle of the states. And Rip Van Winkle it would remain until it repudiated the spirit of Macon.

Chapter 21

THE MURPHEY PROGRAM
FOR STATE DEVELOPMENT

Although to the casual observer North Carolina after 1815 seemed indifferent toward its backward condition and its problems, there was slowly emerging a movement for progress and reform. The ruling class may have been satisfied with the status quo. The mass of the people may have seemed indifferent or apathetic. But North Carolina was not immune to the new spirit abroad in the nation, and there were North Carolinians who were neither satisfied nor indifferent.

A New Era After 1815

The War of 1812 marked the beginning of a new era in the United States. Peace, patriotism, and prosperity after 1815 inaugurated a reform movement throughout the country and witnessed the "rise of American nationality." A general outburst of patriotic pride, nationalism, and economic prosperity made Monroe's first administration (1817–21) an "era of good feelings," when the dominant Republican party, converted by experience from its earlier, negative, state rights policy, embarked upon a constructive nationalistic program of national defense, protective tariff, national bank, and internal improvements designed to meet the needs of the nation.

North Carolina shared in the general spirit of patriotism, political harmony, and liberality toward projects for the general welfare even though they might require greater governmental expenditures. State pride and public spirit were awakened by the war, especially by the heroic exploits of Captain Otway Burns, who engaged in privateering, Captain Johnston Blakeley, of the U.S.S. *Wasp,* and Colonel Benjamin Forsythe. High prices for farm products and low prices for manufactures after the war brought unusual prosperity to agricultural North Carolina and to the entire South and West. The towns experienced a brisk and profitable trade, and speculation in farm lands and projected boom

327

towns became widespread. In 1818 Governor John Branch referred to the "unparalleled prosperity" and urged the state legislature to embark upon a program of state development. Symptomatic of the new spirit and the new era was the unprecedented liberality of the state in making provision for the education at public expense of the orphans of Captain Blakeley and Colonel Forsythe and in purchasing Canova's statue and Sully's protrait of Washington—a total outlay in excess of $20,000. There was a feeble but significant effort to improve agriculture. As early as 1813 the Cape Fear Society of New Hanover was incorporated, followed within a few years by several other county societies and by a state agricultural society in 1818. In 1822 the legislature set aside a small Agricultural Fund to aid the local societies, though scant use of the fund led to its abandonment in 1825. In 1824 Denison Olmsted and in 1827 Elisha Mitchell, both professors at the University of North Carolina, prepared and published reports of a geological survey of the state, the first such publications in the United States. Thus North Carolina, in the years after 1815, responded to the general movement for democratic and humanitarian reform manifested in the United States by the rise of the common man or the spread of Jacksonian Democracy.

Archibald D. Murphey and His Program

The genius, leader, and mouthpiece of the progressive reform movement in North Carolina after 1815 was Archibald D. Murphey, an intelligent, well-educated, public-spirited lawyer of Hillsborough, who represented Orange County in the State Senate from 1812 to 1818. He lamented the poverty, ignorance, and general backwardness of the state, particularly his own western section. He observed that "the Mass of the Common People in the County are lazy, sickly, poor, dirty and ignorant." He collected masses of facts and became the best-informed man on conditions in North Carolina. With brilliant pioneering analysis, he diagnosed the causes of North Carolina's backwardness and formulated an enlightened public policy or program which ultimately revolutionized the political and social thinking of North Carolina and laid the foundations of the present modern commonwealth. To his insurgent leadership rallied a small but able group of rising young leaders, chiefly from the West, including Charles Fisher, Joseph Caldwell, David L. Swain, John M. Morehead, and William A. Graham, and, from the East, Edward Dudley and William Gaston. The most revolutionary feature of the new movement was its repudiation of the prevalent philosophy that government is a necessary evil and its bold acceptance of the concept that a democratic government is the servant of the people and their most effective agency for self-development. The leaders of the new movement also believed that the state government should take the lead in a positive constructive program for the development of the state and for the solution of its problems.

In a series of brilliant reports to the state Senate from 1815 to 1818 Murphey presented his diagnosis of, and prescription for, the sick state—internal improvements, public education, constitutional reform, and the reclamation of swamplands.

State Program of Internal Improvements

To solve North Carolina's greatest need and problem—improved transportation—he urged the state government, under the direction of a state board and with adequate state appropriations, to provide a unified system of land and water transportation adequate for directing domestic and foreign commerce through commercial centers in North Carolina. Only the state government could solve the problem of transportation, for efforts by individuals, private chartered companies, and county governments had failed. The existing inlets at Ocracoke and Beaufort should be deepened and a new inlet should be cut through the coastal sand bar to give to the trade of the Roanoke Valley and Albemarle Sound a direct connection with the markets of the world. A north-south canal connecting the eastern rivers and sounds should direct the trade of the Roanoke, Tar, and Neuse rivers to the ocean at Beaufort, the best harbor on the coast. The navigability of the primary rivers—Roanoke, Tar, Neuse, Cape Fear, Yadkin, Catawba, and Broad—should be improved by the removal of obstructions and the construction of locks and by canals around falls and rapids. An east-west canal should connect the Yadkin, Catawba, and Cape Fear rivers and direct the trade of the southern part of the state through Fayetteville and Wilmington. A system of improved roads should traverse the Mountain and Piedmont regions and lead to centers on the navigable rivers. This unified state system would free North Carolina from economic dependence on Virginia and South Carolina. It would develop Beaufort and Wilmington as large commercial cities where North Carolina products would be collected for export and from which imports could be distributed throughout the state. It would increase the value and productivity of farms and stimulate the rise of manufacturing and merchandising, thus fostering a prosperous middle class. It would reduce freight rates, thereby benefiting the people in their sales and purchases and raising their standard of living, and this, in turn, would check emigration. It would inculcate a spirit of state unity, pride, and patriotism. Finally, by increasing per capita income and wealth, it would produce an expanding state revenue to meet the cost of the program and to provide for a system of public education and other progressive measures.

A State System of Public Education

Murphey was the first North Carolina statesman to envision the democratic goal of state provision for universal education of all white children, "the rich and the poor, the dull and the sprightly." He proposed that the state legislature create a state fund for public instruction and a state board to manage the fund and to administer the state system of schools. This board would have power to create school districts, locate schools, appoint local school boards, fix teachers' qualifications and salaries, prescribe courses of study, and provide examinations to determine promotion from elementary school to high school and to the University of North Carolina. He proposed a system including "a gradation of schools, regularly supporting each other, from the one in which the first rudiments of education are taught, to that in which the highest branches of sciences are cultivated." He urged the establishment of two or more primary schools in each county, ten regional academies, a state school for the deaf and dumb, and generous state support and a broad course of studies for the university. The primary schools should teach reading, writing, and arithmetic to all white children, and the academies should teach classical languages, mathematics, geography, astronomy, and history to prepare selected bright young male graduates of the primary schools to enter the university. The primary schools and academies should be supported in part by the state fund and in part by funds raised locally. The state should pay the teachers' salaries in the primary schools and one-third of the cost of buildings and teachers' salaries for the academies. It should bear the full cost of the school for the deaf and dumb and provide generous support for the university. Poor children should receive free instruction in the primary schools for three years and those selected as superior should be given free education in the academies and the university. But tuition should be charged those who were able to pay. Thus Murphey proposed to meet the educational needs of the white children of the state. His combination of the charity-tuition system and his discrimination against white girls and Negro children made the Murphey plan of public education fall far short of the modern concept and practice of universal free education at public expense for all children. Murphey wrote to Thomas Ruffin about his 1817 Report: "I bequeath this Report to the State as the richest Legacy that I shall ever be able to give it."

Constitutional Reform

Murphey asserted the need for remedying various defects in the Constitution of 1776, chief of which was the undemocratic system of equal county representation in both houses of the General Assembly, which placed the East in control of the state government and discriminated against all of the large, populous counties, most of which were in the West. He proposed that all freemen of the state vote on the question of calling a convention for the purpose of revising and amending the state constitution.

Drainage of Swamplands

Murphey also urged the state to drain the vast areas of swamps and marshes in the East. Rich farming land would be reclaimed, the health of the people would be improved, and the drainage canals would improve the facilities for transportation.

State Response

Such was the ringing challenge of the spirit of Murphey to the dominant spirit of Macon. How was the Murphey program received by the people of North Carolina and how much of it was adopted? Its novelty and its promise of development evoked statewide interest and considerable support particularly in the prosperous period before 1819; but the Panic of 1819 lessened the spirit of liberality and state consciousness and renewed the emphasis on economy, which strengthened the opposition to the program.

Partial Adoption of the Internal Improvements Program

The internal improvements program, heralded as a solution to the acute transportation problem, evoked the widest interest and the strongest support, particularly in the backward Mountain and Piedmont areas, which needed a constructive governmental program designed to end their isolation and give them access to markets. It also had support in the eastern towns and in areas adjacent to the projected improvements. But the General Assembly, dominated by the East, was dilatory and unbusinesslike. Before the end of 1819, however, the state, which had never spent a cent for internal improvements, employed Hamilton Fulton, a competent English engineer, at an annual salary of £1,200 "payable in gold"; procured surveys of rivers and proposed canals and inlets; authorized subscriptions of $112,500 of the stock of navigation and canal companies chiefly in the East; and created a state fund for internal improvements consisting of proceeds from the sale of Cherokee lands, bank stock owned by the state, and the stock in each company equivalent to the amount of the state's subscription; and also created a state board to direct the newly adopted policy. In 1823 the legislature appropriated funds for the construction of the Buncombe Turnpike, the Plymouth Toll Road, the Old Fort–Asheville Road, and the Tennessee River Turnpike. In 1827 the Buncombe Turnpike, connecting Greenville, South Carolina, with Greeneville, Tennessee, via Asheville and Hot Springs, was completed.

The plantation East, which was less in need of improvements and would have to bear the greater share of expense, was skeptical of Murphey's policy, blocked its full adoption, and procured the expenditure of more than half of the state appropriations on projects located in the East. Increasing opposition after the

Panic of 1819 threatened the entire program. The internal improvements program failed to improve greatly the transportation facilities in the state. Funds were insufficient and were poorly invested. Too much money was dissipated on local projects; there was a lack of experienced engineers; and the chief engineer, Fulton, resigned after a few years, because of constant criticism of his high salary, his foreign extraction, and his reports against purely local projects. Before 1836 the state, by purchasing stock in private companies, spent a total of less than $300,000, apportioned in driblets and without relation to a unified state system, among an excessive number of local projects, only three of which yielded any dividends—the Roanoke Navigation Company, the Cape Fear Navigation Company, and the Buncombe Turnpike Company. Bad financing, a sharp decline in the annual income of the funds due to the decline of the dividends from bank stock, hard times, the rivalry of local interests, lack of administrative and engineering skill and experience in the navigation companies, and the coming of the railroad—all these contributed to the failure of the system. But the long agitation revealed the needs and resources of the state, aroused it from its customary lethargy, promulgated the concept of an active government, and inspired greater confidence and hopefulness among the people. It was highly significant that North Carolina had adopted the new policy of state aid to internal improvements. It was the later extension of this policy that finally solved the transportation problem.

Public Education: Literary Board and Fund

Less favorable was the public response to Murphey's program of public education. The legislature quickly killed his bill designed to put his plan into operation. But Murphey had started a movement that gathered momentum. The governors recommended action, and the advocates of schools carried on a vigorous agitation, but the legislature rejected every proposal to establish schools until 1825. In that year it took the first step by creating a Literary Fund "for the establishment of common schools" and a Literary Board, with the governor as president and the state treasurer as treasurer, to manage the fund. The Literary Fund consisted of the following: dividends from state-owned bank stock not already set aside for the fund for internal improvements; dividends arising from state-owned stock in certain navigation and canal companies; excise taxes on auctioneers and retailers of liquors; the unexpended balance of the Agricultural Fund; sales of public lands except the Cherokee lands (lands north and east of the Little Tennessee River and east of the Nantahala Mountains ceded by the Cherokees in 1819); vacant swamp lands; and legislative appropriations. Repeated efforts later to increase the inadequate fund failed. It grew slowly, mainly from dividends on bank stock, in which the board invested it. Total receipts for the years 1825–36 were $243,000 and total expenditures, $239,000, some of which went for schools. The fund suffered from the dishonesty of state Treasurer John Haywood, from poor investments, and from bad faith on the part of the legislature, which borrowed from it for general purposes, including the payment of the salaries of its own members. A legislative committee in 1828 threw the responsibility for the education of North Carolina children upon the Almighty, by reporting its inability to discover any method of educational improvement except to "unite in the prayer that a kind Providence will hasten the time when literary, moral and religious instruction should pervade our country."

Before 1826 the annual interest and dividends from the invested Literary Fund were too small to permit the establishment of a state system of schools. Increasing agitation by the press and from the pulpit, Joseph Caldwell's famous *Letters on Popular Education* in 1832, and the governors' legislative messages urging action could not overcome the indifference of the people and the legislative majority representing property interests. These interests employed the strategy of postponing indefinitely the day when the common people should be educated at public expense. The decade ending in 1835 has been called the "ten unfruitful years" of North Carolina's educational history.

The legislature, with an eastern majority by virtue of the system of equal county representation, would not even consider Murphey's proposal of a convention for constitutional reform, and nothing was done immediately to drain the swamplands.

In his later years Murphey worked on a history of North Carolina to inform the people and arouse their pride and patriotism, but poor health and lack of money kept him from finishing the book. An optimist and a dreamer, with poor business judgment, Murphey invested borrowed money in navigation companies and in real estate that would increase in value if his program of internal improvements were put into effect. Thus he became insolvent, involving some of his friends in financial losses. He suffered the indignity of being put in jail for failure to pay his debts. Waning public confidence in him may have weakened his program.

Failure to Adopt the Murphey Program

Murphey's grand program for revolutionizing North Carolina was defeated by public indifference and by the selfish interests of the East. But his dream was a prophecy. He had drawn a blueprint of state development. With it his followers later erected the magnificent commonwealth of which he dreamed but which he did not live to see. Murphey perhaps ranks first among all of North Carolina's state-builders. Writing in 1860, William A. Graham declared that Murphey's reports "inaugurated a new era in the public policy of the State," and that they constituted "the noblest of monuments of philosophic statesmanship to be found in our public archives since the days of the Revolution."

The Murphey program revealed the basic sectional conflict in North Carolina. The Republican party was the only political party in the state after 1815; but beneath the superficial political unity and harmony there were sectional conflicts arising from the differing interests and needs which grew out of variations in nature's endowment. Each section was primarily concerned with its own self-interest. Sectionalism was accentuated by the Panic of 1819 and eventually split the Republican party. It produced conflicts in North Carolina over the Murphey program and over other public issues, both state and national. There was spirited conflict over five state political and economic issues: internal improvements, constitutional reform, banking and finance, the caucus system, and the general ticket system.

Internal Improvements

The isolated West (Mountain and Piedmont areas), except the southeastern border counties in easy reach of the market town of Fayetteville, gave strong support in the legislature to the Murphey program of internal improvements. The Sound area, having no hope of securing from the state the expensive project of a new inlet to Albemarle Sound and expecting little benefit from the improvement of rivers in other regions, was in determined opposition. The wealthier middle eastern section, less in need of the improvements because of its rivers and knowing that it would have to bear the major cost of the state program, was generally in opposition, though in the towns that would profit commercially and in the valleys of the Roanoke and Cape Fear, whose prospects of improvement were best, there was some support of the policy. In general there was an East-West cleavage on the issue of state internal improvements as revealed by the votes in the legislature.

Constitutional Reform

The growing, more democratic, small-farm, landlocked West, convinced that the legislature would not adopt a program of state development until the dominance of the more wealthy and aristocratic East was broken, demanded a convention to amend the Constitution of 1776, which grossly discriminated against the West in respect to representation and voting power in the legislature. The wealthier slaveholding East stubbornly refused to permit the call of a convention, and thus surrender its complete dominance of the legislature to a poorer section whose economic and social policies might endanger its interests. The sharply defined East-West conflict over constitutional reform assumed a serious aspect after the Panic of 1819. When strong western agitation and legislative efforts failed to secure a state convention, an extralegal western convention of delegates from twenty-four counties met in Raleigh in

1823, but it failed to obtain a call for a state convention from the eastern-controlled legislature.

Banking and Finance

General economic distress after 1819 produced a popular antagonism to banks and a conflict between the debtor and creditor classes. As related in the preceding chapter, the state banks, during the panic of 1819, followed a conservative, deflationary policy with respect to loans and suspended the payment of their notes in specie. They were thought by Governor John Branch and the mass of people to have helped cause the panic or at least to have contributed to its severity. The antibank, inflationary, unsound money sentiment, though widely scattered, was more pronounced in the backward West and in the Sound region. It was not as strong in the West as it might have been, however, because of the strong attachment of that section to the policy of internal improvements, which was financed in part after 1821 by the dividends the state received from its bank stock.

The Caucus System

A caucus of Republican politicians in the General Assembly customarily selected the Republican ticket of electors for which the people would vote in presidential elections, and a caucus of Republicans in the United States Congress chose the presidential candidate for whom the electors would vote. Since the East controlled the General Assembly and furnished the majority of the state's congressmen, the eastern legislators and congressmen determined the role of North Carolina in legislative and congressional caucuses and in presidential elections. The people had no real voice in the selection of a president. A small group of officeholding Republicans, chiefly from the East, controlled the elections in North Carolina by helping the congressional caucus choose the presidential candidate and by choosing the electoral candidates in legislative caucus and securing popular ratification of their electoral ticket by appeals to party loyalty. There was unorganized discontent with the aristocratic eastern control of party machinery. There was also deep concern over the startling loss of public interest in presidential elections, which, in a one-party state, had lost all zest of contest. Of the 60,000 eligible voters in North Carolina, only 9,549 participated in the presidential election of 1816, and in 1820 less than half that number. The Panic of 1819 stimulated a revival of political interest that produced an early division of opinion concerning the person who should succeed Monroe as president and caused an attack on the undemocratic caucus, which would not tolerate party division. The West particularly, restless because of hard times, was in a mood to protest the continued dictation of the state's role in presidential elections by a small band of political leaders.

The General Ticket System

In line with the trend in the nation to insure an undivided Republican electoral vote and to increase the influence of the state in national politics, the General Assembly of 1815 substituted the general ticket system (under which the entire state voted for a ticket containing names equal in number to the state's electoral vote) for the district system (under which one elector was chosen in each district). So attached was the state to the more truly representative district system that for a decade its congressmen were conspicuous in futile advocacy of a federal constitutional amendment establishing it for the entire nation. The general ticket system helped the East to deliver an undivided electoral vote for the Republican candidate for president. A minority of Republicans and surviving Federalists bitterly opposed the general ticket system and worked for the reestablishment of the district system by independent state action. The caucus and general ticket systems were devices for the choice of political candidates and for the control of elections by the dominant group, whose center of power was in the East. Thus, in opposing them, the West was seeking to reduce the political power of the East.

There was sectional division of opinion in North Carolina after 1815 on three important national issues: internal improvements; the protective tariff; and the extension of slavery.

Internal Improvements as a National Issue

After the War of 1812 the national Republican party and the federal government were committed to the policy of internal improvements. John C. Calhoun of South Carolina, congressman and later Monroe's secretary of war, was the foremost advocate of the new policy. Three projected federal projects were of particular interest to North Carolina: a national road from Maine to Louisiana; a new inlet to Albemarle Sound; and an inland waterway from Boston to Savannah. In North Carolina we have seen that the West, which would profit by the projected road to Louisiana, was strongly in favor of internal improvements by the federal government. So too was the coastal Sound region, which would benefit from the inland waterway and the new inlet, hopes for which had been raised by a friendly tour of inspection in 1819 by Monroe, Calhoun, and a group of engineers. But the slaveholding middle eastern area, whose chief spokesman in Washington was Nathaniel Macon, was in bitter opposition because it would be burdened with taxation for projects located elsewhere and because its latent fear of northern attacks on slavery made it regard the federal Constitution, literally and strictly construed, as the chief bulwark of its safety. "If Congress can make canals they can with more propriety emancipate," wrote Macon in 1818. The majority of the national Republican party had been converted, by its long lease of power and by the bitter lessons of the war, to a nationalistic program for the development and strengthening of the nation, based on a broad construction of the Constitution. But a minority was still stubbornly insistent upon strict construction of the Constitution, state rights, rigid economy, and a minimum of federal governmental activity. The majority of North Carolina's congressmen, notably Richard Dobbs Spaight of Craven County, Lewis Williams of Surry County, and Nathaniel Macon of Warren County, were obstructionist; but Charles Fisher of Rowan County and the other congressmen from the undeveloped West and the Sound region were sympathetic with the constructive program of the national party majority.

Protective Tariff

After 1815 the general public was only beginning to realize the economic and sectional implications of the policy of protective tariff. There was some sentiment in North Carolina for the tariff as a stimulus to manufacturing, which was beginning in the South, and as the chief source of federal revenue from which internal improvements might be made. But agricultural North Carolina was generally antitariff. North Carolina's congressmen did not cast a single vote in favor of the tariff bills of 1816 and 1820.

Slavery Extension

In the sectional contest in 1819–20 over the admission of Missouri, ending in the Missouri Compromise, North Carolina cast a solid vote for the admission of Missouri as a slave state, but its senators and congressmen divided equally on the question of excluding slavery from the remainder of the Louisiana Territory north of 36° 30'. The votes favoring exclusion were from the free-labor West, which, though not abolitionist, was willing to restrict but not stop the spread of slavery. The slaveholding East voted solidly in opposition to any restriction on its extension.

The Sectional Alignment in North Carolina

It is clear that there was an insurgent reform movement in North Carolina after 1815, based primarily on sectional needs and self-interest, which was challenging the dominant conservative champions of laissez-faire policy and the status quo. On the issues of state internal improvements, constitutional reform, the extension of slavery, and the reform of party machinery, the cleavage was basically West v. East. But on the issues of federal internal improvements and state financial and banking policy, the cleavage tended to unite the Sound region and the West against the middle eastern section. The undeveloped, underrepresented West was in revolt against the status quo and the negative governmental program of the dominant conservative East. Its most vital need was access to markets, and the public issue with the strongest appeal to the West was internal improvements. It is highly significant that on the issue of federal internal improvements, the East was not united. The Sound region was aligned with the West against the middle eastern section.

Chapter 22

THE STATE'S CHANGING ROLE IN NATIONAL POLITICS, 1824-1835

Eastern Dominance in Politics

The dominance of the conservative East in the General Assembly impeded the adoption of a progressive program of state development after 1815. The East was likewise dominant in determining the role of North Carolina in national politics because of the election of United States senators by the General Assembly, the prestige of Nathaniel Macon, the practice of nominating presidential electors by legislative caucus and presidential candidates by congressional caucus, and the general ticket system of electing presidential electors. In the General Assembly, in state and national campaigns, and in popular interest, national issues completely overshadowed state issues. The Republican party dominated North Carolina politics and the East controlled the state Republican party. Nathaniel Macon was the leading exemplar and spokesman of North Carolina Republicanism. But the decline of popular interest in national elections, which resulted from the absence of party contests, and the resentment of the West at the dominance of the Republican party by the East, which supported a negative, do-nothing program, led to division within the ranks of North Carolina Republicanism over national issues.

The first indication of division came during the struggle over the Missouri Compromise in 1819–20. The North Carolina delegation in each house of Congress split evenly on the compromise of excluding slavery in the Louisiana Territory north of 36° 30′—the West supporting exclusion and the East opposing it.

Presidential Election of 1824

But the first major blow to the unity of the Republican party in the state and to the dominance of the East in national politics was the presidential campaign of 1824.

Macon and the majority of North Carolina congressmen and political leaders favored Secretary of the Treasury William H. Crawford of Georgia for the presidency in 1824 and as early as 1821 were quietly lining up the state for him. Crawford was known to be favorable to a strict construction of the Constitution, state rights, and rigid economy, and hostile to federal internal improvements, protective tariff, and the nationalistic program of the majority of the national Republican party. Customarily the Republicans in the General Assembly, meeting in caucus, nominated the ticket of Republican electors and obtained popular ratification of the ticket by appeals to party loyalty. But the West, aroused by the Panic of 1819 and resentful over the stinging defeat of the Murphey program by the East, was now ready to revolt against the continued dominance of the East in national politics and its delivery of the state's electoral vote to Crawford, whose negative program would not benefit the undeveloped West.

The Calhoun Movement in North Carolina

There was some sentiment for John Quincy Adams of Massachusetts and Andrew Jackson of Tennessee; but before 1824 the only opposition candidate with organized support in the state was Secretary of War John C. Calhoun of South Carolina, brilliant young leader of the nationalistic wing of the Republican party and the most famous advocate of internal improvements. His interest in these improvements—particularly a national road from Maine to Louisiana, a new inlet to Albemarle Sound, and an inland waterway from Boston to Savannah—made him popular in the undeveloped West and in the Sound region, whose economic interests made Crawford unacceptable. The real though secret manager of Calhoun's campaign in the state was Charles Fisher of Salisbury, a well-known champion of western interests. In the General Assembly of 1823 Fisher and other opposition leaders, in an effort to arouse the people, made a spirited attack upon the caucus and the general ticket systems by which the eastern-dominated party machine expected to carry the state for Crawford. The Crawford partisans in control of the legislature easily repulsed these attacks and proceeded in legislative caucus to nominate a "Crawford ticket" of electors. In February, 1824, Crawford was nominated as the Republican candidate for president by a congressional caucus in Washington, which was attended by none of the supporters of the other candidates, and in which North Carolina's nine congressmen formed the third largest state delegation.

The Jackson Movement and the "People's Ticket"

Contemptuous of the opposition, the regular party press and machine boastfully proclaimed that loyal Republican North Carolina was for Crawford. But a secret Calhoun committee, directed by Charles Fisher, began the formation of an opposition "People's Ticket" by the method of nomination by public meetings of voters, granting minority representation to Jackson and Adams men in the hope of capturing for Calhoun and the People's Ticket the entire anti-Crawford vote. By arousing public interest, the Calhoun leaders discovered a spontaneous movement for "Old Hickory," hero of the Battle of New Orleans and of the recent invasion and acquisition of Florida. Sensing that Jackson had the best chance of defeating Crawford because of the appeal of his dramatic personality and military career to the common people who voted more by emotion than intelligence, Archibald D. Murphey of Orange County and William Polk of Mecklenburg took the lead in a systematic campaign for Jackson. This campaign was spreading like wildfire at the time of Calhoun's elimination in March by a compromise in Pennsylvania by which Jackson was nominated for president and Calhoun for vice-president. In North Carolina Jackson leaders completed the People's Ticket, which, in the hope of winning the support of Calhoun's and Adams's friends, was not publicly pledged to anyone, though most of its members were for Jackson. For the most part, the Calhoun following, particularly in the West, shifted to Jackson, though with reluctance and in recognition of the fact that only Jackson and his People's Ticket had a good prospect of defeating the Crawford Ticket in North Carolina. Most of the Adams men also preferred the People's Ticket. Jackson's capture of the People's Ticket in the spring of 1824 made the campaign in North Carolina a contest between Jackson and Crawford.

Crawford's friends attacked Jackson for his crude personality, his lack of education and political experience, and his support in Congress of internal improvements and the tariff; they presented Crawford as the southern candidate and as the regular Republican nominee whose devotion to economy and state rights and opposition to tariff and internal improvements would serve the economic, social, and southern interests of North Carolina.

Victory for "People's Ticket"

Opposition leaders appealed to state pride and the democratic instinct and prejudice of the common people by calling Crawford the "caucus" and the "Virginia" candidate. In 1823 the *Fayetteville Observer* said: "Already has Virginia as a matter of course on the subject of the coming election tacked us to her skirts to follow whither she leads; and without condescending to ask our opinion, placed us on her side of the question. This state of things must be changed. North Carolina must make herself heard and must assert her dignity. She must take an elevated stand and show to the nation and her revilers that she has a will."

Even Murphey thought "Crawford much the greatest and best man" among the candidates, but he would "rather have a weak president than that North Carolina and Virginia should vote together." Crawford, who opposed internal improvements, would not serve the transportation needs of undeveloped North Carolina. Jackson was lauded as the friend of the common people and the brave hero of two victorious wars with England. That he had voted for the General Survey Bill of 1824 and was the alleged personal choice and running mate of Calhoun enabled him to profit by the popularity of the issue of federal improvements in the West and the Sound region.

The innovation of mass meetings, more than a hundred of which were held in the state, at which the common people were entertained and fired with the zeal of a holy crusade for the rights of the sovereign people and polled concerning their choice of candidates, was the basic strategy of the Jackson campaign. "It is very difficult to electioneer successfully against General Jackson," wrote a Crawford elector. "One cup of generous whiskey produces more military ardor than can be allayed by a month of reflection and reason." To the utter dismay of the Republican machine, the People's Ticket swept to a decisive victory in a veritable revolt of the people against the party leaders, which brought the unprecedented number of nearly 36,000 voters to the polls. Crawford received about 15,000 votes and carried most of the heavy slaveholding plantation counties in the middle eastern section and along the Virginia border and also the Quaker counties of Guilford, Randolph, and Chatham. The People's Ticket (Jackson) received some 20,000 votes and carried the undeveloped West and the Sound region, whose self-interest made them favor internal improvements, as well as several counties in the East.

Significance of the 1824 Election in North Carolina

The presidential election of 1824 in North Carolina was a victory for democracy, for the West, and for the movement of revolt against Virginia leadership. No longer could it be said that "North Carolina floats up or down stream as Virginia may or not." The election was something of a political revolution and a successful revolt of the West and the Sound region against the political dominance of the more highly developed and wealthy plantation East. The unity of the Republican party was broken and so was the unity and dominance of the East. The West and the Sound region supported Jackson not only because of his personality and military heroism but also because they thought that he, like Calhoun, would favor a constructive program of internal improvements.

In the nation Jackson led in electoral votes; but, since no candidate received a majority, the president was chosen from the three leading candidates by the

House of Representatives. Despite the popular majority in the state for Jackson, ten of North Carolina's congressmen cast the vote of the state for Crawford in the House election and five of them were defeated for reelection. But Adams was elected president largely because of the support of Henry Clay whom Adams appointed secretary of state. Jackson men charged that their hero was the choice of the people and had been cheated by a "corrupt bargain" between Adams and Clay. In 1825 they began a campaign for the election of Jackson in 1828. The election of 1824 contributed to the split of the Republican party into two factions—the National Republicans led by Adams and Clay with chief strength in New England, the Middle States, and the Northwest, and the Democratic-Republicans, or Jackson men, who were strongest in the South and West.

The East Becomes a Jackson Stronghold

In North Carolina the triumph of the West and the loss of dominance by the East in national politics were short-lived. After 1824, when the only political choice was Jackson or Adams, Macon and the slaveholding East shifted to Jackson as the lesser of two evils. President Adams, a New Englander with nationalistic ideas and policies, was a reputed enemy of slavery. Jackson was a southern slaveholding cotton planter. Though from the democratic West and the hero of the common people, he was identified with the Southwest, which was bound to the Old South by ties of blood and a common interest in Negro slavery and plantation agriculture. His view of the Constitution, though not clearly known, was thought to be not so latitudinarian as Adams's and might be modified by his strong southern support. So in 1828 Jackson had the support of a reunited North Carolina in his victory over Adams, who carried only nine counties. The West and the Sound region continued enthusiastically loyal in the hope that his administration would help solve their problems of transportation and material development. With the state practically solid for Jackson, the East was able to regain its political dominance in national politics because it was still dominant in state politics and had more able and experienced leaders.

As president from 1829 to 1837, Jackson disappointed the West and the Sound region and endeared himself more and more to the plantation East. Originally hostile to Jackson, the East was pleased with his opposition to federal internal improvements in the states as expressed in the Maysville Road Bill veto of 1830 and with his appointment of John Branch of Halifax County as secretary of the navy—the state's first representative in the cabinet. The East was pleased also with his emphasis on economy and the unexpected degree of his devotion to state rights with respect to the Indian problem, internal improvements, banking, and the federal surplus. On the other hand, the West and the Sound region, originally enthusiastic for Jackson, cooled perceptibly during his first term, though National Republican Henry Clay was able to carry only one county against Jackson in 1832.

The dissatisfaction of the West and the Sound region with Jackson reached the stage of open revolt in his second term. Influential eastern leaders with Federalist leanings, among whom were William Gaston of Craven County, Edward B. Dudley of New Hanover, and Edward Stanly of Beaufort, were anti-Jackson. David L. Swain of Buncombe, and perhaps others, had never favored Jackson, even in 1824, and had concentrated their attention on state issues while the Jackson fever was raging in the 1820s. Though South Carolina's nullification of the tariff in 1832 was unpopular in North Carolina, so was Jackson's bold stand against a sovereign state embodied in the Force Bill of 1833 for the use of force against South Carolina because of its nullification of federal tariff laws. This was particularly resented in the southern Piedmont, which was bound closely to South Carolina by geography and trade. Jackson made other enemies by forcing the resignation of John Branch from the cabinet during the tempest over Peggy Eaton.

The unpopularity of Van Buren, who had triumphed over Calhoun and who, after the Calhoun-Jackson break, was Jackson's obvious choice as his successor, decreased Jackson's popularity in North Carolina, especially in the West and the Sound region, where Calhoun had long been popular because of his championship of internal improvements. Van Buren was opposed to internal improvements and was thought to be opposed to slavery. Jackson's effective veto in 1833 of Clay's bill for the distribution among the states of the proceeds of public land sales alienated support in the needy, undeveloped regions of the state. The president's high-handed destruction of the Second Bank of the United States by his veto of recharter in 1832 and his "removal" of the government deposits in 1833 further antagonized the commercial interests of the coastal East, militated against the industrial development of the West, deprived the business interests of a sound circulating medium, and caused Senator Willie P. Mangum and other leaders to break openly with the administration. The growing friendliness of the middle eastern section for Jackson and his state rights policies accentuated the anti-Jackson drift of the West.

Formation of the Whig Party

In the United States Jackson's policies had antagonized many diverse groups. Their common bond of opposition to "King Andrew" and Jacksonian policies, democracy, and the "rise of the common man" was strong enough to draw them together in 1834 into a new opposition party—the Whig party. The dominant wing of this new national organization consisted of the National Republicans, devoted to Henry Clay's nationalistic, constructive program of internal improvements, protective tariff, and national bank. This element was strongest in the North, but it had some support in the South where

Louisiana planters were Whig because of the tariff on sugar. Some backward, isolated areas, such as western North Carolina, were Whig because of that party's support of internal improvements. A second and minority wing of the Whig party consisted of the state rights group of cotton planters in the lower South, antagonized by the principles of Jacksonian democracy and by Jackson's Force Bill of 1833. The Whig party lacked national unity. It contained proponents and opponents of protective tariff, national banks, federal aid to internal improvements, nullifiers, and antinullifiers. The North Carolina elements of opposition to Jackson, chiefly the small-farmer West and the commercial area of the East, identified themselves with the national Whig party whereas the plantation, slaveholding, aristocratic East was staunchly Jacksonian. This cleavage in North Carolina was opposite to that in the lower South with the exception of Louisiana. The North Carolina Whigs obviously belonged to the National Republican, internal improvement wing rather than to the southern state rights wing. The disastrous Panic of 1837, for which the Jackson administration was blamed, and the unpopularity of President Van Buren greatly increased the strength of the opposition Whig party.

The Jackson men gradually dropped other names and became known as Democrats. This Whig-Democratic party cleavage restored the two-party system and dominated American political life for the next twenty years.

The Whig party was formally organized in North Carolina in 1835. In that year it elected a respectable minority in the General Assembly and seven of the state's thirteen congressmen—five from the West and two from the Sound region. The Whig alliance of the undeveloped West and the Sound region against the conservative state rights plantation East seriously challenged the continued dominance of the East in determining North Carolina's role in national politics. Geographically and economically the Whig-Democratic cleavage was similar to the Jackson-Crawford cleavage in 1824.

Whig-Democratic Rivalry

After 1835 there was sharp, bitter rivalry between the North Carolina Whigs and Democrats in both state and national politics. In national affairs the Whigs favored a constructive program of internal improvements, national bank, protective tariff, and distribution—policies that would aid in the economic development of the backward West and the Sound region. The western wing of the Whig party in North Carolina was stronger than the eastern. Among the more prominent Whig leaders, Willie P. Mangum, John M. Morehead, David L. Swain, William A. Graham, George E. Badger, James Graham, Edmund Deberry, Abraham Rencher, Thomas L. Clingman, and Zebulon B. Vance were from the West; William Gaston, W. B. Shepard, Edward B. Dudley, Ebenezer Pettigrew, Edward Stanly, and Kenneth Rayner were from the East.

In national affairs the Democrats championed strict construction of the Constitution, state rights, economy, and a relatively inactive federal government. They opposed the entire Whig program. The strongholds of the Democratic party in North Carolina were the areas of heavy slaveholding and staple-crop farming on a plantation basis—the middle eastern section and two small areas in the Piedmont—the tobacco-growing counties along the Virginia border and the cotton-growing counties along the South Carolina border. Elsewhere the state was predominantly Whig. Among the chief Democratic leaders in North Carolina were John Branch, Bedford Brown, William H. Haywood, Robert Strange, Asa Biggs, David S. Reid, Thomas Bragg, Lewis Williams, John W. Ellis, Romulus M. Saunders, William W. Holden, Burton Craige, L. O'B. Branch, and James C. Dobbin.

Party Machinery and Political Methods

In the quarter-century of partisan conflict after 1835 the Whig party carried North Carolina in the presidential elections of 1840, 1844, and 1848; it also captured half or more of the state's delegation in seven of the thirteen congresses; and it kept its leaders in the United States Senate about half of the time. In the early 1840s the Whigs were at the zenith of their power and strength. They had full control of the state government—governor and legislature—about half of the state's representatives in Congress, both United States senators, William A. Graham and Willie P. Mangum, both from Orange County, and a representative in the president's cabinet, George E. Badger, secretary of the navy. The Whigs greatly surpassed the Democrats in effective party organization, in the number and ability of aggressive leaders, and in the number and influence of party newspapers. In national politics North Carolina was one of the strongest Whig states in the South. National rather than state issues continued to dominate the political campaigns.

After 1835 both the Whigs and the Democrats gradually developed effective party organization and machinery for use in campaigns—the party caucus, the state and district conventions, clubs, state and local committees, the county meeting, and local mass meetings. Party newspapers engaged in violent political warfare, but the Whig papers were more numerous and influential. The *Raleigh Register, Hillsborough Recorder, Fayetteville Observer, Carolina Watchman* (Salisbury), and *Greensborough Patriot* were leading Whig organs, while the Democratic cause was upheld chiefly by the *North Carolina Standard* (Raleigh) assisted by lesser papers including the *Wilmington Journal,* the *Asheville News,* and the *Mecklenburg Jeffersonian* (Charlotte). Opposing candidates plied the voters with addresses, circulars, joint debates, and food and drink. The campaigns dealt chiefly with national public questions and issues but often degenerated into personal abuse, violent partisanship, and petty bickering. Party emblems, campaign slogans and songs, mass meetings, processions, barbecues, and other political devices were used to arouse emotion and woo the voters. A partisan issue which led to spectacular conflict was the right of the legislature to give instructions to the United States senators. The Democrats upheld the right and the Whigs generally opposed it. Whichever party was in control of the state legislature sought to embarrass and force the resignation of a senator of the opposite party. Senators Mangum (Whig), and Brown and Strange (Democrats), were targets of such legislative attack in the 1830s, Mangum resigning in 1836 and Brown and Strange in 1840.

The formation of the Whig party in Jackson's second term definitely split eastern North Carolina politically, aligning the Sound region with the West, and ended the East's easy dominance of North Carolina's role in state and national politics. As a new party, the Whigs were in quest of popular issues. The major state policies supported by the new party were public schools, a school for the deaf and blind, a hospital for the insane, state aid to internal improvements, and revision of the Constitution of 1776. First on the program, and a policy on which all other reforms depended, was the question of constitutional reform.

Chapter 23

THE CONVENTION OF 1835
AND THE TWO-PARTY SYSTEM

The most important and persistent issue in North Carolina for fifty years after the American Revolution was constitutional reform. Dissatisfaction with the Constitution of 1776 first became evident in the 1780s. Repeated demands for reform were stifled until mounting discontent brought the state face to face with revolution in the 1830s and culminated in the Convention of 1835.

It was almost a miracle that the 1776 constitution lasted as long as it did. It was drafted under wartime conditions by a group of men with no experience in constitution making. A good constitution should be flexible. The 1776 constitution was not. As time passed it became more archaic and out of touch with the political realities of life. And there was no provision for amendment. Finally, there were only two alternatives, reform or revolution.

Undemocratic Requirements for Suffrage and Officeholding

The Constitution of 1776 provided an undemocratic government which was increasingly out of harmony with the advance of democracy in the nineteenth century. The people did not participate directly in the choice of county court officials or any state official except members of the General Assembly. All taxpayers could vote for members of the House of Commons, but only owners of at least fifty acres of land could vote for state senators. The General Assembly elected the governor and other state officials. The governor had to own lands worth over £1,000, members of the Senate at least three hundred acres, and members of the House of Commons at least one hundred acres. The landed class had a monopoly of officeholding and special privileges in suffrage. Many people demanded democratic reforms in suffrage and officeholding.

348

Inefficient and Wasteful Government

In some respects the state government was inefficient and wasteful. Elected annually and almost devoid of any real power, the governor was subordinate to the legislature, without the power of veto, and powerless to be a leader and effective administrator. Other state officers were also elected by, and subordinate to, the legislature. Judges held office during good behavior, but the legislature controlled their salaries. The largest expenditure of state government was the cost of the annual sessions of the General Assembly. That body was too large, its sessions too frequent, and its cost too great for the work it accomplished. It spent too much time in discussing unimportant local legislation and in lengthy bickering and balloting for various officials, including the election of militia officers.

Borough Representation

There was discontent with the antiquated, undemocratic system of borough representation by which the boroughs of New Bern, Edenton, Wilmington, Halifax, Fayetteville, Hillsborough, and Salisbury enjoyed the special privilege of electing one member each to the House of Commons. Most of these boroughs were insignificant villages, and their elections were sometimes productive of feuds and scandals.

Illiberal Religious Provisions

There was also dissatisfaction with two illiberal religious provisions of the constitution. The provision that no minister, while in the active discharge of his pastoral duties, could be a member of the legislature or Council of State had been used to expel from the legislature John Culpepper and William Taylor in 1801 and Josiah Crudup in 1820. These expulsions were unpopular; Culpepper and Crudup were elected to Congress. A particularly irritating provision (Article 32) forbade public office to anyone who denied the "being of God or the truth of the Protestant religion, or the divine authority of either the Old or the New Testament or who shall hold Religious principles incompatible with the freedom and safety of the State." This provision of the constitution was in conflict with Article 19 of the bill of rights, which some people felt was superior to the constitution. As a matter of fact, Catholics, Jews, Quakers, and Deists had held public office. An effort to expel from the General Assembly Jacob Henry, a Jew from Carteret County, had failed in 1809. In 1833 William Gaston of New Bern, the most noted Roman Catholic in the state, was elected to the Supreme Court of North Carolina and accepted the office. Nevertheless Gaston and his friends and many people throughout the state desired repeal or modification of Article 32 of the constitution as "out of date, undemocratic, and a relic of English monarchy."

Free Negro Suffrage

As the question of Negro slavery became more acute after 1830, there was a growing demand in the slaveholding East that free Negroes be deprived of the right to vote, which they enjoyed under the constitution.

Representation in the General Assembly

The chief complaint against the constitution was the unjust, undemocratic system of equal county representation which discriminated against all large counties and was particularly unfair to the western half of the state. Murphey said in 1816, "The principal defect [in the constitution] is the inequality of representation in the Legislature," and Governor Swain in 1834 declared, "The great object to be attained is a radical change in the form of representation." Each county, regardless of size, population, or wealth, had one senator and two representatives in the House of Commons. The East had more counties, controlled both houses of every legislature, passed such laws and elected such officials as it wished, blocked laws demanded by the West, and dominated the state government. This system was particularly unjust by 1830, when the more rapidly growing West outnumbered the East in population by 374,092 to 363,896. But the East still possessed the greater wealth, chiefly in land and slaves. Repeatedly the West endeavored to increase its representation by the creation of new western counties; but the dominant East either defeated bills for new western counties or created new eastern counties to offset those created in the West. From 1776 to 1833 eighteen new counties were formed in the West while fifteen were created in the East. The people of the West smarted under this injustice and came to realize that laws for internal improvements and economic development, of basic importance to their backward, landlocked section, could not be enacted until the system of equal county representation was replaced by one which gave to the West more voting power in the legislature. Of course the East opposed any change in the system of representation which would endanger its dominance of the state government.

A Convention Necessary for Reform

But how could the constitution be changed? It contained no provision for amendment. It could be changed only by a constitutional convention called by the General Assembly or by the people. There were precedents for such action in the conventions of 1788 and 1789 to vote on ratification of the United States Constitution. A convention might be called by the legislature, or the proposal could be submitted by the legislature to popular referendum. Either method required action by the General Assembly. But how could the minority West pass a bill calling for a convention in a General Assembly always in control of the East, which was opposed to the whole idea? Obviously a convention bill could not be passed unless some eastern legislators joined the western members in voting for it.

Fifty-Year Campaign for a Convention

Efforts had been made to secure constitutional reform by a convention in 1787, 1788, 1808, and 1811. Murphey reported a convention bill in 1816, but it was defeated. The Panic of 1819 accentuated the grievances of the West and agitation for reform. But to the dismay of the West convention bills were defeated in 1819 and 1821. In 1822 a caucus of western legislators asked the western counties to elect delegates to a western convention and distributed ten thousand copies of an address designed to stimulate and mobilize public sentiment for a convention; and in 1823 twenty-four western counties sent forty-seven delegates to an extralegal western convention at Raleigh, whose proposals for a state convention were rejected by the General Assembly. There followed a temporary decline of the reform agitation, partly because of the intense interest in national politics. But after 1830 the western demand for a convention became so strong and so widespread that the alternatives facing the legislature were reform or revolution. Convention bills were defeated by the legislature in 1831, in 1832, and again in 1833 after an unofficial western plebiscite had resulted in a vote of 30,000 for to 1,000 against a convention. Then a wave of indignation swept the West. There were threats of revolution and secession if the Assembly of 1834 failed to call a convention. The *Carolina Watchman* of Salisbury declared that if the legislature refused to pass a convention bill, "we of the West" will act without legislative authority, that is, revolt and secede. "We admit the experiment is dangerous, but cost what it will the experiment will be made immediately after . . . the next Assembly [1834] if some measure of reform does not pass."

Success in 1834–1835

By 1834 circumstances and events conspired to induce a few eastern legislators to join with the West in passing a law to submit the question of a convention to a statewide referendum.

In the first place, there was some eastern sentiment for a convention to reform the illiberal religious clauses and to abolish free Negro suffrage.

Question of the State Capital—and the New Capitol

In the second place, the question of removing the state capital was used by the West to win some eastern support for a convention. After the capitol at Raleigh burned, June 21, 1831, there was some agitation to remove the capital to Fayetteville. Only a convention could make this change. A legislative coalition of the West and the Cape Fear region in favor of a convention and the removal of the capital to Fayetteville defeated a bill to rebuild at Raleigh in 1831, but was not able to muster enough votes to call the convention. The next year the coalition failed not only to pass a convention bill but also to block the rebuilding bill. In 1833 an appropriation of $50,000 was made and a committee appointed to build a new capitol where the old one had stood. The committee drew plans for a new building somewhat like the first capitol. The cornerstone was laid on June 4, 1833. The building was of stone brought from a quarry just outside the city, over the mile-and-a-quarter "Experimental Railroad," the first railroad in the state. Ithiel Town, noted New England architect, helped the committee make some changes in the plan as the work progressed, and late in 1834 hired David Paton, a young Scottish architect, to take charge and finish the building. Paton made more changes in the plan, hired stone workers from outside the state, and completed the capitol in 1840 at a total cost of $530,000. The capitol was copied in part from the Parthenon and other famous buildings of ancient Greece. It was regarded as one of the most beautiful examples of Greek architecture in the United States. Though Fayetteville failed to become the state capital, the support of the West for removal had won some eastern support for a convention.

Decreasing Differences between East and West

In the third place, diminishing differences between the East and the West had lessened the East's fear of a larger western representation in the legislature. By 1830 the northern Piedmont was growing more tobacco and the southern counties were growing cotton as a staple crop. The westward spread of wealth, Negro slavery, and the plantation system was establishing a similarity of interest and viewpoint in the East and in the Piedmont portion of the West.

In the fourth place, there was some recognition of the necessity of social, economic, and political reform to lessen emigration, which was threatening to depopulate the state. This was the era of Jacksonian democracy and the "rise of the common man." The democratic movement was growing throughout the United States, and six states, including Virginia, had already made constitutional reforms pointing to manhood suffrage and popular elections. Should North Carolina fail to keep pace with the other states and remain the "Rip Van Winkle state"?

Leadership of David L. Swain

In the fifth place, Governor David L. Swain, a western leader of tact and intelligence and statewide popularity, worked diligently for constitutional reform and presented to the legislature of 1834 a compelling argument for a convention. Swain was a leader with sufficient ability, tact, popularity, and practical knowledge of men and affairs to unite the reform forces.

Strategy of the Whig Party

In the sixth place, the Whig party, formed in 1834 in opposition to Jackson, tended to unite the West and the Sound region of the East. The North Carolina Whig leaders, mainly westerners who favored a constructive program for the national government, executed a master stroke for their party and the West by adopting as Whig policies the state issues of internal improvements, public schools, sound currency and banks, and constitutional reform. By this shrewd strategy, the state Whig party captured an almost solid West and the commercial portion of the East, and the West captured some eastern Whig support in its long fight for a constitutional convention.

The Convention Bill and Referendum of 1835

The legislature in January, 1835, passed a law to submit to popular vote the question of calling a convention to consider specified reforms. The House vote was 66 to 62; the Senate, 31 to 30. Thirteen commoners and two senators from the East, including the members from Cumberland and Craven counties, voted for the bill. If called, the convention was to be required to propose amendments reconstructing the Senate and House of Commons and providing a regular method of amendment. It was also to be empowered to propose other specified changes and to be forbidden to consider certain changes.

An unprecedented popular vote in the referendum of 1835 resulted in a convention victory, 27,550 to 21,694. The vote was highly sectional, only 2,701 westerners opposing and 3,611 easterners favoring the convention. At a second election delegates were chosen to meet in convention at Raleigh on June 4, 1835.

The Convention of 1835

The Convention of 1835 met at the height of the national reform movement known as "Jacksonian Democracy" and the "Rise of the Common Man." Most of the original states were revising their antiquated constitutions. (Virginia did so in 1829.) The North Carolina Convention of 1835 contained among its 130 delegates, 2 from each county, the state's leadership in political ability and experience. Three men dominated the convention: Nathaniel Macon, William Gaston, and David L. Swain. The seventy-eight-year-old Macon had spent all of his adult life in public service—largely in Congress. He had known many of the framers of the 1776 constitution, and could speak with authority on what they had intended. Now in retirement and an opponent of sweeping reforms, his selection as president of the convention was a mere personal tribute without much political significance. Gaston, a justice of the state Supreme Court and the leading Roman Catholic layman in the state, was the dominating intellect of the convention. He was considered to be a great liberal, particularly in regard to religious qualifications for office. He opposed free Negro suffrage, though his views on the rights of slaves and free Negroes were liberal for his day. Swain, a native of Buncombe County, governor of the state since 1832, and close personal friend of Gaston, was the floor leader of the reform group, and his skill, tact, and knowledge aided in securing a western victory. But Charles Fisher, John M. Morehead, John Branch, Weldon N. Edwards, John Owen, Daniel M. Barringer, Henry Seawell, and others were also able and experienced.

After more than a month of labor, debate, and conflict between the West and the East, the new order and the old, the conservatives and the liberals, the Convention adjourned on July 11 after having agreed upon a long list of constitutional amendments that should become part of the fundamental law when approved by a vote of the people. There was close division on most of the major problems, and the proposed changes in the constitution were the result of compromise.

Amendments to the State Constitution

Many important amendments to the constitution were proposed by the convention. Borough representation and free Negro suffrage were to be abolished. The poll tax was to be equalized for all persons subject to it. Provision was to be made for the impeachment of public officials. Despite Gaston's two-day address against religious tests for public office, no change was made in the religious tests for officeholding except the substitution of "Christian" for "Protestant," thus removing the test from Roman Catholics but not from Jews and atheists. Two methods of constitutional amendment were proposed: (1) by constitutional convention called by a vote of two-thirds of each House; or (2) by proposal of two successive sessions of the General Assembly and popular ratification at a special election.

The power of the General Assembly to enact private legislation was to be restricted; and its sessions were to be biennial instead of annual. The governor henceforth was to be elected every two years by the adult male taxpayers instead of annually by joint ballot of the two houses of the legislature. He was to be eligible for reelection, but could not serve more than four years in any six, but the most important change was the one that related to the system of representation in the General Assembly. Equal county representation was to be abolished. The Senate would contain fifty members chosen from districts whose inhabitants paid equal amounts of state taxes; the House of Commons would contain one hundred and twenty members distributed to the counties according to federal population ("to be determined by adding the whole numbers of free persons and three-fifths of all other persons"), but with each county guaranteed one representative. By this compromise the East would control the Senate, which represented wealth; the West would control the House of Commons (63 to 57), which represented population. The fifty-acre requirement to vote for state senator was retained, but all adult white male taxpayers were eligible to vote for members of the House of Commons.

Referendum of 1835

A statewide referendum in 1835 ratified the work of the convention by a vote of 26,771 to 21,606. Again the vote revealed the sharp and uncompromising sectionalism which for years had blocked every program of social and economic development—only 2,327 easterners approved the work of the convention and only 3,280 westerners opposed it.

Significance of the Convention's Work

The Convention of 1835 was a turning point in the history of North Carolina. Its achievement was a victory for democracy. Henceforth all white men who paid taxes would elect the governor; the governor, with the backing of the majority of the voters, would have more prestige and influence and might provide effective leadership as the representative of the people; vital state issues could no longer be avoided or stifled without public discussion. For the first time the people of the entire state in biennial statewide campaigns could think, discuss, elect, and play a part in the choice of governor and in the formulation of state policy.

The work of the convention was also a victory for the West. With control of the more democratic house of the legislature, the West might be able to commit the state to a program of social and economic development. Neither section with control of only one house could impose its will on the other, but each could block the will of the other. Sectional negotiation and compromise would play an important part in legislation. The paralyzing East-West sectionalism was undermined but not abolished. But conditions were more favorable for the gradual development of a sense of state unity and state welfare. The Whig party, composed of western and eastern wings, was compelled to minimize sectionalism and was a unifying factor.

Whig-Democratic Rivalry

Highly important and coincident with the constitutional reforms of 1835 was the emergence of the two-party system of government. The Whig and Democratic parties, evenly matched in strength and bitter contenders for control of the state government, found it necessary and desirable in the biennial contests for the votes of the people, to formulate party platforms that would appeal to the "collective will of the people," to develop party machinery, nominate their ablest leaders for public office, and conduct campaigns of debate and publicity. Thus for the first time in 1840 state party conventions, party platforms, and the preelection campaign emerged. Each party held county and state conventions, had county and state committees, and developed newspapers to present its case to the voters. The statewide biennial campaign for governor generated great public interest, discussion, and enlightenment respecting state issues. No longer could national issues monopolize the political scene. State elections were held in August and national elections in November, and this tended to focus more attention on state politics than had been true before.

In the Whig-Democratic rivalry, party feeling and combat reached a new degree of intensity. Party loyalty was the test of character and officeholding. The spoils system of rewarding the faithful, punishing the enemy, and giving public office to the friends of the party in power was in full operation. Party newspapers printed nothing detrimental to their party or complimentary to the opposition. Their editorials were chiefly personal attacks on leading opponents, and were often full of coarse and offensive epithets. Campaign speeches and publicity were violent and defamatory, sometimes resulting in fights and duels.

Zebulon B. Vance, describing the 1844 election, wrote: "I headed a procession on mule back . . . marched sixteen miles to the election precinct through the mountains of Madison County, filled with patriotism, zeal for the Whig cause, and hard cider. . . . Fifteen separate and distinct fights were then and there had, in part of which I participated and for all of which I might be set down as the proximate cause."

Vance was only fourteen at the time, and he was a resident of Buncombe County! Liquor flowed freely at the polls—perhaps more than the hard cider to which the youthful Vance referred. Political discussions and the tactics of vote-getting were often of a low order, disgusting to some of the more intelligent and dignified citizens. John W. Moore said that "a senseless and malignant hostility divided the households and poisoned the intercourse" of Whigs and Democrats. Men who shifted from one party to the other were denounced as "traitors." When William W. Holden shifted from the Whig to the Democratic party, the *Fayetteville Observer* denounced him as a man "diseased with leprosy that has not left a single virtue unconsumed amid his thousand meannesses and vices." Such was the product of the new era of greater democracy, in which a small group of intelligent leaders could no longer determine policy and operate the government without regard to the wishes of the great mass of people. The sovereign people were now in a position to pass judgment upon party leadership and policies.

The Whig Party and Its Program

Under the two-party system, with its healthy rivalry and competition for public office and power, North Carolina experienced a generation of honest, efficient, progressive, and enlightened government after 1835. Seldom if ever in the state's history have so many able men risen to political leadership and distinction as in the years from 1835 to 1860. The Whig party, whose leaders were chiefly from the West, adopted a constructive program of state development, substantially the old Murphey program. It stood for public schools, internal improvements, sound banks and currency, and the promotion of industry. With the pressing issue of constitutional reform achieved by the Convention of 1835, the increased political power of the West and the forces of democracy might inaugurate a program of state development the East might no longer be able to block. Though there were Whig voters in every county, the Whig party was strongest and dominant in the more backward West and the Sound region. It was strongest wherever slaves were fewest. It was preeminently the party of the democratic small farmers, merchants, and businessmen who desired the economic development of the state. Its leaders were not champions of democracy but rather men of wealth, education, and aristocratic philosophy, often interested in railroads and manufacturing. The need of economic development rather than democracy was the determining factor in the allegiance of Whig areas. With its eastern and western wings, the Whig party could not afford to fan the flames of sectionalism; it was an influential deterrent to the sectional spirit and a stimulus to state unity.

The Democratic Party and Its Program

The state Democratic party for several years was merely opposed to the Whig policies. It favored a negative economy, a "do-nothing" program. It held that the state government should tax little, spend little, and do little for the people beyond protecting their life, liberty, and property. Education and internal improvements were matters of individual and local but not of state governmental concern. Eventually the Democratic party was forced by successive defeats to seek more public support by adopting a popular constructive program of state development. Though there were in every county Democratic voters attracted by the principles of Jeffersonian democracy, the Democratic party was strongest in the wealthy plantation-slaveholding counties of the middle eastern section and in the northern and southern staple-growing, slave-holding counties of the Piedmont. It was dominant wherever slaves were numerous. It was preeminently the party of the aristocratic planters and it championed their interests in state and national politics.

Under the influence of greater democracy, the two-party system, and the enhanced political power of the West assisted by the commercial Sound region, a progressive era of unprecedented social and economic development occurred in North Carolina between 1835 and 1860.

Chapter 24

THE WHIGS INAUGURATE AN AGE OF PROGRESS 1835-1850

The constitutional reforms of 1835, which increased the political power of the people and of the West, paved the way for a quarter-century of remarkable development in North Carolina—the first real age of progress in the history of the state. This development was carried on for fifteen years under Whig and then for ten years under Democratic leadership. The state government erected a magnificent capitol, gave financial aid to the building of a state system of railroads and plank roads, provided the major support for a statewide system of public schools, established institutions for the care of the blind and deaf and insane, reformed the system of taxation, and began a liberalization of the criminal law and the legal status of women. The University of North Carolina grew rapidly, and many colleges and academies were established by private and religious agencies. There was an increase in the number and circulation of newspapers and the beginnings of indigenous authorship and literature. Agricultural conditions were improved, factories were established, wealth and trade increased. In no previous generation had there been such progress and development. The state government itself, dominated by the spirit of Murphey rather than the *laissez-faire* spirit of Macon, took the lead in this development.

Whig Control of State Government, 1836–1850

After the constitutional changes of 1835 gave greater political power to the people and to the West, and after the new two-party system linked the backward West and the Sound region in political alliance against the wealthier slaveholding East, social and economic reforms long demanded and overdue were possible. It was logical that the people should entrust control of the state government to the political party with a constructive, reform pro-

359

gram—the Whig party. Though the state was not ready to accept the national program of the Whigs and in 1836 voted for the Democratic candidate for president, Martin Van Buren, the voters elected Whig Edward B. Dudley of New Hanover County as governor and chose a Whig Senate. Dudley and his Democratic opponent had been nominated by the newspapers and by county conventions.

Dudley was an eastern Whig whose interest in internal improvements, public education, and railroad construction made him acceptable to the West. The Whig party had no platform and there was no speaking campaign in this, the first election in which the people voted for governor, but Dudley's views were well known. The keynote of his program was clearly stated in his first inaugural address, in 1837, when he described the state's great natural resources but emphasized the fact that North Carolina was the lowest state "in relative wealth and enterprise," with conditions "daily becoming worse, lands depressed in price," with uncultivated and deserted fields, manufacturing advantages unimproved, "our colleges and schools languishing from neglect and poverty"—a "melancholy picture, and it is our business to prescribe the remedy." He recommended a better banking system to supply the necessary capital for internal improvements and for public schools, and a better transportation system, in order to stop "the torrent of emigration which is desolating our state."

Dudley carried the West and fourteen eastern counties, defeating Democratic Richard Dobbs Spaight, 33,993 to 29,950; almost 22,000 of Dudley's votes came from the western counties. An indication of the decline of sectionalism was the fact that all but two of the twenty-one counties formed from 1835 to 1860 were western. Never after 1835 were East and West so solidly arrayed against each other as they had been on the issue of constitutional reform.

During Dudley's first term the state adopted the epochal new policy of extending financial aid to railroads. In 1838 the Whigs reelected Dudley over Democrat John Branch by a vote of 34,329 to 20,153, and won control of both houses of the legislature, which expanded the program of state aid to railroads and enacted, in 1839, the law providing for the establishment of a statewide system of free public schools. The first two railroads were completed and went into operation in 1840. The Whigs were victorious in the state and national elections of 1840, electing John Motley Morehead of Guilford County as governor over Democratic Romulus M. Saunders, 44,484 to 35,903. They won both houses of the legislature and eight of fourteen seats in the national House of Representatives. Two Whigs, Willie P. Mangum and William A. Graham, were chosen United States senators by the legislature.

The Election of 1840

The campaign of 1840 was memorable for inaugurating the first state party conventions and platforms and the first canvass and joint debates by the gubernatorial candidates. The Whig Convention met in Raleigh on November 12, 1839—almost a year before the election—and the people were so unaccustomed to this new method of selecting candidates that only thirty-four of the sixty-eight counties sent delegates. The Democratic Convention assembled at Raleigh on January 8, 1840, with delegates from thirty-eight counties. Its platform dealt exclusively with national issues, but Saunders's letter of acceptance advocated public schools, internal improvements, and railroads. Saunders stressed, however, the idea of "no state debt." J. G. de R. Hamilton has characterized the joint debates between Dudley and Saunders as "sheer demagoguery of the worst type," but "better than the apathy and localism" of previous elections. Public issues of paramount importance were discussed and this "marked the growth of a new sort of democracy."

The Whigs claimed credit for the two railroads completed in 1840 and rejoiced at the justification of their policies. The electorate endorsed the Whig party's program by reelecting Morehead in 1842 over Louis D. Henry by a vote of 39,343 to 34,411. In 1844 the Whigs elected William A. Graham of Orange County as governor over Michael Hoke, 42,486 to 39,433; two years later Graham was reelected, defeating James B. Shepard by a vote of 43,486 to 35,627. In 1848 Charles Manly of Wake County won over Democratic David S. Reid by the close vote of 42,536 to 41,682—the last Whig victory in a gubernatorial election. Dudley, Morehead, and Graham were very able governors who forcefully urged upon the legislatures constructive programs of internal improvements, public education, railroad construction, and state development.

State Activities, 1836–1850

The era of Whig ascendancy in state politics lasted from 1836 to 1850. Though the biennial elections were generally spirited and close, the margin of victory being usually less than five thousand votes, there was an unbroken succession of Whig governors—Dudley, Morehead, Graham, and Manly. Of the seven legislatures, the Whigs controlled both houses in four. During the years of Whig control the state government embarked upon an unprecedented program of internal improvements, public education, humanitarianism, and fiscal reform that was of great benefit to the state.

The Whigs provided the leadership in the program of state aid to railroads and public education, but the federal government provided the money, without which they might not have been able to launch their program. In Jackson's administration, the last dollar of the federal debt was paid and the federal government was embarrassed by a mounting surplus arising from revenues from the tariff and the sale of public lands in the West. Henry Clay and Jackson's other Whig opponents advocated the distribution of the proceeds from land sales to the states. The popularity of this issue of distribution, even in the Jacksonian states which advocated state rights but were greatly in need of additional revenues, caused Congress to pass Clay's distribution measure in 1833. It was vetoed by President Jackson but the popularity of the idea continued. The Jackson administration solved its political dilemma and also the problem of the surplus by the Distribution of the Surplus Act of 1836 by which the entire federal surplus above $5,000,000 would be distributed in four installments to the states on the basis of their representation in Congress. North Carolina received $1,433,757.39—of a total of $28,000,000 distributed to all the states. The use of this money became a partisan issue in the state. The Democrats, exponents of economy and tax reduction, wanted to use it to pay the state debt and the operating expenses of government; the Whigs wanted to use it for public education and internal improvements. The General Assembly adopted a plan which, though something of a compromise, conformed in the main to Whig ideas; all but $100,000 to meet the current expenses of the state government was to be used for the purchase of bank stock ($600,000), railroad securities ($533,000), and internal improvements, such as the draining of swamp lands ($200,000). Since these investments were assigned to the Literary Fund, the state's share of the federal surplus, except $100,000, ultimately went to the cause of public schools. The passage of this law was of epochal importance because it made possible a new era of economic, social, and cultural development. Most of the Whigs in the legislature voted for it; most of the Democrats voted against it.

Railroad Building

The first significant work of the Whigs was the adoption of the policy of state aid to railroad construction, in an effort to solve the greatest need of the state—an adequate system of transportation. The Whig party inaugurated an era of railroad building which revolutionized the life of the state.

The first railroad engine was built in England in 1825, and the first steam locomotive in America, in 1830. It was not long until America began to construct some railway lines, such as the Baltimore and Ohio, which was started in 1826. The railroad early appeared to be the answer to North Carolina's acute transportation problem. President Joseph Caldwell of the University of North Carolina wrote a series of newspaper articles in 1827, published in 1828 as a book, *The Numbers of Carlton,* in which he discussed the superiority of railroads over canals and turnpikes and advocated that the state government take the lead in building a railroad from Beaufort via New Bern and Raleigh across the state to the Tennessee line. This railroad, to be financed by an increase in the state poll tax and by individual subscriptions of stock, would channel the trade of the state to New Bern and Beaufort.

Railroads now became a subject of wide discussion by individuals, newspapers, and public meetings. Almost every town and community wanted a railroad. After 1830 the legislature chartered many railroad companies that were authorized to sell stock and build railroads. But the state government did not give any aid except the expenditure of $7,000 for railroad surveys in 1832. The one-and-one-quarter-mile Experimental Railroad at Raleigh, built by private capital in 1832–33, over which stone was transported from a quarry in horse-drawn cars for the new capitol, attracted much attention. On Sundays passengers were carried for rides in pleasure cars for "ladies and gentlemen." The Petersburg Railroad, whose line extended nine miles south of the Virginia border to Blakeley, near Halifax, began operation in the late summer of 1833 and allowed Petersburg to tap the Roanoke River Valley trade, especially in tobacco. Internal improvements conventions, meeting at Raleigh the same year, urged the state to aid private capital in railroad construction. There was much public discussion and difference of opinion concerning whether the railroads should be routed east and west or north and south and whether they should be built with state aid or entirely by private capital. The Democrats opposed state aid, while the Whigs tended to favor it. Meanwhile charters were issued to at least ten railroad companies with private capital.

The cost of railroad building was so great and private capital was so scarce and timid about investment in a new enterprise that only two of the railroad companies chartered by the legislature in the period 1830–35 sold enough stock to make construction feasible—the Wilmington and Raleigh and the Raleigh and Gaston companies.

The Wilmington and Weldon Railroad

The Wilmington and Raleigh Railroad Company, chartered in 1834, with an authorized capital of $800,000, later raised to $1,500,000, was chiefly a Wilmington enterprise to connect the state's leading port and largest town with the capital city. Edward B. Dudley, of Wilmington, was its first president. When citizens of Raleigh failed to subscribe their share of stock, the company decided to build the railroad from Wilmington to Weldon on the Roanoke River, where connection could be made with the Richmond and Petersburg railroads, and in 1854 the legislature changed its name to the Wilmington and Weldon. Aroused by the action of the company in changing the terminus of the road from Raleigh to Weldon, Raleigh businessmen organized and got a charter for the Raleigh and Gaston Company, in 1835, to build a road from Raleigh to Gaston on the Roanoke River near Weldon to connect with a railroad from Petersburg. Most of the stock of this road was purchased by Virginia and out-of-state capital. Both companies began construction but exhausted their financial resources before the roads were completed. Both organized and operated as private companies; neither had expected aid from the state; but both were obliged to ask the state for assistance in order to complete their lines.

State Aid to Railroads

At this critical juncture, in order to save the heavy investment of private capital and to complete the much-needed railroads, the Whigs overcame strong Democratic opposition and committed the state to a new policy of state aid to railroads. In 1837 the General Assembly provided for the purchase of over half a million dollars of Wilmington and Raleigh stock, and later extensions of aid made the state's interest in the road nearly a million dollars. In 1838 and 1841 the state endorsed the bonds of the Raleigh and Gaston to the extent of $800,000, secured by mortgages on the road.

With state aid the Wilmington and Raleigh Railroad, 161 miles long—the longest railroad in the world at that time—and the Raleigh and Gaston, 86 miles long, were finished at a cost of $1,300,000 and placed in operation amid great celebration in 1840 as their "iron horses" noisily drew great loads at fifteen or twenty miles an hour over wooden rails covered with iron strips. It is noteworthy that the gauge of the Wilmington and Raleigh Railroad was four feet, eight and a half inches. This later became the "standard gauge" of American railroads.

The Raleigh and Gaston Railroad

The state's first experiment in aid to railroads was not encouraging. Further aid to the Wilmington and Weldon was necessary because of the inability of the road to borrow from private sources for necessary improvements and equipment, particularly the replacement of the worn-out wooden rails with iron rails. After ten years of financial embarrassment, freight and passenger traffic increased so much that from 1850 the road was able to meet its obligations and pay dividends upon its stock. The shorter Raleigh and Gaston road was not so fortunate. After extending further aid in 1841 the state had to foreclose its mortgage and purchase the road in 1845 for $363,000. For six years the state operated the road at a loss. In 1851 a reorganization was made by which the state retained half ownership. From 1854 the road was generally on a profitable dividend-paying basis. But the state had lost nearly a million dollars because of its involvement with the Raleigh and Gaston. Yet so beneficial were the railroads that, in spite of heavy financial losses by the state and sharp Democratic criticism, the people were still favorable to the policy of state aid. They continued the Whig party in power and came to believe that more rather than less state aid was necessary for a statewide network of railroads.

Demands for More Railroads

There was increasing demand for more railroads after the opening of the Wilmington and Raleigh and the Raleigh and Gaston, especially in the landlocked West, where money was so scarce that no railroad had been begun. The disastrous experience of state aid to private companies that had begun railroads, the clamor of the West for railroads, the state's investment of about $2 million in two roads which needed to tap a larger trading area, and the vigorous messages of Governors Morehead and Graham in favor of a state system of transportation, developed sentiment for a different state railroad policy. Morehead told the legislature of 1842 that the state should build a system of roads in order to make North Carolina economically independent of Virginia and South Carolina—that west of Greensboro "Cheraw, Camden, Columbia . . . Augusta, and Charleston are much more familiarly known than even Fayetteville and Raleigh." The state itself should take the initiative in planning railroads and should assume the chief financial burden, allowing private capital to help. Various proposals came to a showdown before the legislature of 1848–49.

Proposals for a State-Owned Railroad

Governor Graham proposed that the state bear half the cost of building an extension of the Raleigh and Gaston to Charlotte, with branches to Goldsboro and Fayetteville. This proposal was defeated by the Democrats, the Wilmington and Weldon interests, and those who regarded the system as a feeder for Virginia and South Carolina markets. A western proposal, championed by Rufus Barringer of Concord and John W. Ellis of Salisbury, to incorporate a company to build a road from Charlotte to Danville and to connect with Columbia, South Carolina, seemed likely to pass because no state aid was asked. The East denounced this project as the "Danville steal" and a "sell-out" to Virginia and South Carolina interests. The westerners, whose main interest was a railroad, were willing to surrender the Charlotte-Danville project and compromise on a measure more acceptable to the East. Such was the origin of the bill for the North Carolina Railroad Company, introduced by W. S. Ashe of New Hanover County, an eastern Democrat, and passed in 1849.

The North Carolina Railroad

The North Carolina Railroad Company was chartered with a capital of three million dollars, two million of which was to be subscribed by the state and the remainder by individuals. It was to build the North Carolina Railroad from Goldsboro through Raleigh to Charlotte. This compromise was satisfactory to the West, and to the two eastern railroads with which the new road would connect. But so close was the legislative contest that its fate depended upon the vote of Speaker Calvin Graves in the Senate, a Democrat from Caswell County, through which the Charlotte-Danville road would have run but the North Carolina Railroad would not. To the surprise of all and to his own political ruin, Graves cast the vote which made the bill become law. One exultant champion of the road said, "Speaker Graves has saved the State—the Railroad Bill has passed," while another called the law "North Carolina's declaration of economic independence."

The North Carolina Railroad Completed

Former Governor John M. Morehead, elected president of the company, was the dominant figure in the sale of stock to individuals, the surveying of the route, and the construction of the road. Political as well as engineering considerations influenced the circuitous routing from Raleigh through Hillsborough (the home of Graham), Salisbury (the home of Ellis), and Concord (the home of Barringer) to Charlotte. Construction proceeded simultaneously from Goldsboro and Charlotte. The 223-mile railroad was opened to trains in January, 1856—the greatest enterprise in whch the government of North Carolina had ever participated. It was the first railroad to traverse the poor, backward Piedmont and to open the West to the markets of the world. Villages and factories sprang up along its route and farmers became more prosperous. Eventually the backward Piedmont area along the route of the North Carolina Railroad became the richest and most highly developed part of the state.

Effect of Railroads

The railroads cut in half the old wagon freight rates. The freight rate on one hundred pounds from Raleigh to Petersburg was reduced from a dollar and a half to seventy cents. This encouraged the production of surplus crops for market, increased the farmer's profit on what he sold, and reduced the price of goods he purchased. Land values and farm productivity increased. There was a marked growth of towns, trade, factories, wealth, and state revenue. There was more travel, more frequent mail service and a higher standard of living for many people. Railroads promoted a spirit of state unity, pride, and patriotism, and tended to check emigration. No phase of North Carolina's life escaped the beneficent effects of improved trade and travel.

Drainage of Swamp Lands

In accordance with the law for the use of the federal surplus, the Literary Board invested $200,000 in the drainage of Mattamuskeet Lake in Hyde County, Pungo and Alligator lakes, and the open savanna lands in Carteret County. This drainage program was ineffective and the investment was almost a complete loss.

The Public School System Begun

While North Carolina under Whig leadership was aiding in the construction of the first important railroads, it established a state system of public schools. Murphey's public school program of 1816–17 had been rejected, though in 1825 a Literary Fund, already mentioned, was created whose income remained too small to permit the establishment of any schools. Poor investments, dishonesty, public indifference, and aversion to taxation kept the fund inadequate, but the legislature repeatedly refused to increase it. For a decade no tangible progress was made toward a public school system. There was some agitation, however, by governors, the press, and the pulpit, and a few legislative leaders and many men educated in the academies and the University of North Carolina added to the growing sentiment for a free public school system which would decrease the state's appalling illiteracy and intellectual degradation.

Joseph Caldwell's Plans for a Public School System

The ablest public discussion consisted of eleven "Letters on Public Education" written and published in the state newspapers in 1832 (later published in book form) by President Joseph Caldwell of the university. He discussed the educational and economic conditions in North Carolina and the great advantages of education, but concluded that it was impossible for the state to provide a system of free public education either by taxation or by the proceeds from the invested Literary Fund. The state should establish and maintain with the proceeds from the small Literary Fund a central school for the training of teachers. Each county should select pupils and pay $100 a year for the expense of each while taking the teacher-training course. These teachers, trained at public expense, would be obligated to teach after the completion of their training. If the state and counties would provide for the training of teachers at public expense, Caldwell hoped or believed that these teachers would organize subscription schools and broaden the opportunity for general education.

Constitutional Reform, 1835, and the Federal Surplus, 1836

By lessening the political power of wealth and of the East and by increasing the political power of the mass of common people, the constitutional reforms of 1835 paved the way for public schools; and the distribution of the surplus federal revenue in 1837 provided the means. As has been stated earlier in this chapter, North Carolina's share was $1,433,757.39. The differences between the Whigs and the Democrats concerning the use of this money were resolved by the compromise already indicated, and all of the surplus revenue from investments of the money, except $100,000, went to the support of education. With a Literary Fund in excess of $2 million, most of which was a gift from the federal government, there was no longer any excuse for the failure to establish a system of public schools.

The Public School Law of 1839

Reports of the Literary Board and legislative reports and bills eventuated in the final passage of the public school law of 1839. The law called for a special election in 1839 in each county on the issue of "schools" or "no schools." If a county voted for schools, the county court should take steps to lay out school districts and appoint district school committees. Any district that supplied a school building for fifty pupils and raised $20 in taxes, which the county court should levy, would receive $40 from the State Literary Fund. With the $60, a teacher might be employed for two or three months a year. In an election characterized by public indifference, sixty-one of the sixty-eight counties voted in favor of schools and later the remaining seven counties (Rowan, Lincoln, Yancey, Davidson, Edgecombe, Wayne, and Columbus) also voted for schools. On January 20, 1840, the first public school in the state was opened in Rockingham County; other counties soon followed suit, and by 1846 every county had one or more public schools, and the state education fund exceeded $2 million. By 1850, 2,657 common schools were in operation, with an enrollment of 100,591 children. For the first time, the white children of the state had an opportunity to receive some education at public expense.

Contrary to most accounts, the chief leaders and legislative support for the school law of 1839 were from the East rather than the West. The bill for the establishment of schools was introduced in the House by Frederic J. Hill of Brunswick County, and in the Senate by William W. Cherry of Bertie. Though the West was more ignorant and in greater need of public education, it never manifested as much support for the public school system as for internal improvements.

The most notable feature of the school system in North Carolina was the complete absence of the charity idea. The schools were free and without tuition to all white children on equal terms. For the first time, there was a legal provision for the primary education of every white child in the state. In achieving a statewide system of free public education, North Carolina took an advanced position among the states of the South and the nation.

Weaknesses of the Public School System

For a decade or more, however, the new school system was a disappointment. The schools suffered from prejudice, inefficiency, poor supervision, and lack of leadership. In 1841 the school law was changed to authorize but not require the county courts to levy taxes amounting to not more than half the allotment from the Literary Fund. Though Negroes did not benefit from the school system, the basis of distributing the Literary Fund was changed from $40 for each school district to allocation among the counties according to federal population—a rank discrimination in favor of the eastern counties having a large slave population and an injustice to the western counties. Federal population was determined by adding the free population and three-fifths of the slave population of the county. Hence a western county with a free population of five thousand whites and no slaves would receive only five-eighths as much for the education of its white children as an eastern county with a free population of five thousand and a slave population of five thousand (federal population, eight thousand). Some counties failed to levy any local taxes and some even failed to spend all their income from the State Literary Fund for schools. There was no state administrative control since the office of state superintendent of common schools was not created until 1852; the county systems lacked uniformity; and local authorities were negligent in making reports. The novelty of public schools, the conservatism of the people and their dislike of taxation, the persistence of the association of public schools with charity, the lack of adequate equipment and trained teachers, and the hostility of the private schools and academies helped to bring discouraging results from the new system. It seemed that the political leaders were willing to allow the school system to drift and disintegrate.

Humanitarian Reforms

While the state under Whig leadership was active in improving transportation and education, it also began to respond to the growing humanitarian sentiment that the state owed an obligation to its dependent, defective, and delinquent citizens. As early as 1817 Murphey had proposed a school for the deaf, but for twenty-five years no steps were taken to translate this proposal into law. Meanwhile the North Carolina Bible Society advocated such an institution, and in 1827 The North Carolina Institution for the Instruction of the Deaf and Dumb was organized to work for the establishment of a school. In the same year President Joseph Caldwell of the University of North Carolina addressed the legislature in advocacy of this idea, but the legislature took no action. In 1842 the General Assembly turned a deaf ear to Governor Morehead's recommendation that a school for the deaf and the blind be established by the state. The next year he made the same recommendation, but this time he convinced many doubting legislators of the possibility of educating the deaf and the blind by bringing to the legislative halls Principal William D. Cooke and some of his pupils from a school operated by Cooke at Staunton, Virginia. This exhibition of what could be done to help such unfortunate children turned the trick, and in 1844 the legislature appropriated $5,000 from the Literary Fund for the education of the deaf and the blind, to be supplemented by county appropriations of $75 a year for each student. A school for the deaf was opened in Raleigh in May, 1845, under the superintendency of William D. Cooke. The legislature appropriated money for buildings in 1847; a "department for the blind" was added in July, 1851; in 1852 the school was incorporated as the North Carolina Institution for the Education of the Deaf and Blind, and the annual state appropriation was increased considerably.

The State Hospital for the Insane

In 1842 Governor Morehead recommended better care of the insane in the state, a proposal repeated by Governor William A. Graham in 1846, but the legislature failed to respond to their requests. Miss Dorothea L. Dix of Massachusetts, nationally famous for her activity in behalf of the insane, prepared a memorial for the General Assembly of 1848 based on her tour of investigation throughout the state, describing in vivid fashion what she had seen of the shocking treatment received by more than a thousand insane in private homes, county poorhouses, and jails. She requested that the state establish a hospital for the proper care and treatment of the insane. The Whigs favored her proposal, but the Democrats, who were in control of the House of Commons, were opposed to any increase in state expenditures. By befriending and enlisting the aid of Mrs. James C. Dobbin, who was in the last days of a fatal illness, Miss Dix achieved a master stroke by winning the help of a Democratic leader, James C. Dobbin of Cumberland County, who made a touching and eloquent speech for the hospital bill and also sponsored an amendment for the small special tax on property and polls for four years with the proviso that the county courts might reduce the local poor tax by the amount of the hospital tax. With Dobbin's support the hospital bill, which avoided the necessity of a tax increase by authorizing the "robbing of the poor for the benefit of the insane," passed the legislature. Construction of the State Hospital for the Insane in North Carolina was begun on January 29, 1849, on a beautiful tree-covered hill in Raleigh, now appropriately called "Dix Hill." In 1852 the state tax of 1848 was continued, and regular state appropriations for maintenance were begun in 1856. The hospital was opened for the care of patients on April 29, 1856, under the directorship of Dr. E. C. Fisher of Virginia. The establishment of this hospital for the insane has been called "the first step in the modern policy of public welfare" in North Carolina.

Poor Relief

Agitation to improve the system for caring for the poor and to establish state institutions for orphans was ineffectual. Doctors, churches, and charitable individuals and organizations helped take care of the poor; but the law placed the responsibility of providing for the poor upon the county overseers and wardens of the poor, who had the power to levy a limited tax and to administer its revenues. In 1831 a state law authorized the county courts to erect poorhouses and purchase lands for the support of the poor. Before 1860 the counties followed four general methods of poor relief: allowances to individual paupers; letting the pauper out under contract; selling the pauper to the lowest bidder; and caring for the paupers in county poorhouses. The state left the matter of orphanages entirely to religious and private enterprise. According to the law, afflicted orphans were placed in the county poorhouse and all other destitute orphans maintained themselves by their own labor as apprentices bound to masters by indenture executed by the county court.

Reform in the Criminal Law

The spirit of reform was largely ineffective in liberalizing the criminal law and the rights of women and Negroes. A long agitation for a state penitentiary—first recommended by Murphey—for the incarceration and reformation of criminals, culminated in the rejection by popular referendum in 1846 of a legislative proposal for a state prison costing $100,000. Before 1860 repeated efforts to humanize the harsh penal code of the state and to mitigate the gruesome methods of punishment inherited from the common law system of England resulted only in the abolition of imprisonment of women for debt (1823), prohibition of the branding and whipping of women (1855), modification of the law to prevent the imprisonment of honest debtors, and a reduction in the number of capital offenses from twenty-eight to seventeen and then to twelve (murder, arson, burglary, rape, duelling, bigamy, stealing a slave, inducing a slave to run away, forgery, horse-stealing, house-breaking, and counterfeiting). Legal punishment by hanging, mutilation, imprisonment, branding, fine, whipping post, ducking stool, pillory, and stocks was still considered by conservative North Carolinians as an essential deterrent to crime. In 1829 former Governor Benjamin Smith died in prison at Smithville (now Southport) while confined for debt, and in 1845 newspapers reported that a man was hanged at Louisburg for the theft of a pair of suspenders. The cruelty of the penal code lessened the number of prosecutions and convictions and increased the number of pardons. The inferior legal status of married women and their subjection to their husbands were slightly improved by a law of 1848 making it illegal for a husband to sell or lease real estate belonging to the wife at the time of marriage without her consent.

Rights of Negroes

Reaction rather than reform characterized the public attitude toward Negroes, both slave and free. The rising value of slave property, fear of insurrection, the growth of the antislavery movement in the North after 1830, and the prominence of slavery as a national political issue led to a restriction of the legal rights of slaves and free Negroes. In August, 1821, it was reported that eighty runaway slaves were hiding in the swamps of Onslow County, causing fear of a general uprising. Exactly ten years later, the Nat Turner Insurrection in Southampton County, Virginia, and an alleged slave plot in North Carolina led to the hanging of two Negroes in Onslow and the killing of about fifteen others, some by mob action. The tightening slave code, partly a result of fear of slave revolts, restricted the slave's mobility, education, emancipation, and privilege of carrying on business. The free Negro was legally restricted in his relations with the whites, his mobility, his association with slaves, and his right to bear arms, vote, trade, teach, and preach. The courts were in general brutally logical in upholding these legal restrictions and the master's ownership and control of the slave. In *State* v. *Mann* in 1829 Chief Justice Thomas Ruffin declared that "the master is not liable to an indictment for battery committed upon a slave. The power of the master must be absolute to render the submission of the slave perfect. I must freely confess my sense of the harshness of this proposition; . . . and as a principle of moral right every person in his retirement must repudiate it." But there were some judicial manifestations of liberality, particularly by Justice William Gaston. In *State* v. *Will,* in 1835, Gaston held that a slave had the right to defend himself against the unlawful attempt of the master to kill him, and in *State* v. *Manuel,* in 1838, that a free Negro was a citizen entitled to the guarantees of the constitution. In 1839 Judge Gaston declared that the courts had the power of reviewing an extenuation from provocation when a master committed a battery upon a slave which resulted in death: "If death unhappily ensue from the master's chastisement of his slave, inflicted apparently with a good intent, for reformation or example, and with no purpose to take life or to put it in jeopardy, the law would doubtless tenderly regard every circumstance. . . . But where the punishment is barbarously immoderate . . . and denotes plainly that the master must have contemplated a fatal termination . . . he is guilty of murder."

Fiscal Reform

Increased state expenditures for railroads, education, humanitarian institutions, and the new capitol necessitated larger revenues and some reform in state taxation and finances. Reassessments of property valuations and reenumerations of polls placed more acres and polls on the tax books but did not add greatly to state revenue because the state tax was only six cents on the hundred dollars valuation of land and twenty cents on each black and white poll. Increased taxation was necessary. Indicative of the rural control and agrarian point of view was the refusal to increase the tax on land and polls and the levying of new taxes in the late 1840s on inheritances, incomes, licenses, and luxuries, which bore more heavily on urban, professional, and business classes. The most glaring inequity of the state tax system was the light tax on slave property as compared with the tax on land, income, and business. Slaves were taxed only as polls, not according to their value. These changes in tax policy raised the state tax revenue from $71,740 in 1835 to $141,610 in 1850.

The increase in taxes was inadequate to maintain the solvency of the state government and to pay its subscriptions to the North Carolina Railroad and other public works from the year 1848 on. In that year the policy of issuing and selling interest-bearing bonds was begun, as a means of acquiring money by borrowing, thus inaugurating the state bonded debt as an enduring feature of state fiscal policy.

Rip Van Winkle Awake

Had Murphey been alive in 1840, he would have known that Rip Van Winkle was awake. In that year two important railroads were completed with state aid; the public school system, supported chiefly by state funds, went into operation; and Governor Morehead occupied the new state capitol. The years of Whig ascendancy from 1836 to 1850 were an era of unprecedented progress and reform. While the state itself was aiding in the construction of railroads, establishing a public school system, inaugurating a system of care for the blind and deaf and insane, building a new capitol, and making some reforms in the fiscal system, the criminal code, and the legal position of women, there was a notable increase in general economic prosperity and a great expansion in the facilities of higher education at the University of North Carolina and at several newly established denominational colleges.

Chapter 25

CONTINUED PROGRESS UNDER THE DEMOCRATS 1850-1860

The decade of the 1850s in North Carolina politics was an era of Democratic ascendancy even more complete than the preceding decade and a half had been one of Whig control. Beginning with the victory of David S. Reid of Rockingham County in 1850, every governor was a Democrat—Reid, Warren Winslow of Cumberland, Thomas Bragg of Northampton, and John W. Ellis of Rowan; and the Democrats controlled both houses of every legislature except that of 1852 in which the Whigs controlled the House of Commons. In national politics the Democrats carried the state in the presidential elections of 1856 and 1860 and dominated the state's delegations in the Congress of the United States after 1853. Why did the voters repudiate the Whig party, which had inaugurated an era of progress and reform, and why did they place in power the Democratic party, which, with no constructive program, had been content merely to oppose the Whig policies?

Decline of the Whig Party

The Whig party was declining in strength, unity, and enthusiasm during the 1840s. Its long lease of power stimulated conservatism, self-confidence, and machine control of the party. Elder statesmen, notably Graham, Morehead, Mangum, and Badger, dominated party machinery and policy, dispensed elective and appointive offices, and made the party inhospitable and unattractive to young men with political ambition. The Whigs relaxed their zeal for the constructive policies that had made them the popular dominant party and became less sensitive to public opinion. Having provided for a public school system in 1839, they failed to improve it and to prevent public disappointment over its operation. Having inaugurated the policy of state aid to

374

railroads under which two roads were completed in 1840, they failed to prosecute the policy after that date—no additional railroad was begun or even chartered until 1849. They lost some of their concern for democracy and the common people, and in an agrarian state pursued policies more in the interest of townspeople, manufacturers, bankers, and merchants than of the great mass of small farmers. The Whigs became the "guardians of wealth, privilege, and culture." Democrats charged that the party was controlled by the "Hillsborough-Raleigh" clique. The Whig leaders were inclined to desire "followers" rather than rivals within the party, and they failed to recruit young, able, and aggressive leaders. The Whigs failed to respond to the growing demand for democratic changes in government, particularly in the qualifications for voting.

On national issues the Whig party lost support in North Carolina. It was weakened by its opposition to the War with Mexico in 1846–48, and to the acquisition of territory from Mexico. Its opposition to the war, "Manifest Destiny," and territorial expansion seemed extremely partisan, unpatriotic if not actually disloyal, and hostile to the peculiar interests of the South in the extension of slavery. Moreover, the party was embarrassingly divided on the question of the right of the state legislature to instruct United States senators and on the increasingly critical issue of the power of Congress to exclude slavery from western territories. The nationalistic "Federal Whigs," comprising Graham, Badger, Morehead, and most of the prominent leaders, believed that Congress under the Constitution had the power to exclude slavery from the territories but should not exercise that power, while "State Rights Whigs," like Willie P. Mangum and Thomas L. Clingman, agreed with the Democrats that Congress did not have this power. As the question of slavery in the territories became the dominant national issue and a serious threat to the Union after the Wilmot Proviso of 1846, the fact that most of the northern antislavery leadership and sentiment was in the Whig party embarrassed the Southern wing of the party and caused many southerners to question the dependability of that party as the friend and defender of slavery and Southern interests. The friendliness of the national Whig party for a national bank, protective tariff, internal improvements, the distribution to the states of the proceeds from the sale of public lands, and the exclusion of slavery from the western territories injured the party in North Carolina and the South.

Growing Strength of the Democratic Party

While the Whig party was losing popularity and strength in North Carolina, the Democratic party was being rejuvenated and strengthened. On national issues it was the more dependable friend of slavery and the interests of the South and of North Carolina. It opposed a national bank, protective tariff, internal improvements, and distribution of the proceeds of the sale of public lands. It was more successful in avoiding the North-South division that plagued the Whigs. It was firmly united in defense of the principle of state rights or local self-government and in opposition to the expansion of federal power and activity and to the power of Congress to exclude slavery from the territories. The Democratic party in North Carolina had been and was preeminently the party of the slaveholders and it was more zealous and united in defense of slavery and southern rights and interests. Because of the growing seriousness of the slavery question after 1846, some State Rights Whigs, notably Clingman, shifted to the Democratic party. The Democratic party patriotically supported the United States in the War with Mexico and received the credit for the victory over Mexico and for the acquisition of California and New Mexico. In North Carolina partisan feeling concerning the war ran high. North Carolina's military contribution of one regiment, which did not become engaged in any important battle, was inconsequential, but the war was a factor in weakening the Whigs and strengthening the Democrats.

Emergence of New Leadership in the Democratic Party

The most important factor in the invigoration of the Democratic party in the state was the emergence of a new leadership of young men—virile, aggressive, sensitive to public sentiment, and determined to commit the party to a constructive, progressive program. It seemed obvious to them that the unbroken succession of defeats since 1836 had been due to the lack of a positive program and to Democratic opposition to the constructive and popular program of the Whigs. Without discounting the ability and influence of David S. Reid, Thomas Bragg, John W. Ellis, Asa Biggs, James C. Dobbin, W. S. Ashe, and other young leaders, it may be stated with confidence that William W. Holden contributed more than any other man to the rejuvenation of the Democratic party. Of obscure and lowly origin in Orange County, Holden worked for several years in the office of Whig newspapers in Hillsborough and Raleigh. Though nominally a Whig, he shifted to the Democratic party because of his resentment at the growing aristocratic tendencies of the Whig leaders, his belief in the principles of Jacksonian democracy, and his conviction that opportunities for political influence and for a newspaper career were better in the Democratic party. In 1843, with the aid of Democratic leaders who recognized his ability, Holden, at the age of twenty-five, became editor of *The North Carolina Standard,* a Democratic newspaper in Raleigh. He brought to North Carolina political journalism an ability and an aggressiveness that soon made *The Standard* recognized as the best and most influential political newspaper in the state. A master of sarcasm and forceful writing, he attacked the Whigs, championed the dignity of labor and the common man, and believed that the Democratic party must cease its opposition to, and even advocate, a constructive program of state development. Holden was interested in youth, new ideas, and a progressive program for the state. He had a great interest in public education and was one of the first men in the state to champion the cause of organized labor. In national affairs Holden and the new leaders emphasized "Southern interests," opposed the protective tariff, advocated the annexation of Texas and Cuba, and favored the extension of slavery into the territories. In 1848 *The Standard* created a sensation by announcing its support of the policy of state aid to internal improvements. By committing the party to the issue of free suffrage in 1848, Holden, David S. Reid, and others, championed democratic constitutional reform and won control of the state government in 1850. Once in power the Democratic party gradually took over and even extended the Whig program of internal improvements, public education, and humanitarian reform.

Reid Leads the Democratic Party to Victory

To the dismay of the party leaders, David S. Reid of Rockingham County wrote Holden a letter declining the gubernatorial nomination by the State Democratic Convention in 1848, but Holden failed to publish the letter and prevailed upon Reid to accept the nomination. In a conference in Raleigh with Holden and other Democratic leaders, Reid decided to make free suffrage the issue in the campaign. He determined to advocate the abolition of the fifty-acre qualification for senatorial suffrage by means of a constitutional amendment by legislative method rather than by convention. The official party platform made no reference to this issue. There was some opposition to Reid's proposal, but Holden endorsed it and wrote many editorials in its defense. He and Reid believed that the party could win with the democratic issue of free suffrage, and the aristocratic eastern leaders acquiesced in the seizure of party leadership by Reid and Holden in the hope that it would end the long period of party defeat.

The Free Suffrage Issue before the Voters

Reid exploded the free suffrage bombshell in 1848 in a joint debate at Beaufort with the Whig candidate, Charles Manly. The surprised Manly committed his party to opposing it, and the issue dominated the rest of the exciting campaign. Free suffrage was popular with the masses. Holden estimated that there were at least 110,000 people in the state—30,000 industrial laborers, 60,000 nonslaveholding small farmers, and 20,000 farm wage-laborers—who were unable to vote for state senators because of the fifty-acre requirement. In 1850 about 40 percent of the farms in North Carolina contained less than fifty acres. But all taxpayers could vote for governor and members of the House of Commons. Free suffrage was particularly popular in the small-farm Whig West. In opposing the free suffrage amendment, Manly and the Whig leaders argued that it would unjustly place thrifty landowners at the mercy of the indolent and landless, remove a stimulus to thrift and land ownership, destroy the symmetry of checks and balances of the constitution, and open the door of innovation to demagoguery and radicalism. The *Raleigh Register* said that free suffrage was a "species of claptrap at variance with common justice." The *Wilmington Journal* made the absurd charge that free suffrage would lead to "the desecration of the Bible and abolition of matrimony." Some Whig leaders said that Reid was activated by personal and party ambition in raising an issue for which there was no public demand as a smoke screen to divert attention from the mistaken policies of the national Democratic party.

The Democrats Win a Moral Victory

Manly's victory by a majority of only 854 votes in contrast to Graham's victory by nearly 8,000 in 1846 was a moral victory for Reid and the Democrats, who carried some normally Whig western counties. Obviously the Democrats had found a popular and perhaps winning issue. After the election of 1848 Reid and the Democrats continued to stand together clearly and strongly for a free suffrage amendment by the legislative method; but the Whigs were embarrassed, divided, and vacillating in their stand. When the issue of suffrage reform was raised by the Democrats, many western Whigs demanded a constitutional convention to provide free suffrage and also other democratic reforms, such as the abolition of all property qualifications for officeholding, the popular election of judges, and the apportionment of county representation in the House of Commons on the basis of white instead of federal population. But the Whigs in the East, where slaves were more numerous and thus increased representation in the House, bitterly opposed a convention and any change in the basis of representation.

Democrats Capture Control of the State Government in 1850

In the gubernatorial election of 1850 Reid and the Democrats, standing squarely for a free suffrage amendment by the legislative method—a three-fifths majority of both houses of the legislature originating the amendment and a two-thirds majority of both houses in the succeeding legislature—defeated Manly and the divided, vacillating Whigs by a majority of nearly three thousand. The Democrats also won a majority of both houses of the legislature. Thus after fourteen years of defeat and demoralization, the Democratic party won complete control of the state government in 1850 chiefly because of the progressive and aggressive leadership of Holden and Reid, the safer position of the Democrats in defending slavery and slavery extension as that issue came to dominate national politics in the late 1840s, and the popularity of the free suffrage issue. The party had learned from long defeat that its traditional policy of a conservative, negative governmental program did not satisfy the majority of the voters or the needs of North Carolina. It was a strange role that the progressive Whig party, strong in the small-farm democratic West, played in opposing democratic constitutional reform and in defending the status quo and property interests from the democratic onslaught of the Democratic party, long dominated by the aristocratic eastern slaveholders.

Free Suffrage Amendment Adopted, 1857

The Democratic legislature of 1850 passed the free suffrage amendment by the required three-fifths vote of each house. But two years later it failed to get a two-thirds majority of each house and thus was killed. The amendment passed the Democratic legislatures of 1854 and 1856 by the required majorities over the opposition of the Whigs, who wanted a state convention, and finally became part of the constitution in 1857 by a vote of 50,007 to 19,397 in a popular referendum, thus settling the important issue Reid had brought forward in 1848. This was the largest majority on any political issue in North Carolina up to that time. The amendment extended the senatorial franchise by an estimated 125,000 voters. The overwhelming majority for free suffrage showed the popularity of the issue; but, significantly, much of the opposition was in the eastern Democratic slaveholding counties. Though rejoicing in party victory in 1850, the aristocratic party leaders in the East were not altogether pleased with the new young leadership and the new progressive policy typified by Reid and Holden and free suffrage.

The Democratic party, rejuvenated and victorious in 1850 and more sensitive to public opinion, gradually adopted the old Whig program of internal improvements, public education, and humanitarian and fiscal reform, and expanded and extended it; and they retained popular support and unbroken control of the state to 1860.

State Aid to Internal Improvements

Governor Reid consistently urged legislative action favorable to railroads and other transportation facilities. He said: "The farmer and other classes need cheap transportation and convenient markets where they can carry their property with safety. They need commercial and manufacturing towns and cities at home, with shipping to do their own importing and exporting, without continuing to pay tribute to the North." The Democratic legislatures of the 1850s responded to the appeals of Reid and succeeding governors (Warren Winslow, Thomas Bragg, and John W. Ellis) by extending millions of dollars worth of state aid to railroads, plank roads, and navigation companies. This reversal of state policy was largely due to the pressure of public opinion and to the influence of Holden's powerful editorials in the *North Carolina Standard.* In the General Assembly of 1852 bills for state aid to railroads were defeated, but public sentiment for such a policy was so strong that in the campaign of 1854 both political parties advocated state aid to transportation. The North Carolina Railroad, completed in 1856, was only the first link in a proposed network of "a great trunk line of railways from the magnificent harbor of Beaufort to the Tennessee Line," with numerous branches and feeders. In the legislative session of 1854–55 the Atlantic and North Carolina Railroad was chartered, with the state pledging two-thirds of the capital stock of $1,600,000. This 95-mile road, from Goldsboro to Beaufort, via Kinston and New Bern, was opened to traffic in June, 1858. The Western North Carolina Railroad Company was chartered in 1855, with a capital stock of $6 million, of which the state subscribed $4 million. Plans called for a road from Salisbury via Statesville and Morganton to Asheville and thence to some point on the Tennessee border. By the summer of 1860 the road had been built to a point about 13 miles east of Morganton—a distance of 67 miles. The Wilmington, Charlotte, and Rutherfordton Railroad Company was chartered in 1855 to build a road from Wilmington via Charlotte to Rutherfordton—a distance of 268 miles. At the outbreak of the Civil War in 1861 the "eastern division" of this road had been completed to within 12 miles of Rockingham—a distance of 100 miles, and the "western division" had been completed 10 miles beyond Lincolnton—a distance of 42 miles. The Wilmington and Manchester Railroad was chartered in 1847 and completed in 1854; about one-third of its 172 miles lay in North Carolina. The Western Railroad Company was chartered in 1852, to build from Fayetteville to the coal regions of Moore and Chatham counties; construction began in 1854, but, because of financial difficulties, the road was completed only to the Egypt mines.

In 1860 North Carolina's railway system comprised 891 miles, constructed at a cost of $17 million, connecting with interstate lines leading north, east, south, and west, and serving every major section of the state except the mountain region. Of the railway network, 641 miles had been built after 1850. The state debt, incurred largely from railroad investments, amounted to almost $9 million.

The state's chief investment was in the purchase of stock in railroads, usually two-thirds of the common stock. In the case of the North Carolina Railroad, however, the state owned three-fourths of the common stock and $100,000 of the preferred stock. The state also made a $400,000 loan to the Atlantic and North Carolina Railroad. There were only two North Carolina–chartered railroads before 1860 in which the state did not own stock—the Western Railroad Company and the Wilmington, Charlotte, and Rutherfordton Railroad Company.

The traffic on the Wilmington and Weldon Railroad consisted largely of naval stores in the 1840s and early 1850s; by 1860 shipments of wheat and cotton surpassed naval stores, with 31,000 bales of cotton and 84,000 bushels of wheat being shipped over this road in that year. The chief freight item on the Wilmington, Charlotte, and Rutherfordton line was turpentine. At first passenger traffic was more important than freight shipments on all of the railroads, but by 1860 the income from freight had taken a commanding lead. For the fiscal year ending June 1, 1860, the freight traffic on the North Carolina Railroad amounted to $225,000, while that from passengers was only $174,000.

The Wilmington and Weldon was the most profitable of the North Carolina railroads before 1860. In the fiscal year 1859–60, it made a profit of 15½ percent on its capital stock. The North Carolina Railroad declared no dividends for years; in 1859 it paid a 6 percent dividend on its preferred stock. After a disastrous first decade the Raleigh and Gaston paid dividends through the 1850s, except for the "panic year" of 1857. Most of the railroad companies maintained shops, the best being those of the Wilmington and Weldon and of the North Carolina Railroad. The present City of Burlington had its beginning as "company shops" for the latter road. New cars and at least one engine were built at the Wilmington and Weldon shops, and in the year 1860 seven new cars were completed in the North Carolina Railroad shops.

The railroad companies employed both free and slave labor. In 1858 the North Carolina Railroad had 139 white employees, 263 slaves, and 13 free Negroes. Slaves were usually hired on a yearly basis by contract with slave owners. Approximately one-third of the employees served as "section hands." In 1860 the Wilmington and Weldon Railroad Company owned about 25 slaves. Only a small number of slaves were employed on any of the other railroads in the state.

Plank Roads, the "Farmer's Railroads"

Few North Carolinians today realize that the first "good roads movement" in the state began a decade before the Civil War and led to the construction of more than five hundred miles of "plank roads," at a cost of more than $1 million. Nor are they aware of the fact that the longest plank road ever built anywhere in the world was the Fayetteville and Western Road, extending from Fayetteville via High Point and Salem to Bethania—a road aptly called the "Appian Way of North Carolina." The state government invested $120,000 in this road alone, and an additional $60,000 in two other roads leading from Fayetteville in other directions—the Fayetteville and Warsaw and the Fayetteville and Albemarle.

The plank road movement which swept North Carolina in the early 1850s was born of the need for an improved system of land transportation. As early as 1842 Governor John M. Morehead declared that there was "no region on the whole earth so destitute of natural or artificial facilities for transportation" as North Carolina. Four years later Governor William A. Graham called the attention of the General Assembly to the "bad conditions of roads," which he thought were a "just reproach to the state," but the legislature refused to take any positive action. The people, notably the farmers and merchants, eager to free themselves from bondage to sand and mud, were determined to have some type of "all weather" roads which would enable them to convey their goods to market and which would serve as "feeders" to the two railroads that had been completed in 1840. Accordingly, farmers in North Carolina, as in other states, began to agitate for the construction of plank roads. Mass meetings were held in several towns in the state, companies were organized, and in 1849 the General Assembly incorporated the first plank road company in the state, the Fayetteville and Western. Sixteen more companies were incorporated by the 1850–51 General Assembly. The plank road fever reached its climax in 1852, when the legislature chartered thirty-two new companies and passed thirty-nine plank road bills. Between 1849 and 1856 some eighty-four plank road companies were incorporated, with a total authorized capital stock of about $6 million. Much of this stock was never paid and some of the companies never built a mile of road. Chapel Hill, for instance, was one of several towns where people anticipated more than they could accomplish. Books were opened at the little university town for subscription to several plank road companies, but little or no construction ever took place. Fayetteville, on the other hand, an "inland port" and the center of the "wagon trade" over a large area, was served by at least six different plank roads, the most important being the Fayetteville and Western, the Fayetteville and Center, and the Fayetteville and Warsaw.

Another prominent and profitable venture was the Greenville and Raleigh Plank Road, which did much to promote the naval stores industry in that section. Several plank roads extended from Wilmington in various directions and there were at least two significant interstate roads, one from Yanceyville to the Virginia line to connect with the road to Danville, and the second from Rocky River, through Wadesboro, to the South Carolina line to tie up with the Cheraw Plank Road.

The "farmer's railroads," as the plank roads were called, were built by private companies, with most of the stock subscriptions coming from farmers who lived along the roads and from businessmen in the towns from which the roads extended. Some companies made profits for a few years and declared dividends. In one six-month period in 1852 the Fayetteville and Western earned $6,000, and the state's dividend that year amounted to $7,800, "the first time the state made any money directly by a subscription to Internal Improvements."

Many people were enthusiastic about plank roads and considered them the best roads imaginable. One contemporary observer wrote: "All classes profited, but the farmer gained most directly. Their peculiar merit was the diminution of friction, by which a horse was enabled to draw two to three times as great a load as he could do on the ordinary road." Speed on a plank road was much greater than on a dirt road. And, instead of being forced to market his crops in good weather, when his labor was needed in the fields, the farmer could deliver his goods to market when bad weather prevented ordinary farm work. The *Raleigh Register* of February 28, 1849, declared that "Plank Roads are the most effectual, at the smallest cost of all forms of transportation." Yet some North Carolinians opposed this "new fangled" type of transportation. They contended the roads cost too much to build, that the lumber and sills being used were of inferior quality, that the planks would wear out and decay in a short time, that the whole plank road idea was "silly," and that the Fayetteville and Western, in particular, was a "monument of folly." The construction of these roads never became a clear-cut political issue. But in the 1849 General Assembly 82 percent of the Whigs voted for state aid to plank roads, while 75 percent of the Democrats opposed.

The law prescribed that the Fayetteville and Western plank road be at least ten feet wide. Most of the other roads were only eight feet wide, the standard used in other states. The roads were surveyed and graded, and then allowed to "settle." Then heavy sills or "stringers," were placed end to end, lengthwise. The planks, usually of heart pine, nine to sixteen inches wide and three to four inches thick, were then laid directly across the sills at right angles to the line of the road. After the planks were properly laid, they were covered with sand, and after the "sanding process," the roads were open to traffic. The cost of construction varied according to the lay of the land, amount of grading required, and local costs of labor and materials, but the average cost was about $1,500 per mile.

According to the laws of incorporation of the plank road companies, "reasonable tolls" were to be charged after five miles of the road was completed. Likewise the companies were not allowed to make more than 20 to 25 percent on their capital stock in any one year! This requirement never worried the directors of the roads, since some of them never made any profits, and only one paid a dividend as high as 4 percent.

The toll levied on the Fayetteville and Western—and perhaps on all of the roads—was one-half cent per mile for a man on horseback; one cent for a one-horse vehicle, two cents for a two-horse team, three cents for a three-horse team, and four cents for a six-horse team. There was a fine of five dollars for riding or driving between toll gates for the purpose of avoiding tolls. Perhaps North Carolinians, like people in other states, had "shunpikes" in order to avoid payments on the "turnpikes." Toll gates and toll houses were located about eleven miles apart on the Fayetteville and Western, the average cost of each house being about $300, and the average salary of the toll collector being about $150 a year.

Plank roads were moderately prosperous for a few years. The original cost of construction was not so great, but the planks wore out rapidly and decayed even more rapidly. The great cost of upkeep discouraged investors and no new plank road companies were chartered after 1857. Bad crops, the Panic of 1857, and the competition of railroads also led to the decline of the "farmer's railroads." They had almost disappeared by 1860.

State Aid to Navigation Companies

The state did less to promote water transportation than it did to encourage railroads and plank roads. Between 1848 and 1854 it purchased $185,000 worth of stock in four "navigation companies"—$40,000 in the Tar Navigation Company; $120,000 in the Neuse River Navigation Company; $20,000 in the New River Navigation Company; and $5,000 in the Yadkin Navigation Company. In 1858 it subscribed $300,000 in the stock of the Cape Fear and Deep River Navigation Company. It also invested $350,000 in the stock of the Albemarle and Chesapeake Canal Company (chartered by the Virginia legislature in 1855 as the great Bridge Lumber and Canal Company), hoping thereby to connect Albemarle, Currituck, and Pamlico sounds with Chesapeake Bay. The state's investments in these water transportation facilities were largely fruitless.

Public Education

While greatly extending the policy of state aid to improved transportation, the Democrats also adopted a liberal policy toward the public school system. This system, created by the Whigs in 1839 and allowed by them to drift and languish in the 1840s, was improved and extended by the Democrats. The chief defect in the disappointing system in the 1840s—lack of effective state supervision—was remedied in 1852 by the creation of the office of state superintendent of common schools and the election of Calvin H. Wiley to fill the position. Wiley, a young lawyer, author of two historical novels and a Whig leader in the legislature for the improvement of the school system, assumed office in 1853 and was so eminently successful in organizing and developing the system that the Democratic legislatures kept him in office until 1865, and he gained preeminence in the history of public education in the state and wide recognition as an educational leader.

Calvin H. Wiley's Administration of Schools

With infinite labor, by travel, speeches, and writings, Wiley overcame opposition to and popularized the public schools. He enforced the state school law, obtained reports from the schools, wrote the *North Carolina Reader* (1851) and sought in other ways to improve the textbooks, and urged the procurement of more interested and efficient school officials and better equipment. He improved the supply and quality of common-school teachers by establishing a system of examinations and certification administered by examining boards in the counties, by establishing county institutes for the training of teachers, by taking the lead in organizing teachers' conventions and the Educational Association of North Carolina, and by editing the *North Carolina Jour-*

nal of Education. He brought about an increase in the number of women teachers, though in 1850 the men outnumbered the licensed women teachers 1,849 to 315. The system grew steadily in both size and quality during the 1850s. In 1850 more than 3,000 common schools were in operation with an enrollment exceeding 118,000, an average term of three and two-thirds months, and an average monthly teacher's salary of $26. The total cost of the system was about $278,000, of which about $100,000 came from local taxes and the remainder from the income of the State Literary Fund distributed to the counties on the basis of federal population. The North Carolina system was the best in the South in 1860—better then than it was between 1860 and 1900, and better in comparison with the systems of other states than it has ever been since 1860.

Humanitarian Institutions

The Democrats expanded and supported, by increasingly liberal appropriations, the state humanitarian institutions for the deaf and blind and for the insane. Appropriations were raised to $10,000 in 1857 for the institution for the deaf, dumb, and blind and to $125,000 in 1858 for the State Hospital for the Insane.

Tax Reform

Increased expenditures for the state government and humanitarian institutions and for interest on the mounting state debt, incurred chiefly for state aid to railroads, made necessary an increase in state taxes. The Democratic party, formerly the advocate of economy and low taxes, did not hesitate in the 1850s to provide sufficient revenue for the popular program of state development. In 1854 the land and poll tax rates, unchanged since 1817, were doubled to twelve cents on a hundred dollar valuation and forty cents, respectively. In 1856 they were increased to fifteen cents and fifty cents and in 1858 to twenty cents and eighty cents. In 1860 the land tax rate was reduced to eighteen cents. State tax revenues rose from $141,610 in 1850 to $667,708 in 1860. Despite rising state taxes and debt, the Democratic majorities in the biennial elections of governor and legislature generally increased after 1850. The people preferred a program of state development, well administered, to low taxes, particularly in the unusually prosperous decade of the 1850s.

Democratic Unity and Dominance Threatened

Internal party dissension and factionalism characterized the 1850s in North Carolina as well as in the nation. Free suffrage divided the

Whigs after 1848. But it was the issue of slavery in the territories that first divided and then destroyed the Whig party. The sectional compromise of 1850, which had been designed to compromise sectional differences, was in reality a stunning defeat for the South because the admission of California as a free state ended the southern veto, or equality of voting power, in the United States Senate. The Whig party generally endorsed the compromise as a savior of the Union, but many State Rights Whigs in North Carolina condemned it. Some, notably Congressman Thomas L. Clingman of Buncombe County, shifted to the Democratic party as the only safe custodian of southern interests, and thereafter supported the national tickets of the Democratic party. The Kansas-Nebraska Act of 1854 and the consequent union of the northern antislavery forces in the new antislavery Republican party destroyed the Whig party in the nation and in North Carolina. It ceased to function as an organized party after 1854. Many Whigs in the nation and the state found temporary abode in the Know-Nothing, or American, party, founded on American opposition to foreign immigration and Roman Catholicism. Maintaining an organization in North Carolina from 1855 to 1859, it attracted chiefly former Whigs—but by no means all—many of whom were without an organized party. Some prominent Whigs who joined the Know-Nothing party were Kenneth Rayner of Bertie County, John A. Gilmer of Guilford, John Pool of Pasquotank, Alfred Dockery of Richmond, and J. M. Leach of Davidson. James B. Shepard was the best-known Democrat who joined the new party. Gilmer, who was the Know-Nothing candidate for governor in 1856 against Thomas Bragg, Democrat, was defeated by a vote of approximately 58,000 to 45,000.

Eastern "Slavocracy" Takes Charge of Democratic Party

More significant were the factors that threatened the unity and dominance of the Democratic party in North Carolina. This party was united in opposition to congressional exclusion of slavery in the territories and largely united in support of the state issue of free suffrage. The very weakness of the opposition—the American party and the disorganized Whigs—stimulated overconfidence, factionalism, and rivalry for office within the Democratic party. Continuing tenure of power promoted conservatism and machine control by a few leaders. Normally the Democratic party had been dominated by the aristocratic slaveholders of the East and the cotton and tobacco counties of the Piedmont. They had relaxed their control during the years 1848 to 1850 to the young, progressive Reid-Holden group on the free suffrage issue in the hope of achieving victory. With their party firmly in power, they again took control of party machinery and policies, showed little concern for democracy and the common people, and made the Democratic party the special guardian of state rights, property rights, the slavocracy, and southern interests. This change of party spirit and leadership threatened the unity and dominance of the party in the state.

Ellis-Holden Contest, 1858, and Its Aftermath

In the gubernatorial campaign of 1858 newspapers, local meetings, and other manifestations of public opinion, especially in the West, indicated clearly that the rank and file of the Democratic party wanted William W. Holden as the party nominee for governor. Holden was the best-known Democratic leader who had not held political office. He had shown interest in democratic reform and in the welfare of the small farmers and working men. His service in the rejuvenation, victory, and conversion to a progressive program of the party had been unsurpassed.

Democratic leaders were willing to use Holden, but not to elevate him to high office. He wanted the nomination for governor, but the eastern conservative Democrats urged the nomination of John W. Ellis of Salisbury. This Holden-Ellis rivalry for the nomination was the first preconvention campaign in North Carolina history and it threatened the unity of the party. The aristocratic eastern leaders of the party refused to accept Holden, a mere editor of lowly origin who had a sincere interest in democratic government and the common people. They decided for the first time to hold the State Democratic Convention in the West, at Charlotte, and they weakened the voting power of the western counties, where Holden was strong, by having the convention adopt the rule that the voting power of each county in the convention be based on the number of Democratic votes cast in the election of 1856. Then the convention, controlled by party leaders rather than by public opinion, nominated Ellis by a close vote. Nearly all the western counties, but only three of the eastern counties, supported Holden. He and his disappointed following were loyal to the party and worked for the election of Ellis as governor. Later in the year the Democratic leaders in the legislature defeated Holden for the United States Senate and elected Thomas Bragg.

This democratic-aristocratic cleavage within the Democratic party was of great importance. Henceforth Holden and many of his followers were lukewarm Democrats. Although he was sympathetic with the reform issue of ad valorem taxation of slave property, which was the chief Whig issue in the state campaign of 1860, in the campaign of that year he avoided an open break with his party by opposing it. But by opposing secession in 1860–61, he broke openly with his party, whose leaders then deprived him of the lucrative office of state printer and thereafter despised him.

In the 1850s a revival of the issue of distributing to the states the public lands, or the proceeds from their sale, created division within the Democratic party. The party officially opposed distribution but a minority favored it. In 1858

Duncan McRae, a Democrat, ran as an independent for governor on the distribution issue. But he was badly defeated by Ellis, the Democratic candidate. McRae's support apparently came more from former Whigs than from Democrats. His defeat ended distribution as an important issue and its threat to the unity of the party.

The Issue of Ad Valorem Taxation

Democratic unity and supremacy were seriously threatened in 1860 by the issue of ad valorem taxation of property, including slaves. Larger state expenditures created pressure for more revenue and there was a glaring inequality in the system of taxation because slaves, the most valuable property in the state, owned by a minority of the white population, were escaping taxation on the same basis as other property. Slaves were taxed not as property but as persons, those of both sexes aged twelve to fifty bearing the same poll tax as free males between twenty-one and forty-five. More than half of the slaves, an estimated 187,500 worth about $113,000,000, escaped taxation altogether, while the remainder, about 160,000 valued at about $140,000,000, were taxed from 1858 at only eighty cents per head per annum. The tax on a $500 slave and one worth $2,000 was the same—forty cents from 1817 to 1856, fifty cents from 1856 to 1858, and eighty cents thereafter. The slave property in the state greatly exceeded the value of land but was taxed far less. Income and savings were also taxed heavily in comparison with slave property. A thousand-dollar slave meant a tax of eighty cents on his owner, while a thousand-dollar cash income in salaries and wages was taxed six dollars, and a thousand dollars worth of land was taxed two dollars. A free mechanic who earned $500 or more a year must pay a five-dollar license tax and eighty cents poll tax; but he often competed with a hired slave mechanic whose owner was taxed only eighty cents. The tax inequality and discrimination in favor of slave property was unjust and potentially an inflammable issue which might arouse the non-slaveholding small farmers and laborers, numbering over two-thirds of the white population, against the minority of more wealthy slaveowners. By 1860 the state's 63,481 laborers, 27,263 tradesmen, and 87,025 farmers, most of whom held no slaves, were beginning to develop class consciousness and to desire a greater influence in public affairs. In a public address to the "workingmen" of Fayetteville in 1859 Holden said, "Let no man be ashamed of mechanical labor. . . . Rather let the mechanic be proud of his skill, of his industry, and of his usefulness to society. . . . Remember that you are now a power in the State . . . and that Common Schools and internal improvements are constantly increasing your intelligence, and your power." The power of workingmen was due in large part to their growing numbers, to the adoption of free suffrage, and to the influence of common schools. Many conservatives had opposed the common school system because of the fear that education would make the masses more articulate. Moreover, North Carolina was out of line with other southern states in respect to the taxation of slaves according to value.

Increasing demand and agitation for ad valorem taxation became a strong movement by 1858, when futile legislative efforts were made for its adoption. The chief ad valorem champion in the General Assembly was Moses Bledsoe, Democratic senator from Wake County. Defeated in the legislature, Bledsoe carried the issue to the people. The Raleigh Workingmen's Association, formed in 1859, conducted a vigorous public campaign. In a resolution written by Holden, the Raleigh association declared that "it becomes the mechanics and workingmen of North Carolina, while respecting the rights and principles of others, to look to their own rights and interests, and to insist upon that political equality and that participation in public affairs to which they as free men are entitled." In the public agitation it was clear that the issue of ad valorem had some support from both Democrats and Whigs, but that the chief opposition was in the Democratic party.

Revival of the Whig Party: The "Pots and Pans Campaign" of 1860

The Whig party, which had not functioned as an organized political body since 1854, was revived and reorganized in the state in 1859 for the purpose of electing unionist congressmen and legislators in an effort to preserve the Union, which was in danger from the attacks of antislavery Republicans in the North and from Southern Democrats, many of whom favored secession. The revived and rejuvenated Whig party, sensing the popularity of ad valorem, shrewdly adopted in its state platform of 1860 the issue of a constitutional amendment by the convention method providing for the taxation of all property according to value. It nominated John Pool of Pasquotank County, an eastern Whig, for the governorship. The Democratic party, dominated by the slaveholding aristocracy rather than by the views of Holden, renominated Governor John W. Ellis. It condemned ad valorem but tried to dodge the issue and to obscure its position by advocating equality of taxation of all types of property as far as was practicable under the state constitution.

An exciting and bitter campaign ensued which tended to cut across party lines. The Whigs were effective in establishing the fact of unjust tax inequality. Their argument against tax favoritism for the wealthy and for justice to the laborers and small farmers tended to inflame the common people against the slaveholding minority. They argued that taxation of slaves according to value was in harmony with the southern view that slaves were property instead of persons, and that it would permit a reduction in the tax on land, furnish needed revenue for internal improvements and other progressive measures, and foster better relations between the East and the West, the rich and the poor. The Democrats were unable to make a well-reasoned defense. They alleged that equal poll taxes were a compromise feature of the constitutional amendments of 1835 and that ad valorem was an attack on slavery and thus an aid to the abolitionists. They promised to reduce the tax on land and resorted to a campaign of misrepresentation and demagoguery, alleging that ad valorem while taxing slave property would oppress the poor by taxing their pots and pans, chickens, furniture, and other property. The Democrats were alarmed at the popular appeal of the ad valorem issue but, aided by the acute sectional issue of slavery in national politics and the general conviction that the Democratic party was the only safe custodian of southern interests, they won a close victory. Compared with the election of 1858, however, they lost several counties to the Whigs and their majority was reduced from sixteen thousand to six thousand.

In ad valorem taxation, the Whig party seemed to have found a popular and perhaps winning issue. The outbreak of the Civil War prevented the party from further exploiting the issue. But during the war the policy of ad valorem was adopted. On this issue the party roles were again reversed. The Democrats in 1860 were defenders of the status quo; the Whigs were aggressive champions of reform. The issues of constitutional reform in 1835, free suffrage in 1850, and ad valorem in 1860, brought political popularity and strength to the party which aggressively championed constructive, democratic reform. In each case the political leaders lagged behind public sentiment.

Chapter 26
ECONOMIC DEVELOPMENT
1835-1860

The era of internal improvements and of political, social, and educational progress before 1860 was in part the cause and in part the result of a coincidental economic development which brought greater income and wealth and a higher standard of living to North Carolinians. North Carolina 'shared in the national economic depression following the Panic of 1837 and in the national recovery and rising prices which made of the late 1840s and the 1850s a period of marked economic development and prosperity. Better and cheaper access to local and national markets by plank roads, railroads, and steamboat navigation enabled North Carolina to share more fully in the national economic upswing. Improving economic conditions and the increase of capital stimulated a spirit of enterprise and optimism. A pronounced movement for agricultural reform contributed to agricultural prosperity. The complex of local and national factors brought notable expansion in agriculture, mining, fishing, manufacturing, transportation, commerce, and urban life in the late 1840s and especially in the 1850s.

Agriculture continued as the chief industry of North Carolina, and the state remained predominantly rural. According to the Census of 1850, North Carolina had a total population of 869,039, of which only 21,109 or 2.4 percent were classified as urban; in 1860 these figures were 992,622 and 24,554, or 2.5 percent. The average size of North Carolina farms in 1850 was 369 acres; this figure had dropped to 316 by 1860.

Rising crop prices and cheaper and better transportation greatly increased the volume of crop production, sales, and profits of farmers, especially those living within reach of railroads, plank roads, and navigable waters. The total value of North Carolina crops increased from $22,900,000 in 1850 to $33,-400,000 in 1860, and land values more than doubled during the "prosperous fifties."

Bright-Leaf Tobacco

There was a remarkable increase in the production of the state's two major staple crops—tobacco and cotton. Tobacco production jumped from 12 million pounds in 1850 to 33 million pounds in 1860, an increase partially due to the discovery of a new type of leaf—the lemon-colored or bright-leaf tobacco and to a new curing process. About 1852 Abisha and Elisha Slade of Caswell County perfected the production of bright yellow or "gold leaf" tobacco by the use of charcoal instead of wood as the fuel for curing tobacco grown on this bright, sandy, and relatively infertile soil. The new flue-curing process had been discovered accidentally by a Slade slave, Stephen, who had a blacksmith shop near the tobacco barns. Here he had a pit where he prepared charcoal for the forge. One rainy night, while he was watching a barn of curing tobacco, he fell asleep and allowed the wood fires to become almost extinguished. When he awoke, he rushed to the charcoal pit, seized several charred butts of logs and placed them on the dying embers. The result was six hundred pounds "of the brightest yellow tobacco ever seen." At first it was thought that this curing process was the secret of producing "bright yellow" tobacco, but later it was found that the soil was the principal factor.

A great part of the North Carolina tobacco crop was marketed at Danville, Virginia. It brought premium prices which stimulated its production in what came to be called the "Bright Leaf Belt" of North Carolina and Virginia. Tobacco was grown in large quantities only in the counties along the Virginia line from Halifax to Stokes. Warren and Granville counties, with more than five million pounds each in 1860, led in the production of the "weed." Tobacco required much hand labor and fertilizer, but it was not uncommon for a farmer to clear from $400 to $700 per worker each year. Land values in the new tobacco belt increased rapidly and the new bright leaf brought "lush prosperity" to the concentrated area in which it was the staple crop.

Cotton, Corn, Wheat, and Other Crops

Cotton production rose from 34,617 five-hundred-pound bales in 1840 to 73,845 in 1850, and to 145,514 bales in 1860. Its production was concentrated chiefly in the block of eastern counties bounded by the towns of Halifax, Goldsboro, and Washington and in the southern counties near the South Carolina line extending from Robeson to Mecklenburg. Edgecombe County led the state in 1860 with more than 15,000 bales. Rice production was concentrated in Brunswick County, which produced about 7,600,000 pounds of the state's 8,000,000-pound crop in 1860. The wheat crop, produced chiefly in the central Piedmont with Randolph, Chatham, and Davidson counties leading, more than doubled in the 1850s—from 2,000,000 bushels to 4,700,000, but corn production experienced only a slight increase from 27,500,000 bushels to 30,000,000. Oats, rye, barley, buckwheat, peas and beans, Irish potatoes, sweet potatoes, hemp, flax, hops, hay, orchard fruits, and vegetables were produced in sizable quantities and indicated a considerable diversification in crops.

Corn production did not increase at such a rapid rate as the other cereals or as cotton and tobacco, but it was nevertheless the state's largest, most widely grown, and most useful crop. The 1859 crop of over 300,000,000 bushels was produced in eighty-four of the state's eighty-six counties, only nine of which had a production of less than 200,000 bushels. Corn constituted an important part of the diet of the people in the form of hominy, hoecakes, grits, corn pone, and mush—not to mention "roasting ears." For the slaves, it was the most important single item of diet. Horses, mules, cattle, swine, and poultry consumed a large part of the corn. Some farmers cut the "green corn" for their livestock, but most of them used the matured grain, tops, fodder, and shucks in feeding. No other crop had such a wide variety of uses. Corn whiskey was an important item of consumption and trade.

Agricultural Journals and Agricultural Societies

Agricultural expansion and prosperity were due in part to a systematic movement to improve farming methods and rural life. For many years the newspapers, which were largely political, had given space to agricultural news and problems and had stressed improved methods, better farm machinery, deep plowing, the use of manures and fertilizers, the adaptation of soil to crops, and better marketing facilities. In the 1830s Edmund Ruffin's *Farmer's Register,* published at Petersburg, Virginia, and several other out-of-state agricultural periodicals had a limited circulation in the state. In 1829 John Christian Blum began publication of the *Farmer's and Planter's Almanac* at Salem. After 1839 and especially in the 1850s several short-lived agricultural journals were published in North Carolina—the *Farmer's Advocate, North Carolina Farmer, Farmer's Journal, Carolina Cultivator, Arator, North Carolina Planter,* and the *Edgecombe Farm Journal.* Surveys of agricultural resources were prepared and published, notably those of State Geologist Ebenezer Emmons, a professor at the University of North Carolina. In 1861 Edmund Ruffin's *Agricultural, Geological and Descriptive Sketches of Lower North Carolina* appeared.

Another phase of agricultural revival and reform was the organization and activity of agricultural societies. Many county societies, through meetings and fairs, enabled farmers to discuss their problems and to receive instruction from speakers and exhibits. The State Agricultural Society, organized at Raleigh on October 8, 1852, began the following year to hold an annual state fair in the capital city. Thomas Ruffin, distinguished jurist and planter and president of the State Agricultural Society, as well as other alert farmers and planters, conducted experiments and published the results of their findings. In 1854 a chair of applied chemistry was established at the university. Agricultural journals, societies, and leaders criticized the prevalent methods of farming and urged crop rotation, deep plowing, hillside terracing, better seeds, improved implements, and the use of fertilizers—stable manure, marl, compost, and commercial fertilizer which was first coming into use in North Carolina. Their objectives were increased production, improved farm life, and the conservation and development of soil resources, which erosion and an improvident system of extensive, frontier agriculture had been depleting for generations. Edgecombe County, with an unusual number of progressive planters, adopted improved methods, greatly increased its production, and acquired wide recognition for its agricultural development and leadership. The decade of the 1850s was a period of unprecedented agricultural expansion and prosperity in North Carolina.

Gold Mining

Mining was an important industry in antebellum North Carolina, though its importance was declining near the close of the period. Endowed by nature with a great variety of minerals, North Carolina possessed few in commercial quantities. Of these, gold experienced the chief commercial development.

Though discovered and mined in small quantities in the colonial period, gold became important in North Carolina with the discovery in 1799 of the Reed Mine in Cabarrus County, where nuggets were later found weighing from one to twenty-eight pounds. Gold was found in stream beds and near the surface throughout the state west of a line joining Warren and Moore counties and was mined crudely with pick, shovel, and pan. Widespread discoveries and publicity generated a gold fever and a gold rush to North Carolina. Scores of gold-mining companies were organized and incorporated by the legislature, systematic searches were made, outside capital and labor were attracted, shafts were sunk, equipment was installed, and mining towns boomed, especially in the region from Charlotte to Gold Hill in Rowan County. In 1848 Gold Hill had five stores, one tavern, four doctors, and one thousand laborers in the nearby mines.

The lure of the precious metal in the "golden state" attracted a total capital investment of perhaps $100 million, mostly from northern states and foreign countries. The total gold production before 1860 has been estimated at sums ranging from $50 million to $65 million. Several of the larger mines operated at a profit, but many of the ventures were relatively unprofitable. At times gold mining employed about thirty thousand men and ranked next to agriculture in importance. The gold was used as a medium of exchange in local trade, exported to Europe, made into jewelry, and coined into money. Before 1829 all of the gold mined in the United States and coined at the Philadelphia mint was from North Carolina, and altogether $9 million of North Carolina gold was coined there. A branch of the United States Mint at Charlotte was authorized by Congress in 1835, built in 1836, and opened in December, 1837, under the superintendency of John H. Wheeler. Up to 1861 this mint had coined $5,059,188. Two Germans, Christopher and Augustus Bechtler, operated a famous private mint and manufactured jewelry in Rutherford County from 1831 to 1857. The Bechtlers minted $3,625,840 into gold coins valued at $1.00, $2.50, and $5.00. Altogether more than $17,000,000 of North Carolina gold was coined before 1860. Until the decline of the industry due to the scarcity of the mineral in easily accessible quantity and to the discovery of far richer gold fields in California in 1848, North Carolina and Georgia were the leading gold-mining states. In 1830 no less than fifty-six mines were in operation in North Carolina, but the Census of 1860 recorded only nine. Despite attempts at revival in the 1850s and years later by scientific methods and machinery, gold mining in North Carolina never regained its lost importance. Nevertheless, in the antebellum period it provided employment, created home markets for the produce of farm and factory, increased the circulating medium, and supplemented agriculture in lean years.

Iron and Coal

Iron mining, which began in the colonial era, grew in importance after 1815. Some iron was produced in Nash, Johnston, and other eastern counties, but most of the iron works, such as forges and furnaces, were in the Piedmont, with Lincoln County leading. Iron was never a major industry of the state, but pig iron production had reached eighteen hundred tons a year by 1830. Corundum was discovered in Madison County in 1847; there was some copper and silver mining, and several mines were operating in the coal fields of the Deep River section after 1855. In 1861 a railroad was under construction from Fayetteville to the "Deep River Coal Fields." One optimistic writer predicted that the Deep River region would become the "Sheffield of America," but only limited quantities of coal were mined and very little manufacturing developed in this area.

Fishing

In 1860 North Carolina ranked second in the South in commercial fishing. Thirty-three fisheries located in the East near the ocean and sounds sold herring, shad, oysters, and other products valued at $120,000.

Manufacturing

While the primitive extractive industries of agriculture, mining, and fishing constituted the chief economic activity of North Carolinians before 1860, the more complex and lucrative pursuit of processing or manufacturing was beginning to develop. Manufacturing was handicapped by poor transportation and by the scarcity of coal, iron, surplus capital, and skilled labor; but abundant water power, cheap labor, and close proximity to cotton and tobacco plantations and forests were definite advantages for the development of manufacturing integrated with agriculture. Many of the planters and farmers, however, had a positive distaste for manufacturing, considering it as not quite respectable and socially inferior to farming. In 1828 Charles Fisher reported to the legislature that "a crisis is at hand when our citizens must turn a portion of their labour and enterprise into other channels of industry; otherwise, poverty and ruin will fall on every class of our community." He pointed out the excellent opportunities for cotton textile manufactures and urged the people of the state to develop that industry, but he admitted that "our habits and prejudices are against manufacturing."

Decreasing Self-Sufficiency after 1815

Despite the auspicious beginnings of manufacturing, North Carolina became increasingly dependent upon the outside world for its manufactured goods. In the years before 1815 the state was for the most part economically isolated and necessarily self-sufficient. It exported only small quantities of agricultural and forest products and few processed articles except naval stores. Consequently, unable to purchase many manufactured goods from England and New England, where the factory system was developing on a large scale, it was compelled to rely upon home and local industries for its scanty needs for brick, flour, meal, lumber, leather, shoes, hats, harness, wagons, whiskey, and a few other articles. Wallace B. Goebel, in his "A History of Manufactures in North Carolina before 1860" (unpublished master's thesis, Duke University) concluded that the year 1810 probably represented the peak of domestic production in North Carolina, that there was a sharp decline in household manufactures from that date to 1825, a more gradual decline from 1825 to 1840, and a swift decline during the next twenty years.

The spinning wheel and the hand loom in the home largely met the demands for thread and cloth. In 1814, 7,500,000 yards of cloth were woven by hand on more than 40,000 looms in North Carolina homes—a production exceeded only by Virginia and New York. There were, mostly in the Piedmont, twenty fulling mills, twenty-three iron works, three paper mills, and eight powder mills. About 24,000 fur hats were made, and over 5,400 small distilleries produced 1,387,000 gallons of whiskey.

As has been indicated earlier, the first cotton factory—a small spinning mill—was established by Michael Schenck and Absalom Warlick near Lincolnton about 1815. But after that date North Carolina became less self-sufficient economically. With the spread of cotton culture agriculture increasingly dominated the economic interest of the state, and there was no serious effort to "bring the cotton mills to the cotton fields." Manufacturing, whether in the home or factory, was unable to compete successfully with staple crop agriculture. Increased export of staple crops, particularly of cotton to England and New England, permitted increased purchases of better and cheaper goods made elsewhere. There was a progressive decline of home manufacturing and a growing colonial dependence upon New England and other commercial areas for cloth and other processed goods, mules, farm implements, whiskey, and even some food and feed stuffs.

But despite this increasing loss of self-sufficiency, there was considerable development of small local factories, especially cotton spinning mills. This development was most rapid in the decade of agricultural depression after the Panic of 1837. In 1840 there were twenty-five textile mills in fifteen counties, thirteen of them in the Piedmont, and the *Raleigh Register* declared that North Carolina "has now more factories than were ten years ago in the whole South." Textile growth was less rapid in the 1850s, when the small factory units had to compete with highly prosperous agriculture, and when the great expansion of cotton and tobacco production and sale permitted the planters to buy from the outside more and more of the things that make life pleasant and comfortable. After 1840 railroads opened a broader market for the small North Carolina factories but also opened North Carolina more easily to the cheaper and better products of more highly industrialized New England and the Middle States. The small North Carolina factories were the product of comparative isolation, were generally side lines or supplementary activities of the owners, served local markets, and prospered most when agriculture was depressed. The foundations of real industrialization of North Carolina, characterized by rapid expansion, specialization, competition in the national market, and relative independence from local economic conditions, were securely laid in the antebellum era. It is unlikely, as some writers have claimed, that the outbreak of war in 1861 postponed for twenty years the industrialization of North Carolina. In 1860, however, planting was still the dominant, most honorable, and most profitable occupation in North Carolina, and the heavy capital investment in land and slaves made capital scarce for the development of manufacturing.

Growth of Industry

According to the United States censuses of 1850 and 1860, there was an increase in the number of manufacturing establishments of all kinds in the state from 2,663 to 3,689; in the invested capital, from $7,500,000 to more than $9,700,000; and in the total value of manufactured products from $9,700,000 to $16,700,000. The number of employees in the manufacturing establishments in 1860 was 14,217.

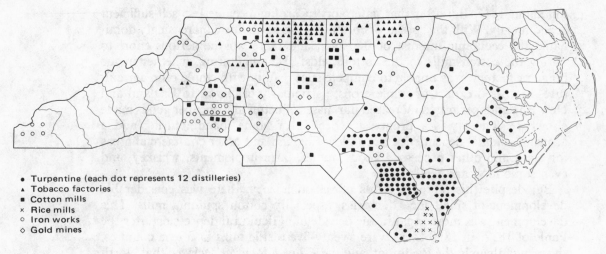

- • Turpentine (each dot represents 12 distilleries)
- ▲ Tobacco factories
- ■ Cotton mills
- × Rice mills
- ○ Iron works
- ◇ Gold mines

North Carolina Industries in 1860
Cartography by the Department of Geography and Earth Sciences
The University of North Carolina at Charlotte

Turpentine, Flour and Meal, Tobacco, and Cotton Textiles

Turpentine, the leading industry in 1860, which was concentrated in Bladen, New Hanover, Cumberland, and nearby counties, was produced by 1,526 establishments. The total production was valued at $5,300,000. More than half of the turpentine distilleries were in Bladen and New Hanover counties. Bladen, with over 500 establishments, led the state. About two-thirds of the turpentine produced in the United States was manufactured in North Carolina and marketed at Wilmington and Fayetteville for export. In fact, turpentine was the only manufacturing industry in antebellum North Carolina that was on an export basis. Its production was very great, but the industry was carried on with the crudest possible techniques, and the only improvement in methods since the colonial era was the introduction in 1834 of copper stills.

The second North Carolina industry in importance was the production of flour and meal, which accounted for 639 mills and a product worth about $4,350,000. Third in importance was tobacco with ninety-seven small factories, chiefly in Rockingham, Stokes, Granville, and Caswell counties. Rockingham led with twenty-five factories. The total value of tobacco manufactures of snuff, plug, and twist for chewing, and pipe tobacco was $1,117,000. Ranking fourth was lumber with 330 saw mills and an annual product of $1,074,000. In fifth place in 1860 was the cotton textile industry with thirty-nine factories, mostly spinning mills, located chiefly in the Piedmont, making goods worth $1,046,-000, and using 41,884 spindles, 761 looms, and 1,764 workers. Only three of the mills employed more than 100 workers each.

Pioneers in the Textile Industry

The Battle family at Rocky Mount and Francis Fries of Salem were pioneers in cotton textiles in North Carolina, but the most outstanding manufacturer in the antebellum period was Edwin Michael Holt. With his profits as farmer, merchant, distiller, sawmill owner, and miller, Holt built his cotton mill and water wheel with slave labor in 1837 on Great Alamance Creek and equipped it with machinery from the North. For several years it was only a spinning mill, the yarn from which was marketed at Hillsborough, Fayetteville, and Philadelphia. Looms were installed in the 1840s and sheeting was produced. In 1853 the Holt Mill became the first factory south of the Potomac to manufacture colored cotton cloth, "Alamance plaids," made by power looms. There were twenty-five cotton mills in the state in 1840 and thirty-nine in 1860, when the state ranked first in the South in the number of mills but third in the value of output. Between 1850 and 1860 the number of workers per cotton mill dropped from fifty-eight to forty-five, and the product per mill from $35,000 to less than $27,000. The leading cotton mill counties in 1860 were Cumberland with seven, Alamance and Randolph with five each, and Gaston with three. There were also seven small woolen mills in North Carolina in 1860.

Many of the early cotton mills were operated in connection with "some other form of manufacture or a store, or perhaps both." Miss Elizabeth Y. Webb has noted that many of the mill owners "kept a store or ran a plantation, tannery or grist mill and managed the factory as one of a number of enterprises." Holt's diary reveals that he ran a gristmill along with his cotton factory, distilled whiskey, and also operated several plantations. The Hoke-Bevens mill near Lincolnton was operated in connection with a store, an axe factory, and other mechanical industries. These early mills were "scarcely more than a step beyond the domestic manufacture with which they were so closely connected." Laborers in the mills did not constitute a distinct labor class, but were usually nearby farmers and their families, who frequently continued to live off the farm, drifted into the mill in bad crop years, and went back to the land in more prosperous times.

Iron Manufacturing

Iron manufacturing in North Carolina declined after 1840 because of competition with richer areas in Pennsylvania with better transportation and more efficient methods of manufacture. In the early nineteenth century, under the leadership of Peter Forney, Alexander Brevard, Joseph Graham, and John Fulenwider, there was a sizable development of the iron industry in Lincoln County. And in 1830 there were four forges in operation in Ashe County. But leadership in the industry was retained in Lincoln, where in 1823 ten forges and four furnaces were making nine hundred tons of bar iron and two hundred tons of castings in the forms of skillets, pots, pans, dog-irons, and ovens for the local trade. The state's peak production of eighteen hundred tons of pig iron in 1830 declined to four hundred tons in 1850 and there was also a decline in the output of castings. The industry had developed because of the isolation of the area; it declined in competition with agriculture and with better and cheaper products shipped from the North. But the Census of 1860 noted forty-nine iron works in the state, most of which were in Lincoln, Cherokee, Cleveland, Surry, and Cumberland counties.

The construction of more than six hundred miles of railroad and some five hundred miles of plank roads in the 1850s employed sufficient labor and capital to take rank as an industry. In 1840 North Carolina produced 1,069,410 gallons of distilled and fermented liquors, which was almost ten times the amount produced in South Carolina.

The development of transportation, agriculture, manufacturing, mining, and fishing greatly increased the internal and external commerce of North Carolina, the growth of towns, the expansion of banking facilities, and the size of the nonagricultural population. To a certain degree, however, as already indicated, manufacturing was inhibited rather than stimulated by the expansion of railroads, which not only opened markets of the nation to North Carolina mills, but also made North Carolina a market for the already established and highly efficient mills of New England and the rest of the North. The major part of exports and imports was not through the ports of the state but overland by roads and railroads to and from other states.

The Growth of Towns

The expanding economic life of the state after 1835 was reflected in an increase in the number and size of towns. The towns had been mere villages on navigable waters, at the junctions of inland roads, and at the seats of county government. Wilmington, the leading seaport and railroad terminus, was the largest town, having more than doubled its 1840 population to 9,552 in 1860; New Bern, with 5,432, was second, Fayetteville and Raleigh had populations in excess of 4,000 each; Salisbury and Charlotte, in excess of 2,000 each; and Henderson, Elizabeth City, Hendersonville, Beaufort, Warrenton, Kinston, and Tarboro, in excess of 1,000 each. Of the twenty-five towns listed in the Census of 1860, twelve had populations of less than 1,000 each. Despite the growth of these towns after 1840 as markets and distributing centers, North

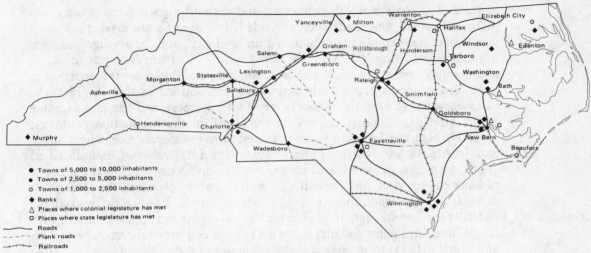

*North Carolina in 1860, Showing Roads, Plank Roads, Railroads,
Cities, Towns, and Banks*

Cartography by the Department of Geography and Earth Sciences
The University of North Carolina at Charlotte

Carolina remained excessively rural with only 2 percent of its population living
in the twenty-five towns. Though farmers bartered and traded with merchants
and relied upon them for credit, the merchants, manufacturers, shippers, and
professional men had increasing need for banks.

Increase in Banks

By 1860 the number of banks had increased to thirty-six. They
were state-chartered with capital stock of less than $7,000,000 deposits of less
than $1,500,000 and loans of bank notes in excess of $12,000,000. Five of the
banks were in Fayetteville, four in Wilmington, three in New Bern, and two
each in Raleigh, Charlotte, and Greensboro.

Though excessively rural in 1860, since 1840 North Carolina had been taking
the first real steps toward a more balanced and diversified economy. Of the total
population there were 87,025 farmers, 63,481 laborers, 27,263 tradesmen, 7,436
professional workers, 3,479 merchants, 1,936 teachers, 1,626 clerks, 1,308
manufacturers, and 4,065 planters (those owning 20 or more slaves each).

Economic Conditions in North Carolina in 1860

Despite notable economic advance after 1840, North Carolina
was still relatively poor and backward in 1860. It was excessively rural and

isolated. The coast was still dangerous and without a good port; ocean commerce was small; the roads and railroads led to out-of-state markets. Money was scarce, trade small, manufacturing undeveloped, and the average standard of income and living low. Most farmers lived too far from railroads to notice much improvement. Agriculture was still retarded by poor transportation, backward methods, crude tools, ignorance, and soil exhaustion. In 1860 the assessed value of land for taxation was $4.41 per acre and the census value $6.03. North Carolina stood first in the South in the production of honey; second in oats, rye, hay, and sweet potatoes; third in tobacco, rice, wheat, hogs, and Irish potatoes; fourth in sheep and in the total value of manufactured goods; fifth in corn, wool, and cattle; sixth in milk cows and in the amount of bank capital stock and deposits; seventh in butter; eighth in the total value of real and personal property; and ninth in cotton. Free labor worked for virtually the lowest wages in the United States—about ten dollars a month with board for a farm hand and fifty cents a day for a common laborer. Low wealth and aversion to taxation restricted the revenue and the ability of local and state governments to render public services. Their total revenue from taxation in 1860 was about $1 million—approximately one dollar per capita for the entire population. Despite its striking economic development before 1860, North Carolina made little improvement in its rank among the states because most of the other states were experiencing equal or greater development.

Chapter 27

AN INTELLECTUAL
AWAKENING, 1835-1860

State System of Common Schools

The greatest social and educational achievement in antebellum North Carolina was the adoption in 1839 of a statewide publicly supported system of free common schools for all white children. Each year after 1840, for the first time in the history of the state, a large portion of the white children went to school to learn such basic skills as reading, writing, and arithmetic. The school system was a disappointment during the 1840s but, as first State Superintendent of Common Schools from 1853 to 1865, Calvin H. Wiley revolutionized the system and made it a credit to North Carolina. As told in an earlier chapter, he stimulated interest and faithfulness among the county boards of education, improved the character and quality of teachers, and brought about more effective organization of the schools. Among the significant changes and improvements were the certification of teachers after examination, improvement in textbooks, better buildings and equipment, the establishment of school libraries, the beginning of graded schools, the formation of teachers' library associations, the organization of the Educational Association of North Carolina, and the publication of the *North Carolina Journal of Education* (1857).

From 1853 to 1860 the number of school districts increased from about 3,000 to 3,500; the number of schools, from 2,500 to 2,854; the number of children in school, from about 100,000 to 118,000; the number of "certified teachers" from 800 to 2,286, and the total school expenditures from $150,000 to $278,000, of which about $100,000 was supplied from local taxes and the remainder from the State Literary Fund. There was much popular indifference to public education, but Wiley allayed opposition, improved the system, and inspired public confidence. His statement that "North Carolina has the start of all her Southern sisters in educational matters" was no exaggeration, and the reduction in the percentage of illiterate voters from 30 percent in 1840 to 23 percent in 1860 was one indication of the state's progress in education. But many of the people were still indifferent; most school buildings were poor and inadequately furnished; the teachers were mostly men unfit for the work; salaries of teachers averaged about $25 per month; the school term was less than four months; textbooks and equipment were scarce and inadequate; the curriculum included only reading, writing, arithmetic, grammar, and geography; and the pupils of all ages studied and recited aloud in the same room. Nearly all of the schools were one-teacher schools. Since the chief support of the system was the proceeds of the Literary Fund, in the nature of an endowment fund, most of which had been granted by the federal government, the average North Carolinian before 1860 was not habituated to the payment of taxes for public education.

Academies and Other Private Schools

Private schools which charged tuition continued to minister to the educational needs of a small group. The subscription, or "old field school," organized by some parent or more often by a teacher, operated irregularly for perhaps the three winter months in villages and rural communities where no public school was in operation or where parents were opposed to or did not wish to send their children to the common school. Private academies, chartered by the legislature and governed by a board of trustees, were more stable and offered a more thorough and advanced type of education than the subscription and common schools. From 1800 to 1860 the General Assembly chartered 287 academies, most of which were short-lived. At some time during the period almost every county had one or more academies, some of which operated as long as ten months a year. The counties that led in the number of incorporated academies were Edgecombe, fifteen; Robeson, thirteen; Wake, twelve; and Anson, Cumberland, Franklin, and Orange, ten each. The academies obtained most of their income from tuition fees charged for the subjects taken. These fees were seldom higher than twenty-five dollars a term—usually two or three months of the year. Some academies obtained money from lotteries, more than forty of which were authorized by the legislature before 1835, at which time lotteries became illegal in the state.

Most of the academies had adequate buildings and equipment, employed superior teachers whose salaries ranged from $400 to $1,000 a year, and often attracted students from other communities who generally boarded and roomed in private homes. As a rule the academies divided the students into classes, and emphasized classical instruction in the more advanced subjects of mathematics, Latin, Greek, rhetoric, logic, moral and natural philosophy, and astronomy. Great stress was placed on memory work, or learning "by heart."

The academy was primarily a school for white boys. Of the 127 chartered before 1825, only 13 were for girls. There were no academies for Negro children, though the well-known preacher and teacher, John Chavis taught white children in Raleigh in a day school and Negroes in an evening school.

The academies emphasized the moral training of students, had many strict rules governing conduct, and followed the current educational philosophy, "Spare the rod and spoil the child." Stokes Community Academy, for instance, had forty-six rules, the infractions of which brought corporal punishment ranging from one to ten "lashes." "Coming to school with dirty face and hands" brought two lashes; "Gambeling or Beting at Schools," four lashes; "Telling Lyes," seven lashes; and "Playing Cards at School," ten lashes.

Most students who went to college or to the state university were prepared by the academies and most of the academy teachers were trained at the University of North Carolina, Yale, Princeton, or William and Mary. The Census of 1860 noted 434 academies and other private schools in North Carolina, with 661 teachers and 13,169 pupils. The "common schools" enrolled nine times as many children as the private schools.

Despite the fact that North Carolina had about 3,500 public and private schools, illiteracy was widespread. In the South only Virginia, with a much larger population, had more illiterates. In 1860 there were nearly 70,000 white illiterates over twenty years of age in a total white population of 629,942. Virtually all Negroes, who comprised 27 percent of the total population, and many whites under twenty years of age were also illiterate. Still the illiteracy rate had shown a marked decrease since 1840.

Special Schools: Law, Medicine, Military, and Manual Labor

At various times and places in antebellum North Carolina there were schools of special types. Archibald D. Murphey, James Iredell, William H. Battle, John Louis Taylor, Leonard Henderson, and Richmond M. Pearson were among the prominent lawyers and judges who conducted well-known law schools. Though most of the doctors were trained in the North, particularly at the University of Pennsylvania, an occasional doctor offered instruction in medicine. As early as 1808 Dr. Joseph Hawkins "established a medical school" at Middleburg, and five years later Dr. John Poytress opened a "private infirmary" at Beaufort, but little is known about these pioneer efforts in medical education. Elijah Graves conducted a Farmers' School near Chapel Hill, and Murphey, D. H. Bingham, Carter Jones, Daniel Harvey Hill, and others conducted military schools that were ordinary academies offering some military training. Another variation of the academy was the manual labor school, where students were required to do manual as well as mental labor, thus earning part of the cost of their education. Manual labor was not popular with the students or successful financially for the schools. In some of the towns there were teachers of penmanship, shorthand, bookkeeping, music, art, and dancing.

The quarter-century before 1860 was memorable for three parallel developments in the realm of higher education. The University of North Carolina grew into one of the large, well-known universities in the South and nation; the leading religious denominations established colleges in the state; and the first colleges for women were founded.

The University of North Carolina

Chartered in 1789, its first building begun in 1793, and opened to students in 1795, the University of North Carolina at Chapel Hill was the oldest and for nearly half a century the only institution of higher learning in the state. Without any regular maintenance appropriations from the state government until 1881, dependent upon tuition fees and escheats—which were difficult to collect and unpopular with the public—early dominated by Presbyterian and Federalist influences, distrusted as a center of aristocracy and conservatism by some, and as a center of radicalism and agnosticism by others, criticized, on the one hand, for the severity of its discipline and, on the other, for its laxity and improper student conduct, and damned by some Republicans as a "school for the rich," the university under its first president, Joseph Caldwell, 1804–12 and 1816–35 (Robert H. Chapman served as president from 1812 to 1816), was small, poverty-stricken, and of limited influence. The Jeffersonian Republicans took charge in 1804 by vesting the election of new trustees in the legislature instead of in the Board of Trustees itself.

Before 1815 the University was a "typical classical college," emphasizing the study of Greek, Latin, and mathematics—subjects that comprised a "gentleman's education." After 1815 more emphasis was placed on natural sciences and studies for public service. Before 1835 Caldwell achieved public confidence as an educational leader and public-spirited citizen. He built up the library, assembled an able faculty, including Denison Olmsted in chemistry and geology and Elisha Mitchell in mathematics, and broadened the curriculum to include natural sciences, literature, and history. A new era began in 1835 with the election to the presidency of Governor David L. Swain, prominent western Whig leader. Swain popularized the institution, built up the enrollment from 104 in 1835 to 456 from many states in 1859, founded the North Carolina Historical Society in 1844, which began the collection of documents relating to the history of the state and shifted the emphasis of the state's first permanent literary magazine, the *University of North Carolina Magazine,* to biography and historical articles on North Carolina. He also added law and modern languages and agricultural chemistry to the curriculum and made the university preeminently a training school for public service. Its alumni included one president of the United States, one vice-president, seven cabinet officials, ten United States senators, forty-one representatives in Congress, fifteen state governors, and many state judges and legislators. From 1814, when a university alumnus first became governor, until 1972, thirty-one of the forty-eight governors of

North Carolina had studied at Chapel Hill.

Wake Forest Founded by the Baptists

To increase the facilities for higher education, to provide a more religious atmosphere than that of the state university in which their young men might be educated, and to train students for the ministry, the religious denominations led by the Baptists established several colleges.

There was a struggle within Baptist ranks over the founding of a college. The Primitive Baptists were opposed to an educated ministry and considered religious education inconsistent with the "divine call to Ministry." They also questioned the state's right to charter a church school, contending that this might give the state the right to control the administration and teaching. The Primitive Baptists split from the main body of the church, the Separate or Missionary Baptists, in 1830, and on March 26 of that year, the latter body organized the Baptist State Convention, with Patrick Dowd as president and Samuel Wait as secretary. The Baptist State Convention urged the establishment of a college, and in 1833 it chartered the Baptist Literary Institute. Professor George W. Paschal, the historian of Wake Forest College, wrote: "Some of the strongest friends of the charter were alumni of the University of North Carolina. Among them were William D. Moseley, the Speaker of the Senate. . . . But for the active support of these men the bill of incorporation would not have passed. No Senator who was a university alumnus opposed the bill." Moseley's affirmative vote broke a tie in the Senate and allowed the bill of incorporation to become law.

The new institution, located in the forest of Wake County, opened with twenty-five students in 1834 under the principalship of the Reverend Samuel Wait. The school began with a combination of manual labor and literary studies, but there was much student opposition to the former, as evidenced by the drop in enrollment from 142 to 51 between 1836 and 1838. In the latter year the legislature chartered Wake Forest College, and the unpopular manual labor feature was abandoned. As a classical school with a liberal arts curriculum Wake Forest prospered under the presidency of Wait and of W. M. Wingate after 1854. An endowment fund was started, which reached $47,500 by 1860; the faculty was expanded and improved; and the enrollment reached 127 in 1856 and then dropped to 76 four years later.

Davidson College Established by the Presbyterians

The Presbyterians were the first denomination to attempt the establishment of a college; they had been responsible for the founding of the short-lived Queen's College, in the 1770s and individual Presbyterians had been prominent in founding and heading the University of North Carolina. But the

Presbyterian Church was not successful in founding a permanent college until 1837, when Davidson College, named in honor of General William Lee Davidson, a hero of the American Revolution, was opened with sixty-five students as a manual labor school by the Concord Presbytery, and under the presidency of the Reverend R. H. Morrison. In 1838 the General Assembly chartered the college. The elimination of the unpopular manual labor feature and its conversion in 1841 to a classical college of the Princeton type resulted in its growth to six professors and 112 students in 1860. It had just spent $1,000 for laboratory apparatus, and classes were meeting in Chambers Hall, "the most imposing college building in the state," built from funds received from the Maxwell Chambers legacy of $200,000.

Trinity College Begun by the Methodists

Not until 1859 did the North Carolina Conference of the Methodist Episcopal Church have a college. About 1838 or 1839 a Methodist minister, the Reverend Brantley York, opened a school in the Methodist-Quaker community of Trinity in Randolph County. This school, which has been considered the forerunner of Duke University, was described in York's autobiography as a "schoolhouse built of round logs, and covered with common boards. The floor was laid with puncheons and slabs. The chimney was made of wood with a little or no clay in it. . . . The hearth was dirt, and the whole in bad repair; for, when it rained, it was with difficulty that the books and paper could be kept dry. The house was entirely too small to accommodate the students, consequently we were necessitated to erect a brush arbor in front of the south door, and part of the students were under the arbor and part in the house."

In spite of its inadequate facilities the school grew and was chartered as Union Institute in 1841. York retired the next year and under the energetic administration of Braxton Craven the Institute began to take on new life. Methodist ministerial students were admitted without charge and in 1851 the institution was rechartered as Normal College "with right to certificate teachers" for the common schools. But there was not enough demand for this type of training and in 1858 the school was transferred to the Methodist Conference and the teacher-training program was abandoned. The institution was rechartered in 1859 as Trinity College, with Braxton Craven as president. The next year it had a faculty of six and a student body of 194.

New Garden Boarding School (Guilford College) Founded by the Quakers

Under the auspices of the North Carolina Yearly Meeting of the Society of Friends, New Garden Boarding School in Guilford County was chartered in 1833. Unlike the University and the denominational colleges, this school was coeducational from the beginning, although the boys and girls recited in separate classrooms. The school opened in 1837 in an imposing brick building, with fifty students, twenty-five of each sex. In 1889 the name of the institution was changed to Guilford College.

Other Denominational Colleges

Among other colleges for men chartered before 1860 were Catawba College at Newton in 1851, Louisburg College in 1857, and North Carolina College at Mount Pleasant in 1859; these were under the influence of the German Reformed, the Methodists, and the Lutherans, respectively.

The Education of Women

Another manifestation of an intellectual awakening was the establishment of institutions of learning for women, though the education of women lagged far behind that of men in antebellum North Carolina. In the common and subscription schools boys and girls were taught in the same classes, but this was the practice in the academies only in the beginners' classes whose students were under ten years of age. Some academies added female departments, and several academies exclusively for girls were established. Salem Female Academy (later Salem College), opened by the Moravians in 1802, was the first boarding school for girls and soon it became one of the best schools for women in the South.

The idea was prevalent that the chief end of education for women, which was skill and grace in the home and a knowledge of household arts, could best be achieved by studies in novel-reading, needlework, dancing, music, drawing, and painting, supplemented by the elementary branches of knowledge. Some academies, however, reflected the growing shift in public thinking by offering to girls substantially the same curriculum as to boys. After 1800 the academy gradually superseded the subscription school for the education of women, but a college education was not available to them—in spite of the statement in the charter of the University of North Carolina about the education of the "rising generation." From the 1830s women's colleges were chartered and ambitious female academies adopted the name "college," though their courses of study did not always justify the title, and a teacher in one of these colleges declared that "the higher female education in North Carolina is not high." The Methodists opened Greensboro Female College in 1838 and Davenport Female College at Lenoir in 1858. Saint Mary's School at Raleigh was founded under Episcopal influences by the Reverend Aldert Smedes in 1842. Chowan Baptist Female Institute was established at Murfreesboro in 1848 and Oxford Female College, sponsored by the Baptists, in 1851. Floral College at Maxton, Statesville Female College and Peace Female Institute at Raleigh were begun by the

Presbyterians in 1841, 1856, and 1857, respectively.

Available statistics for higher education are not altogether reliable, but Governor John W. Ellis in 1860 noted that from 1840 to 1860 the number of male colleges had increased from three to six, the number of female colleges from one to thirteen, the number of students in male colleges from 158 to 900, and the number in female colleges from 125 to 1,500. The United States Census of 1860 reported sixteen colleges in North Carolina with ninety-four teachers and 1,540 students.

Newspapers

Expanding educational opportunity and improved transportation facilities created a greater market for newspapers and magazines. The state was the burial ground of a large number of newspapers whose existence had been brief. Only one newspaper, the *Raleigh Register,* was in continuous existence from 1799 to 1860. The number of newspapers increased slowly from ten in 1810 to twenty-one in 1820; to twenty-seven in 1840, fifty-one in 1850, and seventy-four—including eight dailies—in 1860. The annual circulation of all newspapers rose from 416,000 copies in 1810 to over 2,000,000 in 1850 and to nearly 5,000,000 in 1860. The newspapers were generally small, four-page weeklies; the first regular semiweekly appeared in 1823, the first triweekly in 1846, and the first dailies, the *Raleigh Register* in 1850 and the Wilmington *Daily Journal* in 1851. In all of the papers the type was set by hand and the printing was by hand presses until after 1852, when the first steam press appeared in the state. In 1860 five paper mills in North Carolina were supplying paper made of rags.

The newspapers emphasized state, national, and foreign, rather than local, news. The front page and the headings and advertisements were inconspicuous; the editorials, illustrations, and cartoons, few. Generally the papers were political organs whose major emphasis was on national politics and whose partisan fervor and abuse in election years sometimes involved the editors in fights or duels. Among the oldest and most influential newspapers were the *Raleigh Register,* founded by Joseph Gales in 1799; the *Hillsborough Recorder,* established by Dennis Heartt in 1820; the *Western Carolinian* (Salisbury) founded in 1820; the *Fayetteville Observer,* with which Edward J. Hale was associated from 1825; the *Tarborough Press,* established by George Howard in 1826; the *Greensborough Patriot,* begun in 1826; the *North Carolina Standard,* established by Philo White in 1834 and purchased in 1843 by William W. Holden, who soon became the ablest and most influential editor in the state; and the *Wilmington Journal,* founded by David Fulton in 1844.

Magazines and Other Periodicals

Several literary magazines were launched, but only a few survived for a decade. The *Carolina Law Repository* was published in Raleigh from 1813 to 1816. The state's "first literary magazine," the *Harbinger,* published "under the supervision of the Professors of the University" as a weekly newspaper devoted to "literature, science, and general intelligence," appeared on July 5, 1833, and after a precarious existence was discontinued in 1835. From July, 1833, to October, 1835, Benjamin Swain published *Man of Business* (at New Salem and then Greensboro), a thirty-six-page monthly law magazine, in order "to render every man his own counsellor in matters of ordinary business." In 1838 Leonidas B. Lemay, the nine-year-old son of the editor of the *Raleigh Star,* published the first number of the *Raleigh Microcosm,* devoted to "the flowers of Literature, Science, Commerce, and Agriculture." The *University of North Carolina Magazine,* established by the senior class of the University of North Carolina in March, 1844, and suspended later that year to be resumed in 1852, became the state's first permanent literary magazine. Several agricultural journals, mentioned earlier, were short-lived but indicative of a movement for agricultural progress and reform. The *North Carolina Journal of Education* (1857), edited by State Superintendent Calvin H. Wiley, and the *Medical Journal of North Carolina* (1858), edited by Dr. Edward Warren, were outstanding professional magazines. Temperance papers and religious periodicals appeared for the first time, the most notable "church papers" being the Baptist *Biblical Recorder* (1835) and the Methodist *North Carolina Christian Advocate* (1855). The *North Carolina Presbyterian* began publication in 1858 and the Episcopal *Church Intelligencer* two years later. The *Spirit of the Age* was the only temperance journal that ran for more than a decade.

Though North Carolinians were sometimes called "an unreading people" because of widespread illiteracy and semiliteracy, the dissemination of educational opportunity and a broadening intellectual horizon resulted in the beginnings of native authorship and literature. The almanac, containing information on farming, public affairs, household medicine, and other subjects, and the pamphlet, containing political and literary addresses, biographical sketches, and sermons, were the most numerous, cheapest, and most popular forms of printed matter. Among the better-known and longer-lived almanacs were *Gales' North-Carolina Almanack* (Raleigh, 1815–38), *Henderson's and Boylan's Almanack* (Raleigh, 1813–23), and John Christian Blum's *Farmer's and Planter's Almanac,* published in Salem after 1828. Hundreds of pamphlets, especially those printed after 1835, were an important index and contribution to the literary and cultural life of the times. Joseph Caldwell's *Numbers of Carlton* (1828) and *Letters on Popular Education* (1832) probably excited more interest and exerted greater influence than any other pamphlet literature. Addresses of most of the prominent public figures in the state were printed and distributed as pamphlets, and were not without effect in promoting state pride.

History and Biography

Historical and biographical writing loomed large in antebellum North Carolina. Several general histories of the state appeared: Hugh Williamson, *History of North Carolina* (2 volumes, Philadelphia, 1812); François Xavier Martin, *The History of North Carolina from the Earliest Period* (2 volumes, New Orleans, 1829); John H. Wheeler, *Historical Sketches of North Carolina to 1851* (Philadelphia, 1851), which had a reputed sale of ten thousand copies; and Francis Lister Hawks, *History of North Carolina* (2 volumes, Fayetteville, 1857–58). Plans were also made for the copying of North Carolina documents in English depositories and for the publication of a documentary history of the state. Joseph Seawell ("Shocco") Jones produced two books in defense of the authenticity of the Mecklenburg Declaration of Independence. Many political and military leaders were memorialized in biographical pamphlets and volumes, the most notable of which were *A Sketch of the Life and Character of the Reverend David Caldwell* (Greensboro, 1842) by Eli W. Caruthers and *The Life and Correspondence of James Iredell* (2 vols., New York, 1857–58) by G. J. McRee. At the university, the North Carolina Historical Society, which held its first meeting on June 5, 1844, and the *University Magazine* stimulated interest and writing in North Carolina history. One of the most famous—or notorious—books in the United States was *The Impending Crisis of the South: How To Meet It* (New York, 1857), an attack on slavery written by Hinton Rowan Helper, native of the state. This book was used as a campaign document by the national Republican party in 1860 and reputedly sold several million copies. Though historical writing fell short of the standards of modern scholarship, it had educational, cultural, and patriotic value.

North Carolina educators were beginning to write and publish textbooks for public schools and colleges, the most famous of which was Calvin H. Wiley's *North Carolina Reader* (1851), used in the common schools.

Humor and Fiction

Hamilton C. Jones, John C. Bunting, H. E. Taliaferro, and Johnson Jones Hooper wrote humorous works which attracted considerable attention. Jones's "Cousin Sally Dillard" and "The Quarter Race in Kentucky, or Col. Jones' Fight" received national acclaim, and one reviewer called Bunting's *Life as It Is, or the Writings of Our Mose* "the most amusing work that has been issued in half a century." *Harper's Monthly Magazine* declared Taliaferro's *Fisher's River (North Carolina) Scenes and Characters* "one of the half dozen clever books of American character and humor." Hooper, a native of North Carolina, wrote his famous *Adventures of Captain Simon Suggs* while living in Alabama, but his "quips and quiddities" brought distinction to his native state.

North Carolina drama, fiction, and poetry also began to appear in the antebellum period. Congressman Lemuel Sawyer published two plays, *Blackbeard,* a four-act comedy (1824), and *The Wreck of Honor,* a tragedy. Robert Strange's *Eoneguski,* a story about the Cherokees (1839), and Calvin H. Wiley's *Alamance* (1847) and *Roanoke* (1849) were the best examples of historical fiction. The state's most famous poets were Mary Bayard Clarke, who published *Wood-Notes* (1854), a two-volume anthology of North Carolina poetry including many of her own poems; William Gaston, who wrote "The Old North State"; Adolphus W. Mangum, author of *Myrtle Leaves;* Sarah J. C. Whittlesey, who wrote *Heart Drops from Memory's Urn;* William Henry Rhodes, author of *The Indian Gallows;* and perhaps most famous of all, George Moses Horton, a Negro slave living in Chatham County about ten miles from Chapel Hill, who published three books of poetry. *The Hope of Liberty* (Raleigh, 1829) was the first book published by a Negro in the South and was the first poetic protest by a slave against his status. Horton wrote:

> Must I dwell in Slavery's night
> And all pleasure take its flight
> Far beyond my feeble sight?
>   Forever?

Horton's other books of poetry were *Poetical Works* (1845) and *Naked Genius* (1865). When the Civil War ended, Horton was freed, and when Northern troops came through Chapel Hill in the spring of 1865, he went to Philadelphia with one of the officers. He lived there until his death in 1883.

Though antebellum North Carolina produced no leading poet, dramatist, or historian, and no distinguished literary or agricultural magazine, it did develop a pioneer literary group which marked the beginnings of native authorship and literature of which the state was proud.

Increased wealth and leisure, expanding educational facilities and postal service, the railroad, and the telegraph, which was first available in North Carolina in 1848, facilitated more extensive travel, communication, and intellectual intercourse.

General Educational and Cultural Conditions in the State in 1860

With expanding systems of public and private schools, a growing university, new denominational colleges for men and women, an increase in the number and quality of newspapers and periodicals, and the beginnings of a native authorship and literature, North Carolina, though still backward culturally, experienced an intellectual awakening between 1835 and 1860. After a generation of humiliation over the nationally publicized backwardness of North Carolina the state's public men, newspapers, and writers aggressively boasted of the state's superiority and progress in economic, political, and cultural development, and North Carolina began to acquire a different and more favorable reputation in the nation. Guion Johnson, in her *Ante-Bellum North Carolina,* has summarized the situation very well: "Back of this aggressive spirit which could point with pride to 'the first state university in the Union,' 'the best public school system in the South,' 'the most elegant state capitol in the country,' more than a million dollars invested in manufacturing, a press which had doubled its numbers in the fifties; 'a climate more salubrious than that of any other state in the Union,' 'a soil as plentiful and varied in its agricultural and mineral stores as any in the world,' 'a sturdy, sober, industrious population,' there was a tense localism which forty years of humiliation had produced." The educated political and business leaders had led an ignorant, poverty-ridden people to adopt a program of internal improvements, public education, and social reform, which led to a new spirit of pride in the state.

Chapter 28

RELIGION AND SOCIETY
IN ANTEBELLUM DAYS

Joseph Caldwell, writing in 1797, was surprised to find religion so little in vogue in North Carolina, and Eli Caruthers, a Presbyterian minister, declared, "Men of education and especially the young men of the country thought it a mark of independence to scoff at the Bible and professors of religion." By the opening of the nineteenth century the Deistic influences and writings of the Age of Enlightenment and the Era of the French Revolution had made the small, educated upper class in North Carolina and the nation indifferent or openly skeptical toward orthodox religion, and only a small fraction of the population was actively identified with the churches. Yet "Eusebius," writing in the *Edenton Gazette,* September 29, 1809, maintained that North Carolina "abounded with people, poor but pious, whose religion was their dearest and almost their only patrimony." And before 1860 the various Protestant denominations expanded their organizations and evangelical activities with such success that a large part of the common people was brought into church membership and attendance, and the educated upper class largely ceased to be openly Deistic and skeptical and became church communicants.

The Protestant Episcopal Church

Handicapped by the unpopularity of the established Anglican Church in the colonial period, by its appeal to the aristocratic upper class, and by the Tory leanings of the church and its disruption during the American Revolution, when most of its clergy quietly withdrew from the colony, it grew slowly in North Carolina. The Protestant Episcopal Church in the United States was organized at Philadelphia in 1789, but for many years thereafter it was unorganized in North Carolina. Ministers occasionally held services, and an abortive attempt was made at Tarboro in 1790 to organize the church in the state. But not until 1817 did the Episcopalians organize the Diocese of

415

North Carolina and not until 1823 did John Stark Ravenscroft become its first bishop. Two years later the new bishop wrote concerning the Episcopal Church, "Political feelings were associated with its very name, which operated as a complete bar to any useful or comfortable exercise of duty, by the very few clergymen, perhaps not more than three or four." In 1830 there were eleven ministers and thirty-one congregations in the state, mostly in the East. The second bishop in North Carolina, Levi Silliman Ives, came to the state from New York in 1831 and soon won the affection of his diocese, but his leanings toward Roman Catholicism created dissension. In May, 1853, Bishop Ives renounced the communion of his church and became a Roman Catholic. The Episcopal Church in the state was demoralized by Ives's action: "Her chief shepherd had deserted the fold; he who had for twenty years served in her sanctuary, and had taught, for the greater part of the time, her pure faith to her children, had apostatized from that faith to a false and corrupt communion." Bishop Thomas Atkinson sought with some success to heal the dissension caused by his predecessor's "disaffection," to offer a broader appeal to the masses, and to enlarge the church's membership. By 1860 the number of clergy had increased to forty-four, the number of congregations to fifty-three, and the number of members to 3,036. But the Episcopal Church was far more influential than its small number of communicants would indicate. It drew its membership mainly from the well-to-do, aristocratic planters, professional men, business leaders, and public officials, who lived chiefly in the east and in towns. Their church buildings, located largely in the towns, were the finest in the state, averaging in value nearly $4,000 each in 1860. Avoiding revivals, camp meetings, and emotional devices, esteeming formal services and an educated ministry, appealing to the more aristocratic, educated, and wealthy people in the towns and the plantation East, the Episcopal Church possessed wealth and influence but was unpopular with the common people. Except in the larger western towns, its influence was not great beyond the Coastal Plain.

The Baptists

With its democratic government, simple form of service, emphasis on revivals and emotional religion, and indifference toward an educated ministry, the Baptist Church made rapid strides among the small farmers of the rural districts throughout the state and had more members than any other church in 1860—65,000 in 780 congregations scattered throughout the state. From about 1750 to 1830 doctrinal differences and dissension and the lack of a central authority handicapped the Baptists. The conservative, rigidly Calvinistic Regular (Primitive) Baptists separated from the evangelical Separate (Missionary) Baptists in 1830. Thereafter the Separate Baptists, working through their State Convention, organized at Greenville on March 26, 1830, became more progressive and evangelistic, sponsored the founding of Wake Forest

College to provide an educated ministry, early provided higher education for women, and rapidly outgrew the more conservative Primitive Baptists. Of the 780 churches in 1860, with an average value of $620, only thirty-seven were Primitive Baptist churches and all except about thirty of all Baptist churches were located in rural communities.

The Methodists

The Baptists were hard-pressed in North Carolina by the rapid growth of Methodism. As has been indicated earlier, the Methodist Church evolved from Methodist "societies" within the Anglican Church. Not until 1784, in a meeting at Baltimore, was the Methodist Episcopal Church in the United States organized as a separate denomination, when Francis Asbury and Thomas Coke were chosen as "Superintendents" (a title soon changed to "Bishops"). The first annual conference of the new church was held at Green Hill's home in Franklin County the next year. At first the new church encountered opposition because its ministers criticized slavery, preached to Negroes, and appealed to the emotions. But its efficient organization of ministers, presiding elders, and bishops; its aggressive and constant evangelism; its use of circuit riders; its shift to the defense of slavery; its disregard of ritual; and its emphasis on camp meetings, humanitarianism, and religious reform, prayer, and education won converts and prestige. Internal quarrels led to schisms and the formation of the Christian, Methodist Protestant, and Wesleyan Methodist churches. Methodism rivaled the Baptists in popular appeal. So rapid was its spread in all parts of the state among the common people that in 1860 it had 966 congregations with churches whose average value was $650, and 61,000 members. On the basis of its efficient organization, its youth, and its rapid spread, it perhaps surpassed the Baptists in prestige.

The Presbyterians

The Presbyterian was the third-strongest church in antebellum North Carolina. It had been organized in the colony long before the American Revolution, but its coldness, rigid discipline, austere Calvinism, emphasis on an educated ministry, and indifference toward evangelism offered little appeal to the common people and resulted in slow growth until about 1850. Then, under the stimulus of competition and with a greater emphasis on evangelism, missions, and education, the tempo of growth increased. But in 1860 it had only 15,053 members in 182 congregations with churches whose average value was $2,143. Its membership was drawn mainly from the gentry and middle class, and its chief strength was in the towns of the state and in the Piedmont and Cape Fear Valley where Scottish stock was pronounced. With a prosperous membership and an educated ministry, the Presbyterian Church enjoyed more prestige than its membership would indicate.

Other Denominations

Other religious sects in 1860 with less than 5,000 members each were the Society of Friends, or Quakers, chiefly in Guilford, Randolph, and Chatham counties; the Lutherans and German Reformed churches among the German stock in the Piedmont, with the Lutherans having 38 churches and 3,942 members; the Moravians in the region of Salem; the Disciples of Christ or Christian Church, chiefly in the East; and the Roman Catholics and Jews.

There were 2,117 organized congregations in the ten leading denominations, and the total white and Negro membership was 157,015. Approximately one-half of the adult white population belonged to the churches. Four-fifths of all church members in North Carolina were Baptists and Methodists.

The Great Revival and Camp Meetings

The expansion of church influence and membership among the common people was largely because of the Great Revival, which swept over North Carolina and the United States periodically from about 1800 to 1860. The revival spirit was fostered chiefly by the Methodist and Baptist churches and to some degree by the Presbyterian. Conspicuous was the camp meeting, which attained its highest development among the Methodists. Hundreds of people gathered and camped in tents or log shelters as long as the meeting lasted—frequently a week. From a crude platform the preachers, often un-learned, but powerful, inspired orators and masters of mass psychology, ad-dressed the people seated outdoors on crude seats and usually excited some of the more simple-minded, nervous, and neurotic to shout for joy, jump, jerk, roll on the ground or fall in a faint. The highly emotional sermons, the illiteracy and superstition in isolated rural life were some of the factors of social psy-chology that accounted for the phenomena in the camp meeting and revival.

Nature of Church Work and Influence

The churches in antebellum North Carolina were powerful agen-cies for benevolence, religion, conservatism, social control, and recreation. In different degrees, and with differing success, they promoted home and foreign missions, Bible and tract societies for the distribution of religious literature, the movement for Sunday schools, Sabbath observance, the temperance move-ment, education, and poor relief. Some of the churches tried their members for drunkenness, quarreling, sexual immorality, "disorderly behavior," "neg-lecting church service," "being out of the way," fighting, and other actions that fell short of accepted standards of conduct, though the church courts had lost some of their sternness and effectiveness before 1860. They provided the chief opportunity outside the home for the activity of women. Denominational colleges and academies for men and women were established to provide religious education for ministers and laymen. The church services ministered to the social as well as the religious needs of the people who thronged to them.

The Churches and Slavery

Early in the nineteenth century the churches tended to be critical of slavery, but gradually they shifted to strong defense of the institution and worked for the amelioration of the lot of the slave. The issue of slavery split the Methodist Church into Northern and Southern branches in 1844, and the Baptist churches in 1845. On slavery as well as other social, economic, and moral problems, the churches generally championed the prevailing local attitude.

It would be difficult to overestimate the influence of the churches upon the religious, moral, and social life of antebellum North Carolina. Thousands of people looked to their Protestant ministers as mentors in temporal as well as in spiritual affairs.

Dominant Social Characteristics of North Carolina

So slow is the process of the social evolution of a people that the notable development of wealth, trade, education, political democracy, and religious organization after 1835 had not radically changed the pattern of North Carolina life by 1860. Though somewhat weakened or undermined after 1835, the dominant social characteristics of landlocked, isolated, divided, uneducated, backward, rural North Carolina continued to be (1) provincialism, or an undue emphasis on local affairs growing out of the basic geographic conditions that kept the various parts of the state more isolated from each other than from neighboring states, and also kept the majority of the people from contacts with the outside world; (2) conservatism, or slowness to adopt new ideas and to make changes in government, institutions, and ways of life; (3) sectionalism, or lack of unity, grounded in the geographic, social, and economic differences of East and West; (4) individualism, with overemphasis on individual rights, as shown by unbridled freedom of speech and by resort to physical combat or the duel to settle disputes; (5) impatience toward the orderly process of legal and social control and cooperation; (6) superstition, or a prevailing belief in signs, spells, spirits, and the supernatural; (7) and social stratification, or a division of the population into social and economic classes.

In 1860 North Carolina ranked twelfth in the Union, with a total population of 992,622 (968,068 rural and 24,554 urban), which included 331,059 Negro slaves, 30,463 free Negroes, and 1,168 Indians. The non-native residents numbered slightly less than 25,000, while nearly 300,000 natives were living in other states. The white population was predominantly English with large elements of Scottish and German stocks. The population was heterogeneous, consisting of diverse social, racial, religious and economic groups or classes.

Economic Diversity of the People

Diversity of economic status is indicated by the 1860 census report on occupations in North Carolina. As stated earlier in another connection, there were 87,025 farmers; 63,481 laborers; 27,263 tradesmen; 7,436 professional workers; 3,479 merchants; 1,626 clerks; 1,936 teachers; 1,308 manufacturers; and 4,065 planters (those owning 20 or more slaves each). The upper economic group of planters, merchants, professional men, and manufacturers composed only 6 percent of the total. Agriculture was the chief occupation, and North Carolina was predominantly a state of small farms. Only 311 farms were larger than one thousand acres, while 46,300 were less than 100 acres each, and 2,050 were smaller than ten acres. The average for the whole state was 316 acres. Of every hundred farms in North Carolina, 10 had less than 20 acres, 41 less than 50 acres, 69 less than 100 acres, and only 2 had more than 500 acres. Guion Johnson, in *Ante-Bellum North Carolina,* truly says: "If occupations, land, and slaves be taken as indices of wealth, it is evident that the average per capita wealth in the State was not large. There were few overgrown estates, and the majority of the inhabitants lived upon the produce of their own labors."

E. J. Hale, writing in 1853, declared: "Everybody here knows that very few of the present slaveowners . . . inherited their slaves or other property . . . many began life with nothing, and have made their own fortunes. The man with wealth who inherited it, is the exception. The poor man who made his fortune, is the almost universal rule."

Most of the state's agricultural population consisted, as in the past, of poor, hardworking, nonslaveholding small farmers and farm laborers and tenants who owned no land. Though North Carolina was a slave state, the majority of North Carolina whites never owned slaves at any time. The percentage of slaveholding families in the state was 31 percent in 1790, 26.8 percent in 1850, and 27.7 percent in 1860. The total number of slaveholding families in 1860 was 34,658, divided as follows:

Number of Slaves	Families
1 to 3	16,071
5 to 19	14,522
20 to 49	3,321
50 to 99	611
over 100	133

Of every hundred slaveholding families, 46 owned less than 5 slaves each; 71 owned less than 10; 88 owned less than 20; and only 2 owned as many as 50. In the entire state, according to the United States Census of 1860, only 133 planters owned 100 or more slaves, 15 owned 200 or more, 4 owned 300 or more; and not one owned as many as 500.

Social Stratification

Though social stratification was not so rigid that persons could not rise or fall in the social scale, six reasonably distinct classes or groups were present in North Carolina in the generation preceding 1860. These classes were based primarily on racial and economic differences arising partly from inherited divergences in race, mentality, and ability and partly from differences in environment and opportunity.

The highest social class, the gentry, or planter aristocracy, comprised the owners of large plantations and more than twenty slaves each, as well as the most prominent public officials, professional men, and business leaders. It numbered about 6 percent of the total white population. Much larger than the gentry was the middle class, consisting of small slaveholding farmers owning fewer than twenty slaves each, small merchants and manufacturers, and lesser public officials and professional men, numbering about 20 to 25 percent of the white population. Still larger was the third class of yeomen and mechanics—independent, small, nonslaveholding farmers, naval-stores workers, miners, mechanics, tradesmen, overseers, and some of the farm tenants—number tenants—numbering 60 to 65 percent of the total white population. At the bottom of the social pyramid of the whites were the "poor whites," a group numbering somewhere between 5 and 10 percent of the white people, consisting of landless tenants and laborers who had failed in the struggle of life because of incapacity, laziness, improvidence, or disease. Many of them lived in shacks on the outskirts of towns and villages. The writer of an article in a Raleigh newspaper in 1855 said: "Many hundreds and thousands of poor men with families . . . existing upon half starvation are congregated especially about our towns and villages . . . doomed to drag out a miserable and useless existence." Their inheritance was poor, and many of them suffered from malaria, hookworm, pellagra, and other diseases about which the medical science of the time was largely or completely ignorant. One English observer referred to the southern "poor whites" as "the most degraded people of Anglo Saxon stock in the world." Most of the North Carolina whites were poor, but did not belong to the "poor white" class, which was held in contempt even by many of the slaves. The term "poor white" connoted more than poverty.

Beneath the four classes of whites there were two classes of Negroes—free Negroes and Negro slaves.

Free Negroes

Only Maryland and Virginia in the South and Pennsylvania, New York, and Ohio in the North had more than the 30,463 free Negroes in North Carolina in 1860. The chief source of the free Negro population was manumission, or the granting of freedom to individual slaves by masters and the legislature. But legal restrictions made manumission difficult after 1830, when manumitted slaves were required to leave the state within ninety days (a law not rigidly enforced). Other sources were purchases of freedom by the slaves themselves, births by free Negro and white or Indian mothers, and immigration, though both race-mixing and free Negro immigration were prohibited by law. The rate of increase of free Negroes ranged from 34 to 46 percent for each decade from 1790 to 1830, but dropped sharply thereafter. Seventy percent of the free Negroes in North Carolina in 1860 were mulattoes. There was some concentration of free Negroes in the towns and cities, but most of them were scattered through the rural slaveholding areas. Gradually the free Negro was legally restricted in, or deprived of, his freedom of moving about, associating with slaves, keeping arms, trading, teaching, preaching, and voting. He could not appear as a witness against a white man or compel white debtors to pay their debts to him. However, he retained in North Carolina more rights than in most of the other Southern states. He had the rights of habeas corpus, trial by jury, and the ownership, transfer, devise, and descent of property.

The free Negroes were considered to have a bad influence upon the slaves. Among the free Negroes there was some indolence, poverty, squalor, immorality, disease, and petty criminality, but many were industrious, self-sufficient, and respectable as skilled artisans, businessmen, and farmers.

The following table reveals the great variety of occupations of free Negroes in the state in 1860:

Occupation	Number	Occupation	Number
Barber	25	Mechanic	24
Blacksmith	155	Painter	66
Boatman	43	Planter	24
Cabinet Maker	10	Railroad Hand	37
Carpenters	256	Seaman	61
Common Laborer	1,387	Seamstress	175
Cook	54	Shoemaker	59
Engineer	8	Spinner	244
Factory Worker	17	Tailor	7
Fireman	24	Washerwoman	412
Iron Moulder	19	Wheelwright	23
Mason	120		

In 1860 the average annual wages of a selected number of free Negro artisans were:

Blacksmith	$222	Cabinet Maker	$323
Brickmaker	164	Iron Moulder	202
Carpenter	403	Harness Maker	302
Carriage Maker	285	Shoemaker	316
Cook	306	Wagoner	261

In the towns some of the free Negroes were peddlers, and operators of wood-yards, while others were engaged in hauling and transfer businesses and some worked at livery stables.

In 1860 there were 3,548 free Negroes who owned property, fifty-three of them in amounts ranging from $2,500 to $36,000 each. A few free Negroes owned slaves—in 1790, 25 owned a total of 73 slaves; in 1830, 190 owned 629 slaves; but in 1860, there were only 8 free Negro slaveholders, with a total of only 25 slaves. In 1830 Gooden Bowen of Bladen County and John Walker of New Hanover owned 44 slaves each, and in 1860 James Sampson of New Hanover owned property valued at $36,000. A few free Negroes rose to positions of eminence and influence, notably Ralph Freeman, a Baptist preacher, who was compelled to stop preaching in public by the law of 1831; John Chavis, Presbyterian minister and teacher of Negroes and whites, in separate schools; and Henry Evans, a minister who was the first to introduce Methodism into Fayetteville.

Negro Slaves

The Negro slaves constituted the lowest social class in North Carolina. Numbering in 1860 nearly one-third (331,059) of the total population and increasing in numbers more rapidly than the whites, they varied in density from a small minority in the mountain and other nonstaple areas to more than one-third of the population in the cotton and tobacco counties of the Piedmont and the East. In Anson, Bertie, Caswell, Chowan, Edgecombe, Franklin, Greene, Halifax, Hertford, Jones, Lenoir, Northampton, Perquimans, Pitt, Richmond, and Warren counties, they constituted more than half of the total population. Only five counties—Granville, Wake, Edgecombe, Halifax, and Warren—had more than 10,000 slaves each, the highest ratio of slaves to whites being in the last three, with Warren County having a slave population of 68 percent of its total.

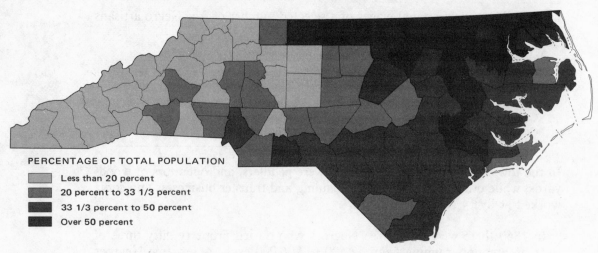

PERCENTAGE OF TOTAL POPULATION

Less than 20 percent

20 percent to 33 1/3 percent

33 1/3 percent to 50 percent

Over 50 percent

North Carolina in 1860, Showing Distribution of Slave Population

Cartography by the Department of Geography and Earth Sciences
The University of North Carolina at Charlotte

Because of the smaller number of large plantations and slaveholdings, North Carolina's slave regime was perhaps milder and more patriarchal than that in most of the southern states. Of the seven major slaveholding states, only Louisiana had fewer slaves in 1860—and that by only four thousand. Of the eleven seceding states in 1860–61, North Carolina ranked eighth in the ratio of slaves to whites. Fewer plantations were owned by absentee landlords and managed by hired overseers than in most slave states. The most intelligent and faithful Negroes worked as slave-drivers, personal and household servants— nurses, cooks, seamstresses, maids, and bodyguards, or as skilled artisans. But the vast majority of the slaves worked as field hands under the supervision of master or overseer, usually "from sun to sun," but occasionally only a nine- or ten-hour stint, tilling an average allotment of about twenty acres per hand, depending on the nature of the crop grown—less for tobacco and more for cotton. Because of the closing of the foreign slave trade in 1808 by act of Congress, and the growing demand for slaves in the cotton areas of Alabama, Mississippi, and Louisiana during their "flush times," the price of a "prime field hand" in North Carolina rose from about $300 in 1804 to $800 in 1840 and to $1,000 in 1860. Slave prices were considerably higher in the new cotton lands of the lower South and the Southwest, thus providing the basis for a profitable domestic slave trade between the upper and the lower South, which flourished after 1830.

Treatment of Slaves

Self-interest as well as humanitarian considerations demanded that the master supply sufficient food and clothing to conserve the strength, health, and happiness of the slave so that he could work regularly and hard. Though marriage of slaves was not recognized by law, masters encouraged slave "marriages," families, and home life. It was to the advantage of the slaveowner to take good care of the slaves. The slaves could not easily be driven beyond their normal pace and quality of labor. Life was easier, happier, and more profitable for the master who won the regard of his slaves by kind treatment and reasonable tasks. The oppressed slave could always retaliate against a cruel or unreasonable master by taking to the woods for a few days. The returning or recaptured runaway would receive a whipping but also perhaps relief from the grievances that had caused the master to suffer the loss of the slave's labor. Legally the master was free to use any punishment or discipline, except murder, that was necessary to secure complete obedience; but more efficacious than harsh punishment were rewards, such as permission to plant patches of land for vegetables and crops and raise pigs and chickens, presents for good behavior and work, and considerable freedom at night and on holidays and weekends. Hunting, swimming, fishing, dancing, games, and visits afforded some recreation for the slaves. Cruel masters and refractory slaves were the exception. Most of the slaves appeared to be contented and well cared for, and often there was real devotion between masters and slaves. Though there was a haunting fear among the whites of trouble from the slaves and free Negroes, there was not a real slave insurrection in North Carolina from 1815 to 1860. There were only a few minor slave conspiracies but many unfounded rumors of conspiracies and insurrections.

Laws Relating to Slaves

The system of laws relating to slaves, known as the slave code, protected the rights of the owner in his valuable property; restricted the mobility and activities of the slave; sought to minimize the possible mental and moral corruption and discontent of the slaves by protecting them from education, preaching, and the writings of free Negroes and antislavery agitators; and provided the machinery for effective white control in emergencies. The slave code was made more harsh and restrictive after 1830 because of the public concern caused by Nat Turner's insurrection in Southampton County, Virginia, in 1831. The missionary efforts of northern abolitionists and the circulation of David Walker's *Appeal in Four Articles,* an incendiary pamphlet written by a North Carolina Negro living in Boston, also aroused concern.

In practice, the lives of the slaves were regulated more by the will of the masters than by law. The slave code was not rigidly enforced in normal periods of quiet, and it portrayed slavery as a harsher institution than it was in actual operation. Though the law frowned upon the education of slaves and prohibited Negroes from teaching and preaching to them, some masters provided rudimentary education for those having unusual ability in order to enhance their usefulness on the plantation, and many masters considered it their duty to provide religious instruction—sometimes on the plantation by the master himself or by a minister, sometimes in the churches of whites where the Negroes sat in their allotted place, and sometimes in separate Negro churches.

Social Life of the Planter Class

Social life among the white classes in North Carolina was largely rural. Some of the gentry lived in stately homes in groves at some distance from the roads or rivers. They had mahogany and other fine furniture; fine linens, china, silver and glassware; fine clothes and jewelry; libraries; Negro servants; tables loaded with an abundance of plain foods—the best in comfort and convenience that life in North Carolina had to offer. The planter was busy most of the time with the complex business of operating the plantation, and the mistress was also busy looking after her home, managing the supplies of food for the plantation population, and caring for the slave families who lived in cabins in the nearby slave quarters. Ebenezer Pettigrew, a successful planter, wrote: "A Plantation to be well managed should never be left but at very short intervals." If a matter of life and death required it, the owner should go away, "but not otherwise." Yet there was time for recreation and pleasure—reading, letter writing, hunting, horse races, cockfights, card games, dances, parties, dinners, visits to neighbors and relatives, trips to town or to the country store or mill or tavern, militia musters, court week at the county seat, political meetings, celebrations, and sometimes in summer a vacation at a resort in North Carolina, Virginia, or the North.

The chief summer resorts in North Carolina were Shocco and the Sulphur Springs in Warren County, the Piedmont in Stokes County, the Warm Springs in Madison, the Sulphur Springs and Warm Springs in Buncombe, the Piedmont in Burke, the Wilson Springs in Cleveland, the Catawba Springs in Lincoln, and the beaches at Nags Head, Ocracoke, Beaufort, Wrightsville, and Masonboro.

Though small in numbers, the gentry or planter class was looked up to by other social groups. Some of the more intelligent, industrious, and thrifty merchants and farmers of the middle class were able to rise to the planter class. It had great influence in county and state politics, and many planters held high political office. It was the dominant class in North Carolina politics before 1835 and in the Democratic party after 1835.

Social Life of the Common People

Less wealthy than the gentry, the middle class lived in smaller and plainer houses, often worked on their farms with their slaves, and led a simpler life. But some of them worked hard, expanded their business, educated their children, achieved political office, and were able to climb the social and economic ladder.

The yeoman class of small farmers and laborers, though a majority in all sections of the state, was predominant in the Piedmont and Mountain regions. Owning no slaves, they lived in poorly furnished log houses of one or two rooms and had simple food and clothes. The father and sons worked the small farm; the wife and daughters did all the housework and often helped in the fields. Though life was rather monotonous and there was little time or money for recreation and travel, they now and then had good times hunting and fishing or at church, camp meetings, weddings, parties, public hangings, horse races, shooting matches, and political meetings. The men sometimes gathered at militia musters, at the county seat during court week, and at country store, church, mill, and tavern. Young men played games requiring physical strength and skill—wrestling, foot races, target shooting, gander pulling. The women enjoyed sewing and quilting parties; and the men helped each other build houses and barns, husk corn, and roll the logs together to be burned when new fields were cleared. Though some of the small farmers and laborers led lives of ignorance, squalor, immorality, and degradation, most of them were honest, industrious, independent, self-respecting persons who had the right to vote, had the respect of their neighbors, and were doing what they could to make a decent living and to be good citizens. More than any other class, the yeomen typified the population of North Carolina.

Town Life

Life in the towns was less monotonous than in the country. Its routine was relieved by visits, gossip, walking through the streets, meeting at tavern, grog shop, store, courthouse, church, academy, or lodge room. The small upper class met at balls, teas, and set suppers, and those who were interested formed benevolent, literary, lyceum, temperance, musical, theatrical, debating, and other organizations.

Family Life

The family was the most important institution of antebellum North Carolina. The husband was head and ruler of the family; by law he had control of his wife's property as well as her person. Woman was idealized, and she had great influence within the limited areas of society in which it was proper for her to express herself—home, church, and charity work. But the wife had virtually no legal rights or personality. She alone could not sue or be sued or own property separate from her husband. She was her husband's subject. Not until 1848 did she gain limited legal rights to own property in her own name. Polite society frowned upon physical labor by white women; but thousands of white women of the middle and yeoman classes worked as field hands and wage earners. Despite a hostile public opinion, surviving records show that divorce, sexual immorality, public houses of prostitution and race-mixing were features of antebellum social life.

Crime and Punishment

Crime was widespread and frequent in antebellum North Carolina, according to sample studies of the records of the county and superior courts. Murder, perjury, grand larceny, burglary, conspiracy, and maiming were the leading major offenses. The most frequent offenses were disturbing the public peace (assault and battery, affray, riot and unlawful assembly); offending public morality and decency (fornication, adultery, and bastardy); being a public nuisance (drunkenness, gambling, and prostitution); and petty larceny. The criminal code was so harsh as to discourage indictments and convictions and to increase pardons. Until 1855 any convicted person who could read might plead "benefit of clergy" and receive a punishment less severe than prescribed by law. In 1817 there were at least twenty-eight crimes for which the legal penalty was death. Execution was by hanging from the gallows. Hangings were public spectacles which attracted great crowds to the county seats. Other legal forms of punishment were dismemberment, branding, pillory, stocks, ducking stool, whipping, imprisonment, and fine. Imprisonment was in county jails, many of which were inadequate, bare, filthy, unheated, and poorly ventilated. A movement and agitation for reform of the criminal code failed to secure a state penitentiary for the imprisonment and reformation of felons, to abolish public hangings, and to eliminate cruel forms of punishment. But the number of offenses punishable by death was reduced from twenty-eight to seventeen; women could not be branded, whipped, or imprisoned for debt; the right to claim benefit of clergy was abolished; and many of the counties improved the condition of their county jails.

Chapter 29

SECTIONAL DIFFERENCES AND CONFLICTS IN THE UNION

Geographical Basis of Sectionalism

Differences in climate, soil, and topography resulted in different occupations, interests, and needs for the people who inhabited the various geographic regions of the United States. Political sectionalism was the inevitable outgrowth of geography and economics. The clashing interests and needs of the sections resulted in political conflict because the representatives in Congress from the various sections sought primarily to adopt laws and policies which served the interests and viewpoints of the constituents who elected them. The Trans-Allegheny West was the center of a critical sectionalism in the late eighteenth century, as New England was in the early nineteenth. But the most enduring and dangerous sectionalism in the history of the United States was that between North and South in the period from 1820 to 1860.

The colonists had discovered that nature made the North especially suitable for fishing and commerce and the South for farming, particularly for the production of the staple crops of tobacco, rice, and indigo. Negro slaves became far more numerous in the South than in the North because only in the tobacco, rice, and indigo fields of the South was their unskilled labor really profitable. Therefore, by 1804, every state north of Maryland had either abolished slavery or, by state law, had put it in process of gradual abolition. South of Pennsylvania no state considered it feasible to abolish slavery because the Negroes were too numerous—exceeding half the total population in some of the tobacco, cotton, rice, and sugar areas. Idleness, crime, race war, and the collapse of white control and civilization might result if freedom were given to the slaves, most of whom were fresh from savage Africa and the West Indies and were therefore ignorant and lacking in self-control and respect for law. Southerners defended

429

slavery as a police system to maintain white supremacy in racial and social relations. To many a southerner, the Negro aspect of the slave was more important than the slave aspect of the Negro. Jefferson Davis once said: "If you kill slavery, what will you do with the corpse?" Slavery was regarded as a necessary police system by which whites controlled the movements, actions, labor, and lives of millions of blacks. Besides, the slaves represented a vast investment and were the basis of Southern prosperity in staple crop production.

Northern Economic Development

The rapid expansion of manufacturing in the North during the period of commercial restrictions from the embargo of 1807 through the War of 1812–15 was stimulated by the adoption of the protective tariff policy after America's "war for commercial independence." By 1830 manufacturing superseded commerce in importance in New England and in most of the Middle States. Growing industry, after 1820, brought to the North greater wealth and economic prosperity, a swelling stream of European immigration—largely Irish, German, and Scandinavian—and the growth of cities and a balanced rural-urban, agricultural-commercial-manufacturing economy. The North bought cotton from the South and sold to the South increasing quantities of thread, cloth, and other manufactured goods. The profits from shipping and manufacturing were greater than those from simple extractive agriculture using unskilled labor. Thus the North outgrew the South in wealth and population; and the South, with respect to commerce, credit, and manufacturers, became an economic dependency or colony of the North. A northern writer, Thomas P. Kettell, diagnosed this situation in a book entitled *Southern Wealth and Northern Profits* (New York, 1860). And many conventions of southern business leaders between 1835 and 1860, particularly the annual Southern Commercial Conventions of the 1850s, advocated railroads to the Pacific Coast, opening up trade with South America, direct trade with Europe, diversification of agriculture and industry, and even the use of southern textbooks as a means of relieving the South's economic dependence on the North. But little was accomplished to carry the resolutions of these meetings into practice before 1860.

Southern Economic Development

Before 1790 the great southern staple had been tobacco. The invention of the cotton gin by Eli Whitney in 1793, the natural suitability of the South for cotton production, and the insatiable demands of the cotton mills of New England and England fixed and spread cotton culture as the major economic interest of a vast southern region. Cotton replaced tobacco as the South's most valuable crop, and the area from North Carolina to Texas came to be called the "Cotton Kingdom." The closing of the foreign slave trade by Congress in 1808, as the demand for labor in the cotton fields increased, raised slave prices, fixed slavery more firmly on the South, and gave rise to a domestic slave trade that transferred thousands of slaves overland and by water from the less profitable tobacco regions of the upper South to the cotton lands of the lower South and Southwest, where their labor was more profitable and their prices higher. Thus the three distinctive and dominant characteristics of southern life became, first, staple crop production, chiefly cotton but also tobacco in Virginia, Maryland, Tennessee, Kentucky, and North Carolina, rice in South Carolina, sugar in Louisiana, Florida, and Texas, hemp in Kentucky and Missouri, and indigo in South Carolina; second, Negro slavery; and third, the plantation system. In the second quarter of the nineteenth century, manufacturing in the North and cotton production in the South brought prosperity to both sections, but made them differ more widely than ever before. And the South became more and more a "conscious minority" section in the Union and an economic colony of the North with respect to manufacturing, commerce, and banking.

The South a "Conscious Minority"

In the United States Congress, where laws were enacted by majority vote, northern and southern congressmen sought to safeguard and promote by legislation the interests of their sections. The slave and free states, generally equal in number before 1850, had the same voting strength in the Senate, but in the House of Representatives, the more populous North was increasingly in the majority. Only in its equal voting power in the Senate did the South have an assured veto of oppressive or dangerous federal laws.

Federal Economic Legislation

For many years the chief dispute between the industrial-commercial North and the agricultural South was over federal economic legislation. Many southern leaders attributed the economic lag and occasional depression of their section to federal laws, which, since the days of Alexander Hamilton, had exploited the South for the benefit of the North. The two Banks of the United States (1791–1811 and 1816–36), fishing bounties, the exclusion of foreign ships from the coastwise trade, and the protective tariff had been of special benefit to northern capitalists, fishermen, shippers, and manufacturers, and had drained the South of wealth in the form of interest charges, high freight rates, and higher prices for manufactures. Moreover, the South contributed more in federal taxes than it recovered in federal expenditures for services and for internal improvement projects such as rivers and harbors, roads, and canals, most of which were in the North and West.

Protective Tariff and Nullification

It was the ever-climbing level of protective tariff rates after 1816 against which the South protested most vehemently. Southern economic depression in the Panic of 1819 was attributed chiefly to the protective tariff, though it was due in part to soil exhaustion, the westward movement of population from the seaboard South, and the disastrous competition of the Southwest, which was better suited to the production and marketing of cotton. Various southern state legislatures protested the tariff laws as oppressive and unconstitutional. A South Carolina convention in 1832, following the suggestion of John C. Calhoun, nullified the tariff laws of 1828 and 1832, and the state took steps to prevent their enforcement in South Carolina. President Andrew Jackson prepared to use military force to execute the federal laws. But an armed clash between South Carolina and the United States was averted when Congress, led by Henry Clay and John C. Calhoun, passed the Compromise Tariff of 1833, which provided for a gradual reduction of rates until they reached the pre-1828 level. In 1842 the rates were raised but from 1848 to 1860 their trend was downward. After 1833 the protective tariff was not a dangerous sectional issue.

Sectional Controversy over Negro Slavery

The most serious conflict between North and South was over Negro slavery. Early in the nineteenth century many people in both sections criticized slavery as a moral, economic, and social evil. The Constitution recognized slavery and left the states with complete authority over the institution within their borders. Though every northern state took action by 1804 to abolish slavery, no southern state followed suit because of economic, social, and racial considerations. Many southerners opposed slavery and realized its dangerous possibilities, but most of the early southern opposition to the "peculiar institution" was conditioned upon the "antislavery" idea of gradual emancipation, compensation to owners, and colonization in Africa or elsewhere. The colonization plan, sponsored by the American Colonization Society after 1816 and championed by various manumission societies, proved impracticable, though Liberia on the African coast was begun as a result of a few thousand Negroes being colonized there by the joint efforts of these societies and acts of the United States Congress. Harassed by internal quarrels and always short on funds, the Colonization Society had sent only about six thousand former slaves to Liberia by 1840, when its activities virtually ceased.

The Principle of Compromise and Division

The principle of compromise and division had been applied, without serious sectional conflict, to slavery in the unorganized territory between the Appalachian mountains and the Mississippi River by the Northwest Ordinance of 1787, which prohibited the introduction of slaves in the region north and west of the Ohio River. Thus slavery in the original area of the United States had been settled by the method of drawing a line separating the free and slave areas. Slavery was illegal north of the Mason and Dixon line (the Pennsylvania-Maryland boundary) and the Ohio River; it was legal south of that line. The Union might have continued thus, half-slave and half-free—Abraham Lincoln's statement to the contrary notwithstanding—without serious sectional controversy except for two new developments in the nineteenth century: first, the rise of the radical abolition movement in the North after 1830; and, second, the perpetual expansion of the United States by the acquisition of territory between the Mississippi River and the Pacific Ocean which repeatedly raised the question of whether slavery could legally expand into new territory.

Rise of the Abolition Movement

The radical abolitionists, whose first leader was William Lloyd Garrison, editor of the *Liberator* (founded in 1831), demanded that the immoral, inhumane, and undemocratic institution of slavery be abolished at once and without compensation or colonization. They heaped abuse and insult upon slaveowners and slavery and even justified theft, insurrection, and murder. Some of the abolitionists seemed to hate slaveowners as much as they did slavery. They distributed vast quantities of incendiary literature in the South designed to incite the slaves to insurrection. Radical abolitionism never won a large following in the North; but under the influence of the churches, abolition societies, newspapers and the leadership of Theodore Weld, the Grimké sisters, and others, the North became hostile to slavery as an evil, immoral, and intolerable institution. Though without the desire or constitutional power to interfere with slavery in any state, the North gradually reached the determination that slavery should not spread from the slave states into the western territories and that there should never be another slave territory or state.

Southern Reaction to the Abolition Movement

The noisy and radical abolition movement excited keen resentment in the South and evoked violent denunciation in and out of Congress by a minority of southern "fire-eaters." Failing to differentiate between abolition and antislavery in the North, the South became fearful as well as resentful of the abolitionists' threat of outside interference and their "meddling" with a serious domestic problem whose complexities were known only by southerners. The bloody Nat Turner insurrection in Virginia in 1831 was regarded in the South as a ghastly result of the abolitionist crusade. Suppose a more populous, abolitionized North should gain control of the Senate as well as the lower

House. Congress might then attack slavery in the South in defiance of the Constitution, or the free states might conceivably, through the amending process, vest Congress with power over slavery in the states. If millions of semicivilized Negroes were set free in the South, would not southern staple crop agriculture and prosperity be ruined; race tension develop into a war between the two races; and peace, order, and white civilization be destroyed? Under outside attack, the South ceased to criticize or apologize for slavery. John C. Calhoun and many other leaders set the new pattern of thought that slavery was legal, moral, and a "positive good" for whites and Negroes. Southern states passed harsher laws relating to Negroes, free and slave, to insure more effective control of the Negroes by the whites in case of emergency, and they united in aggressive defense of their peculiar institution, which was already condemned by most of the civilized world, including the majority of the people of the United States.

Nationalistic Views of the Federal Government

Until after the War of 1812, when Congress, the executive, and the judiciary became frankly nationalistic and broadly constructionist in their policies, sensitive southern leaders, fearing a federal government with expanding powers under the doctrines of implied powers and broad construction of the Constitution, sought to safeguard the interests of the minority South by championing state rights or local self-government, a weak federal government, and strict construction of the Constitution. Then, after the Missouri Compromise of 1820, the South depended upon its equal voting power in the Senate to block any dangerous federal interference. The principle of division along the Mason and Dixon–Ohio River line would have assured a continuation of the southern veto power in the Senate if the United States had not acquired new territory west of the Mississippi. Actually the balance of voting power in the Senate depended on whether slaves might be taken to the western territories and whether these territories were admitted to the Union as free or slave states. It was the sectional quarrel over the extension of slavery, or slavery in the territories, rather than the abolition of slavery in the southern states that brought the North and the South to a parting of the ways.

Acquisition of New Western Territory

During the first half of the nineteenth century the United States acquired the land between the Mississippi River and the Pacific Ocean. As each region was settled Congress provided a territorial government preparatory to its admission as a state with full representation in Congress. Should settlers be permitted to carry slaves into each new territory? Upon the answer to this question depended the southern balance in the Senate and perhaps the ultimate fate of slavery in the southern states.

The Missouri Compromise

The Louisiana territory between the Mississippi River and the Rocky Mountains, purchased from France in 1803, was settled near the mouth of the Missouri River by northerners and southerners, some of whom owned slaves. In 1818, when Missouri applied for admission to the Union as a slave state, the South was shocked by the action of the lower house of Congress in voting to admit it to statehood only on conditions that it take steps to abolish slavery. The South blocked the proposal in the Senate. After months of angry debate the Missouri Compromise of 1820 was adopted, whereby Missouri was admitted as a slave state and Maine as a free state; but slavery was forever prohibited in the remainder of the Louisiana territory north of 36° 30', except in Missouri. The Missouri Compromise was really a defeat for the South because most of the Louisiana territory lay north of 36° 30' and Congress asserted its constitutional authority to exclude slavery from western territory. In this first serious dispute over slavery in the territories, the importance of the South's equality of voting power in the Senate was demonstrated. That equality was maintained for a generation by the custom of admitting new states in pairs—one slave and one free.

Slavery and the Texas-Oregon Questions

Because of geographic factors Texas was settled chiefly by southerners who won independence from Mexico in 1836 and secured the admission of Texas to the United States in 1845 as a slave state. There was strong opposition to the annexation of Texas because of slavery. In 1848, after a war with Mexico over the southern boundary of Texas, the United States forced Mexico to sell the vast region of New Mexico and California stretching from Texas to the Pacific Ocean. Two years before, the United States and Great Britain had divided Oregon along the line of 49 degrees. Over strong southern opposition, Oregon was established as a free territory in 1848. The rush of settlers into California after the discovery of gold in 1848 was so great that application was made to Congress for the admission of California at once as a free state without going through the territorial stage.

The Wilmot Proviso, 1846

The question of whether to admit slavery to these new western regions was far more serious than it had been twenty-five years earlier in the case of the Louisiana territory. The North was more antislavery and determined to prevent the further spread of slavery. Only the South's power in the

Senate had defeated the Wilmot Proviso of 1846 to exclude slavery from the entire Mexican cession. The abolitionists had greatly increased sectional bitterness. Already the Methodist and Baptist churches had split into northern and southern branches. Slavery was more profitable and more firmly entrenched in the South than ever before. Many southerners believed that the North was opposing slavery in the territories in order to gain control of the Senate through the admission of free states and then to attack slavery in the southern states. The South was willing to apply the old principle of division by extending the Missouri Compromise line to the Pacific; but many of its leaders threatened to leave the Union if it lost the Senate veto and failed to obtain its rights in the new lands. Angry debates raged in Congress for months.

Four Possible Methods of Dealing with Slavery in Territories

In the slavery crisis after the Mexican War four methods of solving the question of slavery in the territories had strong support. First, Congress had constitutional power over the territories and should exclude slavery from every territory. This principle of congressional exclusion, as embodied in the Wilmot Proviso, was extreme but it came more and more to have the support of the North. Second, Congress did not have the power to exclude slavery from any territory. The Constitution recognized slavery and followed the flag into newly acquired territories, which were the common property of the states and were in all cases open to slavery. This was the southern solution. Third, the question of slavery in a territory should be decided by the people who inhabited the territory. This solution, embodying the principle of popular sovereignty or local self-government, was advocated most strongly by a Northern Democrat, Stephen A. Douglas of Illinois, and had strong support in the West. Finally, there was the proposal that the line of 36° 30′ be extended westward. This was the old principle of compromise and division by which the question of the extension of slavery had been settled in the past. President Polk (1845–49) strongly favored this solution; and though it did not represent the real thinking and constitutional position of the South, the South as a matter of expediency and compromise was always willing to accept it. The chief danger to a peaceful settlement was the increasing stubbornness of the antislavery North in demanding the adoption of the principle of the congressional exclusion of slavery from every territory. This solution was intolerable to the South.

The Compromise of 1850

Finally, the questions involving slavery were settled by Congress in the Compromise of 1850. To please the North, California was admitted as a free state, and slave trade in the District of Columbia was prohibited. To please the South, a more effective fugitive slave law was passed and the remainder of the Mexican Cession was organized into the territories of New Mexico and Utah with no mention of slavery, whose legality would be decided by the territorial legislatures or courts. The Compromise of 1850 was really a defeat for the South because, by the admission of free California, it lost its equal voting power in the Senate. In June, 1850, several months before the passage by Congress of the various compromise measures, a convention of nine slaveholding states met at Nashville, Tennessee, to consider whether the South should resort to the ultimate act of secession. The convention, controlled by moderates, adopted some tame resolutions and adjourned to await final action by Congress. After the passage of the compromise measures in September an adjourned session of the Nashville Convention met in November, 1850, and condemned the compromise. The North generally accepted the compromise with the exception of the fugitive slave law. Not until 1852 was it certain that the South would accept the compromise and that no southern state would secede from the Union. South Carolina refrained from secession only because no other southern state was willing to leave the Union. Reluctantly the South accepted the compromise and remained in the Union, relying for safety upon northern respect for the guarantees of the Constitution in regard to slavery.

Personal Liberty Laws of Northern States

Both North and South were peaceful and prosperous during the next four years. But the sectional controversy led to the disintegration of the national Whig party, and the Democratic party remained as the strongest bond of union. Contending that Congress had no power over slavery and that slavery should be left entirely to each state and territory, it grew stronger, especially in the South. Personal Liberty laws enacted in northern states and occasional mob action in the North, which obstructed and flouted the new fugitive slave law and the constitutional guarantee of the rendition of runaway slaves, angered the South and caused it to distrust the good faith of the North and the efficacy of constitutional guarantees relating to slavery. Were the interests of the South safe in the Union when the majority North was unwilling to abide by the law and the Constitution?

The Kansas-Nebraska Act, 1854

The Kansas-Nebraska Act of 1854 terminated the four-year period of relative quiet after the Compromise of 1850 and unleashed a sectional storm which was never allayed and which eventuated in war in 1861. As steered through Congress by Stephen A. Douglas, a Northern Democrat, the act repealed the Missouri Compromise of 1820 and divided the remainder of the Louisiana Purchase into Kansas and Nebraska territories, leaving the question of slavery in each to be decided on the principle of popular sovereignty or local self-government—by the settlers themselves. The South was pleased at the possibility that the Kansas territory, which had been closed to slavery since 1820, might become a slave state. The Kansas-Nebraska Act, which legally opened to slavery a region from which it had been excluded since 1820, precipitated a political revolution in the North. Northern Whigs, the free-soilers, and many antislavery Democrats formed the new Republican party, which denounced slavery as a wrong and declared that there must never be another slave territory or state. The new party spread rapidly throughout the Northwest and later to the East. Though it denied any intention or right to attack slavery in the states, one of its leaders, Abraham Lincoln, was saying that the Union could not continue half slave and half free. Alarmed by the popularity of this sectional, free-soil, antislavery northern party, southern leaders openly declared that their states should leave the Union if a Republican were elected president. In 1856 Republican John C. Frémont made a strong race but was defeated by Democrat James Buchanan.

"Bleeding Kansas" and the Slavery Question

The plan of letting the settlers in Kansas and Nebraska decide the slavery question resulted in civil war in Kansas because the question of slavery in that territory was of vital concern to both North and South. Most of the new settlers in Kansas were from nearby states, particularly the slave state of Missouri. But antislavery leaders in the North were determined that the territory should be free soil, and urged northerners to migrate to Kansas. Particularly active in this respect was the New England Emigrant Aid Society, eager to colonize Kansas with free-soilers, and incidentally to make a profit out of selling equipment and supplies to them. It was not long until the free-soilers outnumbered the proslavery settlers in the territory. But the "Blue Lodges" and "Sons of the South" in Missouri were pledged to enter Kansas at a moment's notice to defend slavery at the polls by voting for a constitution that guaranteed their cherished institution. Soon the hostile groups resorted to violence. "Bleeding Kansas" helped to inflame the North and the South and to produce sectional abuse and violence in Congress; and sectional partisans prevented the peaceful solution of the Kansas question.

The Dred Scott Decision, 1857

In 1857, in the Dred Scott case, the Supreme Court of the United States, under the leadership of Chief Justice Roger B. Taney, decided in favor of the South's position that Congress had no constitutional power to exclude slavery from any territory of the United States and that the Missouri Compromise was unconstitutional, null, and void. This decision was applauded by the South and by the Democrats generally; it was denounced as unsound and unacceptable by the North and by the newly formed Republican party.

John Brown's Raid at Harper's Ferry, 1859

In 1859 John Brown, a fanatical abolitionist who had earlier achieved notoriety for a career of pillage, arson, and murder in Kansas, led an armed band of some twenty men against the federal arsenal at Harper's Ferry, Virginia (now West Virginia) in an attempt to seize arms he hoped to use to rally slaves against their masters. The slaves did not respond, and Brown was captured, tried, and hanged. Many northerners considered Brown a martyr, and Emerson referred to him as "that new saint than whom none purer or more brave was ever led by love of men into conflict and death." To many southerners Brown's raid was plain evidence of the desperate plans of "Black Republicans."

The Election of 1860

The Kansas-Nebraska Act and "Bleeding Kansas" caused conflict within the Democratic party between northern and southern factions headed by Stephen A. Douglas of Illinois and President James Buchanan, respectively. The party split became definite when the delegates from the lower South walked out of the Democratic National Convention at Charleston in 1860, when that body adopted an unacceptable platform on slavery and slavery extension. Subsequently the Northern Democrats nominated Douglas for the presidency, and the Southern Democrats nominated John C. Breckinridge of Kentucky. The Constitutional Union party, organized by former Whigs, nominated John Bell of Tennessee; and the Republican party nominated Abraham Lincoln of Illinois. Because of the Democratic split, Lincoln's personality and record, and the broader and more attractive Republican platform (which promised a protective tariff, internal improvements, and homesteads as well as free soil), Lincoln received a majority of electoral votes, though his total popular vote was far below that of the combined vote of his three opponents.

Significance of Lincoln's Election

Though the Republican party controlled neither Congress nor the Supreme Court and denied any intention of attacking slavery in the states, and though the question of the extension of slavery was already nearly settled by the forces of climate and geography, Lincoln's election fired the South to action. The lower South led in setting forth the constitutional doctrine of state rights to give legality and popularity to secession as a means of achieving southern independence, self-government, and safety. South Carolina seceded in December, 1860, followed early the next year by the six other states of the

"Cotton Kingdom"—Georgia, Alabama, Mississippi, Louisiana, Florida, and Texas. These states organized the Confederate States of America in a meeting at Montgomery, Alabama, in February, 1861, and elected Jefferson Davis of Mississippi as president. The states of the upper South and the Democrats in the North sought compromise plans to hold the other slave states in the Union and perhaps to win back the seceded states. But no plan was found to which the extremists in North and South would agree. Although the South was willing to compromise by an equitable division of the territories, the victorious Republican party, on the advice of President-elect Lincoln, was unwilling to compromise. Some recognized that the question of slavery extension, though it involved sectional and partisan sentiment, honor, prestige, and interests, had become largely theoretical because, regardless of law, Negro slavery had already spread as far as geographic conditions and economic forces would permit. It had already "reached its natural limits."

President Lincoln's Views on Slavery and Secession

President Lincoln took office in March, 1861, firm in the belief that no state had the right to secede and in the determination to protect the property of the United States and to preserve the Union. He made the fateful decision to send supplies to Fort Sumter in Charleston harbor, and Confederate forces opened fire on the fort and captured it on April 14, 1861, before the naval forces of the United States arrived. The next day Lincoln called upon the states in the Union for 75,000 men to suppress the southern revolt and preserve the Union. Rather than fight against the South, Virginia, Arkansas, North Carolina, and Tennessee seceded and joined the Confederacy.

Chapter 30

A STATE IN THE CONFEDERACY

North Carolina's location in the upper South made it less southern in its social and economic regime than the states of the lower South. Less suited to the production and marketing of cotton, it had relatively fewer wealthy planters with extensive plantations and large slaveholdings, more small farmers, more public leaders like William Gaston and James Iredell, who before 1830 opposed slavery, more antislavery societies that encouraged masters to emancipate their slaves, and more masters who did free them. The Quakers took the lead in organizing societies to create sentiment in behalf of gradual emancipation. They formed the North Carolina Manumission Society in 1816 and by 1825 this organization had twenty-eight local chapters and more than a thousand members. The society held its last meeting in 1834. The American Colonization Society was also active in the state, having at least forty branches in 1826 and claiming the emancipation of about two thousand slaves in a three-year period.

North Carolina's Relation to the Union

North Carolina was one of the original thirteen states which created the Union and it believed firmly in the preservation of that Union. It was bound firmly to the United States by the ties of commerce and two generations of experience in founding, operating, and developing the nation. Its participation in the highly successful record of the United States in peace and war stimulated a vigorous national patriotism which would strongly resist destruction of the nation by sectional and divisive forces. Despite the conflicts between the North and the South, few North Carolinians seriously contemplated secession before 1860.

But for the most part, North Carolina aligned itself with the South in all disputes with the North. It resented economic vassalage to the industrial and commercial Northeast and believed firmly in slavery as a necessary police system by which the whites might control the Negroes and maintain the peace, safety, and prosperity of the state. Fearful and resentful of the abolition movement, it gradually shifted after 1830 to a strong defense of slavery and enacted more stringent laws for the control of Negro slaves and free Negroes.

The Two-Party System—Whigs and Democrats

After 1835 the Whig and Democratic parties in North Carolina featured national issues and waged unremitting partisan warfare. Both were thoroughly committed to the spoils system. They staged bitter and spectacular, though unimportant, contests over the periodical election of United States senators, the movement to expunge the Senate censure of Jackson, and the right of the state legislature to instruct United States senators. The Democrats upheld and the Whigs generally denounced the right of instruction. Contests involving the right of instruction led to the spectacular resignations from the United States Senate of Willie P. Mangum (Whig) in 1836 and of Bedford Brown and Robert Strange (Democrats) in 1840.

The keen rivalry of two evenly matched and ably led parties made North Carolina a doubtful state and won for it greater recognition in national politics. William A. Graham was the Whig nominee for the vice-presidency in 1852. George E. Badger and Graham, both Whigs, were appointed by Harrison and Fillmore, respectively, as secretary of the navy; and James C. Dobbin held the same post in the Democratic administration of Pierce. Romulus M. Saunders and Daniel M. Barringer were Democratic ministers to Spain. North Carolina Whig and Democratic leaders were active in the national councils of their parties.

Party Views on Protective Tariff, Internal Improvements, and Other Questions

In national politics the North Carolina Whigs supported a constructive program of national bank, internal improvements, moderate protective tariff, the distribution to the states of the proceeds of the sales of public lands, a strong and expanding federal government, and a broad construction of the Constitution. The Democrats were champions of state rights and restricted federal activity based on a strict interpretation of the Constitution. They were content with a negative program of opposition to the Whig policies of protective tariff, internal improvements, national bank, and distribution. As early as 1821 Murphey denounced the branch of the United States Bank at Fayetteville as "a Broker's Shop and kept for this purpose by the Mother Bank . . . the greatest Curse that has befallen us since the Year 1791. . . . We can't bank in this State, with this Monster feeding upon our Vitals."

North Carolina was the only state in the Union that consistently opposed all protective tariff legislation. The North Carolina delegation in Congress was particularly hostile to the 1828 "Tariff of Abominations," and Governor Burton said that "the dignity and interest of the State requires that North Carolina should not be silent." The legislature declared that "manufactures, in the United States, are not an object of *general* but of *local* interest," and that it was "inexpedient for the Congress of the United States to increase the duties on imports." When South Carolina in 1832 adopted an Ordinance of Nullification, declaring null and void the federal tariff laws of 1828 and 1832, the General Assembly of North Carolina called the tariff legislation "impolitic, unjust and oppressive." At the same time it expressed a "warm attachment to the Constitution of the United States," stating that the South Carolina action "is revolutionary in character, subversive of the Constitution of the United States, and leads to a dissolution of the Union."

Though each party sought to impeach the soundness of the other's views on slavery, both defended slavery, denounced abolition, and wanted all western territories open to settlement by any citizen of any state regardless of the kind of property he owned—slave or otherwise.

The Democratic Party, Most Dependable Defender of Slavery

But the Democratic party gradually established itself as the stronger and more dependable friend of slavery and the South. Its northern leaders attacked slavery less often and less violently than did those of the Whig party. In North Carolina its chief strength was in the plantation, slaveholding East. It was united in the belief that Congress had no power over slavery in any state or territory and that any state had the constitutional right of secession. Holden and other Democrats noisily denounced abolition, demanded cessation of attacks on slavery, insisted on protection of slave property by the federal government, urged the South to unite in bold resistance to the North, and questioned the value of a Union in which slavery and other property rights were not secure.

Unionist Whigs and State Rights Whigs

The North Carolina Whigs were more friendly to the Union and sought to allay, avoid, and compromise the slavery issue. But they were not united on the slavery question. Badger, Graham, Morehead, and most of the prominent leaders, who were called Federal Whigs, believed that Congress could, but should not, prohibit slavery in the territories and that no state had the right to secede from the Union. But Mangum, Clingman and others, called State Rights Whigs, agreed with the Democrats on the issues of secession and slavery in the territories. After the Wilmot Proviso of 1846, when slavery began to overshadow all other public issues, Clingman and some other State Rights Whigs joined the Democratic party as the more reliable defender of slavery and of "Southern Rights" generally. The Whig party was strongest in those counties where slavery was relatively weak. Although some of its leaders were large planters and industrialists, it was definitely not the party of the so-called slavocracy. It opposed every trend toward secession, supported the Union, and was the strongest tie in the state binding North Carolina to the Union.

Party Views on the Mexican War

North Carolina Whigs opposed the annexation of Texas in 1845, the war with Mexico in 1846–48 and the acquisition of new territory which would precipitate new controversy over slavery and endanger the Union. They denounced the war as an "unjust war against a weak neighbor" brought on by President Polk and the Democrats in Congress. A Democratic-sponsored resolution in the General Assembly that the war was caused "by action of the Mexican Government" was defeated. The Whigs strongly opposed the Wilmot Proviso, however, and demanded equal rights for the South in the territory acquired from Mexico—in other words, the right to take slave property into this region.

On the other hand, the North Carolina Democrats favored the annexation of Texas, the war with Mexico, and the acquisition of new territory and were even stronger in their denunciation of the Wilmot Proviso and their demands that the new territory be open to slavery. Louis D. Wilson, a leading Democrat of Edgecombe County, went to Mexico in 1847 as colonel of a North Carolina regiment of about one thousand "Volunteers." The regiment took no important part in the war and Wilson died of yellow fever.

For its partisan and seemingly unpatriotic attitude during the war, the Whig party lost some strength in the state. It was further weakened by its moderate, compromising attitude toward slavery in the territories during the crisis of 1849–50, which culminated in the Compromise of 1850. The dynamic leadership of David S. Reid on the free suffrage issue, together with a decline of the Whig progressiveness and leadership, resulted in the overthrow in 1850 of Whig dominance in North Carolina politics. The Democrats were in political control of North Carolina throughout the 1850s.

Party Alignments on the Compromise of 1850

The people of North Carolina were too busy with their own local problems of free suffrage, public schools, farming, railroads, and manufacturing to become greatly excited over the question of slavery in far-away Oregon, California, and New Mexico. Mangum, Badger, and the majority of North Carolina congressmen worked for the Compromise of 1850; and generally the state accepted it gladly, gave little thought to secession, and rejoiced in the belief that the slavery dispute was settled and the Union safe. But some radical Democrats denounced the Compromise as a defeat for the South; and Clingman and some State Rights Whigs joined the Democratic party.

North Carolina was invited to send delegates to the Nashville Convention of June, 1850, called for the purpose of "considering plans to protect southern interests." Holden's *Standard* said that the proposed meeting was "of first importance to the South and the Union and North Carolina ought, by all means, to be represented in it." Several other Democratic newspapers also endorsed the idea. All the Whig papers, except the Raleigh *Star* opposed. Governor Manly, a Whig, refused to call a special session of the legislature to elect delegates, and so the state was not represented at the Nashville Convention.

Party Views on the Kansas-Nebraska Act

The Kansas-Nebraska Act of 1854, opening to slavery a region that had been closed by the Missouri Compromise, came as an agreeable surprise to North Carolina. The North Carolina Whigs feared its effect upon the North but dared not oppose a measure so popular in the South. Even Senator Badger voted for it—the "greatest mistake of his life," he said later. Stirring events quickly followed. The breakup of the national Whig party, the quick rise of the antislavery Republican party, the war in "Bleeding Kansas," and the bitter and violent sectional debates in Congress stirred deeply for the first time the emotions of the people of North Carolina. Many Whigs, left without a party, joined the new American or Know-Nothing party; but this party, which failed to attract all of the Whigs, was temporary and entirely ineffectual in challenging the supremacy of the Democratic party in North Carolina.

North Carolina and the Presidential Election of 1856

In 1856 Holden, Clingman, and the radical Democrats urged the secession of the southern states if Republican John C. Frémont were elected president. The governors of North Carolina, South Carolina, and Virginia met in Raleigh with Holden and other Democratic leaders and discussed the proper course of action in the event of a "Black Republican" victory. But the immediate crisis passed with the triumph of the Democratic candidate, Buchanan, over his two opponents, Frémont and Millard Fillmore, candidate of the American party.

North Carolina's Antislavery Leaders

Mounting hatred of the North, public hysteria, and the arrogance of the Democratic slavocracy were now evident in North Carolina. There were several inflammatory incidents. Benjamin S. Hedrick, a native of Rowan County and a mild-mannered, scholarly professor of chemistry at the University of North Carolina, was deluged with public denunciation, dismissed from the faculty, threatened with mob violence in Salisbury, and forced to flee the state in 1856 when it was learned that he was opposed to the extension of slavery and wanted to vote for Frémont—which he could not do because there was no Republican presidential ticket in North Carolina that year. The alumni of the university had demanded that the "Trustees forthwith expel that traitor to all Southern interests" and Holden insisted that Hedrick be "driven out of the state." In 1857, as already mentioned, Hinton Rowan Helper, also a native of Rowan County, published *The Impending Crisis of the South: How To Meet It,* in which he championed the nonslaveholding southern whites, denounced slave masters as "lords of the lash," and sought to prove by comparative statistics, used in an unfair and unscholarly manner, that slavery had caused the South to lag far behind the North in wealth. This southern attack on slavery gained nationwide notoriety. John Sherman was defeated for the speakership of the national House of Representatives largely because of his endorsement of the book. The national Republican organization printed and circulated at least 100,000 copies of it as a "campaign document" in the election of 1860. Helper had left North Carolina by this time, but a state newspaper said that if he came back he would never be allowed to leave—that "North Carolina would make a home for him in the bosom of his native soil." The law was extended to suppress the book and imprison persons guilty of circulating this "incendiary literature." The most famous victim of the raging hysteria and intolerance was Daniel Worth of Guilford County, an aged minister of the Wesleyan Methodist Church, who opposed slavery. Worth was arrested in 1859 on the charge of circulating Helper's book and preaching unsound doctrines on slavery. He was tried and convicted; and only advanced age, the activity of friends, his flight from the state, and the forfeiture of his bond pending an unsuccessful appeal to the Supreme Court saved him from a public whipping and a year's imprisonment. These incidents revealed a profound change in the attitude of many North Carolinians. Dominated by emotion, fear, and hatred, they would no longer tolerate calm reason, freedom of speech, or division of opinion on sectional and southern interests. Those who did not yield to the mounting hysteria of sectional hatred were suspected as loyal and patriotic southerners and were to be treated as enemies and traitors.

John Brown's raid at Harper's Ferry, Virginia, in 1859 and wild talk about the "forcible overthrow of slavery" added to the popular excitement and anger on the eve of the presidential election of 1860.

The Presidential Election of 1860

The state and presidential campaigns of 1860 in North Carolina were tense, exciting, and close. The former Whigs, who had no party organization after 1854, were alarmed at the danger of disunion and hastily reorganized the Whig party in 1859 in an effort to elect congressmen and other public officials who were friendly to the Union. In state politics they nominated John Pool of Pasquotank County for governor and waged a close contest against Democrat John W. Ellis of Rowan County on the issue of ad valorem taxation. Ellis won by a vote of 59,463 to Pool's 53,123. The Whigs elected four of the state's eight representatives in Congress. In the presidential election they supported John Bell and the new Constitutional Union party whose platform simply endorsed the Constitution and the Union. North Carolina played a moderate role in the events that split the Democratic party. In the national convention at Charleston the state's delegates supported the southern platform that the federal government must protect slavery in the territories; but, led by William W. Holden, they refused to follow the southern delegations in their bolt of the convention when it adopted the northern platform of congressional noninterference with slavery in the territories. The Charleston convention adjourned without nominating a presidential candidate. The North Carolina Democratic delegation bolted the later Baltimore convention, which nominated Stephen A. Douglas as the candidate of the Northern Democrats, and at a later convention in Richmond aided in the nomination of John C. Breckinridge and the adoption of a southern platform. The Republican party, which had nominated Abraham Lincoln, had no electoral ticket in North Carolina.

Breckinridge and the Southern Democrats Carry North Carolina by a Close Margin

Breckinridge was regarded in North Carolina as the nominee of the regular official Democratic party, and he won the entire electoral vote of the state—but by the barest popular majority of 48,539 to 44,990 for Bell and 2,701 for Douglas. In the nation, with four parties in the contest, the Republicans won the solid electoral vote of every northern state except New Jersey and elected Lincoln by a majority of the electoral but a minority of the popular votes. The election of a sectional northern president pledged to prevent the futher extension of slavery created alarm and despair for the future in North Carolina, but it was not considered a sufficient reason for dissolving the Union. Lincoln's election, however, fired the South to action. In the winter of 1860–61, led by South Carolina, the seven states of the "Cotton Kingdom" seceded from the United States and in February, 1861, organized the Confederate States of America. Should North Carolina also secede and join this new nation? This was the dominant issue in North Carolina after Lincoln's election in November.

North Carolina Opposed to Secession in 1860

The election of 1860 showed that the overwhelming majority of North Carolina citizens were unionist—opposed to secession. The entire vote for Bell and Douglas was unionist. Most Breckinridge Democratic leaders in the campaign had denied that Breckinridge was a disunion candidate and the moderate Democrats led by Holden, though voting for Breckinridge, opposed secession. The nationalistic Federal Whigs, led by Graham, Morehead, and Badger, denied the right as well as the expediency and wisdom of secession. The State Rights Whigs and the moderate Democrats, led by Holden, believed in the constitutional right but opposed secession as an inexpedient and unwise course of action. Holden's exhortation that North Carolina "Watch and Wait" within the Union until President Lincoln and the Republican party did something to endanger slavery and the South, represented the view of the large unionist group consisting of moderate Whigs and Democrats. Only a minority group of radical Democrats led by Governor Ellis favored the secession of North Carolina because of Lincoln's election. Governor Ellis recommended to the Democratic legislature in November, 1860, a conference of southern states, the calling of a state convention, and military preparations. Viewing such a convention as unnecessary and as a secessionist scheme to take the state out of the Union, the unionist Democratic legislature declined to call a convention.

But events within and outside North Carolina in the winter of 1860–61 steadily weakened the unionist majority and strengthened the secessionist minority. Disunion was an accomplished fact and it was clear that no compromise proposal could be adopted by Congress because the Republicans opposed every compromise and concession to the South. A congressional committee, headed by Senator John Crittenden of Kentucky, submitted six constitutional amendments and two resolutions to Congress, the adoption of which might have averted or postponed the sectional conflict, but the Republicans in Congress rejected these proposals, largely on President-elect Lincoln's advice. The unionists in North Carolina were divided and on the defensive; the secessionists were united, aggressive, and enthusiastic for a positive program of secession from a nation hostile to slavery and the South and of union with the new, friendly southern Confederacy. Visiting commissioners from the seceded states spoke and worked for secession. An enthusiastic public campaign, characterized by meetings on "southern rights" and secession in the counties, impassioned oratory, editorials and newspaper publicity, military preparations, and petitions to the legislature, greatly strengthened the cause of secession and the demand for a state convention to act on the matter. In January, 1861, the General Assembly passed the Convention Act directing the people on February 28 to vote on the calling of a convention and to elect 120 delegates to serve if the convention referendum carried. The Convention Act passed because the secessionist legislators were joined by some unionists, who reflected the views of Holden, Vance, and Badger that the convention would be controlled by unionists and could serve as a safety valve, a bulwark of the Union, and a preventive of secession.

North Carolina Votes against Convention to Consider Secession

The four-week preconvention campaign was spirited and exciting. Of the 120 delegates chosen in the February 28 election, 42 were secessionists, 28 were conditional unionists, and 50 were unconditional unionists. Of the eighty-six counties, only thirty elected secession delegates. In twenty-two of the thirty secession counties slaves numbered more than 25 percent of the total population. On the issue of secession even the slaveholding area was divided. A secession county was generally a slaveholding county, but several slaveholding counties were opposed to secession because of their Whig strength. The voters were so suspicious and so afraid that a convention might lead to secession that they surprised many people in the state and in the South by voting against the convention, 47,323 to 46,672. They refused to follow the advice of their unionist leaders. Hence the convention, which might have been controlled by unionists, never met.

Failure of the Peace Movement

But the secessionists renewed their public campaign for a convention, and events outside the state played into their hands and brought the triumph of their cause. Various compromise proposals in Congress were defeated. North Carolina sent commissioners to Montgomery, the Confederate capital, in February, 1861, to work for an amicable adjustment of sectional issues; but they encountered no favorable response from the delegates of the seceded states, which were then in the process of organizing the Confederate government. The Peace Conference at Washington in February, called by Virginia and attended by delegates from twenty-one states, presented to Congress a plan of compromise and conciliation consisting of seven proposed amendments to the Constitution, including one for the westward extension of the 36° 30' line, but the plan was opposed by President-elect Lincoln and received scant support in the Senate. The failure of the Peace Conference, in which North Carolina was represented by Judge Thomas Ruffin and others, was a stunning blow to the unionists and a boon to the secessionists. Soon after becoming president in March, 1861, Lincoln decided to send supplies to the federal garrison of Fort Sumter in Charleston harbor. Confederate troops fired on the fort on April 12 and captured it two days later, before the arrival of the naval forces of the United States. Lincoln's decision to relieve Fort Sumter made war inevitable. On April 15 he issued a call to the states in the Union for 75,000 troops to suppress the southern "insurrection."

To the request of the United States secretary of war for two regiments from North Carolina, Governor Ellis replied promptly: "I regard the levy of troops made by the administration for the purpose of subjugating the States of the South as in violation of the Constitution and a gross usurpation of power. I can be no party to this wicked violation of the laws of the country, and to this war upon the liberties of a free people. You can get no troops from North Carolina."

The outbreak of hostilities and Lincoln's call for troops, followed by his proclamation blockading southern ports, unified North Carolina. When the only question was the choice of sides in the war, unionists in every section of the state became secessionists. "We are all one now," said John A. Gilmer, staunch unionist, to George Howard. Former Governor Graham said, "Blood is thicker than water," and unionist Thomas Ruffin urged North Carolinians to "Fight, fight, fight." The fourteen unionist newspapers in the state, led by Holden's *North Carolina Standard* all became secessionist.

Zebulon B. Vance later wrote that he "was pleading for the Union with hand upraised when news came of Fort Sumter and Lincoln's call for troops. When my hand came down from that impassioned gesticulation, it fell slowly and sadly by the side of a Secessionist." He said: "If war must come I preferred to be with my own people. If we had to shed blood, I preferred to shed Northern rather than Southern blood. If we had to slay, I had rather slay strangers than my own kindred and neighbors; and that it was better, whether right or wrong, that communities and States should go together and face the horrors of war in a body—sharing a common fate, rather than endure the unspeakable calamities of internecine strife. . . . The argument having ceased and the sword being drawn, all classes in the South united as by magic, as only a common danger could unite them."

Governor Ellis promptly ordered the seizure of the United States forts—Caswell and Johnston at the mouth of the Cape Fear, the federal arsenal at Fayetteville, and the United States Branch Mint at Charlotte. He called for thirty thousand volunteers and wrote the Confederate secretary of war: "You shall have from one to ten thousand volunteers in a few days, with arms, and I wish them to go as State troops. Many of our men will enlist in the Confederate Army. Will have a regiment in four days." Ellis summoned a special session of the legislature, which called for the election of delegates to a convention to meet in Raleigh on May 20, and made provision for extensive military preparations.

North Carolina Secedes from the Union, May 20, 1861

The convention that assembled at Raleigh on May 20, with 120 delegates present, was "an able body, but their political antipathies were deep and strong." Weldon N. Edwards, an ardent secessionist, was chosen president over William A. Graham, a "revolutionist," by a vote of 65 to 48. There was difference of opinion among the delegates only as to the means by which North Carolina should leave the United States and join the Confederacy. One ordinance, introduced by George E. Badger, Whig leader and unionist at heart, based secession on the right of revolution, and denied by implication the right of secession. The other ordinance, the one that was adopted unanimously, was introduced by Burton Craige, and was based squarely on the right of secession. It declared "that the union now subsisting between the state of North Carolina and the other states, under the title of 'The United States of America,' is hereby dissolved, and that the state of North Carolina is in full possession and exercise of all those rights of sovereignty which belong and appertain to a free and independent state." On the same day, May 20, the convention ratified the Provisional Constitution of the Confederate States of America.

The old secessionists rejoiced at the triumph of their cause and looked forward eagerly to the speedy achievement of southern independence, safety, and prosperity. The old unionists solemnly accepted the tragedy they had tried in vain to avert. As bands played martial airs, guns fired salutes, church bells pealed, and people paraded and shouted for joy, some sober and thoughtful people, like Badger, believed they were celebrating "the death knell of slavery" and eventual defeat. But now that the die was cast, there was general excitement and enthusiasm in the state for the Confederacy and for the cause of "Southern Independence."

Chapter 31

THE WAR FOR SOUTHERN INDEPENDENCE 1861-1865

Now that war had begun between the United States and the Confederate States of America in what has been called the Civil War or the War for Southern Independence, both contestants summoned their resources for the long and bitter struggle. Some optimists predicted a short war and a glorious victory for their side, but more realistic leaders in both North and South thought that the struggle would be long, costly, and devastating. Robert Toombs of Georgia called the South's decision to fight "suicide"—a view that was probably shared, though not openly expressed, by a number of North Carolinians.

Comparative Strength of the Contestants

The United States had the advantage of nearly two and a half times the population of the Confederacy—22,700,000 to 9,000,000, and of the latter figure 3,500,000 were Negro slaves. Thus the odds against the South were five to two, and four to one if the slaves are not considered. This omission is justified, since the Negroes furnished no soldiers to the Confederate armies and 93,000 to the Union armies. Experts estimate the total enrollment of the Confederate armies at about 850,000; that of the union armies, twice that number.

The North had an even greater superiority in material resources. Although southern farm acreage exceeded that of the North, northern farms had a greater gross value. The number of workingmen in northern factories was six times as many as that of the South, and the value of what they produced was five and a half times as great. The North's banking capital of $333,000,000 was seven times as great as that of the South, and the railroad system of the North was twice as extensive. The North possessed more gold, iron, and coal, and more factories to produce textiles, iron and steel, guns, munitions, and other sinews of war. It had a stronger navy and merchant marine, more shipyards, a regular army of 12,000 men (1861), and few natural barriers to hinder its grand strategy of invasion. It also had a government that was functioning, whereas the Confederate government had to "start from scratch." The agricultural South, lacking industrial diversity and economic self-sufficiency, had depended upon the exchange of its surplus of staple crops for supplies from the United States and Europe, particularly England. Deprived of that trade as the northern blockade tightened, the Confederacy would not have the supplies and materials necessary for waging war effectively or supplying the needs of the civilian population. But the Confederacy possessed a greater initial zeal and unity, soldiers more accustomed to outdoor life, and superior military leaders at first. Secessionists boasted that young southern men, trained from childhood in riding and shooting, were far superior to the "plodding farmhand or pale-faced mechanic." Moreover, the South was fighting on shorter, interior lines in defense of home and independence. But the cruel test of war demonstrated that there was not much difference between the valor and fighting ability of the boys in blue from the North and the boys in gray from the South.

Military Strategy and Major Campaigns

A resolution of Congress declared that the primary purpose of the war was to preserve the Union. The North's plan was to split the Confederacy by gaining control of the Mississippi River and its major tributaries in the South; to cut off necessary outside supplies by a blockade of southern ports; to defeat the Confederate armies—especially in the East—to capture Richmond, which had become the Confederate capital soon after Virginia's secession; and to force the seceded states to return to the Union. The primary object of the Confederacy was to maintain its independence—to hold what it had. Its plan was to repel the invading "Yankee armies" and, if possible, to procure aid from England and France. Some unduly optimistic southerners expected England to enter the war on the side of the Confederacy, in order to guarantee a supply of cotton for the English textile industry. Lee said later that he had never had any hope for a southern victory unless foreign powers intervened.

Though unable at any time to halt the invasion in the West, where the North won victories at Fort Henry on the Tennessee River, Fort Donelson on the Cumberland, Island Number 10, and finally New Orleans, the Confederacy, led superbly by Robert E. Lee and Thomas Jonathan ("Stonewall") Jackson, won brilliant victories during the first two years of the war over five superior armies that were sent to capture Richmond. Twice Lee carried offensive war into the North but was defeated and driven back by General George B. McClellan's army at Sharpsburg (Antietam), Maryland, September 17, 1862, and at

Gettysburg, Pennsylvania, early in July, 1863. Lee's defeat at Gettysburg has been called "the decisive battle" of the war.

England and the Confederacy

The Confederacy was unable to obtain commitments of foreign aid. The English aristocracy and the British ministry, under the leadership of Lord Palmerston, assisted by Lord John Russell and William E. Gladstone, were friendly to the South, and English industry suffered from a "cotton famine" as the northern blockade tightened after 1862. But dependence upon the Northwest for wheat, which "outweighed cotton" diplomatically; public hostility to slavery; and the determination of Queen Victoria and her husband, Prince Albert, to stay out of war kept England from coming to the aid of the Confederacy. Britain proclaimed its neutrality on May 13, 1861. Nevertheless it allowed the purchase in England of the *Alabama* and other cruisers as well as a number of blockade-runners, which were used effectively to raid northern commerce and which were extremely helpful to the Confederacy and to individual southern states, especially North Carolina, in the case of the blockade-runners.

Decisive Importance of Sea Power

The North won the war largely because it kept control of the sea. A steadily tightening blockade prevented southern exports of cotton and imports of guns, powder, cloth, medicine, iron, machinery, and other indispensable supplies. Daring blockade-runners carried on an extensive trade through the blockade, especially in the first two years of the conflict, but not enough to save the South. The blockade slowly strangled the Confederacy and paralyzed its morale and its war effort.

The North Splits the Confederacy by Capture of the Mississippi Valley

Before the end of 1863 the United States navy and its armies had cut the Confederacy in half by capturing various forts and towns and gaining complete control of the Mississippi River with the capture of Vicksburg early in July, 1863. Two northern generals won fame and success in the West —Ulysses S. ("Unconditional Surrender") Grant and William Tecumseh ("War is hell") Sherman. Lincoln, eager to put a "fighting general" in the East, ordered Grant to take charge of the campaign against Lee in Virginia, and Sherman was placed in command in the West.

Lincoln's Emancipation Proclamation

The labor of Negro slaves on the farms and with the armies strengthened the Confederacy, though in some parts of the South a few Negroes ran away from their masters. As a war measure designed to weaken the Confederacy—and possibly to gain the good will of England—President Lincoln on September 22, 1862, proclaimed that on and after January 1, 1863, "all persons held as slaves within any State or designated part of a state, the people whereof shall then be in rebellion against the United States, shall be then, thenceforward, and forever, free." This proclamation committed the administration to complete emancipation as soon as possible and weakened English sympathy for the Confederacy, since England had led a crusade for the worldwide abolition of slavery.

The North Wins the War, 1864–1865

The armies of Grant and Sherman delivered the death blow to the Confederacy in 1864 and the early months of 1865. With a superior army and at great loss of life, Grant drove Lee's Army of Northern Virginia southward toward Richmond. Sherman's large western army again cut the Confederacy in half, separating the lower from the upper South and destroying the railroads, factories, livestock, and supplies that were necessary to support Lee's army. Sherman fought his way from Tennessee to Atlanta, laid waste a path sixty miles wide in his famous "March to the Sea," and then marched through South Carolina and into North Carolina on his way to attack Lee from the south. Lee gave up Petersburg on April 3, and two days later Richmond fell into northern hands. Lee knew that it was folly to fight longer and he surrendered to Grant at Appomattox Court House on April 9. A few days later the news spread that President Lincoln had been assassinated in a Washington theater by John Wilkes Booth, a demented actor with southern sympathies. On April 26 General Joseph E. Johnston surrendered his Confederate army to Sherman at the Bennett House, near Durham, North Carolina, and on May 26, General Edmund Kirby-Smith surrendered his Confederate forces in Louisiana. The war was virtually over, with the United States triumphant and the South devastated.

Though North Carolina had been reluctant to secede and did not join the Confederacy until Lincoln called for troops to fight against the South, and though many North Carolinians considered the war an unnecessary and tragic mistake, the state sacrificed mightily for the southern cause. Its troops were in every important battle from Bethel, June 10, 1861, to Johnston's surrender in April, 1865. North Carolinians have liked to boast that its men were "First at Bethel, farthest at Gettysburg, and Chickamauga, and last at Appomattox," and that "North Carolina heroism hallowed and marked every important battlefield."

North Carolina's Contributions to the Confederacy

War spirit was high in the state in 1861 and everybody seemed to feel the stimulus. In May the legislature authorized Governor Ellis to enlist and organize ten regiments of state troops for the duration of the war and fifty thousand volunteers for twelve months' service. It also authorized the issuance of $5 million in bonds. Training camps were established and men swarmed to them; engineers built fortifications and many slaves were used for labor on military works. Under the competent direction of Adjutant General James G. Martin in recruiting, drilling, and organizing troops and in purchasing supplies, North Carolina was converted from a peaceful agricultural state into an armed military camp. All available West Point graduates and others with military training were called upon to convert "thousands of plow-boys and clerks into soldiers." Fortifications were erected along the coast and a small but inconsequential navy was built. Early in the war this "mosquito fleet" was destroyed. A state hospital, medical, and nursing service was organized by Surgeon General Charles E. Johnson of Raleigh. The hospitals, the troops recruited by the state, and the state naval forces were transferred to the Confederacy, but by a special agreement with President Davis and Confederate authorities, North Carolina was the only southern state obliged to clothe its own troops.

North Carolina Soldiers and Officers

North Carolina's greatest contribution to the Confederacy was manpower—the huge number of soldiers who bore the brunt of scores of battles. With one-ninth of the population of the Confederacy, North Carolina furnished about one-sixth or one-seventh of all Confederate soldiers. It furnished 111,000 offensive troops—all volunteers except about 19,000 conscripts —organized into seventy-two regiments; 10,000 reserves organized into eight regiments; and 4,000 home guards—a grand total of 125,000 men, a larger number than its voting population. These troops fought and died bravely on every important battlefield. To the Confederate armies, the state supplied two lieutenant generals (Theophilus H. Holmes and Daniel Harvey Hill); seven major generals (Robert Ransom, Jr., Robert F. Hoke, W. D. Pender, W. H. C. Whiting, Bryan Grimes, Stephen D. Ramseur, and Jeremy F. Gilmer); and twenty-six brigadier generals. Of these officers, nine died in battle or from wounds. The state also lost in battle thirty-six colonels, twenty-five lieutenant colonels, and twenty-seven majors. In the Confederate navy the state's most notable officers were Captain J. W. Cooke of the ram *Albemarle,* Captain J. N. Maffit of the cruiser *Florida,* and Captain James Iredell Waddell of the cruiser *Shenandoah,* which cruised in the Pacific and Arctic oceans destroying commerce and carrying the Confederate flag around the world. This famous ship was turned over to the British government in November, 1865, several months after the war was over.

In President Davis's cabinet, two North Carolinians served for short periods as attorney general—Thomas Bragg (1861–62) and George Davis (1864–65). The state's contribution of prominent Confederate military and civil leaders was not conspicuous in comparison with that of Virginia and some other states, a fact Vance and other North Carolina leaders attributed to President Davis's dislike and distrust of North Carolina because of its reluctance to join the Confederacy.

North Carolina Losses

North Carolinians fought on the sea, in the state, and in the West, but chiefly in Virginia, the "great battlefield of the war." D. H. Hill's regiment won fame by its victory in the first real battle of the war at Big Bethel, Virginia, June 10, 1861, in which Henry L. Wyatt of Edgecombe County was the first Confederate soldier to lose his life in battle. Thousands of North Carolinians were in Lee's army throughout the war. One-fifth of the Confederate lossses in the Seven Days' Battle near Richmond in 1862, one-third at Fredericksburg and Chancellorsville, and one-fourth at Gettysburg were North Carolinians. Of the twenty-seven regiments suffering the highest casualties at Gettysburg, thirteen were from North Carolina; the Twenty-sixth North Carolina regiment suffered casualties of 86 percent, the highest of all the regiments on either side during the war. North Carolina's greatest contribution was made in 1864. While Lee was being pushed back toward Richmond by Grant and when utter defeat seemed imminent, he depended particularly on nearby North Carolina for soldiers, food, supplies, and some of his best young generals. General William R. Cox's brigade fired the last shots of the Army of Northern Virginia, and at Appomattox one-fifth of those who surrendered with Lee were from North Carolina. In the entire war, 19,673 North Carolinians were killed in battle—more than one-fourth of the total Confederate battle deaths, and 20,602 died of disease. North Carolina's total loss in battle and from disease was 40,275, which was greater than that of any other Confederate state. During the course of the war some 23,000 North Carolina soldiers deserted, but 8,000 of these later returned to service. The percentage of desertion, North and South, was about 20, and North Carolina was not out of line in this respect.

Battles and Skirmishes Fought in North Carolina

North Carolina was a secondary though important battlefield of the war. Eleven battles and seventy-three skirmishes were fought on its soil.

Its role in the grand strategy of the war was important. From and through North Carolina, men and supplies went by railroad to Lee's army in Virginia. Near the end of the war, when the West and Gulf South had been cut off, Lee depended on North Carolina for soldiers and for necessary food and supplies, which were run into Wilmington through the blockade and shipped over the vital Wilmington and Weldon Railroad, the "lifeline of the Confederacy." In 1865 the quartermaster general of North Carolina reported that he was feeding half of Lee's army largely with food brought to Wilmington through the blockade. The sounds of eastern North Carolina were of great strategic importance because they opened the way to Norfolk, to the Wilmington and Weldon Railroad, and to the rear of Lee's army in Virginia.

Four military operations of importance were conducted in North Carolina— the Federal conquest and retention of the Sound region, the conquest of Fort Fisher and Wilmington, Sherman's invasion, and Stoneman's raid.

Strategic Importance of North Carolina Sounds and Railroads

Realizing the strategic importance of the Sound region, the North in the first year of the war sent strong and well-equipped naval and military forces, commanded by Generals Benjamin F. Butler and Ambrose E. Burnside, which had little difficulty in capturing poorly defended Fort Hatteras (August 29, 1861), Roanoke Island (February 8, 1862), New Bern (March 14), Washington (March 21), Fort Macon (April 26) and Plymouth (December 13). Meanwhile, on February 20, 1862, a detachment of Federal troops burned the the little town of Winton. This was the first town in the state to be burned during the war. In early November, 1863, General J. G. Foster led his Federal forces on a raid from New Bern to within ten miles of Tarboro. This raid accomplished little other than freeing a large number of slaves and the destruction of much private property. On another raid from New Bern, Foster, with a force of 10,000 infantry, 40 pieces of artillery, and 640 cavalry, set out to destroy the Wilmington and Weldon Railroad in the Goldsboro area. The Federal forces attacked Goldsboro on December 17, but they failed to capture the town. Including the loss of the Neuse River bridge, the damage to the railroad line was only superficial and was repaired in a few days.

The Federal forces occupied the entire Sound region and held most of it throughout the war. In Federal hands, it was the base for possible raids, a factor in the southern evacuation of Norfolk, and a constant threat to the remainder of the state, to the Wilmington and Weldon Railroad, and to Lee's army in Virginia. For two years or more the North was not able to send adequate forces to exploit the strategic value of its bases in North Carolina. The state and the Confederacy were able to insure Lee's safety by holding the Federal forces in check, but they were never able to muster strength enough to drive them from the state. So sharp was the criticism of President Davis in the state for neglecting its defense and so loud the demand for the return of North Carolina troops from Virginia to "drive out the invader" that in 1864 Davis and Lee ordered General Hoke to clear North Carolina of the enemy. Hoke made his plans, sprang a surprise, and in brilliant fashion captured Plymouth on April 20. The ram *Albemarle,* 152 feet long and 45 feet wide, covered with two-inch iron plate, had just been built at Edwards' Ferry, up the Roanoke River. Commanded by Captain J. W. Cooke, it drove the enemy vessels down the river and bombarded the forts, while Hoke's army was taking the town. Hoke then captured Washington and was attacking New Bern when his army was called to Virginia to help Lee in his losing struggle with Grant. On October 27 the enemy sank the *Albemarle* at Plymouth, recaptured the town, and retained control of eastern North Carolina until the close of the war.

Significance of Fort Fisher and the Port of Wilmington

The port of Wilmington held out almost to the very end as the chief Confederate center of blockade-running. It was defended by powerful Fort Fisher at the mouth of the Cape Fear. This fort, called "the Gibraltar of America," had withstood Federal attacks in 1862 and 1864. The fort and the dangerous combination of inlets, shoals, and islands which required a fifty-mile arc of blockading vessels, made it impossible for the northern blockade to stop the running of supplies to Lee's army. The northern leaders determined late in 1864 to cut off these supplies by capturing Fort Fisher and Wilmington. Two attacks were made on the fort by land and naval forces and it capitulated on January 15, 1865, after a brave defense. The Federals occupied Wilmington five weeks later and took over the Wilmington and Weldon Railroad in February, after which they set out for Goldsboro to join the larger army under Sherman, which was about to enter the state from the south. The fall of Fort Fisher and Wilmington sealed the fate of Lee's army.

Sherman in North Carolina

Sherman's army, moving north from Savannah through South Carolina to join Grant in Virginia, reached North Carolina the first week in March, 1865, captured Fayetteville on March 11, destroying the Confederate Arsenal, and set out for Goldsboro to join the Union armies marching from New Bern and Wilmington. Fierce battles took place at Southwest Creek near Kinston and at Averasboro on March 15 and 16. But the chief engagement occurred at Bentonville on March 19–21 where General Joseph E. Johnston and his hastily assembled Confederate army, including some regiments of North Carolina Junior Reserves, sought bravely but in vain to check Sherman in the "bloodiest battle ever fought on North Carolina soil." Confederate casualties were reported as 2,606 and Federal casualties at 1,641. On April 6 "the last grand review" held by any of the Confederate armies was conducted by Johnston, and Governor Vance made one of his most inspiring speeches. But hearing about Lee's surrender to Grant at Appomattox Court House, Virginia, on April 9, Johnston realized that the Confederate cause was lost, and on April 10 he broke camp and the "final retreat" began. Sherman drew closer to Johnston's army when he occupied Raleigh on April 13. Governor Vance, who had fled a few days before, was captured at Statesville on May 14 and was placed for a time in prison at Washington, D.C. Despite President Davis's plea for continued resistance, Johnston surrendered to Sherman on April 18 with 37,000 men, and was granted liberal terms, including unauthorized political concessions disavowed by President Andrew Johnson, who had taken office on April 15, following the assassination of President Lincoln. Final surrender terms along the lines of the Appomattox capitulation were agreed upon at the Bennett place, three miles west of Durham on the Hillsborough Road, on April 26.

Stoneman's Raid

While these developments were taking place in the East, General George Stoneman's army from Tennessee was giving western North Carolina its last taste of war. With a force of seven thousand men, the army swept through western North Carolina seizing or destroying property in a score of counties. On April 12 Salisbury was occupied. Private property in Salisbury was respected by the officers, although there was some minor pillaging. But situated here was one of the most hated Confederate prisons (an enclosure of sixteen acres, which once held ten thousand Federal prisoners) and a vast quantity of government supplies of all kinds brought from Columbia, Charlotte, Richmond, Danville, and Raleigh, as well as an arsenal, a foundry, and a considerable amount of ordnance. All these, along with the public buildings and the railroad depots, were burned.

Millions of dollars' worth of railroad property, factories, bridges, military supplies, and food in the regions of Wilkesboro, Salem, Greensboro, Salisbury, Statesville, Lincolnton, Shelby, Morganton, Rutherfordton, Hendersonville, Asheville, and Waynesville were destroyed. The estimated total destruction wrought by "Stoneman's Raid" was 4 cotton factories; 7,000 bales of cotton; 10,000 stands of arms; 1,000,000 rounds of small arms and ammunition; 1,000 rounds of artillery ammunition; 7,000 pounds of powder; 35,000 bushels of corn; 56,000 bushels of wheat; 160,000 pounds of bacon; 100,000 suits of clothes; 250,000 blankets; 20,000 pounds of leather; 10,000 pounds of saltpeter; large quantities of sugar, salt, and rice; $100,000 worth of drugs; and the machine shops at Salisbury.

At last the war was over. On April 29 General John McA. Schofield became military commander of the state.

Problems of the Home Front

While North Carolina's soldiers were fighting and dying on every battle front, the state government and the people at home were struggling to provide arms, powder, bullets, food, clothes, and other supplies for themselves and the soldiers—a problem made increasingly difficult by the ever-tightening Federal blockade.

Early in the war it was easier to get soldiers than it was to arm and equip them. The state kept most of the 37,000 guns seized in the United States Arsenal at Fayetteville in 1861, and this arsenal, taken over by the Confederacy, became one of the most important military depots of the South. The state government purchased shotguns and rifles from citizens of North Carolina and other states and also established factories for the manufacture of powder, rifles, cartridges, swords, sabres, bayonets, and other weapons. Privately owned factories were encouraged to make rifles and other military equipment. Churches donated their bells to be cast into cannon.

As has been indicated, North Carolina was the only southern state which under a special agreement with the Confederate government clothed its own soldiers. It bought most of the output of the thirty-nine cotton and nine woolen mills in the state; sent agents into other states to buy wool, leather, and other materials; and set up a factory in Raleigh to make uniforms and overcoats. Carpets and quilts from the homes of many people were made to serve as blankets for the soldiers. The acute shortages of goods caused inconvenience and hardship; forced the wide use of substitutes, such as molasses for sugar and parched corn for coffee; stimulated the mechanical and inventive abilities of the people, and revived in thousands of homes the use of hand-operated spinning wheels and looms. But home manufacture of thread and cloth were greatly impeded by the shortage of hand cards used in preparing cotton and wool for spinning. Salt, indispensable to the preservation of each year's production of meat, was a critical problem. The state set up salt factories on the coast for making salt by evaporating sea water, and it also purchased salt in Virginia for resale to the people.

The blockade brought distress and suffering to a people who had few manufactures, and poor transportation hampered the distribution of local products. The maintenance and operation of factories and railroads were made extremely difficult by the lack of oil, iron, machinery, and rails. Prices rose to dizzy heights. Bacon rose from thirty-three cents a pound in 1862 to $7.50 by 1865; wheat from $3.00 to $50.00 a bushel; flour from $18.00 to $500.00 a barrel. By 1865 salt was selling for $70.00 a bushel and coffee for $100.00 a pound. In August, 1864, slave boys from eleven to twenty-one years of age were selling in Charlotte for prices ranging from $4,000 to $5,200.

High prices were due not only to scarcities, state-wide and regional, and to high transportation costs. Selfish merchants, manufacturers, blockade-runners, and farmers charged extortionate prices for goods the people needed and could not get elsewhere. To prevent scarcity of foods and to keep prices down, the state provided by law for an embargo on the export of provisions, for making speculation in the necessities of life a crime, for fixing prices, and for prohibiting the distillation of grain; but poor enforcement made these efforts at economic control ineffective. The steady depreciation of state and Confederate currency was reflected in the steadily rising prices of commodities. The war was financed in part by new and increased taxes, but chiefly by issues of paper currency and the sale of bonds by both state governments and the Confederacy. The currency and bonds depreciated greatly as the prospect of Confederate military victory declined.

Relief of distress and destitution among civilians, especially soldiers' families, was a major problem. During the war the state appropriated $6,000,000 for relief. The state bought and stored provisions for resale to soldiers' families and the poor at low prices through agencies set up in each county. A large portion of the cargoes of state blockade-runners consisted of civilian goods. The county governments also appropriated funds for relief. Charitable individuals and organizations also aided the needy, and Governor Vance was very solicitous of the welfare of the needy civilians as well as the soldiers.

Negroes and the War Effort

The role of the Negro, free and slave, in the war effort has never been fully told. Tragically, for the Confederacy, Negroes were never allowed to formally enlist in the Confederate army, though General Robert E. Lee urged their enlistment in the late days of the war.

Contributions made by southern Negroes directly aided the war effort and indicate that many Negroes did identify themselves with the Confederacy. Negroes were among the first southerners to offer their service to the new government. In New Bern, in April, 1861, "fifteen or twenty free Negroes . . . volunteered their services as laborers and in defense of the city." The *Winston-Salem Press,* in May, 1861, said: "Fifteen free men of color left Salisbury Monday morning for the mouth of the Cape Fear, volunteers for the service of the state. They were in fine spirits and each wore a placard in his hat bearing the inscription, 'We will die by the South.' " The May 7, 1861, *Greenborough Patriot* reported that "a Negro hackman came to his master and insisted with tears in his eyes, that he accept his savings of one hundred dollars to help equip volunteers."

Contemporary North Carolina newspapers contain many accounts of the loyalty of slaves to their masters, especially during the closing months of the war. In March, 1865, a squad of Union cavalry carried off nineteen Negro men from Monroe. Thirteen of the group escaped the night of their capture and returned to their homes. The *North Carolina Standard* of January 11, 1862, noted that "slaves continue to run off to the Yankees in Virginia but when they get a chance to leave they at once return to their masters and declare their disgust at Yankee freedom." The *Raleigh Daily Press* of June 6, 1864, reported that "Negroes as a general rule came to prefer to remain with their masters." Among the troops taken at Hatteras in 1862 by Union forces were two North Carolina Negroes who were offered their release in Boston by the Union commanders. According to a North Carolina newspaper, they politely answered "we radder stick to our Massah, sah." The *Fayetteville Observer* of March 21, 1864, carried the story of a Negro who refused to fire into a Confederate regiment because . . . "My Young Master is thar . . . and I can't shoot thar, for I love my young master still."

Contributions of Women to the War Effort

The women of North Carolina looked after the farms and plantations, many of them working hard in the fields to raise food. They sent their brothers, husbands, fathers, and sweethearts to the army, wrote letters of encouragement to them, and endured loneliness and worry. There was some organized activity of women in the larger towns—sewing circles, knitting associations, hospital aid societies, and nursing clubs—but there was little concerted effort to organize the women of the state for war. Nevertheless women made flags and clothes for soldiers, met troop trains and served refreshments to the soldiers, nursed the sick and wounded in hospitals, and cared for soldiers' families that were in need. They complained about extortionate prices charged by some merchants, and at Salisbury, March 15, 1863, some two hundred women armed with hatchets defied Confederate soldiers and successfully demanded flour from the local merchants.

Blockade-Running

Despite the extraordinary efforts, privations, and sacrifices of the people, there was a steady and increasing shortage of every kind of food, goods, and supplies that were not grown or produced by the excessively agricultural economy of North Carolina. As already stated, the Federal blockade was designed to cut off all trade from and to the Confederacy, to force it to depend upon its own resources, which were inadequate for civilian and military needs, and to bring Union victory by a paralysis of Confederate morale and ability to wage effective war. But it was impossible for the United States navy to establish a perfect blockade of the entire three thousand mile coast of the Confederacy. The huge profits of running the blockade from the Confederacy with a cargo of four- to eight-cent cotton, which sold in Europe for fifty to seventy cents, and returning with a cargo of cheap goods from Europe for sale at high prices in the Confederacy, lured many privately owned ships into the dangerous business of running the blockade. Geographical conditions and man-made fortifications (Forts Fisher, Anderson, Caswell and Campbell) at the mouth of the Cape Fear River made Wilmington the most important blockade-running port in the Confederacy. Except for Galveston, which was not very important, Wilmington was the last Confederate port to be closed. Nearly a hundred daring blockade-runners, over half of which were captured or sunk, made more than four hundred trips from Wilmington to Nassau and other West Indian ports and back, enriching their owners with huge profits and bringing in perhaps $65 million worth of necessary supplies for civilians and soldiers, without which the Confederacy would have collapsed earlier. Near the end of the war half the food for Lee's army came through the blockade to Wilmington and over the Wilmington and Weldon Railroad to the battlefields in Virginia. Early in the war Adjutant General Martin bought supplies for the state from privately owned blockade-runners, but he persuaded Governor Vance that the state government could obtain supplies more effectively and economically by engaging in blockade-running for itself. Governor Vance sent agents to England who purchased for the state a swift steamer which was renamed the *Advance*. Later the state acquired part ownership of several other blockade-runners. Before the capture of the *Advance* it made eleven trips through the blockade, taking out cotton and bringing into Wilmington arms, food, and supplies necessary for civilians and soldiers. Governor Vance regarded the success of the venture of state blockade-running as one of the most important achievements of his administration and it was one of the sources of his great popularity as "war governor." Years later he described the supplies thus obtained by the state: large quantities of machinery supplies, 60,000 pairs of hand cards, 10,000 grain scythes, 200 barrels of bluestone for wheat growers, leather and shoes amounting to 250,000 pairs, 50,000 blankets, woolen cloth for at least 250,000 uniforms, 12,000 overcoats, 2,000 Enfield rifles, 100,000 pounds of bacon, 500 sacks of coffee for hospital use, $50,000 worth of medicines, large quantities of lubricating oils, and many minor supplies of various kinds. The total business on state account was over $12,000,000, of which about $6,000,000 worth of goods were resold to the Confederate government. The state government thus alleviated civilian shortages and suffering, aided in feeding and clothing of the Confederate armies, and fully succeeded in meeting its responsibility of clothing the troops from North Carolina. Whereas near the end of the war Confederate soldiers from other states were ragged and cold, those from North Carolina were well clothed. At the end of the war 92,000 surplus uniforms, ready-made and in cloth, were in the state's warehouses, though the state had sold some of its supplies to the Confederate government.

Chapter 32

INTERNAL DIVISION AND WRECKAGE, 1861-1865

The war for Southern Independence brought political division, bitterness, disaffection, and even disloyalty to North Carolina; destroyed much of the state's wealth; took the lives of some forty thousand of its young men; left a depressing heritage of defeat; blighted almost every phase of the state's life and handicapped its future.

War-Time Politics: Confederates and Conservatives

The political unity in the Secession Convention of May, 1861, and in the early months of the war was abnormal, superficial, and temporary. Writing soon after the adjournment of this convention, Jonathan Worth said: "Abolitionism and Democracy, aided and instigated by the Devil, have forced everybody under the one or the other of their banners. . . . Mr. Lincoln knew his policy would disarm all Union men in the Southern States. He did more than all the secessionists to break up the Union. Lincoln's measures have united the North. They certainly have united North Carolina. There seems to be no alternative in the South, only between independence and humiliation . . . North Carolina would have stood by the Union but for the conduct of the national administration . . . which for folly and simplicity exceeds anything in modern history, as North Carolina is strictly a unit for resistance and everywhere is heard the sound of the drum and fife."

When the pressure of outside events brought secession and war, the secessionists, hitherto a minority, were placed in control of the state government by their prestige of victory and by the initial enthusiasm for the Confederate cause. Before the war was a year old, however, the unity and high enthusiasm of North Carolina were gone. Despite the desperate need for harmony, there arose bitter division and conflict between the newly formed Confederate and Conservative political parties within North Carolina and between North

465

Carolina and the Confederate government.

The Confederate Party and Its Platform

The Confederate party, which was in control of North Carolina when the war began, was composed chiefly of original secessionists, like Governor Ellis, Weldon N. Edwards, and other Democrats, and perhaps some former Whigs and Know-Nothings, who had favored secession even before Lincoln's call for troops. Considering the military success of the Confederacy essential to southern independence, it zealously supported the policies of President Davis and the Confederate administration and was willing to adopt virtually any policy or means to achieve the ultimate goal of Confederate victory and southern independence. Though they had been ardently for state rights in the United States, the Confederates advocated unprecedented centralization and disregard of state rights in the Confederacy.

The Conservative Party

The Conservative party was composed in the main of old Whigs and those Democrats who had been loyal to the Union and hostile to secession until the outbreak of war. Most of the state's prewar leaders, including William A. Graham, Zebulon B. Vance, William W. Holden, George E. Badger, John M. Morehead, and Jonathan Worth were Conservatives. Driven out of the Union and into the Confederacy against their better judgment and wishes, they blamed the tragic war upon northern abolitionists and the mistaken policies of southern secessionists. Now that the war had come, they had no alternative but to "fight to the finish." They favored Confederate military victory and southern independence, but they were unwilling to discard constitutional government for a military dictatorship or surrender the rights and liberties of individuals and states to the Confederate government. Even in war they could not support restrictions on freedom of speech and press, supremacy of military over civil authority, sedition laws, test oaths, and suspension of the writ of habeas corpus. They were determined to preserve freedom, "not only in the end, but also in the means," and they heartily disagreed with the statement of a Richmond newspaper, "The government of the Confederacy is the government of the army; and no citizen has any rights which can interfere with or impede its efficiency." In the United States most of these Conservatives had been nationalistic and friendly to a strong central government; in the Confederacy they were champions of state rights. Because of waning public confidence in the state administration and in the policies of Jefferson Davis and the Confederate government, the Conservative party captured control of the state in 1862 and held it throughout the remainder of the war.

The Conservatives denounced the Confederates as "Destructives," who would destroy the state constitution, state rights and individual liberty, and substitute consolidation and military dictatorship. Regarding unitary direction of meager southern resources as essential to victory over a more powerful enemy, the Confederates denounced the Conservatives as unsound in judgment and devoid of Confederate patriotism. Holden's *North Carolina Standard* was the chief mouthpiece of the Conservatives and the most bitter and outspoken critic of Confederate policies. This powerful paper reflected widespread discontent over the Federal conquest of eastern North Carolina; the heavy casualties of North Carolinians in Virginia; the prospect of a long, costly, and doubtful war; the Confederate Conscription Act of 1862, and other laws and policies of the Confederate government.

The Gubernatorial Contest of 1862

Holden and the Conservatives frustrated the plans of the Confederates to call off the gubernatorial election of 1862. After failing to persuade William A. Graham to run for governor, Holden and other Conservative leaders procured through party newspapers the nomination of Zebulon B. Vance, youthful prewar Whig congressman, Unionist, and popular colonel of the 26th North Carolina Regiment. William J. Johnston, a railroad official and an original secessionist and Davis supporter, was nominated by the Confederates. Neither candidate conducted a campaign—Vance remaining with his regiment on the battlefields of Virginia and Johnston staying at his office in Charlotte, but the eleven newspapers supporting Johnston and the ten backing Vance were active and enunciatory. The Raleigh *Register* said: "Remember that if Zebulon Vance shall be elected governor, the Yankees will claim it as an indispensable sign that the Union sentiment is in the ascendency in the heart of the Southern Confederacy." The Confederates belittled the youthful Vance, called him the "pliant tool of Holden," accused him of antiadministration views, and denounced him as the "Yankee" candidate. Vance's reply was that the "only hope of the South" was "the prosecution of the war at all hazards and to the utmost extremity so long as the foot of an invader pressed the Southern soil." If elected, he promised to "prosecute the war for liberty and independence to the bitter end." The unpopularity of the Confederate party and the public confidence in the ability and loyalty of Vance elected him governor by a vote of 54,423 to 20,448. He captured all but twelve of the state's eighty counties.

Vance as "War Governor"

Some of Vance's opponents had said that Vance would try to restore North Carolina to the Union. Perhaps some of his supporters hoped that he would. Both views were erroneous, and Vance cleared up all doubts on this score in his inaugural address when he declared that secession was the "deliberate judgment" of the people of the state and that he accepted this decision. It meant "a long and bloody war." Victory was the task of the people at home as well as those on the field of battle. There was an imperative necessity for unity and there should "be no dissenting voice."

As war governor Vance endeared himself to the people by his successful efforts to provide necessary supplies of arms, clothing, and food for North Carolina troops and civilians. His warmth of personality, his superb ability as an orator, his sincere sympathy for the people as they suffered from a war which was not of their choosing or making, and his exertions in behalf of southern independence, as well as his sharp tilts with Jefferson Davis and the Confederate government in defense of the rights of North Carolina and its people, won the esteem and support of the vast majority of the citizenry. The widespread dissatisfaction of North Carolina with certain Confederate policies was voiced chiefly by Vance, by editor Holden, and by Chief Justice Richmond M. Pearson. Vance consistently and persistently protested against many Confederate laws and policies which he thought impaired the rights of his state. He objected strenuously to the Confederate conscription laws, the suspension of the writ of habeas corpus, the Confederate impressment of property, and the use of Virginia officers in North Carolina. On one occasion he threatened to "take North Carolina out of the Confederacy" if President Davis did not alter his policies regarding the state.

Vance Charges Confederacy with Discriminating against North Carolina

Vance and other Conservative leaders charged that Davis, in making appointments to high civil and military positions, discriminated against North Carolina in general and against Conservatives and prewar unionists in particular. North Carolinians held no position in the Confederate cabinet, except that of attorney general during the latter part of the war. Discriminations in military appointments were even more offensive to Vance and other state leaders. Of seven full Confederate generals, not one was from North Carolina. Braxton Bragg was born in the state, but he was a resident of Louisiana at the time of his appointment. North Carolina had only 2 lieutenant generals of 19. It had only 7 of 72 major generals and only 26 of 328 brigadier generals. Governor Vance constantly complained that "outsiders," particularly Virginians, were being appointed to command North Carolina troops, and he thought the reason for this was that Davis and other Confederate officials were suspicious of the "loyalty of the great body of our people, because of the great reluctance with which they gave up the old Union." He maintained that there had been a "studied exclusion of the anti-secessionists from all the more important offices of the government, even from those promotions in the army which many of them had won with their own blood." As early as 1861 the North Carolina Convention had registered official complaint against such discriminations.

Vance believed in "patronizing home talent." He thought this would make the war more popular in the state and that it would enable the Confederacy to enforce its unpopular conscription laws in North Carolina. He tried to impress this idea upon Davis, and the Confederate secretary of war, but, failing to make any impression, he laid the matter of officering state troops with North Carolina men before the General Assembly and urged it "to take such steps as would preserve the rights and honor of the state." He declared, "It is mortifying to find entire brigades of North Carolina soldiers in the field commanded by strangers and in many cases our own brave and war-worn colonels are made to give place to colonels from distant states." On January 3, 1863, he informed the Confederate secretary of war that the Confederate government was appointing citizens of other states to important nonmilitary posts in North Carolina. He was especially disgusted that Colonel Thomas P. August had been appointed as commandant for conscripts in North Carolina, and declared that this was tantamount to an announcement "that North Carolina has no man in her borders fit to command her own conscripts" and that such action "smacks of discourtesy to say the least." Colonel August was finally replaced by Peter Mallett, a North Carolinian. Vance protested to Confederate officials against the selection of West Point generals who "ride roughshod over the people, drag them from their homes, and assign them, or rather consign them to strange regiments and strange commanders, without regard to their wishes or feeling." He declared that he "knew more about conditions in North Carolina than all the West Pointers in the service."

North Carolina's Interest in Local Defense

The state's interest in local defense brought it into conflict with the Confederacy early in the war. North Carolina lived in constant fear of an attack upon its coastal region, and in January, 1862, Governor Henry T. Clark was compelled "in view of the immediate and pressing necessity for arms for our defense" to ask the Confederate government for the return of a quantity of arms that had been taken from North Carolina into Virginia. Later in the year Clark issued a proclamation against the purchase of arms or the impressment of any kind of equipment by Confederate agents, and he threatened to use force, if necessary, to protect the citizens against such actions. Goveror Vance pressed these views with even more vigor. He declared that he had originally supported the Confederate Conscription Act of 1862, thinking that this law would "actually be providing for state defense," but that the citizens of North Carolina were being taken from the state, leaving it "stripped and defenseless," and, despite the fact of a vast, unprotected coast, "she has fewer troops given her for its defense" than any other state.

Controversy with the Confederacy over Conscription

One of the most bitter conflicts between the state and Confederate government related to the raising of troops. Before the enactment of the Confederate Conscription Act of 1862, North Carolina officials insisted that all troops furnished to the Confederacy should be "tendered to the Confederate government though the governor or some other authorized state agent." Governor Clark objected to the Confederate policy of "independent acceptance," declaring that it "interfered with the State filling its own quota and that it overreached the Governor and compromised the dignity of the State."

The drastic Confederate Conscription Acts of 1862 and later were extremely unpopular in North Carolina. The soldiers considered them unethical and discriminatory; many lawyers, including Chief Justice Pearson, thought they were unconstitutional; many newspapers condemned them in strong language; the people seemed to think that they were unnecessary, undemocratic, and unjust. Especially unpopular was the provision in the 1862 law which exempted from military service all those who owned as many as twenty slaves. Vance thought the law was "harsh and odious" and, in a letter to President Davis, he said it was "a rich man's war, and a poor man's fight." He admitted that he had "acquiesced in conscription as a matter of necessity," but the enforcement of it in North Carolina was "ruthless and unrelenting," and President Davis, in a letter to Vance in 1863, admitted that North Carolina was "far ahead of all others in the number raised under the conscript law."

Editor Holden, the most caustic North Carolina critic of Confederate conscription, thought that a "military despotism" was making rapid strides in the Confederacy, declaring that "we will be slaves neither to Lincoln, nor Davis, nor France, nor England." On June 3, 1863, Holden wrote in the *North Carolina Standard:* "North Carolina is badly treated. She is ignored. She has no voice in the Cabinet. She is raked for conscripts as with a fine tooth comb. Her troops are always placed in the forefront of the hottest battles. Her sick and wounded are scattered through every hospital in Richmond, and are treated by physicians appointed from other states. A large portion of her people are suspected of being disloyal. The people of North Carolina are long suffering; but Mr. Davis would do well to bear in mind that it is the last straw that breaks the camel's back. . . . North Carolina must be the equal of the other states of the Confederacy, or she will leave it, and endeavor to take care of herself."

Vance insisted that all persons employed by the state, even the most minor officials as well as workers in factories, were necessary to the operation of the state government and therefore exempt from Confederate conscription. He thus secured the exemption of several thousand North Carolinians from military service.

Confederate authorities held that conscript officers should judge whether an individual was subject to conscription. Vance declared that this was the function of the North Carolina courts, and he refused to interfere with the work of "that coordinate branch of the government which intrudes upon nobody, usurps no authority, but is, on the contrary, in great danger of being overlapped and destroyed by the tendencies of the times." Twice he issued orders to militia officers forbidding them to arrest "any man as a conscript who had been discharged by a writ of habeas corpus issued by any judge of competent jurisdiction."

Complaints against Confederate Impressment of Property

The Confederate policy of impressing private property provoked bitter protest in North Carolina, especially in the West where food was scarce, mainly because of the shortage of labor. Vance denounced the "illegal seizures of property and other depredations of an outrageous character" by Confederate cavalry as worse than the plagues of the Egyptians and declared the seizure of food for horses from starving women and children to be a "grievance, intolerable, damnable, and not to be borne." Unless these cavalry horses were removed from the state, the governor said he would be under the "painful necessity" of calling out the militia of the adjoining counties and driving them out. "Unless something can be done," he said, "I shall be compelled in some sections to call out my militia and levy actual war against them." The legislature supported Vance in his stand, denounced the evils of impressment, demanded that the Confederacy "stop all illegal proceedings," and requested the governor to "use every honorable means to retain the remaining provisions in the state."

State and Confederate Taxation

State and local taxes were increased several times during the war. The state property tax jumped from 20 cents on the $100 valuation in 1861 to $1 in 1864, and the state in 1862 adopted an inheritance tax and a tax on all incomes over $100. But it was Confederate taxation that evoked the loudest complaints. The Confederacy levied an occupation tax ranging from $50 to $200 and from 2½ to 20 percent of the gross sales or business of merchants, auctioneers, brokers, lawyers, physicians, butchers, druggists, bankers, and a number of other business pursuits; hotels were taxed from $30 to $500 and theaters, $500. There was an income tax of 1 percent on salaries from $1,000 to $1,500, and a 2 percent on all over $1,500. All trade in bacon, flour, corn, oats, and dry goods during 1862 was taxed 10 percent. All agricultural products in hand on July 1, 1863, as well as salt, wine, and liquors, were taxed 8 percent; all moneys and credits, 1 percent. It has been estimated that North Carolina paid over $10 million in various Confederate taxes. But it was the tax in kind that brought forth the most bitter complaints. This was a tax of 10 percent of the annual farm production, above a specified exemption (fifty bushels of potatoes, twenty bushels of beans and peas, one hundred bushels of corn, and fifty bushels of wheat), which must be delivered by the producer to the nearest railroad station. North Carolina farmers grumbled about this law, but the state was the largest contributor to the tax. By June, 1864, North Carolina farmers had contributed to the Confederacy 3,000,000 pounds of bacon, 770,000 bushels of wheat, 75,000 tons of hay and fodder, and other produce worth $150,000.

Controversy with Confederacy over Supplying North Carolina Troops

Another controversy between state and Confederate authorities arose from the determined effort of the state government to clothe its troops in Confederate service. Believing that the limited resources of the Confederacy should be equitably administered by a central agency, President Davis sought repeatedly but vainly to annul the early agreement that North Carolina clothe its own troops and receive Confederate commutation. The state government monopolized most of the output of North Carolina mills, sent purchasing agents into Virginia, Georgia, Florida, and other states; imported quantities of clothing and cloth beyond its own needs through the blockade (92,000 uniforms were on hand at the close of the war); sold only a small portion of the surplus to the hardpressed Confederacy; resented the presence of Confederate purchasing agents in the state; and tenaciously held to the idea that the resources of North Carolina should be devoted primarily to North Carolina and not to the Confederacy. When the Confederacy sent agents into the state to purchase what goods they could in the open markets, Vance complained that "the country was still swarming with agents of the Confederate government stripping bare our markets and putting enormous prices upon our agents." In January, 1864, a Confederate official, Lawton, complained that North Carolina had forty factories "from not one of which this bureau has realized for years past a single yard of material for the service at large."

Controversy over Blockade-Running

There was considerable controversy between state and Confederate authorities over blockade-running. The Confederacy allowed the states complete freedom to own and use ships for running the blockade; but blockade-runners that were privately owned—as most of them were—or those owned in part by the states, were required to carry one-half their cargoes "on Confederate account." This policy irritated Vance, who accused the Confederate government of hampering his efforts to supply North Carolina soldiers and

A Ship Depicted on a North Carolina Treasury Note of 1866

A Farm Laborer at Work as Depicted on a North Carolina Treasury Note of 1866

citizens with essential goods. He declared that the port of Wilmington was "more effectually blockaded from within than from without," that the Confederate policy would cause blockade-runners "to incur a loss on every voyage," and that in respect to the blockade-runners partially owned by the state, he would "fire the ships" rather than submit to the requirement concerning the carriage of a fixed quota of goods for the Confederacy.

Suspension of the Writ of Habeas Corpus

A Confederate law of February 27, 1862, authorized the suspension of the writ of habeas corpus under certain conditions, and in June of that year President Davis suspended the writ, which resulted in the arrest and imprisonment without trial of about forty North Carolinians suspected of disloyalty. This action aroused Vance's ire and he declared that it was his duty to protect the people of his state "in whatever rights pertain to them." First among these was "the undoubted right of trial for their alleged offenses." The legislature agreed with the governor and passed several resolutions condemning the Confederate policy as a "violation of all the fundamental principles of freedom and liberty, and as destructive of state sovereignty." One Senate resolution declared that "instead of a confederacy of free and sovereign states, we have established the most powerful consolidated military despotism." Finally, the General Assembly passed a law making it mandatory for state judges to issue the writ of habeas corpus. As a result, the Confederate policy was nullified in North Carolina, and the writ of habeas corpus was not suspended to any effective degree.

Writing years later, Vance said: "Neither the losses incurred by the radical and sudden changes in the currency, nor the conscription of the principals or substitutes, nor the extension of it to such as age, and upon such terms as to place the industrial pursuits of the country at the feet of the President, nor the heavy burdens of taxation—none of these, nor all of them together, have so awakened the public feeling as the withdrawal of this time-honored and blood-bought guard of personal freedom, from the people in times when it is most needed for their protection."

The Problem of Desertion

As the war dragged on year after year with increasing suffering and death and with diminishing prospect of southern victory, a numbing war weariness settled upon the people, many of whom longed for an end of the "mistaken, destructive, and futile conflict" which was being fought "chiefly by the common people to preserve the slave property of the wealthy few." Some 23,000 soldiers and 423 North Carolina officers deserted the army. There were many reasons for desertion: strong Union sentiment, especially in the mountain area; resentment at the Confederate Conscription Acts; long absence of soldiers from home; the unsatisfactory furlough policy of the army; appeals from home and the desire to return to suffering wives, children and other loved ones; and, above all, the feeling of futility. Many of the deserters were not disloyal at heart; they were "simply fathers gone mad." Regardless of the causes, civilian indifference and noncooperation became widespread. Vance's eloquent appeals and even his use of the militia were ineffectual in stopping desertion, though some eight thousand North Carolina deserters did return to the service. Whole neighborhoods in "deserter country" were terrorized by deserters, "buffaloes," and "bushwhackers." Proximity to the Virginia battleground and the suitability of the eastern swamps and western mountains as hiding places made North Carolina a haven for deserters from the Confederate armies—and, to a lesser degree, from the Union armies. North Carolina led the Confederacy in the total number of deserters, but it also led in the number "returned from desertion." And its proportion of deserters was about that of the general average for both northern and southern armies—around one-fifth.

Davis and the Confederate authorities blamed Vance, Holden, Judge Pearson, and other Conservative leaders for the "disaffection" in North Carolina; but the people supported their state leaders; they loved Vance, they distrusted Davis, and they resented Confederate suspicion of the loyalty of North Carolina, which was furnishing more than its share of soldiers and making the heaviest contribution of all the states in supplies and Confederate taxes.

Although the "disaffection" in the state may have hampered the Confederacy at times, most of the criticism of the Confederacy fell far short of actual disloyalty. There was some manifestation of open disloyalty to the Confederacy, however. After the Federal capture of Hatteras in 1861 a local convention in November of that year declared secession null and void and "elected" Marble Nash Taylor "governor," but this farcical government was not recognized by the United States. In 1862, after the capture of much of eastern North Carolina, President Lincoln appointed Edward Stanly, a native of North Carolina then living in California, as military governor. Stanley evoked little popular support in the state, and he disagreed with the Federal authorities at New Bern and denounced the action of Federal troops as "guilty of the most shameful pillaging and robbery that ever disgraced an army in any civilized land." Consequently, he resigned his office on January 15, 1863, thus ending the efforts to "reconstruct" North Carolina until after the war.

Holden and the Peace Movement

The disaffection and war weariness manifested themselves after the defeats at Vicksburg and Gettysburg in July, 1863, as a definite peace movement. A hundred or more peace meetings in about forty counties criticized Confederate policies, denounced the war and its conduct, urged the Confederate government to sue for peace, and manifested a growing demand for a North Carolina peace convention. The movement for such a convention alarmed the Confederates and also many Conservatives, as perhaps leading toward North Carolina's secession from the Confederacy and reunion with the United States. Holden published the proceedings of the local peace meetings in the *North Carolina Standard;* the similarity of their phraseology pointed to Holden as the author, and he was bitterly denounced as the leader of a "peace at any price" campaign. He wrote in his newspaper: "Let the people speak. It is refreshing to hear from them." The people took Holden at his word. Some endorsed his actions, many condemned them. On the night of September 3, 1863, a Georgia regiment passing through Raleigh completely demolished his newspaper office, whereupon some two hundred of Holden's supporters demolished the office of the *State Journal,* a Confederate administration paper. Fearful of the peace movement and distrustful of Holden's loyalty, Vance broke with Holden, his erstwhile political ally and fellow critic of the Confederacy. Alarmed at the growing strength of the "peace party," Vance sought to check its growth by denouncing it, by increasing his own criticism of unpopular Confederate policies, and by persuading Davis to placate the state by appointing a North Carolinian to the cabinet, and by ordering General Hoke to drive the Federal forces from eastern North Carolina. On February 10, 1864, a peace meeting nominated Holden for the governorship.

The Gubernatorial Election of 1864

In the Vance-Holden gubernatorial contest of 1864 the peace party denounced Vance and the Confederacy, demanded peace, and called for a state convention without avowing any intention of having North Carolina take separate action in making peace with the United States. Vance wrote E. J. Hale that Holden "is for submission, reconstruction, or anything else that will put him back under Lincoln and stop the war." In the vigorous campaign Vance denounced Confederate encroachment on the rights of North Carolina and its citizens and urged the Confederate government to negotiate with the United States for peace; but he denounced separate state action for peace through a convention, which he insisted was the primary objective of the "peace party," and called for a united southern front until independence was achieved. Vance's platform, personality, and superb campaign oratory (Badger said that Vance was "the greatest stump speaker that ever was") won the support of the Confederate party and the moderate Conservatives. With the support of only the radical wing of the Conservative party, Holden carried only Johnston and Randolph counties, and received only 12,647 civilian votes to Vance's 44,856. The soldier vote was Vance 13,209 to Holden 1,824.

There was no longer—if there had ever been—any danger of North Carolina's desertion of the Confederacy. Early in 1865 a peace group in the Confederate Congress approached Vance to take the lead for peace by separate state action, but Vance "refused to lead the roll of infamy." As Sherman approached Raleigh after the battle of Bentonville, Vance sent Graham and Swain, at their insistence, to open negotiations with Sherman. But North Carolina remained in the war to the bitter end.

Though a caustic critic of Davis and the Confederate government, Governor Vance always urged the state to give support and loyalty to the Confederacy. His policy of "fight the Yankees and fuss with the Confederacy" helped him to hold the confidence of the people and to keep the state loyal to the unpopular policies of the Confederate government. There is no conclusive evidence that Holden wanted North Carolina to desert the Confederacy, but he emerged from the war with the distrust and enmity of the majority of the prewar Democratic and Whig leadership and of the wartime Confederate and Conservative parties. The animosities and divisions accentuated and bred by the war lasted for years and influenced political alignments.

The Devastating Effects of War

Only a terrible war could have transformed the prosperous and progressive North Carolina of 1860 into the divided, defeated, and exhausted North Carolina of 1865. More than forty thousand of its strongest men, ranging in age from sixteen to sixty, lost their lives, slightly more from disease than from battle. Thousands who returned were handicapped for life by the loss of arm, leg, eye, or by other injuries. War conditions also took their toll of civilian deaths, and untold thousands of soldiers and civilians were impaired in strength and health by disease, worry, hard work, and scarcity of food, clothing, and medicine.

The war was likewise a ruthless destroyer of economic resources. The armies of the United States destroyed and carried off millions of dollars worth of property. Railroads, factories, public buildings, bridges, roads, churches, schoolhouses, private homes and barns were destroyed or in need of repair. A capital investment of over $200 million was wiped out by the abolition of slavery—what Charles A. Beard called "the most stupendous act of sequestration in the history of Anglo-Saxon jurisprudence." Millions of dollars in revenue from local, state, and Confederate taxes went for war expenditures and the care of the needy. Citizens, banks, the Literary Fund, the University of North Carolina, colleges, and other institutions, which had loaned money to the state and Confederate governments, faced bankruptcy because Confederate bonds were worthless and state bonds had depreciated greatly in value and might be repudiated. With Confederate and state currency worthless, few people had any cash or credit facilities. Many stores, newspapers, academies, colleges, factories, and banks had closed. The defeat of the Confederacy threatened the collapse of all banks, colleges, the university, the state public school system, and other institutions and businesses. Thousands of citizens were reduced from affluence to poverty. The war had "bled North Carolina white." That North Carolina did not suffer as much as some southern states led Sidney Andrews, a northern newspaper correspondent, to write: "More fire would have made more healthy spirit in the State."

Tired, maimed, hungry, penniless soldiers straggled home to find cattle and stock gone, barns and cribs and smokehouses empty, clothes worn out, farms run down, and buildings, fences, and tools in bad repair. With little but their land, labor, and the memory of defeat, these soldiers and their families courageously went to work to wrest a meager living from the soil and to rebuild their fortunes and their state. They sufficed with what could be grown or made on their farms. Even families accustomed to ease and plenty before 1860 were reduced to penury and hardship. Their broad acres could hardly be worked profitably without slaves or sold to neighbors who had little or no money.

The Social Revolution Resulting from the War

The war brought shocking social revolution to North Carolina and the South. Military defeat resulted in the sudden, total, uncompensated emancipation of slaves and the destruction of the antebellum plantation system. Under the new conditions, could staple crop production prosper? But the greatest problem and worry was the Negro. Would 350,000 North Carolina "freedmen"—poor, ignorant, imperfectly civilized, inexperienced in self-direction—continue to work, obey the laws, and respect the whites, or would they refuse to labor, commit crimes, endanger white women, challenge white control of southern civilization, and precipitate race war? Would the Negroes use or abuse their new freedom? Could 350,000 Negroes and 650,000 whites, many of whom had owned slaves, live side by side in peace and for the good of each other? This problem was especially acute in staple crop areas where Negroes were very numerous.

During the war a few slaves had run away from their masters to nearby Union armies and camps, but generally the slaves had been faithful plantation laborers while the white men were in the army, or servants and workmen with the Confederate armies. The news of freedom had a profound repercussion upon the Negroes. Habituated to bondage, they had no choice but to remain in their old community and work the land for wages or on crop shares. Until harvest the landowner would advance supplies and furnish house, land, tools, and stock. Share-cropping, which had been used in the turpentine industry as early as the 1830s, and in a limited way in farming in the two decades before the war, was now widely adopted in place of the old plantation system as the most convenient arrangement for landless Negroes and landed whites. There was a rapid increase in the number and a decrease in the average size of farms.

But some Negroes left their former masters and made arrangements with other landowners or went to army camps and nearby towns, expecting to receive care, or they simply wandered from place to place. To some Negroes freedom meant the "right of locomotion," and quite a number "took to the open road." They did not like to take orders because that reminded them of slavery. One contemporary declared that "a freedman is a *free man*—so free, indeed, that neither law nor gospel can hold him, when some fancy or whim suggests to him a change of location or service." The freedmen liked the new life of ease and independence and many of them looked forward to receiving "forty acres and a mule" from the federal government. Some exercised their freedom by practicing thievery and insolence to the whites. The feeling of slave days persisted that "what belonged to their masters belonged to them." One northerner in the state in 1865 wrote: "The Negroes are the worst thieves that the Lord ever permitted to live. They steal everything they can lay their hands on . . . hogs, chickens, cattle, horses and mules, and all sorts of vegetables and fruits." The new wine of freedom went to their heads. Freedom from slavery meant freedom from work and freedom to do as they pleased. But soon many of the freedmen were sick, hungry, ragged, or in the toils of the law. When they learned from experience that they had to work in order to live and to fit comfortably into the new social order, most of them were ready to settle down and work for the white landowners for wages or on shares.

The Freedmen and the Freedmen's Bureau

Generally the whites were reasonably kind and helpful to the Negroes; but some exploited them with unfair labor contracts and vented their resentment by abuse and maltreatment. Some Negro leaders, notably James H. Harris, warned the freedmen against expecting too much from the federal government. Harris told his people: "You will not believe the evil-minded men who persuade you that you will get a portion of your master's land." Alfred Moore Waddell was among the small number of whites who thought that "a few of the most intelligent Negroes" might be allowed to vote. A meeting of Negro leaders in Raleigh in 1865 asked not for the ballot but for protection, justice, and schools; they demanded the right to testify in courts, to serve on juries, and to have other "civil rights," saying, "These rights we want, these rights we contend for, and these rights, under God, we must ultimately have." A meeting in Morganton on August 3, 1867, attended by about two thousand Negroes and whites, resolved that "no sensible person of any complexion desires or expects social equality; and that we hereby denounce as a base slanderer, any man who insinuates that it is one of the objects or purpose of the Republican party to bring about social equality between white and colored races."

The governor appointed a committee of prominent lawyers to define the rights of Negroes. Most white people in the state were willing to give the freedmen more rights than they had enjoyed as slaves, but they were not disposed to give them the ballot, legal equality with the whites, or schools. The idea of social equality was repugnant to most whites, and was advocated by very few Negroes. There was some talk about mixed schools, but this proposition did not meet with much approval. In a letter to James A. Garfield, Miss Mary A. Neely, who had come from Ohio to teach school at Jerusalem, near Salisbury, wrote: "For my part I protest against an attempt to compel black and white to mingle more together. I would not consent to our children attending a mixed school; for as the blacks are now, their society would be degrading. . . . I wish they had a country, a pleasant one of their own."

Believing that southern whites were unable or unwilling to give the Negroes sufficient aid in the difficult transition from slavery to freedom, the United States Congress, on March 3, 1865, created the Freedmen's Bureau with a network of local units and officials in each southern state to assist the freedman to find employment, to establish schools, buy or rent land, make fair labor contracts, combat disease and poverty, settle the freedmen's problems with each other and with the whites, and become good citizens. During its three and a half years of existence in North Carolina from the summer of 1865 the Freedmen's Bureau distributed about $1,500,000 worth of food, provided large quantities of clothing, established hospitals and cared for more than 40,000 patients, and organized 431 schools with 439 teachers and over 20,000 pupils. No figures are available on the amount of money spent on these schools, but in 1868–69 it was estimated at $35,000.

By March 31, 1866, some 717 contracts had been approved, and over 6,000 Negroes had been given employment. Their wages averaged between eight and ten dollars per month. Another activity of the bureau was that of apprenticing orphan Negro children to see that they were not illegally "bound out." Some of the bureau agents, ignorant of the problems of the freedmen and resentful of the native whites, gave bad advice to the Negroes, exploited them politically, and stirred up racial hatred. By and large the North Carolina whites resented the bureau as an interference by outsiders, who complicated southern problems that could best be solved by southern people alone. A North Carolinian from Garysburg wrote President Johnson that the teachers in the Freedmen's Bureau schools "conduct themselves in such a way as to disgust our folks, boast what they can do, talk abusingly about the sins of slavery, and glorify the North." According to one contemporary writer, these school teachers left the North with the song on their lips:

> We go to plant the common schools,
> On distant mountain swells,
> And give the Sabbaths of the South
> The ring of Northern bells.

A federal investigation of the bureau in the summer of 1866 found the agent at New Bern exercising "the most arbitrary and despotic power" and "practicing revolting and unheard-of cruelties on the helpless freedmen under his charge."

The Freedmen's Savings and Trust Company, commonly called the Freedmen's Bank, was chartered by Congress on March 3, 1865, to encourage habits of thrift among the Negroes. The bank had thirty-two branches scattered throughout the South, in which the freedmen had deposited almost $20 million before the institution crashed in 1874.

The following table contains some facts about the North Carolina branches of the Freedmen's Bank:

Place	Deposits	Repaid
New Bern	$18,473.67	$11,950.18
Raleigh	16,423.36	10,920.23
Wilmington	22,149.27	14,608.57
Total	$57,046.30	$37,478.98

Before the end of the war Congress passed the Thirteenth Amendment to the Constitution. This amendment, abolishing slavery in the United States, became effective in 1865, when the requisite number of states ratified. Slavery was dead.

The war left North Carolina in defeat, division, confusion, poverty, and seeming ruin for both whites and Negroes. The present was gloomy, and so was the future. Could the state recover economically and solve the race problem? Would North Carolina be allowed peaceably to return to the United States or would it be punished further for secession and war? What changes in state and local government and in the legal rights of Negroes would have to be made? With the collapse of the old state government under Vance at the end of the war, the only governing authority was vested in the United States troops who remained to keep peace and order. No one knew what was going to happen.

Chapter 33

RETURN TO THE UNION

The government of North Carolina and other Confederate states collapsed early in 1865 under military pressure, and on April 29, 1865, General John McA. Schofield took command of the state. Schofield took immediate steps to restore peace and order—and loyalty to the United States. He issued proclamations declaring a cessation of hostilities and the emancipation of slaves, and he made plans for the organization of a police force for each county, placing federal army officers in charge of the three major divisions of the state—General J. D. Cox in the West, General A. H. Terry in the central region, and Generals J. R. Hawley and J. M. Palmer in the East.

The Presidential Plan of Reconstruction

It was essential to the United States and to the people of the state that North Carolina be given a stable government as quickly as possible. In the absence of a constitutional provision for the reconstruction of a state, the president of the United States believed that as commander in chief of the victorious forces of the nation, he had the power to prescribe the conditions under which he would withdraw the military forces and establish civil government. Lincoln and his successor, Andrew Johnson, wanted to make easy and rapid the return of the Confederate states to the Union. Let all southerners, except the leaders, be pardoned as soon as they promised to obey the Constitution of the United States and the laws of Congress. Let them set up a loyal state government in which at least 10 percent of the state's voting population of 1860 had taken the requisite oath to the United States, ratify the Thirteenth Amendment abolishing slavery, and elect representatives to Congress. As soon as peace and order were secure, let the military forces be withdrawn and the southern people left to solve their own problems.

Many southern leaders believed that their states should be allowed to resume their normal place in the Union as soon as they signified their allegiance to the Constitution and their willingness to abide by the laws of Congress. But

Congress was disposed to the view that it, and not the president, had the power to prescribe the conditions of "restoring the lately seceded states" to the Union. Congress was jealous of the powers of the executive and was less disposed to trust the southern people to be loyal to the Union and to treat the Negroes fairly. The Radicals in Congress, led by Thaddeus Stevens in the House and Charles Sumner in the Senate, wanted to disfranchise some of the whites, particularly the leaders, and give the ballot to the Negroes so that they might better protect themselves—and build up a Republican party in the South. There was some talk of "state suicide" and "conquered provinces" and threats of "making treason odious" by hanging a few southern leaders, confiscating their property, and giving it to the freedmen. But the majority of congressmen, and the majority of northerners never held these extreme views.

President Johnson and Reconstruction

The moderate presidential plan of reconstruction pleased the South, and many in the North at first; but before Lincoln had time fully to apply his Ten Per Cent Plan and come to battle with the Radicals in Congress, he was assassinated by John Wilkes Booth, in April, 1865. The new president, Andrew Johnson of Tennessee, did not change Lincoln's plan of reconstruction materially, except to make harsher the provisions towards leaders and wealthier persons in the Confederacy. Johnson was able and courageous, but less adept, tactful, and diplomatic than his predecessor. A southerner and a former Democrat, Johnson and his policies soon became anathema to the Radical Republicans in Congress, though they had thought he was on their side when he took the oath of office as president.

Johnson was born in Raleigh, North Carolina, of poor parents. As a youth he worked in a tailor's shop, ran away from his apprenticeship, and finally located in Greeneville, in East Tennessee. He picked up a little education, married well, and rose to political prominence as a representative in Congress. He remained true to the Union during the war, was made military governor of Tennessee by Lincoln in 1862, and was nominated for vice-president of the United States—at Lincoln's insistence and over Thad Stevens's protest, in 1864. Many southern leaders despised Johnson because he had opposed secession and was more friendly to the farmers and industrial laborers of the South than to the planters.

President Johnson was free to take charge of reconstruction because Congress would not meet until December, 1865, unless he called it into special session—which he did not see fit to do. He first applied his plan of reconstruction to the state of his birth. On May 22, 1865, he launched his plan by two proclamations. In the Amnesty Proclamation, he offered pardon to all southerners who would take an oath of allegiance to the United States Constitution and promise to obey the laws of Congress, except fourteen classes (in contrast to six in the Lincoln plan) including high-ranking military and naval officers, civilian officeholders, and men worth as much as $20,000. These disfranchised classes might obtain pardon by presenting individual applications to the president. By his second proclamation Johnson appointed William W. Holden as "provisional governor of the State of North Carolina, whose duty it shall be, at the earliest practicable period, to prescribe such rules and regulations as may be necessary and proper for convening a convention of the people of the said State who are loyal to the United States, and no others, for the purpose of altering or amending the constitution thereof, and with authority to exercise within the limits of said state all the powers necessary and proper to enable such loyal people of the State of North Carolina to restore said State to its constitutional relations to the Federal Government and to present such a republican form of State government as will entitle the State to the guaranty of the United States therefor and its people to protection by the United States against invasion, insurrection, and domestic violence."

William W. Holden, "Provisional Governor," 1865

Holden's provisional government of North Carolina was in operation from the date of his appointment until December 12. In a proclamation of June 12 he promised to call the convention mentioned in Johnson's proclamation, urged the election of delegates loyal to the Union (voters and delegates had to take the amnesty oath), expressed interest in the Negroes, and congratulated the people upon their "delivery from the Confederate government." Holden worked hard in his temporary position; he made more than 3,000 appointments to state and local offices, examined many applications for pardon, and performed other duties associated with his office. In pursuance of his call, the voters on September 21 elected 120 delegates to meet in convention at Raleigh on October 2.

The Convention of 1865

The Convention of 1865, with Judge Edwin G. Reade presiding, repealed the Ordinance of Secession, declared slavery abolished, provided the machinery for the election in November of a governor, legislators, and representatives in Congress, and repudiated the state's war debt. The first three actions had been anticipated, but the repudiation of the war debt came as a surprise and precipitated a bitter fight in the convention and throughout the state. The majority of the convention seemed to be against repudiation and also against Holden as a candidate for governor in the ensuing election. But a large group of the delegates asked Holden to run for governor and he agreed. His opponents in the convention and throughout the state were advocating the candidacy of Jonathan Worth, an outspoken opponent of repudiation. At a critical juncture in the convention's proceedings, Holden presented a recommendation, supported by a strong written demand from President Johnson, that the convention repudiate the state's war debt. Fearful of incurring the displeasure of the president and of the North, the convention voted for repudiation. This action wrought havoc for the banks, the colleges, the university, the Literary Fund, and for hundreds of citizens who had bought state bonds during the war. The convention adjourned to meet again on May 24, 1866, and the gubernatorial campaign got under way.

Jonathan Worth Defeats Holden for the Governorship, 1865

Neither Worth nor Holden actually campaigned for the governorship, but the election was quite spirited because there were 23 candidates for seven congressional seats and over 500 aspirants for the 170 seats in the General Assembly. The slogan, "William W. Holden and Go Back to the Union, or Jonathan Worth and Stay Out of the Union," might have captured some votes for Holden, but he could not overcome the hostility of the leaders of both old parties which he had incurred over a period of a decade. In an extremely light vote, Worth won by a vote of 31,643 to Holden's 25,704. All representatives elected to Congress were Union men, and the voters ratified the ordinances repealing secession by a vote of 18,257 to 3,696 (only Camden, Currituck, Duplin, Edgecombe, Gates, Jones, and Pitt Counties voting against it). The ordinance abolishing slavery was adopted by a vote of 19,977 to 1,940, not a single county voting in the negative.

Holden's defeat disappointed him and President Johnson and played into the hands of northern Radicals, who regarded Worth's victory as an indication of North Carolina's disloyalty to the Union. Somewhat vindictive over his defeat, Holden urged Johnson to refuse to recognize the election of Worth, advice the president did not heed.

The work of the new General Assembly, with Thomas Settle of Rockingham County as speaker of the Senate and Samuel F. Phillips of Orange as speaker of the House, pleased President Johnson. It elected William A. Graham and John Pool—both unionists—as United States senators, ratified the Thirteenth Amendment, and declared the loyalty of North Carolina to the Union.

Worth assumed the governorship on December 28, 1865, thus putting the presidential plan of reconstruction into full operation. According to some contemporary accounts, "peace and order reigned in the state." But there were other reports that were less optimistic, and that indicated that the "Negroes had not settled down," that Federal troops were interfering with elections, and that General Thomas H. Ruger, in particular, was fomenting trouble. There was some open resentment at the presence of federal troops, the political activities of the Freedmen's Bureau, and the extremely critical and unfavorable reports of northern travelers and newspaper reporters. But the state seemed to be about ready to resume its place as a loyal, if somewhat unhappy, member of the Union and to begin the task of solving the Negro problem and clearing away the ruins of war.

Congress Refuses to Seat Southerners

When Congress convened in December, 1865, it blocked the presidential plan of reconstruction by refusing to seat southern senators and representatives. Under Radical leadership Congress created the Joint Committee on Reconstruction, consisting of fifteen members, that examined conditions in the South and, in a very biased and partisan report, maintained that the South was not loyal to the Union or fair to the freedmen. Hence it would be improper to readmit the southern states to the Union until further changes were made in the governments of the lately seceded states.

The North Carolina legislature of 1866 played squarely into the hands of this committee and of the Radicals in Congress by enacting the so-called "Black Code," defining the legal rights of Negroes. This code, the handiwork of B. F. Moore, W. S. Mason, and R. S. Donnell—a committee appointed by Holden—though more liberal than those of other southern states, did not give the Negroes the right to vote, nor did it give them equal legal rights.

Writing about this significant document, R. D. W. Connor said: "It is true that it did not admit the negro to entire equality before the law with the whites; nevertheless it validated the marriages of former slaves; changed the law of apprenticeship so as to apply, with one minor exception, to both races alike; declared negroes entitled to the same rights and privileges as whites in suits at law and equity; made the criminal law applicable to the two races alike except in the punishment for an assault with intent to rape; provided for the admission of the testimony of the negroes in the courts; and made provision for the protection of negroes from fraud and ignorance in making contracts with white persons."

The "Black Code" of North Carolina and those of other southern states, as well as the reported "Southern Outrages" against Negroes and Union soldiers—many of which were untrue or grossly exaggerated—played into the hands of northern Radicals—and modern "revisionists"—by indicating that the South was determined to "re-enslave the Negro" and to nullify in part the results of the war and emancipation. Surviving war prejudice, the tactlessness of President Johnson, and events in the South so strengthened the Radicals in Congress that they were able to override the presidential veto and pass into law a new Freedmen's Bureau Bill, the Civil Rights Bill, and the Fourteenth Amendment to the United States Constitution. The congressional elections of 1866, following Johnson's ill-fated "Swing Around the Circle," confirmed and strengthened the Radical control of Congress. Johnson was almost helpless—a "president without a party."

The Fourteenth Amendment and North Carolina's Reaction

The Fourteenth Amendment embodied the principle of the Civil Rights Act. Though the word "Negro" does not appear in the amendment, it made Negroes "citizens of the United States and of the States wherein they reside," prohibited states from abridging the "privileges or immunities of citizens of the United States," and prohibited any state from depriving "any person of life, liberty, or property, without due process of law"; provided for a reduction of representation in Congress of any state that "abridged" the right to vote of "any of the male inhabitants of such State, being twenty-one years of age and citizens of the United States"; forbade federal and state offices to any high state or federal officer who had later supported the Confederacy until he received pardon from Congress, and forbade any southern state to pay its war debts. Opposed to Negro suffrage and to the exclusion of their leading citizens from public office, North Carolina and other southern states rejected the Fourteenth Amendment. Before the close of 1866, Holden made another "political shift," broke with President Johnson, and became the head of the Radical party in the state, which bitterly denounced the Worth administration and advocated Negro suffrage and the ratification of the Fourteenth Amendment.

The Congressional Plan of Reconstruction

Rejection of the Fourteenth Amendment by the southern states fired the Radicals in Congress to launch their own revolutionary plan of restoration of the southern state governments, by the passage of the Reconstruction Act of March 2, 1867, followed shortly thereafter by several supplementary laws. Under the provisions of the first and basic Reconstruction Act, the South was divided into five military districts, each in complete charge of a United States general and military forces. North Carolina and South Carolina became Military District Number Two under the command of General Daniel E. Sickles, and later of General E. R. S. Canby, with headquarters in South Carolina. The law required that a convention in each state frame a new constitution which would grant Negro suffrage. In the election of delegates to the convention Negroes could register and vote, but many prominent whites—perhaps 10 percent in North Carolina—were not allowed to vote, since their "political disabilities" had not been removed. When the new constitution was approved by the voters of the state and by Congress, and when the new legislature chosen under the provisions of the new constitution ratified the Fourteenth Amendment, the state would be permitted to return to the Union.

The South and President Johnson and many Northern Democrats were amazed at the drastic plan of the Radicals which, in their opinion, southern conditions did not warrant; but the Radicals were in the saddle with more than a two-thirds majority in each house of Congress. Worth was allowed to remain in the governor's office, but the United States Army was the only "real government in North Carolina." Canby was more radical and unpopular than Sickles had been, more zealous in supervising the Negroes, more ready to interfere with the local and state governmental agencies, more active in removing civil officers, and more successful in stirring up race and party bitterness.

Organization of the Republican Party in North Carolina

Under the regime of military rule and Negro suffrage, the Republican party was organized in North Carolina. Some writers have contended that the party began, without the name, in 1866. But the party was formally launched in North Carolina at a meeting in Raleigh on March 27, 1867, in response to a call issued by a committee appointed by the anti-Worth and anti-Johnson members of the General Assembly. Delegates, Negroes and whites, from fifty-six counties attended the convention, and Robert P. Dick proposed the formal organization of a party, an idea unsuccessfully opposed by Daniel R. Goodloe and B. S. Hedrick.

The newly formed Republican party in the state embraced three elements. First, there were several thousand native whites, called "scalawags" and "squatters" by their enemies, and consisting of democratic, small farmers tired of the rule of the "planter aristocracy"; strong Unionists who welcomed a return to the United States; devoted admirers of Holden; and some who disliked the recent actions of Congress but thought it wiser to submit than to defy and antagonize the northern Radicals any longer. There were a few able leaders among this element—Holden, Robert P. Dick, Alfred Dockery, John Pool, W. B. Rodman, Calvin Cowles, and Thomas Settle. Second, there were the Negroes, who joined the party because it had given them their freedom, the Freedmen's Bureau, and the right to vote. They constituted at least half of the party's membership. On April 4, 1867, Holden had written in the *Standard*: "Let our loyal people, and especially the colored people, trust no man who will not promptly and proudly say he is a Republican." Third, there were the "carpetbaggers"—northerners who had come to the state after the war, supposedly carrying all their worldly goods in a carpetbag. Some came as permanent residents, attracted by economic opportunities; others came with the sincere desire to help the Negroes to useful citizenship; some came to get political power and the spoils of office through control of the Negro vote. Albion W. Tourgée, one of the state's leading carpetbaggers, commenting about the newly formed Republican party, admitted that "ignorance, poverty, and inexperience were its chief characteristics."

Perhaps most of the native whites were Conservatives, as the enemies of the Republicans called themselves, but they were far from united or organized. Old secession Democrats and unionist Whigs were slow to forget the bitter rivalries of the past and to join hands against the Republicans. Disgusted with the entire program of reconstruction, thousands made the mistake of washing their hands of politics and neglecting to register or vote in the election of delegates to the important convention which Canby called, in spite of their strong opposition to Negro suffrage, Reconstruction Acts, and the Fourteenth Amendment. The total registration of voters was 179,653—whites 106,721 and Negroes, 72,932 (with nineteen counties having a Negro majority). In the election of November 19 and 20, 93,006 voted "for convention" and 32,961 against, which means that 53,686 registered voters stayed away from the polls.

The 1868 Convention

In the convention that met in Raleigh, January 14 to March 17, 1868, there were only 13 Conservatives and none of the customary white leadership was present. There were 107 Republicans, including 18 carpetbaggers, 15 Negroes, and 74 native whites, chief among whom were Rodman and Calvin Cowles, who was Holden's son-in-law. The leading carpetbaggers were Lieutenant Albion W. Tourgée, native of Ohio, General Bryan Laflin of Massachusetts and New York, General Joseph C. Abbott of New Hampshire, Major H. L. Grant of Rhode Island and Connecticut, John R. French of New Hampshire and Ohio, and the Reverend S. S. Ashley of Massachusetts. The outstanding Negro delegates were James H. Harris, A. H. Galloway, and J. W. Hood, the latter of Connecticut. The leading Conservatives were Captain Plato Durham and Major John W. Graham. Cowles was president of the convention, though he was not a registered voter and was ineligible even to membership. Carpetbaggers held a majority of the committee chairmanships and exerted an influence far greater than their numbers warranted. The members of the convention took their task seriously and wrote a constitution so modern and democratic that with some changes it has remained effective to this day.

The Constitution of 1868

The state Constitution of 1868, often erroneously called the Canby Constitution and frequently condemned as a radical break with North Carolina traditions made by outsiders, contained a liberal Bill of Rights. Among its provisions were the following:

"Sec. 4. That the State shall ever remain a member of the American Union: that the people thereof are part of the American nation; that there is no right on the part of the State to secede. . . .

"Sec. 5. That every citizen of the State owes paramount allegiance to the Constitution and Government of the United States. . . .

"Sec. 6. To maintain the honor and good faith of the state untarnished, the public debt, regularly contracted before and since the rebellion, shall be regarded as inviolable and never be questioned, but the State shall never assume or pay . . . any debt . . . incurred in aid of insurrection or rebellion against the United States, or any claim for the loss or emancipation of any slave."

Some of the provisions in the constitution were copied from the constitution of Ohio, Tourgée's native state, while others were in line with progressive legislation of other northern states. Many of the changes were modern, progressive, liberal, and democratic. Some of the most significant were: the abolition of slavery; provision for universal manhood suffrage, white and Negro; the elimination of all property and religious qualifications for voting and officeholding, except the disbarment of atheists from public office; popular election of state and county officials; abolition of the county court system and the adoption of the township–county commission form of local government; provision for a Board of Charities and Public Welfare, and for "a general and uniform system of Public Schools" to be open "for at least four months in every year." The University of North Carolina was declared to have "an inseparable connection with the Free Public School system of the State," and as soon as practicable, the General Assembly should "establish and maintain in connection with the University, a Department of Agriculture, of Mechanics, of Mining, and of Normal Instruction." Four new elective state administrative offices were created: lieutenant-governor, auditor, superintendent of public works, and superintendent of public instruction. The elective Council of State was replaced by an *ex officio* one, the two-year term of office for the governor was changed to four years, and the name House of Commons was changed to House of Representatives. The number of capital offenses was reduced to four—murder, arson, burglary, and rape, and it was stated that the purpose of punishment should be "not only to satisfy justice, but also to reform the offender, and thus prevent crime."

The convention had cost the taxpayers about $100,000 and Conservatives denounced the waste of money and pointed out that one member living only thirty miles from Raleigh had collected travel expenses for 262 miles. Josiah Turner, Jr., in the Raleigh *Sentinel,* carried the caption: "THE CONSTITUTIONAL CONVENTION (SO-CALLED) The Disgraceful Closing Scenes! Corn Field Dance and Ethiopian Minstrelsy!! Ham Radicalism in Its Glory!!!"

The Election of 1868

A bitter campaign preceded the election of 1868—held April 21, 22, and 23—in which the people voted on the new constitution and elected new state and county officers and representatives to Congress. A new registration of voters resulted in a total registration of 196,872, of which 117,428 were whites and 79,444 Negroes. The Union League and the Ku Klux Klan were both active in the campaign, and, according to J. G. de R. Hamilton, the first record of a Ku Klux notice appeared at this time. It read:

> K.K.K.
> Attention! First Hour! In the Mist!
> At the Flash! Come. Come. Come!!!
> Retribution is impatient! The grave yawns!
> The spectre bones rattle!
> Let the doomed quake!

The Republicans were well organized and had the support of the Union League and federal troops located in the state. It was reported that the Republicans "sent flocks of Howard Negro students" into the South to make speeches, and applied an extra $200,000 to the campaign in North Carolina through an increase in federal marshals to step up the enforcement of the Ku Klux Act. Accordingly, the Republicans swept to victory, and the new constitution was adopted by a vote of 93,084 to 74,015, which meant that 29,773 registered voters failed to cast their ballots. Holden was elected governor over Conservative Thomas S. Ashe by a vote of 92,235 to 73,594. The Republicans carried fifty-eight of the eighty-nine counties, and the Conservatives elected only one judge, one solicitor, and one representative to Congress.

The Triumph of the Republicans

When the Republican-dominated legislature met, it promptly ratified the Fourteenth Amendment and elected two Republican United States senators, John Pool and Joseph C. Abbott. Governor Worth was forced out of office by General Canby's military order on July 1, and Holden assumed the governor's office the next day. Canby then turned over the powers of government to the newly elected officials. Congress approved the new state constitution and admitted North Carolina representatives and senators on July 20, 1868. North Carolina was back in the Union at last. But the state was in the control of the Republican party whose radical policies and Negro-carpet-bag-scalawag membership were distasteful to the native white majority.

Chapter 34

RECONSTRUCTION POLITICS, 1868-1877

Conditions were such that Governor Holden and the Republican party could hardly give North Carolina satisfactory government. Holden and the Conservative white majority hated each other with implacable bitterness. His enemies would destroy him at the first opportunity. His political friends consisted of a few thousand native whites, the carpetbaggers, and the great mass of ignorant Negroes. As governor and party leader, Holden had to recognize and depend upon his friends—some of whom were of the doubtful variety—and he sought to outwit and intimidate his enemies. He appointed some Negroes to minor public offices, and some of the whites whom he appointed to judgeships and other major offices were primarily self-seeking politicians, lacking in education, ability, sobriety, and integrity.

As has been indicated, Holden's first legislature took the necessary steps for the readmission of North Carolina to the Union. It also authorized the organization of a military force to suppress rebellion—a maximum of nine regiments and artillery battery to be at the disposal of the governor; it passed a resolution declaring the existing state government "valid in every respect"; and it fixed the pay of legislators at $7.00 per diem plus 20 cents mileage. By the time the legislature adjourned, the presidential campaign was gaining momentum.

The Presidential Campaign of 1868 in North Carolina

The presidential campaign of 1868 in North Carolina and throughout the South was characterized by misrepresentations, inflammatory documents, and violent partisanship. The Conservatives inflamed the hatred of whites for Negroes and used the Ku Klux Klan to intimidate Negroes and frighten them from the polls. Republicans denounced the Klan and warned the Conservatives that their treatment of the Negroes might goad them to rapine and insurrection. The Union League redoubled its activities and propaganda.

And the Republicans published and circulated 50,000 copies of an appeal to the conservatives by Chief Justice Richmond Pearson, urging them to vote for Ulysses S. Grant for president, in order to avert civil war. Some party leaders advised their followers to go to the polls armed and ready for any emergency. Yet the election itself was quiet and almost apathetic. Grant carried the state by a vote of 96,939 to Democratic Horatio Seymour's 84,560, and the Republicans won all of the seats in the House of Representatives except one. It is noteworthy that 15,570 more votes were cast in the presidential election than in the gubernatorial contest a few months earlier.

Republican Extravagance and Corruption

The chief blot on the Republican administration was the orgy of extravagance and corruption in the issue of bonds for railroad construction. Before the war the policy of extensive state aid to railroads through the sale of bonds had been effective in building hundreds of miles of road, which had improved trade and contributed to the rapid progress and prosperity of the 1850s. The policy was popular before 1860 and was considered sound and wise. With no cash on hand to repair the worn-out railroads or build new ones at the close of the war, would it not be wise to adopt the tested policy of state aid to railroads as the best and quickest way to restore prosperity to the poverty-stricken state? The presidents and stockholders of the various railroad companies in the state were eager to receive government aid. So the Republican convention of 1868 and the legislatures of 1868 and 1869 authorized $27,-850,000 in bonds (only $17,660,000 were issued), the proceeds of which would be used by various railroad companies to repair and build railroads in various parts of the state. The railroads that stood to receive the largest sums were: the Western Division of the Western North Carolina ($6,387,000), Chatham ($3,200,000), and Wilmington, Charlotte, & Rutherford ($3,000,000). Since bond purchasers began to doubt the ability of the impoverished state government to pay its mounting debt, the price of state bonds dropped steadily and thus reduced the amount of money realized from their sale. After the bond acts were passed, Conservatives began to charge that the railroad bonds and revenues were being wasted and stolen.

Littlefield and Swepson

Later investigations by the Bragg (1870) and the Shipp (1871) legislative committees revealed that large commissions had been paid to lawyers and judges by railroad officials or their lobbyists, and that bribery and fraud tainted a few votes for the bond legislation, though a majority of the legislators perhaps knew nothing of the fraud and voted for the bond laws on the basis of merit. "General" Milton S. Littlefield and the presidents of various railroad companies were largely responsible for the fraud and waste. Littlefield, a carpet-bagger from New York, had located in Raleigh, where he became a prominent banker, lobbyist, and "influence peddler" of the first magnitude. George W. Swepson, a native and president of the Western Division of the Western North Carolina Railroad, employed Littlefield to use his influence to get the legislature to vote bonds for his and other railroads, agreeing to pay him one-tenth of the amounts obtained. Littlefield plied the legislators with food, tobacco, drinks, and other favors and loaned or gave money and bonds to more than a dozen members of the General Assembly, chiefly carpetbaggers and Negroes who voted for the bond laws. Swepson alone paid Littlefield more than $240,000 in cash and bonds, part of which was used to make loans or gifts to legislators. Great sums of the proceeds of the depreciated railroad bonds went into the pockets of lawyers, legislators, railroad presidents, and even a judge.

Never had there been such fraud and waste of public money in the history of the state. When the sordid truth was known, the people were stirred against Holden and the Republican administration; and the Conservative party was given a superb political issue—to "clean up the mess" in Raleigh. Unsold bonds were destroyed, but $13,315,000 was added to the existing $15,000,000 debt of a poverty-stricken state, the tax rate was sharply increased, and no new railroad and little or no trackage built. Swepson, Littlefield, and others, who had had their "hand in the public till" fled the state or otherwise escaped punishment. Holden did not get a dollar and had no connection with the affair, but he and his party, being in control, were blamed for not knowing what was going on and stopping it. A decade later the state government, under Democratic control, repudiated every dollar of these special tax railroad bonds.

Preservation of Law and Order

Conditions in North Carolina were productive of an unusual amount of apprehension, violence, and crime. It was maddening to many whites that Negroes were voting and holding office, attending Union League meetings, and otherwise disporting themselves as the equals of the whites. Thousands of local and state leaders, customarily in control, regarded as intolerable their own supersession by the Republicans, most of whom were newcomers to public life and some of whom were newcomers to the state. The sudden social and political revolution, partially produced and maintained by federal military force, was widely resented, as was the political activity of the Freedmen's Bureau and the Union League, and the very presence of federal troops.

The Ku Klux Klan and Its Activities

To the Union League, of which Holden was the first president and James H. Harris, a Negro, vice-president, the Conservatives replied by secret societies of their own, chief of which was the Ku Klux Klan. This famous organization first appeared in North Carolina in 1867, grew rapidly for a two-year period, then declined and disappeared as a formal organization. Since its activities were shrouded in secrecy, its total membership is a matter of conjecture, but estimates placed it as high as 40,000. By means of warnings, threats, whippings, and an occasional murder, the Klan was a great factor in the "restoration of white supremacy." The reports of a congressional investigating committee reported at least 260 Klan "visitations" in twenty North Carolina counties, 174 of which were directed against Negroes. The reasons given for the rise and spread of the Klan in the state were the effort to combat the Union League and other northern organizations, the desire to "put the Negro in his place," the determination of the whites to regain control of the government, and the desire to "protect Southern womanhood."

The Union League

The Union League induced the Negroes to vote Republican; to memorize the Union League Catechism, which had nothing good to say about Democrats and nothing bad to say about Republicans; and, in effect, to hate their white neighbors. The League brought so much pressure to bear on the Negroes that one leading southern historian has said: "Negroes had exchanged economic slavery with economic security for political slavery without economic security."

Where such groups and racial antipathies existed, an increase of violence and crime was inevitable. To many it seemed that life and property were not safe and that civilization was disintegrating. Conservatives and Republicans accused each other of causing the bad conditions, but both were inflamed, supersensitive, and not without blame. Faced with widespread disorder and crime and with political defeat if the activities of the Ku Klux Klan were not checked, the Republican legislature passed an act making it a felony to go masked, painted, or disguised on the highways and authorized the governor to hire detectives. This law proved ineffective, in spite of the fact that the governor employed about twenty detectives, and the General Assembly, in December, 1869, enacted the Shoffner Act "for the better protection of life and property." This law, which was probably written by John Pool, empowered the governor to protect life and property by placing any county under martial law, if necessary. It did not authorize the suspension of the writ of habeas corpus.

The Kirk-Holden War

The climax of partisan conflict occurred in 1870 with the so-called Kirk-Holden War and the regular legislative and congressional elections. In 1870 a Negro Republican officeholder was murdered in Alamance County, and John W. ("Chicken") Stephens, a state senator and one of Holden's detectives, was murdered in Caswell county. Ku Klux "outrages" were also numerous in Orange, Chatham, and several other counties. Holden did not think that local officers and courts were doing their duty, especially in Alamance and Caswell counties, and on June 8, acting under the authority of the Shoffner Act, he placed these two counties under the rule of "about a thousand plundering soldiers"—according to Josiah Turner, Jr.—commanded by Colonel George W. Kirk, notoriously unpopular Tennessee commander of a regiment of North Carolina Volunteers in the United States army during the war. Holden acted under authority of state law and with the approval of President Grant—which seems strange, in view of the fact that General Canby was in charge of military affairs in North Carolina. Local citizens were placed in jail under military arrest, and both Kirk and Holden refused to recognize writs of habeas corpus for their release issued by state judges. Application was made by William A. Graham, Judge Merrimon, and other prominent people to Chief Justice Pearson for writs of habeas corpus in behalf of A. G. Moore and others arrested by Kirk, but when these writs were served on Kirk, he replied that "such papers had played out" and that he was acting on orders from the Governor. Holden informed Pearson that he was "satisfied that the public interest requires that these military prisoners shall not be delivered up to the civil power." This led Pearson to make his oft-quoted statement: "The power of the judiciary is exhausted, and the responsibility must rest with the Executive."

Josiah Turner, Jr., a native of Orange County, published the following statement in his Raleigh *Sentinel,* on August 3: "Governor Holden: You say you will handle me in due time. You white-livered miscreant. You dared me to resist you; I dare you to arrest me. You villain, come and arrest a man, and order your secret clubs not to molest women and children. Yours with contempt and defiance. Habeas corpus or no habeas corpus. Josiah Turner, Jr."

The governor had been urged not to declare Orange County in a "state of insurrection," and not to have his militia arrest Turner in that county; but disregarding this advice, he telegraphed Kirk to arrest Turner, who was seized at Hillsborough and carried to Yanceyville, the county seat of Caswell, and jailed.

The local situation was desperate. The Conservatives charged that Holden's actions were aimed not so much at the preservation of order and the breakup of the Ku Klux Klan and other secret societies as at the winning of the election of 1870 and the use of military power. Finally, with doubtful power and propriety, federal judge George W. Brooks issued a writ of habeas corpus requiring the prisoners to be brought before him at the coming session of the Salisbury court. Holden at once telegraphed President Grant, denying Brooks's right to issue the writ, and saying that Kirk would be directed to refuse to obey the judge's mandate. Whereupon the President, perhaps on the advice of his attorney general, wired Holden to obey Brooks's writ. Meanwhile the Conservatives won a sweeping victory at the polls. Deserted by Grant and repudiated by the electorate, Holden declared the insurrection at an end, ordered Kirk to "produce his prisoners" for trial before Judge Pearson, and disbanded Kirk's troops.

The record of the Republican administration strengthened Conservative hopes of capturing political control of the state. Prominent lawyers, Conservative leaders, and newspapers boldly attacked the misrule of the Republicans. They pointed to the doubling of the state debt by the corrupt issuance of railroad bonds which were wasted; to increased taxes necessitated by the wholesale waste and extravagance, such as a legislature which had cost almost $350,000 in per diem and mileage allowances, not to mention $50,000 for state printing; to the outrages of the Kirk-Holden war; to Negro voting and officeholding; to Negro-carpetbag-scalawag dominance supported by military force; to widespread crime and violence, and to the poor quality and partisan activity of Republican judges and other officials. All honest, patriotic white men were urged to rally to the Conservative standard and restore "home rule" and "white supremacy" in North Carolina.

In 1870 H. H. Helper, a staunch Republican, wrote: "One of the greatest evils affecting society in North Carolina may justly be set down to the incompetent and worthless State and Federal officials now in power. They are for the most part pestiferous ulcers feeding upon the body politic. Reconstruction for North Carolina as carried out by Congress and the villainous and incompetent State and Federal officials within her borders, has proved a total failure. When the historian comes to write the history of these evil times, truth will impel him to declare that the Ku Klux business of today grew out of things complained of in those statements. The only way to rid the country of these wicked midnight assassins is to first remove the cause which brought them into existence and then apply rigid means for their swift extirpation." D. R. Goodloe, United States marshal and a loyal Republican, expressed somewhat similar views.

The Ku Klux Klan was the most effective weapon of the Conservatives. Its secret meetings, mystic signs, nightly visitations in white hoods and robes, warnings, whippings, and occasional murders spread terror among the Negroes and their white leaders. The Klan was especially active near election time, and it was highly effective in deterring the superstitious, ignorant, and indifferent Negroes from voting. Though many thoughtful, sincere people belonged to the Klan and were able to control its activities at times, it was a secret society enforcing mob law and therefore irresponsible, uncontrollable, and illegal; but to the Conservatives any means was justifiable to intimidate the Negroes, frighten them from political activity, and drive the Republicans from power. The Klan defied the utmost efforts of Holden to enforce the state laws for its destruction. It is noteworthy that the chief Ku Klux activity was not in the East where Negroes were most numerous, but in such Piedmont counties as

Alamance, Caswell, Chatham, Orange, Cleveland, and Rutherford.

By rallying most of the native whites to its standard and keeping many Negroes from the polls, the Conservative party won an overwhelming victory, electing five of seven representatives to Congress and capturing by large majorities both houses of the state legislature. The Conservative majority denied a sufficient number of Republicans their seats to insure a two-thirds senatorial majority necessary for conviction in an impeachment trial. Ever since the outbreak of the Kirk-Holden war, Conservatives had demanded the impeachment of Governor Holden; and some suggested similar action against Chief Justice Pearson. As soon as the General Assembly convened in 1870, many petitions were presented for the impeachment of both. Vance opposed such action, but the majority of his party insisted on impeachment of Holden. The *Standard,* which still reflected Holden's views, said: "In the name of the people of North Carolina, who elected the governor and chief justice, we demand a trial at the bar of the Senate. Innocent or guilty, the matter has reached that point from which there is only one course to pursue and that is—give these men a trial—clear them if innocent and convict them if guilty. If the Democratic party will not try these men, then we denounce the party as being more corrupt and dishonest than has been charged against the Republican party."

The Impeachment of Governor Holden

The Democrats accepted this challenge willingly, and on December 9, Frederick N. Strudwick of Orange County introduced a resolution impeaching the governor. The House "board of managers" and their legal counsel—William A. Graham, Thomas Bragg, and A. S. Merrimon—brought against Holden eight charges of impeachment, among which were the following: that he had proclaimed insurrection; declared martial law; made illegal arrests of eighty-two citizens of Alamance, twenty-two in Caswell, and Josiah Turner, Jr., in Orange; recruited soldiers illegally in the state; and refused to obey the writ of habeas corpus. Holden had three able lawyers as his councillors, who presented answers to the individual charges. The House managers called 57 witnesses; Holden's counsel, 113. After a trial, which lasted from February 2 to March 23, Holden was convicted on six of the eight charges and was promptly removed from office—the only governor of the state ever removed from office by impeachment. Vance's comment about the outcome of the trial was: "It was the longest hunt after the poorest hide I ever saw." Holden was succeeded as governor by Lieutenant Governor Tod R. Caldwell. The legislature that had impeached and convicted Holden also reduced the cost of state government, investigated the charges of fraud in the issuance of railroad bonds, repealed the Shoffner Act, and declared secret political societies illegal.

More Federal Interference in North Carolina Politics

The Republican Congress of the United States, outraged by the activities of the Ku Klux Klan and alarmed at the loss of Republican strength in the South, investigated the Klan and passed the Force Act of 1870, the Federal Election Law of 1871, and the Ku Klux Klan Act of the same year. These laws declared secret societies illegal, provided for suspension of the writs of habeas corpus in disorderly areas, gave military commanders more control over elections, and increased penalties for violations of the Fourteenth Amendment and the recently adopted Fifteenth Amendment (1870), which prohibited any state from denying any citizen the right to vote "on account of race, color, or previous condition of servitude." More United States soldiers were sent into the state, and in September, 1871, a federal grand jury at Raleigh indicted 981 persons for alleged Ku Klux depredations; 37 were convicted, including Randolph A. Shotwell, a Democratic editor, who was sentenced to serve six years in a federal prison. (He was pardoned after two years.) The Ku Klux Klan gradually ceased operations—partly because of federal legislation and partly because of the fact that it had achieved its original objective—the restoration of "white supremacy."

The General Assembly continued to be controlled by the Conservatives, though Caldwell was reelected governor in 1872, defeating A. S. Merrimon by the close vote of 98,132 to 96,234. President Grant carried North Carolina again, defeating Democrat Horace Greeley by a vote of 94,767 to 70,024—a much larger majority than Grant had received four years earlier. A proposed constitutional convention had been voted down by popular referendum in 1871 by a vote of 49,341 to 44,720.

Changes in the North Carolina Constitution

The Conservatives made a few changes in the 1868 constitution by the legislative process in 1873. By action of the General Assembly, approved by the voters in August of that year, the Code Commission and the office of superintendent of public works were abolished; the power to elect trustees of the University of North Carolina was taken from the State Board of Education and vested in the General Assembly; and biennial sessions replaced annual legislative meetings. These changes did not go far enough to suit most people, especially the Conservatives, and there was a mounting demand for a convention to make a thorough revision of the constitution. The Raleigh *Constitution,* the most violent opponent of a convention, declared:

Convention means Revolution.
Convention means the Whipping Post and Pillory.
Convention means Imprisonment for Debt.
Convention means War.

Convention means Apprentice laws, which is one of the worst features of
Slavery.

Convention means Ruin.

Convention means poll-tax qualifications for voting.

But the Conservative leaders and the people generally were not frightened by
such dire prophesies, and the General Assembly early in 1875 adopted a resolution declaring "that the present Constitution is unsuited to the wants of the
people of the State, is a check upon their energy, and impedes their welfare,
and that the people demand that the burdens contained in the same shall be
removed from their shoulders."

The legislature voted to call a convention for this purpose without submitting
the question to a popular referendum, as had been done in 1868. In the election
of delegates to the 1875 convention, the total vote was Republican candidates,
95,191; Conservatives, 95,037. Of the delegates elected, there were 58 Conservatives, 58 Republicans, and 3 Independents, among whom was Dr. Edward
Ransom of Tyrrell County, who became president of the convention.

The convention retained the 1868 constitution as the organic law of the state,
but it added thirty amendments, many of which were the result of the state's
experiences during Reconstruction. Secret political societies were declared illegal; white and Negro schools were to be kept separate; marriages between
whites and Negroes were forbidden; residence requirements for voting were
raised; the General Assembly was authorized to appoint justices of the peace
and given virtual control of county government; henceforth the legislature
should meet in January instead of November; per diem of legislators was fixed
at four dollars and mileage at ten cents; the number of supreme court judges
was reduced from five to three and superior court judges from twelve to nine.
The most significant change was the replacement of popular vote by legislative
control of county government—to insure white and Conservative control, especially in the eastern counties with large Negro populations. The constitutional
amendments were ratified by popular vote.

The Gubernatorial Election of 1876: "Battle of the Giants"

The Conservative party was eager to elect a governor and win
complete control of the state government in 1876. On the national scene, the
"Tidal Wave" of 1874 gave the Democrats control of Congress and pointed
to victory in 1876. The changes made in the State Constitution in 1875 generated optimism among Conservative leaders, who predicted they would "sweep
the state." Radical Reconstruction, Negro domination, and white supremacy
were the issues that placed the Republican party on the defensive. The necessity
of cooperation with the national Democratic party led the state Conservative
organization to adopt the name "Democratic." The Democrats nominated the

man who would make the best race for governor—Zebulon B. Vance, famous political orator, superb stump speaker, and beloved "war governor." The Republicans also nominated a strong candidate, Thomas Settle of Rockingham County. The joint debates in the "battle of the giants" and the general partisan bitterness attracted huge crowds and made the campaign of 1876 stand out as perhaps the most dramatic political contest in the history of the state. The Republican record, both state and national, and Vance's popularity and political oratory carried the Democrats to a narrow victory, Vance defeating Settle by a vote of 118,250 to 103,330—a margin of only 13,928 votes of a total of 233,278. The Democrats also won in the balloting for legislators, congressmen, and president, with Samuel J. Tilden carrying the state over Republican Rutherford B. Hayes, 125,427 to 108,484. There was rejoicing by Democrats "from Manteo to Murphy." The state had been "redeemed," "home rule" had been restored, and "'white supremacy" had been achieved.

The End of Political Reconstruction

By this time, the national Republican leaders had come to realize the difficulties of building up a strong Republican party in the South. To use federal troops to achieve this end was expensive, troublesome, and unsatisfactory in many respects. It had become obvious that the majority of southern whites opposed Republican policies and had a thorough distaste for federal interference in state and local politics. Perhaps the Republicans had done enough for the Negroes; they had set them free and made them citizens. The white people of the South knew the Negroes and had to live with them; perhaps they should be left to handle the Negro problem in their own way. Certainly Negro suffrage should not be forced on the South at the point of the bayonet. The withdrawal of federal troops from the South in 1877—one of the first acts of the Hayes administration—was an outstanding example of statesmanship. And this action marked the end of "the tragic era" of Reconstruction.

The majority of native whites rallied to the Democratic party, which remained in power year after year, though by a closer vote than most historians have realized. More and more the Negroes—unsupported by carpetbaggers and federal troops, indifferent to politics, and reluctant to court the displeasure and discrimination of the dominant whites—ceased to vote. So long as the state was solidly Democratic, the whites could enjoy unchallenged control. In North Carolina, and in the whole South, the Democratic party claimed to be the "white man's party," and there developed the "Solid South," aided and abetted from time to time by national Republican actions.

Reconstruction, though marking a distinct advance in humanitarianism and public education and in some aspects of social, economic, and political democracy, was humiliating to North Carolina and the South generally and was in many ways a worse experience than the war. It produced lasting racial and sectional hatreds; complicated the Negro problem; compelled an abnormal, illogical, and harmful political unity of the whites; made racial and sectional prejudice the basis of political alignment; encouraged lawlessness, political manipulation, and corruption; and diverted political attention from realistic social and economic issues. But after nearly a decade of troublous Reconstruction home rule was established, Negro-Republican dominance was over, "white supremacy" was triumphant; and the state government and most of the local governments were again in charge of the traditional ruling class of whites. Most of the people of North Carolina looked forward to a happier and better future.

Chapter 35

THE INDUSTRIAL REVOLUTION IN NORTH CAROLINA, 1870-1900

The industrial revolution, or the development of factory industry, was the most significant postwar development in North Carolina. Though lacking in coal, iron, and capital for the development of heavy, mechanized industry, the state had a mild climate, abundant and easily developed water power, cheap and abundant labor, and proximity to the raw materials of cotton, tobacco, and lumber—distinct advantages for the development of light industry integrated with agriculture. Before the War for Southern Independence, despite increasing specialization in staple crops and industrial dependence on the North, relative isolation made possible the establishment of many small mills based on local markets; but there was little evidence of the beginnings of real industrialization.

During the war the military and civilian needs and the ever-tightening northern blockade produced high prices and stimulated local industry; the abolition of slavery freed capital of heavy drains for investment in labor. However, invasion, bankruptcy, and plant deterioration closed out many of the cotton mills and tobacco factories before the end of the war.

Postwar Economic Optimism

Though dejected by military defeat, social revolution, and economic collapse, the state was gripped by a buoyant economic optimism during the period of relative quiet in the first two years after the war—before the inauguration of "military reconstruction." The war had demonstrated to many North Carolinians the superiority of diversified northern economy and the weakness of the colonial dependence of the agricultural South. With slavery gone, the plantation system lay in irretrievable ruin. A new thought-pattern began to develop—that a new and greater state and South might come with diversified agriculture, manufacturing, and railroads. The *North Carolina Advertiser* of August 12, 1865, said: "We must keep pace with the giant strides of PROGRESS, and to do this we *must* cast aside every trammel and incumbrance that erewhile left us loitering in its wake."

The *Raleigh Sentinel,* about the same time, commented about "the general recognition of the North's complete superiority" over the South, and asked, "How could it be otherwise when the disposition has been so universal to make nothing and purchase everything?" The editor of this paper went on to say: "The *manufacturing system,* we are convinced, is the policy now to be depended upon to relieve our State of the evils that press upon her. . . . It can be made our greatest means of wealth and prosperity and, once rooted firmly among us, will flourish like a vigorous plant in its native soil."

This economic optimism was premature. Scarcity of capital, experience, and industrial habits caused a return to the prewar regime of staple crop agriculture, and soon Radical Reconstruction gripped the South. The *Raleigh Sentinel* of April 27, 1867, aptly summarized the situation: "Bad as our condition was after the war, earnest and determined as the spirit of our people was to restore their broken fortunes, and stirring as the business marts of the South seemed for awhile, we discover but little real improvement in the condition of the people . . . Thousands of men stand ready to embark in agriculture, mining, manufacturing, and merchandise, but the means for the encouragement of enterprise cannot be had, while the rod of terror, treasured up in the wrath of Congress, is still suspended over our heads."

A little later this paper declared: "There is not as much spirit, vitality or resolution—as much hope, faith, or courage—in the South, this day, we fear, as there were twelve or eighteen months ago." Though the postwar economic optimism was repressed in the decade of "military rule," during which time "the migrating Northerner with his capital was turned away by Southern politics and the cold process of ostracism," one important lesson learned during Reconstruction was that North Carolina must acquire wealth and economic power through the development of industry, natural resources, and railroads. An editorial in the *Raleigh Observer* of September 9, 1869, entitled "How Shall the Aspirations of the Southern Heart Be Realized?" declared: "She [the South] must get power; and to get power she must acquire wealth; and to get wealth she must secure a full development of her resources, varied as they may be and are. Thus, after all, the answer to our question is in a nutshell. The aspirations of the southern heart are to be realized by WORK. Out of Southern soil, out of Southern metals, out of Southern wood, out of Southern fabrics, brought out by intelligence, zeal, and activity, must come the sceptre of our restored power. With us 'to labor is to pray.' "

The Beginnings of Industrial Recovery

Local conditions resulted in the reestablishment of the small prewar units of industry. By 1870 thirty-three cotton mills were making products whose value was in excess of the thirty-nine establishments in 1860. The war advertised and stimulated the consumption of smoking tobacco, made from North Carolina "bright leaf"; and Green, Blackwell, Day, Carr, and Washington Duke were finding tobacco manufacturing profitable in the Durham region. By 1870 tobacco manufacturing had recovered about two-thirds of its prewar status. Prior to 1860 North Carolina "made nearly all the turpentine and other naval stores purchased in the United States"; the state was making "more turpentine than ever before." The United States Census of 1870 reveals the startling fact that, despite the war and its aftermath, North Carolina industry had more than regained its prewar level. By 1870 the state was able to show a "real growth" in flour-milling and a "positive increase" in timber production. Other industries that fell "just short of the million dollar mark" were carriages and wagons, boots and shoes, iron, and leather goods. The 1870 Census listed 3,642 manufacturing establishments in the state, compared to 3,689 in 1860. But those of 1870 had a larger capital and a product almost twice as great as that of 1860.

The decade of the 1870's was marked by transition, expansion, and the real beginnings of the Industrial Revolution in North Carolina. The "gospel of salvation through manufacturing" was preached throughout the state, and profits made the gospel real. In 1880 forty-nine larger cotton mills, chiefly in the prewar textile counties in the Piedmont and owned largely by the same families (Schenck, Fries, Holt, Morehead, Odell, Leak, Lineberger, Battle, and others) were producing goods worth almost $2,500,000—nearly double that of 1870 and more than twice the 1860 product. The prewar mills had trained a large number of textile workers and had created a small class of mill owners and managers who took the lead in postwar textile development. The powerful influence of this class is indicated in Elizabeth Webb's statement that "of the 212 mills listed by the Bureau of Labor Statistics for 1900, at least 130 had the personal supervision over a period of time of at least one, and far more often of several, men who were brought up in the industry or who gained experience with outstanding men who had been in the industry for many years."

The expansion of tobacco manufacturing was more rapid than that of textiles. The first tobacco factory in Winston, established in 1871, manufactured about 20,000 pounds of chewing tobacco that year. In 1874 Richard J. Reynolds began the manufacture of chewing tobacco in Winston, and he, P. H. Hanes, Hamilton Scales, and others built factories in that town. The same year Washington Duke and Sons established their first factory in Durham, for the manufacture of smoking and chewing tobacco and snuff. "Bull Durham" (not made by Duke, but by Green and Blackwell Company), and other North

Carolina brands widely advertised caught the popular fancy. By 1880 North Carolina tobacco was definitely in the national market and entering the export trade. The census of that year noted 126 North Carolina tobacco factories, mainly in Durham and Winston, making products worth $2,300,000—a threefold increase since 1870.

By 1880 North Carolina industry as a whole had surpassed its prewar volume and prosperity. In his message to the legislature in 1879 Governor Vance said, "Remembering that North Carolina is preeminently an agricultural State, your legislation should be directed toward the improvement of that interest mainly." There was no mention here of manufacturing and no suggestion of the dawning industrial revolution. But two years later Governor Thomas J. Jarvis, in his inaugural address, reflected a spirit of optimism about the state's industrial prospects when he said: "The changes introduced by the war are many and various. . . . It is clear that the commonwealth moves with a quicker life now than formerly. The genius of the former state of things was repose; that of the present is activity. . . . The proofs of this meet us on every hand, in the expansion of our old staple crops and in the introduction of new industries; in the erection of cotton mills; in the multiplication of tobacco factories; in the amount of deposits in our banks; in the growth of our towns; in many ways, indeed, without number."

Rapid Industrialization after 1880

The decade after 1880 was marked by rapid industrialization of the state. The gospel of industrialization and of the "New South" was triumphant. With the end of political reconstruction in 1877 came greater political quiet and stability. Business, disturbed by the Panic of 1873, became much more confident after national resumption of specie payments in 1879, and there was a nationwide economic upswing in industry—though not in agriculture. The newspapers of the state began to plead for more industry. "Let us have factories to turn out those things which we need and which will be consumed in the communities where they are made," said the *Raleigh Observer* of January 4, 1880. If local "neighborhood mills" prove to be a success, "we will find stronger wings and soar higher."

The recently founded Raleigh *News and Observer* became the leading exponent of the industrialization of North Carolina. Perhaps its best editorial on this theme was that of November 9, 1880, entitled "our Refuge and Our Strength": ". . . What then is our duty? It is to go to work earnestly to build up North Carolina. Nothing is to be gained by regrets or repinings for Hancock's defeat. No people or State is better able to meet emergencies . . . we have one of the finest countries in the world. And what nobler employment could enlist the energies of a people than the developing of the great resources of our God-favoured States, and having it possessed and enjoyed by an enlightened, law-abiding, peaceful people? But with all its varied and splendid capabilities, it is idle to talk of home independence so long as we go to the North for everything from a toothpick to a President. We may plead in vain for a higher type of manhood and womanhood among the masses, so long as we allow the children to grow up in ignorance. We may look in vain for the dawn of an era of enterprise, progress and development, as long as thousands and millions of money are deposited in banks on four per cent interest, when its judicious investment in manufactures would more than quadruple that rate, and give profitable employment to thousands of now idle women and children. Out of our political defeat we must work out a glorious material and industrial triumph. We must have less politics and more work, fewer stump speakers and more stump pullers, less tinsel and show and boast, and more hard, earnest work. We must make money—it is a power in this practical business age. Teach the boys and girls to work and teach them to be proud of it. Demand a better and more liberal system of public education and if need be, demand increased taxation to obtain it. Infuse into that system practical, industrial education, suited to the wants of the masses, and to the demands of this progressive age. Demand all legislative encouragement for manufacturing that may be consistent with true political economy. Encourage, aid, support, and defend our State Department of Agriculture. . . . Work for the material and educational advancement of North Carolina, and in this, and not in politics will be found her refuge and her strength."

Other newspapers began to proclaim this new gospel in editorials and in special "industrial" editions. Weekly papers carried the message to the small towns and rural communities. Many of the writings and speeches of this period are filled with praise of industrialism, talk of "bringing the cotton mills to the cotton fields," and a veritable "cotton-mill campaign" was carried on in many parts of the state, notably in the Piedmont. The "new spirit" of North Carolina was manifested by the work of such organizations as the Watauga Club of Raleigh and by the famous "Mummy Letters" of Walter Hines Page. The state gradually began to shake itself loose from what Page called the "three ghosts that retarded progress: the Confederate dead, religious orthodoxy, and Negro domination."

The Industrial Balance Sheet

The News and Observer was gratified with the results of its crusade for industry, and in an editorial of June 30, 1885, declared: "Everywhere signs of improvement are becoming visible. The methods of agriculture are becoming more careful, thorough and economical; industries hitherto unknown to our people . . . are springing up at all points; larger manufacturing industries . . . are extending their scope; trade is seeking new and broader channels; the professions are becoming more particular about the standards of admission into their ranks; the educational system is being greatly improved and made more comprehensive."

After 1880 more local and Southern capital was available for investment, and the success of the state's industry began to attract Northern capital. The acceleration of this movement was clearly demonstrated by the census figures on manufactures. All North Carolina industry had an invested capital of $13,-000,000 in 1880; $32,500,000 in 1890; and $76,500,000 in 1900. The total value of manufactured products in 1880 was $20,000,000; in 1890, $40,000,000; and in 1900, $95,000,000. The number of workers in industry was 18,000 in 1880; 33,500 in 1890, and 70,500 in 1900. The increase in capitalization was sixfold; in value of products, fivefold; in number of workers, fourfold. It should be noted, however, that the rate of increase in manufactures in North Carolina from 1865 to 1900 was less than that of the nation, though it was slightly above the national average in the two decades after 1880. The industrial expansion of the state was primarily in three industries—cotton textiles, tobacco, and furniture.

Expansion of Cotton Textiles

During the twenty years after 1880 an average of six new cotton mills were built each year. The number of establishments increased fourfold; the capitalization twelvefold; the value of products elevenfold; the number of workers, ninefold. In 1900 there were 177 cotton mills, capitalized at $33,-000,000, employing 30,273 workers and producing goods valued at $28,000,-000. In 1898 the State Bureau of Labor Statistics declared that "North Carolina today is the Massachusetts of the South and exceeds any Southern state in number and value of manufacturing establishments." But the United States Census of 1900 ranked North Carolina below South Carolina in textiles, and both states were far below Massachusetts.

Approximately 90 percent of the state's cotton mills in 1900 were concentrated in the Piedmont counties. From 1880 to 1900 the average North Carolina cotton mill increased its spindles from 1,885 to 6,400, its capitalization from $58,282 to $186,000, the value of its products from $52,132 to $160,000, and the number of its workers from 66 to 175. Eleven mills exceeded 20,000 spindles each in 1900. A change in the ratio of looms to spindles from 1:52 to 1:44 signified a relative increase in weaving. From 1880 to 1900 the percentage of coarse yarn declined from 93 to 63 of the total output; that of medium quality increased from 7 to 36 percent; and that of fine quality from 0 to 1 percent. There was also an increase in the variety of cotton textile products—plaids, domestics, cheviots, shirting, stripes, hosiery, sheetings, bags, towels, and underwear. In comparison with New England, the North Carolina mills were still small and their products coarse.

The North Carolina textile industry before 1900 was based predominantly on local enterprise, management, capital, and labor. In the 1890's there was a notable movement of northern capital into the state's textile industry, and a small beginning of the exodus of northern mills to the South. Occasionally northern superintendents and members of boards of directors became interested in North Carolina mills. In 1895 Ceasar and Moses Cone opened textile mills in the Greensboro area, and about the same time the Camerons of Pennsylvania established a textile plant at Weldon. A considerable flow of northern capital was lured South by cheaper raw materials and fuel and labor, longer working hours, mild climate, and friendly legislation. The rapid development of the state's textile industry was due largely to reinvestment of the profits of the owners, though some mills were built as patriotic, cooperative enterprises under the leadership of D. A. Tompkins and others.

Unemployed townspeople and small farmers from nearby depressed rural areas constituted the bulk of the textile labor supply. Low wages necessitated the labor of family groups. Women and children workers predominated, the percentages in 1900 being men, 42 percent; women, 34 percent; children, 24 percent. The workers obtained low rent in cheap company-owned houses. Average annual wages in 1900 were $216 for men, $157 for women, and $103 for children.

The use of steam power, which was more economical than water power and did not confine the mills to the stream banks, increased rapidly from 16 percent in 1880 to 48 percent in 1890, and to 64 percent in 1900. In 1898 the Fries Manufacturing and Power Company installed a hydroelectric plant on the Yadkin River—the first in the state, and as early as 1900 2½ percent of textile mill power was electric.

By 1900 the North Carolina textile industry, with its greater commercialization resulting from national competition, increase in the size of its industrial units, and the influence of northern capital and mills, was losing its local characteristics and becoming a vital part of the national textile industry.

Development of the Tobacco Industry

The rise of the tobacco industry in North Carolina is a splendid illustration of the dynamics of private enterprise. In contrast with the cotton textile industry, which had favorable publicity in the press and even from the pulpit, the almost phenomenal development of tobacco manufacturing in the state was almost wholly the result of private initiative and ruthless competitive power. The story of young James Buchanan ("Buck") Duke's going with his father at the close of the war to peddle his "Pro Bono Publico" tobacco from a wagon in order to gain supplies to last through the winter, and of this same Buck Duke's becoming, within thirty years, a multimillionaire and the head of one of America's most powerful trusts, sounds as if it might have come from the pages of Horatio Alger.

In 1860 the state had about a hundred small tobacco establishments, worth about $650,000, employing about 1,500 workers, and producing about $1,-120,000 worth of tobacco products. The average factory employed only fifteen workers and turned out only a little over $11,000 worth of products; most of the factories produced only for a local market. Only two prewar companies became important after the war—Brown and Brother, which began at Mocksville and later moved to Winston, and Robert F. Morris and Son, begun at Durham in 1858. According to the Census of 1870, North Carolina had 98 tobacco factories, located in 12 different counties. Granville was the leader with 39 factories, employing 337 workers, and turning out $143,119 worth of products. Orange [including present Durham] ranked second in value of products, though it had only 7 factories and 98 workers. Rockingham had 12 factories, 223 workers, and $109,562 worth of products. Davie had 5 factories, 105 workers, and a product of $85,026. Stokes had 19 factories, 170 workers, and a product of $34,037. Other counties having factories were Person, with 6; Surry, with 5; Caswell, with 2; and Davidson, Mecklenburg, and Rowan, 1 each.

The war stimulated smoking, and at this time J. R. Green of Durham was producing a popular brand known as "Best Flavored Spanish Smoking Tobacco." Both Confederate and Federal soldiers, passing through Durham, became acquainted with this brand; Northern soldiers ransacked Green's factory, liked his tobacco, and spread favorable reports about it. Within a short time he reopened his factory, took W. T. Blackwell, Julian S. Carr, and John R. Day into partnership, and changed the name of his brand to "Bull Durham Smoking Tobacco," which was soon destined to make North Carolina famous.

In 1865 Washington Duke began the manufacture of tobacco on his farm in Orange (now Durham) County, but in 1874 he moved his business to Durham, where his oldest son, Brodie, had been in business since 1869. Starting with practically nothing, he and his three sons, Brodie, Buck, and Ben, built up one of the greatest tobacco industries in the world. In 1868 Durham had only one tobacco factory; in 1872 it had twelve. Winston, like Durham, witnessed a rapid development of tobacco manufacturing. Hamilton Scales is said to have been, in 1871, the pioneer tobacco manufacturer in Winston, and he was followed shortly thereafter by Pleasant H. Hanes, Bitling and Whitaker, T. L. Vaughan and Company, and Richard J. Reynolds. By 1880 there were 126 tobacco factories in the state, most of them located in Durham and Winston, but with some at Reidsville, Oxford, Henderson, Kernersville, Mount Airy, Statesville, Hickory, and Asheville.

"Buck" Duke and the American Tobacco Company

The capital invested in tobacco manfacturing increased from $1,500,000 to $7,000,000 from 1870 to 1880, the value of products from $2,-

300,000 to $13,800,000, and the number of workers from 3,600 to 6,500. The "U.S. Tobacco Journal Directory, 1881–82" listed 296 tobacco manufacturers in North Carolina. The following counties had the largest numbers: Davie, 29; Rockingham, 26; Forsyth, 25; Vance, 25; Surry, 24; Granville, 22; Yadkin, 14; and Durham, 12. Almost every county, from Cumberland in the East to Buncombe in the West, had one or more manufacturers listed.

By 1890 most of the smaller manufacturers had been squeezed out by the competition of the larger factories, particularly those at Durham, Winston, and Reidsville.

Although expansion was rapid in plug, twist, smoking tobacco, and snuff, it was greatest in cigarettes. In 1882 the Dukes began the manufacture of cigarettes, and they and the Blackwells imported skilled Russian Jewish "rollers" to prepare the tobacco in the convenient popular form of the cigarette. The business acumen of James B. Duke won for the Duke interests supremacy in the cigarette field, first in North Carolina and later in the United States. Duke succeeded in mechanizing the industry by installing Bonsack cigarette-rolling machines in 1884, by advertising widely, and by introducing rigid economy into both production and distribution. An era of over production and cutthroat competition ended with Duke's dominance of the national field through the incorporation of the American Tobacco Company, frequently called the Tobacco Trust, in 1890—the very year of the passage of the Sherman Anti-Trust Act! By efficient, if ruthless, business methods, Duke expanded the American Tobacco Company to a gigantic $274,000,000-business in 1904, controlling an estimated three-fourths of the tobacco industry of the United States. In 1901 he invaded England and forced the organization of the British-American Tobacco Company for control of the world tobacco trade. North Carolinians complained that the "Tobacco Trust" was harming North Carolina by having the state's factories specialize in the manufacture of chewing and plug tobacco rather than cigarettes. After the dissolution of the American Tobacco Company by the United States Supreme Court in 1911, North Carolina regained supremacy in the cigarette field, and Durham became famous for its Chesterfields, Winston for Camels, and Reidsville for Lucky Strikes.

Unlike textiles, the tobacco industry was regarded as a strictly private enterprise. It was highly concentrated geographically, most of the industry centering in the three above-mentioned Piedmont towns; it was more highly competitive and more completely owned by North Carolinians. It relied mainly on the labor of Negroes and white girls, and in 1900 the average annual wage of $136 was $33 less than that of the textile worker.

The Furniture Industry

The furniture industry in North Carolina followed a pattern somewhat similar to that of the tobacco industry. It began in small shops, with little capital, producing chiefly for local markets. It prospered because of an increasing demand, proximity to raw materials, and low labor costs.

In 1881 David A. and William E. White opened a plant at Mebane for the manufacture of spindles, and from this a furniture factory later evolved. But the first furniture factory in the state was the High Point Furniture Company founded in 1888 by M. J. Wrenn, T. F. Wrenn, John H. Tate, and E. A. Snow. Its major products were wooden beds and sideboards. In 1890 there were six factories in the state producing furniture valued at $159,000. All six plants were begun by local men who had had previous experience in making furniture. The financial success of the early factories caused a phenomenal expansion to forty-four factories in 1900 located at High Point and other towns, capitalized at $1,000,000, employing two thousand workers, and producing furniture valued at $1,500,000. The product consisted chiefly of cheap, heavy beds, chairs, and sideboards for local and southern markets. The State Bureau of Labor and Printing in 1902 listed 106 factories, including plants making baskets, coffins, veneers, and upholstery. High Point had 24 of these; Thomasville, 8; Lexington and Winston-Salem, 6 each; Mount Airy and Marion, 4 each; and Statesville, Hickory, Greensboro, Sanford and Dunn, 3 each. Thirty-four other towns had at least one furniture factory.

Capital and labor in the furniture industry were almost exclusively local. The story has been told that "the late Frank Dalton decided one morning that High Point needed a chair plant and that he walked out, called a few friends and thereupon in an hour or so the Southern Chair Company was a realization." In its use of cheap male labor from the town and from nearby farms, the furniture industry afforded a labor market complementary to that of the cotton mills, which employed chiefly women and children.

The Growth of North Carolina Towns

The Industrial Revolution had a wide and profound impact on North Carolina life. It produced a rapid increase in material wealth, in manufacturing development, in the number and size of banks, in the construction of railroads, and in the production of cotton, tobacco, and other crops. The movement of people from farm to factory brought rapid growth of towns and cities as centers of wealth, energy, culture, and political and social influence. From 1870 to 1900, the number of towns in excess of 10,000 inhabitants increased from one (Wilmington) to six (Wilmington, Charlotte, Asheville, Winston, Raleigh, and Greensboro); those from 5,000 to 10,000 population, from two to six; and those from 1,000 to 5,000 population, from fourteen to fifty-two.

In 1880 the urban population was 55,000 and rural, 1,345,000; in 1890 the urban population stood at 116,000 and rural, at 1,502,000; in 1900, the urban population was 187,000 and rural, 1,707,000. The state remained predominantly rural, but the new urban, industrial class of the Piedmont and the western part of the state wrested economic, social, and political leadership from the old rural plantation aristocracy of the East.

Prosperous industry gave North Carolina a new morale and optimism. Rapid material expansion made manufacturing, especially textiles, seem to be a public, patriotic enterprise, and manufacturers were considered philanthropists and public benefactors. Industry received public acclaim, special favors, and legislative protection. This view of private industry as having a quasi-public character hindered the development of a consciousness that the interests of labor, farmer, and the general public might not always coincide with the interests of manufacturers. The glorification of material progress tended to divert attention from the nonmaterialistic aspects of society.

The Social and Cultural Lag

The Industrial Revolution hastened the emergence of many social, economic, and educational problems and at the same time created the needed wealth for their solution. In educational, social, and cultural development, however, North Carolina lagged far behind its economic resources.

Writing of the political leaders of North Carolina at this time, Walter Hines Page said: ". . . these men who ruled by the ghost called Public Opinion held the country and all the people back in almost the same economic and social state in which slavery had left them. There was no hope for the future under their domination. . . . There would be no broadening of thought, because only old thoughts were acceptable; no change in society, because society's chief concern was to tolerate no change. The whole community would stand still, or slip further back."

Historian Holland Thompson, a native of the state, writing in the *New South,* said: "The increasing complexity of this problem is working changes in the manufacturer. Individuals of a type almost unknown in the South, though common in industrial societies generally, appear here and there. They are cold, shrewd, far-sighted. Sentiment in them does not interfere with the strict working of the principle of self-advantage."

Industry was so potent in state development that it became the beneficiary of the dominant Democratic party. Most of the industrial leaders cast their influence with that party, and the party became the guardian of conservatism and the special interests of the industrialists. An abnormal union of the various interests of the white majority—a union enforced by the issue of white supremacy—made the state Democratic party Hamiltonian in philosophy, the guardian of the status quo and of the vested interests of rising capitalism. In national politics, however, some of the manufacturers were Republicans, attracted by the protective tariff and other policies of that party, and alarmed by "unsound economic ideas" of the national Democratic organization.

Capital v. Labor

Slowly the Industrial Revolution caused the emergence of a working class and of class interests and conflicts. The manufacturers were the first to develop class consciousness, solidarity, and "community of interest" ideas. They were the champions of the status quo and of their own interests against agrarianism, the labor movement, and state regulation. Conscious of their own prestige and power as public benefactors, wedded to the large profits arising from their exploitation of labor—and at times of the consuming public —and able to control the Democratic party, they were sensitive toward any attack on their position and amply able to repel it.

Beginnings of Labor Organizations in the State

The class consciousness of labor was slow in developing. Low wages, child labor, night work, long hours, segregation from the rest of the population, exploitation by the "company store," and the identity of employer and landlord did not appear as serious grievances to the first generation of industrial laborers, who remembered their harder lot on the farms during the dark days from 1865 to 1897. But the second generation was dissatisfied and unhappy when it compared its own condition with that of other economic and social classes—or with that of labor in other parts of the nation. Ignorance, fear of the employers, and a sense of dependence upon the employers for home and job discouraged any self-assertiveness on the part of labor. However, on June 18, 1884, the first North Carolina Assembly of the Knights of Labor was organized in Raleigh, and three years later the Knights claimed "assemblies" in most of the counties and a large membership, both white and Negro, male and female. Despite these claims, it can hardly be said that the Knights of Labor made much headway in unionizing labor in the state, although pressure from this organization probably led to the creation of a state Department of Labor Statistics. There was no organized labor in any of the cotton mills, tobacco factories, or furniture plants until near the close of the century. Although "factory labor" was unorganized, there were some organizations among skilled workmen. By the early 1880s the printers of Raleigh, Charlotte, and Wilmington were organized. The 1899 report of the State Department of Labor listed the following organizations in the state: "Bricklayers, Masons and Plasterers Union; Brotherhood of Locomotive Engineers; Typographical Union; Federation of Labor; Order of Railway Conductors; and the Bookbinders Union." All of these were unions of skilled workers and most of them were located in the larger towns.

The American Federation of Labor, organized in the early 1880s, made its first effort to organize North Carolina textile labor in 1898. But it made little progress in the face of opposition by the manufacturers and the ignorance, indifference, and opposition of many of the workers. The general public of North Carolina seemed to have the same attitude as the manufacturers—hostility to organized labor. A minority composed of labor leaders, liberals, and humanitarians was shocked at the conditions of factory workers, especially the long hours of labor of women and children. From 1887 bills were introduced into almost every legislature to limit the hours of work for women and children. Fearing the slightest beginning of government regulation, the manufacturers defeated every important labor bill before 1900. The growing demand for the improvement of labor conditions was successful in only two minor respects before the turn of the century. In 1887 the State Bureau of Labor Statistics was created and empowered to gather information, but only 15 percent of the manufacturers deigned to comply with its requests for data. The Mining Act of 1897, prohibiting the labor of boys under twelve years of age in mines, was not opposed because the mining industry was inconsequential. Public sentiment and the Democratic Party were somewhat amenable to the influence and interests of the manufacturers and were firm believers in the philosopshy of laissez faire. The doctrine of government regulation of private industry was sheer heresy. It was argued that the regulation of manufacturing would retard North Carolina's prosperity by discouraging the establishment of new mills or by driving existing factories to other states whose attitude was more friendly. Thus, until after 1900, the industrialists succeeded in rebuffing efforts at state regulation, in wresting huge profits from labor and the consuming public, and in preserving the fiction that the interests of the manufacturers, labor, and the public were identical and not conflicting.

Transportation

The development of transportation facilities went hand in hand with industrial expansion, partly as a cause and partly as effect. At the end of the war, the railroads from Wilmington to Rutherfordton and from Salisbury to Asheville and the Tennessee line remained incomplete, and the tracks and rolling stock of the completed roads had deteriorated. In spite of the railroad bond scandals of the Reconstruction era, the state government, which was a heavy investor in some of the railway lines, advocated the extension of railroads. The Western North Carolina Railroad was extended from Salisbury to Old Fort in 1869 and much of the work of grading was done to Asheville by 1871. Financial stringency compelled the sale of this railroad at auction in 1875, and it was purchased by the state for $825,000 to protect the state's holdings in the road. From 1875 to 1880 the state owned and operated the road and completed its construction from Old Fort to within seven miles of Asheville.

This, together with the completion of the Carolina Central from Charlotte to Shelby and the construction of the Raleigh and Augusta from Raleigh to Hamlet—a total of less than six hundred miles—was the extent of railroad construction in North Carolina between the close of the war and 1880.

Abandonment of Policy of State Aid to Railroads

The thirty-year-old policy of state aid to railroads was abandoned by the Democratic party after 1870, and railway transportation in North Carolina was relinquished to private development and exploitation. The first step came in 1871 with the leasing of the North Carolina Railroad to Virginia and northern capitalists who acquired the Richmond and Danville Railroad and then the Piedmont Railroad from Danville to Greensboro, and were determined to lease the North Carolina Railroad from Greensboro to Charlotte or to build a road parallel to it, in order to gain control of a through line from Richmond to Atlanta. Since about 70 percent of the North Carolina Railroad's freight was hauled north and south through Greensboro and Charlotte, the road's prosperity and existence might be endangered by the construction of a parallel competing line. Therefore the state leased the North Carolina Railroad for thirty years to the Richmond and Danville at $260,000 a year. In 1894 the Richmond and Danville was reorganized as the Southern Railway Company, and on August 16, 1895, this new company obtained from the state a ninety-nine-year lease of the North Carolina railroad at $266,000 a year for the first six years and $286,000 a year for the remaining ninety-three years.

In 1880 W. J. Best of a New York syndicate proposed to purchase the state-owned Western North Carolina Railroad. The stockholders opposed the sale, and public opinion was sharply divided on the question. But Governor Thomas J. Jarvis threw decisive support in favor of the sale, which was authorized by a special session of the General Assembly. Jarvis contended that the state had been losing money in the operation of the road, that the state treasury was unable to maintain the road and complete its construction, that the withdrawal of the state government would attract private capital and result in more rapid construction of railroads, that the needs of the West for the rapid completion of the road would be met more quickly by private capital, and that the state should focus its limited revenues on the development of its resources and educational system. The state lost its initial investment on the road, but Best assumed an $850,000-mortgage, paid the state $600,000 in cash for its outlay since 1875, and agreed to complete the road to the Tennessee line by 1881 and to Murphy by 1885. Accordingly, the Richmond and Danville road acquired the Western North Carolina, which became a part of the Southern Railway System in 1894. The road was finished to the Tennessee line in 1882 and to Murphy in 1890.

After a turbulent history of financial distress and repeated efforts to lease, the Atlantic and North Carolina Railroad from Goldsboro to Beaufort was leased in 1904 by Governor Charles B. Aycock to the Howland Improvement Company for ninety-one years at an annual rental varying from $54,000 to $108,000. This line and several other small lines were consolidated as the Norfolk and Southern in 1910.

Railroad Consolidation: Emergence of Three Major Systems

Extensive railroad construction characterized the years from 1880 to 1900 in North Carolina and in the nation. In North Carolina .this expansion resulted from genuine economic need, national prosperity and railroad expansion, the influx of Northern capital, and the special favoritism of the Democratic legislatures for railroad companies in the form of tax exemption and freedom from regulation—favors probably influenced by the "free pass evil" practiced by the railroads. The mileage of 1880 more than doubled to 3,001 miles in 1890 and to 3,381 miles in 1900, forming a state-wide network with many interstate connections and tied in which the national network.

The latter part of the nineteenth century was also characterized by railroad consolidation in both state and nation. The Southern Railway Company, formed in 1894, soon obtained trackage rights over the roads from Selma to Tarboro to Norfolk and, with a line from Greensboro to Charlotte, dominated rail transportation in Piedmont and western North Carolina.

In 1900, under the direction of northern capitalists, the Atlantic Coast Line Railroad was formed by a consolidation of the Wilmington and Weldon Railroad with other roads in states to the north and south. The Atlantic Coast Line system thus dominated rail transportation in the Coastal Plain area of the state.

Meanwhile the Seaboard Airline Railway system was being consolidated in the region between the areas served by the Southern Railway and the Atlantic Coast Line. The Seaboard and Roanoke from Norfolk acquired controlling stock in the Raleigh and Gaston in 1873 and built a road from Raleigh to Hamlet on the Carolina Central in 1877. Three years later it acquired control of the Carolina Central. To compete with the expanding Richmond and Danville Company, which leased the Atlanta and Charlotte in 1881, it built a new road from Monroe to Atlanta during the years 1881–92. The combination of these various roads was organized into the Seaboard Air Line Railway in 1900.

Thus by 1900 North Carolina had a network of 3,800 miles of railroads, consolidated into three large systems controlled by private capital chiefly from outside the state. These major lines ran north and south and removed farther from reality the old dream of an East-West trunk line across the state, from a thriving ocean port in the East to Asheville in the West. Although Democratic leaders pointed to the rapid railroad development after 1880 as proof of the wisdom of their abandonment of state aid, there was some belief that the state, which had lost heavily in the pioneer period of railroad construction, should not have turned over its valuable transportation system to private capital just on the eve of a great expansion and prosperity in transportation.

Slow Development of Highways

Railroads so absorbed the interests and resources of North Carolinians that there was little effort to improve waterways and highways, as urged by Murphey and other state leaders of an earlier generation. Highways were essential for internal overland trade; but they were almost impassable in winter's mud, dusty in dry summers, rough at all seasons, and steadily becoming worse under the increasing traffic of the late nineteenth century. The antiquated, ineffective system of county control of highways, dating from the colonial era, prevailed to the close of the century. The people were still "stuck in the mud" with little hope of improvement. In 1881 Governor A. M. Scales told the General Assembly, "We have made little or no progress in our public roads for nearly one hundred years," and he suggested "that at least part of the convicts should be reserved and applied through the counties for this purpose." As early as 1872–73 a law had been passed which provided for the "hire for good roads of convicts to counties other than that in which they were convicted." The provisions of the revised state constitution of 1875 were construed to authorize the employment of convict labor on public works, on highways, or other projects for public benefits. The most important law on this subject was that of 1887 entitled "An act to Provide for the Working of Certain Convicts upon the Public Roads of the State."

These laws, plus favorable editorial comment in the Raleigh *News and Observer* and several other papers, stimulated interest in this method of road building. By 1897 the legislature had authorized forty-two counties to work their convicts on the county roads.

Before 1900 the state government itself had carried out only three assignments in this type of work for its own convict labor. In 1879 it leased 25 state convicts to build a road from Quaker Bridge in Jones County to "a Point Near to a Landing" in Onslow County. In 1883 the number of convicts leased for this project was increased to 36. In 1877 the legislature authorized the use of state convicts to dig a canal and build a road at Angola Bay, in Duplin and Pender counties; in 1885 the State Penitentiary assigned 108 convicts to this task. Beginning in 1887, an average of 89 state convicts worked on the Plymouth turnpike for twenty-two months.

In most of the counties prior to 1900 the local authorities had no resources for road building except that of the "labor tax" of about six days a year from able-bodied male adults and the availability of nearby timber, rock, and dirt for the maintenance of roads. This system accomplished little. As early as 1878 a road law was passed which authorized the county commissioners of Mecklenburg, Forsyth, and Stokes counties to levy a small property tax for the improvement of roads. This law was repealed by the next General Assembly. In 1882, a new law, applicable only to Mecklenburg, was enacted. A few "improved roads" were built in a few communities, but the day when North Carolina would be known as the "good roads state" was far in the future. A few of the towns improved their streets and sidewalks, and on February 1, 1889, the first electric street railway began operation in Asheville. Fayetteville, Salisbury, Charlotte, and several other cities soon followed suit.

Improvements in Communication

During the generation of rapid railway expansion some improvements were made in the field of communication. In October, 1879, the first telephone exchanges in the state were opened at Raleigh and Wilmington, and in the same year long distance telephone service was established between Wilmington and Petersburg, Virginia. By 1898 there were thirteen telephone exchanges and seventeen telephone companies doing business in North Carolina. On October 23, 1896, the first rural free delivery mail route in North Carolina —and one of the earliest in the United States—was established in the China Grove vicinity of Rowan County. The expansion and improvement of transportation and communication facilities were reflected in the increased circulation of newspapers and magazines, and in 1898 there were 279 such publications in the state.

Chapter 36

AGRICULTURAL PROBLEMS AND DEPRESSION 1865-1900

Agriculture continued to be the basic economic pursuit from which most North Carolinians gained their livelihood. Its postwar recovery was made in spite of many handicaps. The war had taken the lives of some forty thousand young North Carolinians, most of whom had come from farm families. It had also caused the destruction of much farm property and considerable quantities of livestock. Barns were in disrepair, tools rusted, fields overgrown, and seed lacking. The war ended in the spring of 1865, too late to "put in a full crop" that year, and, to add to other woes, seasons were unfavorable in both 1865 and 1866. The farmers lacked capital and credit for repairs, replacements, operation, and expansion. Transportation facilities were inadequate and freight costs unduly high. Cotton was bringing a very good price, averaging forty-three cents a pound in 1865 and thirty cents the next year, but the federal government had placed a high tax on cotton, which tended to reduce profits from its production. Most significant of all the problems, however, was the revolution in the labor system produced by the sudden and uncompensated emancipation of approximately 350,000 slaves. Instead of slave labor, which had produced a great portion of the state's cotton and other staple crops before the war, postwar agriculture in North Carolina had to rely on labor from its white farmers and from a Negro population unused to its new status.

Efforts to Procure Labor and Capital from the Outside World

Many North Carolina leaders felt that the state's greatest need was competent labor to develop the immense resources of the state. Writing soon after the end of the war, young Walter Clark said, "Slavery is dead. Let us bring white labor here and capital will follow." The *Wilmington Daily*

520

Journal declared in January, 1866 that North Carolina could never recover "from its present prostration without capital and labor from abroad."

The idea of encouraging immigrants from Europe and from the North was endorsed by a number of county agricultural societies, notably New Hanover; by the State Agricultural Society; by local immigration societies, notably those in Rowan, Forsyth, and Wilmington; by numerous "land companies"; and by railroad companies. Beginning in 1874 the state government became actively interested in promoting immigration and the legislature of that year established an eleven-member Board of Immigration.

Colonel L. L. Polk, the first "Commissioner of Agriculture, Immigration and Statistics" was a strong advocate of immigration. His department hired an agent to solicit immigrants in England. The state also had an immigration agent in New York. The results were disappointing, as only a few immigrants came to North Carolina. In 1887, the State Department of Agriculture declared in its bulletin that the state immigration agency did not exist to bring in "Swedes, Hungarians, Chinese and other foreigners. The people of North Carolina are almost a unit opposed to foreign and promiscuous immigration." By 1890 the state's active work in promoting immigration had come to an end. The movement had accomplished very little. Consequently, North Carolina agriculture had to "lift itself by its own bootstraps" with the white and Negro labor at hand.

The Rapid Recovery of Agriculture

Despite its many handicaps, agriculture quickly reached its pre-war volume of production. Cotton and oats recovered by 1870, and the cotton production of 1880 (389,598 bales) was more than triple that of 1860. There was also recovery in the production of corn, hogs, milk cows, and beef cattle by 1880; of tobacco, in the 1880's, and of potatoes by 1890. Wheat never reached its prewar levels, and recovery in per capita production before 1890 did not occur in any crops except cotton and tobacco.

Certain definite trends characterized North Carolina agriculture in the generation before 1900. There was marked increase in the total production of farm crops and in specialization in the two major staples, cotton and tobacco. In thousands of bales, cotton production in each decade from 1860 to 1900 was 145,145, 390, 336, and 460. The corresponding tobacco production in millions of pounds was 33, 11, 27, 36, and 128. The increase in the production of other crops was not marked after 1880. North Carolina became the only state to become a large producer of both cotton and tobacco. There is little evidence to show that the war and the resultant abolition of slavery were serious long-run deterrents to staple crop production.

The Rise and Spread of Farm Tenancy

Out of the ruins of the antebellum regime developed the share-cropping tenant system as the natural readjustment in a region inhabited by landed proprietors who lacked capital and labor and by Negroes who were experienced in farm labor but lacking in land and capital. The evolution of the share-cropper system was a perfectly natural one, in spite of modern criticisms of the institution of tenancy. The rapid breakup of large plantations is indicated by the increase in the number of farms from 75,203 in 1860 to 93,565 in 1870, to 157,609 in 1880, and to 225,000 in 1900. The corresponding decreases in average acreage per farm were from 316 to 212 to 142 and to 101 acres. In 1880 more than one-third (52,722) of the North Carolina farms were operated by tenants, with share-croppers outnumbering cash tenants in a ratio of five to one; but the number of farms operated by owners (104,877) was much larger than in 1860. The number of farm owners continued to increase—to 117,000 in 1890 and to 132,000 in 1900. In other words, the postwar agricultural readjustment produced a striking increase in farm ownership as well as in tenancy.

Farm tenancy increased both in numbers and in ratio. From 1880 to 1900 the number of tenants in thousands each decade was 53, 61, and 93; and the percentage of farms operated by tenants increased from 33.5 to 41.4. The ratio of share-croppers to cash tenants dropped from 5 to 1 in 1880 to 3.5 to 1 in 1900. Farm tenancy maintained a close association with the regions of cotton and tobacco production and the areas of the richest and highest-priced farm lands.

High-priced land in the staple areas tended to make tenancy necessary, and the high productivity of the soil made the use of unskilled tenant labor economically possible. Contrary to a rather general belief, tenancy was not a racial institution. White tenants outnumbered Negro tenants at all times, though a higher percentage of Negro farmers were tenants than was true of the whites. The percentage of Negro tenancy, however, was on the decrease while that of white tenancy was on the increase.

Advantages and Disadvantages of Tenancy

The system of farm tenancy provided labor and livelihood for a large class of landless, moneyless, unskilled people; it supported agriculture without much operating capital; and for some of the most efficient and ambitious tenants it was a training school for farm ownership. But tenancy tended to decrease the size of the farm and the efficiency of farm operation, deplete soil fertility, discourage the use of machinery, perpetuate the system of money crops and crop liens, discourage a rising standard of living, hinder the growth of rural organization and cooperative enterprise, and hamper intellectual and moral development, good citizenship, a stable rural population, and a healthy political life. Though a serious problem affecting directly nearly half of the farm population in 1900, farm tenancy provoked little or no public or political interest in the state until after the turn of the century. The problem was seldom mentioned by any leader in public life.

Problems of the North Carolina Farmers

There was expansion and prosperity in post war manufacturing, transportation, and banking, but agriculture, despite its quick recovery in volume of production, experienced a generation of chronic economic depression and growing grievances. North Carolina agriculture was definitely a part of the national picture of overproduction, falling prices, shrinking income, less rapidly shrinking expenses and burdens, and waning prestige. This situation, which was acute in the late sixties and seventies, became extremely serious in the eighties and early nineties. The farmer was "gradually but steadily becoming poorer and poorer every year." He always lacked an adequate "reserve" to tide him over a lean year—of which there were many. Prices of things he sold were low and getting lower. Prices of things he bought, such as fertilizer and cotton bagging, were high and, in some instances, getting higher. Industry and commerce seemed to be prosperous, but agriculture was depressed.

An editorial in *The Progressive Farmer* for April 28, 1887, expressed the farmer's plight: "There is something radically wrong in our industrial system. There is a screw loose. The wheels have dropped out of balance. The railroads have never been so prosperous, and yet agriculture languishes. The banks have never done a more profitable business, and yet agriculture languishes. Manufacturing enterprises never made more money or were in more flourishing condition, and yet agriculture languishes. Speculators and incorporations never accumulated fortunes more rapidly, and agriculture languishes. Towns and cities flourish and 'boom' and grow and 'boom,' and yet agriculture languishes. . . . The *News and Observer* 'rejoices in the progress of various towns throughout the state. . . .' Our worthy contemporary sees the languishing condition of agriculture and ascribes it largely to the robbing of people by taxation under the form of law. This is true, but if the towns, railroads, manufacturers, banks and all speculative enterprises flourish so prosperously and agriculture languishes under the same laws imposing these taxes, this is but another proof that something is radically wrong."

In the nation and in North Carolina after the war the farmer lost rapidly and heavily to the urban business and professional classes in social position, wealth, numbers, intellectual progress, and political influence and power. Equality of opportunity and political and economic democracy in America were seriously menaced by the rising power and influence of great combinations of wealth. In 1890 the wealthiest 3 percent of the American population owned

65 percent of the national wealth while the poorest 87 percent owned only 10 percent.

Drop in Prices of Farm Crops

In the postwar generation North Carolina farmers were unable to secure incomes sufficient to meet expenses and provide an attractive standard of living. National overproduction of agricultural staples caused falling crop prices. Larger crops and harder work brought about the same prices or even reduced annual farm incomes. Cotton prices declined from twenty-five cents a pound in 1868 to twelve cents in the 1870's, to nine cents in the 1880's, and to seven cents in the early nineties, finally reaching five cents a pound in 1894. It was difficult for the farmer to "break even" unless cotton sold for as much as ten cents a pound. The farmer had no control over the selling price, which was determined by the world market. He did not understand the law of supply and demand, and he did not have a national government to help him out of his economic difficulties.

With stationary or declining incomes, North Carolina farmers were oppressed by economic obligations and burdens that kept them face to face with hard living conditions, meager net profits, debt, and insolvency. The prices of manufactures, fertilizer, cotton bagging and ties, farm machinery, and other essentials did not decline as much as farm prices—some did not decline at all. Neither did freight rates charged by railroads. Moreover, the railroads, through rebates and other special privileges to corporations and big customers in the towns, discriminated not only against the farmers but also against the small businessmen. The farmers suffered also from the antiquated, unfair, discriminatory system of taxation based primarily on land.

High Taxes

The rate of the state property tax declined irregularly from eighty cents on the hundred-dollar valuation in 1868 to fifteen cents in 1893, but businessmen escaped taxation on their intangible personal property, such as stocks and bonds, and obtained relatively lower assessments on their real property. The railroads enjoyed partial, if not almost complete, exemption from taxation. With the wealthier and more prosperous classes failing to bear their proportionate load of taxation, the farmer's burden was disproportionately heavy. Sales of farms for unpaid taxes forced many owners into bankruptcy and into the ranks of tenancy.

Credit System

Exorbitant credit costs kept the farmers in debt. In the absence of cash reserves, credit was absolutely essential to most tenants and farm owners for the financing of the year's operations. Since farm property and crops were considered inadequate security for loans, banks rendered little or no service in extending credit to the farmers. They were useful indirectly however, through the local merchants who were the farmers' source of credit. The crop-lien system developed as the characteristic relation between the farmer and the merchant. The merchant agreed to "run" the farmer until harvest time, advanced supplies to him at "time prices," about 20 to 50 percent higher than cash prices and assured himself of repayment at harvest time by a farm mortgage requiring the farmer to plant staple crops—tobacco or cotton—readily convertible into cash. "Since the goods were purchased throughout the year and the payments were made in the fall, the average item ran less than six months; so that the farmer paid in effect from 40 to 100 percent annual interest." This crop-lien system helped to perpetuate the one crop system, but the farmer was not without fault on the score. *The Progressive Farmer* attributed the one-crop evil partly to the farmer's ignorance and indifference, and declared: "We may join all the farmers' organizations that can be devised, but hard times will hover around our firesides so long as we buy our meat and bread, hay and fertilizers, and other farm supplies, and attempt to pay for them from the proceeds of one crop."

Exorbitant interest rates and "time prices" were considered necessary to insure the merchants against loss, though generally the "time merchants" prospered under the system. But the heavy credit costs made it impossible for the farmers to pay the year's debts and have enough left to pay cash for the next year's operations. High credit costs kept them in debt to the merchant, and debt compelled them to pay the high credit prices and to grow money crops instead of pursuing a diversified live-at-home economy. Nearly all tenants and most farm owners were always a year behind and seldom could catch up. Sometimes the farmer lost his farm to the merchant and had to become a tenant. *The Progressive Farmer* for August 7, 1888, referring to the crop-lien system, said: "It has proved a worse curse to North Carolina than droughts, floods, cyclones, storms, rust, caterpillars, and every other evil that attends the farmer." It went on to say that the average interest rate paid in the western counties was about 25 percent and that in the East about 40 percent, and observed that "the most profitable business in this country cannot pay such a percent as that, much less farming. . . . It is useless to talk about diversified crops to a man who pays 40 percent for supplies. There is no system of diversified crops that will enable him to pay such a price; it makes no difference what kind of crop may be raised."

The Monetary Problem

The national system of finance and currency was particularly burdensome to the farmers. The medium of exchange consisted, in part, of gold coin whose supply was not subject to rapid increase. But the major source of currency was national bank notes, and their quantity was based on a government debt that was not increasing very much. State banks were prohibited from issuing bank notes, and silver had ceased to be coined into dollars as the result of a federal law of 1873—the so-called "Crime of '73." The farmer was suffering from deflation as the rapidly expanding volume of the nation's business, with a relatively stationary and inelastic supply of currency, tended to make money scarce and to depress the price of farm commodities. Falling crop prices in the eighties and nineties meant that an ever-increasing quantity of cotton, tobacco, corn, wheat, and other crops was necessary to pay off a dollar of indebtedness. The increase of debt due to falling crop prices was about 16 percent during each five-year period for the twenty years after 1875. It became increasingly difficult for the farmer to pay off old debts and increasingly easy for him to incur new ones.

Criticism of the "Money Power"

Under the persecution of unending depression and debt, the farmers developed a deep-seated hatred for those policies and agencies that seemed responsible for bad agricultural conditions. The special objects of the farmers' wrath were the protective tariff, corporations, monopolistic trusts, merchants, and middlemen, railroads, and banks as typified by the power of "Wall Street." The protective tariff, almost exclusively on manufactured goods, raised the price of the farmers' purchases and, by restricting the ability of foreign countries to buy southern staples, tended to depress their prices. The farmer was selling his produce in an unprotected world market and buying in an American market protected by a very high tariff. Middlemen were criticized for dodging their share of taxes, depressing crop prices, exacting inordinate profits, and maintaining excessive prices for goods sold to farmers, especially fertilizers, farm machinery, and cotton bagging. Price wars among competing corporations, though giving a slight temporary relief, seemed always to end in cooperative price-fixing or in monopolies that could raise prices at will.

The Progressive Farmer of August 7, 1888, denounced the "moneyed power of the land, which threatens to impoverish and enslave" the farmers: "It struts into and out of halls of legislation and by bribery or intimidation controls and shapes legislation in its favor. Trusts and combines—names that should be synonymous with highway robbers—are being formed each day to extort through the power of money, exorbitant and ruinous prices from those who are compelled to buy. A few millionaires get together and agree that they will get control of the manufacture or product of a certain commodity—will stop its production if need be, and raise the price to whatever their greed may demand, and thus force the consumer to pay it."

Demands for Railroad Regulation

The prosperous railroads, some of which were paying their stockholders high dividends, were blamed as beneficiaries of unjust tax discriminations and as perpetrators of stockwatering and other unfair practices, poor service, and excessive and discriminatory rates "between persons, places, and things." Farmers' meetings demanded that laws be enacted to "prohibit our public officials from receiving or using free passes or free tickets on our railroads" and that the "Legislature establish a Commission for the regulation of freights and tariff on the railroads of our State"; but it was several years before action was taken to correct these evils.

Banks, "Wall Street," and the "money power" were blamed for the scarcity of money and credit, high interest charges, and the "unholy exploitation of the farmer." Why should control of the nation's currency rest in the hands of the private owners of national banks? Why should not the government itself expand the circulating medium by providing currency and credit by legalizing the free and unlimited coinage of the vast output of western silver mines?

North Carolina farmers contrasted their own lives of toil, penury, and loneliness with those of the prosperous mill owners, bankers, railroad owners, merchants, professional men, and city dwellers. Was the formerly prosperous, independent, small-farmer class—the backbone of North Carolina—destined for extinction or humiliating dependence? Was North Carolina spawning a growing class of tenants whose lot was less attractive than that of the mill workers? A memorial of Chatham County farmers to the legislature in 1889 probably represented the views of most North Carolina farmers, when it said: "Almost every farmer is depressed; many are disheartened; labor is unremunerative; the value of land is depreciating, and there is a growing disposition to abandon the farm and seek other employment. Unless something is done to bring relief, many will be compelled to give up their farms. The boasted progress and wealth in North Carolina is not shared by the farmers. They are gradually but steadily becoming poorer and poorer every year."

The Farmers Begin to Organize

Agricultural leaders urged the farmers to unite for a redress of their many grievances and for the general improvement of rural life. The first major organization of the "embattled farmers" in North Carolina and in the nation was the Patrons of Husbandry, usually called the Grange—the name of its local unit. This national organization of farmers was founded in 1869, but it was not until March 3, 1873, that the first North Carolina grange was organized—at McLeansville, in Guilford County. The Granger movement, which was primarily social and economic in its objectives, spread rapidly, and when the state Grange was incorporated by the General Assembly in 1875, there were 501 local units with a total membership of 15,000. The official report of 1876 revealed that 548 lodges had been organized and that 504 were active, 28 having been consolidated with other lodges and 5 having surrendered their charters. In spite of its auspicious beginnings, the North Carolina Grange did not live up to its early expectations; the condition of the state's rural population seemed to be getting worse; the anticipated reforms were not achieved; and the granges declined in membership and influence. In 1885 there were only 26 granges and approximately 700 members in the whole state.

The most numerous, widespread, and successful farm organization in North Carolina was the Farmers' Alliance which, like the Grange, was part of a nationwide organization primarily concerned with social and economic problems of the farmer. The first subordinate unit of the Alliance was formed at Ashpole, in Robeson county, April 20, 1887; the first county Alliance was that of Robeson, organized on May 28 of that year. The state Alliance was organized at Rockingham on October 4 and by the end of the year there were 12 county alliances, 250 subordinate alliances, and about 30,000 members. In 1890 the Alliance's official report listed 2,147 local units and 90,000 members in North Carolina.

The leading spirit of the Alliance in North Carolina was Colonel Leonidas L. Polk; its leading organ was *The Progressive Farmer.* Polk began publication of this agricultural journal at Winston in 1886. He was soon called to Raleigh to become state commissioner of agriculture, and he moved the paper to Raleigh. Polk was secretary of the state Alliance. Sydenham B. Alexander was its first president. He was succeeded by Elias Carr in 1890. Marion Butler was president from to 1891 to 1894. By this time the Alliance had declined in both membership and influence.

At first the Alliance was not primarily political. Some of its leaders thought an educational program was more important than political activity, so they tried to bring the people of the rural communities together for entertainment and education. Speakers were brought in to discuss seed selection, stock-raising, fertilizer, crop rotation, and other practical matters. Institutes, canning clubs, and agricultural fairs were encouraged and promoted. Active support was given to the movement to establish the schools that are now North Carolina State University and The University of North Carolina at Greensboro.

The act of incorporation of the Alliance conferred upon it "power to conduct mercantile and manufacturing businesses, operate warehouses, stock-yards, grain elevators, and packing establishments, and manufacture fertilizers." Not many of these powers were exercised, but a state agency was created to aid the farmer in buying agricultural implements, fertilizers, and even groceries direct from the manufacturers. Its total business in 1890 amounted to about $325,000, which represented a saving to those who made their purchases through it of from 10 to 60 percent. In general the Alliance was opposed to cooperative stores, though a few were tried.

Although the Farmers' Alliance was a nonpolitical organization, its leaders admitted that it was deeply concerned with the action of the major political parties. *The Progressive Farmer* said, "We don't advise bringing politics into the farmers' organizations, but we do advise taking agricultural questions *into politics.*"

North Carolina farmers demanded of the federal government a reduction in protective tariffs, regulation of railroads and trusts, and expansion of the currency. They began to look to their state government for tax reform, legal limitation of interest rates, railroad regulation, and educational reform. Since most of the farmers were Democrats, they naturally turned to their own dominant party for aid. But they discovered that the Democratic party in North Carolina was indifferent or even hostile to the wishes of the farmers for reform—that the Democratic party had become the guardian of the railroads, manufacturers, and other "special interests," and that agriculture, the state's major economic pursuit, was not one of these interests.

Chapter 37

THE SLOW RECOVERY OF EDUCATION AFTER THE WAR

The war for Southern Independence had a profound effect upon education in North Carolina. Wake Forest closed on May 5, 1862, and from June, 1864, to the close of the war the main college building was used as a Confederate hospital. Trinity managed to remain open by the expedient of admitting girls in 1864, but in April, 1865, all activities were suspended. Davidson established a "preparatory department" on September 25, 1862, to furnish employment to its faculty, but the college was forced to close early in 1865. The New Garden Boarding School (present Guilford College) and most of the colleges for girls managed to keep going throughout the war. Almost all of the academies and many "old field" schools closed for lack of teachers or pupils. The University of North Carolina survived the war as a mere shadow of the robust institution of the previous decade. In 1860 its student body of 376 represented every southern state. In 1864–65 only 65 students matriculated. Of the 15 applicants to the class of 1865, 14 were accepted and the fifteenth was rejected for physical disabilities. Yet the university remained open. "Even after the Confederacy had fallen and the University buildings had been turned into barracks for the 4,000 Michigan Cavalry that occupied Chapel Hill, the college bell was rung daily and the dozen students who had wandered back to their old haunts attended classes." Four students returned to receive their diplomas at the 1865 commencement.

Higher Education during Reconstruction

Even more profound were the changes in North Carolina education during the postwar years of Reconstruction from 1865 to 1877. Several colleges reopened soon after the war—Trinity (January 11, 1866), Wake Forest

530

(January 15, 1866) and Davidson later in the same year. Some of the academies resumed operations, struggled to survive the handicaps of poverty, and closed again. The collapse of the Confederacy and the repudiation of the state war debt wiped out the state's resources of Confederate bonds and bank stock. Handicapped by poverty and the loss of confidence arising from the politics and unionism of its president, David L. Swain, the University of North Carolina was in a desperate condition when the Republicans assumed control of the state government in 1868. The Constitution of that year merged the university with the public school system and the Republican Board of Trustees removed Swain from the presidency and selected a new president, the Reverend Solomon S. Pool of Pasquotank County, and a new faculty. Lack of public confidence, financial support, and students closed the university in 1870. A student expressed it graphically when he wrote on a classroom blackboard: "Today this University busted and went to hell." The capture of state political control by the Conservatives paved the way for a constitutional amendment in 1873 restoring the government of the university to a Board of Trustees chosen by the legislature. The new Conservative Board of Trustees, aided by Mrs. Cornelia Phillips Spencer ("the woman who rang the bell") and other friends, was successful in reopening the university in 1875 under the administration of President Kemp P. Battle and a new faculty. But it remained a weak, struggling, poverty-stricken institution for many years.

Collapse of the State System of Common Schools

The utter collapse of the state system of common schools early in Reconstruction resulted from the general demoralization of the times and the loss of most of the Literary Fund, the main support of the system. The loss of this fund resulted from the sale of its railroad and bank stock at depreciated prices and from the defeat of the Confederacy and the repudiation of the state war debt, which rendered worthless its North Carolina and Confederate securities. During their brief tenure of power from 1865 to 1868, the Conservatives abolished the office of state superintendent of common schools, refused to make state appropriations for schools, and threw the responsibility for public education upon local resources. Towns and counties were empowered to levy taxes for schools, but this failed to solve the problem, since few of the local governments took favorable action. The lack of state aid and the prevalence of poverty, educational apathy and indifference, and popular aversion to taxation forestalled any appreciable achievement in public education.

The Republican Party and Public Education

The state government under radical Republican control from 1868 to 1870 manifested a striking interest in public education. Devoting an entire article to education, the Constitution of 1868 provided for an elective superintendent of public instruction and required the General Assembly at its first session to provide, by taxation and otherwise, a general and uniform system of free public schools for all children between the ages of six and twenty-one. County commissioners were to be subject to indictment if they failed to maintain one or more schools in each district at least four months each year. The powers of making rules for the school system and of managing the educational fund were vested in the Board of Education. The Constitution further provided that the remains of the Literary Fund, the proceeds from the sale of swamp lands and escheats and from fines and penalties, appropriations the General Assembly might make, and at least three-fourths of the proceeds of state and county poll taxes should be used for public schools.

The Public School Law of 1869

In response to Governor Holden's recommendation, the legislature passed the school law of 1869 providing for separate schools for whites and Negroes, a system of administration similar to that of the antebellum period, a four months' term for all children, and the levy by the county commissioners of a sufficient township tax to provide the four months' school if the township failed to make provision therefor. The General Assembly also appropriated $100,000 for the public schools. This school law, a very intelligent and liberal one for its day, might have established an excellent school system had the act been rigidly enforced and the revenues been ample. But the effective school system envisioned by the authors of the 1869 law was only partially established. The fact that the administration of the school law was in the hands of Superintendent of Public Instruction the Reverend S. S. Ashley, a carpetbagger from Massachusetts and an advocate of "mixed schools," and his assistant J. W. Hood, a Negro carpetbagger, created suspicion and lack of public confidence; the state's resources were limited; schoolhouses were few and in bad repair; none of the state's appropriation for schools were immediately available, and in 1870 the Radicals gave the schools only $38,000 of the $136,000 collected for that purpose; the collection of poll taxes was incomplete; and many townships failed to provide schools in accordance with the law. Meager records indicate that in 1870 there were 1,398 schools operating in seventy-four counties at a cost of $43,000 and with an enrollment of 49,999, nearly half of whom were Negroes, though in separate schools from the whites. The total enrollment was only one-fifth to one-seventh of the children of school age. The progress of education in North Carolina was slow during Reconstruction—and it remained slow in the generation of Democratic political supremacy after Reconstruction.

Higher Education and Its Problems

The reopened University of North Carolina struggling with poverty, small enrollment and educational lethargy, began to receive small regular state appropriations for maintenance with a $10,000 grant in 1881; but its state support and its very existence as a university were threatened by the rivalry and opposition of some religious denominations, particularly the Baptists and Methodists. The university fumbled its opportunity to meet the growing need for agricultural and industrial education as it had earlier failed to meet the demand for teacher training. As early as 1866 Daniel Harvey Hill made an appeal for technical education, declaring: "The old plan of education in the palmy days of the South gave us orators and statesmen, but did nothing to enrich us, nothing to promote material greatness. . . . The South must abandon the aesthetic and ornamental for the practical and useful. Is not a practical acquaintance with the ax, the plane, the saw, the anvil, the loom, the plow, and the mattock, vastly more useful to an impoverished people than familiarity with the laws of nations and the science of government? . . . The everlasting twaddle about politics is giving place to important facts in history, in the mechanic arts, in morals, in philosophy, etc."

The Movement for a College of Agriculture and Mechanic Arts

Soon after the readmission of North Carolina to the Union in 1868, North Carolina availed itself of the advantages of the federal Morrill Act, better known as the Land Grant College Act; and the land script for 270,000 acres of public land, which sold for $125,000, was transferred to the University of North Carolina. Although no separate agricultural and mechanical college was established, the university received annually for many years $7,500 (the interest on the original $125,000) for the purpose of giving agricultural and mechanical education. The university offered courses in this type of education, but few or no students enrolled in them. In the early eighties many complaints were made about this situation and there were increasing demands for a separate agricultural and mechanical college—though in many states the land grant college was attached to the state university. The demands for trained men in industry, voiced by Walter Hines Page and the Watauga Club of Raleigh, and the crusade for agricultural education carried on by Colonel L. L. Polk, editor of *The Progressive Farmer,* finally led to the chartering of the State Agricultural and Mechanical College in 1887. It opened two years later.

Other Colleges Established

To satisfy the broadening needs of higher education, the state legislature chartered and established four other new colleges during this period:

the Fayetteville Colored Normal in 1877, the first Negro teacher-training school in the South; the State Normal and Industrial School for white girls at Greensboro in 1891, sponsored chiefly by Charles D. McIver, the Teachers' Assembly, and the Farmers' Alliance; the North Carolina Agricultural and Mechanical College for the Colored Race at Greensboro in 1891; and the Elizabeth City Colored Normal in the same year. The main impetus for these significant achievements in higher education came from outside the ranks of political leaders. Two important denominational colleges were also begun about this time. Meredith College, at Raleigh, founded by the Baptist State Convention and chartered in 1891, opened its doors to students in 1899. Elon College, near Burlington, established under the auspices of the Christian Church, was founded in 1899 and admitted its first students the next year.

Trinity College Moved to Durham

The most significant fact in the realm of the small, struggling, denominational colleges was the removal of Trinity College from Randolph County to Durham in 1892, after Julian S. Carr donated the site and George Washington Duke donated $85,000. Two years later John F. Crowell resigned the presidency and was succeeded by the Reverend John C. Kilgo. At this time the college had a faculty of 9, a student body of 133, and a physical plant worth $135,000.

The Plight of the Public Schools

The chief dependence for secondary education before 1900 was upon the academies, which slowly revived and grew, though they were fewer in number than in the antebellum period. The establishment of a few city graded public schools—with Greensboro and Charlotte taking the lead about 1870—was a significant beginning that would have far-reaching results. But the progress of the public schools was particularly disappointing under the conservative leadership that controlled the Democratic party and the state government for a quarter of a century after 1870. The plain mandatory provisions of the constitution that the General Assembly and the county commissioners provide public schools for four months each year for all children were violated.

The first Democratic legislature of the period (1871) drastically cut the salary of the state superintendent and deprived him of all clerical service and travel funds. This led to Ashley's resignation and his replacement by Alexander McIver. A so-called state tax of 6 2/3 cents on each $100 valuation of property and 20 cents on each poll was levied for the public schools; but the proceeds in each county were to be used by that county. If revenue was insufficient to maintain the constitutional four months' term, the county commissioners were prohibited from levying a special tax to supply the deficiency. In 1873 the tax rate was increased; but if it was insufficient to provide the four months' term in any county, the county commissioners were not empowered to levy a special tax until after a favorable popular referendum. In 1875 the constitution was amended to provide definitely for separate schools for whites and Negroes.

The Beginning of a Teacher-Training Program

Under Governor Vance's leadership, the legislature of 1877 authorized a normal school for each race. Accordingly, as already mentioned, the Fayetteville Colored Normal School was established, and, to carry out this mandate for white teachers, "the first summer school in the United States under the auspices of a college or university" was opened at the University of North Carolina in the summer of 1877. The General Assembly of 1877 also authorized towns of a certain population to vote taxes for public graded schools. In response to the urging of Governor Jarvis, the legislature raised the property and poll tax rates for schools to 12½ cents and 37½ cents, respectively, provided for the holding of four normal schools for each race, and significantly ordered the county commissioners to levy special school taxes to supply any deficiency for the maintenance of four months' schools. In 1889 the normal schools were replaced by teachers' institutes which were held each year in each county by Charles D. McIver and Edwin A. Alderman; and in 1891 the tax rates for schools were raised to 15 cents and 45 cents for property and polls, respectively.

School Statistics

In actuality the public school system did not keep pace with the legislation because the state tax was entirely inadequate to provide a four months' term and the Supreme Court and popular indifference nullified the law and the constitution in respect to the levy of supplementary local taxes. In 1872 the public schools cost $155,000 and enrolled about one-fifth of the children for a few weeks. In 1880 the expenditures were $353,000 for 5,312 schools with 3,266 schoolhouses worth $95 each, running for nine weeks with an average attendence of about one-third of the children and an average teacher salary of $22 per month. In 1890 the cost was $718,000 and the average term sixty days. In 1900 the expenditures were $950,000 for a school term of seventy days, a 58 percent enrollment, a 37 percent average attendance, and a teacher salary average of $25 a month. Illiteracy actually increased in the 1870s. In 1880, a total population of 1,399,750, there were 463,975 persons over ten years of age, more than two-fifths of whom were whites, who could not write. In the 1880s there was some reduction of illiteracy, chiefly among the Negroes. Before 1900 the state failed dismally to live up to the educational provisions of the constitution and the law. In that year its public school system was actually and relatively worse than it had been in 1860. It was perhaps the poorest in the United States. Yet only 19.5 percent of the whites and 47.6 percent of the Negroes were illiterate—a marked decrease since 1880.

Public education in North Carolina was severely handicapped by relative poverty due to war and low income, scattered population, bad roads, a large school population in comparison with the number of taxpayers, and the necessity of maintaining a dual system of schools. The standard explanations for educational backwardness were two: the Negro, with the danger of mixed schools, and poverty resulting from the war. In reality there was no danger of mixed schools either from local demand or outside compulsion. Poverty was a valid explanation for only a portion of the backwardness and relative decline. Economic recovery from the war was achieved long before 1900; the state repudiated most of its debt; the valuations of taxable property were increasing; and the tax rate was decreasing. The per capita school tax in North Carolina in 1890 was 44 cents a year in comparison with the national average of $2.11.

Reasons for the State's Backwardness in Public Education

The real explanations for the state's loss of educational rank, even in the South, were a colossal general indifference to public education and a sterile, reactionary political leadership. The support of public schools mainly by current tax revenue was foreign to the experience and sentiment of the state. The ignorant tax-voting masses were generally indifferent. Some of the wealthy opposed the entire principle of public education and patronized the private schools. The state's political leadership failed to press vigorously for educational improvement; generally it minimized, and sought explanations for, educational backwardness. Though they rendered perfunctory tribute to public education in their messages to the legislature, the governors were in some cases mediocre in ability and in most cases indifferent to education. Vance and Jarvis were more interested than the others (Caldwell, Brogden, Scales, Fowle, Holt, Carr, and Russell). Jarvis frankly faced the need of more revenue and made the startling declaration to the legislature in 1881 that the state tax might be trebled without unduly burdening the state.

Legislative indifference is indicated by the fact that the $600,000 received from the sale of the Western North Carolina Railroad (made partly in response to the argument that the state should withdraw from the railroad field and devote its meager resources to education and state development) was actually used for current state expenses and the state property tax was abolished for a year. This sum exceeded the total value of public school property ($390,000) and the total expenditures for schools ($535,000). Even the state superintendents of public instruction (Ashley, McIver, Stephen Pool, John Pool, John Scarborough, Sidney M. Finger) failed to provide vigorous and effective educational leadership. In fact, no political official in the state made a frank diagnosis of or a crusade for public education. Much of the local management of the schools was bad, ignorant, and political. The economical, unprogressive educational policy of the Democratic party leadership was pleasing to the majority of the tax-hating population, especially the influential property interests.

State Supreme Court Decisions Adverse to Public Schools

In large measure, the responsibility for educational backwardness rested with the reactionary Democratic Supreme Court, which was willing to scrap the law and the Constitution in response to the general opposition to taxation and in defense of the interests and rights of property. The opinions of the court in *Lane* v. *Stanly* in 1870 and *Barksdale* v. *Commissioners* in 1885 made impossible the establishment of the constitutional four months' term; but these opinions provoked no protest or political effort to surmount the legal obstacle raised by the court. These opinions held that neither the township nor the county had the power to levy township taxes for public schools. Though the county might levy a county school tax for the four months' school, it might do so only if the combined county and state taxes did not exceed the constitutional limit of 66⅔ cents on the $100 valuation of property and $2.00 on the poll and then only after a favorable referendum, since education was not a "necessary expense" in the meaning of the constitution. The inadequacy of the constitutional tax rate to provide for both governmental expenses and a four months' school term and the unwillingness of the people to vote additional taxes made it impossible for the counties to have four months' schools, despite the plain constitutional mandate of a four months' term and indictment of county commissioners who failed to provide it. If various constitutional provisions were in conflict, the Supreme Court could have given supremacy to one as well as to another. It sacrificed the educational provisions for those on taxation.

Freedmen's Bureau Schools

The sad plight and the defeated South, particularly the plight of the great mass of ignorant Negroes, elicited educational aid from humanitarian organizations and churches in the North. Their chief interest was in the Negroes, but they also established schools for white children. Though there was keen resentment against the Freedmen's Bureau, it established more than four hundred schools for Negroes in North Carolina with an enrollment of twenty thousand pupils.

The Peabody Fund's Assistance to North Carolina Schools

The most important outside fund for southern education came from the Peabody Fund of about $3 million donated by George Peabody of Boston in 1867 and administered by the Peabody Education Board, of which William A. Graham of North Carolina was a member. Its object was to help only those communities that were willing to provide educational facilities for themselves. It made donations of from $300 to $1,000 a year to free schools for whites or Negroes that raised locally from two to three times that amount and operated ten months with an average attendance of 84 percent of the enrollment. It also gave aid in preparing teachers and purchasing textbooks and to state departments of education, teachers' organizations, and educational periodicals. The Peabody Fund did not meet with much response in North Carolina. It had granted a total of $87,000 by 1877 to a few enterprising North Carolina towns whose schools were already the best in the state. The Peabody Fund stimulated some local school support, helped establish excellent town schools which served as examples to the rest of the state, and tended to break down the bitter southern hatred of the North.

Proposed Federal Aid to Schools: The Blair Bill

In 1881 Senator Henry W. Blair of New Hampshire introduced a bill in the United States Senate calling for a federal appropriation of $120,-000,000 to be distributed to the various states and territories according to their illiteracy rate. One-tenth of the money thus granted was to be used for teacher education, but no part of it was to be used for school buildings. The "Blair Educational Bill" passed the Senate in 1884 and again in 1886, but it failed to pass the House of Representatives. Both senators from North Carolina voted for the bill. Fear of federal control of schools was a major cause of its defeat in the House, and this fear was not limited to the South.

Increasing Sentiment for Public Schools

In spite of the inert political leadership and the vastness of the problem of public education, various forces were laying the foundation for educational advance. A few excellent ten months' town schools, supported by local taxes voted in accordance with the law of 1877 and by the Peabody Fund, were examples which incited an interest in improvement. The public schools themselves, the colleges and normal schools, the teachers' institutes, local and state teachers' organizations, and farm organizations and leaders made gradual inroads on public indifference and slowly developed a public sentiment for greater educational advance. Increasing wealth, particularly in the growing industrial and urban centers, was making the advance economically feasible. Of great importance was the emergence of a group of aggressive, young, interested leaders outside the realm of politics. Walter Hines Page was a flaming critic of the old order through the columns of *The State Chronicle.* Charles D. McIver of the teaching profession, university presidents Kemp P. Battle and George T. Winston, and farm leaders L. L. Polk and Marion Butler were useful in gaining popular support for public education. Public school leaders who were active in the educational crusade included M. C. S. Noble, Alexander Graham, Edward P. Moses, and P. P. Claxton. But the most effective work was one by Charles D. McIver and Edwin A. Alderman, who, as conductors of teachers' institutes in every county from 1889 to 1891, convinced thousands of the value of and necessity for public schools. As for wealth and public opinion, North Carolina was ready and able to provide and maintain better public schools. But the Democratic leadership was so indifferent and dilatory that its failure to make more rapid improvement in public education contributed to the political revolution of the 1890s which drove the party from power.

Chapter 38

CONSERVATIVE DEMOCRACY AND POLITICAL REVOLUTION, 1877-1894

The Democratic victory in the Vance-Settle campaign of 1876 and the recall of federal troops in 1877 marked the end of political and military reconstruction in North Carolina. As already stated, it was fear of a return of Republican-Negro dominance that perpetuated an abnormal unity of the white majority in the Democratic party, and this majority subordinated every issue to the maintenance of "white supremacy" and aided the Democratic party to maintain uninterrupted political control of the state from 1877 to 1894. The emergence of the Democratic "Solid South" thus ended the healthy prewar two-party system which had produced an able political leadership and had divided the voters on realistic social, economic, and political issues.

Impairment of Local Self-Government

By virtue of the constitutional amendments of 1875 and a legislative act of 1876, the victorious Democratic party abolished the choice of county commissioners by popular vote and vested their election in the hands of justices of the peace who were chosen by the legislature, always safely Democratic. Under the guise of eliminating the chance of Negro control in the sixteen eastern Negro counties, these measures ended the possibility of Republican control not only in the eastern counties but also in the white western counties. Even in Democratic counties, the voters lost control of their county government, which generally fell into the hands of "court-house rings" composed of local Democratic leaders. The serious impairment of the principle of local self-government was a mounting grievance against the Democratic party among white voters of the western counties.

540

State Debt Settlement

The Democratic party solved the staggering problem of state finances by repudiating most of the state debt of $30,000,000 in 1870, upon whose interest charges the state had defaulted to the extent of $3,000,000, and about $13,000,000 of which consisted of the special tax railroad bonds issued in 1868–69, during the Republican regime, most of which had been wasted and all of which were generally regarded as fraudulent, unconstitutional, and worthy of repudiation. The remainder of the debt, incurred before, during, and after the war, chiefly for railroad construction, was unquestionably honest and valid. But it was argued that the state, impoverished by a war brought on by the North, whose citizens held many of the bonds, was not able to pay all of the honest debt. For several years there was discussion looking to some fair and obviously needed debt settlement. The cautious Democratic party did not wish to risk the political disfavor or defeat by excessive scaling or repudiation which might dishonor the state and injure local bondholders or by assuming an excessive burden which would necessitate heavy taxes. The bondholders rejected a state offer of settlement in 1875 as too illiberal; and the state rejected the bondholders' proposal of 1877 to settle for 50 percent of the old debt and unpaid interest in new 6 percent thirty-year bonds.

A growing demand for settlement crystallized public opinion rather clearly in favor of complete repudiation of the allegedly dishonest portion of the debt and the heavy scaling down of the honest debt. Governor Vance advocated this policy, and it was enacted by the legislature in the debt settlement law of 1879. The special tax railroad bonds were repudiated completely and a constitutional amendment in 1880 prohibited their future payment without the approval of a majority of the qualified voters. As for the honest debt, all accrued interest was repudiated, and the principal was classified into three groups, each of which was scaled from 60 percent to 85 percent. The state decided to pay $6,500,000 as complete settlement of the entire state debt of about $43,750,000 principal and accrued interest. The bondholders were helpless. Those who owned "honest" bonds, preferring a little to nothing, generally exchanged their bonds for new ones in greatly reduced amounts. A few were not exchanged; and in 1904, as a result of a successful suit by South Dakota before the United States Supreme Court, North Carolina was compelled to pay the entire principal and accrued interest on a few of the old bonds. Various states and foreign countries have endeavored to bring suits before the Supreme Court to compel payment of the repudiated special tax bonds; but no case has ever been tried. The people rejoiced to be free of the heavy burden of taxes and debt under the guise of legality. Many of the repudiationists of 1879 had opposed repudiation of the same war debt in 1865 which was held by North Carolinians. Some people questioned the honesty and fairness of the settlement of 1879, especially the heavy scaling of the debts whose honesty was unquestioned and whose payment to a fuller extent could have been assumed without resort to ruinous taxes. Certainly the debt settlement rendered more feasible the financing of a program of state development.

Conservatives Control Democratic Party

The Democratic party, however, did not commit the state to a progressive program of public education, internal improvements, and state development such as that which the war had interrupted in 1861. Rather, it adopted the policy of stimulating railroad, industrial, mercantile, and banking development by unrestrictive private enterprise protected and aided by the state government. Reversing the traditional policy of state aid to railroads, it leased and sold the state's private capital. Party leaders and public officials held railroad stock, rode on free passes, served as railroad lobbyists and attorneys, and aided the railroads in securing special legislative favors of tax exemption and immunity from public regulation. The railroad companies rapidly expanded their mileage, consolidated, prospered, and met quickly and well the vital transportation needs of most of North Carolina. But they charged rates higher than those in other sections, were haughty and careless in serving the public, inflated their capitalization, indulged in such abuses as the granting of passes and rebates to influential friends and large customers, and waxed arrogant from the possession of security and political influence.

The conservatively controlled Democratic party became the ally and guardian of the railroad and industrial interests which were contributing so powerfully to the economic regeneration of the state and were rising to social, economic, and political dominance. It championed the laissez-faire philosophy of the noninterference of government in private business and the negative policy of maintaining the status quo of Democratic supremacy in politics and the freedom of business from governmental interference. With Hamiltonian devotion to an alliance between business and government, the Democratic party became the custodian and friend of the new business order whose free enterprise would produce a New State and a New South. It opposed a rising demand among depressed farmers, liberals, and reformers for a regulatory railroad commission, lower freight and passenger rates, and the abolition of abuses and favoritism. It opposed also the demands for a readjustment of the discriminatory system of taxation; for social legislation to correct the evil effects of long hours and low wages upon mill workers; and for the expansion of the system of public education. It opposed all such measures of economic and social reform allegedly because they would necessitate higher taxes, would discourage business and perhaps drive it from the state, and would cause discussion that might split the Democratic party and permit the return of Republican-Negro control.

Unwholesome Political Practices

The Democratic party maintained its political supremacy for various reasons as the redeemer of the state from the orgy of Reconstruction and Republican-Negro rule. It presented itself as the party of virtue, economy, patriotism, conservatism, and white supremacy. In recurring political campaigns it drew vivid contrasts between North Carolina under Republican rule and under Democratic rule and cultivated the idea that loyalty to the party was essential to the continuance of white supremacy. If necessary, it admitted the state's backwardness in certain respects but minimized it and attributed it to the Negro and to unavoidable poverty resulting from war and reconstruction. If urged to champion new policies, it cautioned that they might hamper economic development and split the party. Partisan legislation and the manipulation of elections reinforced campaign arguments. The new county government law assured Democratic control of the county governments. Democratic legislatures elected Democratic justices of the peace, who chose Democratic election officials, and these were able to disqualify some Republican voters by using technical requirements concerning name, age, or residence, or enforcing legal regulations for the challenging of voters, or employing other devices. Open threats, or even a show of violence, deterred many Negroes from the polls. If it seemed necessary to party victory, party workers and election officials used their skill in corrupt practices such as ballot-box stuffing and fradulent counting of votes. The end of Democratic victory justified any means. Conditions were conducive to party control in local and state affairs by small groups of leaders. Only the loyal and faithful received appointments; a doubtful party man was a traitor and renegade who must suffer ruthless political destruction. It was an age of low political morality when election laws were framed for their violability, when upright men engaged in political corruption as a necessary means toward what they considered the holy end of saving the state from the Republicans. Under the one-party system, the ability of public officials and party leaders in the generation before 1900 was far less than that in prewar days. They were generally conservative, mediocre, unprogressive, and barren of statesmanship. They seldom faced reality, diagnosed the varied needs of the state, championed constructive policies, or even attempted the role of leadership and statesmanship.

Republican Opposition

Democratic policies, methods, and dominance in the generation after Reconstruction were by no means pleasing to all the people in North Carolina. The Republican party furnished steady, powerful, and bitter opposition to the Democratic regime. In a total state vote of approximately 250,000, the Republicans, from 1876 to 1888, trailed the Democrats in gubernatorial elections by from 6,000 to 20,000 votes, and in presidential elections by from 9,000 to 18,000 votes. The party consisted of those Negroes who cared and dared to vote and a substantial group of whites, chiefly among the mass of common people. It was handicapped by a paucity of able and prominent leaders and by the lack of a vigorous party press. It denounced the Democrats for corruption in elections, the impairment of democratic county self-government, and disregard of the interests of the democratic masses. It was insuperably handicapped by its past record during Reconstruction, by its large contingent of Negro voters, its inability to get out the entire Negro vote because of Negro indifference and Democratic opposition, and by its lack of able leaders. Resigned to recurring defeat in state politics, it failed to champion an aggressive program of liberalism and reform and was content to monopolize the federal postmasterships, judgeships, and revenue jobs that were available because the Republican party was almost constantly in control of the federal government. A minority element sought to curb or eliminate the influence of the Negro in party affairs, offer an attractive program of state reform, and make a real bid for the support of the white voters; but the ring or machine of federal officeholders kept control of the party. With such a record, such leadership, and such a program, the Republican party seemed undeserving of the support of those voters who were not altogether pleased with Democratic rule.

Liberal Democrats

The opposition of a minority of liberal Democrats to the conservative control of their party became evident when the Democratic legislature in 1881, under pressure from the churches, authorized a popular referendum on state prohibition of the manufacture of intoxicating liquor in North Carolina and its sale except in maximum quantities of one gallon for medicinal purposes by druggists on doctor's prescriptions. Liberal Democrats and antiprohibitionists organized the Liberal Anti-Prohibition party, which entered the legislative and congressional elections of 1882 with a platform endorsing individual liberty, restoration of local self-government, the extension of public education, and a pure ballot box. The Republican party denounced prohibition as a Democratic measure and endorsed the Liberal Anti-Prohibition candidates. This third party succeeded in electing only one legislator and one congressman, Tyre York of a mountain district. The referendum resulted in the crushing defeat of state prohibition by a vote of 166,325 to 48,370.

The Democratic party escaped serious damage by the unpopular issue of prohibition because many Democrats announced their opposition to it and strenuously denied that it was a party issue. Zebulon B. Vance, in the United States Senate, pleased the liquor interests, the Democrats, and the great mass of people by denouncing the federal internal revenue system as an agency whereby the Republican party dispensed hundreds of jobs and maintained its strength in North Carolina. The Democrats administered a sharp defeat to Tyre York's candidacy for the governorship in 1884. By impassioned appeals for party loyalty and unity as the only safeguard against the return of Republican-Negro domination, the Democrats prevented any serious party defection and defeated the coalition of liberal Democrats and Republicans. The effectiveness of the Negro issue in securing this decisive victory increased the confidence of the conservative Democratic leadership in its own invincibility.

Intraparty Divisions

The most significant opposition to the Democratic regime in North Carolina came from Democratic small farmers who became disgruntled with the party for its conservatism, its opposition to social and economic reform, its devotion to the special interests of the new business order, and its indifference to the interests of the common people. The business classes in the towns enjoyed political favoritism and economic prosperity, but the farmers suffered under the economic persecution of low crop prices which could not meet high freight rates, discriminatory taxes, high and restricted credits, an inadequate currency, and high prices on nonagriculture commodities. In this dilemma, the first efforts of farmers in North Carolina, as in the nation, were directed toward self-help through farm organizations.

The Agrarian Revolt: The Grangers

The Granger movement in the early 1870s, originating outside the state as a nonpolitical organization to improve the social, educational, and economic conditions of rural life, did not gain great strength in North Carolina, which was still engrossed in the problems of reconstruction. It reached the peak of its strength in the state in 1875–76 with over five hundred Granges and fifteen thousand members. Though relatively weak in North Carolina, it directed the attention of farmers to their deplorable condition and pointed the way to a more attractive rural life. The national political Greenback party movement of the early 1880s elicited little response in North Carolina where the fresh memories of Reconstruction bolstered Democratic solidarity and dominance.

The Farmers' Alliance

But continuing hard times furnished the basis for a powerful nonpolitical Farmers' Alliance in North Carolina. L. L. Polk, a native of Anson County, the first state commissioner of agriculture and for many years editor of *The Progressive Farmer,* had been successful in organizing farmers' clubs which held meetings to provide social diversion for rural families and to teach better methods of farming. In 1887 he organized the North Carolina Farmers'

Association at mass meetings in Raleigh. Polk was interested in an agricultural college and in a more attractive and profitable life for the farmers. The Farmers' Alliance, a national organization, enlisted the support of North Carolina farmers' clubs and of farmers who believed in the benefits of organization. It also enlisted Polk, who became first secretary of the North Carolina alliance. Economic distress caused the Farmers' Alliance to spread like wildfire. By 1890 it had 2,147 local organizations in North Carolina with 90,000 members and a state organization. Polk's ability and success as leader of the North Carolina Alliance resulted in his election as president of the National Farmers' Alliance in 1889.

The Farmers' Alliance was a nonpolitical organization. Its regular meetings were enjoyable social and educational occasions. Through its meetings and its sponsorship of an agricultural college and a more powerful state department of agriculture, it sought to educate the farmers in better methods of production and marketing. In order to reduce prices for the farmer, it organized a few local cooperative stores and a state purchasing agency to eliminate the profits of the middleman. Dealing directly with the manufacturers, the state purchasing agency bought as much as $325,000 worth of produce each year at a considerable saving to the farmers. But poor business management, the small number of farmers who could break away from the crop-lien system and pay cash for their purchases, and the hostility of manufacturers and merchants brought failure to the business enterprises.

Demands of the "Embattled Farmers"

The social, educational, and business activities of the Alliance, important as they were, did not solve the chief problems of the farmers. They wanted railroad regulation, limitation of interest rates, better public schools, higher prices for crops, an expanded currency, an agricultural college, and an inexpensive state-supported college for girls. Though nonpolitical, the Alliance looked to the Democratic party, which was the only agency in North Carolina through which many of its demands could be met. Moreover, most of the Alliance members were Democrats. So powerful was the organization that many Democratic candidates for public office endorsed its program. The legislature of 1887, however, defeated a bill for the establishment of a commission to regulate the railroads. But in 1888, under pressure from the Alliance, the party officially endorsed the railroad commission. To the amazement of the Alliance, the Democratic legislature of 1889, under the influence of conservative Democrats and railroad friends and lobbyists, again defeated a railroad commission bill. This precipitated a veritable agrarian revolt in 1890 in which the Alliance elected many farmers to the legislature and captured control of the Democratic party, to the astonishment and disgust of the conservative party leaders. It was the revolutionary "farmers' legislature" of 1891 that increased the tax rate for public schools; established a normal college for white girls and an agricultural college and a normal college for Negroes; increased the state appropriations to the University of North Carolina and state colleges; and provided state regulation for railroads by forbidding rebates and rate discriminations and creating a railroad commission of three members elected by the legislature and empowered to reduce rates and eliminate the special tax exemptions and low assessments enjoyed by the railroads.

The Political Program of the Farmers' Alliance

Beneficial as were these state reforms, crop prices continued to drop; and the condition of the farmers grew worse in the early 1890s. The main causes of their condition—low prices, scarcity of money, and high credit—were not state problems and could be remedied, if at all, only by the federal government. The national Alliance demanded national currency and financial reform—the free and unlimited coinage of silver at a ratio of 16 to 1 with gold, and the subtreasury plan under which the federal government would establish warehouses for the deposit of farm crops and would issue to the depositors legal tender notes at low interest equal to 80 percent of the value of the crops deposited. When prices rose and the farmers sold their deposited crops, the notes would be repaid and destroyed. These measures, it was urged by the farmers, would increase the supply of money, tide the farmers over the period of low prices, and tend to raise crop prices. Both national parties—Democrats and Republicans—opposed the Alliance program as radical, inflationary, impractical, and unconstitutional. Senator Vance and most of the North Carolina Democratic leaders were hostile.

Formation of the Populist or People's Party

Because both old parties seemed hostile to the farmers' demands, a strong faction of the Alliance (particularly in the western states) decided in 1892 to organize a third political party—the People's party. Faced with the momentous decision of choosing between loyalty to the Democratic party and loyalty to the Alliance as it now sought to achieve its objectives by political means, Polk took the lead in support of the third party; and the more radical half of the North Carolina Alliance followed him out of the Democratic party into the new People's or Populist party. But the more conservative half of the Alliance, led by Elias Carr and S. B. Alexander, fearful that party division might lead to Republican rule, remained loyal to the Democratic party. The formation of the Populist party in 1892 split the Alliance and virtually ended its effective career as a farmers' organization. Before going into politics, it brought social, educational, and business benefits to the farmers and forced the Democratic party to railroad regulation, the establishment of agricultural and normal colleges, and increased support for public education.

The Populist Platform of 1892 and Defeat

In 1892 the Populists entered the national and North Carolina campaigns. Polk died in the same year; if he had not, he might have received the Populist presidential nomination. Marion Butler succeeded him as leader of the North Carolina Populists, and W. P. Exum was nominated for the governorship. The state Populist platform demanded economy, tax reform, election reform, a ten-hour work day for labor, and a limitation of 6 percent on interest charges. The Democrats offered no program of state reform but made a bid for the farmer vote by nominating for governor Elias Carr, conservative former president of the Alliance. Under the skillful management of their party chairman, F. M. Simmons, the Democrats denounced the Populists as traitors, appealed to party loyalty and the fear of Republican-Negro rule, and relied on their control of the election machinery. The Populists were handicapped by Polk's death, the weakness of their nominees, the sympathy of the Republicans, the partisan election laws, and the fear of Democratic division and Republican-Negro domination. With Democratic, Populist, and Republican tickets in the field, the Democrats won an easy victory, capturing the governorship and the legislature. The vote for governor was: Democrats, 135,-519; Republicans, 94,684; Populists, 47,840; Prohibitionists, 2,457. The Populists carried only three counties. But it was of the utmost significance that the combined Republican and Populist vote was larger than that of the Democrats.

Democratic Denunciation of Populists

Conditions and events after 1892 perpetuated the Populist party and developed a Populist hatred of the Democrats so virulent that the party was willing to cooperate with the Republicans in 1894 to drive the Democrats from power. In the first place, falling prices and economic distress, culminating in the Panic of 1893, increased the farmer's grievances. In the second place, the victorious national Democratic party under conservative leadership, arrogantly confident even in the face of two hostile parties that polled a majority of the votes in 1892, refused to conciliate the Populists; denounced them as traitors, "Old Pops," and "Copperheads," led by Marion Butler, the "Sampson County Huckleberry"; punished them by political ostracism; and in the legislature of 1893 not only refused to grant any important agrarian reform but attacked the Alliance by making important changes in its charter.

Republican-Populist Fusion Defeats Democrats

Actuated by a common hatred of the Democrats and the desire for political power, the Republicans and Populists in 1894 avoided their mistake of 1892 and entered into a fusion or cooperative arrangement whereby both would support a single ticket on which both were represented. By a preconvention arrangement, the Populists in making nominations would share the public offices with the Republicans. Their platform called for a four months' public school term, a state reformatory, pure election laws, a nonpartisan judiciary, and the restoration of county self-government. They denounced the Democratic party for its political corruption and subservience to the business interests. The Republican party endorsed the Populist nominations and platform. The Democrats wrote a platform devoted to national issues but devoid of a program of state reform. A campaign of partisan bitterness, vituperation, and prejudice followed. The result was a sweeping fusion victory for the Republicans and Populists. They won virtually all of the state and congressional offices and captured control of both houses of the legislature by large majorities. Since there was no gubernatorial election in 1894, Democratic Governor Elias Carr still had two years remaining in his term of office.

The conservative Democracy, self-confident and arrogant from its long lease of power as guardian of corporate and urban interests in a state predominantly rural, had been conservative and inflexible in the face of mounting demands for reform to meet the changing needs of a growing state, and now, in 1894, to its own amazement, it was repudiated and driven from power by a majority of the North Carolina voters.

Chapter 39

FUSION RULE AND THE RETURN OF A CHASTENED DEMOCRACY TO POWER

The fusion legislature of 1895, anxious to justify the political overturn of 1894 and to keep the Democrats out of power, made a number of constructive reforms. In large measure local self-government was restored to the counties. The voters were given the power to elect justices of the peace and to choose biennially three county commissioners, though as a safeguard against Negro rule in the East two hundred voters in a county might by petition secure the appointment by the superior court judge of two additional county commissioners of a different political party from that of the three elected by the people. A new election law required the following: a new registration of voters; the appointment of local election officials by the elective clerks of court equally from the different parties; the preservation of ballots; and an itemized account of the campaign expenditures of candidates for office. The Farmers' Alliance charter was restored; a legal interest rate of 6 percent was fixed; larger appropriations were made to the University of North Carolina and other state-supported colleges and normal schools; and the state property tax for public schools was increased, though the abolition of the offices of county superintendent and county boards of education and the vesting of local school control in the board of county commissioners could hardly be called a forward step. Some eastern town charters were changed to permit more local self-government. By agreement, Populist Marion Butler and Republican Jeter C. Pritchard were elected United States senators by the Fusion legislature. But there was disagreement between these two men and difficulty between Populists and Republicans generally about distribution of the patronage. The Fusion program resulted in a moderate increase in governmental expenditures and taxes. Though it fell short of the full Populist demands and was denounced by the Democrats, the record of the Fusion legislature was constructive.

550

Increased Negro Political Activity

Fusion rule led to increased political activity by Negroes. The less partisan election law permitted an increasing Negro vote. The restoration of county self-government led to the occasional election of Negroes to minor offices in eastern counties, and the General Assembly, in recognition of the substantial Negro vote, elected a few Negroes to relatively unimportant posts. It also adopted a resolution, following the death of Frederick Douglass, honoring the well-known former slave, orator, and journalist—an action that was strongly denounced by Democratic newspapers. Racial antagonism and political advantage combined to make the Democrats exploit the issue of the Negro in politics. The Fusionists were denounced as "debauchers of governmental efficiency" and as supporters of political and social equality for Negroes and even racial intermarriage. Race relations became more and more strained. The race issue was embarrassing to Populists and to many white Republicans. The Negro was the recipient of increasing Democratic antipathy because he tended to be a Republican in politics.

Despite Democratic allegations of Negro domination of North Carolina politics during Reconstruction and again in the 1890s, the records reveal that at no time did the Negroes constitute more than a small percentage of the total membership of the legislature. Between 1868 and 1900 there were 101 Negroes elected to the lower house of the General Assembly: three from Bertie, one from Bladen, five from Caswell, three from Chowan, fourteen from Craven, two from Cumberland, eleven from Edgecombe, one from Franklin, nine from Granville, nine from Halifax, one from Hertford, fifteen from New Hanover, five from Northampton, three from Pasquotank, one from Richmond, four from Vance, four from Wake, nine from Warren, and one from Washington. During the same period twenty-six Negroes were elected to the state Senate. Most of the counties from which Negroes were elected had a Negro population of 50 percent or more.

Among the most outstanding Negro legislators were Henry Eppes, a Methodist minister of Halifax County, who served a total of ten years (five terms) in the Senate; William P. Mabson, former school teacher, a leader of the Republican party in Edgecombe County, and a member of the Constitutional Convention of 1875; Stewart Ellison of Wake County, Raleigh city alderman for eight years and director of the state penitentiary for four years; James H. Harris of Wake, alderman in Raleigh and a director of the Deaf, Dumb, and Blind School for four years; and George H. White of Bladen, who was elected to Congress in 1896. Four of the Negro legislators were college graduates; two others had attended college and had taught school; one was the business manager of the *Wilmington Record.* Many of them had held public office before their election to the General Assembly. Jonathan Daniels, writing in 1941, declared that "all Negro legislators were not peanut munching apes. . . . There were definitely superior men among the Negro leaders after the war. In politics, however, they were black and that was enough."

Four Negroes from North Carolina served a total of fourteen years in the national House of Representatives: J. A. Hyman (1875–77), J. E. O'Hara (1883–87), Henry P. Cheatham (1889–93), and George H. White (1897–1901). Of the four, only Hyman had not attended college, and only O'Hara was a carpetbagger. North Carolina never had more than one Negro representative in any one session of Congress, and all but Cheatham, of Vance County, were elected from the Second Congressional District, which was almost 70 percent Negro. At least one Negro representative, Cheatham, won the respect of both races. Before his election to Congress White had been a member of both houses of the General Assembly, a solicitor and prosecuting attorney, and a delegate to the 1896 Republican National Convention. White was the last Negro in Congress from the South—and the last Negro in that legislative body for a quarter of a century.

The fact that Negroes held public office from the national to the local level was irritating to Democratic leaders, newspapers, and party members generally. The Raleigh *News and Observer* charged that the Fusionists were trying "to Negroize" the capital city, though only one Negro member was chosen to the Board of Aldermen during the whole Fusion era. The situation in Wilmington and some other eastern North Carolina towns was more critical. Negroes seemed to be gaining in political power and threatening "white supremacy" more than at any time since "the tragic era" of Reconstruction. The state was set for a show-down struggle in the forthcoming election.

The Election of 1896

The campaign of 1896 was of unprecedented bitterness and confusion in state and national politics. In North Carolina both Democratic and Republican leaders negotiated for an alliance with the Populists. On national issues the Democrats and Populists in the state were in close accord in support of William Jennings Bryan for president on a reform program, including the "free and unlimited coinage of silver" at a ratio of 16 to 1; but the Republicans and Populists were more nearly in agreement on state issues. Early efforts at fusion failed and Democrats, Republicans, and Populists nominated separate state tickets, the nominees for governor being Cyrus B. Watson, Daniel L. Russell, and William A. Guthrie, respectively. But in September before the election, following a campaign of extreme bitterness, a complicated Fusion arrangement was worked out. The Democrats and Populists fused in support of Bryan, who was the presidential nominee of four parties: Democrats, Populists, Prohibitionists, and Silver Republicans. Bryan carried North Carolina by a twenty thousand majority over Republican William McKinley, who won the national election. The Republicans and Populists fused in support of a divided ticket of nominees for legislative and congressional offices and for some minor state positions; but each kept its own separate nominee for governor, lieutenant governor, and auditor. Republican Russell carried forty-four of the state's ninety-six counties and was elected governor by a vote of 153,787 over Watson with 145,266 and Guthrie with 31,143. Populist candidates carried only Sampson County and lost 16,000 of their 1892 vote to Republicans and Democrats. Many Fusionist candidates were elected to minor state posts and to seats in the General Assembly and in Congress. The total state vote was the largest on record to that time, and Russell's victory was largely due to the fact that 59,000 more Republicans voted than had four years earlier. Much of this increase—but not all, by any means—was due to the large Negro vote in some of the eastern counties.

Governor Russell's Administration, 1897–1901

The Republicans and Populists, or Fusionists as they were commonly called, were in complete control of the executive, legislative, and judicial branches of the state government from 1897 to 1899. Under the capable leadership of Superintendent of Public Instruction Charles H. Mebane, the Fusionists embarked upon a progressive program of public education. In 1897 the office of county superintendent of schools was restored; every school district was required to vote on the issue of local school taxes and to vote every two years until the taxes should be approved. A legislative appropriation of $50,000 was made to aid schools in those districts that voted for local school taxes. This was the most advanced step in public education since the close of Reconstruction.

To fully restore local self-government, county government was vested in three commissioners elected by the qualified voters of each county. The powers of the railroad commission were enlarged and efforts were made to increase the effectiveness of this regulatory body. In addition to increasing the powers of this commission, the General Assembly wrangled over bills to prohibit the use of free railroad passes by public officials, but it failed to solve this problem. It also failed to annul the ninety-nine-year lease of the North Carolina Railroad made by Governor Elias Carr to the newly organized Southern Railway Company in 1895. Governor Russell, backed by Walter Clark, the "fighting judge" of the state Supreme Court, and a few other "liberals," fought valiantly to secure the annulment of the lease of the state's most valuable piece of property, but was defeated by the influence of the Southern Railway aided by a federal judge.

From the outset there was lack of harmony in the ranks of the Fusionists. In a sense, Fusion was a "marriage of convenience," and it was not long until Republicans and Populists began to quarrel over distribution of the spoils of office, particularly the reelection of conservative Republican Jeter C. Pritchard to the United States Senate. Patronage and other issues split the Fusionists and caused division within Populist ranks. The cleavage increased as Fusion achievements were obscured and Fusion rule discredited by the increased political activity of Negroes. The new election and county government laws resulted in more Negroes voting and holding office in the eastern counties and towns. Several hundred Negroes were chosen as justices of the peace, school committeemen, aldermen, and policemen. Governor Russell made some Negro appointments to institutional boards and state agencies, but only 8 out of 818 in his first two years. The federal government, in control of the Republicans, was responsible for the appointment of a number of Negro postmasters. The number and character of the offices held by Negroes hardly compared with the status of the Negroes as citizens, voters, and taxpayers, or indicated "Negro domination" of the state, but the Democrats seized upon the increased Negro political activity as an issue by which to regain political control. Appeals to racial hatred and prejudice strained race relations and brought about an increase in violence and crime. In lurid colors the Democrats depicted Negro domination as threatening North Carolina civilization with anarchy, violence, and collapse. They talked and wrote about Wilmington, New Bern, Greenville, and other towns in the East being "negroized"—that Negroes "ran the schools, controlled the courts, and dominated county and city politics."

The Spanish-American War, 1898

Political controversies were temporarily forgotten in the "flare of enthusiasm" that followed the American declaration of war against Spain in April, 1898. This armed conflict, which has been called a "comedy of errors," lasted less than six months and ended in the defeat of Spain. By the Treaty of Paris (1898), the United States acquired Puerto Rico in the Caribbean, and the Philippine Islands and Guam in the Pacific. Cuba was also liberated from Spanish rule and, as a result of the Platt Amendment of 1901 [repealed in 1934], it became an American protectorate.

North Carolina's quota of troops under President McKinley's call was two regiments of infantry and a battery of artillery. Three companies of Negro infantry were substituted for the artillery battery and expanded into the Third Regiment of North Carolina Volunteers. The other two regiments consisted of white troops. The First Regiment reached Havana on December 11, after the fighting was over. The other two regiments did not leave the state.

Though state troops saw no military action, two North Carolinians in regular service lost their lives. Ensign Worth Bagley of Raleigh was killed on May 11, "the first American naval officer killed in the war," and Lieutenant William E. Shipp of the army fell in the battle of San Juan near Santiago on July 1.

Party Conventions and Platforms, 1898

The campaign of 1898 had actually been under way long before the outbreak of war. On November 30, 1897, the executive committee of the Democratic party issued an address to the people. Among other things it declared: "We have fallen upon evil days in North Carolina. . . . Too large a number of voters are ignorant for the masses to control. . . . The Democratic party promises the people on its return to power to correct all these abuses." The following month the party leaders worked out the rules for the primaries, and the provision "for exclusion of all negroes from participation" foreshadowed the character of the coming campaign. The Democratic State Convention adopted a platform that condemned Fusion rule for its "corruption, extravagance, and incompetence," denounced the Fusion legislatures for "saddling negro rule upon the eastern towns and for the choice of negro school officials," and condemned the Republican national administration for placing "ignorant, irresponsible, and corrupt men in office." The Populist State Convention endorsed the election law of 1895 and the county government law, again pledged support to public education, demanded an investigation of the lease of the North Carolina Railroad, the reduction of railway rates, and the prohibition of free passes, advocated the initiative and referendum, and urged reform in taxation. The Republican State Convention adopted a platform that was largely devoted to national issues, but contained a strong endorsement of Fusion rule. It declared that state finances had been "wisely, economically, and honestly administered," and that there were "marked and gratifying signs of progress and development in all the material conditions of the State."

The "White Supremacy" Campaign

Under the shrewd leadership of State Chairman Furnifold M. Simmons, the Democrats resorted to unprecedented organization, correspondence, publicity, and stump speaking. Increasingly the campaign centered about the Negro. During August "white government unions" or leagues were organized, especially in the eastern counties. On August 18, there appeared in the Wilmington *Daily Record,* a Negro paper, edited by Alex Manly, "a commentary written in refutation to the Democratic declaration that as long as Fusion reigned Negro men would increase their 'advances' to white women." Manly's editorial said: "We suggest that the whites guard their women more closely . . . thus giving no opportunity for the human fiend, be he white or black. You leave your goods out of doors and then complain because they are taken away. Poor white men are careless in the matter of protecting their women, especially on the farms. They are careless of their conduct toward them and our experience among poor white people in the country teaches us that the women of that race are not any more particular in the matter of clandestine meetings with colored men than the white men with colored women. Meetings of this kind go on for some time until the woman's infatuation or the man's boldness brings attention to them and the man is lynched for rape. Every Negro lynched is called 'a Big Burly Black Brute' when in fact many of these who have been thus dealt with had white men for their fathers and were not only 'not black and burly' but were sufficiently attractive for white girls of culture and refinement to fall in love with them as is well known."

Democratic campaign speakers considered the Manly editorial the "most vile and inflammatory article ever printed in the state," and they proceeded to make the most of it in the closing months of the campaign. Race relations deteriorated and, according to a *News and Observer* editorial, private homes were being "fortified against possible attack." Several years later Governor Aycock declared that "more guns and pistols were sold in the State between 1896 and 1898 than had been sold in the previous twenty years." In a dramatic but somewhat exaggerated statement, he said that "lawlessness walked the state like a pestilence—death stalked abroad at noonday—'sleep lay down armed'— the sound of the pistol was more frequent than the song of the mockingbird—the screams of women, fleeing from pursuing brutes, closed the gates of our hearts with shock."

The "Red Shirts" and the 1898 Campaign

An organization known as the Red Shirts appeared in the closing days of October. "Men wore flaming red shirts, rode horses, carried rifles, paraded through Negro communities, and appeared at political rallies, especially Republican rallies." The Red Shirts were most active in New Hanover, Brunswick, Columbus, Robeson, and other counties in the southeastern portion of the state. Some of the Red Shirts had come into the state from neighboring counties in South Carolina. A newspaper report from Wilmington on November 3 read: "The first red shirt parade on horseback ever witnessed in Wilmington electrified the people today. It created enthusiasm among the whites and consternation among the negroes. The whole town turned out to see it. It was an enthusiastic body of men. Otherwise it was quiet and orderly."

Governor Russell's Advice

Governor Russell was alarmed about the whole situation. On October 26 he issued a proclamation warning the people against acts of violence. He declared that the state constitution guaranteed the people the "inherent right to regulate their own internal government, and that no turbulent mob using the weapons of intimidation and violence should usurp the authority of the courts." He said that some counties had been "actually invaded by armed and lawless men from another state; that political meetings had been broken up and dispersed by these armed men; that citizens had been fired on from ambush and taken from their homes at night and whipped; and that peaceful citizens were afraid to register preparatory to voting." He advised "all law-abiding citizens not to allow themselves to become excited by appeals made to their passions and prejudices; all officers of the law to apprehend and bring to speedy trial all offenders against the political and civil rights of any person; and all persons who have entered this state from other states, in pursuance of any unlawful purpose, to disperse instantly and leave the state."

"White Supremacy" as a Factor in the Election

Shortly before the election, Simmons, chairman of the state Democratic Executive Committee, issued an "Appeal to the Voters of North Carolina," asking them to "restore the state to the white people." He said: "The most memorable campaign ever waged in North Carolina is approaching its end. It has been a campaign of startling and momentous developments. The issues which have overshadowed all others have been the questions of honest and economical State government and WHITE SUPREMACY. . . . A proud race, which has never known a master, which has never bent to the yoke of any other race, by the irresistible power of fusion laws and fusion legislation has been placed under the control or dominion of that race which ranks lowest, save one, in the human family. . . .

"WHITE WOMEN, of pure Anglo-Saxon blood, have been arrested upon groundless charges, by negro constables, and arraigned, tried and sentenced by negro magistrates. . . .

"NEGRO CONGRESSMEN, NEGRO SOLICITORS, NEGRO REVENUE OFFICERS, NEGRO COLLECTORS OF CUSTOMS, NEGROES in charge of white institutions, NEGROES in charge of white schools, NEGROES holding inquests over white dead. NEGROES controlling the finances of great cities, NEGROES in control of the sanitation and police of cities, NEGRO CONSTABLES arresting white women and white men, NEGRO MAGISTRATES trying white women and white men, white convicts chained to NEGRO CONVICTS, and forced to social equality with them. . . .

"The battle has been fought, the victory is within our reach. North Carolina is a WHITE MAN'S STATE, and WHITE MEN will rule it, and they will crush the party of negro domination beneath a majority so overwhelming that no other party will ever again dare to establish negro rule here."

As election day approached, Republicans and Populists were definitely on the defensive. They deplored the excesses of the Democratic campaign and warned that a Democratic victory would lead to a constitutional amendment setting up an educational test for voting. The Democratic leaders denied the charge and declared that they would never agree to take from any man his right to vote. The Populists split hopelessly over the Fusion issue—one faction wishing to join the Democrats and the other the Republicans. The Democratic party, violently hostile to the Populists and confident of victory, spurned the offer of Fusion.

The election of November 8 was much more quiet and orderly than might have been expected. Many Negroes refrained from voting, perhaps because of Red Shirt activities or other pressures exerted to keep them from the polls. The Democrats elected 134 members of the General Assembly, the Republicans 30, and the Populists only 6. Of the Representatives to Congress, the Democrats elected 5, the Republicans 3, and the Populists 1.

The Role of Business Interests in the 1898 Election

It has been customary to interpret the 1898 campaign almost wholly in terms of the struggle for "white supremacy." But there were other factors in this memorable election. One of the state's Republican leaders declared soon after the election that "the negro was only the torch light which the voters have observed, while the tar beneath that produces the light has been obscured." The *Charlotte Observer* declared editorially that "the business men of the State are largely responsible for the victory. Not before in years have the bank men, the mill men, and the business men in general—the backbone of the property interest of the State—taken such sincere interest. They worked from start to finish, and furthermore they spent large bits of money in behalf of the cause. . . . Indeed North Carolina is fast changing from an agricultural to a manufacturing State."

Democratic leaders sought and most likely received heavy financial support from business interests. At the request of Simmons, former governor Thomas J. Jarvis approached the "large corporations" and promised that "in the event of Democratic victory their taxes would not be increased." Josephus Daniels, writing years later, said that Simmons "promised denominational leaders that appropriations to State institutions of higher learning would not be increased by the legislature during the 1899 session." In later years Simmons admitted that "in order to win the campaign I felt it necessary to make two promises which later became somewhat embarrassing." It is significant that a year before the election Marion Butler wrote in his newspaper, the *Caucasian:* "There is but one chance and but one hope for the railroads to capture the next legislature, and that is for the 'nigger' to be made the issue," Yet he found the Raleigh *News and Observer* and the *Charlotte Observer,* representing the liberal and conservative factions in the Democratic party, respectively, "together in the same bed shouting nigger." A few years later, North Carolina's beloved poet, John Charles McNeill, wrote:

> I cannot see, if you were dead,
> Mr. Nigger,

How orators could earn their bread,
  Mr. Nigger,
For they could never hold the crowd,
Save they abused you long and loud
As being a dark and threatening cloud,
  Mr. Nigger.

The Wilmington Race Riot

A tragic aftermath of the 1898 election was the race riot at Wilmington on November 10. Inflamed by Republican-Negro rule of the city and the "inflammatory editorials" of the local Negro newspaper, a band of "600 armed white citizens" destroyed the printing material of editor Manly and "in some unaccountable way, the building took fire and burned to the ground." The city was placed under armed guard, ten Negroes were reported killed, ten or more Negroes were "lodged in jail on the charge of being implicated in the instigation of a riot," and "bumptious negro political leaders" were "made to leave the town on almost every train." Mayor Silas Wright fled to New York, Negro officials resigned, and a new city government was set up with former Congressman A. M. Waddell as mayor. The *News and Observer* of November 13 announced that "Negro rule is at end in North Carolina forever. The events . . . at Wilmington and elsewhere place that fact beyond all question."

The Democratic Legislature of 1899

In control of the General Assembly, the Democrats determined to complete their political conquest and to eliminate the Negro as a factor in North Carolina politics. The legislature repealed the school law of 1869, but appropriated $100,000 for public schools. It reasserted legislative control over county government, established a department of insurance, made the commissioner of agriculture an elective office, and replaced the railroad commission with a corporation commission of three members, appointed by the governor and empowered to supervise railroads, banks, telegraph and telephone companies, street railways, and express companies. A new election law provided for a new registration of voters and the election by the General Assembly of a state board of elections to choose county election boards, which in turn should choose the local election officials. The most significant action of this legislature was the passage of the suffrage amendment.

The Suffrage Amendment and the "Grandfather Clause"

Despite the campaign pledge that no man would be deprived of the right to vote, the Democrats, tired of repressing the Negro vote by intimidation, election manipulation, and fraud, determined to secure the permanent legal elimination of the Negro from North Carolina politics. But how could they eliminate the Negro voter legally without disfranchising illiterate white voters or coming into conflict with the Fifteenth Amendment to the federal Constitution? Following, in part, plans devised by Mississippi, South Carolina, and Louisiana, the General Assembly proposed a constitutional amendment containing a requirement that any applicant for registration must have paid his poll tax and be able to read and write any section of the Constitution. A so-called "grandfather clause" provided that no person who was entitled to vote on or before January 1, 1867, or his lineal descendant, should be denied registration by reason of his failure to possess the educational qualifications, provided that he shall have registered prior to December 1, 1908. The literacy test would disfranchise illiterate Negroes and whites; but illiterate whites who registered before December 1, 1908 would be permitted to vote. This provision was thus an enfranchising clause. The proposed amendment must be voted on by the people at a state election in August, 1900.

Candidates and Platforms, 1900

The Democratic state convention of 1900 nominated by acclamation as the party candidate for governor Charles B. Aycock, former schoolteacher and lawyer who had won statewide renown as a political orator able to convince the mind and stir the emotions. A platform was adopted calling for a minimum school term of four months in each district, more liberal care for the insane, a statewide direct primary election law, and the ratification of the suffrage amendment.

A small Populist convention, seriously split by factionalism and by the suffrage amendment, nominated a complete state ticket headed by Cyrus Thompson; but later, as part of a fusion arrangement with the Republicans, Thompson withdrew from the race. The Populist party was dead, and apparently many Populists voted the Democratic ticket.

The Republican convention nominated a state ticket with Spencer B. Adams at its head. The platform denied the charge of Negro domination of the state, endorsed Fusion rule, and denounced the suffrage amendment as undemocratic and in conflict with the federal Constitution.

The 1900 Election

The Negroes were generally silent and quiescent during the campaign that aimed to take from them by state constitutional amendment the voting privilege guaranteed them by the Fifteenth Amendment to the federal Constitution; but a small group of prominent, educated Negroes issued a respectful address appealing for justice and the retention of the right of suffrage as beneficial to both Negroes and whites.

Democratic strategy, again directed by Simmons, featured the suffrage amendment and white supremacy. Appeals were made to the intellect and to the passions of voters. Aycock was merely the ablest of a large corps of campaign orators who advocated the disfranchisement of illiterate Negroes as constitutional, beneficial to Negroes and whites, conducive to political peace and purity as well as material prosperity and general advancement, and promotive of a wholesome division of the whites on current questions. Aycock asserted the superiority of the whites, demanded the disfranchisement of illiterate Negroes, justified the "grandfather clause" on the ground that illiterate whites had political intelligence by inheritance, and pledged justice to the Negro. When it appeared that the amendment might be endangered by the fear of disfranchisement of illiterate whites, Aycock injected a note of statesmanship and turned the white supremacy campaign into a crusade for public education. He pledged his administration to the development of public schools for whites and Negroes, so that after the registration of 1908 no white man need be disfranchised because of illiteracy.

The Republicans maintained that the proposed amendment was undemocratic, violative of the United States Constitution and of the 1868 act of Congress readmitting North Carolina to the Union, and certain to disfranchise thousands of illiterate whites in the state. Many Populists and some Republicans, desirous of eliminating the Negro and making the party "lily white," endorsed the amendment.

Despite the popular view that the only "Red Shirt" campaign was the one that existed in 1898, that organization was probably more active and effective in 1900 than it had been two years earlier. In July and August of that year the newspapers reported that Aycock was met in Orange County by "two bands and a thousand horsemen in red shirts," that he had an escort of Red Shirts from Duplin, Pender, and Sampson counties when he spoke at Clinton, that five hundred Red Shirts attended a rally at Burlington, and that Red Shirt activity was in evidence at Henderson, Smithfield, Greensboro, and other places. One Republican speaker found "Red Shirts waiting for him all along the line" from Wilmington to Weldon, and finally cancelled his tour.

Democrats Win a Decisive Victory

Aycock, white supremacy, Negro disfranchisement, and public education brought a sweeping Democratic victory. The suffrage amendment carried by a vote of 182,217 to 128,285. Thirty-one "white counties" in the central and western part of the state voted against it. The counties with a heavy Negro population gave the amendment a huge majority. This could either mean that the Negro did not vote or that his ballot was counted for the amendment regardless of how it was cast. It is noteworthy that forty-five registrars were arrested on various charges of misconduct in connection with the election. One Republican leader, Z. V. Walser, claimed that 50,000 votes were stolen.

Aycock defeated Adams for the governorship by a vote of 186,650 to 126,-296; the Democrats won an overwhelming majority of seats in the General Assembly, and seven of nine in the national House of Representatives, the two successful Republican candidates being from Wilkes and Haywood counties. William Jennings Bryan, Democratic candidate for president, carried the state over Republican William McKinley by a vote of 157,733 to 132,997. Bryan's vote was almost 29,000 smaller than that received by Aycock, and it was 17,000 less than Bryan had received in 1896.

The Political Revolution of 1900

The adoption of the suffrage amendment deprived the Republican party of about 50,000 voters, confirmed Democratic dominance of state politics, and strengthened the one-party system. The Negro ceased to vote in large numbers; but the "race question" continued to be used effectively by the Democrats against the Republicans and at times against "insurgent Democrats." The adoption of the amendment did not put an end to corrupt ballot practices when they were needed against Republicans or even against insurgent elements within the Democratic party. Neither did it result in frank and open discussion of public issues by the two parties. The chief discussion of and division on current issues was henceforth between factions within the Democratic party, though such discussion and division was deplored by Democratic leaders in power.

The political revolution was highly significant for its effect upon the Democratic party. Defeated by its stubborn resistance to reform, its adherence to conservatism and its championship of the special interests of the business classes and chastened by its experience of defeat, the Democratic party returned to power with a more virile, youthful, progressive leadership; a program of public education and state development; a concern for the welfare of the common man; and a greater responsiveness to the changing needs of a growing state. Moreover, Aycock and the Democrats took control at a time when economic conditions were much better than they had been in the "dark days" of the eighties and nineties. Conditions were propitious for notable progress and achievement. Many "reforms" in government were long overdue.

Chapter 40

A NEW ERA IN NORTH CAROLINA POLITICS, 1901-1920

Democratic Monopoly of Public Offices

The completeness of Democratic supremacy after 1900 was amazing. There was an unbroken succession of Democratic governors from Aycock (1901–5) to Robert W. Scott (1969–73). (See Appendix A.) Democratic majorities in the gubernatorial contests averaged about 50,000 from 1900 to 1916, when the total vote ranged from 200,000 to 300,000. The total Republican vote ranged from about 80,000 in 1904 to about 200,000 by the 1920s.

Though the Republican vote was substantial in both totals and percentages, that party succeeded in electing no governor, no state officer, no United States Senator, and only three representatives in Congress between 1900 and 1920. The state delegation in the national House of Representatives, numbering ten from 1903 to 1933, was solidly Democratic in every election from 1910 to 1920. Even in the state Senate of fifty members, there were usually only two or three Republicans. Their number in the House of Representatives of 120 members averaged about 5 or 6. In the General Assembly the minority Republican members had little influence and at times were not even accorded the usual legislative courtesy of controlling local legislation for the counties they represented. After 1900 the Republican party, to which one-third or more of the state's voters belonged, was almost completely without representation, influence, or power in the state government.

Republicans in Control of National Government, 1901–1913

While the Democratic party dominated the political life of North Carolina, the Republican party was in control of the United States government

563

from 1861 to 1913, with the exception of the two terms of President Grover Cleveland (1885–89 and 1893–97). Since the state and nation were ruled by hostile and unsympathetic parties, North Carolina had little part or influence in the federal government. Even during the Cleveland administrations, Senator Vance and many North Carolina Democrats were not sympathetic toward the policies and leadership of the national Democratic party. North Carolina had a feeling of estrangement from the federal government and resented its exclusion from, and unsympathetic treatment by, the Republican-controlled national administration. Federal patronage in North Carolina was controlled by the Republican party. Federal revenue agents, postmasters, customs officials, judges, and other officers appointed in Washington represented the United States government and performed their official duties in a state which was resentful and politically hostile.

This situation caused bad feeling between the state and federal governments and friction between state and federal officials. The federal courts, presided over by Republican judges sympathetic with railroad and other corporate interests and sometimes overruling the state courts, were regarded as alien tribunals and were distrusted by North Carolina Democrats, who feared that their own political control might be threatened by attacks of Republican courts upon the constitutionality of the suffrage amendment of 1900.

Divisions within the Democratic Party

Within the Democratic party "conservatives" and "liberals" fought for control. The conservatives, who dominated the party most of the time, sought to stimulate business as the most direct means of state development and were reasonably responsive to the demands for educational, humanitarian, and social reform. The liberals painted the conservatives as subservient to the special interests—tobacco and power companies, cotton mills, railroads, and the business and urban classes—and neglectful of the interest of the mass of farmers, industrial laborers, and the common people generally. The liberals depicted themselves as democratic, progressive, sympathetic to farm and labor interests, desirous of making business bear a greater share of the tax burden, and friendly to the common man. The East, predominantly agricultural, was the chief center of liberal strength; the Piedmont was the chief stronghold of the conservatives.

The Policies of the Two Democratic Factions

The conservatives pointed with pride to the remarkable economic development of the state after 1900, and to the record of honest and progressive government. They asserted their friendliness to all classes of the people and charged that the liberals, if placed in control, would frighten business and hamper economic growth and general progress. The conservatives, supported by the industrial interests of the Piedmont and West as well as the business interests and many of the large-scale farmers of the East, usually had the advantages that went with control of election machinery, greater financial backing, more numerous and able leaders, and more efficient organization and publicity. They functioned so smoothly and effectively that their opponents charged "machine control" and "boss rule." Until his defeat for reelection in 1930 because he refused to support Alfred E. Smith, Catholic and antiprohibition Democratic nominee for the presidency in 1928, United States Senator Furnifold M. Simmons was the boss of the Democratic machine.

Regularly state Democratic campaigns after 1904, except in 1912 and 1928 when Locke Craig and O. Max Gardner, respectively, were unopposed for nomination for the governorship, assumed the character of contests for party control between conservatives and liberals, "the machine" and "the people," the "administration" and "anti-administration," the "special interests" and "the people." The insurgent liberals were led by Robert Glenn in 1904, by William W. Kitchin in 1908 and 1912, by Thomas W. Bickett in 1916, by Gardner and Robert N. Page in 1920. The most spectacular battle against the "Simmons machine" was the futile effort of Kitchin and Judge Walter Clark in 1912 to defeat Simmons for reelection to the United States Senate, a contest in which Clark, the state's best-known liberal, failed to carry a single county. Simmons, conservatism, and party regularity held sway from 1912 until Simmons violated party loyalty and regularity by refusing to support the Democratic presidential nominee in 1928.

Division within the Republican Party

The Republican party, weakened in voting strength by the suffrage amendment of 1900, was likewise beset by internal division and was unable to reap the advantage from the friction and division within the ranks of its opponent. Convinced of the relative unimportance of the Negro vote after 1900 and of the stigma arising from the party's historic connection with the Negro, the "lily white" Republicans made their party a "white man's party" by excluding Negroes from party affairs and by ceasing to appeal for their votes. But the party was largely controlled by federal officeholders who were satisfied to control federal patronage in North Carolina, which was at the disposal of the conservative Republican party, usually in control of the federal government before 1933. They did not care to risk control of federal patronage by waging an uphill battle to wrest control of the state from the conservative Democrats. Though a minority desired the party to manifest an aggressive interest in state problems and seek to become a strong state party, the federal officeholders and those primarily interested in national politics retained their control of party machinery. With such leadership and policies, the Republicans took no real part in state politics, attracted virtually none of the discontented Democrats, and failed to serve effectively as an opposition party. During the years of Democratic control of the United States government under Woodrow Wilson (1913–21) the North Carolina Republican party, without the federal patronage and a substantial state program, was in a sad plight.

Generally, after 1900, the Republican party was stronger in national than in North Carolina politics. In each election from 1900 to 1932 the Republican candidate for president polled a larger vote in the state than the Republican candidate for governor. This indicated that a considerable number of people—industrialists and other conservatives—attracted by the conservative policies of the national Republican party, or fearful of "socialistic policies" of the national Democratic party, were Democrats in state politics and Republicans in national elections.

Democratic Partisanship

The fact that Aycock's party was not free from partisanship was amply demonstrated by the General Assembly of 1901. This body enacted legislation which provided for a permanent registration of voters under the "grandfather clause" and which permitted the dominant party to practice intimidation, fraud, and corruption. The legislature also rearranged the state senatorial and Congressional districts by a process of gerrymandering which all but deprived the Republican voters of representation, and it rejected a proposed statewide primary law the Democratic platform of 1900 had promised.

The Impeachment of Two Republican Judges

The Democratic party, victorious in the executive and legislative branches of the state's government, now sought to complete its conquest and gain control of the judiciary. Immediately after the 1901 General Assembly convened, impeachment charges were brought in the House of Representatives against two Republican members of the state Supreme Court—Chief Justice David M. Furches and Associate Justice Robert M. Douglas. It was charged that these two judges had violated Article IV, Section 9 of the state Constitution because they had issued mandamuses upon the state auditor and state treasurer to pay the sum of $851.15 to Theophilus White, state inspector of shell fish. White was a Populist and the Democratic legislature of 1899 had transferred the functions of his office to a Democratic commission. White, however, tested the title to his office and was upheld both by the Superior Court and the state Supreme Court. The impeachment charges against Furches and

Douglas involved a technical violation of the Constitution. After a trial lasting fourteen days, and one which "took on the appearance of a puny political performance," the less partisan state Senate acquitted the judges on all five articles of impeachment.

The Off-Year Election of 1902

The Republican state convention of 1902 excluded Negro delegates, thus committing that party to the "lily white" movement. It pledged a four month's school term, generous support to charitable institutions, more liberal Confederate pensions, and legislation designed to attract capital investments to the state. It did not specifically pledge its acceptance of the suffrage amendment, but declared that its adoption had eliminated the Negro from politics. But the Democrats were not to be denied. They made a clean sweep of all congressional and state offices. With the appointment by the legislature in November, 1902, of Lee S. Overman to succeed Republican Jeter C. Pritchard in the United States Senate, every North Carolinian in both houses of Congress was a Democrat.

The 1902 contest for Chief Justice of the state Supreme Court overshadowed all others and "precipitated a fight which for bitterness has never been surpassed in the political annals of the state." Walter Clark had been an associate justice since 1899, and he was "now universally regarded as the ablest man on the Court, and his critics charged that he dominated it." In various dissenting opinions, public addresses, and articles in magazines and newspapers, Clark had established himself as an ardent liberal and an outspoken critic of many evils he thought were sapping the lifeblood of democracy and good government. His biographer wrote: "Here was a lone judge without money and without political organization fighting the most powerful vested interests in North Carolina." He faced the bitter opposition of the railroads because he had denounced their practices of issuing illegal free passes, charging exorbitant and discriminatory passenger and freight rates, obtaining unfair tax valuations, legislative lobbying, and interfering in the politics of both parties. The American Tobacco Company was also out for Clark's scalp because he had condemned it as a violator of the Sherman Anti-Trust Act and he had stated that it should be criminally prosecuted under the law for destroying innocent competitors and robbing the farmers of their tobacco. Josephus Daniels's *News and Observer* was Clark's chief supporter, standing behind him "like a brick wall in all of his fights against monopolies, trusts, combines, and railroad domination."

Clark also faced the opposition of some very influential Methodist and Baptist leaders. His quarrel with John C. Kilgo, president of Trinity College, had alienated some Methodists, and Josiah W. Bailey, editor of the Baptist *Biblical Recorder,* had already shown his animosity to the judge. The Democratic political machine, headed by Simmons, had no love for an "independent" like Clark, who had the courage to attack big business interests which supplied most of the funds for the Democratic campaign chest. Despite the opposition of many powerful interests, the state Democratic Convention nominated Clark by an overwhelming majority; in the general election he defeated his Republican opponent by more than 60,000 votes and with the loss of only two counties.

The South Dakota Bond Case, 1904

In the decade after 1900 there were frequent conflicts of jurisdiction between state and federal courts, in which the latter usually overrode the former. Professor Connor aptly wrote: "The Federal courts were notoriously under the influence of railroad and allied interests. To the average North Carolinian they were alien tribunals, feared by lawyers, avoided by litigants, and distrusted by the people." There was widespread resentment in North Carolina over the decision of the United States Supreme Court in the South Dakota bond decision in 1904, in which the state of North Carolina was ordered to pay $27,400 covering principal and accrued interest upon ten state railroad construction bonds which had not been turned in for settlement at twenty-five cents on the dollar in accordance with the state debt settlement in 1879. Marion Butler and former governor Daniel L. Russell, both of whom were anathema to Democratic leaders, were attorneys for Schafer Brothers, New York brokers, who had 250 of these bonds, 10 of which they donated to South Dakota, which could bring suit against another state. The Supreme Court of the United States ordered the sale of sufficient stock of the state-owned North Carolina Railroad to satisfy the judgment. Some Democratic leaders, especially lawyers, urged resistance and insisted that the Court had no way of enforcing its decision. Governor Aycock thought that the decision was unjust and that the Court's jurisdiction "had been secured by chicanery." Yet he recommended to the General Assembly that the judgment be paid in full and that other outstanding bonds of the same issue be settled promptly. A direct clash between state and federal governments was averted when the General Assembly voted to follow the governor's recommendation. Democratic leaders condemned Butler and Russell for their connection with the case and charged that they were scheming to aid the holders of millions of dollars worth of fraudulent repudiated Reconstruction bonds to sue for their payment. Butler vigorously denied this accusation, pointing out the difference between the "honest bonds" involved in the South Dakota case and the "fraudulent bonds" of the Reconstruction era.

The "Attempted Larceny" of the Atlantic and North Carolina Railroad

While the South Dakota case was pending, Republican District Judge Thomas R. Purnell was the object of bitter attack in the state because, at the behest of V. E. McBee and other outside financial interests who were trying to get control of the Atlantic and North Carolina Railroad, he threw the road into receivership on two different occasions. The state, which owned 12,660 of the road's 18,000 shares of stock, had been trying to lease the unprofitable road; but Governor Aycock, who first learned of the receivership by reading the newspapers, determined to resist the "conspiracy" to force the state to accept an unfavorable lease. He upset the first receivership when the state's attorney-general, on order of the governor, applied to Chief Justice Walter Clark for a bench warrant against McBee charging him with "fraud and conspiracy in an effort to acquire the road by unlawful means" and placing McBee, the receiver, under arrest. Aycock upset the second receivership by securing a writ from Chief Justice Fuller of the United States Supreme Court and by ousting the receivers with a threat of military force. Judge Purnell expressed "serious doubts" concerning the validity of this order, but wisely decided not to resist it. The receivers, however, refused to vacate until they read a telegram from Aycock to the superintendent of the road which read: "Put receivers out of office. If necessary call on sheriff to put them out. If military is needed notify me. Order of Chief Justice Fuller shall be obeyed." The receivers "vacated" immediately, and within an hour the superintendent of the road wired Aycock: "We are in quiet possession of the road."

This railroad "conspiracy"—the attempt to "steal a railroad"—created a sensation in the state. For harsh criticism of Judge Purnell, Josephus Daniels was cited for contempt of court, fined, and ordered to jail until the fine was paid. Daniels refused to pay the fine and was "imprisoned" in the Yarborough Hotel in Raleigh until he was ordered discharged by the first official act of the new United States Circuit Court Judge, Jeter C. Pritchard. Later in the year, Governor Aycock leased the Atlantic and North Carolina Railroad to the Howland Improvement Company. This completed the transfer by sale or lease of all the state's railroad holdings to private enterprise.

The Election of 1904

Despite the fact that Aycock's administration had been outstanding, the Democrats were not well united as the 1904 election approached. Sectional rivalries were apparent and the race question, though not as bitter as it had been a decade earlier, was still in evidence. Some Democrats from the western counties complained about Negro domination and pointed out that Halifax County had forty-four votes in the State Convention, while the nine western counties with the smallest percentage of Negro votes had only a total of forty-three votes. The *Union Republican* of August 7, 1902, had declared that by the use of the Negro vote one eastern county "waved the sceptre of power over a great mountain belt, with twice its intelligence, with ten times its population, and with twenty times its wealth. This is the machine against the people. The East against the West."

Simmons, who again directed Democratic strategy, played down differences of opinion within the party. He maintained that the Democrats had "rescued the State from the fusion combination with its one thousand office holders, and put it in the hands of the responsible white people of the State." He claimed that his party was responsible for "a school house in every school district in the State," with sufficient funds "to run it for four months in the year."

The leading contenders for the Democratic nomination for governor were Robert B. Glenn of Forsyth County and Charles M. Stedman of Guilford. Glenn, who was considered an "anti-organization" man, and had been called "Aycock's chief critic," challenged his opponents to a primary, championed the cause of organized labor, and "struck a popular chord by opposing the use of taxes paid by whites for the education of Negroes." Glenn won the nomination on the fifth ballot. In the general election he defeated Republican C. J. Harris by a vote of 128,761 to 79,505. Democrat Alton B. Parker carried the state for president over Republican Theodore Roosevelt by a vote of 124,121 to 82,442.

The "Progressively Conservative" Administration of Governor Glenn, 1905–1909

The Raleigh *News and Observer* characterized the 1905 General Assembly as "progressively conservative." The 1907 legislature was even more progressive. Several acts were passed that conservatives criticized as "detrimental to business." Chief among these was the act reducing passenger rates "to a point which conservatives declared would bankrupt the railroads." Federal Judge Pritchard championed the railroads in their resistance to the new state law reducing passenger rates to two and one-fourth cents per mile. He issued an injunction restraining state officials from enforcing penalties against the Southern Railway for disobedience to the law, and, by writs of habeas corpus, he discharged from punishment two railroad agents who had been convicted in the state courts. In one case Superior Court Judge B. F. Long had fined the Southern Railway $30,000. Railroad attorneys urged Pritchard to cite the state judges for contempt, and Governor Glenn announced that he would resist such action with the full power of the state. This threatened clash between state and federal authorities was serious and attracted national attention. President Theodore Roosevelt intervened and helped to arrange a compromise whereby the state and the railroads agreed upon a compromise passenger rate of two and a half cents a mile.

North Carolina Adopts Statewide Prohibition

The best-known act of the Glenn Administration was the adoption of statewide prohibition. The temperance forces before 1900 had eliminated the legal sale of liquor from many of the towns by local option elections; and hundreds of rural communities had become "dry" by obtaining acts of incorporation from the General Assembly. The Democratic-dominated legislature, sensing the popularity of the issue and responsive to the urging of the newly organized North Carolina Anti-Saloon League enacted the Watts Act in 1903. This law prohibited the manufacture and sale of spirituous liquors except in incorporated towns and was calculated "to get rid of the county distilleries," which Simmons called "Republican recruiting stations." Two years later the Ward Law, by forbidding the liquor traffic in all communities except incorporated places of at least one thousand inhabitants, dried up all except eighty of the state's 328 incorporated towns. Sixty-eight of the ninety-eight counties thus had prohibition. The Anti-Saloon League launched an intensive campaign for statewide prohibition in 1907. The following year the General Assembly responded to the urging of Governor Glenn by providing for a statewide referendum on May 26, 1908, to determine whether statewide prohibition would become effective on July 1, 1909. After a strenuous campaign led by Glenn, who was a powerful and persuasive orator, the people adopted statewide prohibition by a vote of 113,612 to 69,416. Twenty-one counties voted against prohibition, the largest majorities against it being in Johnston, Martin, Onslow, Wake, and Wilkes counties. Statewide prohibition became effective with the passage of the Turlington Act in January, 1909. The Webb-Kenyon Interstate Shipment Act of Congress in 1913 forbade the transportation of liquor from wet states into North Carolina and other dry states.

The Election of 1908

The liberal elements in the Democratic party, with the backing of Governor Glenn, attempted to break the power of the "machine" by the passage of a primary law in 1907. But this law did not achieve their objectives because it provided that there should be no primary "unless the executive committee or county conventions of the party . . . require a primary election to be held," and limited its operations to certain specified counties. The factional struggle within the party reached a climax in the gubernatorial campaign of 1908, when the Democratic State Convention nominated William W. Kitchin of Person County on the sixty-first ballot over Locke Craig of Buncombe County. Kitchin was considered the "people's choice," the "challenger of the machine," and the "enemy of trusts and monopolies." In the general election, Kitchin won over J. Elwood Cox by a vote of 145,102 to 107,760. Bryan carried the state for president over his Republican opponent, William Howard Taft, by a vote of 136,928 to 114,887—the smallest majority North Carolina gave a Democratic candidate for president between 1896 and 1924. The Republicans captured three Congressional districts in the Piedmont and mountain regions.

The Election of 1912

In 1912 there was no contest for the selection of a Democratic gubernatorial candidate, since the State Convention nominated Locke Craig by acclamation. The primary contest for the United States senatorship, however, produced one of the most prolonged and bitter political fights in the state's history. The candidacy of Woodrow Wilson for the Democratic nomination for president was now looming upon the horizon. The liberal Democrats felt that it would be unfortunate to reelect Simmons, who was opposed to Wilson, and had a voting record on the tariff and some other issues that was distasteful to them. As the campaign opened, a tragedy occurred in the sudden death of one of the candidates, Charles B. Aycock, thus leaving Simmons, William W. Kitchin, and Judge Walter Clark in the race for the nomination. The election returns gave Simmons 84,687 votes, Kitchin 47,000, and Clark only 16,418. The Simmons victory was not too surprising, "but its crushing force astounded friends and foes alike." Historian S. A. Ashe interpreted it as an expression "of confidence in the Senator and satisfaction with his record." Wilson carried North Carolina by a vote of 144,407 to 70,272 for Theodore Roosevelt (Progressive), and 29,129 for Taft (Republican). The vote for governor was Craig, 149,975; Iredell Meares (Progressive), 49,930; and Thomas Settle (Republican), 43,625.

North Carolinians in the Wilson Administration, 1913–1921

In the conduct of the federal government North Carolina had little influence before 1913. But during the eight years of Wilson's presidency North Carolinians played a prominent role in the national administration. Josephus Daniels, editor of the Raleigh *News and Observer,* and an advocate of Wilson's nomination long before 1912, was secretary of the navy for the whole eight years. David Houston, another Cabinet member, had been born in North Carolina, though he was a resident of another state at the time of his appointment. In Congress, many of the most powerful committees were headed by North Carolinians. In the Senate, Simmons was chairman of the Finance Committee and Overman of the Rules Committee. In the House of Representatives, Claude Kitchin was Democratic leader; E. W. Pou headed the Rules Committee and E. Yates Webb the Judiciary committee. Walter Hines Page was the United States Ambassador to England. Never before had so many North Carolinians held influential positions in any national administration.

The Quiet Election of 1916

The contest for the Democratic nomination for governor in 1916 was relatively quiet and largely devoid of bitterness. This was the first election held under the statewide primary law of 1915. It also occurred at a time when American entry into World War I seemed imminent. Though some liberal leaders declared that E. L. Daughtridge was the "machine" candidate, the battle lines were not too clearly drawn. Attorney General Thomas W. Bickett of Franklin County defeated Daughtridge for the nomination by a vote of 63,121 to 37,017—an extremely small vote. In November Bickett defeated Republican Frank A. Linney, 167,761 to 120,157. Wilson carried the state over Republican Charles Evans Hughes by a vote of 168,383 to 120,890.

North Carolina's Role in World War I

Soon after Bickett became governor in 1917 the United States was drawn into the World War, which had been raging since 1914 between the "Allies"—England, France, Russia, Italy, and many smaller nations—on the one side, and the "Central Powers"—Germany, Austria-Hungary, Turkey, and Bulgaria—on the other. Sincere sympathy, Allied propaganda, heavy financial stakes in the forms of loans and sales of supplies, the sinking of American ships, with the loss of American lives by German submarines, and the desire for national self-defense and safety caused the United States to declare war on the Central Powers in April, 1917.

North Carolina turned its attention from local politics and problems to do its part in the war. Altogether the state contributed to the armed services 86,457 men, 20,350 of whom were Negroes. The state's losses were 629 killed in action, 204 deaths from wounds, and 1,542 deaths from disease. There were no military units composed entirely of North Carolinians; but two army divisions containing many North Carolinians became famous—the Thirtieth or "Old Hickory" Division, which helped to break the strong "Hindenburg Line," and the Eighty-First or "Wildcat" Division, which took part in the Meuse-Argonne offensive near the close of the war. One major general, three brigadier generals, and three rear admirals were North Carolinians.

A number of training camps for soldiers were established in the state. The largest of these were Camp Greene, at Charlotte, begun in July, 1917, as a training center for the infantry; Camp Polk, at Raleigh, established in September, 1918, as a tank camp; and Fort Bragg, near Fayetteville, begun in 1918 as a field artillery training center. The first two of these camps were discontinued after the war. Bragg was continued and became the largest camp of its kind in the nation.

The civilian population on the "home front" was thoroughly organized for the war effort. The women at home worked through the Red Cross, the YMCA, the YWCA, the Knights of Columbus, and other organizations to furnish clothes and supplies for the men in service. One hundred and ninety-five North Carolina women acted as nurses for the armed services. The people economized on food and fuel, worked in shipyards and munitions plants, contributed over $3 million to the Red Cross and other organizations, and oversubscribed the state's quota of war bonds by some $10 million. In October, 1918, an influenza epidemic swept the nation, causing 9,686 deaths in the state, and closing many schools, churches, and theaters. In this crisis the Red Cross performed splendid service. The war came close to North Carolina on August 6, 1918, when the Diamond Shoals Lightship was shelled and sunk by a German submarine. Ten days later the British tanker *Mirlo* was torpedoed and sunk by a German submarine off Rodanthe.

North Carolinians also played a prominent role in the national government during the war. Claude Kitchin was Democratic leader in the House of Representatives and Furnifold M. Simmons was chairman of the Senate Finance Committee. Josephus Daniels, as secretary of the navy, was responsible for the transportation to Europe of more than two million American troops. Not a single soldier in a ship commanded by an American naval officer lost his life on the way to France. One American ship, the *President Lincoln,* commanded by Captain Percy W. Foote, native of Wilkes County, was torpedoed and sunk returning from Europe. Foote was "highly commended for his coolness in saving a large number of the crew."

The war ended on November 11, 1918, in victory for the United States and the Allies. Speaking to the General Assembly, Governor Bickett said: "Lest we forget, I write it down in this last chapter and certify to all the generations that the one stupendous, immortal thing connected with this administration is the part North Carolina played in the World War. Everything done in the field of taxation, of education, of agriculture, of mercy to the fallen, of the physical and social regeneration of our people—all of it is but 'a snowflake on the river' in the gigantic and glorified presence of the eighty thousand men who plunged into the blood-red tide of war."

Changes in the State's Tax Structure

The World War created many problems for the nation and the individual states. Monetary expenditures, inflation, and recurring state deficits compelled drastic changes in the North Carolina tax structure. The first significant change was a revaluation of property, the so-called "Bickett Revaluation" of 1920, which increased the assessed value of all property in the state from $1,099,000,000 to $3,139,000,000.

Governor Bickett told the General Assembly in its extra session of August, 1920, that "the dollar we receive and the dollar we pay is relatively worth about forty cents." He insisted that discriminations and inequities in taxation should be eliminated as far as possible and that property that had been escaping taxation should be placed on the tax books. The legislature adopted his recommendations and "an entire change in the plan of ordinary administration." In the general election three months later the voters of the state approved constitutional amendments that had been proposed by the General Assembly to tax incomes at a graduated rate not to exceed six percent and limited the general property tax [except for school purposes] to fifteen cents on the $100 valuation. In the early 1920s the state government ceased to levy a general property tax, leaving property as the exclusive and main source of revenue for local governments. Other amendments adopted in 1920 reduced residence requirement for voting from two years to one year in the state, and to four months in the voting precinct.

Woman Suffrage

The adoption of the Nineteenth Amendment to the United States Constitution in 1920 gave women the right to vote and doubled the electorate of North Carolina. During the previous decade there had been considerable agitation in the state for "Women's Rights." In 1913 the "Equal Suffrage Association" was organized in North Carolina, and in the same year a bill providing for woman suffrage was introduced in the General Assembly. This bill was defeated, as were similar bills in succeeding legislatures. In 1918 the state Republican platform endorsed woman suffrage, but the Democrats declined to give it their approval, though some party leaders, notably Walter Clark, A. L. Brooks, Josephus Daniels, and O. Max Gardner endorsed it. In 1919 Congress submitted the Woman Suffrage Amendment to the states. When the Democratic State Convention met in April, 1920, the proposed amendment had been ratified by so many states that its adoption seemed certain. Accordingly the party platform endorsed woman suffrage, over the opposition of Cameron Morrison and some other leaders. Yet the special session of the General Assembly in August rejected the proposed amendment. Meanwhile the Nineteenth Amendment had become effective with the ratification by the requisite three-fourths of the state legislatures. Accordingly the General Assembly ate crow and made provision for the registration and voting of women in the forthcoming election.

Chapter 41

A QUARTER CENTURY OF ECONOMIC GROWTH

In the quarter century after 1900 North Carolina's economic development followed the dominant trends of national growth. General economic expansion and prosperity, improved transportation facilities, and the development of hydroelectric power combined with mild climate, abundant and cheap labor, and proximity to the raw materials of cotton, tobacco, and lumber to speed the process of industrialization. Agriculture expanded greatly and continued as the chief support of most North Carolinians, though its development was slower than that of manufacturing, trade, and finance.

Population Trends

The total population of the state increased from 1,893,810 in 1900 to 2,206,287 in 1910 and to 3,170,276 in 1920. The rural population, living in the country or in incorporated towns of less than 2,500 inhabitants, increased from 186,790 in 1900 to 318,474 in 1910 and to 490,370 in 1920. In 1900 less than 10 percent of the state's population was classified as urban; by 1920 it had risen to more than 19 percent. The movement from farm to town was caused by higher wages and the social appeal of the towns, the relatively low prices of farm crops, soil exhaustion and erosion, and the extensions of city limits to include suburban areas. But the urbanization and industrialization did not cause an actual decline in agriculture or rural population. Throughout this period North Carolina had one of the largest rural populations in the nation.

A State of Small Farms

North Carolina continued to be a state of small farms. This trend was even more pronounced after 1900. The number of farms increased steadily from 224,637 in 1900 to 283,482 in 1925. This was the result of a reduction in the size of farms rather than an extension of the farm area. In fact, the acreage of farmland in the state declined from 22,749,356 acres in 1900 to 18,593,670 in 1925. During these years the average size farm declined from 101.3 acres to 65.6 acrs. The value per acre of land increased from $6.24 in 1900 to $42.84 in 1920 and then dropped to $36.92 in 1925.

The majority of North Carolina farmers were white, though from 1910 to 1925 the percentage of farms operated by Negroes increased from 25.8 to 28.5, and the number of farms operated by Negroes from 65,656 to 80,966. The percentage of all farms operated by tenants was 41 in 1900; by 1925 it had risen to 45. The total number of tenants rose from 93,000 in 1900 to 107,000 in 1910, to 117,000 in 1920 and to 128,000 in 1925. The majority of tenants were sharecroppers, though there were more than 9,000 cash tenants and more than 6,000 "standing renters" in the early 1920s.

The counties with the largest tenant ratios were in the areas producing cotton and tobacco—ideal tenant crops which utilized unskilled hand labor, produced crops readily convertible into cash, and hence were good security for the supply-merchant or crop-lien system of credit. In 1925 there were more than thirty counties in which more than one-half of the farmers were tenants. The lowest tenant ratio counties were those in the central Piedmont, Mountain, and Tidewater areas that were outside the cotton and tobacco belts. In some of the mountain counties fewer than 10 percent of the farmers were tenants.

Tenancy has never been a racial problem in North Carolina. At all times the number of white tenants was greater than that of Negro tenants, but the percentage of all white farmers who were tenants was less than that of the Negroes. In 1920 33 percent of all white farmers were tenants, while the percentage of all Negro farmers who were tenants was 71.

North Carolina's Cash Crops: Tobacco, Cotton, and Others

The major cash crops in North Carolina during the first quarter of the twentieth century were tobacco, cotton, corn, hay, and peanuts. From these crops most of the cash farm income was derived, with cotton usually furnishing the largest single source prior to 1920 and tobacco after that date. The annual production of cotton rose from about 460,000 bales in 1900 to 1,102,000 in 1925, raising the state from eighth to seventh among the cotton-producing states. The quality of North Carolina lint was above average, and the yield per acre was usually the highest of all the states, because of the well-cultivated farms, greater use of commercial fertilizer than any other state, and relative freedom from the ravages of the boll weevil. The leading cotton counties were usually Robeson, Mecklenburg, Johnston, Wake, Edgecombe, Union, Anson, Halifax, Wayne, Cleveland, Pitt, Scotland, Wilson, and Nash.

North Carolina's rank as a tobacco producer was higher. In 1900 the state produced 127,503,000 pounds, valued at $8,038,691, on 203,023 acres. In 1925 these figures were 380,165,000, $87,438,000, and 547,000, respectively. Only Kentucky surpassed North Carolina in tobacco production, but North Carolina led the nation in bright-leaf production.

Corn was grown extensively throughout the state, especially in the cotton and tobacco areas, primarily as a food and feed rather than as a "cash crop." The acreage in corn dropped from 2,720,200 in 1899 to 2,009,000 in 1924, though per acre production increased slightly, the number of bushels dropping only from 34,819,000 to 30,548,000. The value of the state's corn crop in 1910 was $31,286,000; five years later it had increased to $49,318,000.

Few states grew a larger variety of crops than North Carolina, but their value and volume was small in comparison with cotton, tobacco, and corn. Peanuts became a commercial crop after 1900, with more than 200,000 acres being devoted to that crop by 1920. Wheat cultivation before World War I was declining. The value of the crop in 1910 was less than $5 million, though it rose to almost twice that figure by 1925. The farmers of the state also produced sizable quantities of hay, the crop being valued as high as $14 million in 1927. Irish potatoes became an important crop, especially after World War I, the 1927 crop being valued at more than $11 million. The state ranked high in sweet potato production, the 1927 crop being worth more than $8 million. By the mid-twenties North Carolina led all other states in the production of soybeans, the 1927 crop being valued at almost $5 million. In the production of peas, strawberries, peaches, and rye the state usually ranked among the top five to ten in the nation.

Livestock

Before 1929 there was probably no state in which livestock played so small a part in the system of agriculture as in North Carolina. In 1920 the value of all livestock per farm was only $442—only one dollar more than that of Alabama, which ranked lowest among all the states. If only meat and milk animals are considered, on a per farm basis, North Carolina ranked lowest of all the states. In 1925 the state had an average of only .74 milk cows per farm and ranked forty-sixth among the states. The 1920 census reported 100,000 farms in North Carolina with no dairy cow, and nearly 100,000 farms with no cattle of any description. As late as 1930 the state did not produce one-sixth of the beef it needed and only about one-third of the milk and butter needed, based on the national consumption of these articles.

Values of Farm Property

According to the 1925 Census of Agriculture, the farm property of the state was valued at $1,050,015,960, some $200,000,000 less than in 1920, which was a time of inflationary prices. The value of all North Carolina farm property per farm in 1925 was $3,704, compared to the national average of $8,949; the state's rank was forty-first in this respect.

E. C. Branson, noted rural economist, wrote: "Living from hand-to-mouth as most of our farmers live—both tenants and operating owners—the problems of farming as a business are well-nigh insolvable. They can not or will not act together in group production, group buying, group processing, group credit, and self-defensive group action in farm policies. Furthermore, in the lonely life of isolated farms, there is developed an economic and social inertia that is stubbornly resistant to change of any sort."

The North Carolina Farmers' Union

North Carolina Farmers in the early twentieth century faced most of the same problems the Grange and the Farmers' Alliance had grappled with at an earlier period. Realizing that organization was necessary to achieve many of the reforms they desired, thousands of North Carolina farmers joined the Farmer's Educational and Cooperative Union of America. This organization, ordinarily called the Farmers' Union, was organized in Texas in 1902 and entered North Carolina in 1905; three years later the North Carolina Farmers' Union was established. Like previous farm organizations, it tried to "keep out of politics" but was not opposed to using its influence to secure legislation for public schools, banking reform, trust regulation, and other progressive measures. Its speakers and writers were severe in their denunciation of trusts, the crop-lien system, exorbitant interest rates, and the low prices paid for tobacco by warehouse buyers, and the high prices charged by fertilizer dealers. One Union leader declared that "a flock of sheep girded by ravenous wolves, would not be in much worse fix than are the farmers of the land, surrounded by the predatory trusts." Another said that "farmers stand alone as the only class of producers who work fifteen hours a day in competition with each other and sell their products at auction upon the streets." Still another denounced those men who go into the tobacco warehouse business "as poor as a church mouse and . . . strut out as big as a king." And the *Carolina Union Farmer* declared that "we are the most thoroughly trust-ridden people on the face of God's green earth," and that the fertilizer "trusts" were causing the farmers to pay "three million dollars for sand, brick dust, and dirt."

The state Farmers' Union began in 1908 with 938 members, but by 1911 it had over 25,000 members, and when it reached its peak in 1912–13 it had 1,783 local units and over 33,000 members, which was 37.1 percent of the national membership. By 1920 membership had dropped to 12,348; by 1928 there were only 1,364 members. It is difficult to assess the positive accomplishments of this organization, but it is a significant fact that the Farmers' Union had a larger percentage of its total national membership in North Carolina than any other farm organization in American history.

Other Efforts to Solve Farm Problems

Meanwhile other efforts were being made to solve some of the state's farm problems. In 1908 and the following years, under the leadership of Hugh McRae, farm colonies of European immigrants were established in Pender, Columbus, and New Hanover counties. The best known of these communities were St. Helena (Italian), Castle Hayne and Van Eden (Dutch), and New Berlin (German). In 1909 the first 4-H Club was organized in the state in Hertford County. In 1914 the Tobacco Experiment Station was established at Oxford. The General Assembly of 1915 enacted the Credit Union Law and the first credit union in the state was organized at Lowe's Grove in Durham County in the same year. During and after World War I North Carolina farmers sought to extend and develop their credit facilities by organizing credit unions and to obtain more favorable prices by forming associations for cooperative marketing. In 1920 the Tobacco Growers Cooperative Marketing Association of North Carolina, South Carolina, and Virginia was organized. There was considerable opposition to its objectives. Many members broke their contracts, resulting in court actions. The organization gradually declined, its assets were liquidated, and in June, 1926, the United States District Court appointed receivers for the "Tobacco Co-op," which thus came to an end.

Federal Aid to Agriculture

The federal government continued increasing financial support to aid the Agricultural and Mechanical College (now North Carolina State University) in its Agricultural Experiment Station and extension work and to supplement state and local funds for vocational education in agriculture, home economics, and trade and industries in the public schools—a federal policy inaugurated under authority of the Smith-Hughes Act of 1917.

Remarkable Development of Manufactures

During the first quarter of the present century a remarkable development of manufactures took place in North Carolina. The rapidity of industrialization is indicated by the more than twofold increase in the volume of manufactures from approximately $95 million in 1900 to $217 million in 1910, and by the more than fourfold growth during the next decade to $944 million. As early as 1900 the value of manufactures exceeded that of agriculture, but by a small margin. By 1920 it was almost double that of agriculture. In 1927 the value of all North Carolina manufactures was $1,154,617,000, while that of agriculture was only $361,605,000.

The number of industrial laborers did not increase as rapidly as did the total value of manufactures. The number of wage earners in industry in 1899, 1919, and 1927 was 72,422, 157,659, and 204,767, respectively. The total amount of wages increased from $14 million in 1899 to $134 million in 1925. North Carolina became the leading industrial state of the Southeast and the nation's largest producer of cotton textiles, tobacco products, and wooden furniture. Manufacturing superseded farming as the state's chief source of wealth. But the leading manufactures were all closely associated with the local abundance of raw materials produced on the farm.

The Development of Electric Power

One of the factors that contributed to North Carolina's rapid industrialization was the development of electric power. From one small Yadkin River plant in 1898, the state's production of electricity grew until in 1935 only nine states exceeded North Carolina in total kilowatts of electricity and only three in hydroelectric capacity. The Duke Power Company, organized as the Southern Power Company in 1904 and developed by James B. Duke, tobacco tycoon, became the largest utility producing and distributing electric power in North Carolina. By 1927 it had developed into a $200 million corporation which had built on the Catawba River at least ten hydroelectric plants with a total capacity of 850,000 horsepower. It served the Piedmont region, and it was in this area that most of the factories were located. Other major utilities were the Carolina Power and Light Company, the Tidewater Power Company, and the Virginia Electric and Power Company. A large number of towns owned and operated their own electric plants, but only a few of these owned their generating plants.

An expanding network of power lines stimulated the growth and spread of factories and made possible the rapid industrialization of North Carolina. Power transmission lines carried electricity into nearly every county and town to run factories, street cars, lighting systems, refrigerators, irons, sewing machines, and many appliances that made business, home, and farm life easier and richer. Factories could be built anywhere at a distance from stream banks, and they utilized electricity as cheaper and more convenient than steam power. The generation and distribution of electric power has been a primary factor in the economic and social life of modern North Carolina.

The Textile Industry

Because of its decentralization, its extensive employment of labor, and the value added by manufactures, textile manufacturing has been the most important industry in the state. In the first quarter of the twentieth century North Carolina came to lead the nation in the manufacture of cotton goods and to rank first in the South in the production of all knit goods. Its chief textile products in this period were denim, damask, towels, underwear, hosiery, yarns, and blankets. The state ranked high in dyeing and finishing men's work clothes such as overalls, woolen goods, and cordage and twine. Only in overalls, underwear, and hosiery was there extensive manufacture of wearing apparel. The state boasted of the largest towel mill in the world at Kannapolis, the largest denim mill at Greensboro, the largest damask mill at Roanoke Rapids, the largest men's underwear factory at Winston-Salem, and the world's "combed yarn capital" at Gastonia.

The total value of textile manufactures increased over fifteenfold from about $30 million in 1900 to $450 million in 1930. The number of textile workers increased four times from 32,000 in 1900 to 125,000 in 1930. By 1927 the state had 579 mills, with a total spindleage of 6,388,160 and 94,957 looms. There were 129 knit goods factories, with 27,269 knitting machines; more than 170,-000 workers; and a product valued at $61,000,000. During this era the state's textile mills, averaging about 10,000 spindles each, were considerably smaller than the mills of New England. Most of the mills were in the Piedmont area between Durham and Shelby.

Tobacco Manufactures

North Carolina has been aptly called "Tobaccoland." The state grows more tobacco than any other state, and it is the leader in the manufacture of tobacco products. The value of tobacco manufactures, largely cigarettes and pipe tobacco, increased from $16 million in 1900 to $413 million in 1927. Intensive mechanization caused the number of workers to increase at a much slower pace—from seven thousand in 1900 to sixteen thousand in 1927. Before the 1950s almost the entire output of the state's tobacco factories came from three cities—Winston-Salem, Durham, and Reidsville, the location of R. J. Reynolds, Liggett-Myers, and American Tobacco Companies, respectively.

By 1920 North Carolina was paying more taxes into the United States Treasury than any other state except New York, Pennsylvania, Illinois, and Ohio. This was largely due to taxes on tobacco manufacturers. For the fiscal year ending June 30, 1928, North Carolina paid to the federal government a total tax of $204 million on tobacco products—52 percent of the entire tobacco tax paid by all the states in that year.

Furniture Manufactures

The third largest industry in the state during this period was that of wooden furniture. The total value of furniture products rose from $1,547,000 in 1899 to $54,000,000 in 1929, while the number of workers increased from 1,909 to 14,821, and wages and salaries from $725,000 to $14,418,000. By 1925 the state had become the nation's leading producer of wooden furniture, and it ranked fifth in the production of all furniture. High Point was the chief center of furniture manufacture and marketing, but the industry became important in Thomasville, Lexington, Statesville, Lenoir, Hickory, Newton, Conover, Morganton, Mount Airy, Sanford, and a number of other towns, particularly in the Piedmont area.

Other Industries

Although textiles, tobacco, and furniture accounted for almost three-fourths of the value of North Carolina manufactures in the first quarter of the century, a large number of other industries were becoming important. Among these were lumber, including planing mill products; flour and meal; cottonseed oil and meal; fertilizer; leather; railway car construction and repair; printing and publishing; and paper. In 1908 the Champion Fiber Company began the manufacture of wood pulp at Canton. In 1914 the state had fourteen fertilizer factories with a product of over $10,000,000. In 1927 the state had 2,249 "miscellaneous manufacturing plants," employing 50,439 workers, who received $45,000,000 in wages, used $153,000,000 worth of raw materials, and turned out products valued at $262,354,000.

Slow Growth of Organized Labor

Rapid industrialization produced some problems and controversies between laborers and mill management. The workers showed an increasing tendency to organize unions for the purpose of bargaining collectively and striking if necessary in their efforts to get higher wages and better working conditions. But many of the employers opposed labor unions, refused to bargain collectively, insisted on their unimpaired control over wages and employment and working conditions, and maintained that wages, though lower than in the North, were as high as they could afford in order to compete successfully in the national market. The hostility of manufacturers, the indifference or hostility of the state government and of public opinion to organized labor, the high percentage of unskilled laborers, and the division of industrial workers among many scattered factories greatly handicapped the development of a strong labor movement in North Carolina.

The earliest, most enduring, and most successful labor unions in the late nineteenth and early twentieth centuries were those of skilled laborers, such as printers, carpenters, engineers, machinists, and railway workers in the larger cities. These unions in the more limited and skilled trades were largely responsible for the formation of the North Carolina State Federation of Labor in 1905 and for its continuance thereafter. From 1899 to 1901 the American Federation of Labor first turned its attention to the South. In 1900 there were eighty-two labor unions in the state, including sixteen in the textile industry. But the failure in that year of textile strikes at Gibsonville, Durham, Raleigh, and Fayetteville, led to the decline of the labor movement for more than a decade. The United States Department of Labor in 1908 reported union activity at only one place in the state. The efforts of the United Textile Workers to unionize the South during the years 1913 to 1918 "were not extended to North Carolina because of its strong anti-union sentiment."

The next period of union activity in the state began in 1919, when the United Textile Workers organized forty-three unions with an estimated membership of thirty thousand. Rising prices and lagging wages after World War I stimulated labor activity. In 1919, one of the greatest "strike years" in American history, a strike and lockout in the Charlotte area, which continued for three months, was partially successful. It was finally settled by committees of the unions and manufacturers "on an open shop basis, with reinstatement without discrimination, a fifty-five hour week with the old sixty hours' pay, abolition of the bonus, and free house rent during . . . the lockout." Wage cuts and the recession of 1921 caused several strikes in the textile centers and involved an estimated nine thousand workers. Governor Morrison sent the National Guard to the striking centers. The failure of the strikers to achieve their objectives "so crippled the union that not a substantial local was left at the end of the year." In the summer of 1922 a strike by railway shopmen, clerks, and station employees also failed. The failure of these strikes brought another lapse of union activity, and it was not until 1929 that labor organization on a significant scale began to manifest itself in North Carolina.

Mining

About seventy minerals of commercial importance occur in North Carolina, but industrial minerals and building materials are the most valuable. The total value of the state's mineral production increased from $1,604,078 in 1901 to $12,569,000 in 1927. Building materials accounted for more than four-fifths of this amount—granite, $4,563,000; brick and tile, $3,-834,000; sand and gravel, $871,000, cement products, $671,000; and limestone and marble, $477,000. In 1927 the state's 803 brick-making establishments gave North Carolina third rank in the nation in the manufacture of common brick. After 1911 the production of feldspar rose from almost nothing to first place in the nation by 1927, when the state produced $612,214 worth of this article. Though North Carolina had ceased to be the "gold state," some of the precious metal was still mined—$126,000 worth in 1916. Among other minerals produced on a commercial scale were kaolin, mica, pyrophyllite, and talc. The state produced most of the nation's primary kaolin, 70 percent of its mica, and about 35 percent of its titanium. The state usually ranked about eight in clay products.

Commercial Fisheries

A 1925 report revealed that "approximately 15,000 persons are engaged in fishing activities incident to the production and marketing of sea foods in North Carolina; and a population of around 50,000 is estimated to be dependent upon the industry for a livelihood." The value of all sea food products in 1908 was $1,716,000; by the 1920s the average annual value was about $3,000,000. Of the food fish in North Carolina the most important were shad, trout, herring, croakers, mullet, rock, bluefish, and mackerel. In addition to food fish, there was an enormous catch of nonfood fish, chiefly menhaden, used for oil in manufacturing process. The annual yield of oysters in the 1920s was about 500,000 bushels, the average annual value of shrimp about $60,000, and of escallops about $20,000.

Total and Per Capita Wealth

The total estimated wealth of North Carolina rose from $682,000,000 in 1900 to $1,648,000,000 in 1912, and to $6,458,000,000 in 1920. The per capita wealth of the state in 1922 was $1,703, a rank of forty-second in the nation.

Banking and Insurance Progress

The quarter century after 1900 was one of accelerated growth of banking institutions. In 1900 the state had 120 banks with resources of $33,000,000; in 1918 these figures had increased to 543 and $288,000,000; in 1920 the total bank resources of North Carolina amounted to $456,000,000, of which $272,000,000 belonged to state banks and $184,000,000 to national banks. Only five states had smaller per capita bank resources than North Carolina's $176.77. The state had 2½ percent of the nation's population, but only four-fifths of 1 percent of the nation's bank resources.

In 1919 there were 141 building and loan associations in the state; in 1924 the number was 247, with 71,301 white shareholders and 10,173 Negro shareholders. By the mid-twenties, almost 10,000 new homes, at a total cost of $25,000,000, were being built each year through the building and loan plan.

In 1900 there were twenty-eight life insurance companies doing business in North Carolina, all of them from outside the state except one—the North Carolina Mutual Life Insurance Company, organized by Negroes in Durham, April 1, 1899. The Security Life and Annuity Company of Greensboro began business in 1901. This company was later merged with the Jefferson Life Insurance Company, which was organized in 1907, and the Greensboro Life Insurance Company, which was formed in 1905, to form Jefferson Standard, which became the largest insurance company in the state. The Pilot Life Insurance Company of Greensboro began business in 1903. State-chartered fire insurance companies increased from five in 1900 to twenty-five in 1928.

Railroad Construction and Consolidation

Improved transportation facilities were both a cause and an effect of the economic development of the state. Railroad expansion, which resulted in the construction of 3,831 miles of track before 1900 in the organization of the Southern, Seaboard Air Line, and Atlantic Coast Line systems and in the development of railway property valued at $12,322,000, continued at a much slower pace after 1900. In 1906 the Norfolk Elizabeth City-Edenton line was consolidated with several other short lines connecting with Raleigh, Morehead City, New Bern, and other towns in the East to form the Norfolk and Southern Railway Company. In 1910 it was reorganized as the Norfolk Southern Railroad Company. In 1911 this company acquired control of the Aberdeen and Asheboro Railroad, with 106 miles of track; the Durham and Charlotte Railroad, extending sixty miles south of Durham; and a sixty-four mile line connecting Raleigh and Fayetteville. Thus the Norfolk Southern had a line connecting Charlotte and Raleigh with Norfolk. Besides the four large systems, more than thirty companies operated short lines in the state.

The total railroad mileage in North Carolina increased to 4,932 in 1910 and to 5,522 in 1920. Two new railroads were built during this period. The Winston-Salem Southbound, completed from Wadesboro to Winston-Salem in 1911, and the Carolina, Clinchfield and Ohio, constructed with great engineering skill across the Appalachian mountains from Kentucky via Marion and to Bostic, North Carolina. This road, completed between 1910 and 1914, also provided a route for traffic between North Carolina and the Middle West.

A Passenger Train Depicted on a North Carolina Treasury Note of 1865

North Carolina Collection, The University of North Carolina at Chapel Hill

The Movement for State Regulation of Railroads

Before and after 1900 there was strong antirailroad sentiment in North Carolina as in other states. The railroads were accused of charging excessive and discriminatory freight and passenger rates; giving poor service to shippers and passengers; dodging taxes; making excessive earnings; stock-watering, pooling, and giving rebates; charging more for a short haul than for a long haul over the same road; acquiring undue influence over legislators by the use of skillful lobbyists and the issuance of free passes; and even influencing judges.

After 1900 the regulatory power of the Corporation Commission was extended to electric light, power, and gas companies; and it was further empowered to require the adjustment of train schedules, to order the provision of adequate warehouses, and to promote improved handling of freight. The broadening powers of the federal Interstate Commerce Commission (created in 1887) subjected the railroads to increasing federal regulation and probably lessened the influence and power of the various state regulatory commissions. Yet between 1899 and 1911 the North Carolina Corporation Commission heard 4,230 complaints—consisting in the main of overcharges, discriminations, poor freight service, failure to provide adequate cars for shipment of freight, storage charges, and petitions for depots and sidings. In 1923 the Corporation Commission was authorized to require the adjustment of train schedules, to order the provisions of adequate warehousing facilities, and to promote the more expeditious handling of shipments of less than carload lots. In 1923 supervision was extended to motor vehicles.

Highways and Motor Cars

As the twentieth century progressed, highways became more important than railways. Under the old system of county control, highway improvement was too slow to meet the growing needs of travel, transportation, and trade, particularly with the increasing use of automobiles whose numbers in the state rose from 2,400 in 1910 to 150,000 in 1921. Under the Mecklenburg County plan of assessing a county road tax, the wealthier and more progressive counties built improved roads, but as late as 1911 there were only 1,175 miles of macadamized, 1,502 miles of sand-clay, and 683 miles of gravel roads in a total mileage of about 48,000 in the whole state. As early as 1901–2 a "good roads train" under the combined auspices of the United States Department of Agriculture and the Southern Railway operated throughout the state "stimulating interest in highway improvement." In 1902 the North Carolina Good Roads Association was organized, with P. H. Hanes as president. This organization favored the establishment of a state highway commission and provision for highway maintenance by the state.

In 1915 the General Assembly created the State Highway Commission to cooperate with the counties in road building. The next year Congress passed the Federal Highway Act and began to allocate funds to the states on a matching basis to improve major interstate federal roads. In 1917 the State Highway Commission was authorized to receive federal funds and to receive the state automobile license fees for the purpose of maintaining roads and bridges. Some progress was made in highway construction during the next four years, but it was not until the passage of the Highway Act of 1921 that North Carolina began to emerge as the "Good Roads State."

Chapter 42

EDUCATIONAL AND CULTURAL GROWTH

General economic prosperity, an awareness of intellectual backwardness, and more enlightened and progressive leadership of the dominant Democratic party brought phenomenal educational development to North Carolina in the twentieth century. Aycock turned the partisan gubernatorial campaign of 1900 into a crusade for public education, and he pledged his administration to the promotion of this cause.

In his inaugural address of 1901, Governor Aycock said: "On a hundred platforms, to half the voters of the State, in the late campaign, I pledged the State, its strength, its heart, its wealth to universal education. I promised the illiterate poor man bound to a life of toil and struggle and poverty, that life should be brighter for his boy and girl than it had been for him and the partner of his sorrows and joys. I pledged the wealth of the State to the education of his children. . . . We are prosperous as never before—our wealth increases, our industries multiply, our commerce extends, and among the owners of this wealth, this multiplying industry, this extending commerce, I have found no man who is unwilling to make the State stronger and better by liberal aid to the cause of education. . . . I declare to you that it shall be my constant aim and effort, during the four years that I shall endeavor to serve the people of this State, to redeem this most solemn of all our pledges."

The Crusade for Public Schools

Realizing that the people must be convinced of the necessity for better schools, Aycock and the newly elected Superintendent of Public Instruction, Thomas F. Toon, began a canvass of the state in behalf of education. Toon died a year after taking office and was succeeded by James Y. Joyner, then a professor at what is now The University of North Carolina at Greensboro. The task of arousing public opinion in a predominantly rural state lacking in large

589

cities and having inadequate transportation facilities was simplified in 1902 by a gift of $4,000 annually by the Southern Education Board for campaign expenses. At the suggestion of Charles D. McIver, Aycock called a conference of educational workers. This conference issued "A Declaration against Illiteracy," calling upon all patriotic citizens to aid in promoting "free public schools, open to all, supported by the taxes of all its citizens, where every child, regardless of its condition in life, or circumstances of fortune, may receive that opportunity for training into social service which the constitution of this and other great states of the age demand."

A Central Campaign Committee for the Promotion of Public Education in North Carolina, composed of Aycock, McIver, and Joyner, with Eugene C. Brooks as executive secretary, launched the most remarkable educational campaign in the history of North Carolina. Men and women of every business, profession, religious denomination, and political party addressed hundreds of educational rallies throughout the state. Newspapers gave extensive publicity, ministers preached on education, and "politics yielded first place in public interest to education." For the first time Superior Court judges instructed grand juries "that it was quite as much their duty to investigate the condition of school buildings as it was to investigate jails and poorhouses." Aycock and other speakers inspired the people with a vision of a developing, prosperous state and convinced them of the wisdom and economy of voting local school taxes, consolidating school districts, and providing for more and better schoolhouses, longer terms, and higher salaries for teachers. Hundreds of school districts responded favorably, and the educational movement continued to spread and gain momentum. The people of North Carolina became convinced of the value of public education, spent increasing amounts for schools, and came to consider education their most important public activity.

Reversal of the Barksdale Decision by the State Supreme Court

The Barksdale decision, discussed earlier (p. 537) "remained undisturbed in its career of promoting illiteracy" until 1907. In that year the commissioners of Franklin County levied a one-cent special property tax beyond the 66⅔ cents state and county limit and a three-cent special poll tax for the purpose of maintaining a four-months school during the forthcoming school year. Opponents of this tax levy claimed that it was in violation of Article I, section 5 of the state constitution and obtained an injunction to prevent its collection. In the case of *J. R. Collie* v. *Commissioners* the state Supreme Court held that the county commissioners had the right to levy special taxes beyond 66⅔ cents on a $100 valuation, if such taxes were necessary to maintain the four-months school term required by the constitution. This reversal of the Barksdale decision was a great victory for public education. "The dead hand of reaction was no longer to prevail."

Achievements of a Decade

During the first decade of the century nearly three thousand schoolhouses were built, an average of about one a day; the total annual cost of public schools rose from about $1 million to more than $3 million; the total value of school property increased from about $1 million to more than $5 million, and the annual state appropriation for equalizing the school term among the counties more than doubled. In 1903 the state government began the policy of loaning money to aid counties in building and improving schoolhouses—a sum that averaged about $250,000 a year for the next decade. The services of the office of superintendent of public instruction were greatly expanded, particularly in the distribution of educational bulletins and in school supervision; the number of special local tax districts increased from 18 to 1,167, and rural school libraries from 472 to 2,272. Nearly a month was added to the length of the public school term, and enrollment and average daily attendance were increased, as well as teachers' salaries. A compulsory school law was enacted in 1907; the percentage of illiteracy among persons ten years old and over dropped from 28.7 to 18.5; and, as a means of training more and better teachers, the state took steps to improve the normal schools for Negroes and established three normals for white teachers—the Appalachian Training School at Boone in 1903, the Cullowhee Normal and Industrial School in 1905, and the East Carolina Teacher's Training School at Greenville in 1907.

Before 1907 high school subjects were taught in many of the public schools, especially in the cities. In that year the General Assembly passed "an act to stimulate high school instruction in the public schools" and appropriated $45,-000 annually for this purpose. In 1909 this amount was increased to $50,000 and in 1911 to $75,000. Under the 1907 law not more than four high schools in any one county could receive aid, no school was to get less than $250 nor more than $500 state aid a year, and high schools in towns of more than 1,200 people could receive no aid whatever. This law "laid the basis for the development of a system of public rural high schools." By 1911 some two hundred rural high schools had been established in ninety-three of the state's one hundred counties.

Continued Progress of the Public Schools

Even more rapid was public school expansion and improvement in the decade after 1910. The General Assembly of 1913 levied a statewide property tax of five cents (on a $100 valuation) to enable schools to lengthen the terms to as much as six months; it also enacted an improved compulsory school law requiring "all children between the ages of eight and twelve to attend school for at least four months in each year"; it passed a law prohibiting children under twelve from being employed in factories except as apprentices and only after having attended school for the four months required, and it made provision for the teaching of agriculture and domestic science in high schools. In 1915 the per capita cost of state government in North Carolina was only $1.46—among the lowest of any state—and of this amount 71 cents went for public education and 39 cents for charities, hospitals, and corrections.

The General Assembly of 1917 created a State Board of Examiners and Institute Conductors, to be appointed by the governor, and to have power to examine and certify all applicants for teaching positions in the public schools, and also to direct the teachers' institutes. It also created an Educational Commission "to make a thorough study of the entire public school system." Largely as a result of the work of this commission, which received financial assistance from the General Education Board, "improvements were made in the support of public education, in the training and certification of teachers, in the development of the county unit in school administration, and in the consolidation of school districts."

In 1918 the voters of the state approved a constitutional amendment extending the minimum school term to six months. For the school year 1918-19, total school expenditures amounted to $6,786,000; value of school property, $16,-295,000; the number of teachers, 15,037; the average monthly salary of teachers, $56.83, and the average number of days of pupils in school, 112. The average monthly salary of white teachers was $62.00, that of Negro teachers, $37.18.

Negro Education

Improvements in Negro public schools followed the same pattern as in white schools, though they were less expensive and poorer in every respect. But gradually better buildings and equipment and greater facilities for teacher training were provided by the state. The Jeanes Fund, the Slater Fund, the Rosenwald Fund, and the General Education Board cooperated with the state and counties in the improvement of Negro schools. Between 1906 and 1928 these agencies contributed $1,877,000 to promote the education of the Negro in North Carolina.

Progress of Higher Education

The development of higher education in North Carolina kept pace with that of the public schools. In 1900 the state and denominational colleges were struggling with few buildings, little equipment, inadequate income, small enrollments, small libraries, inadequate laboratories, and poorly paid teachers. Largely dependent upon tuition and fees—which were very low compared to what they are today—for financial support, and upon poorly equipped preparatory schools for students, "the colleges were forced by circumstances to maintain low academic standards."

The state government, educational foundations, churches, and philanthropic individuals rapidly revolutionized the facilities of higher education. Work in this direction was stimulated by the Carnegie Foundation for the Advancement of Teaching, whose 1907 report on standards of admission proved of great value to college administrators. Some years later the General Education Board began to appropriate funds to colleges on condition that the institutions themselves would raise additional sums. By 1914, five denominational colleges in the state had received gifts amounting to $387,500, conditioned upon their raising additional funds. Accordingly Trinity College raised $1,000,000; Davidson College, $300,000; Salem Academy and College, $300,000; Wake Forest College, $150,-000, and Meredith College, $150,000.

The state increased its annual appropriations for maintenance of its colleges and the University of North Carolina from $155,000 in 1901 to over $2,000,000 in the early 1920s, and for permanent improvements from $95,500 to about $2,000,000. In 1911 legislative appropriations for the university alone amounted to $200,000. Increased state appropriations resulted in a remarkable expansion of physical plants, teaching staffs, and breadth and quality of educational program. In the first two decades of the century, more than a dozen buildings were erected on the campus at Chapel Hill; funds for at least three of these arose from outside sources.

During the administration of Francis P. Venable (1900–14) the university's financial condition improved, the physical plant was greatly expanded, student enrollment greatly increased, athletics were encouraged, creative scholarship was required of the faculty, graduate and professional schools increased and improved in quality, and some of the institution's departments achieved national distinction. The brief administration of Edward K. Graham (1914–18) was notable for the enlargement of the university's service to the state at large, increased resources for administrative and building purposes, and a strengthening of student morale and honor standards. President Harry W. Chase (1919–30) guided the university through a period of rapid physical expansion, and during this period the university achieved a national and international reputation for high standards of scholarship and freedom in research and teaching.

The Agricultural and Mechanical College at Raleigh also witnessed considerable physical expansion. Four buildings were erected on the campus between 1900 and 1912. One of the most notable achievements during this era was the organization of the Department of Agricultural Extension in 1909. Under the capable leadership of presidents George T. Winston (1899–1908), D. H. Hill (1908–16), and W. C. Riddick (1916–23), student enrollment increased from 301 in 1901 to 1,040 in 1920.

In this period biennial legislative appropriations for the maintenance of normal schools and teachers' colleges were greatly increased—from $32,000 in 1901 to over $500,000 by 1920. Appropriations for permanent improvement jumped from $5,000 to approximately $500,000. Upon the death of Charles D. McIver in 1906, Julius I. Foust became president of what is now The University of North Carolina at Greensboro. Robert H. Wright headed the East Carolina Teachers' College at Greenville from its establishment in 1907 until after 1920, and B. B. Dougherty was president of the Appalachian Training School from its founding in 1903 to 1955. (Its name was changed to Appalachian State Normal School in 1925, to Appalachian State Teachers' College in 1929, and to Appalachian State University in 1967.) In 1925 Cullowhee Normal and Industrial School became Cullowhee State Normal School, and in 1929 Western Carolina Teachers' College. In 1951 the name "Teachers' " was dropped from the title, and in 1967 it became Western Carolina University.

The denominational or church-related colleges of the state witnessed a similar record of growth and expansion. Between 1900 and 1925 the enrollment of Davidson College increased from 173 to 639, its faculty from 8 to 83, and its endowment from $90,000 to $667,000. Its presidents were Henry Louis Smith (1901–12) and William J. Martin.

When Charles E. Taylor resigned from the presidency of Wake Forest College in 1905, that institution had 7 professors, 150 students, and an endowment of about $300,000. Under the leadership of President William Louis Poteat (1905–27), the college's enrollment increased to 716, its faculty to 37, and its endowment to more than $2,000,000. During this period the student body of Meredith College more than doubled, and its endowment rose from nothing to $465,000.

Trinity College, headed by John C. Kilgo (1894–1910), and then by W. P. Few, made the greatest progress of any of the denominational colleges. When Kilgo assumed the presidency the college had a faculty of nine, a student body of 153, and a physical plant worth only $135,000. But Kilgo "won for the college the closer friendship of the Dukes, father and sons, who together bore the financial burden of the college of twenty-five years." Shortly before his death Washington Duke gave the college $500,000 and his sons "Buck" and Ben together had given the college more than $1,250,000 before 1919. As early as 1916 the faculty had increased to 30 and the student body to almost 600.

One of the most notable contributions made by Trinity College in the field of scholarship was the founding in 1902 of the *South Atlantic Quarterly*. This scholarly journal, with history professor John Spencer Bassett as editor, was established as "a medium through which the younger generation of the South could express their thought." In October, 1903, Bassett published an article in which he expressed the view that Booker T. Washington, a Negro, was "the greatest man, save General Lee, born in the South in a hundred years." This "advanced view" provoked a storm of criticism throughout the state. Trinity College was attacked and there were demands that Professor Bassett be fired.

Josephus Daniels was among those who called for dismissal. President Kilgo rose to Bassett's defense, and every member of the faculty advised Kilgo that they would resign if Bassett was dismissed, and every member signed a public statement which said:"Money, students, friends are not for one moment to be weighed in the balance with tolerance, with fairness, and with freedom. . . . We urge you to say of Trinity College what Thomas Jefferson, the founder of American democracy, said of the institution which he established [the University of Virginia]: 'This institution will be based upon the illimitable freedom of the human mind. For here we are not afraid to follow truth where-ever it may lead, nor to tolerate error so long as reason is left free to combat it.' "

The Board of Trustees voted 18 to 7 not to dismiss Bassett. This decision represented "one of the greatest victories for academic freedom ever won in the United States." Walter Hines Page, writing before the trustees voted, said that they had the opportunity to make a decision that would be "the most important event in the history of North Carolina in our time; for free speech and free teaching will be won there for all time to come."

North Carolina's Backwardness in Library Facilities

In 1897 Walter Hines Page said, "There are no great libraries in the state, nor do the people yet read, nor have the publishing houses yet reckoned them as patrons, except the publishers of school books." In that year Durham established the first tax-supported public library in the state. Greensboro, Charlotte, and Winston and Salem followed suit in 1902, 1903, and 1906, respectively. At that time school libraries were almost nonexistent and college libraries were far from adequate. The state government took the lead in library development. It maintained the century-old State Library, though not until 1921 did legislative appropriations for it reach as much as $3,000. The state also began to offer limited funds to aid communities in establishing public school libraries, made more liberal appropriations for libraries in institutions of higher learning, and established the Library Commission of North Carolina. This agency, with Louis R. Wilson as chairman, took the lead in the reorganization and improvement of existing libraries and the establishment of new ones, the operation of "package libraries" for the use of students and book clubs, and traveling library service to the people of communities where no other library service was available. By 1922 thirty-five of the state's sixty-two largest towns had public libraries. But the total expenditures for all public libraries were only $83,031, or 3¼ cents per capita.

Newspapers and Magazines

In the first quarter of the century, there was a decrease in the number of state newspapers, but there was an improvement in quality, and a great increase in the size and circulation of papers due largely to the development of rural free delivery, the building of good roads, and the general improvement of transportation facilities. Newspaper circulation increased from 612,000 in 1901 to over 2,000,000 by 1926. Leading dailies, such as the *Charlotte Observer,* the *Greensboro Daily News,* and the Raleigh *News and Observer* increased their size from eight to sixteen pages. Under the able editorship of Joseph P. Caldwell, the *Charlotte Observer* achieved a wide reputation for its liberalism. The Raleigh *News and Observer,* edited by Josephus Daniels, was a powerful force, especially in eastern North Carolina. Virginius Dabney, prominent Virginia editor, declared that it "is probably the most fearless paper in the South in its attitude toward economic and industrial questions. The textile and tobacco interests, the two most powerful groups in North Carolina, are treated as cavalierly by Mr. Daniels as if they controlled no advertising." Dabney also said that the *Greensboro Daily News* was "notable for the enlightenment of its views no less than for the urbanity of the language in which those views are expressed. When Gerald W. Johnson was on its editorial staff the *News* held undisputed sway in the State, and was the mouthpiece of North Carolina liberalism."

North Carolina Writers

In the twentieth century, for the first time, the literary production of North Carolinians began to achieve more than local distinction in quantity and quality. During the first quarter of the century the chief interest and activity were in the fields of history and biography. Most of the authors were not trained in methods of research but wrote or edited historical works from patriotic impulse. Among this group were Samuel A. Ashe, best known for his two-volume *History of North Carolina* (1908 and 1925) and his eight-volume *Biographical History of North Carolina* (1905 and 1917); Kemp P. Battle for his two-volume *History of the University of North Carolina* (1907 and 1912); Walter Clark as editor of the five-volume regimental histories (1901) and the sixteen-volume *State Records of North Carolina* (1895–1905); Charles L. Coon for editing documentary books on North Carolina public schools and academies; Marshall DeLancey Haywood for his *Governor William Tryon* (1903), his *Lives of the Bishops of North Carolina* (1910), and many other historical studies. Other writers of history and biography were Edwin A. Alderman, Episcopal Bishop Joseph B. Cheshire, Horace Kephart, and Walter Hines Page.

For the first time there appeared a group of historians trained in modern scientific historical research. Chief among these professional historians were: John Spencer Bassett, William K. Boyd, R. D. W. Connor, William E. Dodd, J. G. de R. Hamilton, C. L. Raper, Holland Thompson, Henry M. Wagstaff, and Stephen B. Weeks. All of these men made distinctive contributions to

North Carolina and American historiography. These trained scholars devoted more attention to social, economic, and cultural factors than did earlier writers. The achievements of the "new school of North Carolina historians" were due in part to the establishment of the North Carolina Historical Commission (1903) whose activity in collecting, preserving, and publishing the state's historical sources made North Carolina history an attractive field for research and writing.

Novels, Poetry, and Drama

Production of other forms of literature was not impressive. The best known poets were John Henry Boner, John Charles McNeill, and Henry Jerome Stockard. McNeill, who has been called "the Robert Burns of the South," is best known for *Songs, Merry and Sad* (1906) and *Lyrics from Cotton Land* (1907).

In the field of the novel, Thomas Dixon was the state's most prolific writer. Among more than a score of his novels, the best known were *The Leopard's Spots* (1902) and *The Clansman* (1905). From the latter novel was made the "Birth of a Nation," one of the greatest landmarks in motion picture history. Charles W. Chesnutt, a Negro, wrote three novels between 1899 and 1905 and numerous short stories with North Carolina settings. In 1928 he was awarded the Spingarn Medal for his work in depicting the true life and struggles of the Negro. In the field of the short story North Carolina–born William Sidney Porter, better known as "O. Henry," achieved worldwide recognition. Approximately three hundred of his short stories were published in contemporary periodicals. Among his best-known books were *Cabbages and Kings* (1904), *The Four Million* (1907), *The Voice of the City* (1908), and *Rolling Stones* (1912).

One of the state's most versatile writers was Olive Tilford Dargan, better known as "Fielding Burke." A North Carolinian by adoption (she was born in Kentucky), she published four books of plays (1904–22), three books of poetry (1914–22), and many short stories and sketches in the *Atlantic Monthly* and other national periodicals. She published three novels (1932–47). Frances Christine (Fisher) Tiernan of Salisbury, who wrote under the name "Christian Reid," published forty-two books, chiefly novels, eleven of which appeared between 1900 and her death in 1920. One of her early books, *Land of the Sky* (1876) a novel of the North Carolina mountains, gave to that part of the state its picturesque name.

Chapter 43

POLITICS, 1920-1932: GOVERNORS MORRISON, McLEAN, AND GARDNER

The joy and enthusiasm that greeted the armistice of November 11, 1918, gave way all too soon to controversy, unrest, and disillusionment. North Carolina shared in some degree the social and moral degeneration, the gross materialism, and the speculative economic prosperity of America in the postwar years. In the following years World War I many Americans reacted against domestic reforms, which had prevailed during the previous decade. They reacted more strongly against internationalism and became "excessively nationalistic and intolerantly patriotic." Unconventional political doctrines were attacked and there was much talk about "100 percent Americanism." Between 1917 and 1936 twenty-two states adopted teachers' oath laws. North Carolina, however, was not one of these.

The Ku Klux Klan

There was also a revival of "nativism," best illustrated by the rise to a position of influence of the second Ku Klux Klan (not to be confused with that of the Reconstruction era). The Klan was not as strong in North Carolina as in some states, notably Georgia and Indiana, yet it was quite active in some portions of the state.

The Fundamentalist Movement

Another aspect of the postwar reaction was the fundamentalist movement in both religion and economics. The religious fundamentalist remained faithful to the literal interpretation of the Bible; the economic fundamentalist clung to the sacred formulae of individual liberty and property rights.

The religious fundamentalists opposed all efforts to reconcile the teachings of Christian religion with modern scientific thought. In particular, they opposed the teaching of the theory of evolution and succeeded in getting a number of state legislatures to enact antievolution laws. Heroic work by Harry W. Chase and William Louis Poteat, presidents of the University of North Carolina and Wake Forest College, respectively, defeated antievolution legislation in North Carolina, the fight ending finally in the defeat of the so-called "Monkey Bill" in 1927.

The "Noble Experiment" of Prohibition

Another problem of the 1920s was the "Noble Experiment" of prohibition. The Eighteenth Amendment (1919) prohibited the manufacture, sale, or transportation of intoxicating liquors within the United States. To enforce this amendment, the Volstead Act defining "intoxicating" liquors as that containing as much as .5 percent alcohol, was passed over the veto of President Wilson, but it was soon discovered that it was easier to put a dry amendment in the Constitution than actually to enforce prohibition. Since North Carolina had been legally dry for many years, there was less evasion of the prohibition law than in some states, and there were certainly less gangsterism and racketeering than prevailed in Chicago and some other large cities. But there was bootlegging in many communities. The price of liquor jumped considerably and its quality declined. The majority of North Carolinians, however, believed in prohibition. Humorist Will Rogers, speaking in Raleigh, wisecracked that the "North Carolina voters would vote dry as long as they could stagger to the polls." This view was hardly correct, but the fact remains that the prohibition law was not rigidly enforced. Finally, in 1933, the Twenty-First Amendment repealed the Eighteenth Amendment and national prohibition came to an end. Under the new amendment the federal government was pledged to protect the "dry states," and North Carolina remained dry legally until 1937.

The Election of 1920

The presidential campaign of 1920 furnished a splendid illustration of America's postwar disillusionment. In an election in which the *New York Times* advised the electorate to "Hold Your Nose and Vote," Republican Warren G. Harding won over Democrat James M. Cox by a landslide vote of 16,141,536 to 9,128,488. North Carolina gave Cox 305,367 votes to 232,819 for Harding. Republicans controlled the national administration for the next twelve years. In striking contrast to the national picture, North Carolina during these twelve years had three of the ablest governors in its history—Cameron Morrison, Angus W. McLean, and O. Max Gardner. In the Democratic gubernatorial primary of 1920 Morrison received 49,070 votes; Gardner (then Lieutenant Governor), 48,983, and Congressman Robert N. Page, 30,180. Morrison won the second primary over Gardner, 70,353 to 61,073. In the general election Morrison defeated Republican John J. Parker, 308,151 to 230,175.

Morrison, "Good Roads Governor," 1921–1925

In his inaugural address Governor Morrison promised that education and every other material interest of the people were to be advanced, but he placed particular stress on highway development. Under his capable leadership the Highway Act of 1921 enlarged the personnel and powers of the Highway Commission, directed the building and maintenance of a state system of almost six thousand miles of improved roads "connecting all county seats, state institutions and leading towns," and authorized a bond issue of $50 million for highway construction. Harriet Morehead Berry, secretary of the North Carolina Good Roads Association, was most active in securing the approval of this bond issue, as she had been in procuring the passage of highway legislation. Under the energetic leadership of Frank Page, chairman of the state Highway Commission, an era of unprecedented construction of asphalt, concrete, sand-clay and gravel roads began which soon brought fame to North Carolina as a "Good Roads State," and to Morrison, the "Good Roads Governor." The initial burst of speed in building improved roads was due in large part to the state's policy of building with borrowed money—from the sale of bonds—and letting the roads "pay for themselves" later, by the income from state taxes on automobiles, trucks, and gasoline.

In Morrison's administration, state ad valorem property taxes were abolished; income taxes were increased; the North Carolina College for Negroes at Durham became a full-fledged state institution, and the Gastonia Orthopedic Hospital for children came under state control.

Remarkable Improvements in Higher Education

Under Morrison's leadership the state greatly increased its appropriations for support of its colleges and university. The General Assembly now "entered on a scheme of permanent improvement of remarkable scope." For the fiscal year 1921 the legislature appropriated $445,000 for the maintenance of the University of North Carolina, $275,000 for the State College of Agriculture and Engineering, and $270,000 for the Woman's College. Appropriations for 1922 were substantially the same.

In the 1920s, with increased financial support and under the capable leadership of President Harry W. Chase, the University of North Carolina achieved a national reputation for high standards of scholarship and freedom in research and teaching, student enrollment increased greatly, and maintenance appropriations reached $894,000 in 1928–29, the high point to that time. Increasing emphasis was given the social sciences and graduate work. The Graduate School was reorganized in 1920. The Institute of Government was founded in the 1920s. The University of North Carolina Press was incorporated in 1922, and the Institute for Social Research was begun in 1924. Professional schools of law, medicine, pharmacy, engineering, education, and commerce attained a standing that gave the university its widening reputation. The other state-supported institutions of higher learning also made great progress, though not as spectacular as that of the university.

The Rise of Duke University

The most notable development in denominational higher education was the transformation of Trinity College into Duke University. In 1924 James Buchanan ("Buck") Duke, tobacco and power magnate, created the Duke Endowment of $40 million for aid to educational institutions, hospitals, orphanages, and superannuated Methodist preachers. At Duke's death the next year this endowment was more than doubled, and a large portion of the more than $80 million was assigned to Trinity College, which changed its name to Duke University. Davidson College, Furman University at Greenville, South Carolina, and Johnson C. Smith University for Negroes at Charlotte also received smaller portions of the income from the Duke Endowment, which was the largest benefaction ever made for any purpose in the South.

Progress of the Public Schools

The public schools also made great strides. Under the administration of E. C. Brooks as superintendent of public instruction, (1919–23) the six-months school term was made effective; salary schedules were adopted for teachers, principals, and superintendents; certification regulations were strengthened; special building funds totalling $10 million were loaned to the counties for the erection of schoolhouses; many small rural schools were consolidated "in accordance with a countywide plan of school organization"; the school bus transportation system was begun, and vocational education in the schools was extended.

When Brooks resigned to become president of North Carolina State College, he was succeeded by Arch T. Allen, who continued in office until his death in 1934. Under Allen's leadership the building program was continued under the stimulation of special building funds (1925 and 1927) totalling $7,500,000; greater emphasis was placed on the standardization of schools; the school curriculum was revised; *State School Facts,* a monthly paper for "the dissemination of information about the schools," was begun in 1928; increased emphasis was placed upon library facilities; improvements were made in the training of teachers; and the State Equalization Fund was increased.

By 1930 the total value of public school property was $110 million—a twenty-twofold increase since 1900—and total annual school expenditure amounted to $33 million—an eleven-fold increase. In 1930 there were 747 white and 119 Negro high schools, 676 of which—largely white—were accredited. The number of elementary schools was 3,110 white and 2,364 Negro. Public school enrollment increased from 691,000 in 1920 to 867,000 in 1930. In this decade the average annual salary of teachers rose from $465 to $850, and the average school term from 134 to 154 days. The annual current expense per pupil rose from $20.21 in 1920 to $42.53 in 1930.

Attempts to Develop North Carolina Ports

North Carolina's economic development was handicapped because of higher freight rates than those charged Virginia competitors, a situation partially due to the state's lack of adequate ports and water transportation. The freight rate problem caused a strong agitation in the early 1920s for state-owned ports, terminals, and ships, and for an east-west trunk line railroad to the Middle West. Governor Morrison, ardent advocate of the plan to provide water transport competition for railroads, called a special session of the legislature in 1924 which submitted to popular vote the proposal of appropriating $8,500,000 for the above-named purposes. The referendum resulted in the defeat of the proposal by a vote of 127,000 to 184,000, with most of the Piedmont counties voting against it.

Writing about the Morrison administration as it came to a close, historian S. A. Ashe said: "It was Governor Morrison's happy fortune to be at the helm of State affairs at a period when the shackles that had bound the people had been severed; when poverty was giving place to prosperity; when the resources of the banks were $474,000,000; when the value of manufactured products was $781,000,000; that of the principal agricultural products had increased to $430,000,000, and incomes were far beyond the dream of the previous generation. Weakness had given place to strength. The future now seemed assured. . . . Higher education for the thousands, the welfare of the unfortunate, the enlargement of all activities were in the air."

The Expanding Functions of Government

The unprecedented application of private initiative, capital, and industry to the utilization of natural resources and to economic development was becoming a conspicuous feature of North Carolina. Equally impressive was the increasing role of governmental agencies at all levels. Individuals and an ever-increasing number of business, professional, and social organizations turned more and more to their local and state governments as common agencies of all the people for the solution of common problems.

By the 1920s the broad modern social concept of government as a service agency for community development had triumphed. The word "commonwealth" was coming to mean "common wealth." As the people demanded more and better services from government, its structure expanded, its costs increased, and taxes became heavier. This trend, opposed by some but apparently approved by the majority, was an inevitable result of the increasing number and complexity of social and economic problems of public interest arising from an expanding population brought closer together by improving transportation and communication facilities.

The Election of 1924

In the Democratic state gubernatorial primary of 1924, Angus W. McLean of Robeson County defeated Josiah W. Bailey by a vote of 151,197 to 83,594. In the general election McLean won over Republican Isaac M. Meekins, 294,441 to 185,627. In the presidential election the state gave Democrat John W. Davis 284,000 votes to 190,754 for Republican Calvin Coolidge and 6,651 for Progressive Robert M. LaFollette. Coolidge, who had succeeded to the presidency upon the death of Warren G. Harding in 1923, won the national election.

Achievements of the McLean Administration, 1925–1929

Progress continued under McLean, but at a less spectacular rate than during Morrison's governorship. North Carolina, one of the leading agricultural states, did not share as fully in "Coolidge Prosperity" as did the more industrialized regions of the nation. Prices for farm products had dropped sharply between 1920 and 1922, then they took an upward turn, but they did not increase as much as did those of manufactured articles purchased by the farmers. The cost of living of industrial workers also increased more rapidly than did their wages. When McLean, "the business man's governor," took office the state debt was $113,868,000—one of the heaviest per capita in the United States.

Creation of the Budget Bureau

Economy became the watchword. The state government could not afford to halt the various programs Governor Morrison had undertaken, but it had to economize. Perhaps the most far-reaching law of the McLean administration was the act of 1925 creating the Budget Bureau. This law vested in the governor "a more direct and effective supervision over all agencies and institutions, and for the initiation and preparation for each session of the General Assembly, of a balanced budget of the state's revenues and expenditures." The governor became ex officio director of the budget and head of the Budget Bureau. The Advisory Budget Commission, created by the same act, was to consist of the chairmen of the Appropriations and Finance committees of the House and Senate, and two other persons to be appointed by the governor.

The state government also sought to reduce expenses by consolidating some departments. The collection of all state taxes was vested in the Revenue Department; and since the number of state employees had greatly increased and there were some inequities in their compensation, the General Assembly provided for a Salary and Wage Commission, with power to fix salaries. A state Sinking Fund Commission was established. The Geological and Economic Survey, created in 1905, was replaced by the Department of Conservation and Development. A Transportation Advisory Commission was created to study the problem of freight rate differentials and "to recommend a remedy." The General Assembly of 1925 also authorized a $20 million bond issue for highways, increased the tax on gasoline to four cents a gallon, and placed the operation of bus lines under control of the Corporation Commission. Liberal appropriations were made to institutions of higher learning and to various state agencies. And an Educational Commission was established and authorized "to make a complete survey" of public schools and state-supported institutions of higher learning, "to investigate the State equalizing fund," and "to collect and disseminate educational data on the costs and results of the State's educational activities."

The General Assembly of 1927 created three important state agencies: (1) the Tax Commission, which was authorized to make a thorough study of taxation and "assemble, classify, and digest all available data on taxation, to the end that it may be submitted to the Governor and General Assembly"; (2) the County Government Advisory Commission, which was "to study the whole subject of county government and to advise with county commissioners as to the best methods of county administration; to prepare and recommend simple and efficient methods of accounting and the proper forms and books; to suggest needed changes; to make recommendations to the Governor"; (3) the State Board of Equalization, which was empowered "to determine the true value of all property subject to taxation in each county . . . and also to determine the cost of maintaining the six months' school term in each county," and "to distribute the equalizing fund to the counties."

Use of the Equalization Fund for Public Schools

The General Assembly of 1927 broke all precedents by making an annual appropriation of $3,250,000 for distribution to public schools during the next biennium. In 1928 ninety counties received sums from the Equalization Fund, ranging from $88,705 for Wilkes to $1,791 for Rowan. The ten counties that received no funds from this source, since their schools were less in need of them, were Buncombe, Cabarrus, Durham, Forsyth, Gaston, Guilford, Mecklenburg, New Hanover, Wake, and Wilson.

The Election of 1928

The presidential election of 1928 was a bitter one, particularly in the South. The Republican nominee, Herbert Hoover, then Secretary of Commerce, was a man of experience and culture, a Protestant, and an advocate of prohibition. The Democratic candidate, Alfred E. Smith, had been an outstanding governor of New York, had risen from the New York "East Side," had been associated with Tammany Hall, was a Roman Catholic, and a "wet" who believed that national prohibition had been a failure.

Senator Simmons, the most influential political leader in North Carolina, had opposed Smith's nomination. Many Democrats refused to support the Democratic nominee and joined the "Anti-Smith" forces, led by Frank McNinch of Charlotte. To counteract this movement Smith made a number of speeches in the state and attracted large audiences. But North Carolina, along with four other southern states, refused to vote for him.

Hoover carried North Carolina by a vote of 348,923 to 286,227 for Smith, the latter winning in only thirty-seven counties. The counties containing the largest cities (Charlotte, Winston-Salem, Durham, and Greensboro), gave Smith his most severe trouncing, while some predominantly rural counties gave him his most significant majorities. The state elected two Republicans to Congress: Charles A. Jonas and George M. Pritchard, from the Ninth and Tenth districts, respectively. In the election for governor, O. Max Gardner, who had been unopposed for the Democratic nomination, defeated Republican H. F. Seawell by a vote of 362,009 to 289,415. The Democrats also retained control of all state offices and both houses of the General Assembly, though the Republicans won more seats than they had held for many years.

The Administration of O. Max Gardner, 1929–1933

The administration of any governor is conditioned to a great degree by the current state of economic affairs. This was particularly true of Gardner. When he assumed office in January, 1929, the nation seemed to be prosperous, but there were already signs of impending economic disaster, which finally came with the stock market crash in October, followed by the Great Depression. Even before Gardner took office farm prices were dropping sharply and there were rumblings of industrial unrest. The state debt had increased from $13,000,000 in 1920 to $178,264,000, but the credit of the state was still good and taxes were adequate "to meet all the demands of current expenses, bond interest and retirement if collected." Some people felt that government expenditures should be cut and the state debt reduced. Others felt that the state should continue its "progressive program," even if this meant increased taxes. In his inaugural address Gardner advocated reforms in election laws, including the secret (Australian) ballot; the short ballot, whereby only a small number of state officers would be elective; a workmen's compensation law; a reduction of property taxes, but an additional one-cent tax on gasoline. The 1929 General Assembly adopted the Australian ballot, but the short ballot was defeated. One of the major achievements was the passage of the Workmen's Compensation Act and the creation of the Industrial Commission to administer it. A long legislative struggle over an eight months' school law failed to pass. All state agencies were placed under the Budget Bureau, and some county road relief measures were enacted.

Beginnings of the Great Depression

The complex national economic structure with its maldistribution of wealth, overproduction, overexpansion of credit and mountainous debts in comparison with income, reduced exports, and inflated prices, crashed in 1929.

Prices dropped sharply and continued to drop until 1933. Wages and salaries were slashed. Many businesses closed and thousands of individuals and companies went bankrupt. Mills could run only part time, and some closed entirely. Many farmers lost their farms and townspeople their homes and businesses. Thousands of unemployed walked the streets in vain looking for work. Thousands of people could not pay their taxes. Cash farm income in the state dropped from $283,000,000 in 1928 to $97,000,000 in 1932; value added by manufactures declined from $603,000,000 in 1929 to $384,000,000 in 1931; retail trade dropped from $1,155,000,000 in 1928 to $878,000,000 in 1933; and income payments to individuals declined from $1,046,000,000 in 1929 to $603,-000,000 in 1932. There were eighteen bank failures in the state in 1929, and considerably more each year between that date and 1933.

As income and property values declined, the amount of taxes collected by the state and counties and cities fell also. Counties and towns were not able to maintain the schools, roads, and other services as they had been doing. They cut the salaries of school teachers and public officials, neglected the roads, reduced their services, and were even in danger of having to close the schools. The state government also sharply reduced salaries and services.

All over the state arose the cry, "Reduce the Taxes." Early in 1930 "tax relief associations" began to demand a special session of the General Assembly to cope with the tax problem. By the end of that year delinquent property taxes in the state amounted to more than $7,500,000 with more than 150,000 pieces of property being advertised for sale for taxes. Governor Gardner was concerned about this problem, but he refused to yield to the demands for a special session of the legislature. He was determined that the next General Assembly "would have all the information possible to begin on the state's business as soon as it assembled." With this in mind he ordered a number of investigations, one of which was an authorization to the Brookings Institution of Washington to make "a complete study of State and county government in order to make recommendations for improvement."

Meanwhile, in the summer of 1930 the state had witnessed a bitter fight in the United States senatorial primary between the incumbent, Simmons, and Josiah W. Bailey. The refusal of Simmons to support "Al" Smith for the presidency in 1928 had turned many Democrats against him. Bailey had been one of Smith's earliest champions and had stumped the state for him. Most of the Democratic leaders supported Bailey, as did most of the daily newspapers. Many strange and bitter campaign pamphlets were circulated. The election, however, went off rather quietly, with Bailey carrying all but sixteen counties and winning by a majority of 68,000 in a total vote of 333,000.

Gardner's Program

Late in December the Brookings Institution made its report to the governor. Among its recommendations, some of which shocked North Carolinians were proposals for the elimination of all but three of the state's thirteen elective administrative offices, the governor, lieutenant governor, and auditor; the reduction of the number of separate state agencies from ninety-two to fourteen; the creation of a Central Purchasing Agency; the consolidation of some counties; and the consolidation of the University of North Carolina, State College, and the Woman's College. By the time the General Assembly of 1931 convened, Gardner "had reached the conclusion that centralization of power was the only answer to the imperative needs of the hour." In his message to the legislature, he said: "Of one conclusion I am absolutely certain—taxes on property must be reduced." Accordingly he presented a comprehensive program which included a 10 percent cut in salaries of state, county, and city officials "except those cut since December, 1929, and those receiving less than fifty dollars a month"; the consolidation of the University of North Carolina, State College, and the Woman's College; the establishment of a Division of Purchase and Contract; the appointment instead of election of the Corporation Commission, Commissioner of Agriculture, and Commissioner of Labor; a general reorganization of state government; the mandatory consolidation of some counties; the reduction of property taxes; and the establishment of an eight months' school term.

The General Assembly of 1931

Some of these proposals met with strong opposition in the legislature, which was in session for 141 days, but Gardner emerged with most of his program enacted into law. He failed to get his goal of the short ballot, the consolidation of counties, and control of the Department of Agriculture in a board rather than a commissioner.

The General Assembly spent many days discussing a general sales tax as well as a luxury tax. Thousands of farmers descended on Raleigh on March 13 to urge a luxury tax. Ten days later Gardner told the legislature that he did not consider a sales tax to be reasonable taxation, because it was "based on human needs and not on the ability to pay," and that "it violates every tenet of the Democratic party in that it taxes the weak to relieve the strong." Furthermore, he believed that its adoption would drive business out of the state. The legislature of 1931 failed to enact either a general sales tax or a luxury tax. The revenue bill, as finally passed, "represented a victory for the Governor and for the opponents of the luxury tax, but at the same time business and industry, which had fought so hard against the luxury tax, had to pay a heavy price." Corporate income taxes were increased by about $2,000,000 and corporation franchise taxes by about $2,250,000. On the local and county levels, however, taxes would be reduced as a result of the state operation of roads.

As Gardner's administration drew to a close, he published an article in the *Saturday Evening Post* showing how North Carolina had "cleaned house." He wrote: "In 1931, North Carolina passed four acts of legislation largely without precedent in the nation. Each was revolutionary, but each was designed to meet the situation prevailing under changed economic conditions. North Carolina is traditionally a conservative state . . . but it is not afraid to stand by itself. . . . At any rate, it pioneered in road legislation, in public-school legislation, in legislation for control of public debt, and in university consolidation.

"The most advanced legislation enacted was embraced in the administration bill for the state to take over the county roads. . . . The transfer involved the state's assumption of an expenditure that was costing $8,250,000 a year.

"The act . . . that attracted widest attention, that stabilized the credit of North Carolina counties and towns, that increased the confidence of the holders of North Carolina securities, that gave a new meaning to the phrase 'local self-government,' was the Local Government Act. . . . Until 1927 we did not know what the local governments owed. When it was figured up, the sum staggered us, but it did not check our bond issues.

"The act . . . that will have the deepest and most enduring effect on the future of this commonwealth was the consolidation and merger of the three major state educational institutions into a greater University of North Carolina.

"The legislation which brought about the largest decrease in the cost of government and the greatest reduction in taxes on property was the public-school legislation. . . . In 1931 the General Assembly . . . boldly stepped up and embraced the principle of state responsibility for the constitutional school term. It enacted the MacLean Law, which provided that the six months' constitutional term should be supported by the state from sources other than ad-valorem taxes.

"The most substantial contribution of the 1931 General Assembly was to tackle and stop in its tracks the advancing tax burden for the first time in the modern history of North Carolina. . . . The total cost of government was reduced $7,000,000, but the tax burden on property was reduced by more than $12,000,000 by the school and road legislation alone."

The Election of 1932

The 1932 Democratic campaign for the governorship was a close and bitter contest between J. C. Blucher Ehringhaus of Elizabeth City, Lieutenant Governor Richard T. Fountain of Edgecombe County, and A. J. Maxwell, State Commissioner of Revenue. Ehringhaus championed the Gardner administration; he accused Fountain of "making Republican speeches," and he declared that the chief evil of the state was "tax colic brought on by prescriptions of 'Doctors Fountain and Maxwell.' " In the June primary Ehringhaus polled 162,498 votes; Fountain, 115,127 and Maxwell 102,032. In the second primary Ehringhaus defeated Fountain by a vote of 182,055 to 168,971.

The second gubernatorial primary was overshadowed by the contest for the Democratic nomination for the United States Senate between Robert R. ("Our Bob") Reynolds and Cameron Morrison, who had been appointed by Governor Gardner in 1930, following the death of Senator Overman. Reynolds charged that Morrison had used "his wife's money to defeat Senator Simmons: and then at the first opportunity played the part of the demagogue and embraced Senator Simmons' first lieutenant [Frank McNinch] in the campaign of 1928." Reynolds's strategy was to ridicule Morrison and to portray himself as a poor man (which he was not) and the "champion of the people." In his speeches Reynolds "would mimic the absurd postures and pompous stride of the millionaire Presbyterian Cam Morrison. His stage props were a red carpet, a big menu from Cam's hotel [the Mayflower in Washington], and a container of caviar." Reynolds would show his audiences the menu; he would hold up a jar of caviar, and then he would say: "Fish eggs that's what he eats. And fish eggs from Red Russia at that. . . . North Carolina hen eggs ain't good enough for him. Now fellow citizens let me ask you, do you want a senator who is not too high and mighty to eat good old North Carolina hen eggs?"

The vote in the first primary was Reynolds, 156,548; Morrison, 143,179; Tam C. Bowie, 37,748; and Frank D. Grist, 31,010. In the second primary, Reynolds defeated Morrison by the overwhelming vote of 227,864 to 120,428—the largest majority in a North Carolina primary up to that time. The man whom Robert M. Hanes had called "a clown, and a playboy, and a wisecracker" had virtually laughed Morrison out of the United States Senate.

In the general election Ehringhaus defeated Republican Clifford Frazier by a vote of 497,657 to 212,561; Reynolds won by an overwhelming vote. And North Carolina gave the Democratic candidate for president, Franklin Delano Roosevelt of New York, 498,006 to 208,345 for Republican Herbert Hoover, and 5,549 for Socialist Norman Thomas.

Chapter 44

THE NEW DEAL TO THE OUTBREAK OF WORLD WAR II, 1933-1941

When Governor Ehringhaus took office in January, 1933, economic conditions were at their worst. Cotton had dropped to five cents a pound, tobacco to eight cents, and other crop prices also reached new lows. Many farmers could not pay their taxes or pay off mortgages on their property. Accordingly many of them lost their farms. Industrial workers were also in a sad plight as wages continued to drop and unemployment reached an all-time high. Wholesale and retail trade, which had been declining since 1929, continued to drop. Bank failures multiplied. In the eight years before 1929 there had been bank closures in the state, with assets of $22,936,000. Between October of that year and March 15, 1933, there were 215 bank failures, with assets of $110,854,000. The resources of state banks dropped from $263,000,000 in 1931 to $212,000,000 the next year. Many county and municipal governments could not meet their financial obligations because of the inability of citizens to pay their taxes. In January, 1933, forty counties and 125 municipalities were in default on bond payments.

Efforts of the Ehringhaus Administration to Cope with the Depression

The financial situation of the state government was also critical. During the last three years of the Gardner administration the cost of state government had run far ahead of tax collections. The state had failed by about $7,000,000 to balance the budget for 1931–32, and had to borrow money—at a rate of 6 percent. The total state and local bonded debt in the latter year was $532,747,000, which was about one-ninth of the estimated total wealth in the state. Governor Ehringhaus declared that the state "had reached the cross roads of its financial destiny." Both he and the Democratic party were pledged to the removal of the fifteen cents ad valorem tax for the support of public schools. In the Democratic primary, Ehringhaus had called both the general sales tax and the luxury tax "economically unsound," "ethically debatable," and the "last expedient of desperation." The Tax Commission also considered the sales tax as "unsound, unfair and unwise," and recommended that no new taxes be imposed and that a program of rigid retrenchment be followed because it would be "unthinkable to place a ten million dollar additional tax burden upon the people of the State." To balance the budget the Tax Commission proposed a reduction in every item, except debt service, of about 15 percent, which would reduce general fund expenditures by about $3 million; a temporary diversion for the next two years of $2 million from the highway fund to the general fund; refunding of the general fund bonds for the next two years; repeal of the fifteen cents ad valorem tax, the loss to be compensated for by increasing existing income, franchise, and license taxes by about 20 percent.

Ehringhaus failed to endorse and the the General Assembly failed to follow these recommendations, but the governor's proposals for a revaluation of property and for the end of the fifteen cents ad valorem property tax were enacted by the 1933 legislature. His proposals to bring about economy by reorganizing and consolidating state agencies and functions ran into more difficulty, but most of these became law. A Parole and Pardon Commission was created; the State Board of Equalization was replaced by a State School Commission; the State Highway and Prison Departments were merged, and the Corporation Commission was replaced by a Utilities Commission, consisting of an elective commissioner and two associates, appointed by the governor.

Adoption of the 3 Percent General Sales Tax

The major fight in the 1933 General Assembly centered around taxation, particularly the sales tax. Industrial leaders maintained that any new taxes or higher taxes would wreck business. Insurance men insisted that North Carolina already collected the largest insurance tax in the nation. Tobacco company representatives pointed out that in the previous year that industry had paid 57 percent of all state income taxes. Merchants declared that further taxes would put them out of business.

It soon became obvious that the legislature was not going to raise taxes on business or impose a luxury tax. The friends of education stood ready to battle further cuts in school expenditures. Josephus Daniels, ardent foe of a general sales tax, declared he would "put a mortgage on this capitol" before he would "close the doors of learning to a single boy or girl in North Carolina." On January 31 about four thousand people assembled in Raleigh to urge the legislature not to default on the schools. Five days later, the *News and Observer* carried a huge headline: "Sales Tax Plans Now Linked with School Policies."

And on March 13 Governor Ehringhaus told a joint-session of the General Assembly, "If it is a choice between a sales tax on the one hand and a decent school on the other, I stand for the school," and declared that the state should "establish a state-wide uniform state-controlled school system with an eight months' term." The Merchants' Association bombarded the legislature with anti-sales tax petitions, declaring such a tax "the last resort of despotism" and the "badge of a bankrupt state." The *News and Observer* led the crusade for a luxury tax but to no avail. By a close vote the General Assembly rejected the luxury tax and passed a law placing a sales tax of 3 percent on all articles sold in the state, except a few necessities such as bread, flour, and meat. There was an outcry against the sales tax as a tax on the poor man—a "tax on poverty," as Commissioner of Revenue A. J. Maxwell called it. Nevertheless it became the largest source of revenue for the general fund and made possible the balancing of the state budget, which was now heavily burdened by the cost of roads and schools. To permit further reduction of local taxes and to maintain the public schools, the state government took over from the localities almost the entire support of the public schools and at the same time extended the minimum school term from six to eight months. The salaries of teachers and state employees, as well as all of the state services, were again reduced.

The End of Statewide Prohibition

The 1933 General Assembly also authorized a statewide referendum on prohibition at the coming November election. Though it was reasonably clear that the Eighteenth (Prohibition) Amendment would be repealed regardless of North Carolina's action, the organized dry forces were determined to retain legal prohibition. On the vote "to call a convention to consider the proposed amendment to the Constitution repealing the 18th Amendment," 120,190 voted "for Convention," and 293,484 voted "No Convention." Despite this overwhelming victory for the "drys," the antiprohibition forces were not willing to surrender. The 1935 legislature passed a bill to exempt Pasquotank County from the prohibition law and to establish an Alcoholic Beverage Control Board. The "Pasquotank Act," as amended and passed, granted local option to Pasquotank and fifteen other counties. On July 2, 1935, the first county-operated liquor store was opened at Wilson.

The New Deal

In March, 1933, while the General Assembly was still in session, Franklin D. Roosevelt became president of the United States. This was the beginning of the New Deal—the most far-reaching program of social and economic reform ever enacted into law in the United States.

Roosevelt's inaugural address gratified those who wanted promise of action to deal with one of the greatest crises that had ever faced the American people. To meet the emergency, he promised economy in government, relief for the unemployed, and assistance to the farmers. He said, "There must be a strict supervision of all banking and credits and investments; there must be an end to speculation with other people's money, and there must be provision for an adequate but sound currency." He would urge all these matters upon Congress, but should Congress fail to respond, he would use the executive power "to wage a war against the emergency, as great as the power that would be given to me if we were in fact invaded by a foreign foe." His insistence that "the only thing we have to fear is fear itself" gave hope to millions of listeners.

Coping with the Financial Crisis

In general the New Deal aimed at recovery, relief, and reform. And, as Roosevelt said "first things should come first." By the day he assumed office, March 4, 1933, every state had restricted banking operations or had invoked bank holidays. The day after inauguration, while awaiting the opening of a special session of Congress, he declared a national bank holiday and an embargo on the transportation and withdrawal of gold or silver. On March 9 Congress passed the Emergency Banking Act, which provided for the opening of sound banks when their solvency was assured. The Reconstruction Finance Corporation (RFC), which had been established in the Hoover Administration, might assist banks that were members of the Federal Reserve System by loaning them money on preferred stock, or it might even purchase such stock. The banks were eventually stabilized by government loans, by the separation of investment banking from commercial banking (under the Glass-Steagall Act of June, 1933), and by the insurance of all bank deposits up to $5,000 (by the Federal Deposit Insurance Corporation), and vast sums of money were loaned to banks and businesses by the RFC so that they could get on their feet again. Between October, 1932, and May, 1933, North Carolina received nearly $6 million in RFC grants.

Another emergency measure, approved by Congress in March, 1933, was the Economy Act, a feeble effort to carry out the pledge to balance the budget. Salaries of all government employees were cut 15 percent for a year, and veterans' pensions were readjusted to bring an estimated savings of $500 million. The amount actually saved was less than half that amount. The next year, however, Congress restored the former wage and pension scales over the president's veto. A third measure legalized the sale of "light" wine and beer with 3.2 percent alcoholic content. On May 1 the sale of light wine and beer became legal in North Carolina. Mention has already been made of the repeal of national prohibition.

Relief Measures and Agencies

The first relief agency created was the Civilian Conservation Corps (CCC), designed as both a relief and conservation agency. Approximately 300,000 men between the ages of seventeen and twenty-eight, inclusive, were recruited for work on such projects as flood control, reforestation, and road-building. CCC camps were established in North Carolina at many places. By the end of 1935 there were sixty-six such camps in the state and up to October of that year, nearly 27,000 men had been enrolled or reenrolled.

In May, 1933, the Federal Emergency Relief Administration (FERA) was set up to dispense both direct relief and work relief. Eventually this agency granted about $3 billion to local and state agencies for distribution. More permanent than FERA was the Public Works Administration (PWA). This agency eventually expended $4,250,000,000, chiefly before 1939, on some 35,-000 projects, including slum-clearance, low-cost housing, hospitals, public schools and other buildings, playgrounds and recreational facilities, highways, improvement of rivers and harbors, and conservation. A report of FERA, covering the period August 8, 1933, to December 5, 1935, shows that the average number of North Carolinians on relief during 1934 was 76,175 (11.8 percent of the population). In the first six months of 1935 the average was 68,907 (10.7 percent). The total grants for relief purposes in the state from FERA funds June 1, 1933 to December 5, 1935, amounted to $39,898,184; from PWA funds, $12,155,000.

The National Youth Administration (NYA), a relief agency created in June, 1935, provided funds to pay for part-time work of young people in high school and college and for vocational training for others. By June, 1936, some 475 projects were being carried on in the state; in the previous year 25,000 youths had been given part-time jobs and another 13,000 had been give jobs to aid in the continuance of their education.

The relief agency that caused the most controversy was the Works Progress Administration (WPA) established in April, 1935. This agency superseded FERA and eventually took over the relief aspects of PWA. Its numerous and varied projects included road and bridge building; constructing airfields; serving school lunches, conducting nursery schools; collecting historical data; decorating public buildings; and giving plays and concerts. The pay varied with the profession, skill, and locality, from $19 to $94 a month. Altogether WPA expended some $10,500,000,000; the total number of persons given work during the seven years of its existence was in excess of 8,500,000 persons. North Carolina shared in the program of public works, agricultural aid, and in various relief and construction projects. In the first five years of the New Deal, 1933–38, the state received $428,053,000 in "federal aid." Though this figure seems large, it is noteworthy that North Carolina received the lowest per capita amount of all the states—only $123.82 as contrasted with $1,114 for Nevada, $202 for

Mississippi, and $180 for South Carolina.

Although critics admitted the validity of the purpose and major phases of the WPA, they also asserted that many of the projects were foolish, encouraged laziness and "boondoggling," and resulted in shabby work, especially construction. Costs were alleged to be all out of proportion to benefits. The most serious charge was that "politics trafficked in relief needs," especially in election years—a charge upheld by a Senate Committee on Campaign Practices, of which the majority were Democrats.

Aid to the Farmer

To solve the critical farm problem, loans were made to farmers to save farms and finance crops. The Agricultural Adjustment Administration (AAA), created by a law of May, 1933, made "benefit payments" to farmers for limiting tobacco, cotton, wheat, and some other crops and for soil conservation. In January, 1936, the Supreme Court of the United States declared the Agricultural Adjustment Act unconstitutional on two counts. The regulation of agriculture was "a purely local activity," and therefore it was a right reserved to the states, and, secondly, the processing tax to raise money for "benefit payments" was an improper use of the taxing power. This decision caused the national administration to shift its emphasis to soil conservation. Under the Soil Conservation Act of February, 1936, the federal government allocated $5 million for conservation and flood control projects. Processing taxes were not revived. Instead the government made "benefit payments" to farmers who improved the fertility of their lands. Crop control reduced production and raised prices; rural electrification was extended, largely through the Rural Electrification Administration (1935); and, through the Farm Security Administration (1937), financial aid was extended to a selected number of tenants in order that they might become landowners. Under the New Deal program of controlled production, crop prices rose and the total income of North Carolina farmers increased from $150,081,000 in 1932 to $305,122,000 in 1935. The amount of "federal benefits" received by North Carolina farmers during the years 1933–40 totalled $99,351,000. Lured by high prices and irked by government regulation, southern farmers voted in 1938 to end federal control of tobacco production, though they voted to retain cotton control. North Carolina farmers voted against both tobacco and cotton control.

The New Deal and Business and Labor

Roosevelt called the National Industrial Recovery Act of June, 1933, "the most important and far-reaching legislation ever enacted by the American Congress." This law, usually called NRA, had many aims: to relieve unemployment, to curtail industrial production, to raise minimum wages and reduce hours of labor to protect the rights of labor to organize and to strike (Section 7-a of the law), to eliminate child labor, and to check the waste of competition without aiding the growth of monopolies. Each industry was required to draw up a "code of fair competition" to govern the conduct of that industry's business.

Within a short time complaints were raised against the NRA, especially by small businessmen, who claimed that the "codes" favored "big business." Wages increased, but prices advanced more rapidly. On May 27, 1935, the Supreme Court killed NRA when by a unanimous vote it declared that "Congress cannot delegate legislative power to the President to exercise an unfettered discretion to make whatever laws he thinks may be needed or advisable for the rehabilitation and expansion of trade or industry," that the fixing of wages and hours of labor for firms engaged in intrastate manufacturing was not a phase of interstate commerce and that therefore the federal government had no authority.

Congress quickly acted to pass the Wagner Act, the basic purpose of which was the same as Section 7-a of the NRA—that workers had the right to bargain collectively, that there must be no discrimination against union members, and that employers must sponsor company unions. Employers were no longer free to discharge workers for union activity or interfere unfairly with the rights of labor, without running the risk of punishment. The organization of labor unions in North Carolina proceeded with remarkable rapidity. Under direct federal stimulus, North Carolina established the Unemployment Compensation Commission in 1936 to maintain a statewide employment service and to administer a fund collected from taxes on employers' payrolls, from which unemployed workers might draw compensation during limited periods of unemployment. The federal Wages and Hours Act of 1938 established a minimum wage beginning at twenty-five cents an hour and maximum hours beginning at forty-four per week for all industries making goods for interstate commerce.

Under the direct stimulus of the federal Social Security Act of 1935, North Carolina embarked upon a system whereby the aged needy, the needy blind, and dependent children received monthly payments from federal, state, and local funds. Beginning in 1940, participants in the program who had reached the age of sixty-five were paid monthly pensions ranging from $10 to $84 a month. Some employers complained that Social Security forced them to pay taxes that were detrimental to business and that the whole plan was unconstitutional, but the Supreme Court upheld the law, and many people considered it one of the most liberal and beneficial measures of the New Deal.

The New Deal also took steps to protect investors from exploitation by sellers of stocks and other securities; placed heavier taxes and more stringent regulations upon business; manufactured cheap electricity (particularly through the Tennessee Valley Authority, commonly known as TVA) and brought the privately owned power companies under stricter control, pressing them to lower their rates; brought the telegraph, telephone, and radio under federal regulation; and did many other things of importance.

The New Deal measures and the expenditures of millions of dollars of federal money helped many North Carolinians—farmers, industrial workers, merchants, bankers, manufacturers, and professional men. The great improvement of conditions by 1935 enabled the state government to increase the salaries of teachers and state employees and to make larger appropriations for all the state's services. By 1939 every important state service had been more than restored to the 1930 level of financial support except the public schools and institutions of higher learning. North Carolina was well out of the depression, but many of its political leaders showed little enthusiasm for the liberal social and economic reforms of the New Deal, and some of them thought that the nation was enjoying an artificial and "phony" prosperity. Yet more North Carolinians held high posts in the national administration under Roosevelt than ever before. Among these were Robert L. Doughton, chairman of the Ways and Means Committee of the House of Representatives; Lindsay Warren, comptroller general of the United States; Josephus Daniels, ambassador to Mexico, 1933–41; R. D. W. Connor, first archivist of the United States, 1934–41.

The Election of 1936

In the first Democratic primary of 1936 Clyde R. Hoey of Shelby, brother-in-law of former governor O. Max Gardner, received 193,972 votes to 189,504 for Dr. Ralph McDonald, and 127,000 for Lieutenant Governor A. H. Graham. In the second primary, Hoey won over McDonald by a vote of 266,354 to 214,414. In the general election Hoey defeated Republican Gilliam Grissom, 542,139 to 270,843. J. W. Bailey was re-elected to the United States Senate, and Franklin D. Roosevelt carried the state over Republican Alfred M. Landon by a vote of 616,141 to 223,284. Two years later Robert R. Reynolds was re-elected to the United States Senate.

The Administration of Clyde R. Hoey, 1937–1941

The General Assembly of 1937 rejected the proposed federal Child Labor Amendment, but it raised the prohibitory age for employment of children in industry to sixteen years, and to eighteen for certain hazardous occupations. It also enacted a general law limiting the hours of industrial labor to forty-eight for women and fifty-five for men, with many exceptions. This legislature enacted a statewide county option liquor bill and created a State Board of Alcoholic Beverage Control. Under the new system Alcoholic Beverage Control (ABC) stores were established in more than one-fourth of the counties, largely in the East.

The General Assembly of 1939, in response to the public demand for cleaner elections—as Governor Hoey said, "to stop racketeering at the ballot boxes," —repealed the absentee ballot laws for primaries. A law was passed authorizing free textbooks in public schools for elementary grades and textbook rental system for high schools. To meet the issue of graduate and professional education for Negroes, two state-supported Negro colleges were authorized to establish graduate and professional schools in liberal arts, agricultural and technical studies, law, pharmacy, and library science.

The Election of 1940

In the 1940 Democratic gubernatorial primary J. Melville Broughton of Raleigh led the field of seven candidates, receiving 147,386 votes to 105,916 for Lieutenant Governor W. P. Horton, 102,095 for A. J. Maxwell, and a total of 134,000 for four other candidates. Broughton became the nominee when Horton failed to demand a second primary. In the November election, Broughton defeated Republican Robert H. McNeill, 609,015 to 195,402—the largest majority ever given a candidate for governor in North Carolina history. President Roosevelt carried the state over Republican Wendell Wilkie, 608,744 to 213,633.

Chapter 45

WORLD WAR II AND AFTER: PROGRESS AND PROBLEMS, 1941-1952

The administration of Governor J. Melville Broughton began with unusual political harmony and a spirit of liberality, especially in regard to public education and various state services. The General Assembly of 1941 greatly increased appropriations to state agencies and public schools, doubled the support for vocational education, made a beginning toward the addition of a twelfth grade, increased salaries of public school teachers, established a pension and retirement system for teachers and other state employees, and greatly increased appropriations for institutions of higher learning. Because of the increase of the state's population (to 3,571,623), as revealed by the 1940 Census, a twelfth Congressional district was created, and representation in the national House of Representatives was reapportioned.

Preparations for National Defense

By the time the 1941 legislature adjourned people in North Carolina and throughout the nation had become vitally concerned about national defense and the possibility of American entry into World War II, which had been raging since Hitler's German armies invaded Poland in September, 1939. In May, 1940, Congress had answered President Roosevelt's request for 50,000 planes with an appropriation of $1 billion; by the end of the summer $5 billion had been voted. By November a total of $18 billion had been authorized for a "two-ocean navy," an army of 1,200,000 men, and an increase in the staff of federal "G-men," and for production of war materials. In September the first peace-time draft law in American history was passed.

As early as May, 1940, Roosevelt had appointed an agency to coordinate production, the National Defense Advisory Commission; in December this agency was supplemented by the Office of Production Management. To deal with labor problems, the National Defense Mediation Board was established in March, 1941. Because the wartime boom tended to force prices up, the president, in April, established the Office of Price Administration and Civilian Supply, better known as OPA. In May the Office of Civilian Defense was established, with citizens serving on a voluntary basis, to take care of problems of home defense as they affected local communities.

The United States Becomes "The Arsenal of Democracy."

As the plight of England and France became more desperate, war came closer to the United States. In the language of Winston Churchill, British prime minister, "England stood alone," and only Britain and her navy stood guard. To safeguard British lifelines along the supply routes, more warships were desperately needed. On September 3, 1940, President Roosevelt announced that he had completed negotiations with Great Britain for a ninety-nine year lease of bases in Newfoundland and Bermuda without rental, but as "gifts—generously given and gladly received," and a number of lesser ones in exchange for fifty "over-age" American destroyers. In March, 1941, Congress passed the Lend-Lease bill, by the provisions of which the United States would manufacture military supplies that could be transferred to Britain without cash payments. Congress allotted $7 billion to finance this program. The United States was now openly and deeply committed to a policy of supporting the enemies of the Axis (Germany, Italy, and Japan) throughout the world.

On May 27, 1941, Roosevelt proclaimed the existence of an "unlimited emergency." German and Italian merchant shipping in American harbors had been seized by the end of March; in June the German and Italian consulates in the United States were closed. By midsummer the United States was fully committed to assist Great Britain "in all means short of war." On November 13 Congress repealed that section of the neutrality laws which forbade arming merchant ships. The United States was engaged in war at sea in everything except name.

Finally, on December 7, 1941, while two Japanese representatives were engaging in "peace talks" at Washington with Secretary of State Cordell Hull, planes from Japanese carriers swooped down in a "sneak attack" on the American naval base at Pearl Harbor, Hawaii. Nearly 4,500 Americans were killed or wounded, eight battleships were sunk or severely damaged along with a number of smaller craft, and about 250 planes were destroyed. On the next day President Roosevelt appeared before Congress to inform that body that on "December 7, 1941—a date which will live in infamy—the United States of America was suddenly and deliberately attacked." Congress approved the declaration of a state of war, with only one dissenting vote. Three days later Germany and Italy fulfilled their obligations to their Axis partner, Japan, by declaring war on the United States. Immediately Congress responded with similar declarations—and without a dissenting vote.

North Carolina's Role in World War II

The national defense program and World War II had important effects on North Carolina. Fort Bragg, near Fayetteville, was greatly enlarged, so that with its 122,000 acres and 3,135 buildings and a maximum load of nearly 100,000 men, it was "the most comprehensive of Army installations, performing more different functions than any other camp." More than one hundred army, navy, marine, and coast guard stations were established in the state. Camp Lejeune was the second largest marine base in the nation, Cherry Point one of the largest marine air bases. Camp Butner was one of the largest infantry camps as was Camp Davis. At Camp Mackall, the second largest airborne training center in the nation, the famous 82nd and 101st Airborne Divisions were trained, as well as the 11th and 13th. There were large air-installations at Elizabeth City and Edenton, and the navy receiving station and center at Wilmington. In these various installations, more than two million fighting men were trained for combat. Supporting all the services were thousands of volunteers in the Red Cross, the Civilian Air Patrol, the Coast Guard Reserve, and the United Service Organization (USO), which dispatched entertainers to troops in battle areas, and set up recreational facilities at home and abroad.

The total number of men registered by local draft boards in North Carolina as of June 1, 1945, was 1,137,276. The percentage of rejection for all physical causes in the state was 27.8, in contrast with the national percentage of 23.9. Many of the registrants were given either "agricultural deferment," "non-agricultural occupational deferment," or "deferment to prevent extreme hardship in home."

From the state's total population of about 3,600,000, some 362,000 young North Carolinians, including more than 7,000 women, entered the various armed services—258,000 in the army, 90,000 in the navy, 13,000 in the marines, and most of the remainder in the Coast Guard. Approximately 4,000 North Carolina women served in the Women's Army Auxiliary Corps (WAAC or WAC); the Women Accepted for Volunteer Emergency Service (WAVES), a navy subsidiary; the Women's Auxiliary Ferrying Service (WAFS), associated with the marines; and the SPARS (from *Semper Paratus*), a branch of the Coast Guard. Many others served as nurses, medical technicians, and in other capacities.

North Carolinians served around the world in every important battle zone. In the war against Japan they participated in the Philippine campaigns, the conquest of the East Indies, the naval battles of Coral Sea and Midway, the bloody victory at Guadalcanal, the invasion and capture of Iwo Jima and of "bloody Okinawa," and many other battles in the Pacific. They took part in the fighting along the China-India-Burma front. They served under General Dwight D. Eisenhower in the invasion of North Africa in November, 1942, and under General Mark Clark in the invasion of Italy in the summer of 1943. They also took part in the invasion of France on "D-Day," June 6, 1944. Many North Carolinians fought in the Third Army of General George B. Patton and the First Army of Courtney Hodges, as these and other fighting units swept across France, Belgium, and Luxembourg, defeating the Germans in the battle of the "Bulge," and finally driving on to the Rhine. Finally, on May 8, 1945, "V-E Day," the German armies surrendered. On September 2, "V-J Day," the Japanese surrendered in formal ceremonies aboard the U.S.S. *Missouri* in Tokyo Bay. Thus ended the most costly and destructive war in all history.

In World War II more than 291,000 Americans were killed, five times the battle deaths of World War I. More than 7,000 North Carolinians lost their lives, and many thousands were wounded. Secretary of War Kenneth C. Royall of Goldsboro, writing in May, 1946, said: "But in World War II North Carolina could not be associated primarily with any particular division or unit. North Carolinians served in every unit which fought in Africa and Europe under Eisenhower, or Patton, or Hodges, or Bradley—or, in the Pacific under MacArthur, Kreuger, Nimitz, or Vandergrift. . . . Our State paid with the lives of between 7,000 and 8,000 of her young men. Many others were casualties—who will carry grievous wounds of war the remainder of their lives. No North Carolina city, no town, no rural section escaped. These boys, the dead and living wounded, are the real heroes of this war—these boys and those living who were awarded decorations for valor. These are the men to whom our State and every part thereof should never fail to pay tribute."

World War II did more to bring the nation out of the depression than had "pump priming" and the various nostrums of the New Deal. The fact that North Carolina had more than a third of a million men in service had a significant bearing on its unemployment problem. Huge expenditures by the federal government for war materials further reduced the number of unemployed; they also caused taxes, wages, and prices to rise. Men, women, and children "on the home front" worked hard to produce enough war and civilian supplies to meet the emergency situation. In eight war and victory bond drives, North Carolinians purchased $1,811,000,000 worth of United States savings bond. Teachers and students in the state's schools and colleges sponsored millions of dollars' worth of planes, jeeps, ships, ambulances and hospital equipment, both by purchasing and selling $43,074,000 in War Bonds and Savings Stamps.

The State's Industrial Contributions to the War

Almost $2 billion was spent in North Carolina directly by the armed forces in connection with the purchase of manufactured war supplies and materials; this did not include subcontracting, that is, the amounts sold by North Carolina industries to producers, who, in turn, sold directly to the government. Eighty-three of the state's industrial plants manufactured and sold directly to various defense agencies $1,358,000,000 worth of war materials. North Carolina delivered to the Quartermaster Corps more textile goods than did any other state—sheets, blankets, clothing, tents, bandages, parachutes, tire cords and fabrics, and other materials. At Kure Beach, the Ethyl-Dow Plant manufactured all the tetraethyl lead used by the United States in the war, and the state supplied more than 50 percent of all mica. North Carolina ranked fourth in the production of lumber for the armed forces. Many North Carolina products became symbols of good workmanship. Twenty-eight of the industrial plants in the state received a total of 72 army-navy "E" awards for outstanding war production records. An "M," or Maritime award, was made to the North Carolina Ship Corporation at Wilmington, which turned out 126 Liberty ships and 232 other ships, having a total value of more than $475,000,000. One of the North Carolina plants producing war materials employed more than 5,500 workers; one employed only 68. The construction industry in the state produced almost a half billion dollars in army and navy cantonments, airfields, and military installations, and "also produced for defense homes, and housing projects, and public works therewith—many more millions of dollars."

Politics during the War Years

The major objective of North Carolinians and all loyal Americans was winning the war. But this did not mean that they forgot politics or the activities of state and local governments. In the Democratic primary in June, 1942, Senator Josiah W. Bailey defeated Richard T. Fountain by a vote of 211,000 to 95,000. In November the voters elected a solid Democratic delegation to Congress and an overwhelming majority of members of the General Assembly. They also adopted a constitutional amendment to centralize authority over the public schools in an appointive State Board of Education.

The first wartime legislature in the state since 1865 adjourned on March 19, 1943, after a short and harmonious fifty-five-day session. Emergency war powers were granted to the governor and council of state; provision was made for a nine months' school term; a state school for delinquent Negro girls was authorized; appropriations were made to the North Carolina Art Society and to the North Carolina Symphony Society (organized at Chapel Hill in March, 1932)—the first instance of the state's giving financial aid to art and music; provision was made for unified administrative control of public schools, of state correctional institutions, and of state institutions for mental defectives; a fund of $20 million was set aside for use by the state government after the war, and record-breaking appropriations were made for public schools, institutions of higher learning, and various state agencies—without any increase in taxes.

Governor Broughton took the lead in working out plans for a statewide medical care program, whose ultimate purposes, he said, "should be that no person in North Carolina shall lack adequate hospital care or medical treatment by reason of poverty or low income." In February, 1944, he appointed a commission to survey the hospital and medical care needs of the state and to recommend a program to the next General Assembly. After many months of study and investigation, a program emphasizing the need for more doctors, more hospitals, and more insurance was adopted by the legislature.

The 1944 Election

In the Democratic primary of 1944 R. Gregg Cherry of Gastonia won the gubernatorial nomination over Dr. Ralph McDonald, 185,027 to 134,461. Clyde R. Hoey, the incumbent, won the senatorial nomination over Cameron Morrison by a vote of 211,049 to 80,154. In the November election, Cherry defeated Republican Frank C. Patton, by a vote of 528,095 to 230,998; Hoey won over A. L. Ferree 534,000 to 226,000, and President Roosevelt carried the state for the fourth time, by a vote of 527,390 to 263,155 for Republican Thomas E. Dewey.

The Administration of Governor Cherry

Cherry's administration (1945–49) was marked by political harmony, continued economic prosperity, and caution in view of the future, which was uncertain because of the war and its aftermath. The 1945 legislature made large appropriations to state agencies and the public schools. Salaries of state employees and public school teachers were increased, and the compulsory school attendance age was raised from fourteen to sixteen years. The legislature left intact the $20 million postwar reserve fund set up in 1943, with the exception of earmarking $5 million for aid to veterans of World War II. About $52 million were set aside from the surplus in the treasury to pay off the entire general-fund debt of the state government. Record-breaking annual appropriations of $116 million were held within estimated revenues. The 3 percent general sales tax was removed from some items, but the tax on wines was sharply increased. A new State Board of Education was established and given control over public school funds. Important beginnings were made for a four-year medical school (there had been a two-year one for many years) and teaching hospital at the University of North Carolina at Chapel Hill and a statewide system of hospitals, health centers, and clinics designed to provide better service for the people. The Five-Year Hospital Plan, inaugurated on July 8, 1947, was virtually completed by 1953, some 127 projects having been authorized at a cost of over $68 million. Under this plan approximately five thousand new hospital beds had been provided or contracted for, making North

Carolina second only to Texas in the number added in the five-year period after July 1, 1947. Of the $68,000,000, over $24,000,000 came from federal funds, over $29,000,000 from local funds, and a little more than $14,000,000 from state revenues.

The Election of 1948

The Democratic primary contests of 1948 were close and bitter. In the first gubernatorial primary Charles M. Johnson, state treasurer, received 170,141 votes; W. Kerr Scott, Alamance County dairy farmer and former commissioner of agriculture, 161,293; R. Mayne Albright, Raleigh attorney, 76,281; and Oscar Barker, Durham lawyer, 10,871. In the second primary Scott scored a surprising victory over Johnson by a vote of 217,620 to 182,684. J. Melville Broughton won the Democratic senatorial primary nomination over William B. Umstead of Durham, who had been appointed by Governor Cherry in 1946 to fill out the unexpired term of Josiah W. Bailey, who had died in office. In November Scott defeated Republican George M. Pritchard, 570,995 to 206,166. Harry S. Truman, who had succeeded to the presidency upon the death of President Roosevelt in April, 1945, carried the state by a vote of 459,070 to 258,572 for Republican Thomas E. Dewey, 69,652 for Strom Thurmond (State Rights party), and 3,915 for Progressive Henry Wallace.

The Scott Administration (1949–1953)

Under the forceful, aggressive leadership of W. Kerr Scott, the General Assembly and the voters, by popular referendum, adopted the governor's "Go Forward" program and voted a bond issue of $200 million for secondary road construction, accompanied by an increase in the state tax on gasoline from six to seven cents a gallon, and $25 million to be allocated to the counties on the basis of average daily school attendance to aid in the construction and repair of school buildings. It seemed strange to some people that Governor Scott advocated a bond issue of such magnitude, because in the Democratic primary contests of 1948 he had criticized Charles Johnson's proposal for a bond issue of $100 million. It was apparent that the people, and especially the farmers, were in favor of improved county roads, which would "get them out of the mud" and enable them to take their produce to market with more ease.

The General Assembly of 1949 made record-breaking appropriations for the biennium of $401,417,791 to operate the state agencies and institutions, another $25,000,000 to be distributed equally among the counties to aid in the construction or repair of public school buildings, and $72,827,734 for buildings and other improvements at state institutions and agencies. The legislature authorized the issue of $7,500,000 in bonds for the construction and improvement of North Carolina port facilities, and it made the state a party to the compact of southern states for the development and maintenance of regional educational services in the South in professional, technological, scientific, literary, and other fields. It also authorized the university at Chapel Hill to establish and operate a standard dental school in connection with the four-year medical school. The salaries of teachers and other state employees were raised again.

During the remainder of Scott's administration the state felt the impact of the Go Forward program for greater progress in rural road construction, public education, rural electrification, and public health and welfare. There was also marked progress in port development, terminal facilities equipped to handle ocean shipping at Wilmington and Morehead City being completed in 1952. A significant development occurred in higher education when, on May 27, 1951, the Fourth United States Circuit Court of Appeals, reversing a 1950 District Court decision, ruled that Negroes must be admitted to the University of North Carolina's law school if they met standard requirements. In the summer and fall sessions of 1951 Negroes were admitted to the law, medical, and graduate schools at Chapel Hill, and the 162-year-old university broke its long-standing policy of racial segregation. Another important event in higher education occurred a few months later when, on October 15, President Truman made the principal address at the ground-breaking ceremony in connection with the removal of 117-year-old Wake Forest College to a four-hundred-acre estate, formerly belonging to R. J. Reynolds, just outside Winston-Salem.

United States Senator Broughton died soon after taking office in March, 1949, and Governor Scott surprised many people by appointing as his successor the state's best known liberal, Frank P. Graham, president of the University of North Carolina. In the Democratic primary on May 27, 1950 Graham received 303,605 votes; Willis Smith, Raleigh lawyer, 250,222; former Senator Robert R. Reynolds, 58,752; and Olla Ray Boyd, 5,900. The total vote, 619,479, established an all-time record in a state Democratic primary. In a heated second primary, Smith defeated Graham, 281,114 to 261,789, in a contest involving state rights and the social, economic, and civil rights policies of President Harry Truman's Fair Deal administration—and perhaps the policies of the state administration as well. The race issue—desegregation of public schools— projected into the limelight by a United States Supreme Court decision was of major importance for the first time since the white supremacy campaign of 1900. In the general election in November Smith defeated Republican E. R. Gavin, 364,912 to 177,753, and Senator Clyde R. Hoey won over Republican H. B. Leavitt by a vote of 376,472 to 171,804.

North Carolinians in the Truman Administration

The election returns from 1932 to 1952 seemed to indicate that North Carolinians were losing their enthusiasm for the New Deal of President

Roosevelt and the Fair Deal of his successor, Harry Truman. The total popular vote in the state for Roosevelt showed a steady decline from 1936 to 1944, and Truman's 1948 vote was 157,000 less than that received by Roosevelt in 1936. Despite this apparent cooling off to the policies of the Democratic administration by the state's electorate, more North Carolinians held important positions in the Truman administration than at any time in history. In 1947 Kenneth Royall of Goldsboro became secretary of war, the last man to hold that position before the creation of the Department of Defense, in which Royall served as secretary of the army, 1947–49. He was succeeded in this position by Gordon Gray of Winston-Salem, who served until mid-1950, when he resigned to become president of the University of North Carolina. O. Max Gardner became under secretary of the treasury in 1946, and the next year Truman appointed him ambassador to England, but Gardner died eight hours before the scheduled sailing time to assume this important post. James Webb of Oxford became director of the budget in 1946 and under secretary of the treasury in 1949. John S. Graham of Winston-Salem was assistant secretary of the treasury in 1948. Dan Edwards of Durham became assistant secretary of defense in 1951. Judges F. Donald Phillips of Rockingham and Richard Dillard Dixon of Edenton, were members of the International Military Tribunal that tried the German war criminals at Nuremberg in 1946–47, while Carlisle Higgins of Winston-Salem helped prosecute the Japanese war criminals. T. Lamar Caudle of Wadesboro was assistant attorney general, 1945-51. George Allen, a career diplomat from Durham, was ambassador to Iran, 1946–50, ambassador to Yugoslavia, 1950–53, and then ambassador to India. Capus Waynick of High Point served as Ambassador to Nicaragua, 1948–50, and then became ambassador to Colombia. Luther H. Hodges was chief of the Economic Cooperation Administration's industry division in West Germany in 1950–51. Robert Hanes of Winston-Salem was chief of ECA's mission to Belgium and Luxembourg in 1949 and was assistant to the United States high commissioner in Germany in 1949–50. For a short period Jonathan Daniels was press secretary to President Truman, and later published *The Man of Independence,* one of the best biographies of Truman. The *Official Register of the United States* for 1952 listed some three hundred North Carolinians holding "top federal jobs."

The Election of 1952

In the Democratic gubernatorial primary of 1952 William B. Umstead, who had served in both houses of Congress, defeated Judge Hubert E. Olive, who had the open support of Governor W. Kerr Scott, by the narrow margin of 294,170 to 265,175. But the apparent split in the party was soon healed and in November Umstead was elected governor by a tremendous majority, 796,306 to 383,329 for his Republican opponent, H. F. ("Chub")

Seawell, Jr. North Carolina gave the Democratic candidate for president, Adlai E. Stevenson 652,803 votes to 558,107 for Republican Dwight David Eisenhower—a majority of only 94,696, as compared to a majority of 412,977 for Umstead.

Chapter 46

THE MODERN INDUSTRIAL REVOLUTION AFTER 1930

As has been indicated in Chapter 41, North Carolina in the 1920s became the leading industrial state in the Southeast and the nation's largest producer of textiles, tobacco products, and wooden furniture. It retained that supremacy after 1930 despite the phenomenal industrial development of many other states, notably those in the South.

Increase in the Value of Manufactures

The Great Depression reduced the total value of North Carolina manufactures from $1,312,000,000 in 1930 to $878,000,000 in 1933, but recovery brought it to $1,112,000,000 in 1935 and to $1,421,000 in 1939. Inflation and economic expansion during and following World War II increased the total value of manufactures to $5,031,000,000 in 1950; to $9,161,000,000 in 1959; and to $15,129,600,000 in 1967. The total value of North Carolina manufactures and leading industries is revealed in the table on page 631.

Between 1939 and 1967 the number of manufacturing establishments in the state increased two and a half times from 3,225 to 8,266. The net gain of more than 5,000 new industrial plants was not matched by any other southern state. In 1971 North Carolina ranked first in the nation in the value of textile, tobacco, and furniture manufacture. Although the total value of manufactures was increased fifteen times from 1900 to 1930, the number of wage earners increased less than four times, from 70,570 to 270,210, and the total wages about fourteen times, from $14,000,000 to 199,000,000. The number of wage earners and their total wages greatly increased in the prosperous—and inflationary—forties to 350,000 and $6,000,000, respectively, in 1947; to 402,631 and $788,812,000, respectively in 1951; and to 648,300 and $3,066,100,000, respectively, in 1967.

630

	1939	*1949*	*1959*	*1967*
Textiles	$ 549,700,000	$1,913,700,000	$3,104,000,000	$5,935,100,000
Tobacco	538,400,000	841,000,000	2,321,000,000	2,354,000,000
Foods	69,200,000	293,300,000	723,000,000	1,309,000,000
Chemicals	50,700,000	162,500,000	410,000,000	702,000,000
Lumber	45,800,000	167,800,000	275,000,000	386,000,000
Paper Pulp	26,000,000	158,800,000	431,000,000	487,000,000
Furniture	58,800,000	180,800,000	520,000,000	945,000,000
Others	82,700,000	361,500,000	1,377,000,000	3,011,500,000
Total	$1,421,300,000	$4,079,800,000	$9,161,000,000	$15,129,600,000
Employees	270,210	380,700	505,000	648,300
Establishments	3,225	5,414	7,300	8,266

Although modern North Carolina manufacturing is decentralized and tending to become more so each year, with cotton mills and other industrial plants located in many counties, before 1950 there was a notable concentration in the Piedmont and to a lesser degree in the Mountain region, because of the accessibility of cheap labor and hydroelectric power. At mid-century twelve of the fifteen leading manufacturing counties were in the Piedmont and three in the Mountain region. After 1950, however, a number of large industrial plants were established in Lenoir, New Hanover, and several other counties in the Coastal Plain area.

The Textile Industry

Because of its decentralization, its extensive employment of labor, and the total value of its product, textile manufacturing has long been the major industry of North Carolina. The total value of textile manufactures increased over fifteen times, from about $30,000,000 in 1900 to $459,000,000 in 1930; it was $549,700,000 in 1939, $1,913,700,000 in 1949 and $5,935,-100,000 in 1967. The number of textile workers increased over four times, from 32,000 in 1900 to 125,000 in 1930; in 1939 there were 175,000 textile workers and in 1967, 257,200. In 1940 there were 609 textile mills in the state; in 1967 there were 1,262.

North Carolina has more textile mills than any other state, employs more textile workers, has one-fourth of the spindles in the entire industry, leads in the production of synthetic fibers, leads the South in the production of all knit goods and rayon, and has more knitting mills than any other state. The School of Textile Design at North Carolina State University has the largest textile research department in the nation. North Carolina has long led the nation in the manufacture of cotton goods and, in recent years, of nylon hosiery. One of the earliest and largest producers of rayon and nylon has been the American Enka Corporation, near Asheville, which began operation in 1939.

The chief textile products of the state have been cotton goods, consisting mainly of yarns and cloth, concentrated in about a dozen counties, with Gaston, Mecklenburg, and Guilford being the leaders; knit goods consisting chiefly of hosiery and underwear; silk and rayon products; dyeing and finishing; men's work clothes, such as overalls; woolen goods, cordage and twine. Recent tendencies are toward the production of finer quality yarns and goods and an increase in the size of the manufacturing unit. Overalls, underwear, and hosiery have been the most extensive manufacture of finished wearing apparel. In 1967 the state had 473 plants manufacturing wearing apparel and other textile products, with 64,000 workers, and a product valued at $473,000,000. The manufacture of hosiery, synthetics, and woolens rose rapidly after 1945, and a number of Northern mills either moved to North Carolina or established branches in the state. Vast new factories were established after 1950 to produce DuPont Dacron at Kinston and Union Carbide Dynel at Eden.

North Carolina has many "firsts" in the textile industry. It boasts the largest towel factory in the world at Kannapolis, the largest hosiery mill at Durham, the largest denim mill at Greensboro, the largest damask mill at Roanoke Rapids, the largest men's underwear factory at Winston-Salem, the largest producer of woolen blankets at Elkin, and "the world's combed yarn capital" at Gastonia. Gaston County has more cotton mills than any county in the United States.

Consolidation of Textile Mills

In addition to the phenomenal growth of textile manufactures; the rapid increase in the production of rayon, nylon, dacron, orlon, and various synthetics; and the expansion of woolen manufactures, the textile industry spread over a wider area. One of the most significant developments in North Carolina textiles after 1930 was the purchase of many smaller mills by some of the larger companies, notably Burlington Mills and Cone Mills, and the growth of "textile empires." The rise of Burlington Mills (now called Burlington Industries) was litttle less than spectacular. Founded in 1924 and employing only 200 workers that year, by 1934 this company was the largest weaver of rayon fabrics in the United States. By 1942 it was the largest single producer of rayon yarns in the nation and had 44 plants and 16,000 employees. During World War II it produced more than fifty different products for the government; it entered the foreign field in 1944, with plants in Cuba and Australia; and in 1971 it had 132 plants in ninety-two communities in fifteen states and eleven foreign countries and Puerto Rico, with about 87,000 employees and an annual product of approximately $1,832,539,000.

The "Passing of the Mill Village"

Another significant trend in the North Carolina textile industry has been the gradual "passing of the mill village." As Harriet Herring wrote, "The company-owned village has been a conspicuous adjunct of the cotton mill whenever and wherever this branch of textiles has sprung up." But since 1934 North Carolina mill owners, for one reason or another, have been selling their "company houses" to the employees. By 1950 more mills in the state, both in actual members—83—and in percentage—21.8—had sold their dwellings than in all of the other southern states combined. This trend continued after 1950, but at a slower pace. In contrast with many mill towns in other states, the highways leading to many of North Carolina's industrial towns are lined with houses of mill workers, and have been called "stringtowns," a development closely related to the building of good roads, which enabled mill owners to draw labor "from the countryside for miles around."

Tobacco Manufacturing

For a few years in the late 1920s tobacco replaced textiles as the leader in total value of products, but since 1939 the textile industry has always held first place. By the 1950s the annual value of textile products was usually about twice that of tobacco. The value of tobacco manufactures, consisting chiefly of cigarettes and pipe tobacco, increased more than thirty times from $16,000,000 in 1900 to $480,000,000 in 1951. By 1967 some forty-five plants turned out a product valued at $2,354,500,000. The number of workers increased from 16,500 in 1939 to 39,000 in 1959. Intensive mechanization caused a drop in the number of workers to 27,300 in 1967. In contrast with textile manufactures, tobacco manufacturing has been concentrated in four cities and in four gigantic companies—R. J. Reynolds Tobacco Company of Winston-Salem (Winston, Camel, and Salem cigarettes); Liggett and Myers Company of Durham (Chesterfield and L and M); the American Tobacco Company of Reidsville (Lucky Strike and Pall Mall); and P. Lorillard and Company of Greensboro (Kent and Old Gold).

The Ecusta Corporation, in operation near Brevard since August, 1939,"manufactures from flax the paper for most of the cigarettes of America." Growing about two-fifths of the nation's tobacco and manufacturing more than one-half of the nation's tobacco products, North Carolina is truly "Tobacco-land" and the tobacco center of the United States and of the world.

Forest Products Industries

Textiles and tobacco accounted for more than half the dollar value production of North Carolina manufactures in the twentieth century, but some other industries reached major proportions, particularly after 1940.

The forest products industries—chiefly lumber, paper, and furniture—ranked third among the states' manufactures. The total value of products of these industries increased seven times from $19,000,000 in 1900 to $139,-000,000 in 1930, to $788,000,000 in 1951, and to $1,848,500,000 in 1967. The state became the leading producer of wooden furniture, with particular emphasis on furniture for bedroom, dining room, and kitchen. In recent years it has entered the field of fine upholstered furniture. High Point has been the chief center of furniture manufacturing and marketing from the start, but the industry is important in Thomasville, Lexington, Statesville, Lenoir, Hickory, Newton-Conover, Mount Airy, Sanford, and a number of other towns, particularly in the Piedmont.

For many years furniture was the leading branch of the forest products industry, but by 1951 lumber ranked first, paper pulp second, and furniture a close third. By 1954, however, "furniture and fixtures" had regained first place; in 1967 the state had 558 establishments manufacturing household furniture, with 58,500 workers, and a product valued at $945,400,000. The Champion Paper and Fibre Company at Canton, which began operation in 1908, is one of the world's largest paper mills, and at Acme, in Columbus county, a $25,000,000 plant of Reigel Corporation manufactures a great variety of paper products. In 1967 the state had 119 establishments, with 25,000 workers, manufacturing "paper and allied products," such as containers and boxes, valued at $487,000,000. By the mid-forties the state's annual lumber production averaged about one and one-half billion feet, a record exceeded by only four other states, and constituting over 4 percent of the nation's total. In 1967 the state had 2,299 lumber plants, with 25,000 employees, and a product valued at $386,100,000.

Other Industries

Other significant industries, some of which grew at phenomenal rates, were food products, largely flour, bread, foodstuffs, and butter; chemicals, notably fertilizers, medicines, and cottonseed oil; electrical machinery, and machinery other than electrical; and printing and publishing. In 1969 the state had 793 food-processing plants, with 36,200 workers, and a product of $1,308,500,000. In that year the chemicals industry in the state had 227 plants, 17,700 employees, and a product of $702,200,000.

The construction industry rose from $76,000,000 in 1939 to more than $800,000,000 in 1971. North Carolina has three of the largest construction companies in the United States. They are J. A. Jones Construction Company of Charlotte, Nello Teer Company of Durham, and H. L. Coble Construction Company of Greensboro. These firms operate not only throughout North Carolina, but also in many other states and in foreign countries.

Two of the largest concerns of their kind in the nation are the Carolina Aluminum Company of Badin and Vick Chemical Company of Greensboro, "world famous drug and cosmetics manufacturers."

North Carolina in recent years has "many examples of industries which step completely beyond the pattern of our traditional industry." The Ecusta plant, already mentioned, is an illustration. So is the rubber plant at Marion, the piano factories at Granite Falls, Hickory, Granite Quarry, and Morganton, and the factory of Proctor Company at Mount Airy—the "largest plant in the world completely devoted to the manufacture of automatic toasters." But perhaps the best example of all is seen in the state's rapid rise as a producer of electrical and electronic equipment. Before World War II this industry was almost nonexistent in North Carolina; in 1939 there were 3 such plants and they employed only 66 people. In 1955, after an investment of almost $42,000,000, there were at least 40 plants making electrical or electronic equipment and employing some 22,000 persons. According to the 1967 Census of Manufactures, the state had 517 establishments manfacturing "machinery, except electrical," with 21,800 employees, and a product of $552,400,000. At the same time, it had 119 establishments making "electric equipment and supplies," with 34,300 employees, and a product valued at $831,700,000. In 1971 Western Electric with plants at Winston-Salem, Greensboro, and Burlington employed more than 14,000 workers. Among other large national concerns with plants in the state are Westinghouse, General Electric, National Carbon, Great Lakes Carbon, and Sylvania.

To encourage the development of small industries in North Carolina, in 1955 the state government sponsored the North Carolina Business Development Corporation, first headed by Capus Waynick, and with $500,000 capital provided by interested citizens.

The Tourist Industry

The most spectacular growth of all, though not considered as a manufacture, has been the tourist or "travel-serving" industry, which by 1970 had an estimated value of $802 million. In that year an estimated 40 million people from out of state visited North Carolina. The state has three superlative features that have tended to make it "Variety Vacationland": the most unusual coastline and some of the finest beaches in the eastern United States; the mild, dry Sandhills area, which has become a mecca for golfers; and the largest and most varied mountain area in the East. Since 1950 the Great Smoky Mountains National Park has been the most visited park in America and the beautiful Blue Ridge Parkway has been the "most traveled facility of the National Park Service." For many years Asheville, Hendersonville, Brevard, Waynesville, and many other places in the mountain region were well known as summer resorts. Since 1951, when skiing was introduced at Catalooche, near Maggie Valley, other slopes have been opened, including Beech Mountain, Appalachian Ski Mountain, Seven Devils, Hound Ears, Sapphire Valley, High Meadows, and Sugar Mountain. In the twelve-week ski season of 1970–71 an estimated 250,-000 skiers spent $10 million in North Carolina. The skiing industry represents a capital investment of more than $40 million, which has had a profound effect on the mountain country.

Mineral Production

Despite the fact that about seventy minerals of commercial importance occur in the state, North Carolina in recent years has usually ranked thirty-third among the states in mineral production. Yet it produces almost 100 percent of the nation's supply of primary kaolin (china clay), 70 percent of its mica, and 35 percent of its feldspar. North Carolina has approximately 93 percent of the nation's known reserves of lithium. It leads the nation in the production of pyrophyllite and spodumene. The "new demand for the lithium which occurs in a gigantic belt of spodumene running through North Carolina" resulted in two new establishments, including a $7 million plant at Bessemer City. Slate, heretofore considered of little value, is now being used to make light-weight aggregate [Solite] at Aquadale, in Stanly County, "at the most modern plant of its kind in the South."

The stone, sand and gravel, and clay and related industries are the most important in terms of value of product. North Carolina leads the South in the production of dimension and crushed stone. The largest "open-faced" granite quarry in the world is at Mount Airy; it is nearly a mile long and 1,800 feet wide, and turns out about 3,000 carloads a year. The largest tungsten mine in the United States is near Henderson. In 1967 some 351 establishments, employing 12,800 workers, turned out stone, clay, and glass products valued at $262,-800,000. The state has usually ranked about eighth in the manufacture of clay products, and in recent years it has ranked first or second (Ohio being the other state) in brick manufacture. The 1957 Census of Manufactures placed the "value added by manufactures" of stone, clay, and glass products in North Carolina at $90,200,000. Recently one of the largest deposits of phosphate rock in the world was discovered in the eastern part of Beaufort County. In 1964 the Texas Gulf Sulphur Company invested $45,000,000 in a mining operation that produced 1.6 million tons of phosphate concentrate in 1968.

Commercial Fisheries

Fishing has been a sizable industry in the North Carolina coastal region for many years. In the 1920s the average annual value of all seafood products was about $3 million. By 1969 this figure had risen to over $12 million.

Of the food fish in North Carolina, the most important have been shad, trout, herring, croakers, mullets, rock, bluefish, and mackerel. The shellfish industry has also been sizable, with shrimp, oysters, and crabs being the most important products. In addition to food fish, the state has an enormous catch of nonfood fish, chiefly menhaden, used for making oil and fertilizer.

Total and Per Capita Wealth of North Carolina

The total estimated wealth of North Carolina rose from $682,-000,000 in 1900 to $6,458,000,000 in 1920, and then dropped chiefly because of the agricultural depression to $4,719,000,000 in 1930. It rose sharply during the inflationary era after 1939, to over $12,000,000,000 in 1953, and to $14,-687,150,000 in 1969. The per capita annual income of the state rose from $255 in 1930 to $732 in 1945, to $1,052 in 1951, to $1,562 in 1960, to $2,987 in 1969, and to $3,188 in 1970. This increase has closed the gap between state and national per capita average, but each Tar Heel was still $722 shy of the national average of $3,910 in 1970. However, the state is one of three states (with South Carolina and Mississippi) whose per capita income more than doubled in the decade after 1960.

In wage rates North Carolina has consistently ranked near the bottom among the fifty states, a condition that has been attributed to the fact that the textile and tobacco industries everywhere have wage scales lower than those of the more highly skilled and specialized manufactures. In January, 1971, the total average weekly earnings of industrial workers in North Carolina was $100.33, in comparison with the national average of $137.86. The average hourly earnings of all industrial workers was $2.54, compared to $3.49 for the nation.

It is unlikely that the state's per capita income is as low as the above figures indicate. Each year thousands of North Carolina farmers work one hundred days or more off the farm, and "many of these report only the cash income received in that off-the-farm employment period." By 1950 approximately one-third of the state's population was classified as urban, one-third as rural, and one-third as "rural non-farm." Many, perhaps a majority of those in this third category, "live on small tracts and produce vegetables, meat, dairy products, chickens, eggs, honey, and other commodities. While it adds measurably to their income, none of this product of their time and labor is counted in these statistics." Another factor that has a bearing on North Carolina's low per capita income is its extremely large percentage of people under twenty-one and over sixty-five years of age. One authority in this field of investigation has written, "When variations in age make-up are taken into consideration, the difference in per capita income between the states tends to become smaller."

Population Trends

Though North Carolina received an insignificant number of foreign immigrants and continued to contribute more people to other states than it received from them, it maintained a rate of population growth from 1890 to 1930 slightly in excess of that of the United States. The rate of population growth dropped sharply after 1930. The state's population in 1920, 1930, 1940, 1950, 1960, and 1970 was 2,559,123; 3,170,276; 3,571,623; 4,061,929, 4,556,-155, and 5,082,059. From 1950 to 1960 North Carolina's population increased 12.2 percent, while that of the United States as a whole increased 18.5 percent. From 1960 to 1970 the state population increased 525,904, or 11.5 percent over the 1960 figure.

In recent years North Carolina has been losing population to other states to an extent that many people do not realize. During the years 1950–54 North Carolina's natural gain in population—births minus deaths—was 352,000, but the total net gain was only 163,000 because 189,000 people moved out of the state. The *Greensboro Daily News,* of December 27, 1955, said:

"1. The massive exodus of population from rural areas, brought on by agricultural mechanization and industrialization, hits North Carolina a real blow because this state is heavily agricultural. In 1940, 34 per cent of the state labor force was employed in agriculture compared with only 25 per cent in 1950 (and only one in five workers in 1955.).

"2. Whites and Negroes are leaving the state's agricultural regions in droves, in about the same ratio, but the net effect of their departure is hidden to some extent by the large natural birth rate.

"3. But the significant fact is this: While a huge percentage of the white migrants are moving to rural non-farm areas of towns and cities *inside* North Carolina, well over half of the Negro migrants are moving *outside* the state, continuing a trend of the last 30 or 40 years.

"Within the next 10 or 20 years North Carolina's Negro percentage of population may fall from the neighborhood of 20 to, say, 10 per cent or less."

The industrial areas grew far more rapidly than the rural counties, especially those which produced cotton and tobacco on a large scale. Twenty-two of the state's 100 counties had fewer people in 1954 than they had in 1950—and fewer even than in 1940. There was close coordination between industrialization and urbanization as economic and social opportunity attracted many farm families to the factory towns.

The United States Census of 1960 revealed that the vast majority of North Carolinians were no longer "rural farm" people. Of the state's total population of 4,556,155, some 1,945,852 (42.7 percent) were classified as "rural nonfarm"; 1,801,921 (39.5 percent) as "urban," and only 808,379 (17.8 percent) as "rural farm."

From 1890 to 1930 the state's urban population increased from 7.2 percent to 25.8 percent of the total population, the number of towns with a population of 25,000 increased from none to eight, two of which were in excess of 75,000; the number with a population of from 10,000 to 25,000 increased from four to thirteen; and the number with a population from 5,000 to 10,000, from three to thirty. The urban population increased at a rate ten times that of the rural. The white population grew more rapidly than the Negro, and the chief gain of Negro population was in the urban areas. These population trends continued after 1930. The urban population increased to 27.3 percent in 1940, to 33.7 percent in 1950, to 39.5 percent in 1960, and to 45.0 percent in 1970. Between 1950 and 1960 thirty-four counties (twenty-three in the East and eleven in the mountains) lost population. This trend was even more pronounced in the sixties. The 1970 census revealed that thirty-eight counties had lost population during the previous decade. All but seven of these (Ashe, Cherokee, Clay, Madison, Mitchell, Swain, and Yancey) were in the East. Every county in the Piedmont gained population, as did a few eastern counties, notably Cumberland and Onslow.

In 1950, only one city, Charlotte, had over 100,000 population (134,000); Winston-Salem had 87,811; Greensboro, 74,389; Durham, 71,311; Raleigh, 65,679; Kannapolis (unincorporated), 28,448; and Rocky Mount, 27,679. The state had 475 places incorporated as cities or towns, and 48 unincorporated places of 1,000 or more inhabitants.

The largest North Carolina cities in 1960 were Charlotte, 201,5564; Greensboro, 119,574; Winston-Salem, 111,135; Raleigh, 93,931; Durham, 78,302; High Point, 62,063; Asheville, 60,192; Fayetteville, 47,106; Wilmington, 44,-103; and Gastonia, 37,276. The state had thirty-five unincorporated places of 10,000 or more.

Urbanization and the growth and expansion of metropolitan areas was even more pronounced in the sixties. The state's twelve largest cities in 1970 were Charlotte, 241,178; Greensboro, 144,076; Winston-Salem, 132,913; Raleigh, 121,577; Durham, 95,458; High Point, 63,204; Asheville, 57,681; Fayetteville, 53,070; Gastonia, 47,412; Fort Bragg, 46,995; Wilmington, 46,169, and Kannapolis 36,293. There were thirty other towns in the state with a population of over 10,000 each.

Increasing Importance of North Carolina Cities

The growing cities were the centers of wealth, greater and more diversified economic and social opportunity, education, culture, progress, a growing class of workers, and political influence. The cities provided opportunities for capitalists, bankers, business and professional men and women, and industrial laborers, and helped North Carolina to attract capital and labor from other states. From 1939 to 1954 the number of national banks in the state increased from 41 to 61, the state banks from 186 to 388, and total bank deposits from $400,000,000 to $2,011,225,000. Charlotte became the leading banking center between Richmond and Atlanta, and was gaining on these two cities. Winston-Salem, Greensboro, Durham, and Raleigh were among other important banking centers. As of June 30, 1970, the state had 22 national banks

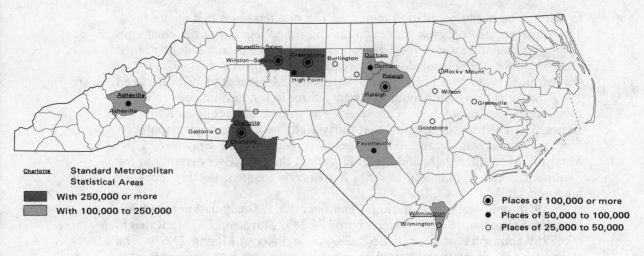

Places of 25,000 or More, and Standard Metropolitan Statistical Areas in 1970

Cartography by the Department of Geography and Earth Sciences
The University of North Carolina at Charlotte

and 82 state banks, with total bank deposits of $6,261,327,000. On that date Wachovia Bank and Trust Company, the largest bank in the Southeast and thirty-ninth largest in the nation, had deposits of $1,244,906,156 and total resources $1,662,457,725. Eight other banks in the state had deposits of over $100,000,000 each. In 1970 there were 141 state and 39 federal building and loan associations in the state with total assets of $3,117,907,318. In 1969 there were 22 life insurance companies having their home offices in North Carolina, and there were 276 other companies doing business in North Carolina. The total ordinary life and annuity insurance in force by the North Carolina companies in 1969 was over $4,407,073,706 and by "out-of-state" companies over $9,804,838,763; group life insurance of all companies was over $9,737,195,050; and "industrial business" of all companies over $1,780,940,916. The grand total of all insurance in force amounted to $25,730,048,035. The six largest North Carolina companies were Jefferson Standard, Security Life and Trust, Pilot Life, State Capital, Home Security Life, and Durham Life.

Growth of the Labor Movement in North Carolina

In the main North Carolina has had a record of peaceful labor-management relations, though there have been "labor troubles" at various times and places. From 1929 to 1934 there were several serious disputes. Discontented with lagging wages and unsatisfactory working conditions, many workers in the Gastonia-Marion area in 1929 responded to the organizing efforts of Fred Beale, who was sent into the state by the radical National Textile Workers Union. Several "leftist" unions were formed, and the leaders preached radical, if not communistic doctrines. In a raid on union headquarters during a strike at Gastonia, the local chief of police was killed, and the community was in a state of hysteria for several days. Some union members were treated with violence and Ella Mae Wiggins, a mill worker, was killed. Beale and six associates were convicted in a questionable, albeit dramatic, manner and were given long prison sentences for the murder of the chief of police; but local sentiment was such that not one was convicted for outrages against the strikers. Nine persons were accused of having a hand in the slaying of Mrs. Wiggins but all were freed by the grand jury. Bloodshed also resulted from a strike at Marion, where eight deputies accused of slaying a striker were acquitted by a jury. Governor Gardner sent troops to both towns.

Drastic wage cuts and hard working conditions caused workers to strike in several cotton mills, particularly at High Point, Rockingham, and other places in 1932. The strikers achieved some success at High Point but not in the other towns. In these strikes, in contrast with those at Gastonia earlier, the workers had local instead of outside leadership; the unions persisted after the strike; and the strikers had the sympathy of a considerable part of the community.

On September 3, 1934, almost one hundred textile mills in the state closed as workers joined a nationwide walkout. A week later twenty-eight companies of the National Guard were placed on "strike duty." On September 23 the strike was called off in response to an appeal by President Roosevelt.

Labor Policies of the New Deal and the Fair Deal

The weak and lagging labor movement in North Carolina was vastly stimulated by the "New Deal" policies of the federal government during the administrations of Franklin D. Roosevelt (1933–45) and the "Fair Deal" policies of his successor, Harry S. Truman (1945–53). The various New Deal laws relating to labor have been discussed in Chapter 44. Suffice it to say here that the National Labor Relations Board could order the dissolution of "company unions," receive complaints, and order the reinstatement of discharged workers, issue "cease and desist" orders against employers who violated the law (Wagner Act), conduct hearings, and supervise the elections held by the workers.

The State Department of Labor

Meanwhile the state government was becoming more responsive to the demands and interests of management and labor. Though slow in acquiring adequate powers, financial support, and personnel, the state Department of Labor, headed by an elective commissioner, was rendering valuable services by the 1930s. It collected labor statistics, sought to settle strikes and other industrial conflicts, directed a public employment service, ministered to the needs of unemployed children of working age, and to deaf and blind persons, assisted war veterans in prosecuting claims for disability compensation and hospitalization, enforced labor legislation, inspected factories, stores, and other places of employment (6,185 places in 1935), and, through the state Industrial Commission, administered the Workmen's Compensation Act under which were adjusted about forty thousand claims a year involving compensation and medical charges of about a million and a half dollars.

Growth of Organized Labor

In 1937 the national Committee on Industrial Organization (CIO), headed by John L. Lewis, began an aggressive campaign to unionize the southern textile industry and many unions were organized in North Carolina. The active intervention of the New Deal administration in behalf of the rights of labor presaged the successful unionization of labor in the state, the cessation of the use of state troops in strikes, the supplanting of violent strikes by peaceful collective bargaining as the means of settling industrial disputes, the growing influence of labor, and the decline of industrial autocracy and "paternalism." After 1937 the union movement grew with rapidity and with little open strife. Some employers hailed the federal law as a boon to better and more peaceful relations between management and labor; some accepted it with sullen resentment; some utterly hated it and sought to disregard or defy it, only to find themselves in some cases subject to federal disciplinary action. Some of the Democratic leaders of the state were not very sympathetic to the labor policies of Roosevelt and Truman. The General Assembly rejected the proposed Child Labor Amendment to the Constitution, and in 1947 made it illegal to enter into a labor contract providing for a closed shop, a union shop, the checkoff of union dues or the maintenance of union membership. This legislature also defeated a mild wages and hours bill.

North Carolina's Labor Force

Total nonagricultural employment in the state averaged 1,745,-900 in 1970. The average employment and hourly earnings for five of the leading industries were textiles, 272,900 and $2.35; tobacco, 27,200 and $3.19; furniture, 65,400 and $2.41; paper, 16,700 and $3.27; electronics, 40,000 and $2.61.

Employment in North Carolina agriculture averaged 416,000 during 1960. This figure included all hired and family farm workers in the state. It is noteworthy that annual average farm employment in North Carolina dropped from 590,000 in 1950 to 416,000 in 1960, and to 241,000 in 1970.

Labor-Management Relations

Though organized labor made some headway in the state in the period after World War II the vast majority of North Carolina's labor force has remained unorganized. In 1953 some 83,800 workers were members of labor unions, and the number in 1968 was 124,000, or less than 7.5 percent of the total industrial labor force. Labor-management relations in North Carolina industry have been much more peaceful than those in the nation as a whole. In the two decades, 1941–60, inclusive, the number of strikes ranged from 57 in 1943 to 12 in 1960; the number of workers idle, from 24,300 in 1951 to 1,885 in 1960; the number of man-days idle, from 542,000 in 1947 to 9,833 in 1960, and the North Carolina percentage of the national total of man-idle days from 2.2 in 1951 to 0.08 in 1960. The most prolonged strike in the state's history occurred at a large textile mill at Henderson in 1959. The strike was finally settled, although not until after intermittent outbursts of violence caused the National Guard to be ordered to the scene in May. In July eight textile union members were sentenced to prison terms following convictions for conspiring to blow up mill installations. In 1961 the state had eleven strikes, 1,601 workers idle, and 5,468 man-days idle. The year 1961 was the sixth consecutive year during which North Carolina's total of man-days idle as a result of strikes amounted to only a fraction of 1 percent of the national total—a very remarkable record. In 1970 there were thirty-seven strikes in the state; the number of workers idle, 14,429, and 128,023 man-days idle.

Chapter 47

AGRICULTURE, TRANSPORTATION, AND TRADE IN RECENT YEARS

Though agriculture developed more slowly after 1930 than industry, trade, and finance, it expanded greatly and continued as the primary occupation of North Carolinians. From 1930 until after 1950 there was an increase in the number of farms and farmers, a decrease in per acre yield and total production, particularly of cotton and tobacco, a marked increase in the production of cattle and poultry, and a striking decrease in tenancy. As more and more farms became mechanized the number of work animals decreased. The number of mules on North Carolina farms in 1954 was only 190,000—the lowest since 1912, and 28 percent less than the average for the decade 1944–53. By 1969 the number of mules was "so negligible" that they were not listed in the census.

Profound Changes in North Carolina Agriculture After 1954

In an article in the *Greensboro Daily News* of July 2, 1961, Professor S. H. Hobbs, Jr. pointed out the following "basic trends in North Carolina agriculture, 1954–1959": a rapid decline in the number of farms; a large gain in the size of farms; tremendous gains in mechanization; a rapid trend toward large-scale agriculture; a great decline in farm tenancy; and large increases in the value of farms, both per farm and per acre. Hobbs concluded that the changes were "the most pronounced of any period during the last 100 years."

The number of farms in the state dropped from 267,906 in 1954 to 190,567 in 1959—a decline of 77,339 farms; the loss "due to change of definition" of farms in the census reports amounted to 14,885, thus leaving a net decline of 62,454 farms. It is also significant that every county in the state lost in the number of farms—the first time in history that this had happened. The percentages of losses ranged from 13.2 in Washington County to 49.6 in Cherokee and Polk.

North Carolina, a State of Small Farms

The percentage of rural population in North Carolina dropped steadily after 1930. According to the U.S. Census of 1960, only 17.8 percent (808,379 of 4,556,635) of the state's total population was classified as "rural farm." In 1970 this figure was 17.7. In that year the state had the second largest number of farms (148,202) in the nation, exceeded only by Texas. The average size of farms dropped from 101.3 acres in 1900 to 64.5 in 1930, then rose to 67.7 in 1940, to 83.4 in 1959, and to 103 in 1969. In the latter year the state had 2,227 farms in the 500 to 999 acreage range and 743 farms containing more than 1,000 acres each.

From 1910 to 1925 the percentage of farms operated by Negroes increased from 25.8 to 28.5, and the rate of increase of Negro farmers was more than three times the rate of increase of white farmers. Then a striking reversal of trend occurred during the depression years, which decreased the percentage of farms operated by Negroes to 23 in 1935. In 1964 the percentage of farms operated by nonwhites was only 20.2 (29,926 farm operators).

"King" Tobacco

From 1930 to the present tobacco has been "king" in North Carolina agriculture. Its production in millions of pounds dropped from 454 in 1930 to 399 in 1935 and then increased to 746 in 1948 and to 815 in 1969. North Carolina usually produced about two-fifths of the nation's crop—chiefly bright-leaf, flue-cured tobacco used in the manufacture of cigarettes and pipe tobacco. The cash income of $125,000,000 from tobacco in 1939, $309,000,000 in 1949, $523,000,000 in 1959, and $575,711,000 in 1969, was greater than all other crops combined. It has been truly said that the North Carolina tobacco crop is worth more than "all the wheat in Kansas, or all the pigs in Iowa, or all the cotton in Mississippi." The chief areas of production have been the northern Piedmont (the old Bright Belt), the Central Coastal Plain (the new Bright Belt), the South Carolina Belt of border counties in the Coastal Plain, and the Burley Belt in the mountains. Some Turkish tobacco has been grown in a few of the mountain counties in recent years.

Cotton and Corn

World overpopulation and falling prices brought a vast reduction in cotton acreage and yield in the late twenties and early thirties. The average annual production in the state for the decade after 1929 was 658,000 bales. Its production increased to 740,000 bales in 1948, dropped to 428,000 bales in 1945, increased to 550,000 bales in 1951, then dropped to 319,000 bales in 1959 and to 160,000 bales in 1970. The state's cash income from cotton in 1953 was $84,214,000; in 1959 it was $49,708,000; and in 1969 it was only $9,357,000 ($7,756,000, lint; $1,601,000 cotton, seed). The quality of North Carolina lint was above average, and the yield per acre was usually the highest in the South, but because of its difficulty in competing with the states of the Lower South and Southwest, North Carolina appeared destined for a decreasing role as a cotton-producing state. The middle East and the southern Piedmont were the areas of most extensive cotton production.

The third major North Carolina crop was corn, grown extensively throughout the state, especially in the cotton and tobacco areas, primarily as a food and feed rather than as a "money crop." Its production in millions of bushels was 45 in 1937, 56 in 1945, 71 in 1959, and 67 in 1970 (plus 1,656,000 tons for silage). The cash income from corn after 1949 was usually between $90,-000,000 and $100,000,000 a year, reaching the figure of $112,000,000 in 1951, and dropping to $92,000 in 1959, and to $59,000,000 in 1969.

Other Cash Crops

Few states grow a larger variety of crops than North Carolina, but the volume and value are small in comparison with tobacco, corn, and cotton, although the cash income from peanuts in 1969 amounted to $42,-000,000. In 1959 the state's hay crop was valued at $21,000,000, but this figure had dropped to only $2,305,000 in 1969. The state also ranked high as a producer of soybeans, Irish potatoes, sweet potatoes, and a great variety of vegetables and fruits. Prominent developments occurred after 1920 in the production of apples in the mountains, peaches in the Sandhills, berries in the southeastern counties, and truck crops in the Coastal Plain and near the city markets.

Livestock, Cattle, Poultry, Pigs

The table on page 647 reveals the amazing progress of North Carolina agriculture in recent decades. Among other things, it shows that Tar Heel farmers had started diversifying the old row-crop economy by increasing production of livestock, cattle, poultry, and swine. Before 1930, or even 1940, North Carolina ranked very low in quantity, quality, and value of livestock and cattle. Excessive emphasis on nonfood cash crops and inadequate attention to food and feed crops and livestock caused enormous expenditures for fertilizer, food and feed, dairy products, poultry products and meat produced in other states. Low crop prices in the depression years compelled an increase in diversified, live-at-home, and livestock farming. The total value of "livestock and livestock products" in the state increased from $93,533,000 in 1940, to $173,084,000 in 1950, to $243,190,000 in 1959, and to $581,383,000 in 1969. The cash income from dairy products for these years was $9,534,000, $26,-277,000, $49,677,000, and $91,650,000 respectively. The cash income from hogs during these years was $5,748,000, $19,461,000, $31,715,000, and $118,-614,000. In 1954 the state's cash income from poultry (chiefly broilers) and eggs was only $17,680,000; by 1969 this figure had increased to $335,660,000.

The 1969 cash income from agriculture in North Carolina had reached $1,406,161,000 ($812,810,000, crops; $581,383,000, livestock products; $69,-572,000, government payments).

	Cash Income from Agriculture		
	1940	1959	1969
From all farming	$328,695,232	$944,514,014	$1,406,161,000
Farm crops	225,627,682	651,643,594	812,810,000
Livestock	93,533,140	243,189,609	502,477,000
Dairy products	9,534,410	49,676,811	91,650,000
	Principal Crops		
Tobacco	$109,358,911	$372,846,433	$ 515,711,000
Cotton	26,279,120	49,707,528	9,357,000
Corn	34,948,916	92,042,647	58,732,000
Hay	8,005,780	20,916,243	2,305,000
Peanuts	10,546,885	27,971,340	41,783,000
Irish potatoes	5,552,788	9,048,899	4,339,000
Sweet potatoes	5,461,591	5,461,591	9,981,000
Vegetables	3,650,399	8,475,809	27,867,000
Fruits and berries	5,985,973	7,317,250	20,630,000
	Livestock, Hogs, and Poultry		
Cattle	$ 79,918,258	$112,087,083	$ 45,619,000
Poultry and eggs	7,866,964	99,387,098	335,660,000
Hogs	5,747,918	31,715,428	118,614,000
Number of farms	278,276	190,567	161,000
Value of land and buildings, average per farm	$ 2,647	$ 14,685	$ 33,390

Rapid Decline in Farm Tenancy

One of the greatest social and economic problems of North Carolina and the rest of the South has been farm tenancy. But there was a rapid decline in tenancy after 1940. The percentage of all North Carolina farms operated by tenants was 49 in 1930, 44 in 1940, 30.4 in 1959, and 27.1 in 1964. The total number of tenants was 142,158 in 1935; 123,476 in 1940; 110,485 in 1950; and 40,115 in 1964. All of the heavy tenant counties were in the areas producing tobacco and cotton—ideal tenant crops, which utilized hand labor, produced crops readily convertible into cash and hence were good security for the supply-merchant or crop-lien system of credit. It is noteworthy, however, that the number of tractors on farms—many of them on farms operated by tenants—increased more than 90 percent between 1945 and 1970. During the depression years of the 1930s, there was a decrease in the number of farms and tenants in the tobacco counties—the decrease in Negro farm operators being particularly conspicuous. An even greater decrease occurred in the "prosperous fifties."

Tenancy has never been a racial problem in North Carolina. At all times the number of white tenants was greater than that of Negro tenants, though the percentage of Negro tenants was higher than that of the whites. In 1920, 50 percent of all tenants were white; the percentage rose to 58.5 in 1930, to 65.5 in 1935, 66 in 1940, dropped to 55 by 1959, and was estimated at 59 percent in 1964. The percentage of all white farmers who are tenants was 33 in 1920, 40 in 1935, 21.1 in 1959, and 59 in 1964, while the percentage of all Negro farmers who were tenants in these years was 71, 79, 52.9, and 41. The numbers of white and Negro tenants, respectively, were 63,542 and 53,197 in 1920; 93,173 and 48,985 in 1935; 61,468 and 49,000 in 1950; 32,667 and 25,236 in 1959; and 23,577 and 16,358 in 1964.

Migrant Labor

With the decline of farm tenancy after 1940 many farm owners began to depend upon migrant labor during the growing and harvesting seasons. This was particularly true in the tobacco producing areas and on truck farms. In 1965 it was estimated that from ten to thirteen thousand migrant agricultural workers were employed in the state each year. The season begins in mid-April in the southeastern counties and the laborers follow the season across the state until work for them reaches its peak in July. Most of them are Negroes from Florida, Georgia, South Carolina, Mississippi, and Alabama, but in recent years they have been joined by Spanish-speaking whites. The welfare of these people has become the concern of the state Employment Security Commission, the Department of Social Services, and the North Carolina Council of Churches. Legislation has been enacted which was designed to provide greater safety on the highway, better housing and working conditions, fairer pay, care for the sick and aged, and for child care.

Federal Government Aid to North Carolina Farmers

The federal government continued in increasing amounts to aid what is now North Carolina State University in its agricultural and extension work and to supplement state and local funds for vocational education in agriculture, home economics, and trade and industries in the public schools. Expenditures for vocational education declined from 1930 to 1934 and then increased rapidly. In 1937–38 there was a total expenditure of nearly $1,250,000, one-half of which came from federal funds. In the year 1969–70 there were 475 teachers giving instruction in agriculture to approximately 45,000 high school students and 15,000 adults.

As has been indicated in Chapter 44, the New Deal brought great benefits to North Carolina farmers in the form of loans and "benefit payments" for limiting tobacco, cotton, and other crops and for soil conservation, with resultant crop price increases. Direct federal benefits to North Carolina farmers in 1935 exceeded $16,000,000 and in 1939 were about $20,000,000. They declined from $15,000,000 in 1940 to $8,000,000 in 1948; rose to $8,800,000 in 1950; dropped to $3,926,000 in 1953; increased to $12,800,000 in 1960; and to $69,-800,000 in 1969.

Under stimulus of the federal government, the state created the North Carolina Rural Electrification Authority (REA) in 1935 to stimulate the building of rural power lines. Within ten years the percentage of electrified farms in the state rose from about 3 percent to 12 percent due to the construction of 5,250 miles of power lines chiefly by existing utility companies. By 1939 over fifty counties had electric service available to 20 percent of their farms and thirty-nine counties had more than 30 percent of their farms electrified. On July 1, 1951, the state REA reported 261,440 farms with electric power and the state ranked second in the nation in the number of farms electrified—85 percent. By 1954 this percentage had risen to 96.9 percent (279,625 of 288,508 farms). The 1971 figure was slightly higher, some estimates being as high as 99 percent.

The state government rendered aid to the farmers through its expanding Department of Agriculture, which supplied information on farm problems; operated test farms; worked for the extermination of insects; analyzed foods, feeds, fertilizers, seeds and soil; inspected fruit trees offered for sale; kept a record of leaf tobacco sales; and rendered many other valuable services.

Much of the progress of agriculture in twentieth-century North Carolina has been due to the heavy use of fertilizer and from the use of more and more improved farm machinery, more careful seed selection, crop rotation, better plowing, terracing, and other improved farming techniques. These improved methods were constantly urged upon farmers by various agencies of the state and federal governments, county agents, home demonstration agents, teachers of agriculture in the public schools, 4-H Clubs, Future Farmers of America, radio and television programs, and farm journals, especially *The Progressive Farmer* (owned and edited by Clarence Poe of Raleigh), which boasted the largest circulation (1,103,956 in December, 1971) of all farm papers in the South and second largest in the nation.

As farm production and income expanded and brought higher living standards, the public consolidated school, telephone, electricity, the automobile, rural free delivery, the radio, and television broadened the farmer's social and intellectual horizon and decreased the isolation, unattractiveness, and burdens of rural life. Good roads and the automobile broadened the farmer's markets and solved his transportation problem. The growth of cities provided local markets for the sale of a greater variety of food crops and other products. Rural life in modern North Carolina had undergone a far-reaching transformation in its economic, social, and cultural aspects.

A New Era in Transportation and Communication

The period after 1930 witnessed a revolution in transportation and communication. As has been indicated in Chapter 43, North Carolina became a "Good Roads State" in the 1920s. By 1936 the state government had a total investment of over $210,000,000 in state roads; of this sum, $115,000,000 had been borrowed by the sale of bonds and about $42,000,000 had been contributed by the federal government. In 1949 there were 10,351 miles in the state highway system and 51,031 miles of county roads maintained by the state, of which 14,635 were hard-surfaced. More and better bridges were built, many roads were relocated, and many railroad grade crossings were eliminated by underpasses and overpasses.

North Carolina was the only state that maintained all public roads without resort to a state tax on property. Revenues from automobile, bus, and truck licenses, from gasoline taxes and from the federal government held up so well that highways suffered less curtailment of financial resources than other state services during the decade after 1929. By 1945 the state had spent more than half a billion dollars in the construction and maintenance of highways—a great portion of it on "primary roads." During the administration of Governor Scott (1949–53) the state paved approximately 12,000 miles of "secondary" or rural roads and "stabilized" for all-weather travel more than 15,000 miles. Under the provisions of the Powell Bill of 1951, the state government was required to turn over to municipalities for street work an increased amount equal to the revenue from one-half of one cent of the seven cents tax on motor fuels. The state was also required to construct and maintain city streets that formed part of the state highway system. At the close of the Scott administration the state highway system embraced 66,547 miles of roads, of which 26,864 were paved and most of the remainder stabilized for all-weather travel. In 1969–70 total state and federal disbursements for North Carolina roads amounted to $112,-566,698. On January 1, 1971, the state highway system embraced 73,026 miles, of which 48,911 were paved. It also had 522 miles of interstate highway completed and 90 more miles under construction. In 1971 North Carolina had the largest highway system in the nation under state administration and, according to its population and area it had more miles of paved road than any other state.

Motor Bus and Freight Lines

Improved highway transportation made possible the development of statewide motor freight and passenger service. As of January 1, 1971, there were 60 regulated motor passenger carriers operating 1,838 buses, and there were 16,090 trucks registered with the State Utilities Commission. The motor bus and freight lines offered serious competition to the railroads and served many communities which the railroads did not reach. By 1941 North Carolina had 50 percent more truck-tractors than any other state of the Southeast, and by 1948 the wholesale trade of the state was $800 per capita, compared to Virginia's $680. In that year the wholesale trade of Charlotte exceeded that of Richmond by 55 percent and was gaining rapidly on Atlanta, the only southeastern city that surpassed it in this respect. By 1954 the trucking industry of the state was the fourth largest in the nation, and North Carolina had "more Class I motor carriers domiciled within her boundaries than any other state." In Winston-Salem the McLean Trucking Company—one of the top ten in the nation—"operates the largest individually-owned truck terminal in the world." Trucks made it possible to disperse industry throughout the state and to do this in an atomic age when the goal of "accessible isolation" is vitally important. At long last North Carolina products were being shipped outward from the state's cities, towns, and farms "by a means of transport that required no immediate port," and the state was released from the economic bondage to cities of other states.

Death on the Highways

Much has been said and written about "death on the highways." Traffic fatalities for the period 1960–70 averaged over 1,500 a year. Violations of the law on the part of the driver played a part in more than half of the accidents, and speeding was the one law violation more responsible than any other. Accidents were the third leading cause of death in North Carolina, being exceeded only by heart disease and cancer, and of the accidents more than 40 percent were automobile accidents.

Railroads

The railroads, with an operating total track mileage of 4,349 in 1970, were also contributing to ease transportation handicaps. They still played a significant role in the state's economic life, though they were less important relatively than they had been in the era before automobiles and aviation. In 1957 the Southern Railway acquired the 94-mile Atlantic and East Carolina Railway. In 1967 the Atlantic Coast Line and the Seaboard Air Line systems merged to form the Seaboard Coast Line, with a total trackage of 9,707 miles.

Development of Ports

In 1949 the General Assembly authorized the issue of $7,500,000 in bonds for the construction and improvement of seaports. In 1952 terminal facilities equipped to handle ocean-shipping at the ports of Wilmington and Morehead City were completed, and two new storage warehouses at the latter port were leased to the navy. The Ocean Shipping Port Terminal at Morehead City is accessible to large ocean-going ships as well as freight-carrying barges of the Intracoastal Waterway. The volume of exports and imports handled through this port has increased rapidly. The same is true of Wilmington, with its $5,000,000 river-front terminals. In 1970 these two ports handled 2,455,154 tons of cargo, and the gross revenue amounted to $3,774,413.

Recent Developments in Aviation

By the 1940s air transportation had become a significant factor in North Carolina life. By 1960 six regularly scheduled commercial air lines served the state and there were 102 airports and airfields (62 commercial and municipal, 9 military, 26 private, and 5 others).

Improvements in Communication

In recent years communication facilities have been greatly expanded and improved by a large number of radio broadcasting and television stations and by direct distance dialing telephone facilities. In 1971 the state had 18 commercial television stations in operation and 2 noncommercial stations. The Charlotte-Mecklenburg school system operates one; The University of North Carolina, the other. In 1971 the state had 231 commercial and seven noncommercial radio stations in operation.

Wholesale and Retail Trade

By the 1950s North Carolina had become the leading state in the South Atlantic region in wholesale and retail trade. The following tables indicate the magnitude of this important aspect of the state's economic life, as indicated by the 1967 Census of Business:

A.   Wholesale Trade, 1967

Number of establishments	7,010
Sale	$9,530,398,000
Payroll, entire year	460,991,000
Merchant wholesalers	
Establishments	4,461
Sales	$3,599,076,000
Other operating types	
Establishments	2,549
Sales	$5,931,322,000

Kind of Business	*Sales*	*Establishments*
Farm products	$1,134,202,000	450
Groceries and related products	1,271,682,000	966
Petroleum products	1,002,000,000	1,003
Motor vehicles	1,077,950,000	809
Drugs, chemicals, allied products	1,008,654,000	256
Machinery, equipment, supplies	894,833,000	1,032
Electrical goods	598,307,000	330
Lumber, construction materials	392,724,000	327
Dry goods	512,938,000	222
Hardware, plumbing, heating	296,958,000	284
Metals, minerals, etc.	215,844,000	85
Tobacco products	119,395,000	84
Furniture	166,150,000	157
Farm supplies	133,368,000	138
Paper, paper products	189,319,000	160
Scrap, waste materials	87,877,000	147
Beer, wine, etc.	135,585,000	98
Amusement and sporting goods	52,525,000	85
Other products	643,389,000	377

B.   Retail Trade, 1967

Number of establishments	41,296
Sales	$6,648,359,000

Kind of Business	*Sales*	*Establishments*
Food stores	$1,160,000,000	10,401
Automotive dealers	$1,369,598,000	3,179
General Merchandise	776,000,000	2,483
Food stores	1,453,407,000	10,401

Gasoline service stations	563,604,000	7,010
Lumber, building materials	427,205,000	1,789
Apparel, accessory stores	364,643,000	2,682
Furniture, home furnishings	343,947,000	2,636
Eating, drinking places	339,478,000	5,451
Farm and garden supply stores	163,928,000	722
Drug stores	229,920,000	1,154
Fuel, ice dealers	113,702,000	801
Liquor stores	140,912,000	364
Jewelry stores	48,685,000	593
Florists	26,980,000	800
Antique stores	20,736,000	585
Book, stationery stores	7,932,000	80
Sporting goods stores	14,983,000	293
Other stores	3,590,000,000	610

Chapter 48
TOWARD A FINER
NORTH CAROLINA

As economic conditions improved from 1934 to 1939, the state's public services were more than restored to their 1930 basis of public support, with the exception of public schools and institutions of higher learning. The state government in the 1930s did not manifest the zeal for public education that had been characteristic of the previous twenty years. Enrollment in public schools increased steadily until 1934 and then began to taper off, but that in the institutions of higher learning continued to increase. In 1939 the state was maintaining the "Consolidated University of North Carolina" with an enrollment of about 15,000 students as well as twelve standard colleges for whites, Negroes, and Indians. In 1952–53 state appropriations to all of these institutions amounted to about $14 million annually, By 1954–55 this figure had increased to approximately $20 million, which was about 10 percent of the total state expenditures from the General Fund. In 1960–61 the three units of The University of North Carolina had 17,595 students and a faculty and staff numbering 8,206. At that date North Carolina had thirty-eight senior colleges, twelve of which were state supported, and twenty-six junior colleges, five of which were state supported. As of October, 1960, the total enrollment in all institutions of higher learning in the state was 67,183.

Progress of the Public Schools

Between 1933 and 1955 expenditures for public school operations alone increased eight times; the value of school property more than quadrupled; teachers' salaries increased nearly six times, and public school libraries grew from one and a half million volumes to five million. Progress of the schools was even more phenomenal after 1955. North Carolina's public school property, listed in terms of buildings and equipment, increased in value from $1,695,250 in 1900 to $282,558,115 in 1951, to $480,051,815 in 1955, to

655

$711,454,884 in 1961–62, and to $1,215,388,433 in 1969–70. During this period the number of schoolhouses decreased from 7,166 to 3,456, to 3,190 respectively, and then increased slightly to 3,202 in 1959–60 (2,206 whites; 996 Negroes). The number of one- and two-teacher schools declined from 917 to 288 between 1949 and 1954, and by 1962 this type of school had been eliminated from about half of the counties.

In the school year 1971–72 the state had 2,054 public schools, of which 1,546 were elementary (first eight grades) and 508 were high schools. The total number of pupils enrolled amounted to 1,197,797; there were 52,421 teachers; and average daily attendance was 1,082,650. The average annual salary for teachers was $8,604. School bus transportation by "the world's largest bus system" cost $24,410,659 in state funds; the cost per pupil was $33.38; and the daily miles traveled, 417,760.

In 1970–71 the expense of the public schools amounted to an estimated $725,349,166.55, of which $492,774,184.63 (67.9 percent) came from state funds, $126,156,877.44 (17.4 percent) from local funds, and $106,418,549.48 (14.7 percent) from federal funds. Per pupil expenditures, which had been only $29.65 in 1934–35 and $72.80 ten years later, had increased to $662.81. The three major sources of state public school funds for 1970–71 were income taxes, $413,596,745 (42.8 percent); sales taxes, $285,893,056 (29.6 percent); and franchise taxes, $61,924,665 (6.4 percent). Approximately $110,358,229 (87.5 percent) of the local funds came from property taxes. In 1971 North Carolina ranked fourth among the states in the proportion of public school costs borne by the state. During the decade 1959–69 more than 6.69 percent of the state's per capita income was spent for public education.

Much progress was made during the 1960s and early 1970s. Governor Terry Sanford (1961–65) placed great emphasis on "quality education" and his successors, Dan K. Moore (1965–69) and Robert W. Scott (1969–73) carried on most of the Sanford educational policies. In the school year 1969–70 there were 1,220,619 pupils in the public schools, with 48,834 teachers. Public school expenditures had increased to $675,722,000 ($609 per pupil), and the average teacher's salary was $7,444.

Some significant innovations of recent years have been special training for physically handicapped pupils; a lunch program embracing over 1,600 schools; a public school insurance program; and an annual appropriation of approximately a half-million dollars for a school health program. It is also noteworthy that a larger percentage of seniors graduated from high school in 1959–60 than a decade earlier.

State-Supported Institutions of Higher Learning

Under President Frank P. Graham (1930–49) The University of North Carolina continued to make progress. The consolidation of the university at Chapel Hill, the North Carolina College of Agriculture and Engineering at Raleigh, and the Woman's College at Greensboro into the "Consolidated University of North Carolina" was put into effect. Some schools were discontinued, such as the Engineering School at Chapel Hill and the School of Science and Business at State College. But more schools, divisions, and departments were added at all three branches of the "Greater University" between 1931 (the date of the legislative act of consolidation) and 1962 than ever before. Among those added at Chapel Hill were Library Science (1931), General College (1935), Public Health (1936), and the Communication Center (1945). The Institute of Government became a part of the University in 1942; the School of Education, discontinued in 1933, was reinstituted in 1948. Many new departments were added—City and Regional Planning (1946), Radio (1947), Religion (1947), and Astronomy (1950) in connection with the $3 million Morehead Building and Planetarium (the only Zeiss planetarium on a college campus), which was completed in 1949. The Division of Health Affairs, which includes the schools of Medicine, Public Health, Nursing, Pharmacy, and Dentistry was organized, and Memorial Hospital was built and put into operation. In 1950 a School of Journalism and a School of Social Work were established, and the School of Commerce became the School of Business Administration. The University of North Carolina Library, with almost two million books in 1971, ranked second among state university libraries in the South.

A perusal of the catalogs of what are now North Carolina State University and The University of North Carolina at Greensboro reveals the same sort of "proliferation of courses" and additions of departments, schools, and "divisions" as that which took place at Chapel Hill—and in colleges throughout the nation.

By 1950 eleven of the departments at Chapel Hill had gained national ranking. By 1971 this number had increased to twenty-four, twelve of which were ranked as "distinguished." Among the unique organizations which have brought national and international distinction to Chapel Hill have been the Carolina Playmakers, founded by "Proff" Frederick H. Koch; the Institute of Government, organized by Albert Coates; the Institute for Research in Social Science, largely the handiwork of Howard W. Odum; and the Southern Historical Collection, consisting of some five million manuscripts, built up through J. G. de Roulhac Hamilton (its founder and director, 1930–48), and his successors. For the past two decades the Graduate School at Chapel Hill has been one of the largest in the nation. The university's Schools of Pharmacy, Dentistry, and Journalism were the only ones of their kind in a vast area of the Upper South.

North Carolina State University has boasted of having one of the nation's largest engineering schools; an outstanding School of Agriculture; a textile school, called "the foremost in the nation"; a School of Design, "regarded as one of the nation's six top schools of its kind"; the only Pulp and Paper

Technology Center in the South; the "first furniture manufacturing and management curriculum and research program in the nation"; the "largest research forest in the world," the 80,000-acre Hofmann Forest Tract in Jones and Onslow counties; and the "first college-owned Nuclear Reactor in the world, the first to be used entirely for peacetime teaching and research." Between 1950 and 1955 State College "received over 6½ million dollars from sources other than appropriations and student fees."

The growth of what is now The University of North Carolina at Greensboro was not as rapid or dramatic as that of the other two branches of the university, but it made steady progress and while it was the Woman's College of the University of North Carolina it boasted "the largest on-the-campus enrollment of any woman's college in the nation."

Expansion of the University of North Carolina

For more than two decades the University of North Carolina had only three campuses—at Chapel Hill, Raleigh, and Greensboro. The General Assembly of 1965 added a fourth campus, at Charlotte, and the legislature of 1969 added two more units: Asheville-Biltmore and Wilmington. In the fall of 1970, over 45,000 students were enrolled in the "Consolidated University" of whom more than 18,000 were at Chapel Hill and more than 13,000 at Raleigh. The book value of the physical plant of the six units of the university was $335,843,766.

Regional Universities

Perhaps the most significant educational development in recent years was the creation of an enlarged system of regional universities out of the state's system of four-year senior colleges. The General Assembly of 1967 created four regional universities outside the Consolidated University system: East Carolina at Greenville, Western Carolina at Cullowhee, Appalachian State at Boone, and North Carolina Agricultural and Technical University at Greensboro. The 1969 legislature created five more regional universities: Pembroke State at Pembroke, North Carolina Central at Durham, Elizabeth City State, Fayetteville State, and Winston-Salem State. In 1971 the North Carolina School of the Arts at Winston-Salem was the only state supported institution of higher learning without university status. In 1970–71 the total enrollment in the nine regional universities was 34,985, with East Carolina having 10,007 of that number.

Private Institutions of Higher Learning

North Carolina has long been noted for its large number of church-related colleges. In 1970–71 there were twenty-nine of these senior nonpublic colleges and universities, with a total enrollment of about 39,000 students, and there were twelve nonpublic junior colleges, with a total enrollment of about 8,000.

The total enrollment in North Carolina's colleges and universities in the fall of 1970 was 140,485. (This figure does not include extension, adult education, and noncredit enrollment or technical and vocational enrollment in community colleges).

The Growth and Expansion of Duke University

Duke University made steady progress in many fields of activity. By January 1, 1971, its endowment and other invested funds had increased to $98,195,615, and its greatly enlarged physical plant had a book value of $172,-146,892. Its Law School achieved national distinction. Its School of Forestry was the first in the United States to offer the doctor's degree. Duke Hospital and Medical School have national distinction, and Duke scientists have made pioneering studies in high blood pressure, cancer, heart disease, pellagra, and many other human ills. Many new departments have been added since 1960, as well as a School of Engineering and a Graduate School of Business Administration.

On July 1, 1930, the Duke University Hospital and Medical School opened their doors. As of January 1, 1971, the hospital had admitted 916,000 patients, who came from all of the state's one hundred counties, all the states of the Union, and about fifty foreign countries. In 1971 Duke Hospital was "the second largest private general hospital in the South." The Duke University Library, with more than 2,128,524 volumes in June, 1970, was the largest in the Southeast, the second largest in the South, and the nineteenth largest in the nation. The collections of the Duke and Carolina libraries make the Durham–Chapel Hill area a national research center for southern history.

The Transfer of Wake Forest College to Winston-Salem

Wake Forest College was the beneficiary of several large bequests in the 1940s. The first of these led to the establishment of the Bowman Gray Medical School at Winston-Salem in the summer of 1941. In 1946 the Zachary Smith Reynolds Foundation announced its offer of the income from $10,-500,000 to Wake Forest contingent upon the college's moving to Winston-Salem. Charles Babcock offered a site of 350 acres and an anonymous donor promised $2,000,000 if the Baptists would raise an additional $3,000,000, which they did by the end of 1953. On October 15, 1951, President Harry S. Truman participated in the ground-breaking ceremonies for the new Wake Forest at

Winston-Salem. The college began operation at its new site in the fall of 1956. In 1967 Wake Forest achieved university status. By 1971 the book value of its endowment had increased to $26,500,000. The old buildings at Wake Forest were transformed into a seminary for the training of Baptist ministers.

Other Church-Related Colleges

During the past forty years Davidson, Meredith, Greensboro, Elon, Guilford, Catawba, Lenoir Rhyne, and other church-related colleges made steady progress. Endowments increased, physical plants expanded, the size of student bodies and facilities increased, and all of the colleges greatly expanded their activities; Guilford, for example, established a night school in Greensboro. A number of colleges were founded between 1931 and 1971. The first Greek college and orphanage in the United States was dedicated at Gastonia on September 18, 1932. Two new Methodist colleges began operation in the fall of 1960: North Carolina Wesleyan at Rocky Mount and Methodist College at Fayetteville. St. Andrews, a Presbyterian institution at Laurinburg (a merger of the resources of three small colleges in the state) was opened to students in 1961.

Community Colleges and Technical Institutes

A significant development in higher education in the state in recent years has been the establishment and rapid growth of two-year community colleges and technical institutes. These schools were established to bridge a gap in educational opportunity between the high schools and four-year colleges and universities. Thirty-nine technical institutes and seventeen community colleges were in full operation in the state in 1972. The 293,602 students enrolled in 1970 represented a considerable increase over the 240,851 enrolled the previous year and more than thirty-six times the 8,000 enrolled in 1963, the year the system was established. In 1972–73 the total state appropriations for these schools was $58,154,909, with over $6,308,000 for equipment. In 1972 more than 403,000 persons attended one or more classes in a technical institute or a community college in North Carolina.

Another notable trend in higher education was the increasing number of two-year junior colleges that were converted into four-year senior colleges. Among these were Pfeiffer at Misenheimer, Mars Hill in Madison County, and Campbell College at Buies Creek.

Expansion of Public-Library Facilities

As indicated in an earlier chapter, North Carolina made considerable progress in the promotion of public libraries after the establishment of

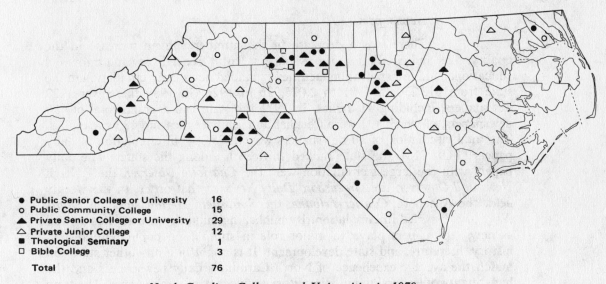

● Public Senior College or University	16
○ Public Community College	15
▲ Private Senior College or University	29
△ Private Junior College	12
■ Theological Seminary	1
□ Bible College	3
Total	76

North Carolina Colleges and Universities in 1970

Cartography by the Department of Geography and Earth Sciences
The University of North Carolina at Charlotte

the Library Commission in 1909. The commission merged with State Library on July 1, 1956, to form the present North Carolina State Library. More rapid progress was made after 1935. In 1937 there were twelve county and seventy city public libraries with 781,973 books and 3,945,116 circulation, and there were nine Negro public libraries. At this date forty-three counties were appropriating money for public libraries, but no public library in the state met the minimum standards of the American Library Association, and 54 percent of the state's population was without library service. Public libraries had only one-third of a book per capita and a total annual income of only ten cents per capita for the state.

The three decades after 1940 witnessed a great expansion of library facilities. On January 1, 1970, the state had 313 public libraries (15 regional, 53 county, 34 municipal, and 211 branch). On that date the total number of volumes in these libraries was 5,697,443 and total circulation, 13,906,899. Total income of these libraries amounted to $8,826,574 for the fiscal year 1969–70. Of this amount $6,270,089 came from local funds, $1,293,125 from the state, $520,584, federal aid, and $742,736 from other sources. Thirty counties and fourteen towns had voted bond issues for libraries. "Population with access to public library service" was 100 percent. In 1971 North Carolina had 85 "bookmobiles," giving it high rank in the nation in this respect.

Newspapers

There was a decrease in the number and an increase in the quality, size, and circulation of newspapers. Rural free delivery and improved educational and transportation facilities expanded newspaper circulation in the state from 612,230 in 1901 to 2,025,926 in 1926. In 1939 there were 227 newspapers, including 41 dailies. In 1971 the state had a grand total of 179 newspapers, of which 131 were weeklies and semiweeklies and 48 were dailies. The total circulation of all newspapers was 1,475,084; in circulation of daily papers (1,691,718), the state ranked thirteenth among the states. The daily papers with the largest circulation were the *Charlotte Observer,* the Raleigh *News and Observer,* the *Greensboro Daily News,* in that order. In the weekly field, the Asheboro *Courier-Tribune,* the *Smithfield Herald,* and the *Stanly News and Press* led in circulation. By publishing many feature articles as well as news, the papers played a major role in stimulating popular interest in history, literature, and state development. It is doubtful if any other state can match the average excellence of North Carolina's daily newspapers and the high quality of leadership in their editorial advocacy of public issues. The state also has at least a dozen weekly and semiweekly papers that would rank among the best in the nation. In 1952 the courageous editorials against the Ku Klux Klan by W. Horace Carter, editor of the *Tabor City Tribune,* won for him and his paper the Pulitzer Prize "for outstanding public service by an American newspaper." This was the first and only time a weekly newspaper ever received this award. The semiweekly Whiteville *News Reporter* won a similar award in 1953.

Book Publishing

The University of North Carolina Press at Chapel Hill and the Duke University Press in Durham achieved national and international distinction for the quality and quantity of their production of scholarly books possessing great value but having little appeal for commercial publishers. The University of North Carolina Press had published approximately fifteen hundred books by 1971. These two outstanding presses also published several of the nation's leading scholarly journals. Among the growing list of commercial publishing concerns are John F. Blair, Publisher, in Winston-Salem and Heritage Printers, Inc., in Charlotte.

North Carolina Writers: Nonfiction

The educational progress of North Carolina after World War I produced an intellectual awakening of great significance and promise. No longer was the state a "literary desert" and one whose "only culture was agriculture." North Carolina was becoming a vital part of the intellectual life of the nation. After 1920 many volumes of history, biography, and autobiography—some scholarly and some popular—were published by native or adopted North Carolinians. Among the significant authors and editors in this field whose works related to North Carolina were John G. Barrett, W. L. Blythe, A. L. Brooks, R. D. W. Connor, C. C. Crittenden, Josephus Daniels, Jonathan Daniels, Chalmers Davidson, Alonzo Dill, Adelaide L. Fries, Burke Davis, Fletcher M. Green, J. G. de R. Hamilton, Archibald Henderson, Guion G. Johnson, Frontis Johnston, Hugh T. Lefler, Sarah M. Lemmon, Joseph L. Morrison, A. R. Newsome, G. W. Paschal, William S. Powell, Hugh F. Rankin, Blackwell P. Robinson, Joseph C. Robert, Phillips Russell, Joseph Steelman, J. C. Sitterson, David Stick, Nannie M. Tilley, and D. J. Whitener.

Before 1950 few adequate histories had been published about the state's counties or cities. After that date an awakened interest in this aspect of the state's history was manifested by the large number of local historical societies and a rapidly increasing number of books and other publications relating to local history. The one publication that has done most to stimulate interest in this field of local history was a popular magazine, the *State,* published in Raleigh by Bill Sharpe and Carl Goerch.

Among the state's distinguished writers were E. C. Branson, S. H. Hobbs, Jr., Howard Odum, and Rupert Vance in sociology; Richmond P. Bond, Hugh Holman, Jay Hubbell, Richard Walser, and N. I. White in literature; R. E. Coker, W. C. Coker, Z. P. Metcalf, and B. W. Wells in science; E. McNeill Poteat and W. L. Poteat in religion, Louis R. Wilson in library science, and Edgar W. Knight in the history of education.

Three of the most prolific North Carolina writers in recent years have been Harry Golden, Carl Sandburg, and Glenn Tucker—all adopted Tar Heels. Golden, a resident of Charlotte and editor of an unusual paper, the *Carolina Israelite* (published from February, 1944, to February, 1968), had three books on the best seller-list—two of them (*Only in America* and *For 2¢ Plain*) at one time. Sandburg was well known for his biography of Abraham Lincoln, but was more noted for his poetry. Tucker published many volumes, chiefly biographies of national figures and military history.

North Carolina Novelists

After 1920 a number of North Carolina novelists achieved national distinction. Among these were James Boyd, Inglis Fletcher, Bernice Kelly Harris, Robert Ruark, Betty Smith, James Street, and Thomas Wolfe. Boyd's *Drums* is one of the best novels about the American Revolution; his *Marching On* dealt with the Civil War era. Between 1940 and 1960 Mrs. Fletcher published nine novels, all of which related to early North Carolina history. In her numerous and beautiful novels, Mrs. Harris recorded her "deeply felt impressions of scenes and people in terms of their universality." Two adopted North Carolinians, Betty Smith, a native of Brooklyn, and James Street, a native of Mississippi, were novelists of national renown. Mrs. Smith's *A Tree Grows in Brooklyn* was on the best-seller list for a long time and was made into a movie. Street published many well-known novels and also short stories and popular books about the Revolution and the Civil War. Wolfe, whose "prose had force and beauty unsurpassed," wrote a "series of novels which represents the closest approach to a North Carolina or an American epic that any writer has yet produced." In the brief decade of adult-writing time allotted him, he wrote millions of words, "not a series of books but one book—a highly autobiographical story of one young man's deep and persistent sense of loneliness and his intense and unsophisticated obsession with the flight of time." His *Look Homeward, Angel* (1929) opened this series and made him famous. *Of Time and the River* continued the story of the early years of maturity. *The Web and the Rock* "restated and reshaped the story" and *You Can't Go Home Again* stressed the matured Wolfe's faith in democracy: "I believe we are lost here in America, but I believe we shall be found." On this note, Wolfe, perhaps the greatest of all North Carolina writers, died.

Among the state's outstanding novelists in recent years are Ovid Pierce, Frank B. Hanes, Richard McKenna, Reynolds Price, Doris Betts, Frances Gray Patton, Guy Owen, William M. Hardy, Ben Haas, John Ehle, and Daphne Athas.

North Carolina Poets, Playwrights, and Folklorists

James Larkin Pearson, "Poet Laureate" of North Carolina, Thad Stem, Jr., Guy Owen, Sam Ragan, and several other natives were publishing poetry of some distinction, but the two poets of greatest renown in the state were both adopted sons, Carl Sandburg and Randall Jarrell. Sandburg has been recognized for many years as one of the great poets of America. Jarrell, who taught at The University of North Carolina at Greensboro, won the 1961 National Book Award for Poetry for his book *The Woman at the Washington Zoo*.

Among other noted writers in North Carolina after 1920 were Noel Houston, Frances Gray Patton, William T. Polk, and Max Steele, in the field of the short story, and Paul Green and Laurence Stallings in drama. The Carolina Playmakers, founded in 1918 by Frederick H. Koch at The University of North Carolina, produced many notable original plays on North Carolina life. Its most distinguished product, Paul Green, was awarded the Pulitzer Prize in 1927 for his *In Abraham's Bosom.* Green also achieved national recognition for his outdoor historical pageants, or symphonic dramas, especially *The Lost Colony* and *The Common Glory,* as did Kermit Hunter for *Unto These Hills* and *Horn in the West.* Carl Goerch, John Harden, Bill Sharpe, Manly Wade

Wellman, and others wrote entertaining stories about interesting events and personalities in the state—past and present—and Charlotte Hilton Green wrote interesting and valuable books on the birds and trees of North Carolina. Robert Ruark, a native of Southport, achieved a national reputation for his syndicated column, which appeared in 145 different newspapers, and for his essays, chiefly humorous, in the *Saturday Evening Post, Esquire,* and other magazines; some of his books, notably *Something of Value* (1955), had phenomenal sales.

Among those who published books and articles on North Carolina folklore were Richard Chase, John Harden, A. P. Hudson, Guy B. Johnson, Howard W. Odum, Cecil J. Sharp, and Newman I. White. The *Frank C. Brown Collection of North Carolina Folklore,* in seven volumes (Duke University Press, 1952–62) has been called "the most imposing monument ever erected in this country to the common memory of the people in any single state." The North Carolina Folklore Society (founded in 1912) and the North Carolina Folklore Council (founded in 1937) have fostered the organized study of the state's folklore. *North Carolina Folklore,* a journal founded in 1948, has been published at Chapel Hill and more recently at Raleigh under the joint auspices of the two organizations.

Increasing Interest in Art

North Carolina made great progress in art after the mid-twenties. The mainspring of this movement was the North Carolina Art Society, which was started by Mrs. Katherine Pendleton Arrington and a few others who were determined to make North Carolinians art conscious. This organization was founded for the purpose of promoting art appreciation and education, and eventually of establishing a state art museum. In 1929 the General Assembly placed the Art Society under the patronage and control of the state, incorporating it and giving it legal power to receive donations. In 1943 the State Art Gallery was opened in Raleigh and it has consistently broadened its activities.

The 1947 General Assembly, at the exhortation of Robert Lee Humber, Greenville attorney and former international lawyer, appropriated $1 million for the purchase of paintings for a proposed state art museum. This marked the first instance in the nation's history that a state allocated such a sum for the purchase of art objects. This appropriation was contingent on its being matched by another million dollars, which seemed at the time most unlikely. But the Samuel H. Kress Foundation, at Humber's urging, did match the amount with paintings mainly of the Renaissance period, valued at a million dollars or more.

In 1951 a State Art Commission was appointed and it purchased with the million dollars appropriated for that purpose some two hundred paintings by various "old masters," including Rubens, Reynolds, Rembrandt, Van Dyck,

Sully, Copley, Gainsborough, Frans Hals, and many other famous artists. The North Carolina Museum of Art, which was opened at Raleigh on April 6, 1956, is in many respects the outstanding art collection in the United States south of Washington.

Music in Modern North Carolina

North Carolina has made tremendous strides in music in the past thirty years. One of the most significant developments has been the North Carolina Symphony Orchestra. Organized by Dr. Benjamin Swalin of Chapel Hill and supported partly by the state and partly by private subscription, this fine orchestra carries good music to all the people of the state. In the school year 1969–70 it travelled over 13,000 miles to give 140 concerts. In that year 219,644 school children heard 85 free concerts in school and civic auditoriums, recreation centers, and gymnasiums.

Other symphony orchestras in the state are located in Charlotte, Greensboro, Winston-Salem, Fayetteville, and Asheville, in addition to college orchestras.

Another notable development in recent years has been the Transylvania Music Camp at Brevard, started in 1936 by James Christian Pfohl, and operated primarily as a summer school for musicians. Each year, however, it puts on a music festival that attracts some of the most renowned lecturers and performers in the country.

The Grass Roots Opera Company, organized by Mr. and Mrs. A. J. Fletcher of Raleigh, "takes both grand and light opera in English translation to North Carolinians in town and countryside, without benefit of scenery or much costuming," for a nominal charge.

In 1959 the North Carolina Civic Ballet Company was chartered as a nonprofit organization by a group of interested citizens headed by E. N. Richards of Raleigh. The company, originally based in Raleigh, became affiliated with East Carolina University in 1967 but performs throughout the state.

For many years Bascom Lamar Lunsford of South Turkey Creek near Asheville, conducted an annual Mountain Dance and Folk Festival at Asheville. It was held "about sundown the first week in August." For a decade or so, Lunsford also put on a Carolina Folk Festival at Chapel Hill.

North Carolina composers of distinction include Lamar Stringfield, who won a Pulitzer Prize in Music in 1928 for his suite *From the Southern Mountains;* Charles G. Vardell, who composed *Carolina Symphony;* Hunter Johnson, who won the Prix de Rome in 1938; Nathaniel Dett; and William Klenz.

Church Membership

While North Carolina was witnessing an intellectual revolution, church membership was increasing at a rapid rate. According to a report of the North Carolina Council of Churches, the total church membership in the state in 1960–61 was 2,434,720 (the latest available figure), a numerical gain of 438,088 over the 1950 figure. In 1960 approximately 53 percent of the state's population belonged to a church. Slightly more than 50 percent of the church members were Baptist; more than 26 percent were Methodists and almost 8 percent were Presbyterians.

Denominations	Membership
Baptist—State Convention	913,176
Baptist—General	300,000
Baptist—Free Will	50,160
Methodist Church (N.C. and W.N.C. Conferences)	455,460
African Methodist Episcopal Zion	155,902
Methodist (Central Jurisdiction)	14,834
Methodist Wesleyan	5,708
Christian Methodist Episcopal	5,631
Presbyterian, U.S. (Synod of N.C.)	144,784
Presbyterian, U.S.A. (Catawba Synod)	14,149
Presbyterian, Assoc. Reformed	9,070
Presbyterian—other	15,000
Lutheran-United (Baptized Members)	69,093
Lutheran-Missouri Synod	7,500
Disciples of Christ	50,932
Protestant Episcopal Church	44,533
Roman Catholic Church	42,080
Congregational Christian Churches	22,037
Moravian Church	21,032
Evangelical and Reformed Church	17,050
Church of God	14,615
Society of Friends	14,260
Pentecostal Holiness	13,011
Jewish	6,000
Salvation Army	4,218
Seventh Day Adventist	3,873
Church of Christ	3,443
Pilgrim Holiness	3,257
Church of the Nazarene	2,355
Church of the Brethren	2,247
Assembly of God	2,000
Christian Missionary Alliance	1,800
Greek Orthodox	510
Other groups not listed, estimated	5,000
Total Members, All Denominations	2,434,720

Chapter 49

THE NEW COMMON-WEALTH—FOR THE PUBLIC WELFARE

In the twentieth century, particularly after World War I, the broad modern social concept of government as a service agency for community development triumphed for the first time in North Carolina. As the people demanded more and better services from government, its structure expanded, its cost increased, and taxes became heavier. This trend was an inevitable result of the increasing number and complexity of social and economic problems of public interest arising from an expanding population brought closer together by improving transportation and communication facilities.

Organization and Functions of Local Government

North Carolina counties and municipalities are created and largely controlled by the state. Their governments exist to serve the people of the county and city in respect to such needs as roads and streets, water supply, health and sanitation, education, public welfare, maintenance of law and order, protection of life and property, and public morals. Their officials are elected by and responsible to the people.

The North Carolina county is governed by a board of commissioners (usually three or five) whose authorities and rulings are enforced by the sheriff. Other elective county officials are the register of deeds, treasurer, surveyor, coroner, clerk of superior court, constables, and magistrates. The district superior court, meeting periodically at the county seat, is the chief judicial authority; but, to relieve the increasing congestion of litigation in recent years, several new types of county courts have been authorized, such as the county recorder's court.

General state law authorizes four plans for the organization and government of municipalities: (1) mayor and council elected at large; (2) mayor and council elected by districts and at large; (3) commission; and (4) mayor, council, and

668

city manager. The mayor is the executive head; the council is the legislative body and also the administrative agency except in the managerial plan, under which a manager chosen by the council is the administrator. The council acts as a unit in administrative matters except in the commission plan, where administration is divided among the members. The municipal recorder's court is the major city court, but others such as domestic relations, juvenile, and justice of the peace courts are authorized.

The Structure and Services of the State Government

State government also became of greater and increasing significance to the citizens of the state. Its executive and administrative functions are exercised by an elective governor; an ex officio council of state; several elective constitutional officers—lieutenant governor, secretary of state, treasurer, auditor, superintendent of public instruction, attorney general, commissioner of agriculture, commissioner of labor, and commissioner of insurance; and a host of departments, boards, and commissions established by the legislature. Legislative authority is exercised by the biennially elected bicameral General Assembly consisting of a Senate of 50 members and a House of Representatives of 120 members. Before 1956 the General Assembly met in regular session on Wednesday after the first Monday in all odd-numbered years. By a constitutional amendment adopted in that year, this date was changed to the corresponding day in February.

The North Carolina House of Representatives

Until 1967 the unit of representation in the House of Representatives was the county, with each of the state's one hundred counties having at least one representative. The extra twenty seats were distributed among the most populous counties. In the 1961 General Assembly the additional twenty seats were allotted as follows: Mecklenburg, three; Guilford, three; Buncombe, two; Forsyth, two; Wake, two; and Cabarrus, Cumberland, Durham, Gaston, Johnston, Pitt, Robeson, and Rowan, one each. The inequitable distribution of seats—a characteristic feature of North Carolina throughout its long history—caused bitter complaints in some of the more populous counties. The state constitution (Article 2, Section 5) requires the General Assembly to reapportion seats in the House of Representatives after each federal census. Throughout the decade of the 1950s the legislature failed to obey this mandate. The General Assembly of 1961 made a slight "reapportionment," and, as a result, in the General Assembly of 1963 Mecklenburg, Alamance, Cumberland, and Onslow counties gained an additional member, while Buncombe, Cabarrus, Pitt and Johnston lost one member each. Under this "reapportionment," the twelve most populous counties, with a 1960 population of 1,735,000—and growing much more rapidly than most of the counties—had a total of thirty-six

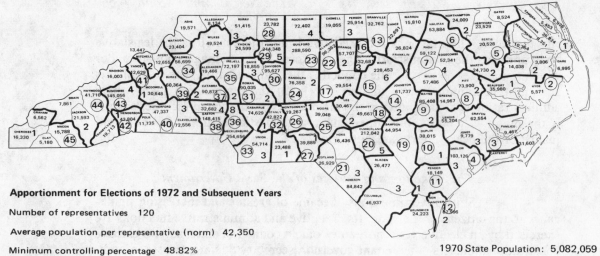

Apportionment for Elections of 1972 and Subsequent Years

Number of representatives   120

Average population per representative (norm)   42,350

Minimum controlling percentage   48.82%

Largest to smallest ratio   1.21 to 1

Range of deviation from norm   -10.24% to +8.22%

Average relative deviation per representative   4.07%

1970 State Population: 5,082,059

Sess. Laws 1971, Chap. 483

① District number

3   Number of representatives per district

North Carolina House of Representatives, 1972

Cartography by the Department of Geography and Earth Sciences
The University of North Carolina at Charlotte

seats in the House of Representatives, while the twelve least populous counties, with a 1960 population of only 84,780—and growing very slowly, or not at all—had twelve representatives. This apportionment amounted to "government by acreage," and it was obviously not in line with the "one man, one vote" required by the federal courts. Accordingly, in a special session of the General Assembly of 1966, the county ceased to be the unit of representation, being replaced by "county districts." Under this new plan there were forty-nine "districts," with Mecklenburg having seven representatives; Guilford, six; Forsyth, five; Wake, four; Durham, three; Alamance, Pitt, Wayne, New Hanover, Davidson, Rowan, and Catawba, two each; Duplin, Moore, Richmond, Stanly, and Henderson, one each. In the remaining thirty-one "districts" two or more counties were grouped together. For instance, the First District (Camden, Chowan, Currituck, Gates, Pasquotank, and Perquimans) was given two representatives; the Second District (Beaufort, Dare, Hyde, Tyrrell, and Washington) also had two representatives; the Third District (Carteret, Craven, and Pamlico) was allotted three seats; and the Forty-ninth District (Cherokee, Clay, Graham, and Macon) was given only one representative.

The State Senate

The fifty state senators are elected by the voters in twenty-seven districts. Article 2, Section 4 of the state constitution reads: "The Senate

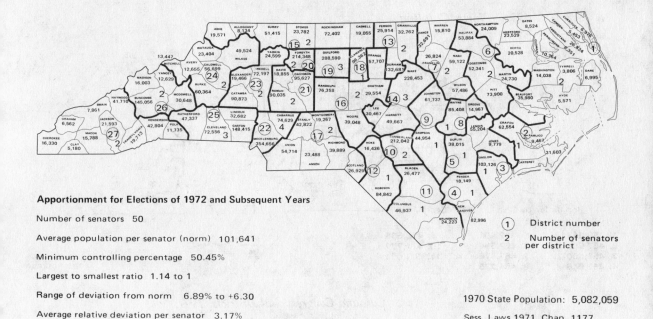

Apportionment for Elections of 1972 and Subsequent Years

Number of senators 50

Average population per senator (norm) 101,641

Minimum controlling percentage 50.45%

Largest to smallest ratio 1.14 to 1

Range of deviation from norm 6.89% to +6.30

Average relative deviation per senator 3.17%

1970 State Population: 5,082,059

Sess. Laws 1971, Chap. 1177

①	District number
2	Number of senators per district

North Carolina Senate, 1972

Cartography by the Department of Geography and Earth Sciences
The University of North Carolina at Charlotte

Districts shall be so altered by the General Assembly, at the first session after the return of every enumeration by order of Congress, that each Senate District shall contain, as near as may be, an equal number of inhabitants, excluding aliens and Indians not taxed, and shall remain unaltered until the return of another enumeration, and shall at all times consist of contiguous territory; and no county shall be divided in the formation of a Senate District, unless such county shall be equitably entitled to two or more Senators."

The General Assembly of 1961 failed to carry out this constitutional mandate. On the basis of population some districts were overrepresented while others were greatly underrepresented. In one district, for instance, there was an average of one senator for 51,355 people, and in four other districts the average was one for less than 60,000 population each. In five of the most populous districts the average was as follows: District 20 (Mecklenburg County), one senator for 272,111 people; District 17 (Guilford), one for 246,-520; District 22 (Forsyth), one for 189,428; District 31 (Buncombe), one for 130,074; and District 26 (Gaston), one for 127,074.

On March 25, 1962, the Supreme Court of the United States ruled that "lower federal courts may determine whether city voters are unconstitutionally discriminated against in the apportionment of legislative seats." The long-range effect of this decision led to a shift in control of the General Assembly to urban areas. The urban voters of America had won a momentous first-round victory in their long fight against rural domination of state legislatures. It was not until

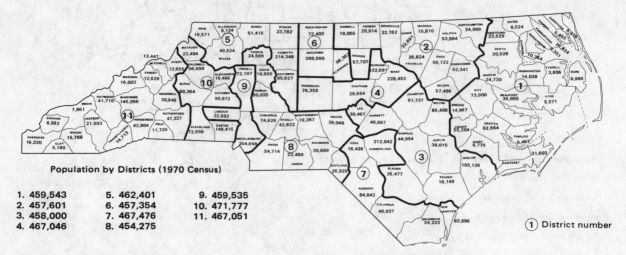

Population by Districts (1970 Census)

1. 459,543	5. 462,401	9. 459,535
2. 457,601	6. 457,354	10. 471,777
3. 458,000	7. 467,476	11. 467,051
4. 467,046	8. 454,275	

North Carolina Congressional Districts, 1971

Cartography by the Department of Geography and Earth Sciences
The University of North Carolina at Charlotte

a special session of the North Carolina General Assembly in 1966, however, that seats in the Senate and House were reapportioned in line with federal court rulings of "one man, one vote." Under this new plan, the urban districts gained many seats in the Senate, and the rural areas lost many. For instance, District 23 (Mecklenburg) was to elect three senators; District 18 (Guilford and Randolph), three; District 12 (Wake), two; District 22 (Forsyth), two; District 1 (Bertie, Camden, Chowan, Currituck, Gates, Hertford, Northampton, Pasquotank, Perquimans, and Washington), two; and District 33 (Cherokee, Clay, Graham, Jackson, Macon, Swain, and Transylvania), one.

The 1971 General Assembly reapportioned seats in both houses in line with the 1970 census figures.

Congressional Districts

Neither the United States Constitution nor the state constitution currently prescribes specific standards the General Assembly must follow in laying out Congressional districts. From 1842 to 1850, and again from 1872 to 1929, there were federal statutory requirements that members of the national House of Representatives be chosen from single-member districts, consisting of compact area and contiguous territory, and equal in population to every other congressional district in the same state. All of these requirements were repealed in 1929, however. After that date these districts in North Carolina gerrymandered to the advantage of the dominant Democratic party, and glaring inequities resulted. The following table is self-explanatory.

Populations of Congressional Districts

	1950	1960
First District	247,894	253,511
Second District	306,904	313,728
Third District	308,470	382,124
Fourth District	401,913	442,059
Fifth District	355,088	408,992
Sixth District	398,351	487,159
Seventh District	394,214	455,630
Eighth District	369,455	396,369
Ninth District	338,907	364,561
Tenth District	360,318	452,732
Eleventh District	295,724	307,575
Twelfth District	284,691	291,715

As a result of North Carolina's relative decline in population, as revealed by the federal Census of 1960, the state delegation in the national House of Representatives was reduced from twelve to eleven. The 1961 General Assembly set up the eleven congressional districts effective for the 1962 elections. Not one of the Republican members of the legislature was permitted to serve on the Committee on Congressional Districts and all Republicans in the General Assembly opposed the formations enacted into law. The accompanying map reveals large population discrepancies and flagrant gerrymandering, a situation not peculiar to North Carolina or to the Democratic party, but, nevertheless, one which evoked considerable criticism.

Population of Congressional Districts
(After redistricting of 1961)

	1961	Democratic voting strength based on 1960 returns for governor. Percentage of vote cast.
First District	277,861	80
Second District	350,135	79
Third District	430,360	63
Fourth District	460,795	53
Fifth District	454,261	49
Sixth District	487,159	47
Seventh District	448,933	70
Eighth District	491,461	55
Ninth District	404,093	44
Tenth District	390,020	56
Eleventh District	361,077	49

The map on page 672 shows the North Carolina congressional districts as laid out by the General Assembly of 1971—in line with the "one man, one vote" mandate of the federal courts.

The State's Judiciary

The judicial branch of the state government is made up of the following parts: the Supreme Court, the Intermediate Court of Appeals, the Superior Courts, the District Courts, and the magistrates of the District Courts. The Supreme Court consists of a chief justice and six associate justices. These judges are elected by the voters of the whole state for a term of eight years, with privilege of reelection. When a vacancy occurs, by death or resignation, the governor appoints a person to fill the unexpired term. Unlike other courts in the state, the Supreme Court does not try original cases. It is a court of appeal. The Intermediate Court of Appeals, which hears certain appeals from the lower courts, consists of one chief judge and five other judges elected by the voters of the whole state for eight-year terms, with privilege of reelection. The Superior Court judges (there were thirty in 1970), who try civil and criminal cases, are also elected by the voters of the entire state for eight-year terms, with privilege of reelection. The solicitors for the Superior Courts are elected by the voters of their solicitorial districts (there were twenty-one in 1970) for four-year terms.

Until 1965 the justice-of-the-peace court was the lowest court in the state. This court, consisting of one justice of the peace, might try cases of common assaults and fights where no deadly weapon was used and no serious damage was done. The justice of the peace also tried civil cases where the amount of money involved did not exceed two hundred dollars. Ordinarily this court had no jury. Instead of being paid a fixed salary, the justices of the peace received fees. They were elected by voters in townships and in cities and towns, while others might be appointed by the governor.

Increasing criticism of the justice-of-the-peace system led to the passage of the Judicial Department Act of 1965. This law abolished the office of justice of the peace. In its place, the office of magistrate was created. Magistrates are nominated by the clerk of Superior Court of the county in which they are to serve. The regular resident Superior Court judge of the district then appoints the magistrate for a term of two years from the list of nominees. Magistrates operate under the direct control of the chief district court judge, retaining some of the old functions of the justice of the peace in criminal matters but with even more power in civil actions.

Protection of Life and Property

The oldest and most basic function of government—protection of life and property—has been the objective of the increasing number of criminal and civil laws, courts, and branches of the state and local governments. This protection was also the objective of the old adjutant general's department, which provided military force in emergencies, most commonly in strikes and labor disturbances; of the Driver License Division in the Department of Motor Vehicles, which examined applicants and issued licenses to automobile drivers, and of the State Highway Patrol in its efforts to enforce highway laws and safety.

The state government's most important service to the people, that of public education, has been discussed in earlier chapters. Especially important and most expensive among the state's services are the construction, maintenance, and control of highways. This subject has also been covered in other portions of this volume. The role of the state government in the development of agriculture, industry, trade, and finance has also been discussed in earlier chapters. In the remaining sections of this chapter the many and varied services of the state government for the general welfare of the people of North Carolina will be discussed.

Protection for Consumers

The state government found it necessary to serve its citizens by protecting them as consumers of services and goods purchased chiefly from private individuals and corporations. Many examining and licensing boards were created to safeguard the health of citizens and to guarantee high quality of service by lawyers, physicians, pharmacists, dentists, veterinarians, nurses, embalmers, optometrists, barbers, beauticians, architects, engineers, plumbers, and other trades and professions. Mention has already been made of the Utilities Commission, which superseded the Corporation Commission in 1933, and which has power to require efficient service at reasonable rates from railroads, telegraph, telephone, bus, electric light, power, water, and gas companies, and other public utilities. The Insurance Department, headed by an elective commissioner, has sought to safeguard purchasers of insurance and patrons of building and loan associations. Mention has been made in other chapters of state regulation of banking, labor legislation, rural electrification, and control of the sale of alcoholic beverages through the ABC stores.

Public Welfare Program

A consistent and popular policy of the state government in the twentieth century was the care of its unfortunate citizens—the dependent, defective, and delinquent. In 1917 the state created the Board of Charities and Public Welfare and began the development of a statewide system of public welfare based on the counties, each of which should have a public welfare board, a juvenile court, and a whole or part-time superintendent of public welfare. The State Board supervised all state charitable and penal institutions, assisted counties in their public welfare work, inspected county penal and charitable institutions, and administered benefit payments under the Social Security Act to the aged needy, the needy blind, and dependent children. The board sought on behalf of the state to secure for the insane, feeble-minded, poor, crippled, orphan, criminal, neglected, dependent, and delinquent the protection and care demanded by their own needs and the public welfare. Among the board's supervisory services which touch the lives of many thousands and which do not involve direct financial aid are that of child adoption procedures and the inspection of private organizations receiving and placing children, juvenile delinquency, boarding homes for the aged, mental testing services, school attendance, and child labor certification.

For a long time North Carolina's charitable and correctional institutions were almost disgraceful. Since 1920, thanks to some strong leadership, great improvements have been made. The facilities of the old institutions for criminals, insane, blind, and deaf were greatly expanded, and new institutions were established for mental defectives, cripples, victims of tuberculosis, dependent Confederate soldiers and their widows, and delinquents of both sexes and races. The state contributed to some orphanages, though it did not maintain any.

State appropriations to charitable and correctional institutions rose to more than $2 million in 1939, when the state maintained or aided twenty such institutions containing about 25,000 patients and inmates. By 1952 the number of these institutions had increased to twenty-eight, with total state appropriations of over $15 million. A bond issue of $22 million, adopted by popular vote in October, 1953, was used for permanent improvements at the state's mental institutions. During the fiscal year 1969–70 public assistance to the aged, dependent children, the permanently and totally disabled and the blind, and general assistance totaled $104,218,964. The average monthly number of recipients was 194,693.

In 1971 the state was maintaining four hospitals for the mentally ill (at Butner, Morganton, Raleigh, and Goldsboro); four schools for the mentally retarded (at Kinston, Butner, Goldsboro, and Morganton); three alcoholic rehabilitation centers (at Butner, Greenville, and Black Mountain); four sanitoriums for the tubercular (at Black Mountain, McCain, Wilson, and Chapel Hill); one hospital for crippled children; a home for Confederate veterans' widows; five correctional schools for boys (at Butner, Rocky Mount, McCain, Hoffman, and Concord) and two for girls (Eagle Springs and Kinston); a juvenile evaluation center at Swannanoa; a two-campus school in Raleigh attended by both deaf and blind children, and schools in Wilson and

Morganton for the deaf; four prisons and one prison farm; sixty-one field units (formerly "camps"); and six youth centers. During 1969–70 the state spent $68,676,918 for the operation of mental institutions.

The War Against Disease: Work of the State Board of Health

The early activities of the State Board of Health have been discussed in a previous chapter. After World War I the functions and effectiveness of this important agency increased. Its most significant activity during the past quarter of a century has been the extension and strengthening of the local health program. By 1949 all of the state's one hundred counties had local health departments. Annual state appropriations for the State Board of Health had expanded to nearly $500,000 by 1940; to more than $2,000,000 by 1950; to $4,047,277 in 1961–62; and to $8,600,344 in 1969–70. Expenditures by the board from all sources amounted to $14,886,873 in 1969–70. Of this sum, $2,535,759 came from federal funds.

The budget for "Local Health Services" in North Carolina for 1970-71 was:

Total state funds	$2,028,834
Total federal funds	120,000
Total local funds	15,112,714
Total budget, local health	$17,261,538

Under the leadership of the State Board of Health, the state almost eliminated typhoid fever, diptheria, smallpox, malaria, hookworm, and rabies as deadly diseases, and greatly reduced the ravages of tuberculosis, polio, and syphilis by distributing serums, vaccines, antitoxins, and medicine and by a campaign of health education. Since 1913 the board has kept records of all births and deaths, and in recent years has investigated industrial plants with dust and other hazards to health. As early as 1919 it began the inspection and ratings of hotels, and later this policy was extended to all public eating places. Other services of the Board of Health have been the dissemination of literature on communicable diseases; prenatal care and clinical supervision of orthopedic clinics and provisions for surgical and medical care for crippled children; mouth-health programs of lectures, free examinations, and minor treatment by state dentists in many cooperating counties; construction of sanitary privies in rural areas; and supervision and advice in respect to public problems relating to water supply, sewage disposal, and sanitary conditions in malarial areas, public eating places, hotels, schools, swimming pools, jails, and camps. The board succeeded in stimulating many counties to appropriate money for the employment of health officers, inspectors, and nurses, and for the promotion of public health. In 1938 the first state-sponsored birth control clinics in the United States were opened by the State Board of Health, in collaboration with local health authorities. In 1955 and 1956 the Board of Health played a prominent part in the distribution of the Salk polio vaccine to local boards of health and physicians, whereby thousands of children were given anti-polio "shots." On March 31, 1959, North Carolina passed the first state law in the nation pertaining to poliomyelitis, making inoculation for this disease mandatory for all children "between the ages of two months and six years."

A significant development, though not associated directly with the Board of Health, was the establishment in December, 1937, of the Zachary Smith Reynolds Foundation for the control of venereal diseases.

The State's Hospital and Medical Care Program

On January 31, 1944, Governor Broughton presented to the Board of Trustees of The University of North Carolina a report from "a committee of distinguished physicians," which pointed out that "North Carolina is now the 11th most populous state in the Union but is 42nd in number of hospital beds per 1,000 population . . . and 45th in number of doctors per 1,000 population." This committee joined the governor in recommending "the expansion of the two-year medical school at the University of North Carolina into a standard four-year medical school with a central hospital of 600 beds or more" and "a hospital and medical care program for the entire state with this noble objective as expressed by Governor Broughton: 'The ultimate purpose of this program should be that no person in North Carolina shall lack hospital care or medical treatment by reason of poverty or low income.' "

By unanimous action, the Board of Trustees approved this program, whereupon Governor Broughton appointed a State Hospital and Medical Care Commission, with Clarence Poe as chairman. In its report, based on eight months of careful study, this commission declared that "three things are supremely needed: MORE DOCTORS, MORE HOSPITALS, MORE INSURANCE." It went on to say, "We cannot have enough doctors without more hospitals . . . nor enough hospitals without greater popular ability to pay for hospital service . . . and such ability to pay on the part of the poorer half of our population is impossible without insurance." The commission recommended that "the State encourage in every practicable way the development of group medical care plans which make it possible for people to insure themselves against expensive illness, expensive treatment by specialists, and extended hospitalization. The Blue Cross Plan of hospital and surgical service with some modifications can meet the needs of that part of the state's population able to pay all their medical costs. It is recommended that the Blue Cross organizations be asked to expand their services to include the general practitioner and prescribed drugs."

Blue Cross–Blue Shield in North Carolina

The idea of group insurance was not new in the state. As early as 1933 the Hospital Care Association had been organized at Durham. And, in March, 1934, the Hospital Saving Association of North Carolina was organized as a nonstock, nonprofit, public service corporation, with headquarters at Chapel Hill. The program of the association met with prompt success. By the end of 1961 it had a total of 639,452 subscribers and had paid a total of over $145 million in claims. Hospital Care had more than 400,000 subscribers and had paid over $75 million in claims.

The Five-Year Hospital Plan inaugurated on July 8, 1947, was virtually completed on schedule, 127 projects having been authorized at a cost of over $68 million. Under this plan for a statewide system of hospitals, health centers, and clinics designed to provide better medical and health service for the people, approximately five thousand new hospital beds had been provided for, making North Carolina second only to Texas in the number added in the five-year period after July 1, 1947. Of the $68 million mentioned above, over $24 million came from federal funds, over $29 million from local funds, and a little more than $14 million from state revenues. As of January 1, 1971, there were 160 hospitals in the state, with 34,835 beds.

When James B. Duke wrote the Trust Indenture creating the Duke Endowment in 1924, he said, "I have selected hospitals as another of the principal objects of this trust because I recognize that they have become indispensable institutions, not only by way of ministering to the comfort of the sick but in increasing the efficiency of mankind and prolonging human life." Between December 11, 1924, and December 31, 1970, the Duke Endowment, which at the latter date had an approximate market value of $503,437,506, had given $59,669,181 to North Carolina hospitals.

Development of the State's Resources

To coordinate and expand its services in conserving, developing, and utilizing its natural resources, the state created the Department of Conservation and Development in 1925. This department enforced the fish and game laws, issued hunting and fishing licenses, operated fish hatcheries, maintained game and wild life preserves and sanctuaries, and sought to protect and develop the fish and game resources of the state. It supervised state parks and the work of forest wardens, tried to save forests from destruction by fire, and operated forest nurseries for reforestation. It maintained stream-gauging stations and carried on studies of water resources, power development, beach erosion, stream pollution, flood control, and other conservation projects. Under the direction of the state geologist, it collected data on mineral deposits and mining operations and worked toward the development of a wider use of mineral resources. Finally, it publicized the scenic, commercial, and industrial attractions of North Carolina to draw tourists and industry. Beginning in 1937, large appropriations were made for state advertising. This policy helped attract industry as well as tourists. By 1952 the tourist or "travel-serving industry" in North Carolina amounted to over $300 million a year. In 1970 it was estimated at $802 million, making it the state's third largest industry. In 1970 tourists spent an estimated $518 million in North Carolina, which was 6 percent of the state's total trade.

The rich and varied forest resources of the state are important in relation to industry, wild game, recreational facilities, and the protection of watersheds. The United States government helped to preserve its forest resources by establishing four National Forests, upon which only mature timber is cut and scientific management is practiced. These forests are Pisgah and Nantahala in the mountains, Uharie in the Piedmont, and Croatan in the Coastal Plain.

State Parks and Historic Sites

Climate, scenery, flora and fauna, topography, historic places, good roads, modern hotels and motels, and advertising combined to make North Carolina attractive for recreation, sports, and health. Summer resorts along the Atlantic coast and the inland sounds and in the mountains and winter resorts in the Sandhills were developed extensively with the aid of individuals and corporations. But the state itself contributed to recreational development by its program of good roads, conservation, advertising, and state parks. In 1971 the state had seventeen state parks: Cliffs of the Neuse (Wayne County); Duke Power (Iredell); Fort Macon (Carteret); Hammocks Beach (Onslow); Hanging Rock (Stokes); Jones Lake (Bladen); Masonboro (New Hanover); Morrow Mountain (Stanly); Mount Jefferson (Ashe); Mount Mitchell (Yancey); Pettigrew (Washington and Tyrrell); Pilot Mountain (Surry); Raven Rock (Harnett); Singletary Lake (Bladen); Sandhills Nature Preserve (Moore); William B. Umstead (Wake); Stone Mountain (Wilkes and Alleghany).

In accordance with an act of the 1955 General Assembly seven state historic sites were transferred to the State Department of Archives and History for administration. By 1971 the number of "State Historic Sites" under the administration of this department had grown to fifteen: Alamance Battleground (Alamance); Charles B. Aycock Birthplace (Wayne); Historic Bath (Beaufort); Bennett Place (Durham); Bentonville Battleground (Johnston); Brunswick Town (Brunswick); Richard Caswell Memorial (Lenoir); C.S.S. *Neuse* (Lenoir); Fort Fisher (New Hanover); James K. Polk Birthplace (Mecklenburg); Somerset Place (Washington and Tyrrell); Town Creek Indian Mound (Montgomery); Tryon Palace (Craven); and Zebulon B. Vance Birthplace (Buncombe). Two other properties owned by the state and under the indirect control of the Department of Archives and History but administered by local organizations are the House in the Horseshoe (Philip Alston House) in Moore County and the James Iredell House in Edenton.

Historic Fort Macon remained under the administration of the Department of Conservation and Development, and the beautiful Elizabethan Garden at Manteo is administered by the Garden Clubs of North Carolina.

In addition to state-owned sites, other historic places have been or are being restored with small amounts of assistance from the state. Notable among these are the Boggan-Hammond House (Anson); Hope Plantation (Bertie); Cupola and Barker Houses (Chowan); Blandwood (Guilford); Carson House (McDowell); Fort Defiance (Caldwell); Hezekiah Alexander House (Mecklenburg); and Joel Lane House (Wake). Old Salem, one of the most important historic preservation districts in the South, is administered by the privately endowed Old Salem, Incorporated.

By 1971 thirteen historic places in North Carolina had been designated as "Registered National Historic Landmarks": Palmer-Marsh House (Beaufort); Biltmore Estate (Buncombe); Reed Gold Mine (Cabarrus); Chowan County Courthouse and Cupola House (Chowan); Duke Homestead and Tobacco Factory (Durham); Old Salem Historic District, Salem Tavern, and Single Brothers House (Forsyth); Carl Sandburg Home (Henderson); Town Creek Indian Mound (Montgomery); Fort Fisher (New Hanover); and Old East Building of the University of North Carolina (Orange). Designation as a landmark does not affect the ownership and administration of these properties.

National Parks, Sites, and Memorials

In 1926 the national government established the Great Smoky Mountains National Park containing about a half-million acres in North Carolina and Tennessee. One of America's most magnificent highways, the Blue Ridge Parkway, connects this park and the Shenandoah National Park in Virginia—a distance of about 480 miles. Since 1955 the Great Smoky Mountains Park has attracted more visitors each year than any national park in the country. The Cape Hatteras National Recreational Area composed of some 28,500 acres in public beach and dune lands was the first and largest unit of such character in the National Park Service. The Cape Lookout National Seashore is in the process of being established. In 1941 Fort Raleigh National Historic Site was established "to commemorate the earliest attempt at English colonization within the limits of the continental United States and the birthplace of Virginia Dare, first white child of English parentage born in the New World." Nearby on top of Kill Devil Hill is the Wright Brothers National Memorial erected by the United States government in 1932, "in commemoration of the conquest of the air by the brothers Wilbur and Orville Wright conceived by Genius, achieved by Dauntless Resolution and Unconquerable Faith." There are two National Military Parks in North Carolina, both commemorating battles of the American Revolution: Guilford Court House (March 15, 1781) near Greensboro, and Moore's Creek Bridge (February 27, 1776) near Wilmington.

State Department of Archives and History

One of the most important and effective state agencies is the State Department of Archives and History (formerly the North Carolina Historical Commission). This department, which has been considered one of the best of its kind in the nation, collects and preserves valuable public archives and other historical records so that family, local, and state history can be investigated and written; issues historical publications, such as books, pamphlets, and a quarterly magazine, the *North Carolina Historical Review,* one of the leading state historical journals in the nation; administers the North Carolina Museum of History; and marks historic sites. The General Assembly of 1935 authorized a statewide historical marker program. This program is conducted jointly by the Office of Archives and History and the State Highway Commission. Between 1935 and January, 1971, more than a thousand "North Carolina Historical Highway Markers" had been written and erected, plus a number of special Civil War markers, erected by this department in cooperation with the Civil War Centennial Commission. Under the Civil War Marker Program, the Battles of Roanoke Island, Averasboro, New Bern, Fort Macon, and others have been or will be marked.

The Increasing Cost of Government

The vast expansion of the service of government—federal, state, and local—necessitated constantly increasing expenditures and heavier taxes. State expenditures rose slowly but steadily from 1900 to World War I, then increased rapidly until the advent of the New Deal in 1933, and in recent years have reached "almost astronomical heights." Annual state expenditures in North Carolina in millions of dollars rose from 2 in 1900 to 3¾ in 1916, 7½ in 1922, 20¾ in 1926, 49¾ in 1932, 53⅓ in 1935, 75 in 1939, 85 in 1941, 271 in 1951, 330 in 1955, 443 in 1961, and 913 for the fiscal year 1969–70. These figures do not include expenditures from special funds, from institutional earnings, from federal aid, and for permanent improvements other than roads. Highway expenditures from federal aid for the fiscal year 1969–70 amounted to $76,487,000,000. Ordinary legislative, executive, administrative, and judicial costs of the state government increased steadily. By the 1960s North Carolina had the largest number of state government employees per one thousand population of any state in the nation. This high ratio was due to the fact that all public school employees and public highway workers are state employees in North Carolina, whereas they are local employees in most of the other states.

The mounting state expenditures were largely due to the expanding program of economic activities for the public good. The greatest increases were for highways, which in the 1920s came to exceed all other state government expenditures combined and amounted to nearly half of the state budget in 1939, and for public schools, which required about one-third of the state budget in that year, almost two-fifths in 1955–56, and almost one-half in 1960–61.

The state's "General Fund Revenue," which is derived largely from income taxes, sales taxes, franchise taxes, license taxes, beverage taxes, insurance taxes, and inheritance and gift taxes, increased from $23,000,000 in 1933–34, to $90,453,171 in 1944–45, to $224,614,000 in 1955–56, and to $878,550,034 in 1969–70. During these same years the "Highway Fund Revenue," largely from gasoline taxes and motor vehicle registrations, jumped from $31,499,621 to $33,855,933 to $139,378,567, and to $307,854,223 in 1969–70. The states "Agriculture Fund Revenue," derived largely from a tax on fertilizer, has never been large. In 1933–34 it was only $308,667. By 1949–50 it had reached the million-dollar mark, and by 1969–70 it was $2,540,541.

In the fiscal year ending June 30, 1972, approximately 69½ cents of every dollar from the state's "General Fund" went for education, more than 15 cents for human resources, and about 4 cents for social rehabilitation and control. In other words, approximately 88½ percent of these expenditures were for the state's "general welfare." The following table shows the sources and percentages of state revenues and expenditures for the fiscal year ending June 30, 1972.

Revenues

General Fund (75.62%)	$1,093,453,065	
Income		
Individual	361,816,480	(25.02%)
Corporate	122,034,298	(8.44%)
Sales and use	324,824,018	(22.46%)
Franchise	71,073,722	(4.92%)
Beverage	60,583,412	(4.19%)
Insurance	35,927,677	(2.48%)
Interest	24,325,582	(1.68%)
Inheritance and gift	23,214,697	(1.61%)
Soft drink, cigarettes, and license	48,021,967	(3.32%)
Bank, building and loan, and others	21,631,212	(1.50%)
TOTAL GENERAL FUND	1,093,453,065	
Highway Funds (24.38%)	352,488,454	
Gasoline	253,898,033	(17.56%)
Motor vehicle registration	81,575,756	(5.64%)
Interest and miscellaneous revenue	13,014,273	(.90%)
Other	4,000,392	(.28%)
TOTAL HIGHWAY FUND	352,488,454	
TOTAL REVENUES	1,445,941,519	

Expenditures

General Fund (74.11%)	1,028,634,601	
Education		
Public schools	526,575,641	(37.94%)
Higher education and		
related activities	188,734,109	(13.60%)
Human resources	156,297,465	(11.26%)
General government	55,075,340	(3.97%)
Social rehabilitation and control	40,881,783	(2.94%)
Debt service	18,171,391	(1.31%)
Agriculture	19,826,920	(1.43%)
Natural and economic resources		
and miscellaneous services	23,071,952	(1.66%)
TOTAL GENERAL FUND	$1,028,634,601	
Highway Fund (25.89%)	359,377,957	
Construction and maintenance	255,142,972	(18.38%)
Administration	59,087,815	(4.26%)
Debt service	32,617,500	(2.35%)
State aid to municipalities	12,529,670	(.90%)
TOTAL HIGHWAY FUND	359,377,957	
TOTAL EXPENDITURES	1,388,012,588	

State and Local Government Debt

The combined state and local bonded debt as of June 30, 1972, was $1,627,859,149, or $328.08 per capita, compared with the national average of $1,806.24 per capita for the fiscal year 1970.

Chapter 50

IN THE MAINSTREAM:
AN ERA OF GREAT
GROWTH AND CHANGE

Greater social, economic, and political changes occurred throughout the world in the past quarter century than had ever taken place in any similar period in history. North Carolina and the nation were entering a vastly different world from any they had ever known. During this short span of years "the beginning of a major turn was made in the life of North Carolina, turning toward the mainstream. It is a beginning, but its nature seems to be fundamental and general in the life of the state."

As has been indicated in earlier chapters, North Carolina has been a rural, agricultural state moving toward industrialization. During the early 1940s the demand and prices for farm products increased and the state's industrial plants "were humming at increased wages." But this was a prosperity based on wartime needs. There was "no automatic industrial and general economic growth in North Carolina during the postwar period." The state continued to make progress but slowly, losing ground relatively. It was this situation that produced the crisis of the early 1950s. This situation was well summarized by George L. Simpson, Jr., in the May, 1960, issue of The University of North Carolina *News Letter*. He wrote: "The state, which in 1945 was several times the largest industrial state in the Southeast and one of the largest in the Nation, was not making satisfactory progress in industrial growth. Ground was being lost in manufacturing wage rates. The per capita income situation had worsened. Agricultural income was beginning to level off. Out-migration was picking up. The demand for public services was growing far faster than tax receipts. It was to this crisis that the two administrations of Governor Luther Hodges have addressed themselves, to the particular need of industrial growth as the basic answer." Hodges, as lieutenant governor, had become the state's chief executive upon the death of Governor William B. Umstead in November, 1954.

685

The Administration of Umstead

The 1953 General Assembly demonstrated its belief in the "Go Forward" program for North Carolina by authorizing the issuance of $14,-250,000 of state bonds for permanent improvements at the state's institutions of higher learning, correctional and charitable institutions, and departments. It also authorized a special election on a $50,000,000 bond issue to aid counties in construction of school buildings, and a $22,000,000 issue for permanent improvements at the state's mental institutions. In October the voters approved both proposals by an overwhelming vote, not a single county voting in the negative.

The "Bryant Committee's" Report on Higher Education

The General Assembly also adopted a joint resolution providing for the appointment by the governor of a commission to make a study of all institutions of higher education supported by state funds. After a lengthy and careful study the Commission on Higher Education, headed by Victor S. Bryant, and commonly called the "Bryant Committee," made its report to Governor Hodges in January, 1955. Among its other "findings," the commission reported that:

"In 1950, North Carolina ranked 47th among the 48 states as to the proportion of its population in college. Only 15.3 per cent . . . The national figure . . . was 28.4 per cent. . . .

"North Carolina does not rank 47th in *support* of higher education. In 1950, North Carolina ranked 32nd among the states in the funds received by institutions of higher education from the State for operating purposes per capita . . .

"North Carolina is not getting the results in higher education which might be expected in view of the amount of money being spent . . . In studying this problem, the Commission has discovered a number of situations which may account for it.

"One is the unjustified duplication of program and functions by the institutions. Such duplication in specialized areas of learning is expensive and wasteful. There is no provision for an effective allocation of functions at the present time.

"Another situation lies in the present method of appropriating funds for the support of the institutions. Accurate analysis of financial requests from institutions requires that uniform systems of student and fiscal accounting be installed so that valid data on which to base decisions concerning the wise division of available funds may be secured. . . .

"Among the state supported institutions of higher learning there exist a number of divergent and, in some instances, conflicting educational policies concerning which the Commission feels that a measure of uniformity would be highly desirable . . ."

The commission made fifteen specific recommendations and concluded its report by recommending the passage by the General Assembly of "an act creating a State Board of Higher Education, and providing for its members, their qualifications, selection, appointment, powers, duties, and financing."

Politics and the 1954 Off-Year Election

Senator Willis Smith died on June 26, 1953, and many North Carolinians were surprised when Governor Umstead appointed as his successor Alton A. Lennon, Wilmington attorney and former state legislator. On May 29, 1954, former Governor W. Kerr Scott defeated Lennon for the senatorial nomination by a vote of 312,053 to 286,730, in a very bitter contest in which the race question played a major role. Meanwhile Senator Clyde R. Hoey died on May 12, and Governor Umstead appointed Supreme Court Justice Sam J. Ervin, Jr. as his successor. In the general election, Ervin was elected without opposition for the remaining two years of Hoey's term. Scott defeated Republican Paul C. West by a vote of 408,312 to 211,322. Five days later, Governor Umstead died and, on November 9, Lieutenant Governor Luther H. Hodges of Leaksville took the oath of office to fill out the remaining twenty-six months of the late governor's term. In 1956 Hodges was elected to the governorship "in his own right." He thus served as governor for more than six years—a longer period than any other chief executive of North Carolina as an independent state.

The First Administration of Hodges, 1954–1957

Hodges inherited some difficult problems from the previous administration. One of the most critical was that of "integration" or "desegregation" of the public schools. The governor and the General Assembly moved slowly and cautiously in implementing the May 17, 1954, decision of the United States Supreme Court in outlawing racial segregation in the public schools. On June 3 the State Board of Education with Hodges as chairman (he was then lieutenant-governor) had voted to continue racial segregation for the school year 1954–55. On July 22 Hodges appointed a committee to study the legal aspects of the problem. On August 4 Governor Umstead appointed a nineteen-member committee, headed by Thomas J. Pearsall of Rocky Mount, and including three Negroes, to work out "a policy and a program which will preserve the state public school system by having the support of the people." On November 15 Attorney General Harry McMullan filed the state's brief with the United States Supreme Court, declaring that decrees calling for public school desegregation "forthwith" would be illegal and might lead to chaos. The next move was up to the 1955 legislature.

The 1955 General Assembly

The regular session of the 1955 General Assembly (January 5–May 26) set a record by enacting 1,376 laws. Some minor changes were made in the state's tax structure, and several new state agencies were created, the most important of which was a nine-member State Board of Higher Education. In accordance with an enabling act of the General Assembly, followed by a referendum in October, some 65,000 members of the state retirement system "went on Social Security" by voting overwhelmingly to integrate their retirement systems with Federal Old Age and Survivor's Insurance. But the paramount problem confronting the legislators was that of public school desegregation.

Faced with the problem of desegregation or integration, as a result of federal court decisions, the General Assembly made the following basic changes in the state school laws: (1) elimination from the laws of any reference to race; (2) transfer of authority over enrollment and assignment of pupils from the State Board of Education to local boards; (3) transfer of ownership, operation, and control of the state's 7,200 school buses to local units; and (4) substitution of yearly contracts for teachers and principals in lieu of continuing contracts. By unanimous vote the General Assembly resolved that: "The mixing of the races in the public schools within the state cannot be accomplished and if attempted would alienate public support of the schools to such an extent that they could not be operated successfully."

On August 8 Governor Hodges urged the people of the state to operate the public schools "in accordance with the policies set out by the General Assembly and at the same time avoid defiance or evasion of the opinion of the United States Supreme Court" by having the children of both white and Negro races "voluntarily attend separate public schools." This proposal drew praise from many of the state's newspapers, but it was denounced by the National Association for the Advancement of Colored People (NAACP) and by some individuals and groups. On August 22 the Patriots of North Carolina, an all-white organization aimed at maintaining "the purity of the white race and of Anglo-Saxon institutions," was incorporated. With only a few exceptions the public schools opened in September without incident—and without integration.

Meanwhile three Negro graduates of Durham High School applied for admission to The University of North Carolina at Chapel Hill. On May 23 the University Board of Trustees resolved that "applications to undergraduate divisions will be rejected." Whereupon the NAACP announced it would take the case to the federal courts if the applicants were denied admission. The three Negro applicants were admitted in the fall, the first in the university's 160-year history, after three federal judges ruled that the university must "process their applications without regard to race or color." The judges also declined a stay of judgment while appeal of the case to the Supreme Court was pending.

The 1956 Primaries

In the democratic primary of 1956 Governor Hodges won the gubernatorial nomination by a vote of 401,082 to 65,752 for his three opponents, and Senator Sam Ervin, Jr. defeated Marshall Kurfees, 360,967 to 65,512. Seven of the state's twelve representatives in Congress were renominated without strong opposition, but there were bitter contests in four districts, with the Southern Manifesto having an important bearing on the outcome. Thurmond Chatham was defeated by Ralph J. Scott, Ertel Carlyle by Alton A. Lennon, and C. B. Deane by Paul Kitchin. Representative Harold D. Cooley was the only nonsigner of the Southern Manifesto to win renomination, defeating W. E. Debnam, an ardent champion of state rights. In the Eleventh District Basil Whitener won over Ralph Gardner in a second primary, 22,442 to 21,064.

The "Pearsall Plan"

To cope with the problem of public school desegregation, Governor Hodges convened a special session of the General Assembly on July 23. After two days of televised hearings, this body, with only a few dissenting votes, enacted six laws, one resolution, and a proposed constitutional amendment recommended by the "Pearsall Committee." This amendment, adopted by an overwhelming majority at a special election on September 8, was designed as a safety valve, so that parents who did not desire to send their children to schools with members of another race might withdraw them and receive private tuition grants from the state. As it turned out, little or no use was made of the Pearsall plan. It was declared unconstitutional by the federal courts in April, 1966.

The 1956 Election

The Democrats carried the state in the election of November 6, electing all state officials, and eleven of twelve representatives in Congress. Charles R. Jonas, the state's sole Republican congressman, was reelected by a larger majority than he had received two years earlier. Democrat Adlai E. Stevenson won the state's fourteen electoral votes by an extremely small margin of 15,468 popular votes, while President Eisenhower received the largest total vote (575,062 to 590,530 for Stevenson) ever cast for a Republican in North Carolina. Luther Hodges was elected governor by a vote of 760,480 to 375,379 for Republican Kyle Hayes.

The 1957 General Assembly

The General Assembly of 1957 did much to reorganize the state government. It created a Department of Administration, consisting basically of two divisions—a Budget Division and a Purchase and Contract Division, and headed by a director appointed by and solely responsible to the governor. The Board of Public Buildings and Grounds was replaced by a Director of General Services under a director appointed by and responsible to the governor. The State Highway and Public Works Commission was abolished and replaced by a seven-member State Highway Commission, and the state prison system was separated from the Highway Department and established as the State Prison Department.

In an effort to attract out-of-state industries to North Carolina, many changes were made in the tax laws for multistate corporations. Revisions were made in the method of determining the proportion of net income of corporations taxable by North Carolina, and in that of determining the franchise tax payable by corporations manufacturing, producing, or selling tangible property. Partly as a result of these changes, and partly as a result of an extensive advertising campaign, new industries worth over $100 million had been brought to the state by the close of the year.

The Research Triangle

Under the leadership of Governor Hodges efforts were begun in 1955 to develop a state and regional center of industrial, governmental, and academic research laboratories and programs in what has come to be called the "Research Triangle." This triangle is formed by The University of North Carolina at Chapel Hill; Duke University in Durham; and North Carolina State University in Raleigh. Taken together these three institutions constitute "The heaviest concentration in the South of scientists, research resources, and cultural activity—a concentration of value to the location of new industrial and governmental laboratories." The location of such laboratories in the triangle area, it was felt, would enrich the work of the universities, provide jobs for young scientists at home, and provide for the development of new products for the state and region.

Robert M. Hanes became the first chairman of the Research Triangle Committee, which initiated the program. George L. Simpson, Jr. was executive director. Among other active supporters of the program were: George Watts Hill, university presidents William C. Friday and Hollis Edens, Karl Robbins, and Archie K. Davis. The latter led a fund-raising drive that brought in nearly $1.5 million for initial development.

By 1961 a good start had been made. A five-thousand-acre Research Park had been established in the middle of the Triangle. The Chemstrand Corporation had built its main research center there, employing some four hundred people in a laboratory of nearly 200,000 square feet. The United States Forestry Service had also built a laboratory. In addition, the Research Triangle Institute, a contract research organization, had been established and was employing one hundred researchers in several fields of work. The institute occupied two buildings in the Research Park, the Hanes Building and the Camille Dreyfus Memorial Laboratory. The latter building was constructed to carry on fundamental research in polymer chemistry, supported by a grant of $2.5 million dollars from the Camille and Henry Dreyfus Foundation. In more recent years a number of other national and international concerns have either transferred their main operations here or opened important research facilities. Among them are the National Environmental Protection Agency, the Burroughs Wellcome Company, the National Institute of Environmental Health Sciences Center, International Business Machines, and the medical research facilities of Becton, Dickinson and Company.

The 1958 Election

In the 1958 election the Democrats won eleven of twelve seats in the national House of Representatives. In the Tenth District Republican incumbent Charles R. Jonas defeated Democrat David Clark, 56,465 to 52,438. B. Everett Jordan, textile manufacturer of Saxapahaw, whom Governor Hodges had appointed to the United States Senate following the death of Senator W. Kerr Scott (April 16, 1958), defeated Richard C. Clark by an overwhelming majority. Republican ranks in the General Assembly were cut from sixteen to five—the lowest number in the state's history.

North Carolina's Rapid Recovery from the Recession of 1957–1958

North Carolina agriculture and industry witnessed a rapid recovery from the recession of late 1957 and early 1958. Governor Hodges's program to attract industry to the state was gaining momentum. Many new industries were established, and some old ones were expanded. Industrial investment in the state for the fiscal year 1957–58 amounted to a record high of $244,000,000. The next year it rose to $247,371,000, and in 1959–60 to $256,505,000.

Industry was becoming more diversified, and there was a marked development of food processing and other industries related to agriculture. The most spectacular industrial expansion was in electronics and chemicals. The Research Triangle Park was making substantial progress. The Chemstrand Research Center laboratory began operation in August, 1960; the Hanes Memorial Building, which houses administrative and desk-type research was completed in December of that year, and in 1961 the Dreyfus Laboratory was dedicated. Plans were also underway for a biology laboratory for the United States Forestry Service.

Governor Hodges, the state Department of Conservation and Development, and business leaders carried on an intensive campaign of advertising North

Carolina throughout the nation. In the fall of 1959 Hodges and some sixty business and professional leaders visited western Europe in an effort to promote the industry and trade of North Carolina.

The 1959 General Assembly

The General Assembly of 1959 adopted a biennial budget of $1.2 billion, the largest in the state's history to that time. It also proposed several bond issues for capital improvements, which were later approved by the voters, and which totalled $34,050,000 ($18,891,000 for higher educational institutions; $12,053,000 for state mental institutions; $1,500,000 for community colleges; $500,000 for state hospitals; $500,000 for state ports; $466,000 for state training schools; and $140,000 for a state rehabilitation center for the blind). The General Assembly also took steps to provide for the erection of a long-needed legislative building. The huge budget was adopted without the addition of new taxes, though a law was passed which provided that beginning in January, 1960, state personal income taxes were to be withheld by all employers.

The General Assembly passed a minimum hourly wage law of seventy-five cents for employees in companies hiring more than five people, thus becoming the first legislature in the South to enact such a measure. It also enacted a law making polio vaccination for children compulsory—the first state in the nation to enact such legislation. Facing up to a problem of increasing magnitude, that of water, the assembly provided for a Department of Water Resources to formulate policies to coordinate the conservation and use of water in the state. In an effort to cope with another critical problem, that of death on the highways, it passed a law providing for a penalty point system for violations of motor vehicle laws. The legislators rejected recommendations for court reform submitted by a study committee on this matter. Attempts to reapportion representation in the General Assembly on the basis of the 1950 census failed, as they had in every legislature since 1951.

The Elections of 1960

The Democratic primaries of 1960 were hardfought and bitter, and the general election was more closely contested than any since 1900. In the Democratic gubernatorial primary in May, Terry Sanford, Fayetteville attorney, received 269,463 votes; I. Beverly Lake, Raleigh lawyer and former professor of law at Wake Forest, 181,692; Malcolm Seawell, former attorney general, 101,148; and John Larkins of Trenton, lawyer and legislator, 100,757. In the second primary, in which integration in the schools was a major issue—as it had been in the first—Sanford defeated Lake, outspoken opponent of integration, by a vote of 352,133 to 275,905. In the general election Sanford defeated Republican Robert L. Gavin, Sanford attorney, by a vote of 735,248 to 613,975. All other state officials on the Democratic ticket won by overwhelming majorities. In some of the congressional districts, the contests were close but the Democrats won all except the Tenth District, where Republican Charles R. Jonas was reelected. The Republicans gained nine extra seats in the General Assembly. In the presidential race Democrat John F. Kennedy defeated Republican Richard M. Nixon by a vote of 713,318 to 655,648.

The 1961 General Assembly

In Sanford's vigorous campaign for the governorship he had advocated a "Go Forward" policy and a "New Day" for North Carolina; he had endorsed Kennedy's promise of a "New Frontier," and he had placed major emphasis on a program of "quality education" for the people of the state. As governor he moved swiftly and energetically to translate these promises into action. The 1961 General Assembly enacted more far-reaching legislation than any similar body in the twentieth century. It also adopted a biennial budget of $1,070,000,000, second in size to the $1.2 billion for the previous biennium. It made many changes in the state's administrative machinery. Ten new state agencies were created; three new boards were established in connection with existing agencies; three agencies, among them the State Art Commission, were abolished; and many agencies underwent some statutory change, ranging from the addition or deletion of a board member to complete reorganization, as in the case of the Highway Commission, which was increased from seven to nineteen members.

For the biennium 1961–63, the General Assembly appropriated $460,694,-183 for public schools (enough to increase teachers' salaries 21.8 percent—to new ranges of $3,600 to $5,600), $60,503,169 for higher education, and $44,-489,781 for state mental institutions. To finance this program all exemptions —including food, but excepting prescription drugs, school books, and a few other items—were removed from the 3 percent sales tax. The General Assembly also authorized a $61,500,000 "Capital Improvement Bonds" issue to be submitted to the voters in November. The ten items, each to be voted on separately, included $31,008,000 for educational institutions; $13,500,000 for the "construction, acquisition, and improvement of State Ports facilities"; $7,396,000 "for the construction of needed Capital Improvements at the State's mental institutions"; $2,858,000 "for construction of needed buildings for State purposes in the Capital area"; $2,560,000 "for construction of a building to house the Department of Archives and History and the State Library"; $1,483,000 "for grants-in-aid for community college Capital Improvements"; and $1,110,000 "for needed Capital Improvements at the State's correctional schools."

The General Assembly amended the state Minimum Wage Act, thus bringing an additional nineteen thousand workers under this law. It enacted a stringent law against gamblers and point-fixers in college athletic contests—a result of the recent scandals in college basketball. For the first time in twenty years the state House of Representatives was reapportioned, though efforts to redistrict the state Senate failed. Because North Carolina lost one of its twelve seats in the national House of Representatives as a result of the 1960 census, the General Assembly created the new Eighth Congressional District in a neat job of gerrymandering, which appeared to some observers to be an effort to defeat Charles R. Jonas, the state's only Republican in Congress.

The legislature also adopted six proposed constitutional amendments to be submitted to a popular referendum in November, 1962. If adopted, these would provide for a uniform system of inferior courts; require automatic reapportionment in the state House of Representatives after each federal census; clarify succession to the governorship; reduce the residence requirement for voting in presidential elections; and allow the General Assembly to set a uniform schedule of classifications on property for tax purposes by counties.

The Economic Situation in 1961

A bright spot in North Carolina's economy in 1961 was an increase in farm income of about 5 percent, or about $54,000,000 over the 1960 record of $1,800,000,000. This increase was primarily due to larger receipts from tobacco, corn, peanuts, broilers, dairy products, hogs, and eggs. The new governor, Terry Sanford, continued the policy of his predecessor, Hodges, in trying to attract industry to the state. Among the steps taken to promote industry and trade were a more extensive campaign of advertising, continued growth of research activities in the Research Triangle, and the North Carolina Trade Fair at Charlotte, October 12–21, the first of its kind in the state's history. Investments in new industries and expansions in 1961 reached a record high of $279,447,000, an increase of $44,000,000 over that of the preceding year. Shipments through the two state ports of Wilmington and Morehead City also reached an all-time high, the total revenues from the ports, $1,135,000, being almost double the revenues four years earlier.

North Carolinians in the Kennedy Administration

Among the many North Carolinians appointed to high posts in the Kennedy administration were former Governor Luther H. Hodges, secretary of commerce; Voit Gilmore of Southern Pines, director of the first United States Travel Service in history; and J. Spencer Bell of Charlotte, judge of the Fourth Circuit Court of Appeals. (After Kennedy's assassination on November 22, 1963, and Vice-President Lyndon B. Johnson's accession to the presidency, Hodges continued to serve as secretary of commerce until 1964.)

Public School Desegregation

North Carolina escaped many of the problems encountered by some southern states in the matter of public school desegregation. There was a peaceful adjustment to "integration" under the "Pearsall plan," or Pupil Assignment law, enacted in 1956. North Carolina was the first state in the Southeast to move voluntarily toward integration when the school boards at Charlotte, Winston-Salem, and Greensboro voted on July 23, 1957, to admit twelve Negro pupils to formerly all-white schools. Despite some protests by segregationists, most Negro pupils who entered all-white schools in September continued to attend integrated classes. The three above-mentioned schools admitted a few additional Negro pupils the next year and in June, 1958, a Negro girl in Greensboro became the first person of her race to graduate from what had been an all-white school. In 1959 local school boards in Craven and Wayne counties admitted Negroes to formerly all-white schools, and in October of that year fifty-four Negro pupils were attending integrated schools in seven of the state's cities and towns. In 1960 Chapel Hill, Durham, and several other towns and a few additional counties admitted Negroes to formerly all-white schools without incident. In 1961 the state added an eleventh desegregated school district (Asheville), and the number of Negro students in desegregated schools increased to more than two hundred.

Integration at Eating Places and Theaters and Civil Rights

Beginning in Greensboro in February, 1960, and spreading rapidly to many cities and towns throughout North Carolina and other southern states, many sit-in lunch-counter demonstrations were conducted, the object being to gain for the Negro the privilege of eating in these places on a desegregated basis. Most of these demonstrations were peaceful and without incident, though some arrests were made under the state trespass law. Many efforts were made to solve the problem by peaceful methods and, in many instances, lunch counters began to serve their patrons on an integrated basis. On the other hand, some establishments discontinued lunch-counter service, while others began to operate them on a stand-up basis. In many places the Negroes had won their fight to eat at lunch counters on an equal basis with the whites, but in many of the smaller towns, especially in the eastern counties, eating establishments continued to operate on a segregated basis. Meanwhile, many theaters in the state were being picketed as a protest against segregation, and eventually some of them, chiefly in the Piedmont cities, began to operate on a desegregated basis. By this time, largely because of action by the federal government, segregation had been virtually eliminated on buses, trains, and airplanes, and at bus terminals, railway stations, and airports. Meanwhile, a campaign for civil rights for Negroes was being waged, spearheaded by the NAACP, CORE (Congress on Racial Equality), and other groups, with particular emphasis on voting and voter registration. The United States government seemed more concerned about this problem than did the state government. On October 4, 1959, the federally appointed "North Carolina Advisory Committee to the United States Commission on Civil Rights" made its first report on "Equal Protection of the Law in Respect to Voting in North Carolina." A June 4, 1961, report of this committee stated: "In 1958, about 90 per cent of the registered voters in North Carolina were white and 10 per cent non-white. The situation has changed very little since. Of the new names added to the voter lists during the last two years, about 87 per cent were white and 13 per cent non-white. The registered electorate of North Carolina remains overwhelmingly and disproportionately white." This committee estimated that in 1958 the total proportion of potential voters registered was 71.2 percent; in 1960 it was 76.4 percent. For these two years, the percentage of white potential voters registered was 84 and 90.2, respectively; that of nonwhites was 30.9 and 31.2, respectively.

Defeat of Capital Improvements Bond Issue, 1961

On November 7, 1961, the voters of the state by an overwhelming majority, defeated every one of the proposed "Capital Improvements Bonds"—the first instance since 1924 of the state's electorate rejecting a statewide bond issue. Only twenty-seven counties—many of them small ones—voted in favor of the educational bonds; only twenty for the port bonds, and only forty-eight for the mental institutions bonds. The defeat of the bonds came as a surprise and a great disappointment to many of the state's political, business, and educational leaders, and many explanations were offered for what appeared to be a backward step on the part of the state. Perhaps the voters were showing their resentment of the so-called "food tax" enacted by the recent General Assembly. Perhaps they felt that government expenditures were already too high. Perhaps the friends of the bonds did not work hard enough to educate the state's citizenry to the need for the proposed bonds. Perhaps the voters thought they were being pushed too hard and too fast, and they asserted their independence—or even stubbornness—as North Carolinians have done at various times in the past.

Despite the defeat of the bond issues and what might appear to be a temporary setback to the state's "Go Forward" program, the people of the state, as well as its leaders, seem to be committed to the idea of progress and North Carolina will most likely continue to move forward. It is significant that in February, 1962, the leading article in the *National Geographic* was entitled "North Carolina, Dixie Dynamo."

In some respects, notably in the area of economic development, North Carolina probably merited this flattering title. In other respects, however, the state was still relatively backward. The problem of inequitable representation in the General Assembly was as serious as it had been in the period when North Carolina was known as the "Rip Van Winkle State." And in the field of public education illiteracy was "a state disgrace." The census figures of 1960 reveal that 697,432 North Carolinians were, on the date of enumeration, "functionally illiterate"; that 60,827 had never completed one year of school; that 300,000 had completed one to four years; that 35,000 children in the seven-to-fifteen-year age group were not enrolled in school. The *Greensboro Daily News* of March 20, 1962, editorialized:

"North Carolinians, parents, citizens and leaders, have had shocking statistics presented to them years on end. Selective service rejections in both world wars showed North Carolina at the very bottom of the list. School study after school study has emphasized the unbelievably high dropout rate. Less than half the children who enter first grade graduate from high school; and the percentage who quit school during the compulsory attendance age limits is a severe indictment in and of itself.

"So far, however, for all its educational progress, its tremendous investment in schools and its addiction to "quality education," the state as such has done woefully little to curb the loss in human resources and social problems which largely stem from ignorance. . . .

"The immediate answer is strict and effective enforcement of the school attendance law. It may be the law needs to be strengthened; but first of all is the responsibility of enforcing the law that we already have. And the shame of existing conditions is darkened by the knowledge that some form of compulsory attendance law has been on the statute books for nearly 50 years. . . .

"Surely the point has been reached where North Carolina can no longer afford to permit such waste of brain- and earning-power. The figures are there for all to see and heed. May the concern and shock generated by the latest recitation of shameful statistics bring results which, to the state's disgrace, have not been obtained years ago."

Constitutional Changes Approved, 1962

On November 6, 1962, the state's electorate by overwhelming majorities approved six amendments to the state constitution. The first of these, the so-called "court reform" amendment, provided for a General Court of Justice, which "shall constitute a unified judicial system for purposes of jurisdiction, operation, and administration; and shall consist of an appellate division, a Superior Court division, and a District Court division." Judges of the District Courts are to be elected for four-year terms, and "the senior resident Judges, upon nomination by the Clerk of the Superior Court, shall appoint one or more Magistrates for each county who shall be the officers of the District Court to serve for a term of two years." The General Assembly was also authorized to "establish a schedule of court fees and costs which must be uniform throughout the State," and operating expenses of the judicial depart-ment were to be paid from state funds. In no case would the compensation of any judge or magistrate be dependent upon his decision or upon the collection of costs. The General Assembly "must complete its job of creating District Courts by January 1, 1971, and on that date all previously existing inferior courts shall cease to exist." This amendment thus called for the most sweeping change of the state's court system that has occurred in the twentieth century.

The other five amendments provided for a procedure for the automatic reapportionment of the state House of Representatives by the Speaker after each federal census; a clarification of the "constitutional provisions controlling succession to the office of Governor and Lieutenant-Governor upon death, resignation or removal from office, or temporary physical or mental in-capacity"; authorization for the General Assembly to reduce the residence requirement for voting in presidential elections; authorization for the General Assembly to fix and regulate the salaries of elective state officers constituting the Council of State and the Executive Department during their terms of office, and a clarification of the General Assembly's powers to provide for a uniform, statewide classification and exemption of property for taxation.

The Election of 1962: A Republican Upsurge

For the first time in many years, the Republican party waged an intensive campaign for offices at all levels. In three congressional districts there were closely contested Republican primaries. In the Democratic primar-ies the only close contest was in the new Eighth District, where incumbent A. Paul Kitchin defeated the "liberal candidate," John P. Kennedy, 33,277 to 31,446. In the general election Republican Charles Raper Jonas, incumbent representative from the old Tenth District, defeated Kitchin by a vote of 63,991 to 49,845. In the Ninth District James T. Broyhill defeated incumbent Hugh Q. Alexander by slightly more than a thousand votes. Thus, for the first time in thirty years, North Carolina was to have two Republicans in Congress. The Democratic effort to gerrymander Jonas out of Congress had backfired and had contributed to Kitchin's defeat. Alexander's defeat was also due to the fact that two Republican counties had been added to his district.

The Republicans boosted their strength in the 120-seat House of Representa-tives from 15 to 21 seats; in the state Senate Republican strength remained at 2 seats. There were many surprises in some of the county elections, notably in Guilford, where Republicans captured the Senate seat and all 4 seats in the House of Representatives. Republicans also scored gains in Mecklenburg, Forsyth, Buncombe, and several other counties, notably in the Piedmont. It seemed to many observers of the political scene that North Carolina had finally developed a real two-party system. There were even predictions that the Repub-licans might win the gubernatorial election of 1964.

The General Assembly of 1963

The General Assembly of 1963 met for the first time in the new Legislative Building. This legislature adopted one of the largest budgets in the history of the state and passed more laws relating to public welfare than any other legislature in North Carolina history. It increased schoolteachers' salaries again and passed many laws relating to "education beyond the high school." Among these laws was a provision for the establishment and operation of a state system of community colleges, industrial education centers, and technical institutes. The legislature also changed the name and status of the three branches of The University of North Carolina. North Carolina State of The University of North Carolina became North Carolina State University at Raleigh; the Woman's College became The University of North Carolina at Greensboro; and the original university became The University of North Carolina at Chapel Hill. In addition to this basic change in the "Consolidated University," three two-year colleges—Asheville-Biltmore, Wilmington, and Charlotte—were made into four-year colleges.

The "Speaker Ban Law"

The most widely discussed action of the 1963 legislature was the "Speaker Ban Law," which provided that no state-supported college or university "shall permit any person to use the facilities of such institution for speaking who (A) Is a known member of the Communist party; (B) Is known to advocate the overthrow of the United States or the State of North Carolina; (C) Has pleaded the Fifth Amendment to the Constitution in refusing to answer any question with respect to Communist or subversive connections or activities, before any duly constituted legislative committee, any judicial tribunal, or any executive or administrative board of the United States or any state." This law was praised by some, but it was denounced by many, especially educational leaders. There were predictions that the General Assembly of 1965 or some later legislature would modify this law or repeal it altogether.

The 1964 Elections

In 1964 there were three major candidates for the Democratic gubernatorial nomination: Federal Judge Richardson L. Preyer, of Greensboro, the "liberal" candidate; former Superior Court Judge Dan K. Moore of Canton, the "moderate" candidate, and I. Beverly Lake, the leader of the conservatives. The vote in the first primary was Preyer, 281,430; Moore, 257,872; Lake, 217,172. In a bitter second primary, Moore defeated Preyer, who had the open support of Governor Sanford, by a vote of 480,431 to 293,863. In the general election Moore defeated Republican Robert L. Gavin 790,343 to 606,165. In the presidental race President Johnson defeated Republican Barry Goldwater, 800,139 to 624,844.

The Administration of Governor Dan K. Moore

Dan Moore came into office following a decade of dynamic gubernatorial leadership. Luther Hodges (1954–61) and Terry Sanford (1961–65) had set a fast pace. In his inaugural the new governor labeled his program "Total Development." In his own words that meant "developing all the state's resources without emphasizing one field to the detriment of others." In his quiet, unostentatious way he went about putting his program into effect.

The General Assembly of 1965

Moore's first legislature adopted the largest budget in the history of the state up to that time. Salaries of state employees were increased by 10 percent, and schoolteachers' salaries were also raised. Charlotte College was made a branch of the "Greater University" and renamed The University of North Carolina at Charlotte. The 1965 General Assembly was the most safety-minded legislature in many years. Fifty-nine laws were passed relating to motor vehicles and highway safety, one of which requires annual inspection of all motor vehicles registered in the state.

The General Assembly sent two proposals to the voters for their approval or disapproval in the November 2 general election. One of these was a proposed constitutional amendment to create an intermediate Court of Appeals between the State Supreme Court and the Superior Courts. The second proposal was a $300 million highway bond issue. The voters approved both of these proposals by a three-to-one majority.

The Special Session Modifies the "Speaker Ban Law"

One of the most serious problems confronting Governor Moore when he took office in January, 1965, was the "Speaker Ban Law," which had been passed by the legislature of 1963. There was widespread criticism of this law, especially on college campuses, on the ground that it was a violaton of free speech and might cause the colleges and universities to lose their "accreditation." Faced with the threat that the Southern Association of Colleges and Schools would take away this accreditation, the governor set up a nine-member commission, headed by David Britt, to make a careful study of this problem. This commission held two days of televised hearings in August and two more in September, before reporting on November 5 to the governor. Governor Moore called a special session of the legislature to meet November 15. The legislature, following the advice of the "Britt Commission," modified the Speaker Ban Law by returning to the institutions' boards of trustees control of visiting speakers. In 1968 the original Speaker Ban Law of 1963 was declared to be unconstitutional by a federal court.

The 1967 General Assembly

In the longest legislative session in the state's history to that time (February 8 to July 6) the General Assembly settled more major controversial issues than any other legislature in modern times. It legalized "brown bagging" —a custom of thirty years' standing in North Carolina in which people carry liquor to restaurants and clubs for consumption there—but bills to permit the sale of liquor by the drink were defeated.

New antiterror laws making it a felony to burn crosses or wear masks for the purpose of frightening people or to burn down occupied dwellings were passed. Many laws of major significance to the courts and court officials were also enacted. Thirteen new state agencies were added. The old State Prison Department was replaced by a Department of Correction. The legislature passed a 20 percent pay increase for public school teachers. Four new regional universities were created: Agricultural and Technical University of North Carolina (Greensboro), Appalachian State University (Boone), East Carolina University (Greenville), and Western Carolina University (Cullowhee). All of these were outside the "consolidated university" system. In spite of the record-breaking $2.8 billion biennial budget, the legislature revised the state's income-tax base, giving taxpayers an immediate $23.5 million income-tax cut.

The 1968 Elections

In the Democratic primary contest for the nomination for governor, Robert Scott of Haw River, son of former Governor W. Kerr Scott, received 337,368 votes; Melville Broughton of Raleigh, also a son of a former governor, received 223,924 votes; and Dr. Reginald Hawkins, a Charlotte dentist and the first Negro candidate for governor in the history of the state, received 129,808 votes.

The Republicans waged their most intensive campaign in this century for governor and for the state's seats in Congress. Representative Jim Gardner of Rocky Mount, who two years earlier had defeated Harold Cooley, long-time congressman from his district, won the nomination for governor, defeating John Stickley of Charlotte.

In the general election in November, North Carolina cast a majority of its votes for Republican presidential candidate, Richard M. Nixon (627,192), with George Wallace of the American party running second (496,188), and Democrat Hubert Humphrey coming in third (464,113). Only once before in the twentieth century (1928, when North Carolina cast its electoral vote for Herbert Hoover), had the Democratic presidential candidate failed to carry the state. Humphrey carried only twelve of the state's one hundred counties.

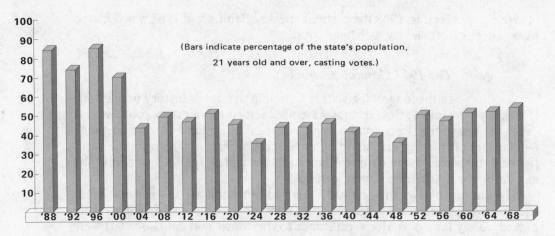

(Bars indicate percentage of the state's population, 21 years old and over, casting votes.)

Women excluded from potential electorate prior to 1920

Participation by North Carolina Voters in Presidential Elections, 1888–1968

Department of Geography and Earth Sciences, The University of North Carolina at Charlotte

The Republicans also elected four of the state's eleven candidates for Congress—a gain of two seats.

At the state level Scott defeated Gardner for the governorship, 821,232 to 737,075. All Democratic candidates for the state's constitutional office won. The Republicans gained a few seats in the state legislature. A Negro Democratic candidate, Henry Frye of Greensboro, won a seat. He was the first Negro to be elected to the General Assembly in this century.

The General Assembly of 1969

The General Assembly of 1969 was the longest legislative session in the state's history to that time. It adopted a biennial budget of $3.5 billion, by far the largest in North Carolina's history to that time. For the first time taxes were placed on cigarettes (two cents a package), on soft drinks (one cent a bottle), and on syrup for soft drinks (one dollar a gallon). Taxes on beer and liquor were also increased, and the state gasoline tax went up two cents, to nine cents a gallon.

The 1969 legislature built a substantial record of conservation legislation. One of these laws provided for the protection of coastal estuaries and $500,000 was appropriated for "estuarine land acquisition." Another law increased the powers of local governments to control air pollution.

Seven constitutional amendments were approved by the legislature which were later adopted by the voters. One authorized a general revision of the

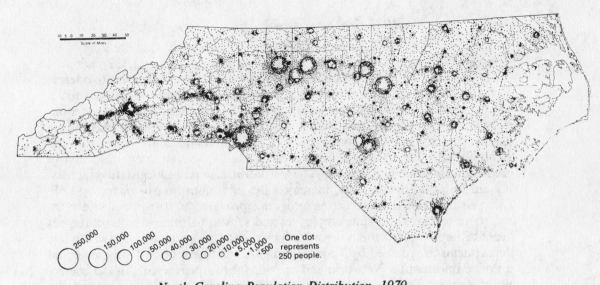

North Carolina Population Distribution, 1970

*Cartography by Dr. Richard Kopec & Ann Watkins, Department of Geography, The University
of North Carolina*

state and local government provisions of the constitution. Another authorized
the General Assembly to reduce the more than three hundred "administrative
departments, agencies, and offices of the state" to not more than twenty-five
by July 1, 1975.

The 1969 legislature voted more money for schools than any previous legislature. It voted public schoolteachers a pay boost of 12 percent and an 8 percent
increase for teachers in institutions of higher learning. The Asheville-Biltmore
and Wilmington colleges were made branches of The University of North
Carolina. Five colleges were made into "regional universities" —Elizabeth City
State University, Fayetteville State University, North Carolina Central University (Durham), Pembroke State University, and Winston-Salem State University—in addition to the four created by the legislature of 1967 (see p. 701),
making a total of nine altogether. The legislature also appropriated $250,000
as the first step in the establishment of a state zoo.

The 1969 legislature voted a great deal of money for medical education,
including some $350,000 to aid North Carolina students at Duke and Bowman
Gray Medical Schools. The legislature passed a number of laws designed to
prevent riots and "civil disorders" on college campuses. It also strengthened
the powers of the governor by making him chairman of some important agencies, notably the Board of Higher Education.

In the closing days of the session the legislators voted themselves a salary
increase—retroactive to the beginning of the session. They also established a
pension plan for legislators.

The 1971 General Assembly

The 1971 session of the General Assembly was the longest on record (136 days), introduced the most bills and resolutions (2,589), adopted the largest biennial budget ($4.3 billion), and was the most expensive to operate (over $2.2 million). It completely reorganized state government; created a "watchdog" legislative fiscal research agency; enacted legislative reapportionment and congressional redistricting legislation; approved eighteen years as the age of maturity; adopted comprehensive environmental controls; rewrote the alcoholic beverage control laws; and established new consumer protection in credit and automobile insurance. The legislature also passed legislation increasing aid to local governments; increased the minimum hourly wage to $1.60; enlarged the state's kindergarten program; provided a 10 percent salary increase for teachers and state employees and substantial increases in retirement benefits; implemented the reorganization of state government into twenty-five departments as required by a constitutional amendment of 1970; implemented a Police Information Network; and provided for improvements in the correctional system. The legislature also appropriated $3.3 million to expand the highway patrol and $1.2 million to improve operations of the State Bureau of Investigation. The North Carolina Drug Authority was established in the Department of Administration to coordinate all state efforts related to drug abuse, prevention, education, control, treatment, and rehabilitation.

The 1971 legislature made substantial appropriations for agencies and new programs in the field of health. Recognition of new needs in both social services and health took the form of state appropriations for Medicaid, the licensing of day-care facilities, a child-abuse reporting law, and the establishment of the Governor's Advisory Commission on Children and Youth.

An adjourned session of the General Assembly in October "restructured" the system of state-supported higher education. The Consolidated University of North Carolina (six campuses) was abolished, and, effective July 1, 1972, all sixteen public higher education institutions (including the School of the Arts at Winston-Salem) were placed under a thirty-two-member governing board which has almost complete planning, program, and budget control.

The 1972 Elections

Only 65 percent of the registered voters of the state participated in the November 7 elections, but Republican hopes, which had been rising for several years, were finally realized. James E. Holshouser of Boone was elected as the first Republican governor since 1896, defeating Hargrove Bowles, the Democratic candidate. Republican Jesse Helms won the United States Senate seat vacated by B. Everett Jordan, Democrat. Voters approved five constitutional amendments, one of which lowered the voting age to eighteen years and provided that only persons twenty-one or older should be eligible for elective office.

APPENDIXES

CHAPTER BIBLIOGRAPHIES

INDEX

Appendix A

CHIEF EXECUTIVES OF NORTH CAROLINA

Governors of the Original Virginia Colony

1585–86	Ralph Lane	Appointed by Walter Raleigh
1587	John White	Appointed by Walter Raleigh

Commander of the Southern Plantation

1662–64	Samuel Stephens	Appointed by council in Virginia

Governors of "Albermarle County" under the Lords Proprietors

1664–67	William Drummond	
1667–70	Samuel Stephens	
1670–72	Peter Carteret	
1672–77	John Jenkins	President of the Council
1676–78	Thomas Eastchurch	
1677	Thomas Miller	Deputy
1678	[John Jenkins?]	President of the council
1679	John Harvey	Deputy
1680–81	John Jenkins	President of the council
1682–89	Seth Sothel	

Governors under the Lords Proprietors of "That Part of the Province of Carolina That Lies North and East of Cape Fear"

1689–91	Philip Ludwell	
1691–94	Thomas Jarvis	Deputy of the governor of "Carolina"
1694–96	John Archdale	Deputy of the governor of "Carolina"
1696–99	Thomas Harvey	Deputy of the governor of "Carolina"
1699–1704	Henderson Walker	President of the council
1704–5	Robert Daniel	Deputy of the governor of "Carolina"
1705–6	Thomas Cary	Deputy of the governor of "Carolina"
1706–8	William Glover	President of the council
1708–11	Thomas Cary	President of the council
1711–12	Edward Hyde	

Governors of "North Carolina" under the Lords Proprietors

1712	Edward Hyde	
1712–14	Thomas Pollock	President of the council
1714–22	Charles Eden	
1722	Thomas Pollock	President of the council
1722–24	William Reed	President of the council
1724–25	George Burrington	
1725–29	Richard Everard	

Governors of North Carolina under the King

1729–31	Richard Everard	Held office until Burrington, the royal governor, arrived from England
1731–34	George Burrington	
1734–52	Gabriel Johnston	
1752–53	Nathaniel Rice	President of the council
1753–54	Matthew Rowan	President of the council
1754–65	Arthur Dobbs	
1765–71	William Tryon	
1771	James Hasell	President of the council
1771–75	Josiah Martin	

Presidents of the Council under the Revolutionary Government

1775–76	Cornelius Harnett
1776	Samuel Ashe
1776	Willie Jones

Governors of the State of North Carolina

(Elected by joint ballot of the two houses of the General Assembly for one-year terms during the period 1776–1835; elected by the qualified voters for two-year terms in the period 1836–68; elected by the voters for four-year terms since 1868).

		Home County
1776–80	Richard Caswell	Dobbs (Lenoir
1780–81	Abner Nash	Craven
1781–82	Thomas Burke	Orange
1782–84	Alexander Martin	Guilford
1784–87	Richard Caswell	Dobbs (Lenoir)
1787–89	Samuel Johnston	Chowan
1789–92	Alexander Martin	Guilford
1792–95	Richard Dobbs Spaight	Craven
1795–98	Samuel Ashe	New Hanover
1798–99	William R. Davie	Halifax
1799–1802	Benjamin Williams	Moore

1802–5	James Turner	Warren
1805–7	Nathaniel Alexander	Mecklenburg
1807–8	Benjamin Williams	Moore
1808–10	David Stone	Bertie
1810–11	Benjamin Smith	Brunswick
1811–14	William Hawkins	Warren
1814–17	William Miller	Warren
1817–20	John Branch	Halifax
1820–21	Jesse Franklin	Surry
1821–24	Gabriel Holmes	Sampson
1824–27	Hutchins G. Burton	Halifax
1827–28	James Iredell	Chowan
1828–30	John Owen	Bladen
1830–32	Montfort Stokes	Wilkes
1832–35	David L. Swain	Buncombe
1835–36	Richard Dobbs Spaight, Jr.	Craven
1836–41	Edward B. Dudley	New Hanover
1841–45	John M. Morehead	Guilford
1845–49	William A. Graham	Orange
1849–51	Charles Manly	Wake
1851–54	David S. Reid	Rockingham
1854–55	Warren Winslow	Cumberland
1855–59	Thomas Bragg	Northampton
1859–61	John W. Ellis	Rowan
1861–62	Henry T. Clark	Edgecombe
1862–65	Zebulon B. Vance	Buncombe
1865	William W. Holden	Wake
	(Appointed by Andrew Johnson, president of the United States)	
1865–68	Jonathan Worth	Randolph
1868–71	William W. Holden	Wake
	(Impeached and removed from office in 1871; succeeded by Lieutenant Governor Tod R. Caldwell)	
1871–74	Tod R. Caldwell	Burke
1874–77	Curtis H. Brogden	Wayne
1877–79	Zebulon B. Vance	Mecklenburg
1879–85	Thomas J. Jarvis	Pitt
1885–89	Alfred M. Scales	Rockingham
1889–91	Daniel G. Fowle	Wake
1891–93	Thomas M. Holt	Alamance
1893–97	Elias Carr	Edgecombe
1897–1901	Daniel L. Russell	Brunswick

1901–5	Charles B. Aycock	Wayne
1905–9	Robert B. Glenn	Forsyth
1909–13	William W. Kitchin	Person
1913–17	Locke Craig	Buncombe
1917–21	Thomas W. Bickett	Franklin
1921–25	Cameron Morrison	Mecklenburg
1925–29	Angus W. McLean	Robeson
1929–33	O. Max Gardner	Cleveland
1933–37	J. C. B. Ehringhaus	Pasquotank
1937–41	Clyde R. Hoey	Cleveland
1941–45	J. Melville Broughton	Wake
1945–49	R. Gregg Cherry	Gaston
1949–53	W. Kerr Scott	Alamance
1953–54	William B. Umstead	Durham
1954–61	Luther H. Hodges	Rockingham
1961–65	Terry Sanford	Cumberland
1965–69	Dan K. Moore	Jackson
1969–73	Robert W. Scott	Alamance
1973–	James E. Holshouser	Watauga

Appendix B

NORTH CAROLINA COUNTIES

Name	Date of Formation	Named For	County Seat	Land Area in Square Miles	1970 Population
Alamance	1849	Indian name	Graham	434	96,362
Alexander	1847	William J. Alexander	Taylorsville	255	14,466
Alleghany	1859	Indian name	Sparta	230	8,134
Anson	1750	Lord Anson	Wadesboro	533	23,488
Ashe	1799	Samuel Ashe	Jefferson	427	19,571
Avery	1911	Waightstill Avery	Newland	247	12,655
Beaufort	1712	Duke of Beaufort	Washington	831	35,980
Bertie	1722	James and Henry Bertie	Windsor	693	20,528
Bladen	1734	Martin Bladen	Elizabethtown	879	26,477
Brunswick	1764	The House of Brunswick	Southport	873	24,223
Buncombe	1791	Edward Buncombe	Asheville	645	145,056
Burke	1777	Thomas Burke	Morganton	506	60,364
Cabarrus	1792	Stephen Cabarrus	Concord	360	74,629
Caldwell	1841	Joseph Caldwell	Lenoir	476	56,669
Camden	1777	Earl of Camden	Camden Courthouse	239	5,453
Carteret	1722	Sir John Carteret	Beaufort	532	31,603
Caswell	1777	Richard Caswell	Yanceyville	435	19,055
Catawba	1842	Indian name	Newton	406	90,873
Chatham	1771	William Pitt, Earl of Chatham	Pittsboro	707	29,554
Cherokee	1839	Indian name	Murphy	454	16,130
Chowan	1670	Indian name	Edenton	180	10,764
Clay	1861	Henry Clay	Hayesville	213	5,180
Cleveland	1841	Benjamin Cleveland	Shelby	466	72,556
Columbus	1808	Christopher Columbus	Whiteville	939	46,937
Craven	1712	William, Lord Craven	New Bern	725	62,554

County	Year	Named for	County seat	Area	Population
Cumberland	1754	Duke of Cumberland	Fayetteville	661	212,042
Currituck	1670	Indian name	Currituck Courthouse	273	6,976
Dare	1870	Virginia Dare	Manteo	388	6,995
Davidson	1822	William Lee Davidson	Lexington	546	95,627
Davie	1836	William R. Davie	Mocksville	264	18,855
Duplin	1750	Lord Duplin	Kenansville	822	38,015
Durham	1881	Town of Durham	Durham	299	132,681
Edgecombe	1741	Baron Edgecombe	Tarboro	511	52,341
Forsyth	1849	Benjamin Forsyth	Winston-Salem	424	214,348
Franklin	1779	Benjamin Franklin	Louisburg	494	26,820
Gaston	1846	William Gaston	Gastonia	358	148,415
Gates	1779	Horatio Gates	Gatesville	343	8,524
Graham	1872	William A. Graham	Robbinsville	289	6,562
Granville	1746	Earl Granville	Oxford	542	32,762
Greene	1799	Nathanael Greene	Snow Hill	269	14,967
Guilford	1771	Lord North, Earl of Guilford	Greensboro	651	288,590
Halifax	1759	Earl of Halifax	Halifax	722	53,884
Harnett	1855	Cornelius Harnett	Lillington	606	49,667
Haywood	1808	John Haywood	Waynesville	543	41,710
Henderson	1838	Leonard Henderson	Hendersonville	382	42,804
Hertford	1760	Earl of Hertford	Winton	356	23,529
Hoke	1911	Robert F. Hoke	Raeford	326	16,436
Hyde	1712	Edward Hyde	Swanquarter	634	5,571
Iredell	1788	James Iredell	Statesville	591	72,197
Jackson	1851	Andrew Jackson	Sylva	495	21,593
Johnston	1746	Gabriel Johnston	Smithfield	795	61,737
Jones	1779	Willie Jones	Trenton	467	9,779
Lee	1907	Robert E. Lee	Sanford	255	30,467
Lenoir	1791	William Lenoir	Kinston	391	55,204
Lincoln	1779	Benjamin Lincoln	Lincolnton	308	32,682
McDowell	1842	Joseph McDowell	Marion	442	30,648
Macon	1828	Nathaniel Macon	Franklin	517	15,788
Madison	1851	James Madison	Marshall	456	16,003
Martin	1774	Josiah Martin	Williamston	481	24,730
Mecklenburg	1763	Princess Charlotte of Mecklenburg	Charlotte	542	354,656
Mitchell	1861	Elisha Mitchell	Bakersville	220	13,447
Montgomery	1779	Richard Montgomery	Troy	488	19,267
Moore	1784	Alfred Moore	Carthage	760	39,048
Nash	1777	Francis Nash	Nashville	552	59,122
New Hanover	1729	The House of Hanover	Wilmington	194	82,996

Northampton	1741	The Earl of Northampton	Jackson	539	24,009
Onslow	1734	Arthur Onslow	Jacksonville	756	103,126
Orange	1752	William of Orange	Hillsborough	398	57,707
Pamlico	1872	Indian name	Bayboro	341	9,467
Pasquotank	1670	Indian name	Elizabeth City	229	26,824
Pender	1875	William D. Pender	Burgaw	857	18,149
Perquimans	1670	Indian name	Hertford	261	8,351
Person	1792	Thomas Person	Roxboro	400	25,914
Pitt	1761	William Pitt	Greenville	656	73,900
Polk	1855	William Polk	Columbus	234	11,735
Randolph	1779	Peyton Randolph	Asheboro	801	76,538
Richmond	1779	Duke of Richmond	Rockingham	477	39,889
Robeson	1786	Thomas Robeson	Lumberton	944	84,842
Rockingham	1785	Marquis of Rockingham	Wentworth	572	72,402
Rowan	1753	Matthew Rowan	Salisbury	517	90,035
Rutherford	1779	Griffith Rutherford	Rutherfordton	566	47,337
Sampson	1784	John Sampson	Clinton	963	44,954
Scotland	1899	Scotland	Laurinburg	317	26,929
Stanly	1841	John Stanly	Albemarle	399	42,822
Stokes	1789	John Stokes	Danbury	459	23,782
Surry	1771	Earl of Surrey	Dobson	537	51,415
Swain	1871	David L. Swain	Bryson City	530	7,861
Transylvania	1861	Latin words	Brevard	379	19,713
Tyrrell	1729	Sir John Tyrrell	Columbia	399	3,806
Union	1842	Made from parts of two counties	Monroe	643	54,714
Vance	1881	Zebulon B. Vance	Henderson	249	32,691
Wake	1771	Margaret Wake	Raleigh	864	228,453
Warren	1779	Joseph Warren	Warrenton	443	15,810
Washington	1799	George Washington	Plymouth	336	14,038
Watauga	1849	Indian name	Boone	320	23,404
Wayne	1779	Anthony Wayne	Goldsboro	555	85,408
Wilkes	1778	John Wilkes	Wilkesboro	765	49,524
Wilson	1855	Louis D. Wilson	Wilson	373	57,486
Yadkin	1850	Indian name	Yadkinville	335	24,599
Yancey	1833	Bartlett Yancey	Burnsville	311	12,629
			TOTAL	49,067	5,082,059

POPULATION OF NORTH CAROLINA

(Figures for population before 1790 are estimates; those since 1790 are the official United States Census returns.)

DATE	TOTAL POPULATION	URBAN	RURAL	PERCENT URBAN
1675	4,000			
1701	5,000			
1707	7,000			
1715	11,000			
1729	35,000			
1752	100,000			
1765	200,000			
1786	350,000			
1790	393,751			
1800	478,103			
1810	555,500			
1820	638,829	12,502	626,327	2.0
1830	737,987	10,455	727,532	1.4
1840	753,409	13,310	740,109	1.8
1850	869,039	21,109	847,930	2.4
1860	992,622	24,554	968,068	2.5
1870	1,071,361	36,218	1,035,143	3.4
1880	1,399,750	55,116	1,344,634	3.9
1890	1,617,947	115,759	1,502,190	7.2
1900	1,893,810	186,790	1,707,020	9.9
1910	2,206,287	318,474	1,887,813	14.4
1920	2,559,123	490,370	2,068,753	19.2
1930	3,170,276	809,847	2,360,429	25.5
1940	3,571,623	974,175	2,597,448	27.3
1950	4,061,929	1,238,193	2,823,736	30.5
1960	4,556,155	1,801,921	2,754,234	39.5
1970	5,082,059	2,285,168	2,796,891	45.0

Twelve Largest Cities in 1970

Charlotte—241,178
Greensboro—144,076
Winston-Salem—132,913
Raleigh—121,577
Durham—95,438
High Point—63,204
Asheville—57,681
Fayetteville—53,510
Gastonia—47,142
Fort Bragg (Unincorporated)—
  46,995
Wilmington—46,169
Kannapolis (Unincorporated)—
  36,293

Appendix D
SIGNIFICANT DATES

1524	Verrazzano, Florentine navigator in the service of France, explored North Carolina coast.
1526	Spanish expedition, led by D'Ayllón, attempted settlement in Carolina coastal area.
1540	Expedition, headed by De Soto, explored portions of western North Carolina.
1584	Amadas and Barlowe, sent out by Walter Raleigh, explored Roanoke Island and surrounding vicinity. Land was named Virginia in honor of Queen Elizabeth.
1585–86	Ralph Lane's colony at Roanoke Island. First English colony in the New World.
1587	John White's "Lost Colony" at Roanoke Island. August 18, birth of Virginia Dare, first child of English parents in New World.
1607	English planted first permanent colony in the New World at Jamestown, Virginia.
1622	John Pory of Virginia explored Chowan River region.
1629	Charles I granted Carolana to Robert Heath.
1653	Virginia legislature granted lands along Roanoke and Chowan rivers to Roger Green.
1653–60	(?) Settlers from Virginia began to move into the Albemarle Sound area.
1662	Oldest recorded land grant in North Carolina.
1663	Charles II granted Carolina to eight Lords Proprietors.
1664	Plans formulated for three counties in Carolina: Albemarle, Clarendon, and Craven. William Drummond appointed governor of Albemarle.
1665	Charles II granted second charter to Lords Proprietors. Boundaries of Carolina extended northward and southward. Sir John Yeamans appointed governor of Clarendon. Albemarle County Assembly had its first meeting.
1667	Clarendon County abandoned.
1669	Fundamental Constitutions of Carolina promulgated.

1672	William Edmundson and George Fox, Quaker ministers, preached in Albemarle Sound region.
1677	John Culpeper and George Durant headed revolt against acting governor Miller; "rebels" controlled government for a year.
1689	Albemarle County ceased to exist. Government of Carolina "north and east of Cape Fear" established.
1700 (?)	First "public library" in North Carolina at Bath.
1701	Vestry Act, the first church law in North Carolina. December 15, Chowan Parish organized.
1705 (1706 n.s.)	Town of Bath incorporated. First town in North Carolina.
1705–08	Charles Griffin taught school in Pasquotank County. First recorded schoolteacher in North Carolina.
1710	New Bern founded under leadership of Christoph von Graffenried and John Lawson.
1711	Cary's Rebellion. Tuscarora War began. Aid sent from South Carolina.
1712	Edward Hyde became first governor of North Carolina as a separate province. Christopher Gale appointed first chief justice of North Carolina.
1713	Tuscarora War resumed. More aid sent from South Carolina. First paper money authorized by colonial legislature. Town of Beaufort laid out.
1717	Reservation, later known as "Indian Woods," created for Tuscaroras still remaining in North Carolina.
1718	Piracy along coast reached its climax. Blackbeard killed near Ocracoke Inlet and Bonnet and many other pirates hanged at Charleston.
1722	Law passed to build courthouse and assembly house at "Fork of Queen Ann's Creek," later known as Edenton.
1725 (?)	Settlement begun in Brunswick area. Beginning of town of Brunswick about 1727.
1728	Survey of North Carolina–Virginia boundary line begun. Line was run 220 miles westward from Knott's Island, Currituck County.
1729	George II purchased shares of seven of the eight Lords Proprietors. Carteret share was not sold and later became Granville District.
1734	St. Thomas Church at Bath, oldest church building in North Carolina, was constructed.
1735	North Carolina–South Carolina boundary survey was begun.
1738–39	First post road in North Carolina over which mail was regularly carried.
1739–48	England at war with Spain and France.
1740	North Carolina troops were in action for the first time as part of the British army.
1739–46	Scottish Highland migration to the Cape Fear Valley began on large scale.
1744	Granville District created, but only portion of boundary line was surveyed.
1747–48	Spanish attacked Beaufort and Brunswick.
1749	First printing press in North Carolina was installed at New Bern by James Davis. First publication was the "Journal of the House of Burgesses."

1751   First newspaper in the colony, the *North Carolina Gazette,* was printed at New Bern by James Davis.

1753   Moravians purchased about 100,000 acres of land from the Earl of Granville. Tract was named Wachovia. Bethabara founded. Bethania and Salem were begun a few years later.

1754   The "Great War for Empire" (French and Indian War) broke out.

1755   Sandy Creek Baptist Church, the "Mother of Southern Baptist Churches," was founded.

1755–56 Fort Dobbs built to protect western counties from the Indians.

1760   An academy was opened at Wilmington.

1763   Treaty of Paris concluded the "Great War for Empire." Britain inaugurated its "New Colonial Policy," which embodied the idea of taxation of the colonies.

1765   Parliament passed the Stamp Act. Protest at Wilmington and other places.

1766   North Carolina "Sons of Liberty" offered armed resistance to the Stamp Act at Brunswick. The Stamp Act repealed by Parliament.

1767   David Caldwell opened his "Log College" in Guilford County.

1768   Farmers of Orange County organized the Regulator Association. Movement spread to other counties in the backcountry.

1770   "Tryon's Palace," colonial capitol at New Bern, was completed. It was considered the finest "government building" in English America.

1771   January 15. North Carolina's first college, "Queen's College in the Town of Charlotte," chartered by the legislature.
         May 16. Regulators defeated at Battle of Alamance by North Carolina militiamen led by Governor William Tryon.

1774   August. First Provincial Congress met at New Bern. Nonimportation policy adopted. Delegates chosen to First Continental Congress.
         Oct. 25. Edenton Tea Party held at home of Mrs. Elizabeth King.

1775   Apr. 19. The American Revolution began with the battles of Lexington and Concord, Mass.
         Governor Martin dissolved legislature.
         May 20. "Mecklenburg Declaration of Independence."
         May 31. Mecklenburg patriots adopted Mecklenburg Resolves.
         Governor Martin took refuge on British man-of-war.
         Provincial Congress at Hillsborough put North Carolina on a war footing.

1776   Feb. 27. Tories were defeated by Whigs at Moore's Creek Bridge, first battle of the Revolution in North Carolina.
         Apr. 12. Provincial Congress at Halifax authorized North Carolina delegates in Continental Congress to "concur in independency."
         This was first action of this kind taken by any state.
         Aug. 2. National Declaration of Independence was signed by North Carolina delegates—William Hooper, Joseph Hewes, and John Penn.
         Dec. 18. Provincial Congress at Halifax adopted Bill of Rights and Consti-

tution. Richard Caswell was chosen as governor.

1777 Inauguration of Caswell as first governor of independent state of North Carolina.

1777 and 1779 State Legislature passed laws confiscating Tory property.

1778 Articles of Confederation ratified by North Carolina.

1780 October 7. Decisive American victory at Battle of King's Mountain.

1781 Mar. 15. Cornwallis won technical victory over Greene at Battle of Guilford Courthouse, but began retreat toward Wilmington.

   Sept. 12. Tories, led by David Fanning, captured Governor Thomas Burke at Hillsborough and took him to Charleston.

   Oct. 19. Cornwallis surrendered to Washington at Yorktown, Virginia.

1783 Treaty of Paris between England and the United States. Official end of the war.

1784 North Carolina legislature ceded its western lands to the United States; later in year it revoked this cession.

1785 "Lost State of Franklin" was created in Tennessee country.

   First annual conference of the Methodist Church in the United States was held at the home of Green Hill near Louisburg.

1787 Constitution of the United States drawn up at Philadelphia. Signed for North Carolina by William Blount, Richard Dobbs Spaight, and Hugh Williamson.

   Case of Bayard vs. Singleton, early precedent for judicial review.

1788 Convention at Hillsborough refused to ratify United States Constitution, but suggested many amendments to be incorporated into a Bill of Rights. Convention voted to locate permanent capital of state "within ten miles of Isaac Hunter's plantation" in Wake County.

1789 Convention at Fayetteville ratified United States Constitution. Legislature, meeting in same town, chartered University of North Carolina and also ceded state's western lands to the United States.

1790 Dismal Swamp Canal, to connect Albemarle Sound and Chesapeake Bay was begun.

1791 President Washington visited many communities in North Carolina on his "southern tour."

1792 Capital was located at Raleigh.

1793 Cornerstone of first building (Old East) was laid at University of North Carolina.

1794 New statehouse completed. General Assembly met in new capitol, December 30.

   Judge Iredell's strong state rights opinion in case of Chisholm vs. Georgia.

1795 The University of North Carolina opened its doors to students.

1797 Asheville was incorporated.

1799 Gold was discovered in Cabarrus County. North Carolina became the "Golden State."

1804	The Bank of Cape Fear and the Bank of New Bern chartered. First banks in the state.
1810	The Bank of North Carolina was incorporated.
1812–15	Second War with Great Britain.
1813	July 12–16 British fleet occupied Portsmouth and Ocracoke.
1813–16	(?) Earliest known date of a cotton mill in North Carolina—in Lincoln County.
1815–17	Archibald D. Murphey made his famous reports on education to the legislature.
1817	Diocese of North Carolina organized by Episcopalians.
1818	Cotton mill was begun at Rocky Mount by the Battle Family.
	State Supreme Court was reorganized.
1819	Murphey made report to the legislature on internal improvements.
	Boundary disputed by North Carolina, South Carolina, and Georgia was settled by confirmation of the 35th parallel.
	Cherokees ceded a large tract of land to North Carolina.
1824	In the presidential election North Carolina refused to support William H. Crawford, the "caucus," and the "Virginia candidate."
1825	State Literary Board and Fund were established.
1827	The first toll gate was installed for the Buncombe Turnpike from Saluda Gap through Asheville to the Tennessee Line.
1828	Aug. 1. First public meeting to promote railroads in North Carolina was held in William Albright's home in Alamance County.
1830	First cotton mill in the state operated by steam.
	Baptist State Convention was organized.
1831	Statehouse at Raleigh was destroyed by fire.
	Christopher Bechtler established a private mint at Rutherfordton.
1833	The one and one-fourth mile "Experimental Railroad" was built to convey granite from the quarry to the site of the new capitol.
	New Garden Boarding School (later Guilford College) was begun.
1834	Wake Forest Institute (later Wake Forest College) was opened.
1834–35	Whig party was formed in North Carolina.
1835	State Convention at Raleigh added many amendments to 1776 Constitution.
1837	Jan. 1. Edward B. Dudley, first governor elected by popular vote, was inaugurated.
	Davidson College was started.
	United States Branch Mint open at Charlotte.
1838	Greensboro Female College, first girl's college in state authorized to grant degrees, was established.
	Majority of Cherokees removed from North Carolina to "Indian territory."
1839	Union Institute was begun at Trinity, in Randolph County. It became Normal College in 1851; Trinity College in 1859; moved to Durham in

1892; and became Duke University in 1924.

First public school law passed by the state legislature.

1840	Wilmington and Weldon and Raleigh and Gaston Railroads were completed.

New Capitol was finished.

First public schools were opened.

1845   State School for the Deaf was established at Raleigh; department for the blind was added in 1851.

1846–48   Mexican War.

1849   State Hospital for the Insane was begun at Raleigh; opened for patients, 1856.

North Carolina Railroad was chartered by the General Assembly.

Beginning of Fayetteville and Western and other plank roads.

1850–51   First daily newspapers in the state, the Raleigh *Register* and the Wilmington *Daily Journal,* began publication.

1852 (?)   First bright leaf tobacco produced in North Carolina.

1853   Calvin H. Wiley became first Superintendent of Common Schools.

Holt mill manufactured "Alamance plaids," first colored cotton cloth in the South.

First North Carolina State Fair was held in Raleigh, October 18–21.

1856   North Carolina Railroad was completed from Goldsboro to Charlotte.

1857   State adopted free suffrage amendment and thus eliminated fifty-acre requirement to vote for state senators.

1859   Raleigh Workingmen's Association organized.

1860   North Carolina voted for the Southern Democratic presidential candidate, John C. Breckinridge.

1861   May 20. North Carolina Convention at Raleigh adopted ordinance of secession.

Aug. 29. Forts Hatteras and Clark captured by Federal forces.

1862   Federal forces, led by Generals Butler and Burnside, captured Roanoke Island (Feb. 8), New Bern (March 14), Washington (March 21), Fort Macon (April 26), and Plymouth (Dec. 13).

Zebulon B. Vance elected governor.

1864   Apr. 24. General Hoke recaptured Plymouth.

Oct. 27. Ram *Albemarle,* Confederate iron-clad, blown up at Plymouth by Federal forces.

1865   Jan. 15. Fort Fisher, the "Gibraltar of America," fell to Federals.

Wilmington, last important Confederate port, captured.

Mar. 11–14. General Sherman occupied Fayetteville.

Mar. 19–21. Sherman defeated Johnston at Bentonville.

Apr. 13. Sherman occupied Raleigh.

Apr. 26. Johnston surrendered to Sherman at Bennett House, near Durham.

March-April. "Stoneman's Raid" in Western North Carolina.

May 6. General J. G. Martin surrendered last Confederate forces in North Carolina, near Waynesville.

Slavery was abolished by state action and by the 13th Amendment to the United States Constitution.

Ordinance of secession repealed by North Carolina Convention.

May 22. President Johnson appointed W. W. Holden as provisional governor of North Carolina.

1867   March 2. Congress passed Reconstruction Act. North Carolina became part of a "Military District."

1868   New state constitution was ratified by popular vote. North Carolina was readmitted to the Union.

1869   The state legislature ratified the 15th Amendment to the United States Constitution.

1870   Governor Holden, acting under provisions of the Shoffner Act, proclaimed Alamance and Caswell counties in a state of insurrection and sent troops there. The "Kirk-Holden War" followed.

1871   Holden was impeached and removed from office.

1873   Eight amendments to state constitution were approved by popular vote.

1874   R. J. Reynolds built his first factory in Winston-Salem. Washington Duke and Sons built their first factory in Durham.

1875   Thirty amendments were added to the state constitution.

State Grange incorporated by the General Assembly.

1876   Vance was elected governor and Democrats regained control of the state government.

1877   Political reconstruction ended when President Hayes withdrew federal troops from the South.

First state normal for Negroes in the South was established at Fayetteville.

State Board of Health was created.

State Department of Agriculture was organized.

1881   Statewide prohibition was defeated by an overwhelming vote.

1887   North Carolina College of Agriculture and Mechanic Arts was established at West Raleigh; opened for students in 1889.

Pembroke State College, normal school for Indians, was begun in Robeson County.

First unit of Farmers' Alliance in North Carolina.

1888   First furniture factory at High Point.

1890   James B. Duke incorporated the American Tobacco Company.

Congress passed the Sherman Anti-Trust Law.

1891   State Normal and Industrial School (later the Woman's College of the University of North Carolina and now The University of North Carolina at Greensboro) was established at Greensboro; opened for students in 1892.

Normal School for Negroes at Elizabeth City.

North Carolina School for the Deaf and Dumb at Morganton.

1892   Formation of Populist (People's) Party.

1893   State motto, "Esse Quam Videri," was adopted by the General Assembly.
Waldensians, a religious group from French Alps, founded town of Valdese in Burke County.

1894   Populists and Republicans gained control of the legislature.
Southern Railway Company was organized.

1896   Republican D. L. Russell was elected governor on Fusion ticket.
First Rural Free Delivery of mail in North Carolina.

1898   "Red Shirt" Campaign. Democrats regained control of the legislature.
Race riots occurred at Wilmington.
Spanish-American War began and ended.
The American Federation of Labor made its first efforts to organize North Carolina labor.

1900   "White Supremacy" Campaign. State added a suffrage amendment to the Constitution, providing for a "literacy test" and including the "grandfather clause."
Charles B. Aycock was elected governor.
Atlantic Coast Line Railroad was organized.
Seaboard Air Line Railway Company was formed.

1903   North Carolina Historical Commission (now the State Department of Archives and History) was created by the General Assembly.
December 17. Wilbur and Orville Wright made the first flight of a power-driven airplane at Kill Devil Hill.
First state child-labor law was enacted.

1904   James B. Duke organized the Southern Power Company.

1906   Norfolk and Southern Railway Company was organized.

1908   Statewide prohibition law was passed.

1911   Winston-Salem Southbound Railway Company was organized.

1914   Carolina, Clinchfield and Ohio Railroad was completed.

1915   State Highway Commission was created.

1916   Federal Highway Act inaugurated policy of federal aid for highway construction.

1917–18   The United States in World War I.

1918   The state increased school term from four to six months.
Fort Bragg, United States field artillery training center, was established. Named for Confederate General Braxton Bragg, native of North Carolina.

1921   State highway system was established. Program of statewide highway construction led North Carolina to become the "Good Roads State."

1924   Trinity College in Durham was endowed by James B. Duke and changed its name to Duke University.

1925   State Department of Conservation and Development was created.

1928   North Carolina voted for Herbert Hoover, Republican candidate for president, but went overwhelmingly Democratic for state and local officers.

1929   Beginning of the "Great Depression."

1931   State government assumed control of entire highway system.

The General Assembly passed act consolidating the University of North Carolina at Chapel Hill, State College at Raleigh, and the Woman's College at Greensboro.

1933   The General Assembly adopted a program for financing an eight-months public school term.

President Franklin D. Roosevelt inaugurated the New Deal.

1935   Statewide prohibition was ended. Under special legislation sixteen eastern counties voted to establish liquor stores.

1936   Inland Waterway was completed.

1937   First general law passed to limit hours of labor in industry.

County local option for establishment of liquor stores was adopted by General Assembly.

Old-age pensions and unemployment insurance established.

1939   Free textbooks provided in public schools for elementary grades and textbook rental system established for high schools.

World War II began in Europe and Asia.

1941   United States entered World War II.

A retirement system for teachers and state employees was established.

1943   Ninth month in public school system was added.

1945   World War II ended.

1946   Reynolds's bequest was made to Wake Forest College, and plans were made to transfer the college to Winston-Salem.

1947   State inaugurated good health program.

1949   State bond issue voted $200 million for secondary road construction. $50 million program for public school buildings.

1951   Legislature appropriated a record-breaking budget of $506 million October 15. President Harry Truman participated in the ground-breaking ceremonies for the new Wake Forest College plant at Winston-Salem.

1953   Legislature authorized special election for approval of $50 million state bond issue for public schools and $22 million state bond issue for mental institutions. On October 3 state electorate approved both by an overwhelming vote.

1954   Governor William B. Umstead died; Lieutenant Governor Luther H. Hodges became governor.

1955   Governor Hodges took lead in development of the Research Triangle.

Board of Higher Education was established.

State school laws were changed in order to cope with problem of desegregation.

1956   "Pearsall Plan" was approved by popular vote. North Carolina Museum of Art was opened at Raleigh.

1957   Changes were made in state's administrative structure.

Revisions were made in tax laws relating to multistate corporations.

Research Park was begun in the Research Triangle.

1959   General Assembly made record-breaking appropriations. Voters approved $34,050,000 bond issue for capital improvements.

1960   Terry Sanford elected governor on a "Go Forward" program, with emphasis on "quality education."

1961   February 1. First sit-in lunch counter demonstration in the United States began at Greensboro.

General Assembly enacted much far-reaching legislation and removed the food exemption from the 3 percent sales tax.

Teachers' salaries were given a big boost.

Voters overwhelmingly defeated a $16,500,000 capital improvements bond issue.

The 35,000-ton battleship *North Carolina* was berthed at Wilmington, where it will serve as a museum and war memorial.

1962   Governor Sanford appointed Superior Court Judge Susie Sharp to the State Supreme Court, the first instance of a woman serving on the state's highest court.

For the first time in thirty years North Carolina elected two Republicans to the national House of Representatives.

The state's electorate approved six amendments to the state constitution. The "court reform" amendment provided for the most sweeping change of the state's court system that has occurred in the present century.

1963   General assembly met for first time in the new Legislative Building, first building ever constructed by a state for the sole use of its legislature.

Legislature made provision for establishment of a state system of community colleges, industrial education, and technical institutes.

"Speaker Ban Law" enacted to prevent "known" Communists from speaking on campuses of state-supported institutions of higher learning.

1964   Dan K. Moore (Democrat) elected governor.

1965   Charlotte College became The University of North Carolina at Charlotte. Names of the other three campuses of University changed.

Legislature enacted a one-dollar-per-hour minimum wage law.

State's judicial system reorganized. Court of Appeals created; justice of the peace system abolished, and replaced by magistrates.

1966   Special session of General Assembly reapportioned seats in both houses.

Legislature modified "Speaker Ban Law." Federal courts declared it unconstitutional in 1968.

1967   General Assembly legalized "brown bagging."

Four new "regional universities" created.

1968   North Carolina gave its electoral vote to Republican Richard Nixon. Robert Scott, (Democrat) elected governor. Republicans elected four of the state's eleven representatives in Congress. First Negro candidate for Democratic gubernatorial nomination.

1969 For the first time the legislature placed taxes on cigarettes and soft drinks. Many other taxes were increased, including a two-cent-per-gallon hike on gasoline. Five more colleges made into "regional universities."

1970 State's population exceeded five million for the first time. Census revealed that thirty-eight counties had lost population between 1960 and 1970. Democrats gained seats in the General Assembly.

1971 The General Assembly reapportioned the state's eleven congressional districts, in accordance with federal court requirement of "one man, one vote." The legislature adopted the largest budget in the state's history.

Chapter Bibliographies

   North Carolina is rich in materials for the writing, teaching, and study of the state's history. It has several of the best manuscript collections in the nation, notably that of the Southern Historical Collection in the library of The University of North Carolina at Chapel Hill, the Flowers Collection at Duke University, and the official manuscript archives in the Office of Archives and History at Raleigh. The state's one hundred counties also have local manuscript archives of varying importance and value. An excellent guide to these local records is to be found in *The Historical Records of North Carolina,* 3 vols. (Raleigh, 1938–39), edited by C. C. Crittenden and Dan Lacy.

   The most valuable of all collections of printed sources for North Carolina history are the *Colonial Records of North Carolina,* 10 vols. (Raleigh, 1886–90), edited by W. L. Saunders, and the *State Records of North Carolina,* 16 vols. (Winston, Goldsboro, Charlotte, 1895–1905), edited by Walter Clark, with four index volumes (Goldsboro, Charlotte, Raleigh, 1909–14), edited by Stephen B. Weeks. These two collections, among the best published by any state, include legislative journals; laws; royal instructions to governors; letters of governors, missionaries, and others; the Census of 1790; lists of taxables; extracts from newspapers; official documents of various kinds; and a great variety of miscellaneous papers. The *Colonial Records of North Carolina* has been out of print for many years. Under the auspices of the State Department of Archives and History, a new set of colonial records is being published. This new collection will contain many new documents; it will correct the numerous errors in the older set, it will be better organized, more carefully edited, and better indexed. The first volume of this new series, *North Carolina Charters and Constitutions, 1578–1698,* edited by Mattie Erma Edwards Parker, was published in 1963. The second volume, *North Carolina Higher-Court Records, 1670–1696,* also edited by Mrs. Parker, was published in 1968, while a third volume, *North Carolina Higher-Court Records, 1697–1701,* was published in 1971. The *Records of the Moravians in North Carolina,* edited by Adelaide L. Fries (vols. 1–7), Douglas Rights (vol. 8), Minnie J. Smith (vol. 9), and Kenneth G. Hamilton (vols. 10 and 11) contain a wealth of information on the economic, social, religious, and cultural life of the North Carolina backcountry for more than a century and a quarter (1752–79). J. Bryan Grimes, ed., *Abstract of North Carolina Wills* (Raleigh, 1910) and *North Carolina Wills and Inventories* (Raleigh, 1912) are useful for social and economic history, particularly for the colonial era, since

729

they give detailed lists of the worldly goods of many North Carolinians, especially those of the planter class.

Two indispensable books for a study of North Carolina history are Richard E. Lonsdale, comp. and ed., *Atlas of North Carolina* (Chapel Hill, 1968), and William S. Powell, *The North Carolina Gazetteer* (Chapel Hill, 1968). The twenty thousand entries in Powell's geographical dictionary make it a unique reference work for North Carolina. All types of geographical features are listed—counties, towns, cities, rivers, creeks, lakes, mountains, gaps, ridges, bays, sounds, inlets—and in many cases the derivation of the name and additional historical data are presented to give a complete and authoritative picture.

The role of the North Carolina delegates in the Continental Congress (1774–89) may be traced in E. C. Burnett, ed., *Letters of Members of the Continental Congress,* 8 vols. (Washington, D.C., 1921–36), while the activity of the state's delegates in the Constitutional Convention of 1787 may be followed in Max Farrand, ed., *The Records of the Federal Convention of 1787,* 4 vols. (Washington, D.C., 1911, 1937). Jonathan Elliot, ed., *The Debates in the Several State Conventions on the Adoption of the Federal Constitution,* vol. 4 (Washington, D.C., 1836) contains the proceedings of the convention at Hillsborough in 1788. There are no extant records of the debates in the Fayetteville Convention of 1789, which ratified the Constitution.

The North Carolina Historical Commission (now the Office of Archives and History) has published scores of documentary volumes, including the papers of John Steele, Archibald D. Murphey, Thomas Ruffin, John Gray Blount, William A. Graham, Willie P. Mangum, Zebulon B. Vance, and the official papers of many of the recent governors. Many of these volumes are listed at the proper place in the chapter bibliographies below. The *North Carolina Manual* for 1913, edited by R. D. W. Connor, is an invaluable source for a study of North Carolina political history, since it lists governors, state legislators, congressmen, and other public officials from 1664 to 1913 and gives election returns for president and governor, 1836–1912, and votes on various conventions and constitutional amendments.

Hundreds of North Carolinians have had biographical sketches written about them, though extremely few have had full-length biographies. Some two hundred of the state's most prominent citizens have had sketches in the authoritative *Dictionary of American Biography,* 22 vols. (New York, 1928–58). A few of the most outstanding colonial figures have been written up in the English *Dictionary of National Biography,* 63 vols. (London, 1885–1901). There is a short sketch of every North Carolinian who ever served in the Congress of the United States in the *Biographical Directory of the American Congress, 1774–1961* (Washington, D.C., 1961). S. A. Ashe, ed., *Biographical History of North Carolina from Colonial Times to the Present,* 8 vols. (Greensboro, 1905–17) is the most ambitious undertaking of its kind in the state's history. It contains hundreds of biographical essays—some good, some bad, some indifferent. Scores of biographical sketches have also appeared in the *North Carolina Booklet,* a periodical no longer being published.

Some very good biographical studies and many excellent articles on almost every aspect and period of North Carolina history have appeared in the *North Carolina Historical Review,* which has been published under the auspices of the North Carolina Historical Commission (now the Office of Archives and History) since 1924. This quarterly periodical, one of the best state historical journals in the nation, is indispensable for a thorough study of North Carolina history. Many splendid articles on North Carolina history have also appeared in the Trinity College Historical Society Papers; in the James Sprunt Studies in History and Political Science at The University of North Carolina at Chapel Hill; in the Johns Hopkins University Studies; in the *Journal of Southern History;* and in the *American Historical Review.* Many short articles on various phases of North Carolina history are found in J. T. Adams, ed., *Dictionary of American History,* 5 vols. (New York, 1940).

The following bibliography is designed to meet the needs of college students in North Carolina history and general readers who have access to libraries containing standard works and a judicious selection of monographs. Authors and titles are grouped under the titles of the respective chapters.

Books listed above the asterisks are considered basic reading for students taking North Carolina history courses. The other books listed are in the nature of "suggested reading" for either the college student or the general reader.

To save space and to avoid repetition, the following abbreviations have been used:

AHA—American Historical Association.

JSHP—James Sprunt Historical Publications.

TCHS—Trinity College Historical Society.

NCB—North Carolina Booklet.

NCHR—North Carolina Historical Review.

1. Explorations and Attempts at Settlement

Lefler, Hugh T., ed. *North Carolina History Told by Contemporaries.* Chapel Hill, 1934, 1948. Pp. 1–15.

Connor, R. D. W. *North Carolina: Rebuilding an Ancient Commonwealth.* Chicago, 1929. 1: 63–72.

———. *History of North Carolina: The Colonial and Revolutionary Periods.* Chicago, 1919. 1: 1–31. Hereafter cited as *History of North Carolina.*

Ashe, S. A. *History of North Carolina.* Greensboro, 1908. 1:1–49.

* * *

Brown, Alexander. *Genesis of the United States.* 2 vols. Boston, 1890. 1:1–22.

Corbitt, D. L., ed. *Explorations, Descriptions, and Attempted Settlements of Carolina, 1584–1590.* Raleigh, 1953. Pp. 1–154.

Craven, W. F. *The Southern Colonies in the Seventeenth Century.* Baton Rouge, La. 1949. Pp. 27–59.

Fletcher, Inglis. *Roanoke Hundred.* Indianapolis, 1948. Pp. 1–492.

Green, Paul. *The Lost Colony.* Chapel Hill, 1938. Pp. 1–80.

Harrington, J. C. "Archeological Explorations at Fort Raleigh National Historic Site." *NCHR* 26 (April 1949): 127–49.

————. "The Finding of Fort Raleigh." *Southern Indian Studies* 1 (April 1949): 18–19.

————. *An Outwork at Fort Raleigh: Further Archeological Excavations at Fort Raleigh National Historic Site.* Philadelphia, 1966. Pp. 1–66.

————. *Search for the Citie of Raleigh.* Washington, D.C., 1962. Pp. 1–63.

Hulton, Paul, and David B. Quinn, eds. *The American Drawings of John White, 1577–1590.* 2 vols. London and Chapel Hill, 1964.

Lonsdale, Richard E., comp. *Atlas of North Carolina.* Chapel Hill, 1967. Pp. 1–168.

Lowery, Woodbury. *The Spanish Settlements within the Present Limits of the United States.* New York, 1911. Pp. 168, 230, 355, 449.

Pearce, H. J., Jr. "The Dare Stones." *Brenau College Bulletin* 30 (March 1939): 1–8.

————. "New Light on the Roanoke Colony." *Journal of Southern History* 4 (May 1938): 148–63.

Quinn, David B. *Raleigh and the British Empire.* New York, 1949. Pp. 47–129.

————, ed. *The Roanoke Voyages, 1584–1590.* 2 vols. London, 1955.

Rights, Douglas L. *The American Indian in North Carolina.* Durham, 1947. Pp. 6–27.

Sams, C. W. *The Conquest of Virginia: The First Attempt.* Norfolk, Va., 1924. Pp. 1–367.

Sparkes, Boyden. "Writ on Rocke." *Saturday Evening Post* 213 (April 26, 1941): 9–11, 118, 120–22, 124–26, 128.

Vigneras, L. A. "A Spanish Discovery of North Carolina in 1566." *NCHR* 46 (October 1969): 398–407.

Wallace, D. D. *South Carolina: A Short History.* Chapel Hill, 1951. Pp. 15–22.

Weeks, S. B. "The Lost Colony: Its Fate and Survival." *AHA* Papers. Washington, D.C., 1891. 5: 439–80.

2. Natural Setting and Native Peoples

Connor, R. D. W. *North Carolina: Rebuilding an Ancient Commonwealth.* 1: 3–61.

* * *

Barton, Lew. *The Most Ironic Story in American History: An Authoritative Documented History of the Lumbee Indians of North Carolina.* Pembroke, N.C., 1967. Pp. 1–142.

Bassett, J. S. "The Influence of Coast Line and Rivers on North Carolina." *AHA Annual Report.* Washington, D.C., 1908. 1: 58–61.

Bleeker, Sonia. *The Cherokee Indians of the Mountains.* New York, 1952. Pp. 1–159.

Brickell, John. *The Natural History of North Carolina.* Dublin, 1737; reprint, Raleigh, 1910. Pp. 277–408.

Brown, D. S. *The Catawba Indians: The People of the River.* Columbia, S.C., 1967. Pp. 1–400.

Bryson, Herman. *Gold Deposits in North Carolina.* Raleigh, 1936. Pp. 1–157.

————. *The Story of the Geologic Making of North Carolina.* Raleigh, 1928. Pp. 1–42.

Camp, Cordelia. *The Influence of Geography Upon Early North Carolina.* Raleigh, 1963. Pp. 1–31.

Crane, V. W. *The Southern Frontier, 1670–1732.* Durham, 1929. Pp. 1–46.

Crittenden, C. C. *The Commerce of North Carolina, 1763–1789.* New Haven, Conn., 1937. Pp. 1–20.

Cumming, William P. *North Carolina in Maps.* Raleigh, 1966. Pp. 1–36.

———. *The Southeast in Early Maps.* Princeton, N.J., 1958, and Chapel Hill, 1962. Pp. 1–356.

Dunbar, Gary S. *Geographical History of the North Carolina Outer Banks.* Baton Rouge, La., 1955. Pp. 1–249.

Hobbs, S. H., Jr. *North Carolina: Economic and Social.* Chapel Hill, 1930. Pp. 13–25.

Hodge, F. W. *Handbook of American Indians North of Mexico.* Washington, D.C., 1907–10. Pt. 2, pp. 841–53.

Holmes, J. S. *Common Forest Trees of North Carolina: A Pocket Manual.* Chapel Hill, 1922. Pp. 1–76.

Johnson, F. Roy. *The Tuscaroras.* 2 vols. Murfreesboro, N.C., 1962.

Lee, E. Lawrence, Jr. *The Indian Wars in North Carolina, 1663–1763.* Raleigh, 1963. Pp. 1–94.

Lefler, Hugh T., ed. *John Lawson's "A New Voyage to Carolina."* Chapel Hill, 1967. Pp. 1–305.

Lemert, B. F. "Geographic Influences in the History of North Carolina." *NCHR* 12 (October 1935): 297–319.

Lonsdale, Richard E., comp. *Atlas of North Carolina.* Chapel Hill, 1967. Pp. 2–32.

McCall, W. A. *Cherokees and Pioneers.* Asheville, 1952. Pp. 1–106.

McNeill, Ben Dixon. *The Hatterasman.* Winston-Salem, 1958. Pp. 1–276.

McPherson, O. M. *Indians of North Carolina.* Washington, D.C., 1905. Pp. 58–148, 180–84.

Merrens, Harry Roy. *Colonial North Carolina in the Eighteenth Century: A Study in Historical Geography.* Chapel Hill, 1964. Pp. 1–293.

Milling, J. C. *Red Carolinians.* Chapel Hill, 1940. Pp. 3–34, 266–85.

Mooney, James. *The Aboriginal Population North of Mexico.* Washington, D.C., 1928. Pp. 4–6.

———. *Myths of the Cherokees.* Washington, D.C., 1902. Pp. 11–20.

Rights, Douglas. *The American Indian in North Carolina.* Pp. 28–61, 113–210.

Ross, Malcolm. *The Cape Fear.* New York, 1965. Pp. 1–340.

Royce, C. C. *The Cherokee Nation of Indians.* Washington, D.C., 1887. Pp. 129–44.

———. *Indian Land Cessions in the United States.* Washington, D.C., 1889. Pp. 545–62, 624–30.

South, Stanley A. *Indians in North Carolina.* Raleigh, 1959. Pp. 1–69.

Stick, David. *Graveyard of the Atlantic.* Chapel Hill, 1952. Pp. 1–276.

———. *The Outer Banks of North Carolina, 1584–1958.* Chapel Hill, 1958. Pp. 1–352.

Stuckey, Jasper L. *North Carolina: Its Geology and Mineral Resources.* Raleigh, 1965. Pp. 1–550.

Wells, B. W. *The Natural Gardens of North Carolina.* Chapel Hill, 1932; reprint, 1967. Pp. 1–458 (original edition).

3. The Carolina Proprietary: Albemarle County

Lefler, Hugh T., ed. *North Carolina History Told by Contemporaries.* Pp. 15–31.
Connor, R. D. W. *North Carolina: Rebuilding an Ancient Commonwealth.* 1:73–107.
_____. *History of North Carolina.* 1: 32–63.
Ashe, S. A. *History of North Carolina.* 1: 55–140.

* * *

Albertson, Catherine. *In Ancient Albemarle.* Raleigh, 1914. Pp. 1–53.
Andrews, C. M. *The Colonial Period of American History.* 4 vols. New Haven, Conn., 1937. 3: 182–267.
_____, ed. *Narratives of the Insurrections.* New York, 1915. Pp. 145–64.
Bassett, J. S. *The Constitutional Beginnings of North Carolina.* Baltimore, 1894. Pp. 9–73.
_____. "The County of Clarendon." *NCB* 2 (February 1903): 1–20.
_____. "The Naming of the Carolinas." *Sewanee Review* 2 (1894): 343–52.
Butler, Lindley S. "The Early Settlement of Carolina: Virginia's Southern Frontier." *Virginia Magazine of History and Biography* 79 (January 1971): 20–28.
_____. "The Governors of Albemarle County, 1663–1689." *NCHR* 46 (July 1969): 281–99.
Cumming, W. P. "Naming Carolina." *NCHR* 22 (January 1945): 34–42.
Dodd, W. E. *The Old South: Struggles for Democracy.* New York, 1937. Pp. 208–34.
Guess, W. C. *County Government in Colonial North Carolina. JSHP* 11 (1911): 7–39.
Hall, Louise. "New Englanders at Sea: Cape Fear Before the Royal Charter of 24 March 1662/3." *New England Historical and Genealogical Magazine* 124 (April 1970): 88–108.
Lapsley, G. T. *The County Palatine of Durham.* New York, 1900. Pp. 1–310.
McCain, Paul M. *The County Court in North Carolina before 1750.* Durham, 1954. Pp. 1–147.
McPherson, Elizabeth G. "Nathaniel Batts, Landholder on Pasquotank River, 1660." *NCHR* 43 (January 1966): 66–81.
Parker, Coralie. *The History of Taxation in North Carolina during the Colonial Period: 1663–1776.* New York, 1928. Pp. 68–96.
Parker, Mattie E., ed. *North Carolina Charters and Constitutions, 1578–1698.* Raleigh, 1963. Pp. i–xxii, 1–247.
_____. *North Carolina Court Records, 1670–1696.* Raleigh, 1968. Pp. xiii–xc, 1–533.
Powell, William S. *The Carolina Charter of 1663.* Raleigh, 1954. Pp. 1–79.
_____, ed. *Ye Countie of Albemarle in Carolina: A Collection of Documents, 1664–1675.* Raleigh, 1958. Pp. 1–101.
_____, *The Proprietors of Carolina.* Raleigh, 1963. Pp. 1–70.

Rankin, Hugh F. *Upheaval in Albemarle, 1675–1689: The Story of Culpeper's Rebellion.* Raleigh, 1962. Pp. 1–87.

Raper, C. L. *North Carolina: A Study in English Colonial Government.* New York, 1904. Pp. 1–26.

Rights, Douglas L. *The American Indian in North Carolina.* Pp. 62–70.

Salley, A. S., ed. *Narratives of Early Carolina, 1650–1708.* New York, 1911. Pp. 65–73, 137–76.

Wager, Paul W. *County Government and Administration in North Carolina.* Chapel Hill, 1928. Pp. 1–16.

Wertenbaker, T. J. *The Old South: The Founding of American Civilization.* New York, 1942. Pp. 1–21.

4. The Emergence of North Carolina, 1689–1729

Lefler, Hugh T., ed. *North Carolina History Told by Contemporaries.* Pp. 30–51.

Connor, R. D. W. *North Carolina: Rebuilding an Ancient Commonwealth.* 1: 108–48.

———. *History of North Carolina.* 1: 64–142.

Ashe, S. A. *History of North Carolina.* 1: 141–223.

* * *

Ashe, S. A. "Our Own Pirates: Blackbeard and Bonnet." *NCB* 2 (June 1902): 3–23.

Boyd, W. K., ed. *William Byrd's Histories of the Dividing Line Betwixt Virginia and North Carolina.* Raleigh, 1929. Pp. 1–341.

Crittenden, C. C. "The Surrender of the Charter of Carolina." *NCHR* 1 (October 1924): 383–402.

Dill, Alonzo. "Eighteenth Century New Bern." *NCHR* 22 and 23 (January 1945–October 1946): 1–21, 152–75, 292–319, 460–89; 47–48, 142–71, 325–59, 495–535.

———. *Governor Tryon and His Palace.* Chapel Hill, 1955. Chaps. 1–2.

Faust, A. B. *The German Element in the United States.* 2 vols. New York, 1909. 1: 212–16.

Hodge, F. W. *Handbook of American Indians North of Mexico.* Pt. 2, Pp. 841–53.

Howell, A. J. *The Book of Wilmington.* Wilmington, 1930. Pp. 1–31.

Hughson, S. C. *Carolina Pirates and Colonial Commerce.* Baltimore, 1894. Pp. 1–134.

Jameson, J. F., ed. *Privateering and Firacy in the Colonial Period.* New York, 1923. Pp. 535–48.

Karraker, Cyrus. *Piracy Was a Business.* Rindge, N.J., 1953. (Use index for N.C. references.)

Lee, E. Lawrence, Jr. *The Indian Wars in North Carolina, 1663–1763.* Raleigh, 1963.

———. *The Lower Cape Fear in Colonial Days.* Chapel Hill, 1965. Chaps. 1–5.

Lonsdale, Richard E. *Atlas of North Carolina.* Pp. 41–43.

McCrady, Edward. *South Carolina Under the Proprietary Government.* New York, 1897. Pp. 506–96.

McPherson, O. M. *Indians of North Carolina.* Pp. 180–96.

Milling, C. J. *Red Carolinians.* Pp. 113–35.

Oliver, David D. *The Society for the Propagation of the Gospel in the Province of North Carolina.* JSHP 9 (1910): 1–23.

Paschal, Herbert R., Jr. *A History of Colonial Bath.* Raleigh, 1955. Pp. 1–69.

Pascoe, C. F. *Two Hundred Years of the S.P.G.* 2 vols. London, 1901. 1: 20–25.

Rankin, Hugh F. *The Golden Age of Piracy.* Williamsburg, Va., 1969. Pp. 105–51.

———. *North Carolina Pirates.* Raleigh, 1960. Pp. 1–72.

Sprunt, James. *Chronicles of the Cape Fear, 1660–1916.* Raleigh, 1914. Pp. 1–40.

Todd, V. H., and Goebel, J., eds. *Christoph Von Graffenried's Account of the Founding of New Bern.* Raleigh, 1920. Pp. 35–76.

Weeks, S. B. *Church and State in North Carolina.* Baltimore, 1893. Pp. 1–25.

———. *The Religious Development in the Province of Carolina.* Baltimore, 1892. Pp. 1–65.

Wright, Louis B., ed. *The Prose Works of William Byrd of Westover: Narratives of a Colonial Virginian.* Cambridge, Mass., 1966. Pp. 1–438.

5. The Coming of the Highlanders, Scotch-Irish, and Germans

Connor, R. D. W. *North Carolina: Rebuilding an Ancient Commonwealth.* 1: 149–63.

———. *History of North Carolina.* 1: 162–79.

Ashe, S. A. *History of North Carolina.* 1: 247–58.

* * *

Adam, Margaret. "The Highland Emigration of 1770." *Scottish Historical Review* 16: 280–93.

Baker, Howard F. "National Stocks in the Population of the United States as Indicated by the Surnames in the Census of 1790." AHA *Annual Report.* Washington, D.C., 1931. 1: 126–34.

Bolton, C. K. *Scotch-Irish Pioneers in Ulster and America.* Boston, 1910. Pp. 285–95.

Clewell, J. H. *History of Wachovia in North Carolina.* New York, 1902. Pp. 1–120.

Connor, R. D. W. *Race Elements in the White Population of North Carolina.* Raleigh, 1920. Pp. 7–112.

Dunaway, W. F. *The Scotch-Irish of Colonial Pennsylvania.* Chapel Hill, 1944. Pp. 28–49, 102–17.

Faust, A. B. *The German Element in the United States.* Pp. 212–33.

Fries, Adelaide, ed. *Records of the Moravians in North Carolina.* 8 vols. Raleigh, 1922–54. Vols. 1 and 2.

———. *The Road to Salem.* Chapel Hill, 1944. Pp. 3–215.

Gehrke, W. H. "The Transition from the German to the English Language in North Carolina." *NCHR* 12 (January 1935): 1–19.

Graham, Ian C. C. *Colonists from Scotland: Emigration to America, 1707–1783.* Ithaca, N.Y., 1956. Pp. 1–213.

Green, Paul. *The Highland Call.* Chapel Hill, 1941. Pp. 2–203.

Greene, E. B., and Virginia D. Harrington. *American Population Before the Census of 1790.* New York, 1932. Pp. 156–71.

Hammer, Carl, Jr. *Rhinelanders on the Yadkin.* Salisbury, N.C., 1943. Pp. 11–63.

Hooker, Richard J., ed. *The Carolina Backcountry on the Eve of the Revolution: The Journal and Other Writings of Charles Woodmason, Anglican Itinerant.* Chapel Hill, 1953. Pp. 1–305.

Klees, Frederic. *The Pennsylvania Dutch.* New York, 1950. Pp. 72–121.

Leyburn, James G. *The Scotch-Irish.* Chapel Hill, 1962. Sec. 3, pp. 157–326.

Lonsdale, Richard E. *Atlas of North Carolina.* Pp. 37–38.

McKelway, A. J. "The Scotch-Irish of North Carolina." *NCB* 4 (March 1905): 3–24.

Maclean, J. P. *The Scotch Highlanders in America.* Cleveland, 1900. Pp. 100–45.

Meyer, Duane. *The Highland Scots of North Carolina, 1732–1776.* Chapel Hill, 1961. Pp. 3–165.

Nixon, J. R. *The German Settlers in Lincoln County and Western North Carolina.* JSHP 11 (1912): 29–62.

Oates, John A. *The Story of Fayetteville and the Upper Cape Fear.* Fayetteville, 1950. Pp. 1–868.

Ramsey, Robert W. *Carolina Cradle: Settlement of the Northwest Carolina Frontier, 1747–1762.* Chapel Hill, 1964. Pp. 1–251.

Wittke, Carl. *We Who Built America.* New York, 1939. Pp. 3–97.

6. Agriculture and Industry, 1729–1775

Lefler, Hugh T., ed. *North Carolina History Told by Contemporaries.* Pp. 62–82.

Connor, R. D. W. *North Carolina: Rebuilding an Ancient Commonwealth.* Vol. 1. (Use index.)

Ashe, S. A. *History of North Carolina.* Vol. 1. (Use index.)

Hawks, F. L. *History of North Carolina.* 2: 216–334.

* * *

Bassett, J. S. "Landholding in Colonial North Carolina." TCHS *Papers,* ser. 2 (1898): 44–61.

Bond, B. W. *The Quit Rent System in the American Colonies.* New Haven, Conn., 1919. Pp. 61–82, 113–18, 286–318.

Carrier, Lyman. *The Beginnings of Agriculture in America.* Pp. 195–99.

Cathey, C. O. *Agricultural Developments in North Carolina, 1783–1860.* Chapel Hill, 1956. Pp. 3–29.

Coulter, E. M. *The Granville District.* JSHP 13 (1913): 35–56.

Franklin, W. N. "Agriculture in Colonial North Carolina." *NCHR* 3 (October 1926): 539–74.

Gray, L. C. *History of Agriculture in the Southern United States to 1860.* Washington, D.C., 1933. Vol. 1. (Use index for N.C. references.)

Lefler, Hugh T., ed. *John Lawson's "A New Voyage to Carolina."* Pp. 81–120.

Lonsdale, Richard E. *Atlas of North Carolina.* Pp. 39–40.

Parker, Coralie. *History of Taxation in North Carolina During the Colonial Period, 1663–1776.* New York, 1928. Pp. 39–67.

Pittman, T. M. "Industrial Life in Colonial North Carolina." *NCB* 7 (July 1907): 50–58.

7. *Transportation, Trade and Communication, 1715–1775*

Crittenden, C. C. *The Commerce of North Carolina, 1763–1789.* Pp. 1–170.

Connor, R. D. W. *North Carolina: Rebuilding an Ancient Commonwealth.* Vol. 1. (Use index.)

Ashe, S. A. *History of North Carolina.* Vol. 1 (Use index.)

Andrews, E. W., and C. M. Andrews, eds. *The Journal of a Lady of Quality.* New Haven, Conn., 1923. Pp. 144–79.

Bassett, J. S. "The Influence of Coast Line and Rivers on North Carolina." AHA *Annual Report.* 1: 58–61.

Clonts, F. W. "Travel and Transportation in Colonial North Carolina." *NCHR* 3 (January 1926): 16–35.

Crittenden, C. C. "Means of Communication in North Carolina, 1763–1789." *NCHR* 8 (October 1931): 373–83.

———. "Overland Travel and Transportation in North Carolina, 1763–1789." *NCHR* 8 (July 1931): 239–57.

Keith, Alice B., ed. *The John Gray Blount Papers.* 2 vols. Raleigh, 1952–59. Vol. 1.

Lonsdale, Richard E. *Atlas of North Carolina.* Pp. 39–40.

Merrens, Roy H. *Colonial North Carolina in the Eighteenth Century.* Pp. 142–72.

Moody, Robert E. "Massachusetts Trade with Carolina, 1686–1709." *NCHR* 20 (January 1943): 43–53.

Scott, Kenneth. "Counterfeiting in Colonial North Carolina." *NCHR* 34 (October 1957): 467–82.

Wallace, Wesley H. "Property and Trade: Main Themes of Early North Carolina Newspaper Advertisements." *NCHR* 32 (October 1955): 451–82.

8. *The Social Order*

Lefler, Hugh T., ed. *North Carolina History Told by Contemporaries.* Pp. 35–38, 48–81.

Connor, R. D. W. *North Carolina: Rebuilding an Ancient Commonwealth.* 1: 164–218.

———. *History of North Carolina.* 1: 180–209.

Ashe, S. A. *History of North Carolina.* 1: 377–95.

* * *

Allcott, John. *Colonial Homes in North Carolina.* Raleigh, 1963. Pp. 1–100.

Andrews, E. W., and C. M. Andrews, eds. *The Journal of a Lady of Quality.* Pp. 148–204.

Ashe, S. A. *Slavery and Servitude in the Colony of North Carolina.* Baltimore, 1896. Pp. 11–86.

———. "Social Conditions in North Carolina in 1783." *NCB* 10 (April 1911): 200–222.

Bassett, John S. *Slavery and Servitude in the Colony of North Carolina.* Baltimore, 1896. Pp. 11–86.

Bridenbaugh, Carl. *Myths and Realities: Societies of the Colonial South.* Baton Rouge, La., 1952. Pp. 119–96.

Franklin, John Hope. *The Free Negro in North Carolina.* Chapel Hill, 1943. Pp. 1–13.

Grimes, J. Bryan. "Some Notes on Colonial North Carolina: 1700–1750." *NCB* 5 (October 1905): 90–149.

Johnson, Guion G. *Ante-Bellum North Carolina.* Chapel Hill, 1937. Pp. 52–114.

Johnston, Frances, and Thomas J. Waterman. *The Early Architecture of North Carolina.* Chapel Hill, 1941. Pp. 1–290.

Lauber, A. W. *Indian Slavery in Colonial Times within the Present Limits of the United States.* New York, 1913. (Use index.)

Padgett, J. S. "The Status of Slaves in Colonial North Carolina." *Journal of Negro History* 14 (July 1929): 300–327.

Raper, Charles L. "Social Life in Colonial North Carolina." *NCB* 3 (September 1905): 5–21.

Smith, A. E. *Colonists in Bondage.* Chapel Hill, 1947. Pp. 226–306.

Spruill, Julia C. *Women's Life and Work in the Southern Colonies.* Chapel Hill, 1938. Pp. 1–366.

Taylor, Rosser, H. *The Free Negro in North Carolina.* JSHP 17 (1920): 5–26.

———. *Slaveholding in North Carolina: An Economic View.* JSHP 18 (1926): 9–29.

Wootten, Bayard, and Archibald Henderson. *Old Homes and Gardens of North Carolina.* Chapel Hill, 1939. Pp. 1–264.

9. Religious and Cultural Development, 1730–1776

Lefler, Hugh T., ed. *North Carolina History Told by Contemporaries.* Pp. 41–62, 118–22.

Connor, R. D. W. *North Carolina: Rebuilding an Ancient Commonwealth.* 1: 177–84.

Bernheim, G. D. *Historical Sketch of the Evangelical Lutheran Synod and Ministerium of North Carolina.* Philadelphia, 1902. Pp. 9–27.

———. *History of the German Settlements and the Lutheran Church in North and South Carolina.* Philadelphia, 1872. Pp. 67–148, 175–85, 239–62.

Biggs, Joseph. *A Concise History of the Kehukee Baptist Association.* Tarboro, N.C., 1834. Pp. 1–130.

Caruthers, Eli W. *A Sketch of the Life and Character of the Rev. David Caldwell.* Greensboro, 1842. Pp. 1–109.

Cheshire, J. B. *Sketches of Church History in North Carolina.* Wilmington, 1892. Pp. 43–90.

Clapp, J. C., and J. C. Leonard. *Historic Sketch of the Reformed Church in North Carolina.* Philadelphia, 1908. Pp. 11–29.

Connor, R. D. W. "The Genesis of Higher Education in North Carolina." *NCHR* 28 (January 1951): 1–14.

Coon, Charles L. *The Beginnings of Public Education in North Carolina: A Documentary History, 1790–1840.* 2 vols. Raleigh, 1908. 1: 1–9.

Corbitt, D. L. "The North Carolina Gazette." *NCHR* 12 (January 1936): 45–61.

Crittenden, C. C. *North Carolina Newspapers Before 1790.* JSHP 20 (1928): 1–83.

Cross, A. L. *The Anglican Episcopate in the American Colonies.* New York, 1902. Pp. 1–225.

Foote, W. H. *Sketches of North Carolina.* New York, 1846; reprint, Dunn, N.C., 1912. Pp. 77–83, 125–36, 158–243.

Grissom, W. L. *History of Methodism in North Carolina.* Nashville, 1905. Pp. 1–49.

Haywood, M. de L. *Lives of the Bishops of North Carolina.* Raleigh, 1910. Pp. 1–40.

―――. "Story of Queen's College or Liberty Hall." NCB 11 (January 1912): 169–75.

Jones, Rufus M. *The Quakers in the American Colonies.* London, 1911. Pp. 265–353.

Klain, Zora. *Quaker Contributions to Education in North Carolina.* Philadelphia, 1924. Pp. 17–57.

Knight, E. W. *Public School Education in North Carolina.* Boston, 1916. Pp. 1–41.

―――. *A Documentary History of Education in the South Before 1860.* Chapel Hill, 1949. 1: 36, 51, 55–57, 84–90, 369–70, 661–64, 703–26.

Lemmon, Sarah M. "Genesis of the Protestant Episcopal Church in North Carolina, 1701–1823." *NCHR* 28 (October 1951): 426–62.

McMurtrie, D. C. *A Bibliography of Early North Carolina Imprints.* Chapel Hill, 1938. Pp. 1–188.

―――. "The First Twelve Years of Printing in North Carolina, 1749–1760." *NCHR* 10 (July 1933): 214–34.

O'Connell, J. J. *Catholicity in the Carolinas and Georgia.* New York, 1878. Pp. 395–499.

Oliver, D. D. *The Society for the Propagation of the Gospel in the Province of North Carolina.* JSHP 9 (1909): 9–23.

Noble, M. C. S. *A History of the Public Schools of North Carolina.* Chapel Hill, 1930. Pp. 3–24.

Paschal, G. W. *History of the Baptists in North Carolina.* Vol. 1, 1663–1805. Raleigh, 1930. 1: 1–445.

―――. *A History of Printing in North Carolina.* Raleigh, 1946. Pp. 1–27.

Paschal, Herbert R. "Charles Griffin: Schoolmaster to the Southern Frontier." *East Carolina Publications in History* 2 (1965): 1–16.

Pennington, Edgar L. *The Church of England and the Reverend Clement Hall in Colonial North Carolina.* Hartford, Conn., 1937. Pp. 1–51.

Powell, William S., ed. *Clement Hall, A Collection of Many Christian Experiences.* Raleigh, 1961. Pp. 1–25, [3]–[51].

―――. *The Journal of the House of Burgesses of the Province of North Carolina, 1749.* Raleigh, 1949. Pp. ix–xix, 1–14.

Purefoy, George W. *History of the Sandy Creek Baptist Association.* New York, 1859. Pp. 42–47.

Raper, C. L. *The Church and Private Schools in North Carolina: A Historical Study.* Greensboro, 1898. Pp. 1–70.

Turner, Herbert S. *Church in the Old Fields: Hawfields Presbyterian Church and Community in North Carolina.* Chapel Hill, 1962. Pp. 4–78.

Weeks, S. B. "Libraries and Literature in North Carolina in the Eighteenth Century." AHA *Annual Report.* Washington, D.C., 1895. 1: 169–267.

————. "Pre-Revolutionary Printers in North Carolina—Davis, Steuart, and Boyd." *NCB* 15 (October 1915): 104–22.

White, Julia S. "The Quakers of Perquimans." *NCB* 7 (April 1908): 278–89.

Williams, Charles B. *History of the Baptists in North Carolina.* Raleigh, 1901. Pp. 1–50.

10. The Royal Governors and Their Problems, 1730–1775

Lefler, Hugh T., ed. *North Carolina History Told by Contemporaries.* Pp. 31–36, 70–77.

Connor, R. D. W. *North Carolina: Rebuilding an Ancient Commonwealth.* 1: 219–42.

————. *History of North Carolina.* 1: 210–38.

* * *

Alden, John R. *John Stuart and the Southern Colonial Frontier.* Ann Arbor, Mich., 1944. Pp. 115–85.

Boyd, W. K., ed. *Some Eighteenth Century Tracts Concerning North Carolina.* Raleigh, 1927. Pp. 57–100.

Bullock, C. J. *Essays in the Monetary History of the United States.* New York, 1900. Pp. 125–55.

Corbitt, D. L. *Formation of North Carolina Counties, 1663–1943.* Raleigh, 1950. (Use index for particular counties.)

Coulter, E. M. *The Granville District.* JSHP 13 (1913): 35–56.

Greene, Jack P. "The North Carolina Lower House and the Power to Appoint Public Treasurers, 1711–1775." *NCHR* 40 (January 1963): 37–53.

————. *The Quest for Power: The Lower Houses of Assembly in the Southern Royal Colonies, 1689–1776.* Chapel Hill, 1963. (Use index for N.C. references.)

Guess, W. C. *County Government in Colonial North Carolina.* JSHP 11 (1911): 7–39.

Haywood, M. de L. *Governor William Tryon and His Administration in the Province of North Carolina, 1765–1771.* Raleigh, 1903. Pp. 9–103.

Lanning, John T. *The Diplomatic History of Georgia: A Study of the Epoch of Jenkin's Ear.* Chapel Hill, 1936. Pp. 186–206.

London, L. F. "The Representation Controversy in Colonial North Carolina." *NCHR* 11 (October 1934): 255–76.

McCain, Paul M. *The County Court in North Carolina before 1750.* Durham, 1954. Pp. 43–99.

McKinley, A. E. *The Suffrage Franchise in the Thirteen English Colonies in America.* Philadelphia, 1905. Pp. 79–121.

Nash, Francis. "The Borough Towns of North Carolina." *NCB* 6 (October 1906): 83–102.

North Carolina Manual, 1913, ed. R. D. W. Connor. Raleigh, 1913. Pp. 320–413.

Parker, Coralie. *History of Taxation in North Carolina during the Colonial Period: 1663–1776.* Pp. 36–97.

Powell, William S. "Tryon's 'Book' on North Carolina." NCHR 34 (July 1957): 406–15.

Raper, C. L. *North Carolina: A Study in English Colonial Government.* Pp. 27–100.

Robinson, Blackwell P. *The Five Royal Governors of North Carolina.* Raleigh, 1963. Pp. 1–74.

Skaggs, M. L. *North Carolina Boundary Disputes Involving Her Southern Line.* JSHP 25 (1941): 1–166.

Waddell, A. M. *A Colonial Officer and His Times, 1754–1773.* Raleigh, 1890. Pp. 1–242.

Wager, P. W. *County Government and Administration in North Carolina.* Pp. 1–98.

11. Sectional Controversies

Lefler, Hugh T., ed. *North Carolina History Told by Contemporaries.* Pp. 67–73, 87–93.

Connor, R. D. W. *North Carolina: Rebuilding an Ancient Commonwealth.* 1: 264–88.

_____. *History of North Carolina.* 1: 287–320.

Ashe, S. A. *History of North Carolina.* 1: 247–79, 326–76.

* * *

Bassett, J. S. "The Regulators of North Carolina." AHA *Annual Report.* Washington, D.C., 1895. Pp. 141–212.

Boyd, Julian P. "The Sheriff in Colonial North Carolina." *NCHR* 5 (April 1928): 151–80.

Boyd, W. K. "Early Relations of North Carolina and the West." *NCB* 7 (1908): 193–209.

_____, ed. *Some Eighteenth Century Tracts Concerning North Carolina.* Pp. 175–413.

Bridenbaugh, Carl. *Myths and Realities: Societies of the Colonial South.* Pp. 159–63.

Dill, Alonzo T. *Governor Tryon and His Palace.* Chapel Hill, 1955. Pp. 103–54.

Haywood, M. de L. *Governor William Tryon and His Administration in the Province of North Carolina, 1765–1771.* Pp. 9–194.

Henderson, Archibald. "Origin of the Regulation in North Carolina." *American Historical Review* 21 (January 1916): 320–32.

Hudson, A. P. "Songs of the Regulators." *William and Mary Quarterly,* ser. 3, vol. 4 (October 1947): 470–85.

Lazenby, Mary E. *Herman Husband, A Story of His Life.* Washington, D.C., 1940. Pp. 25–123.

Lefler, Hugh T. "Orange County and the War of the Regulation," in *Orange County, 1752–1952,* ed. Hugh T. Lefler and Paul Wager. Chapel Hill, 1953. Pp. 22–40.

London, L. F. "The Representation Controversy in Colonial North Carolina." *NCHR* 11 (October 1934): 255–76.

Miller, Helen, *The Case for Liberty.* Chapel Hill, 1965. Chap. 9, "Freedom from Extortion," pp. 203–26.

Powell, William S., James K. Huhta, and Thomas J. Farnham. *The Regulators in North Carolina, A Documentary History, 1759–1776.* Raleigh, 1971. Pp. 1–626.

––––––. *The War of the Regulation and the Battle of Alamance, May 16, 1771.* Raleigh, 1949. Pp. 1–32.

12. The Approach of the American Revolution

Lefler, Hugh T., ed. *North Carolina History Told by Contemporaries.* Pp. 82–98.

Connor, R. D. W. *North Carolina: Rebuilding an Ancient Commonwealth.* 1: 289–313.

––––––. *History of North Carolina.* 1: 321–37.

Ashe, S. A. *History of North Carolina.* 1: 310–25.

* * *

Andrews, E. W., and C. M. Andrews, eds. *The Journal of a Lady of Quality.* Pp. 180–215.

Boyd, W. K., ed. *Some Eighteenth Century Tracts Concerning North Carolina.* Pp. 101–95.

Connor, R. D. W. *Cornelius Harnett: An Essay in North Carolina History.* Raleigh, 1909. Pp. 30–119.

––––––. *Revolutionary Leaders of North Carolina.* Greensboro, 1916. Pp. 3–125.

Davidson, Philip G. *Propaganda and the American Revolution, 1763–1783.* Chapel Hill, 1941. (Use index for N.C. references.)

De Mond, Robert O. *The Loyalists in North Carolina During the Revolution.* Durham, 1940. Pp. 1–62.

Harrell, I. M. "North Carolina Loyalists." *NCHR* 3 (October 1926): 575–90.

Haywood, Robert C. "The Mind of the North Carolina Opponents of the Stamp Act." *NCHR* 29 (July 1952): 317–43.

Hoyt, W. H. *The Mecklenburg Declaration of Independence.* New York, 1907. Pp. 1–284.

Lee, E. Lawrence, Jr. "Days of Defiance: Resistance to the Stamp Act in the Lower Cape Fear." *NCHR* 43 (April 1966): 186–202.

Morgan, Edmund S., and Helen M. Morgan. *The Stamp Act Crisis.* Chapel Hill, 1953. Pp. 38–39, 156, 165–201.

Nevins, Allan. *The American States During and After the Revolution, 1775–1789.* New York, 1924. Pp. 17–18, 41–42, 61–65, 74–78.

Rankin, Hugh F. "The Moore's Creek Bridge Campaign, 1776." *NCHR* 30 (January 1953): 23–60.

Sellers, Charles G., Jr. "Making a Revolution: The North Carolina Whigs, 1765–1775," in *Studies in Southern History,* ed. J. C. Sitterson. Chapel Hill, 1957. Pp. 23–46.

Sikes, E. W. *The Transition of North Carolina from Colony to Commonwealth.* Baltimore, 1898. Pp. 2–41.

Waddell, A. M. *A Colonial Officer and His Times, 1754–1773.* Pp. 73–130.

13. Transition from Colony to Statehood

Lefler, Hugh T., ed. *North Carolina History Told by Contemporaries.* Pp. 105–11.

Connor, R. D. W. *North Carolina: Rebuilding an Ancient Commonwealth.* 1: 314–46.

———. *History of North Carolina.* 1: 389–410.

Ashe, S. A. *History of North Carolina.* 1: 377–416.

Connor, R. D. W. *Cornelius Harnett: An Essay in North Carolina History.* Pp. 152–78.

———. "North Carolina's Priority in the Demand for Independence." *Journal of Southern History* 8 (July 1909): 235–54.

Green, Fletcher M. *Constitutional Development of the South Atlantic States.* Chapel Hill, 1930. (Use index for N.C. references.)

McNitt, Virgil V. *Chain of Error and the Mecklenburg Declaration of Independence.* Palmer, Mass., 1960. Pp. 1–134.

McRee, G. J., ed. *The Life and Correspondence of James Iredell.* 2 vols. New York, 1857–58. 1: 282–339.

Nevins, Allan. *The American States During and After the Revolution.* Pp. 15–170.

Sikes, E. W. *The Transition of North Carolina from Colony to Commonwealth.* Pp. 42–84.

Thorpe, F. N. *American Charters, Constitutions, and Organic Laws.* Washington, D.C., 1909. 5: 2787–94.

14. The New State and Its Problems

Lefler, Hugh T., ed. *North Carolina History Told by Contemporaries.* Pp. 111–15.

Connor, R. D. W. *North Carolina: Rebuilding an Ancient Commonwealth.* Pp. 372–437.

Boyd, W. K. *History of North Carolina: The Federal Period.* Chicago, 1919. Pp. 1–20.

Ashe, S. A. *History of North Carolina.* 1: 497–512.

* * *

Bullock, C. J. *Essays in the Monetary History of the United States.* Pp. 193–200.

Connor, R. D. W. *Revolutionary Leaders of North Carolina.* Pp. 3–125.

Crittenden, C. C. *The Commerce of North Carolina, 1763–1789.* Pp. 116–70.

Harrell, I. M. "North Carolina Loyalists." *NCHR* 3 (October 1926): 575–90.

McRee, G. J., ed. *The Life and Correspondence of James Iredell.* 1: 340–564.

Morris, Frances S., and Phyllis Mary Morris. "Economic Conditions in North Carolina about 1780." *NCHR* 16 (April and July 1939): 107–33, 296–327.

Nevins, Allan. *The American States During and After the Revolution.* Pp. 358–543.

Wagstaff, H. M. *State Rights and Political Parties in North Carolina, 1776–1861.* Baltimore, 1906. Pp. 14–31.

15. The State at War

Lefler, Hugh T., ed. *North Carolina History Told by Contemporaries.* Pp. 115–19.
Connor, R. D. W. *North Carolina: Rebuilding an Ancient Commonwealth.* 1: 347–71.
———. *History of North Carolina.* 1: 437–94.
Ashe, S. A. *History of North Carolina.* 1: 396–497.

* * *

Alden, John R. *The South in the Revolution, 1763–1789.* Baton Rouge, La., 1957. (Use index for N.C. references.)
Bailey, Ralph E. *Guns over the Carolinas: The Story of Nathanael Greene.* New York, 1967. Pp. 1–224.
Connor, R. D. W. *Revolutionary Leaders of North Carolina.* Pp. 3–125.
Davidson, Chalmers. *Piedmont Partisan: The Life and Times of Brigadier-General William Lee Davidson.* Davidson, N.C., 1951. Pp. 91–123.
Davis, Sallie. "North Carolina's Part in the Revolution." *South Atlantic Quarterly* 2 (October 1903): 413–24; 3 (January and July 1904): 27–38, 154–65.
Draper, Lyman. *King's Mountain and Its Heroes.* Cincinnati, 1881. Pp. 191–309.
Greene, G. W. *The Life of Nathanael Greene, Major General in the Army of the Revolution.* 3 vols. Boston, 1890. 3: 148–218.
King, Clyde L. "Military Organization of North Carolina During and After the Revolution." *NCB* 8 (July 1908): 41–55.
Lee, Henry. *Memoirs of the War in the Southern Department of the United States,* ed. Robert E. Lee. New York, 1870. Pp. 194–297.
Miller, John C. *Triumph of Freedom, 1775-1783.* Boston, 1948. Pp. 546–53.
Newsome, A. R., ed. "A British Orderly Book, 1780–1781." *NCHR* 9 (January and April 1932): 57–58, 163–86, 273–98, 366–92.
Quarles, Benjamin. *The Negro in the American Revolution.* Chapel Hill, 1961. (Use index for N.C. references.)
Rankin, Hugh F. *The North Carolina Continentals.* Chapel Hill, 1971. Pp. 3–428.
———. *North Carolina in the American Revolution.* Raleigh, 1959. Pp. 1–75.
Robinson, Blackwell P. *William R. Davie.* Chapel Hill, 1954. Pp. 1–495.
Ross, Charles, ed. *Correspondence of Charles, First Marquis Cornwallis.* 3 vols. London, 1859. 1: 84–98, 501–10.
Schenck, David. *North Carolina, 1780–1781.* Raleigh, 1889. Pp. 199–426.
Wallace, Willard M. *Appeal to Arms: A Military History of the American Revolution.* New York, 1951. Pp. 89–91, 228–45.

16. Aftermath of the Revolution

Lefler, Hugh T., ed. *North Carolina History Told by Contemporaries.* Pp. 125–33, 157–62.

Connor, R. D. W. *North Carolina: Rebuilding an Ancient Commonwealth.* 1: 372–400.

Boyd, W. K. *History of North Carolina: The Federal Period.* Pp. 1–46, 66–82.

* * *

Amis, Moses N. *Historical Raleigh from Its Foundation in 1792.* Raleigh, 1902. Pp. 11–77.

Battle, K. P. *History of the Supreme Court of North Carolina.* Raleigh, 1899. Pp. 5–39.

————. *History of the University of North Carolina.* 2 vols. Raleigh, 1907. 1: 1–162.

Chamberlain, Hope. *History of Wake County.* Raleigh, 1922. Pp. 17–115.

Clark, Walter. "History of the Superior and Supreme Courts of North Carolina." *NCB* 2 (October 1918): 79–104.

Coon, Charles L., ed. *North Carolina Schools and Academies, 1790–1840: A Documentary History.* 2 vols. Raleigh, 1915.

Corbitt, D. L. "Judicial Districts in North Carolina, 1746–1934." *NCHR* 12 (January 1936): 45–61.

Crittenden, C. C. *The Commerce of North Carolina, 1763–1789.* Pp. 155–70.

De Mond, Robert O. *The Loyalists in North Carolina During the Revolution.* Pp. 170–201.

Henderson, Archibald. *The Campus of the First State University.* Chapel Hill, 1949. Pp. 1–71.

Keith, Alice B., ed. *The John Gray Blount Papers.* 1: 13–563.

Nevins, Allan. *The American States During and After the Revolution.* Pp. 606–78.

17. North Carolina and the Federal Union, 1777–1789

Lefler, Hugh T., ed. *North Carolina History Told by Contemporaries.* Pp. 120–25. 133–39.

Connor, R. D. W. *North Carolina: Rebuilding an Ancient Commonwealth.* 1: 378–408.

Boyd, W. K. *History of North Carolina: The Federal Period.* Pp. 1–46, 66–82.

* * *

Boyd, W. K., ed. "Letters of Sylvius" [Hugh Williamson]." TCHS *Papers,* ser. 11 (1915): 5–46.

Burnett, E. C. *The Continental Congress.* New York, 1941. Pp. 669–721.

————, ed. *Letters of Members of the Continental Congress.* 8 vols. Washington, D.C., 1931–36. Vols. 2–7 for North Carolina references. (Use index.)

Douglass, Elisha P. "Thomas Burke, Disillusioned Democrat." *NCHR* 26 (April 1949): 150–86.

Driver, Carl. *John Sevier, Pioneer of the Old Southwest.* Chapel Hill, 1923. Pp. 16–116.

Elliot, Jonathan, ed. *The Debates in the Several State Conventions on the Adoption of the Federal Constitution.* Washington, D.C., 1836–45. 4: 1–251.

Jensen, Merrill. *The Articles of Confederation: An Interpretation of Social-Constitutional History of the American Revolution. 1774–1781.* Madison, Wis., 1940. Pp. 25–28, 84–85, 102, 147–49, 172, 185–86, 195, 216–17.

————. *The New Nation: A History of the United States During the Confederation, 1781–1789.* New York, 1950. Pp. 132, 263, 286, 299–305, 319–20, 328–34.

Lefler, Hugh T., ed. *A Plea for Federal Union, 1788.* Charlottesville, Va., 1950. Pp. 7–73.

Lester, W. S. *The Transylvania Colony.* Spencer, Ind., 1935. Pp. 1–83, 255–75.

McRee, G. J., ed. *The Life and Correspondence of James Iredell.* 1: 340–564.

Masterson, William H. *William Blount.* Baton Rouge, La., 1954. Pp. 110–70.

Neal, John W. "Life and Public Service of Hugh Williamson." TCHS *Papers,* 13 (1919): 62–111.

Nevins, Allan. *The American States During and After the Revolution.* Pp. 544–65.

Newsome, A. R. "North Carolina and the Ratification of the Federal Constitution." *NCHR* 17 (October 1940): 287–301.

Raper, C. L. "Why North Carolina at First Refused to Ratify the Federal Constitution." AHA *Annual Report.* Washington, D.C., 1895. 1: 99–108.

Robinson, B. P. "Willie Jones of Halifax." *NCHR* 18 (January and April 1941): 1–26, 133–70.

Trenholme, Louise Irby. *North Carolina and the Ratification of the Federal Constitution.* New York, 1932. Pp. 1–282.

Wagstaff, H. M. *State Rights and Political Parties in North Carolina, 1776–1861.* Pp. 14–31.

Williams, S. C. *History of the Lost State of Franklin.* Johnson City, Tenn., 1924. Pp. 1–378.

18. Politics and Personalities, 1789–1800

Lefler, Hugh T., ed. *North Carolina History Told by Contemporaries.* Pp. 139–42.

Connor, R. D. W. *North Carolina: Rebuilding an Ancient Commonwealth.* 1: 426–34.

Boyd, W. K. *History of North Carolina: The Federal Period.* Pp. 47–65.

Ashe, S. A. *History of North Carolina.* Vol. 2, chaps. 8–12.

* * *

Dodd, W. E. *The Life of Nathaniel Macon.* Raleigh, 1903. Pp. 1–100.

Elliott, Robert N., Jr. *The Raleigh Register, 1799–1863.* Chapel Hill, 1955. Pp. 1–133.

Gilpatrick, D. H. *Jeffersonian Democracy in North Carolina, 1789–1816.* New York, 1931. Pp. 11–127.

Henderson, Archibald. *Washington's Southern Tour 1791.* Boston, 1923. Pp. 70–125.

Lycan, Gilbert. "Alexander Hamilton and the North Carolina Federalists." *NCHR* 25 (October 1948): 442–65.

McRee, G. J. *The Life and Correspondence of James Iredell.* 2: 1–277.

Powell, William S. ed. "The Diary of Joseph Gales, 1794–1795." *NCHR* 26 (July 1949): 335–47.

Wagstaff, H. M. *Federalism in North Carolina.* JSHP 9 (1910): 3–44.

———, ed. *The Papers of John Steele.* 2 vols. Raleigh, 1924.

———. *State Rights and Political Parties in North Carolina, 1776–1861.* Pp. 1–31.

19. Triumphant Jeffersonian Democracy, 1801–1815

Lefler, Hugh T., ed. *North Carolina History Told by Contemporaries.* Pp. 140–46.

Connor, R. D. W. *North Carolina: Rebuilding an Ancient Commonwealth.* 1: 382–94, 428–59.

Boyd, W. K. *History of North Carolina: The Federal Period.* Pp. 83–104.

Ashe, S. A. *History of North Carolina.* Vol. 2, chap. 3 and pp. 216–38.

* * *

Boyd, W. K. "Currency and Banking in North Carolina." TCHS *Papers* 10 (1914): 52–86.

Connor, R. D. W. *Documentary History of the University of North Carolina, 1776–1799.* 2 vols. Chapel Hill, 1953.

Dodd, W. E. *The Life of Nathaniel Macon.* Pp. 100–250.

Gilpatrick, D. H. *Jeffersonian Democracy in North Carolina.* Pp. 127–239.

Henderson, Archibald. *The Campus of the First State University.* Chapel Hill, 1949. Pp. 5–82.

Knight, E. W., ed. *A Documentary History of Education in the South Before 1860.* Vol. 3, *The Rise of the State University.* Chapel Hill, 1952. Pp. 1–528.

———. *Public School Education in North Carolina.* Pp. 1–101.

Morgan. J. A. "State Aid to Transportation in North Carolina—The Pre-Railroad Era." *NCB* 10 (January 1911): 122–54.

Newsome, A. R. "Udna Maria Blakeley." *NCHR* 4 (April 1927): 158–71.

Pratt, J. W. *Expansionists of 1812.* New York, 1925. Pp. 1–409.

Wagstaff, H. M. *State Rights and Political Parties in North Carolina, 1775–1861.* Pp. 32–155.

Weaver, C. C. *History of Internal Improvements in North Carolina Previous to 1860.* Baltimore, 1903. Pp. 1–94.

Wilson, E. M. *The Congressional Career of Nathaniel Macon.* JSHP 2 (1900): 1–115.

20. The "Rip Van Winkle State"

Lefler, Hugh T., ed. *North Carolina History Told by Contemporaries.* Pp. 140–46.

Connor, R. D. W. *North Carolina: Rebuilding an Ancient Commonwealth.* 1: 438–46, 455–74, 498–506.

Boyd, W. K. *History of North Carolina: The Federal Period.* Pp. 105–38.

* * *

Brown, C. K. *A State Movement in Railroad Development.* Chapel Hill, 1928. Pp. 1–14.

Cathey, C. O. *Agricultural Developments in North Carolina, 1783–1860.* Chapel Hill, 1956. Chaps. 1–4, pp. 3–29.

Connor, R. D. W. *Ante-Bellum Builders of North Carolina.* Greensboro, 1914. Pp. 3–31.

Dodd, W. E. *The Life of Nathaniel Macon.* Pp. 291–369.

Hamilton, J. G. de R. *Party Politics in North Carolina, 1835–1860.* JSHP 15 (1916): 17–29.

Hobbs, S. H., Jr. *North Carolina: Economic and Social.* Pp. 67–87.

Johnson, Guion G. *Ante-Bellum North Carolina.* Chapel Hill, 1937. Pp. 3–51.

Poe, Clarence. "Nathaniel Macon, the Cincinnatus of America." *South Atlantic Quarterly* 37 (January 1938): 12–21.

Wager, P. W. *County Government and Administration in North Carolina.* Pp. 1–31.

21. The Murphey Program for State Development

Lefler, Hugh T., ed. *North Carolina History Told by Contemporaries.* Pp. 146–48, 150–52, 164–77, 198–212.

Connor, R. D. W. *North Carolina: Rebuilding an Ancient Commonwealth.* 1: 474–97.

Boyd, W. K. *History of North Carolina: The Federal Period.* Pp. 91–104.

* * *

Boyd, W. K. "The Finances of the North Carolina Literary Fund." *South Atlantic Quarterly* 13 (October 1914): 361–70.

———. "The North Carolina Fund for Internal Improvements." *South Atlantic Quarterly* 15 (January 1916): 52–67.

Caldwell, Joseph. *Letters on Popular Education, Addressed to the People of North Carolina.* Hillsborough, 1832. Pp. 1–102.

Connor, R. D. W. *Ante-Bellum Builders of North Carolina.* Pp. 32–60.

Coon, Charles L., ed. *The Beginnings of Public Education in North Carolina.* 1: ix–xxxvii, 99–282.

Haywood, M. De L. "Canova's Statue of Washington." *South Atlantic Quarterly* (1902): 278–87.

Knight, E. W. *Public School Education in North Carolina.* Pp. 13–111.

Konkle, B. A. *John Motley Morehead and the Development of North Carolina, 1796–1866.* Philadelphia, 1922. Pp. 63–101.

Morgan, J. A. "State Aid to Transportation in North Carolina: The Pre-Railroad Era." *NCB* 10 (January 1911): 122–54.

Newsome, A. R. *The Presidential Election of 1824 in North Carolina.* JSHP 23 (1939): 1–44.

Noble, M. C. S. *A History of the Public Schools of North Carolina.* Pp. 25–55.

Weaver, C. C. *History of Internal Improvements in North Carolina Previous to 1860.* Pp. 9–75.

22. The State's Changing Role in National Politics, 1824–1835

Lefler, Hugh T., ed. *North Carolina History Told by Contemporaries.* Pp. 148–50.
Connor, R. D. W. *North Carolina: Rebuilding an Ancient Commonwealth.* 1: 506–17.
Boyd, W. K. *The History of North Carolina: The Federal Period.* Pp. 166–84.

* * *

Cole, A. C. *The Whig Party in the South.* Washington, D.C., 1913. (Use index for N.C. references.)
Hamilton, J. G. de R. *The Papers of William A. Graham.* 3 vols. Raleigh, 1957–60. 1: 144–246.
Konkle, B. A. *John Motley Morehead and the Development of North Carolina.* Pp. 170–98.
Newsome, A. R. *The Presidential Election of 1824 in North Carolina.* Pp. 45–173.
Shanks, Henry T., ed. *The Papers of Willie P. Mangum.* 5 vols. Raleigh, 1950–56. Vol. 1.
Williams, Max R. "The Foundations of the Whig Party in North Carolina." *NCHR* (April 1970): 115–129.

23. The Conventions of 1835 and the Two-Party System

Lefler, Hugh T., ed. *North Carolina History Told by Contemporaries.* Pp. 152–54.
Connor, R. D. W. *North Carolina: Rebuilding an Ancient Commonwealth.* 1: 518–40.
Boyd, W. K. *The History of North Carolina: The Federal Period.* Pp. 139–65.

* * *

Connor, H. G. "The Convention of 1835." *NCB* 8 (October 1908): 89–110.
Connor, R. D. W. *Ante-Bellum Builders of North Carolina.* Pp. 60–92.
Dodd, W. E. *The Life of Nathaniel Macon.* Pp. 370–401.
Green, F. M. *Constitutional Development of the South Atlantic States.* Chapel Hill, 1930. Pp. 176–79, 183–87, 200, 204–8, 224–33, 265–72.
Hamilton, J. G. de R. *Party Politics in North Carolina, 1835–1860.* Pp. 1–16.
Konkle, B. A. *John Motley Morehead and the Development of North Carolina.* Pp. 144–69.
Schauinger, Joseph H. *William Gaston, Carolinian.* New York, 1949. Pp. 1–242.
Smith, M. P. "Borough Representation in North Carolina." *NCHR* 7 (April 1930): 177–91.
Wagstaff, H. M. *State Rights and Political Parties in North Carolina, 1776–1861.* Pp. 60–69.

24. *The Whigs Inaugurate an Age of Progress, 1835–1850.*

Lefler, Hugh T., ed. *North Carolina History Told by Contemporaries.* Pp. 185–89, 212–16, 236–43, 264–77.

Connor, R. D. W. *North Carolina: Rebuilding an Ancient Commonwealth.* 1: 541–55, 581–90; 2: 7–48.

Boyd, W. K. *History of North Carolina: The Federal Period.* Pp. 225–62.

* * *

Betz, Ezra. *William Gaston, Fighter for Social Justice.* New York, 1964. Pp. 1–190.

Brown, C. K. *A State Movement in Railroad Development.* Pp. 15–94.

Caldwell, Joseph. *The Numbers of Carlton.* New York, 1828. Pp. 3–232.

Connor, R. D. W. *Ante-Bellum Builders of North Carolina.* Pp. 93–149.

Coon, C. L., ed. *Beginnings of Public Education in North Carolina.* 1: xxxvii–xlvii; 2: 545–613.

Hamilton, J. G. de R. *Party Politics in North Carolina, 1835–1860.* Pp. 30–135.

———, ed. *The Papers of William A. Graham.* Vols. 2 and 3.

Hoffmann, William S. *Andrew Jackson and North Carolina Politics.* Chapel Hill, 1958. Pp. 1–134.

Johnson, Guion G. *Ante-Bellum North Carolina.* Pp. 259–82, 493–521, 560–81, 613–73.

Knight, E. W. *Public School Education in North Carolina.* Pp. 113–56.

Konkle, B. A. *John Motley Morehead and the Development of North Carolina.* Pp. 199–344.

McCulloch, Margaret C. "Founding the North Carolina Asylum for the Insane." *NCHR* 13 (July 1936): 185–201.

Marshall, Helen. *Dorothea Dix, Forgotten Samaritan.* Chapel Hill, 1937. Pp. 1–298.

Noble, M. C. S. *A History of the Public Schools of North Carolina.* Pp. 56–129.

Norton, C. C. *The Democratic Party in Ante-Bellum North Carolina, 1835–1861.* Chapel Hill, 1930. Pp. 3–106.

Shanks, Henry T., ed. *The Papers of Willie P. Mangum.* Vols. 4 and 5.

Sellers, Charles G., Jr. *James K. Polk, Jacksonian, 1795–1843.* Princeton, N.J., 1957. (Use index for N.C. references.)

Wagstaff, H. M. *State Rights and Political Parties in North Carolina, 1776–1861.* Pp. 69–80.

Waugh, Elizabeth. *North Carolina's Capital: Raleigh.* Raleigh, 1967. Pp. 1–216.

25. *Continued Progress under the Democrats, 1850–1860*

Lefler, Hugh T., ed. *North Carolina History Told by Contemporaries.* Pp. 228–36.

Connor, R. D. W. *North Carolina: Rebuilding an Ancient Commonwealth.* 2: 49–90.

Boyd, W. K. *History of North Carolina: The Federal Period.* Pp. 288–97, 308–22, 344–53.

* * *

Bassett, J. S. "The Congressional Career of Thomas L. Clingman." TCHS *Papers,* ser. 4 (1900): 48–63.

Boyd, W. K. "Ad Valorem Slave Taxation." TCHS *Papers,* ser. 5 (1905): 1–11.

————. "William W. Holden." TCHS *Papers,* ser. 3 (1899): 39–78, 90–130.

Brown, C. K. *A State Movement in Railroad Development.* Pp. 95–147.

Carr, J. W. "The Manhood Suffrage Movement in North Carolina." TCHS *Papers,* ser. 11 (1915): 47–77.

Hamilton, J. G. de R. *Party Politics in North Carolina, 1835–1860.* Pp. 136–210.

Knight, E. W. *Public School Education in North Carolina.* Pp. 158–216.

Noble, M. C. S. *A History of the Public Schools of North Carolina.* Pp. 133–229.

Norton, C. C. *The Democratic Party in Ante-Bellum North Carolina.* Pp. 109–257.

Wagstaff, H. M. *State Rights and Political Parties in North Carolina, 1775–1861.* Pp. 81–119.

Weeks, S. B. *The Beginnings of the Common School System in North Carolina, or Calvin Henderson Wiley and the Organization of the Common Schools of North Carolina.* Washington, D.C., 1898. Pp. 1379–1474.

26. Economic Development, 1835–1860

Lefler, Hugh T., ed. *North Carolina History Told by Contemporaries.* Pp. 226–28.

Boyd, W. K. *The History of North Carolina: The Federal Period.* Pp. 331–53.

* * *

Cappon, L. C. "Iron-Making—A Forgotten Industry of North Carolina." *NCHR* 9 (October 1932): 331–48.

Cathey, C. O. *Agricultural Developments in North Carolina, 1783–1860.* Chapel Hill, 1956. Pp. 30–205.

Gray, L. C. *History of Agriculture in the Southern United States to 1860.* 2 vols. Washington, D.C., 1933. Vol. 1. (Use index for N.C. references.)

Green, F. M. "Gold Mining in North Carolina." *NCHR* 14 (January and April 1937): 1–19, 135–55.

Olmsted, F. L. *A Journey in the Seaboard Slave States.* New York, 1858. Pp. 305–76.

Phillips, U. B. *American Negro Slavery.* New York, 1918. Pp. 81–82, 126.

————. *Life and Labor in the Old South.* Boston, 1929. Pp. 45, 252–54.

Robert, J. C. "The Tobacco Industry in Ante-Bellum North Carolina." *NCHR* 15 (April 1938): 119–30.

————. *The Tobacco Kingdom, Plantation, Market and Factory in Virginia and North Carolina, 1800–1860.* Durham, 1938. Pp. 3–52.

Taylor, Rosser H. *Slaveholding in North Carolina: An Economic View.* JSHP 18 (1926): 8–98.

Stampp, Kenneth M. *The Peculiar Institution: Slavery in the Ante-Bellum South.* New York, 1956. (Use index for N.C. references.)

Tilley, Nannie May. *The Bright-Tobacco Industry.* Chapel Hill, 1948. Pp. 3–36.

27. An Intellectual Awakening, 1835–1860

Lefler, Hugh T., ed. *North Carolina History Told by Contemporaries.* Pp. 179–85, 189–94.

Connor, R. D. W. *North Carolina: Rebuilding an Ancient Commonwealth.* 1: 590–613.

Boyd, W. K. *The History of North Carolina: The Federal Period.* Pp. 354–92.

* * *

Battle, K. P. *History of the University of North Carolina.* 1: 423–723.

Chaffin, Nora. *Trinity College, 1839–1892: The Beginnings of Duke University.* Durham, 1950. Pp. 22–117.

Coon, Charles L., ed. *The Beginnings of Public Education in North Carolina: A Documentary History, 1790–1840.* 2 vols. Raleigh, 1908.

_____. *North Carolina Schools and Academies, 1790–1849: A Documentary History.* Raleigh, 1915. Pp. 1–846.

Dormon, James H., Jr., *The Theater in the Ante-Bellum South, 1815–1861.* Chapel Hill, 1967. (Use index for N.C. towns.)

Eaton, Clement. *Freedom of Thought in the Old South.* Durham, 1940. Pp. 200–217.

Gilbert, Dorothy. *Guilford, A Quaker College.* Greensboro, 1937. Pp. 11–79.

Gobbel, L. L. *Church-State Relationships in Education in North Carolina Since 1776.* Durham, 1938. Pp. 1–251.

Henderson, Archibald. *The Campus of the First State University.* Pp. 83–178.

Joint Committee of the North Carolina English Teachers Association and the North Carolina Library Association. *North Carolina Authors: A Selective Handbook.* Chapel Hill, 1952. (Use index for particular authors.)

Paschal, George W. *History of Wake Forest College.* 3 vols. Wake Forest, N.C., 1935–43. 1: 1–653.

Raper, C. L. *The Church and Private Schools in North Carolina.* Greensboro, 1898. Pp. 9–247.

Shaw, Cornelia. *Davidson College.* New York, 1923. Pp. 1–98.

28. Religion and Society in Antebellum Days

Lefler, Hugh T., ed. *North Carolina History Told by Contemporaries.* Pp. 195–98, 216–25.

Connor, R. D. W. *North Carolina: Rebuilding an Ancient Commonwealth.* 2: 152–73.

Boyd, W. K. *The History of North Carolina: The Federal Period.* Pp. 185–224.

* * *

Bassett, J. S. *Anti-Slavery Leaders of North Carolina.* Baltimore, 1898. Pp. 7–74.

_____. *History of Slavery in the State of North Carolina.* Baltimore, 1899. Pp. 7–109.

Franklin, John Hope. *The Free Negro in North Carolina, 1790–1860.* Pp. 14–271.

Johnson, Guion G. *Ante-Bellum North Carolina.* Pp. 331–467, 522–59, 582–612.

Lemmon, Sarah M. "The Genesis of the Protestant Episcopal Diocese of North Carolina, 1701–1823." *NCHR* 28 (October 1951): 426–62.

Owsley F. L. *Plain Folk of the Old South*. Baton Rouge, La., 1949. Pp. 45–51, 58–61.

Stroupe, Henry S. "The Beginnings of Religious Journalism in North Carolina, 1823–1865." *NCHR* 30 (January 1953): 1–22.

Taylor, Rosser H. *The Free Negro in North Carolina*. JSHP 17 (1920): 5–26.

_____. "Humanizing the Slave Code of North Carolina." *NCHR* 42 (July 1965): 323–31.

_____. "Slave Conspiracies in North Carolina." *NCHR* 5 (January 1928): 20–34.

29. Sectional Differences and Conflicts in the Union

Barck, O. T., Jr.; Walter Wakefield; and Hugh T. Lefler. *The United States: A Survey of National Development*. New York, 1950. Pp. 307–29, 405–31.

Hicks, J. D. *The Federal Union*. Boston, 1937. Pp. 371–90, 493–507, 532–47, 575–625.

* * *

Carpenter, J. T. *The South as a Conscious Minority*. New York, 1930. (Use index for N.C. references.)

Craven, Avery. *The Coming of the Civil War*. New York, 1942. Pp. 21–25, 58, 96, 153–54, 213, 262–70, 352, 414.

Johnston, Clifton. "Abolitionist Missionary Activities in North Carolina." *NCHR* 40 (July 1963): 295–320.

Morison, S. E., and H. S. Commager. *The Growth of the American Republic*. New York, 1950. 1: 420–46, 494–548.

Randall, J. G. *The Civil War and Reconstruction*. New York, 1937. Pp. 3–258.

Sitterson, J. C. "Economic Sectionalism in Ante-Bellum North Carolina." *NCHR* 16 (April 1939): 134–46.

Sydnor, C. S. *The Development of Southern Sectionalism, 1819–1848*. Baton Rouge, La., 1948. (Use index for N.C. references.)

30. A State in the Confederacy

Lefler, Hugh T., ed. *North Carolina History Told by Contemporaries*. Pp. 262–89.

Boyd, W. K. *The History of North Carolina: The Federal Period*. Pp. 263–87, 297–330.

Hamilton, J. G. de R. *North Carolina Since 1860*. Chicago, 1919. Pp. 1–6.

* * *

Bassett, J. S. *Anti–Slavery Leaders of North Carolina*. Pp. 7–74.

Hamilton, J. G. de R. *Benjamin Sherwood Hedrick*. JSHP 10 (1910): 1–42.

_____. *Reconstruction in North Carolina*. Raleigh, 1906. Pp. 1–36.

Hill, D. H. *North Carolina in the War Between the States: Bethel to Sharpsburg.* 2 vols. Raleigh, 1926. Vol. 1, chap. 1.

Holt, Bryce R. "The Supreme Court of North Carolina and Slavery." TCHS *Papers,* ser. 17 (1927): 7–77.

Hoffman, William S. *North Carolina in the Mexican War, 1846–1848.* Raleigh, 1959. Pp. 1–48.

Johnston, Frontis, ed. *The Papers of Zebulon Baird Vance, 1843–1862.* Raleigh, 1963. 1: xvii–xxiv, 1–100.

Lefler, Hugh T. *Hinton Rowan Helper: Advocate of a "White America."* Charlottesville, Va., 1935. Pp. 5–42.

Sitterson, J. C. *The Secession Movement in North Carolina.* JSHP 23 (1939): 24–249.

31. The War for Southern Independence, 1861–1865

Lefler, Hugh T., ed. *North Carolina History Told by Contemporaries.* Pp. 296–304, 308–14.

Connor, R. D. W. *North Carolina: Rebuilding an Ancient Commonwealth.* 2: 232–60.

Hamilton, J. G. de R. *North Carolina Since 1860.* Pp. 7–38.

Ashe, S. A. *History of North Carolina.* 2: 620–1012.

* * *

Barrett, John G. *The Civil War in North Carolina.* Chapel Hill, 1963. Pp. 3–392.

———. *North Carolina as a Civil War Battleground, 1861–1865.* Raleigh, 1960. Pp. 1–99.

———. *Sherman's March Through the Carolinas.* Chapel Hill, 1956. Pp. 1–325.

Brooks, A. L., and Hugh T. Lefler, eds. *The Papers of Walter Clark.* 2 vols. Chapel Hill, 1948. 1: 49–146.

Clark, Walter, ed. *Histories of the Several Regiments and Battalions from North Carolina in the Great War, 1861–'65.* 5 vols. Raleigh, 1901.

Corbitt, D. L., and Elizabeth W. Wilborn, eds. *Civil War Pictures.* Raleigh, 1961. Pp. 1–90.

Coulter, E. M. *The Confederate States of America, 1861–1865.* Baton Rouge, La., 1950. Pp. 3, 40, 98, 271, 366, 398, 426, 493, 519, 534–36.

Hesseltine, W. B. *Civil War Prisons: A Study in War Psychology.* Columbus, Ohio, 1930. (Use index for references to Salisbury Prison.)

Hill, D. H. *North Carolina in the War Between the States: Bethel to Sharpsburg.* Vols. 1 and 2.

Lonsdale, Richard E. *Atlas of North Carolina.* Pp. 49–51.

Tucker, Glenn. *Front Rank: A Story of North Carolina in the Civil War.* Raleigh, 1962. Pp. 1–83.

———. *Zeb Vance: Champion of Personal Freedom.* Indianapolis, 1965. Pp. 1–564.

32. *Internal Division and Wreckage, 1861–1865*

Lefler, Hugh T., ed. *North Carolina History Told by Contemporaries.* Pp. 296–301, 306–8, 314–15, 324–31.

Connor, R. D. W. *North Carolina: Rebuilding an Ancient Commonwealth.* 2: 183–92, 204–31.

Hamilton, J. G. de R. *North Carolina Since 1860.* Pp. 39–55.

* * *

Black, Robert C., III. *The Railroads of the Confederacy.* Chapel Hill, 1952. (Use index for N.C. references.)

Dowd, Clement. *Life of Zebulon B. Vance.* Charlotte, 1897. Pp. 62–101.

Hamilton, J. G. de R. *Reconstruction in North Carolina.* Pp. 36–80.

Hesseltine, W. B. *Civil War Prisons: A Study in War Psychology.* Columbus, Ohio, 1930. (Use index for Salisbury Prison.)

Klingberg, Frank W. *The Southern Claims Commission.* Berkeley and Los Angeles, Calif., 1955. Pp. 157–69.

Lonn, Ella. *Desertion During the Civil War.* New York, 1928. (Use index for N.C. references.)

Massey, Mary E. *Ersatz in the Confederacy.* Columbia, S.C., 1952. Pp. ii, 18, 21–29, 83–88, 101–5, 161–63.

Moore, A. B. *Conscription and Conflict in the Confederacy.* New York, 1924. Pp. 47, 79, 95–97, 107, 148, 187, 202–3, 279–96, 317–20.

Owsley, F. L. *State Rights in the Confederacy.* Chicago, 1925. (Use index for N.C. references.)

Smith, Mary Shannon. *Union Sentiment in North Carolina During the Civil War.* Raleigh, 1915. Pp. 1–21.

Spencer, Cornelia Phillips. *The Last Ninety Days of the War in North Carolina.* New York, 1866. Pp. 1–287.

Robinson, W. M. *Justice in Grey: A History of the Judicial System of the Confederate States of America.* Cambridge, Mass., 1941. Pp. 18, 78, 82, 92–96, 115, 116, 128, 193–95, 414, 547, 586–87, 595, 616.

Tatum, Georgia Lee. *Disloyalty in the Confederacy.* Chapel Hill, 1934. (Use index for N.C. references.)

Yates, Richard E. *The Confederacy and Zeb Vance.* Tuscaloosa, Ala. 1958. Pp. 1–132.

33. *Return to the Union*

Lefler, Hugh T., ed. *North Carolina History Told by Contemporaries.* Pp. 306–24, 331–40.

Connor, R. D. W. *North Carolina: Rebuilding an Ancient Commonwealth.* 2: 261–74, 280–305.

Hamilton, J. G. de R. *North Carolina Since 1860.* Pp. 56–113.

* * *

Brooks, A. L., and Lefler, Hugh T., eds. *The Papers of Walter Clark.* 1: 145–93.

Coulter, E. M. *The South During Reconstruction, 1865–1877.* Baton Rouge, La., 1947. Pp. 2, 207, 348–50.

Evans, William McKee. *Ballots and Fence Rails: Reconstruction on the Lower Cape Fear.* Chapel Hill, 1967. Pp. 4–102.

Hamilton, J. G. de R. *Reconstruction in North Carolina.* Pp. 81–342.

_____, ed. *The Papers of Randolph Abbott Shotwell.* 3 vols. Raleigh, 1929–36.

Russ, W. A., Jr. "Radical Disfranchisement in North Carolina, 1867–1868." *NCHR* 11 (July 1934): 271–83.

Winston, R. W. *Andrew Johnson: Plebeian and Patriot.* New York, 1928. Pp. 3–14, 325–454.

34. Reconstruction Politics, 1868–1877

Lefler, Hugh T., ed. *North Carolina History Told by Contemporaries.* Pp. 341–45, 350–55.

Connor, R. D. W. *North Carolina: Rebuilding an Ancient Commonwealth.* 2: 305–52.

Daniels, Jonathan. *Prince of Carpetbaggers* (Milton S. Littlefield). New York, 1958. Pp. 1–319.

Hamilton, J. G. de R. *North Carolina Since 1860.* Pp. 114–60, 170–91.

Boyd, W. K. "William W. Holden." TCHS *Papers,* ser. 3 (1899): 39–78, 90–130.

_____, ed. *Memoirs of W. W. Holden.* Durham, 1911. Pp. 31–130.

Evans, William McKee. *Ballots and Fence Rails: Reconstruction on the Lower Cape Fear.* Pp. 103–75.

Ewing, C. A. M. "Two Reconstruction Impeachments." *NCHR* 15 (July 1938): 204–30.

Hamilton, J. G. de R. *Reconstruction in North Carolina.* Pp. 343–608, 631–67.

Olsen, Otto H. *Carpetbagger's Crusade: The Life of Albion Winegar Tourgée.* Baltimore, 1965. Pp. 1–395.

_____. "The Ku Klux Klan: A Study in Reconstruction Politics and Propaganda." *NCHR* 39 (July 1962): 340–62.

Smith, Samuel D. *The Negro in Congress, 1870–1901.* Chapel Hill, 1940. (Use index.)

Tourgée, A. W. *A Fool's Errand.* New York, 1880. Pp. 1–521.

Whitener, D. J. "Public Education in North Carolina During Reconstruction, 1865–1876," in *Essays in Southern History Presented to J. G. de R. Hamilton,* ed. Fletcher M. Green. Chapel Hill, 1949. Pp. 67–91.

35. The Industrial Revolution, 1870–1900

Lefler, Hugh T., ed. *North Carolina History Told by Contemporaries.* Pp. 357–66, 391–93.

Connor, R. D. W. *North Carolina: Rebuilding an Ancient Commonwealth.* 2: 353–75, 420–22, 450–53.

Hamilton, J. G. de R. *North Carolina Since 1860.* Pp. 384–403.

* * *

Boyd, W. K. *The Story of Durham, City of the New South.* Durham, 1925. Pp. 1–96.

Davidson, Elizabeth H. "The Child-Labor Problem in North Carolina." *NCHR* 13 (April 1936): 105–21.

Evans, William McKee. *Ballots and Fence Rails: Reconstruction on the Lower Cape Fear.* Pp. 176–210.

Jenkins, J. W. *James B. Duke, Master Builder.* New York, 1927. Pp. 1–98.

Logan, Frenise A. *The Negro in North Carolina, 1876–1894.* Chapel Hill, 1964. Pp. 3–219.

McGuire, P. S. "The Seaboard Air Line." *NCHR* 11 (April 1934): 94–115.

Mitchell, Broadus. *The Rise of Cotton Mills in the South.* Baltimore, 1921. (Use index.)

Thompson, Holland. *From the Cotton Field to the Cotton Mill: A Study of the Industrial Transition in North Carolina.* New York, 1906. (Use index.)

———. *The New South.* New Haven, Conn., 1920. (Use index.)

Webb, Elizabeth Y. "Cotton Manufacturing and State Regulation in North Carolina, 1861–1865." *NCHR* 9 (April 1932): 117–37.

Winston, G. T. *A Builder of the New South, Being the Story of the Life Work of Daniel Augustus Tompkins 1920.* Pp. 3–403.

36. Agricultural Problems and Depression, 1865–1900

Lefler, Hugh T., ed. *North Carolina History Told by Contemporaries.* Pp. 356–57, 372–79.

Connor, R. D. W. *North Carolina: Rebuilding an Ancient Commonwealth.* 2: 356–58, 420–28.

Hamilton, J. G. de R. *North Carolina Since 1860.* Pp. 376–84.

* * *

Buck, S. J. *The Agrarian Crusade.* New Haven, Conn., 1921. (Use index.)

———. *The Granger Movement.* Cambridge, Mass., 1913. (Use index.)

Hicks, John D. "The Farmers' Alliance in North Carolina." *NCHR* 2 (April 1925): 162–87.

———. *The Populist Revolt.* Minneapolis, 1931. Pp. 36–95.

Lockmiller, David A. "The Establishment of the North Carolina College of Agriculture and Mechanic Arts." *NCHR* 16 (July 1939): 273–95.

Noblin, Stuart. *Leonidas LaFayette Polk, Agrarian Crusader.* Chapel Hill, 1949. Pp. 73–108.

Taylor, Joseph H. "The Great Migration from North Carolina in 1879." *NCHR* 31 (January 1954): 18–33.

37. The Slow Recovery of Education after the War

Lefler, Hugh T., ed. *North Carolina History Told by Contemporaries.* Pp. 304–6, 345–49, 366–72, 382–91.

Connor, R. D. W. *North Carolina: Rebuilding an Ancient Commonwealth.* 2: 376–98, 414–20, 449.

Hamilton, J. G. de R. *North Carolina Since 1860.* Pp. 347–475.

* * *

Battle, K. P. *History of the University of North Carolina.* 2: 1–589.

Bowles, Elisabeth A. *A Good Beginning: The First Four Decades of the University of North Carolina at Greensboro.* Chapel Hill, 1967. Pp. 3–28.

Chaffin, Nora C. *Trinity College, 1839–1892: The Beginnings of Duke University.* Durham, 1949. Pp. 1–584.

Garber, Paul N. *John Carlisle Kilgo, President of Trinity College, 1859–1910.* Durham, 1937. Pp. 84–287.

Holder, Rose Howell. *McIver of North Carolina.* Chapel Hill, 1957. Pp. 1–283.

Knight, E. W. *Public School Education in North Carolina.* Pp. 238–327.

Noble, M. C. S. *A History of the Public Schools of North Carolina.* Pp. 233–439.

Paschal, G. W. *A History of Wake Forest College.* 2: 3–308.

Whitener, D. J. "The Republican Party and Public Education in North Carolina." *NCHR* 37 (July 1960): 382–96.

Wilson, L. R., ed. *Selected Papers of Cornelia Phillips Spencer, 1865–1900.* Chapel Hill, 1953. Pp. 612–728.

38. Conservative Democracy and Political Revolution

Lefler, Hugh T., ed. *North Carolina History Told by Contemporaries.* Pp. 372–82.

Connor, R. D. W. *North Carolina: Rebuilding an Ancient Commonwealth.* 2: 399–414.

Hamilton, J. G. de R. *North Carolina Since 1860.* Pp. 192–246.

* * *

Daniels, Josephus. *Tar Heel Editor.* Chapel Hill, 1939. Pp. 247–505.

Hendrick, B. J. *The Earlier Life and Letters of Walter Hines Page.* New York, 1922. 1: 1–444.

Hicks, John D. "The Farmers' Alliance in North Carolina." *NCHR* 2 (April 1925): 162–87.

————. *The Populist Revolt.* Pp. 96–339.

Noblin, Stuart. *Leonidas LaFayette Polk, Agrarian Crusader.* Pp. 109–298.

Ratchford, B. U. "The North Carolina Public Debt, 1870–1878." *NCHR* 10 (January 1933): 1–20. "The Adjustment of the North Carolina Public Debt, 1879–1883." *NCHR* 10 (July 1933): 157–67. "The Conversion of the North Carolina Public Debt After 1879." *NCHR* 10 (October 1933): 251–72.

Whitener, D. J. "North Carolina Prohibition Election of 1881 and Its Aftermath." *NCHR* 11 (April 1934): 71–93.

———. *Prohibition in North Carolina, 1715–1945.* Chapel Hill, 1946. Pp. 50–132.

Woodward, C. Vann. *Origins of the New South, 1877–1913.* Baton Rouge, La., 1951. Pp. 46–54, 80–81, 87–89, 129–37, 159–63, 170, 178–79, 191, 203, 244.

———. *Reunion and Reaction: The Compromise of 1877 and the End of Reconstruction.* Boston, 1951. Pp. 43–46, 49, 84, 173–174, 187, 217, 228, 233.

39. Fusion Rule and the Return of a Chastened Democracy to Power

Lefler, Hugh T., ed. *North Carolina History Told by Contemporaries.* Pp. 396–402.

Connor, R. D. W. *North Carolina: Rebuilding an Ancient Commonwealth.* 2: 445–98.

Hamilton, J. G. de R. *North Carolina Since 1860.* Pp. 445–98.

* * *

Connor, R. D. W., and Clarence Poe, eds. *The Life and Speeches of Charles Brantley Aycock.* New York, 1912. Pp. 1–89.

Daniels, Josephus. *Editor in Politics.* Chapel Hill, 1941. Pp. 85–157, 202–64, 381–439.

Delap, Simeon A. "The Populist Party in North Carolina." TCHS *Papers,* ser. 14 (1922): 40–74.

Durden, Robert F. *Reconstruction Bonds and Twentieth Century Politics: South Dakota V. North Carolina, 1904.* Durham, 1962. Pp. 3–62.

Hicks, John D. *The Populist Revolt.* Pp. 340–423.

Johnson, Guion. "The Ideology of White Supremacy, 1876–1910," in *Essays in Southern History Presented to J. G. de R. Hamilton,* ed. Fletcher Green. Chapel Hill, 1949. Pp. 124–56.

Mabry, W. A. "Negro Suffrage and Fusion Rule in North Carolina." *NCHR* 12 (April 1935): 79–102.

———. "White Supremacy and the North Carolina Suffrage Amendment." *NCHR* 13 (January 1936): 1–24.

Morrison, Joseph L. *Josephus Daniels Says. . . . : An Editor's Political Odyssey from Bryan to Wilson and F.D.R., 1894–1913.* Chapel Hill, 1962. Pp. 1–339.

Woodward, C. Vann. *Origins of the New South, 1877–1913.* Pp. 239, 260, 261, 276–77, 282–84, 321, 331–34, 348–55, 380–82.

40. A New Era in North Carolina Politics, 1901–1920

Lefler, Hugh T., ed. *North Carolina History Told by Contemporaries.* Pp. 407–14.

Connor, R. D. W. *North Carolina: Rebuilding an Ancient Commonwealth.* 2: 490–541.

Hamilton, J. G. de R. *North Carolina Since 1860.* Pp. 316–46.

* * *

Arnett, A. M. *Claude Kitchin and the Wilson War Policies.* Boston, 1937. Pp. 47–300.

Brooks, A. L. *Walter Clark: Fighting Judge.* Chapel Hill, 1944. Pp. 129–92.

_____, and Hugh T. Lefler, eds. *The Papers of Walter Clark.* 2 vols. Chapel Hill, 1948, 1950. Vol. 2.

Daniels, Josephus. *Editor in Politics.* Chapel Hill, 1941. Pp. 1–644.

_____. *Tar Heel Editor.* Chapel Hill, 1939. Pp. 1–544.

_____. *The Wilson Era.* 2 vols. Chapel Hill, 1944.

Heard, Alexander. *A Two-Party South?* Chapel Hill, 1952. (Use index for N.C. references.)

Lemmon, Sarah M. *North Carolina's Role in the First World War.* Raleigh, 1916. Pp. 1–91.

Lonsdale, Richard E. *Atlas of North Carolina.* Pp. 52–53.

Orr, Oliver H., Jr. *Charles Brantley Aycock.* Chapel Hill, 1961. Pp. 1–394.

Tindall, George B. *The Emergence of the New South, 1913–1945.* Baton Rouge, La., 1967. (Use index for N.C. references.)

Watson, Richard L., Jr. "Furnifold M. Simmons: Jehovah of the Tar Heels." *NCHR* 44 (April 1967): 166–87.

Whitener, D. J. *Prohibition in North Carolina, 1715–1945.* Chapel Hill, 1946. Pp. 133–83.

41. A Quarter Century of Economic Growth

Lefler, Hugh T., ed. *North Carolina History Told by Contemporaries.* Pp. 427–37, 445–50.

Connor, R. D. W. *North Carolina: Rebuilding an Ancient Commonwealth.* 2: 548–621.

Hamilton, J. G. de R. *North Carolina Since 1860.* Pp. 376–403.

* * *

Arnett, Ethel Stephens, and W. C. Jackson. *Greensboro, North Carolina: The County Seat of Guilford.* Chapel Hill, 1955. Pp. 1–51.

Blythe, W. L. *William Henry Belk: Merchant of the South.* Chapel Hill, 1950. Pp. 1–81.

Boyd, W. K. *The Story of Durham: City of the New South.* Durham, 1925. Pp. 1–345.

Brown, C. K. *The State Highway System of North Carolina.* Chapel Hill, 1931. Pp. 1–260.

_____. *A State Movement in Railroad Development.* Chapel Hill, 1928. Pp. 245–53.

Fries, Adelaide, and others. *Forsyth: A County on the March.* Chapel Hill, 1949. Pp. 169–96.

Hobbs, S. H., Jr. *North Carolina: An Economic and Social Profile.* Chapel Hill, 1958. Pp. 85–177.

Jenkins, J. W. *James B. Duke, Master Builder.* New York, 1927. Pp. 98–184.

Lemert, B. F. *The Cotton Textile Industry of the Southern Appalachian Piedmont.* Chapel Hill, 1953. Pp. 1–120.

Waynick, Capus. *North Carolina Roads and Their Builders.* Raleigh, 1952. Pp. 1–308.

42. Educational and Cultural Growth

Lefler, Hugh T., ed. *North Carolina History Told by Contemporaries.* Pp. 407–11, 436–37.

Connor, R. D. W. *North Carolina: Rebuilding an Ancient Commonwealth.* 2: 639–95.

Hamilton, J. G. de R. *North Carolina Since 1860.* Pp. 347–75.

* * *

Cash, W. J. *The Mind of the South.* New York, 1941. Pp. 89, 224, 322–26, 341, 354, 372–76.

Gatewood, Willard B., Jr. *Eugene Clyde Brooks: Educator and Public Servant.* Durham, 1960. Pp. 1–279.

Harlan, Louis R. *Separate and Unequal: Public School Campaigns and Racism in the Southern Seaboard States, 1901–1915.* Chapel Hill, 1958. Pp. 45–74, 102–34.

Henderson, Archibald. *The Campus of the First State University.* Pp. 216–94.

Hobbs, S. H., Jr. *North Carolina: An Economic and Social Profile.* Pp. 247–79.

Holder, Rose Howell. *McIver of North Carolina.* Chapel Hill, 1959. Pp. 1–283.

Joint Committee of the North Carolina English Teachers Association and the North Carolina Library Association. *North Carolina Authors: A Selective Handbook.* (Use index.)

Jones, H. G. *For History's Sake: The Preservation and Publication of North Carolina History, 1668–1903.* Chapel Hill, 1966. Pp. 3–287.

Knight, E. W. *Public School Education in North Carolina.* Boston, 1916. Pp. 1–384.

Linder, S. C. *William Louis Poteat: Prophet of Progress.* Chapel Hill, 1966. Pp. xiv, 1–224.

Orr, Oliver T., Jr. *Charles Brantley Aycock.* Chapel Hill, 1961. Pp. 189–334.

Polk, William T. *Southern Accent: From Uncle Remus to Oak Ridge.* New York, 1953. Pp. 1–264.

43. Politics, 1920–1932: Governors Morrison, McLean, and Gardner

Lefler, Hugh T., ed. *North Carolina History Told by Contemporaries.* Pp. 417–24, 431–36.

Connor, R. D. W. *North Carolina: Rebuilding an Ancient Commonwealth.* 2: 490–549.

Corbitt, D. L., ed. *Public Papers and Letters of Cameron Morrison, Governor of North Carolina, 1921–25.* Raleigh, 1927. Pp. 1–365.

————. *Public Papers and Letters of Angus Wilton McLean, Governor of North Carolina, 1925–1929.* Raleigh, 1931. Pp. 1–921.

————. *Public Papers and Letters of Oliver Max Gardner, Governor of North Carolina, 1929–1933.* Raleigh, 1937. Pp. 1–788.

Gatewood, Willard, B., Jr., *Preachers, Pedagogues & Politicians: The Evolution Controversy in North Carolina, 1920–1927.* Chapel Hill, 1966. Pp. 1–268.

Morrison, Joseph L. *Josephus Daniels: The Small-d Democrat.* Chapel Hill, 1966. Pp. 1–316.

_____. *Josephus Daniels Says.* Chapel Hill, 1962. Pp. 1–339.

_____. *O. Max Gardner: A Power in North Carolina Politics and New Deal Washington.* Chapel Hill, 1971. Pp. 1–356.

Puryear, Elmer L. *Democratic Party Dissension in North Carolina, 1928–1936.* Chapel Hill, 1962. Pp. 3–155.

Tindall, George B. *The Emergence of the New South, 1913–1945.* (Use index for N.C. references.)

Watson, Richard L., Jr. "A Political Leader Bolts—F. M. Simmons in the Presidential Election of 1928." *NCHR* 37 (October 1960): 516–43.

44. The New Deal to the Outbreak of World War II, 1933–1941

Connor, R. D. W. *North Carolina: Rebuilding an Ancient Commonwealth.* 2: 622–64.

Henderson, Archibald. *North Carolina: The Old North State and the New.* 2 vols. Chicago, 1941. 2: 540–99.

* * *

Corbitt, D. L., ed. *Addresses, Letters, and Papers of John Christopher Blucher Ehringhaus, Governor of North Carolina, 1933–1937.* Raleigh, 1950. Pp. 1–509.

_____. *Addresses, Letters, and Papers of Clyde Roark Hoey, Governor of North Carolina, 1937–1941.* Raleigh, 1944. Pp. 1–869.

Lonsdale, Richard E. *Atlas of North Carolina.* Pp. 70–75 (election maps).

Whitener, D. J. *Prohibition in North Carolina, 1715–1945.* Pp. 184–228.

45. World War II and After: Progress and Problems, 1941–1952

Lefler, Hugh T., ed. *North Carolina History Told by Contemporaries.* Pp. 464–79.

Henderson, Archibald. *North Carolina: The Old North State and the New.* 2: 617–43.

* * *

Corbitt, D. L., ed. *Public Addresses, Letters, and Papers of Joseph Melville Broughton, Governor of North Carolina, 1941–1945.* Raleigh, 1950. Pp. 1–718.

_____. *Public Addresses and Papers of Robert Gregg Cherry, Governor of North Carolina, 1945–1949.* Raleigh, 1950. Pp. 1–1058.

_____. *Public Addresses, Letters, and Papers of William Kerr Scott, Governor of North Carolina, 1949–1953.* Raleigh, 1957. Pp. 1–626.

King, Spencer, B., Jr. *Selective Service in North Carolina in World War II*. Chapel Hill, 1949. Pp. 1–360.

Lemmon, Sarah M. *North Carolina's Role in World War II*. Raleigh, 1964. Pp. 1–69.

46. The Modern Industrial Revolution after 1930

Lefler, Hugh T., ed. *North Carolina History Told by Contemporaries*. Pp. 469–74, 510–18.

Hobbs, S. H., Jr. *North Carolina: An Economic and Social Profile*. Pp. 3–9, 75–83, 98–130, 157–77.

* * *

Herring, Harriet. *The Passing of the Mill Village*. Chapel Hill, 1949. Pp. 3–131.

————. *Welfare Work in Mill Villages*. Chapel Hill, 1929. (Use index.)

Lemert, Ben F. *The Cotton Textile Industry of the Southern Appalachian Piedmont*. Pp. 120–75.

————. *The Tobacco Manufacturing Industry in North Carolina*. Raleigh, 1939. (Use index.)

Lonsdale, Richard E. *Atlas of North Carolina*. Pp. 56–60, 116–39.

Mitchell, G. S. *Textile Unionism and the South*. Chapel Hill, 1931. (Use index.)

Morris, J. A. *Woolen and Worsted Manufacturing in the Southern Piedmont*. Columbia, S.C., 1952. (Use index.)

47. Agriculture, Transportation, and Trade in Recent Years

Hobbs, S. H., Jr. *North Carolina: An Economic and Social Profile*. Pp. 85–97, 138–42, 146–47.

* * *

Blythe, W. LeGette. *William Henry Belk: Merchant of the South*. Chapel Hill, 1950. Pp. 81–219.

Brown, Aycock. *The Birth of Aviation: Kitty Hawk, North Carolina*. Winston-Salem, 1953. Pp. 1–63.

Lively, R. A. *The South in Action: A Sectional Crusade Against Freight Rate Discrimination*. Chapel Hill, 1949. (Use index.)

Lonsdale, Richard E. *Atlas of North Carolina*. Pp. 61–69, 100–115, 140–58.

Noblin, Stuart. *The Grange in North Carolina, 1929–1954*. Greensboro, 1954. Pp. 1–59.

Taylor, Rosser H. *Carolina Crossroads: A Study of Rural Life at the End of the Horse-and-Buggy Era*. Murfreesboro, N.C., 1966. Pp. 1–172.

Waynick, Capus. *North Carolina Roads and Their Builders*. Raleigh, 1952. Pp. 1–308.

48. Toward a Finer North Carolina

Connor, R. D. W. *North Carolina: Rebuilding an Ancient Commonwealth.* 2: 665–98.

Henderson, Archibald. *North Carolina: The Old North State and the New.* 2: 644–833.

Hobbs, S. H., Jr. *North Carolina: An Economic and Social Profile.* Pp. 219–47.

* * *

The Frank C. Brown Collection of North Carolina Folklore. 5 vols. Durham, 1952–62.

Hamilton, William B. *Fifty Years of the South Atlantic Quarterly.* Durham, 1952. Pp. 1–397.

Holman, Hugh. *Thomas Wolfe.* Indianapolis, 1960. Pp. 1–47.

Hoyle, Bernadette. *Tar Heel Writers I Know.* Winston-Salem, 1956. Pp. 1–215.

Joint Committee of the North Carolina English Teachers Association and the North Carolina Library Association. *North Carolina Authors: A Selective Handbook.* (Use index.)

Knight, Edgar W. *Public School Education in North Carolina.* Pp. 329–66.

Lonsdale, Richard E. *Atlas of North Carolina.* Pp. 76–94.

Noble, Alice. *The School of Pharmacy of the University of North Carolina.* Chapel Hill, 1962. Pp. 3–222.

Polk, William T. *The Fallen Angel and Other Stories.* Chapel Hill, 1956. Pp. 1–188.

Walser, Richard. *Literary North Carolina: A Brief Historical Survey.* Raleigh, 1970. Pp. 1–137.

————, ed. *North Carolina Poetry.* Richmond, 1951. Pp. 1–166.

————. *Picture Book of Tar Heel Authors.* Raleigh, 1960. Pp. 1–46.

————. *Short Stories from the Old North State.* Chapel Hill, 1959. Pp. 1–288.

Wilson, Louis R. *The University of North Carolina, 1900–1930: The Making of a Modern University.* Chapel Hill, 1957. Pp. 1–633.

49. The New Commonwealth—For the Public Welfare

Brown, Roy, M. *Public Poor Relief in North Carolina.* Chapel Hill, 1929. Pp. 1–84.

Cheek, Roma S. *Sleeping Tar-Heels.* Durham, 1956. Pp. 1–95.

Jolly, Harley E. *The Blue Ridge Parkway.* Knoxville, Tenn., 1969. Pp. xxiii, 1–290.

Wager, Paul W., ed. *County Government Across the Nation.* Chapel Hill, 1950. Pp. 408–20.

50. In the Mainstream: An Era of Great Growth and Change

Lefler, Hugh T., ed. *North Carolina History Told by Contemporaries.* Pp. 487–510.

* * *

Burgess, M. Elaine. *Negro Leadership in A Southern City* (Durham). Chapel Hill, 1962. Pp. 1–231.

Corbitt, D. L., ed. *Public Addresses, Letters, and Papers of William Bradley Umstead, Governor of North Carolina, 1953–1954.* Raleigh, 1957. Pp. 1–414.

Fleer, Jack. *North Carolina Politics.* Chapel Hill, 1968. Pp. 1–163.

Hamilton, William B. "The Research Triangle of North Carolina: A Study in Leadership for the Common Weal." *South Atlantic Quarterly* 65 (April 1966): 254–78.

Hodges, Luther H. *Businessman in the Statehouse.* Chapel Hill, 1962. Pp. 1–336.

Mitchell, Memory F., ed. *Messages, Addresses, and Public Papers of Terry Sanford, Governor of North Carolina, 1961–1965.* Raleigh, 1966. Pp. 1–792.

Patton, James W., ed. *Messages, Addresses, and Public Papers of Luther Hartwell Hodges, Governor of North Carolina, 1954–1961.* 3 vols. Raleigh, 961–63.

Ross, Malcolm. "North Carolina, Dixie Dynamo." *National Geographic* 121 (February 1962): 141–83.

Sanford, Terry. *Storm Over the States.* New York, 1967. (Use index for N.C. references.)

Index of Persons

Index of Subjects

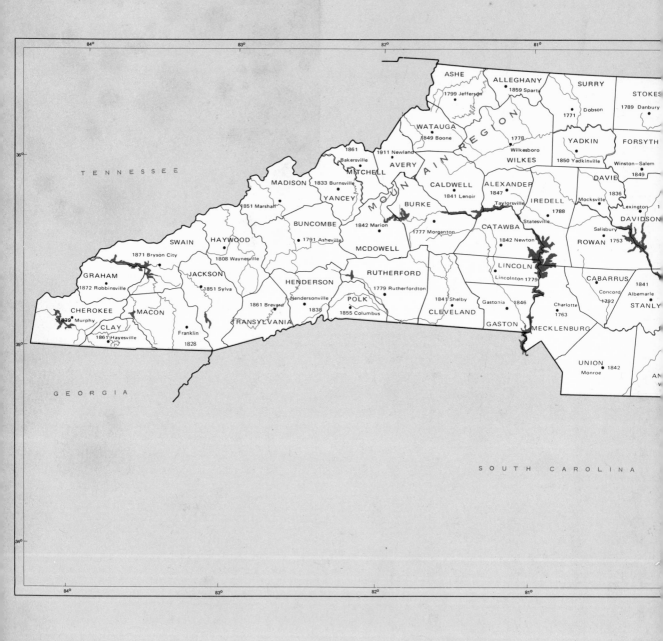